April 18, 2004

Dear Readers of *A Persian Letter:*

For me, the pleasure of reading *A Persian Letter* was equal to finding a treasure. It takes you by the hand and leads you down a delightful path of memory, history and the meaning of Iranian culture. For anyone wanting to get to know the depth of the Iranian mentality this book provides amazing insight in an entertaining way.

It should be read by every Iranian, but it should also be read by every Canadian as well as other nationalities. This book is truly perceptive in the accounts of Persian life from the memories of an Iranian immigrant in Canada. It is written in an effortless manner, simple yet complex in what it is conveying. Once you start reading it you can't put it down. It is original, entertaining and educational about a truly unique culture in the world.

Dr. Shojania is a remarkably talented physician, a specialist in biology, but he has now proven that he is also an exceptional writer. I would highly recommend this book to anyone wanting to have a better understanding of Persian immigrants in Canada, and the world that they have come from.

Sincerely,

F. Kasravi

Dr. Frederic (Fereydoun) Kasravi

Frederic J. Kasravi
6455 Spooner Way, Victoria, B.C., Canada V8M 1W7
Tel 250 544-2071 Fax 250 544-2073
Email fred.kasravi@sympatico.ca
www. fredkasravi.com

About this book

Authors who publish through Trafford Publishing can publish their work through other means as well. I have printed this copy through Island Blue Print, in a hurry, for those friends and readers who cannot wait anymore. Some of these friends have previously read or heard parts of this book. Here are some of their remembered comments.

"A Persian Letter is not a Greek tragedy. It is a tragedy, nevertheless, if you don't finish it."

Don Boult, editor of the Camosun Gyro Club newsletter,
encouraging me to complete the writing of this book

"I am dying to see your book."

Margaret, an old friend and a long term cancer survivor,
after numerous delays in the publication of this book

"I have learned about so many topics in your multilayered book, and have been pleasantly entertained."

Faye Ford, after reading and partially editing the manuscript

"This is fantastic!"

Dr. van der Westhuizen, my learned friend and esteemed colleague at work

"I learned about philosophy, Persian literature, my roots, you, and many more topics. It is great to learn while one is entertained."

Dr. Nima Shojania, a new rheumatologist in Vancouver,
after proof-reading the manuscript for his father

"After reading once again the completed version to see how it sounds, I see that it sounds neither like any of the more than hundred letters I had written to my mother in Farsi, nor like any of the more than one thousand postmortem reports I have dictated in English. In fact it sounds better than both, as if written by someone else."

Dr. Nasser Shojania, a pathologist in Victoria,
and the author of A Persian Letter

To Mitra (Mithra) a Persian god of sun

and my radiating wife

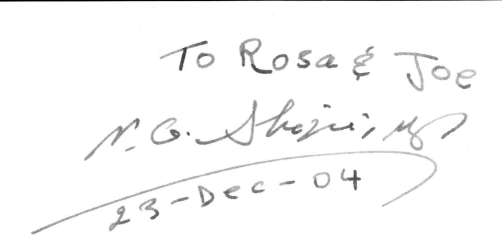

A
PERSIAN LETTER

TO A PIOUS MOTHER
FROM AN AGNOSTIC SON

Dr. Nasser Shojania

Printed in Canada

Design and typesetting: Roy Diment, VRG.
www.members.shaw.ca/vrg
Cover: Roy Diment

Note for Librarians: a cataloguing record for this book that includes Dewey Decimal Classification
and US Library of Congress numbers is available from the National Library of Canada.
The complete cataloguing record can be obtained from the National Library's online database at:
www.nlc-bnc.ca/amicus/index-e.html

ISBN 1-4120-3075-7

Printed in Victoria, BC, Canada

TRAFFORD

Offices in Canada, USA, Ireland, UK and Spain
This book was published *on-demand* in cooperation with Trafford Publishing. On-demand publishing is a unique
process and service of making a book available for retail sale to the public taking advantage of on-demand
manufacturing and Internet marketing. On-demand publishing includes promotions, retail sales, manufacturing,
order fulfilment, accounting and collecting royalties on behalf of the author.
Book sales in Europe:
Trafford Publishing (UK) Ltd., Enterprise House, Wistaston Road Business Centre,
Wistaston Road, Crewe CW2 7RP UNITED KINGDOM
phone 01270 251 396 (local rate 0845 230 9601)
facsimile 01270 254 983; info.uk@trafford.com
Book sales for North America and international:
Trafford Publishing, 6E–2333 Government St.,
Victoria, BC V8T 4P4 CANADA
phone 250 383 6864 (toll-free 1 888 232 4444)
fax 250 383 6804; email to bookstore@trafford.com

www.trafford.com/robots/04-0902.html

10 9 8 7 6 5 4 3 2 1

What is to be done, O Moslems? For I do not recognize myself.

I am neither Christian, nor Jew, nor Gabr, nor Moslem.

I am not of the East, nor of the West, nor of the land, nor of the sea;

I am not of Nature's mint, nor of the circling heavens.

I am not of this world, nor of the next, nor of Heaven, nor Hell;

I am not of Adam, nor of Eve, nor of Eden and Paradise.

My place is the placeless, my trace is the traceless;

It is neither body nor soul, for I belong to the soul of the beloved.

Rumi

Translated by R. A. Nicholson

CONTENTS

PREFACE

A PERSIAN LETTER is a segmented letter addressed to my dead mother in Iran. It is written in English so that non-Iranians can read it. It simulates the letters I used to write to her in Farsi from the summer of 1965, when I came to Canada to specialize in pathology, till the fall of 1989 when she died a natural death in Tehran. It particularly simulates the last letter I had written to her, somewhat tongue-in-cheek, with the broad-tipped reed pen that I had plucked from the reed yard of my neighbour in Victoria and the rehydrated black ink that I had brought with myself when I came to Canada. Without planning, the book has become long, segmented and hollow. Perhaps, unconsciously, it wants to imitate the stem of reed from which it is made.

The Persian name for reed is *nay*. Not only the famous mystic Rumi has begun his book of Mathnavi by the sound of *nay* — complaining about the pain of separation from its origin —but every literate Persian child has used a reed pen in calligraphy classes in elementary school in Iran. Furthermore, since *nay* rhymes with *kay,* and *kay* means "when?" in Farsi, whenever the Persian children asked their parents, "When are you going to buy me a bicycle?" they heard the disappointing but rhyming reply, "At the time of flowering of nay" meaning, of course, never. It is interpreted as never, not because nay also means "no" in Farsi, but because the Iranian parents erroneously believed that reed never flowers.

This is why, when my neighbour saw me looking at the row of flowering reeds that he had planted along the wall-less junction of our yards and apologized for planting them without prior discussion with me, I had to interrupt his apologies to thank him for planting them. I told him that I had grown up with reeds when I was growing up in Iran, and to prove to him that I was telling the truth, with his permission, I plucked a dried stem of the row of reed, broke it into nine pen-sized segments through its gouty joints, and shaved them the way our calligraphy teacher would do and began writing a letter to my mother with the one with the broadest tip.

Besides being a letter to my dead mother, *A Persian Letter*, by bringing together other letters from my family and friends, becomes a commentary on the dying art of letter writing and the importance of friendship among the Iranians. The book can be considered a little window as well, to the subconcious, if not the unconcious, of the people of Iran, at least those I was associating with.

Even though the words are in English, the thoughts are in Persian. In other words, without trying to translate my thoughts from Farsi to English, I have tried to think in English. It is a very personal letter, yet it is not my biography. To fill the pages, I have made extensive use of my remembered memoirs, yet this is not my memoirs either. I have written down the relevant thoughts that have come to my mind when I was sitting in my office, looking into my microscope or into the drawers of my desk, if not out of the three shut windows, as well as the thoughts that have come to my mind while performing postmortem examinations in the windowless morgue of the same hospital.

Even though my thoughts are very personal, they are brought here for their universal effects. My thoughts are mainly about the middle class Moslem family with secular tendencies and progressive western thoughts that I grew up in, from 1930, when I was born, till the present time. These thoughts can be found in many middle class Iranian families who grew up in the second half of the last century.

I have been told that when one wants to write a book about people, one should either write about the extraordinary things that happen to ordinary people, or ordinary things that happen to extraordinary people. My book is an exception in the sense that it is about ordinary things that happen to ordinary people. It is a plotless book with no extraordinary events. It does contain crimes and punishments, vices and virtues, but, like everything else in the book, they are not outstanding and all easily fall within the normal limits of an ordinary life. The ordinary events, however, when they happen in an extraordinary location, or expressed in a different language, become ironical or entertaining. Besides, when I talk about myself, I do so in order to illuminate the associated social events. When I talk about the time when I was four years old, living in the religious city of Mashad in Iran, for example, I want to spotlight the significant event of the unveiling of women in Iran that occurred in 1934 and a mosqueful of men who were *Shaheed* (martyred) to prevent it from happening.

In my office, whenever I play back the dictating machine to hear what I have dictated, I always dislike my voice. But, when I read my manuscript back to myself to see how it sounds, to my surprise, I note that it resembles neither any of the more than one hundred letters that I had written to my mother in Farsi, nor any of the more than a thousand postmortem reports I have been dictating in English. In fact, it sounds better than both, as if written by someone else.

Perhaps one writes differently when one employs different stationery. Of course one is forced to choose different words when one writes with a smooth Waterman fountain pen and purple ink on a white sheet of paper than with a hammer and chisel on the gravestone of one's mother, in cuneiform script. Perhaps it is not the content, but the stationery which is the message of this book.

The intended message of this book, however, was to entertain. I hope, like my mother who enjoyed my letters so much that she lost a few minutes of her life while reading them the reader will enjoy this book so much and will not notice the passage of time during the few hours of reading it.

ACKNOWLEDGMENTS

I DON'T KNOW THE GESTATIONAL PERIOD OF A BOOK SUCH AS THIS. It took about seven years to finish this, so long that several who had heavily contributed to its conception and production died during the process. Some were dead from the beginning. Luckily, most are alive. I would rather acknowledge the dead first. The order in which they appear, however, depends on the order that they come to my mind, rather than the magnitude of their contribution to the book. The amount of contribution, of course, is always difficult to measure. Some, with a single encouraging word, have made the entire work possible, while some contributed to it just by being alive and anxiously waiting for it.

A—Among the dead, I would like to acknowledge the following and hope that I have not forgotten some more important ones.

1—Nayyer Ashraf Shojania, my mother and the recipient of *A Persian Letter*. Among many other things, she is responsible for the name of the book and the voice of its author.

2—Colonel Abdollah Khalvati, nicknamed Sharabi, meaning the wine-stricken, who is the older brother of my mother. He wrote a book during the Second World War and named it *SOS*. He did so because he thought humanity was in danger and the world needed something like the future United Nations. He stayed all his life in a rented house and sold his unfinished house to self-publish his book to send to the heads of nations who could do something for the world. I have borrowed some pictures and many words from the prologue and epilogue of his book. I might decorate the back of my book with the design of the cover of his book.

3—Ezzat Rastegar nicknamed Arefeh Khamoosh (Silent Mystic) by his sister after his death. He is my mentor and my self-exiled friend from Iran to France who has enriched my book by his personal letters and his writings in the political and literary *Magazine of Sahand*, published in France in Persian.

4—Dr. Massoud Meer-baha, my psychiatrist friend who shared my political views and ignorance of youth and suffered more from his subsequent repentance than me. His absence is compensated for by the presence of several chapters in the book about him and his sayings.

5—Peter Gzowski, the host of the long-lasting radio program by the name of Morningside in Canada. His question on the morning of March 11, 1986, "Do you feel you are a Canadian now?" has given some direction to the evolution of this book. My book, in fact, is the expanded version of my reply at that time. At that time, I replied like this: "Peter, twelve years ago when we moved from Winnipeg to Victoria, I planted three small trees, smaller than the smallest of our three sons, in our backyard. Now those trees are taller than the roof of our house. As those trees grow, I feel that it is me who is growing roots in this land."

6—Daryush Ja'far-zadeh, my perfectionist, half-Persian, half-German friend in Victoria, perhaps the first person who died in the intensive care unit of the new D and T building of the Royal Jubilee Hospital. He did survive, however, for a week or two after his open heart surgery to read the "Sneak Preview" of my book, published in the Victoria Medical Society newsletter as well as its first chapter, "A Faraway Lullaby," and the last chapter, "An Agnostic's Prayer," published in the bilingual *Persian Heritage* magazine in New York in 2002.

7—Dr. Victor, my Scottish colleague in Victoria who saved me from insanity by going insane first.

8—Mahmood Shojania, my youngest brother, whose letters after his release from prison became part of my book.

9—Mr. Amir-jalal Khazaei, my father-in-law, who was waiting so eagerly for this book and died from the fastest growing tumour I had seen in my long life as a pathologist. "Whatever you decide to do, it will turn out to be the best," he used to say to me about the book. I regret that I rarely believed in his cocksureness and confidence in me. I hope he is right about the book.

10—Fred Kasravi. He is not dead yet but he will be in less than six months. He lived long enough, however, to read the chapter about him, play backgammon with Mitra and fall in love with an angelic Irish lady. He expired after he read the first copy of the book and wrote the testimonial about it.

B—Among the living:

Since the names of many with significant contribution do appear in the book, I don't have to repeat their names here. This, of course, does not mean that those whose names are not mentioned here won't appear in the book.

1—Mitra Shojania, my wife, without whose help this book would not exist. All the ideal conditions, such as a quiet location and magnificent view, required for writing this book were provided by her. She did not agree with all the changes and editing, but she was quite happy with the few initial samples I read for her. At the beginning, she was a little worried that I might lose my job if I went deep into writing. To alleviate her worry, I extended my work beyond the normal age for retirement by ten years. Paradoxically, that extension increased my contact with my colleagues and co-workers in the hospital, and that in turn increased the length and the depth of my book through a sort of biofeedback.

2—Kamran, Keyvan and Nima, our sons, who enjoyed, improved and corrected my occasional essays long before I had any intention of writing a book. I thank each of them twice, once for not being ashamed of the writing of their father, once for their encouragement for writing more.

3—All the physicians of the Royal Jubilee Hospital, Victoria General Hospital and the members of the Victoria Medical Society who have made encouraging comments after reading my essays in the newsletters of the hospitals or of the VMS, particularly Dr. Arthur Macgregor who gave me a book with the unfamiliar Greek name of *Eothen*—one of the favourite books of Mr. Churchill— as an example of good English writing.

4—Faith Gildenhuys, the professional editor of the book who made many corrections without changing my voice and taught me how to edit my own work.

5—Dr. Doug Cavers, my learned colleague who knows many of my friends from Winnipeg and knows books, for his constructive comments after reading the manuscript twice.

6—Dr. Seamus Kelly, my Irish colleague and friend, for his partial reading of the manuscript and editing the early chapters as well as his constructive advice for the rest of the book.

7—Dr. Nick Van Der Westhuizen, my knowledgeable colleague who informs me of any informative talk taking place in the University of Victoria or on the Ideas program on CBC radio. Also I thank him for his appreciation of my writing and his high expectations for its success. He is the friend who was looking –in vain of course—at several issues of *The New Yorker* after I told him that I had submitted my poem about the implosion of the Twin Towers, "An Agnostic's Prayer," to them. The same poem he had liked so much that made a copy of it for his son, Michael, who was to write an essay on the side effects of terror on their school.

8—Doctor Grace Kho, our only lady colleague, who said my writings make her sometimes cry and sometimes laugh and is impatiently waiting to see them in print.

9—Mr. Khatami, President of Iran, who when he was asked, "When are you going to make up with the West and the rest of the world?" replied, "It is first up to the Iranians living outside of Iran to demonstrate their culture and learn from other cultures before the officials can negotiate to find a way. "

Introduction

A FARAWAY LULLABY

Once there was someone

Then there was no one

Except for the omnipresent God

There was no one....

Let me begin again.

ONCE UPON A TIME, in a dusty distant parcel of land, blessed with motionless waters and running sand, located within the light brown zone of a blue planet, far away from the crushing sound of falling waters and the foaming lips of rushing rivers, in a mud-made town, a Persian widow with seven fearless sons and two daring daughters was singing a melancholy lullaby to her insomniac son.

The name of that mud-made town was Torbat, and *Torbat* is an Arabic noun, meaning *Khaak* in Persian. And *Khaak* is that pluripotential powdery matter from which the adjective *khaki* is derived. It can be blown away simply by breathing beside it, or it can be compacted to make round or rectangular praying stones, the *Mohr of Namaaz*, so that Moslem men or women from all over the world, whether Arab or Persian, may kiss it with their forehead or touch it with their lips.

Torbat was populated by many poets, peasant and artisans, making it sometimes difficult to differentiate between the poets and the artisans. It had many potters, some of them believing that the handle at the neck of their *Khaak*-made *Koozeh* was the arm of the wine worshipper, Omar Khayyam, at the neck of his beloved, now turned to dust. It was a thirsty town with little water; nevertheless the poets advised its population not to look for water but to look for more thirst.

The land of my childhood was a tool-less town, but had many craftsmen: lazy-looking lean men, working with all their limbs, fingers and toes, making smooth, slippery jack-knives in the shape of fish. The knife handles were made of the horns of slaughtered rams, the blades, of iron scraps left over from the long-forgotten wars in the rusty mountains of nearby Afghanistan. The barefooted children of that land made their faceless dolls and limbless camels out of mud and baked them in the sunshine.

Copper was still the king of the metals, more precious than gold. Thieves preferred to steal the copper watering cans from the edge of pools than the sterling silver spoons nestled in their velvet-lined boxes in closets.

It was a compassionate place. Malaria was not yet eradicated and its regular bouts of chills and fever embraced its fatherless children much more intimately and frequently than their fathers ever did.

Even though the blessed land was located in a temperate zone of the planet, it had an extreme climate, extreme men, and extremely moderate women. Some of the women, when they became mothers, did not expect anything from their children except for remembering their lullabies.

In that dusty parcel of dry land, there lived a crownless Persian prince who, of all the precious jewels of the world, possessed only a blue marble and kept it in his closed hand all the time, day or night.

It was night but not quite dark. The inside of the room was darker than outside. Outside, under the transparent tent of the moonlight, if one were awake, one could see the shadowless fragments of fractured earthenware scattered everywhere, resembling an abandoned pottery shop. Inside was dimly illuminated by a smouldering blue lamp with a constricted waist, projecting grotesque shadows on the wall. The mother was sitting firmly on the ground, cross-legged—the way she always sat—like those pregnant Russian dolls that contain multiple similar but smaller ones inside. Her parted black hair had narrowed her porcelain face to an oval moon. The magnified shadows of her spidery lashes on the wall touched each other every now and then to send cryptic messages to the son that the horrific story he was hearing was true, while her almond-shaped eyes, pretending to be sleepy, opened and closed as she sang, meaning the story was a tragedy if he looked at it from the ground, and a comedy if he looked at it from the sky.

Except for the monotonous breathing of his sleeping siblings, it was a silent night. One could not tell if the wind was blowing because there were no trees in sight. One could not tell if it were a false nirvana or a true mirage. What was deepening the silence was her voice that, coming through closed lips, was low as if coming from a well.

The son was all ears.

To further obscure her voice, the mother made extra, metallic sounds, like the chirping of well-pigeons, by turning the handle of her Singer sewing machine—that omnipresent man-made machine that had crossed all the international borders to reach her house so that she could make hundreds of shorts for her sons and tens of skirts for her daughters.

On that particular night, however, the mother, for the first time, was making something for herself, and in a hurry: a frilly blue dress to get ready for the official opening day of the unveiling of women in that land.

The son, bare-bottomed, was straddling the lid of the sewing machine next to the mother, like a legless little donkey. He was repeating the words of his mother, more like the loose-legged, cheeky doll of a ventriloquist than a parrot. One could not repeat those words, word by word, unless one had heard them a hundred times, or one had a good memory. The son was endowed with both. Despite his multiple congenital anomalies and numerous god-given deficiencies, the son was lucky to have an elephantine memory.

Time was passing rapidly and uneventfully, since the son was having a good time watching his mother. Sometimes, like flames of fire going upward, sometimes, like running water going down, the wavy blue material was forced to pass under the narrow bridge of the sewing machine, leaving the son to wonder if he was day-dreaming at night or if he was watching a colour movie in the morning.

The somniferous sound of the breathing of his sleeping siblings, instead of making him sleepy, awoke in him a few lines from the father of the new Persian poetry, Nima Yousheej, who declared with regret—like the rude awakening by a rooster—when he arrived at a sleepy village in his homeland, "with a knapsack on his back and a walking stick in his hand," early in the morning:

The sorrow of these fallen few

Breaks the desire of sleep in my eye

That tall and tender stem of flower

That I once planted in my soul

And irrigated with my blood

Pity! It is breaking within my flesh.

When the mother saw the white of the eyes of the son was still glowing in the darkness of the room, she grew irritated and began to include advice in her lullaby:

Pretend, at least.

Pretend to be asleep my little son

Try to close your beady eyes for a moment

And see

My little prince

That no one is going to take your marble away

As long as I am awake.

It is yours

Everybody knows

Don't be a tight-fisted miser

My dear Nasser.

The son got so upset that his mother, usually so patient and wise, was teaching him pretence and imitation, that he decided then and there that he should leave his mother and his country and go somewhere so far away that he could not hear her anymore. As he was thinking and planning how to escape from his mother and his country he lost the sense of time and repeated one of the lines of the lullaby once—only once—slightly ahead of his mother. She became truly upset and quoted the Persian proverb which is always used against those who do not act as they preach: "If you know the lullaby, then why can't you sleep?"

The mother uttered that line and fell backward on the carpet, where she was sitting. Whether she was dead, asleep or *Ghahr*, the son could not tell because the cardinal sign of the three is silence.

Ghahr is something that, when it happens, the two who have *ghahred* with each other do not communicate, either by speech or gesture. They ignore the presence of each other. The son could not verify in which of the three states the mother was because he too had *ghahred* with her because of her unkind words. *Ghahr*, of course, happens always between two friends, and therefore it is a temporary interruption, but the son, who rarely *ghahred* with anybody, believed that he would never make up whenever he *ghahred*.

More than being *ghahr*, it was the lack of love and logic in her last line that made the entire lullaby a false story, and helped the son to make up his mind to leave the loveless house of his mother and the semi-arid land of his father.

Time passed again. The son grew up, grew a moustache, wore glasses and left his country. Unlike the caged bird-man in the lullaby, however, he did not have to suffer, nor did he require seven iron shoes and seven iron canes to reach the land where a half-truth was considered a double lie. He travelled long and far, sometimes walking with a wooden stick like a human, sometimes flying like a bird. When he was walking like a human, he wished he was a bird. When he was flying like a bird, he wished he was a human. He landed on an island the shape of a boat, anchored at the foaming lips of the Pacific Ocean where it kisses the corrugated west coast of a county named Canada, the place to where salmon are attracted when they want to spawn, proliferate and die.

The grown son lived on that island for the rest of his life, happily, like an exiled king, with his pretty Persian wife and their three normal sons.

Except for the night of the last lullaby, the stories of the mother always terminated with the following disclaimer:

We went up; there was Maast, (yogurt)

Our story was Raast. (true)

We went down; there was Doogh, (diluted yogurt)

Our story was Doroogh. (false)

But, let me end this lullaby differently, as I have begun differently, different than the ending of Persian stories.

When a hairless Buddhist with orange robe saw the prince was praying with the rosary of his mother that was given to him in compensation for his lost marble, he asked him why he did not subscribe to the religion of his mother himself. The son repeated the same meaningless line of the lullaby that had ended his relationship with his mother, "because I know the lullaby, but cannot sleep."

"I will never forget this line," the Buddhist man said, and wrote it down to murmur it a thousand times or more, when turning the handle of his praying wheel with one hand.

1

THREE SHUT WINDOWS

If you wish to see the real Canada

Don't look at it through the window of television;

Look at it through an open window.

– A Morningside guest in conversation with Peter Gzowski

MY OFFICE HAS THREE WINDOWS, one looking towards the south, and two towards the east. My colleagues' offices have only one or two windows. I can see more of the outside world than they can. This privilege, of course, is not because I am the oldest or the most important among the seven anatomic pathologists of this department. It is rather due to the fact that the lab is located at the upper top corner of this five-storey hospital, and my office happens to be at one of its corners.

The single window looks towards the snow-streaked Olympic Mountains to the south. Those mountains belong to the United States of America. They occupy the entire length of my horizon. Between me and those seagull-stained mountains, there is a begging seagull on the window sill, a canopy of trees, and occasional slanted roofs the colour of an arbutus tree.

The double windows look towards the mainland of Canada, separated from this island by a narrow band of green water. The water is of course colourless, but it looks green because of the plethora of inverted images of evergreen trees in it.

My windows, like all the windows of our hundred-year-old brown brick hospital, are old-fashioned. They are the vertical type, the kind that I have never learned the English name of and do not wish to learn. I have seen them in Iran, too. Our high school had them in the main hall where conferences were held. In Iran they called them *Orossi*, meaning Russian, because, like many new or European things, such as modern leather shoes which were also called *Orossi*, they were introduced to Iran from Russia. Unlike the ordinary windows that open sideways like the wings of a bird, they open by sliding vertically over each other.

They have two overlapping segments; the lower one is designed to move easily upward with the lightest touch of a finger, but mine do not move. All three are shut, permanently stuck with layers of hospital-white paint. One can see, if one looks closely, the dried droplets of paint on the wooden frame, like the artificial teardrops on the face of a clown.

On the first day that this office was given to me I almost compressed several of my intervertebral discs when I tried to open them. The second time I tried to open them was several years later when two inmates from the nearby mental institute climbed the fire escape stairs and came up to the window ledge threatening to commit suicide by throwing themselves down. By the motions of their hands and fingers, I thought they wanted cigarettes, because in Iran, some of the mental patients always asked for a cigarette whenever I visited them. So, with the additional muscular power that one acquires in emergencies, I tried once more to open one of the windows. It did not open, of course, but the glass made such a cracking sound that it startled the two women and they almost fell to their deaths on the hospital grounds

Years have passed and I have not looked at these windows or through them. The reason I am doing it today is because when I was driving to work today—elongating my way to see more of this garden city, as usual—I heard on the CBC radio a guest on the Morningside program, in conversation with Peter Gzowski said, "To see Canada one should look at it through an open window rather than the window of a television." And Peter said that that reply was the most important reply he had heard during the 15 years that he was running that program.

So today, I gave the windows a third chance, and when they didn't open, I decided to look through them, and see how much of real Canada I could see through my closed windows. These windows are transparent. They let the light in and let me see outside as far as my eyes can see. The snow-streaked chain of the Olympic Mountains in the south reminds me of the snow-streaked chain of Alborz Mountains, north of Tehran, in Iran. On the sill is a begging seagull that used to sit outside Janet's window, the secretary to our boss, the one whose husband bred dogs and owned a pair of peacocks. She could give it bread through her functioning window, but she is retired now and her small office is vacant. She believed that seagulls were the incarnation of dead sailors.

Through the double window I can see the cubical building of the psychiatric institute staring at my office with hundreds of rectangular blind eyes. Beyond that is the low roof of a modern shopping centre with large neon signs. Next to this is the Oak Bay Recreation Centre where I sometimes go to recreate myself. Next to it is the sturdy, stony building where some seniors live and it recently was decorated with a new silver bow on its wall to celebrate the Year of Seniors.

Invisible beyond these buildings is water that separates this island from the mainland. Also invisible from my office is the tall chimney on the north side of the hospital on the shady side of the parking lot that glows like a disrupted orange pill in the sky when I approach the hospital through the back door on sunny mornings.

There is so much light in my office that when I close my eyes I see a red night.

When I open my eyes, I see a thin Persian book, *Red Wisdom*, sent from Paris by my wise friend, Ezzat Rastegar, waiting on the dusty top of my filing cabinet. I have not read this book yet because it arrived only yesterday.

I look at the cork clipboard screwed on the wavy plaster of the wall near the entrance door. On the roster, the days of the week are arranged in vertical columns, the tasks and duties along a horizontal bar. The heading on the task bar is like the menu of a computer. From left to right it reads cellular pathology, tissue pathology, and post-mortem examination, alternating with days of microscopic work. The duties are arranged by the size of the specimen in ascending order. As a general rule, the smaller the specimen, the more difficult it is to make a diagnosis; this is why the books about smaller specimens are much thicker than the books about bigger specimens.

I find my initials under the column for post-mortem. It is too early to phone the morgue to find out how many autopsies I have to do today. It could be none or one or more. Sometimes, on bad days, it can be as many as four. But the good thing about being on autopsy is that there is no rush.

I go to the doctors' lounge on the same floor as the lab for half a cup of coffee and talk with the surgeons. The corridor of the lab smells of dry formalin dust. The technicians with their white coats are at the bench, all bent, blowing and pulling at the uncooperative ribbon of paraffin containing a slice of tissue thinner than a snowflake hanging from the cutting edge of their microtome. They are preparing microscope slides. They will stain them red and purple before taking them to the offices of pathologists. It takes time to make colourful translucent images out of the colourless fragments of dead or dying tissue. This is why I have a lot of time on my hands in the mornings.

Sometimes I go to the cafeteria for coffee with my colleagues, sometimes I go alone to the doctors' lounge, the latter more often since it is located near the operating rooms on the same floor as the lab. One can get information about the specimens from the surgeons if they happen to be there. The more information one receives about a specimen, the easier it is to interpret.

Only a single swinging door separates the lab from the semi-sterile, semi-lit corridor leading to the operating rooms. One has to be careful pushing or pulling this door, for at any moment an amputated leg in a plastic bag may appear from the opposite direction. Or one may run into a cart loaded with tubes of blood and urine and specimen containers. The refrigerator for big specimens is the only object that sings in the lab this early in the morning.

Two wheeled stretchers are parked against the wall beside the operating rooms for small surgeries like circumcision or cystoscopy. Each stretcher is occupied by an old man, each with grey hair and both slightly ashamed of being in bed, horizontal, while everybody else is vertical and walking. They are both holding the backs of their heads above the pillows, not on them, as if to show that they are not completely supine. A nurse is looking at the wristband of one of the two for identification while talking to him with a voice louder than necessary, as if the old man were hard of hearing or his mother tongue were not English. She is asking if he knew what kind of operation the doctor was going to perform on him. The man seems reluctant to give a clear-cut answer. He mumbles and murmurs something that the nurse does not understand. I accelerate my steps so as not to appear to be listening to their confidential conversation. The nurse is doing her job. She has to make sure that the patient knows what kind of operation he is having and to make sure he is the right patient.

In the lounge I see the urologist having coffee and reading the headlines of the newspaper in his hand. His coffee-coloured skin accentuates his silvery hair. His angulated profile would suit the back of an ancient silver coin. He is upset by the recurrent war between India and Pakistan. He seems to think I am always on the side of Pakistan. Just to have something to say, I tell him semi-jokingly, "Paul! Your patient does not know what kind of operation you are going to inflict upon him."

"He knows."

"Then how come he couldn't tell the nurse?"

"He can, but he is reluctant to state it."

"Why?"

Paul seems to be as hesitant to tell me the name of the operation as the patient was about telling the nurse.

"Why?" I repeat.

"He is going to have a circumcision and because he is German he is not proud of it, and naturally does not wish to shout it in the corridor, even though he speaks perfect English."

Paul's reply also explained why he too was hesitant. A circumcision is nothing to brag about when one is sitting with surgeons waiting to open a heart or remove a brain tumour.

I pour half a cup of coffee for myself and sit on the green vinyl sofa with radiating sunken buttons. I know I will be back several times before the day is over. So I drink with measure, not by measure, the way my only civilian uncle used to drink vodka when he visited my military uncle, Colonel Sharabi. Anytime Sharabi had a shot for himself, he offered his older brother one as well. The older brother never refused his offer, but as soon as the level of vodka reached the middle of the glass, he would hurry to say, "Enough, enough!" After this happened several times, near the end of the bottle, Sharabi commented, "Brother! You seem to drink *with* measures, not *by* measure!"

I look for milk. The plastic cream and milk jars are not easily distinguishable because the labels on the lids are worn out. I don't try to distinguish them. I add from the container closer to my hand. I tell myself that as long as it does not have a bluish hue when I pour it into my cup, it is all right.

I do not like blue milk and I never buy it. Whenever my wife sends me to buy skim milk, I always buy normal milk. And when she objects I always tell her that I do not like blue milk because I come from Iran.

"What is the connection between milk and coming from Iran?" she asked me the first time I said this. I told her that in Iran, when I was there, the milkmen sometimes added so much water to the milk that it acquired a blue hue. She said that she is from Iran too but has never seen blue milk.

"That is because you are thirteen years younger than I," I said. "By the time you began putting milk in your tea or coffee, you got pasteurized milk in sealed bottles." She said, "You are more than thirteen years older than me, almost fourteen."

Adding water to milk was so common that our professor of infectious diseases, Dr. Mojdehi, said that even though typhoid is predominantly due to consumption of contaminated water, one should always be suspicious of milk as well because the dishonest milkman may have added contaminated water to the milk.

Among the doctors in the lounge there are a few non-doctors too, but no less important than the doctors. They are not nurses. They are all male, and all in green gowns similar to the surgeons. They are perfusionists. They keep the body and brain irrigated with oxygenated blood while the surgeon is working on the non-beating heart.

The atmosphere of the room resembles the indifferent atmosphere of a waiting room of a busy doctor's office, but doctors are not good at waiting, especially the surgeons who are used to doing two things very quickly: *decision* and *incision*. They are often made to wait because their case is bumped from the operating room by a more urgent one. Everybody reads a page of a shared newspaper, the *Times Colonist*, and occasionally the *Globe and*

Mail, the *National Post*, or the *Vancouver Sun*. The last is a misnomer because everybody knows that Victoria gets more sunshine than Vancouver, so much so that when clouds appear on sunny days in Victoria, they say they are the empties coming from Vancouver.

A friendly perfusionist, Michael, who knows by now which section of the newspaper I am looking for, finds it, folds it four times, and hands it to me with the bridge problem showing.

The bridge puzzle and the horoscope are always on the same page, and I read my horoscope every day before I begin the bridge problem. Now, having read the horoscope religiously every morning, I am beginning to believe in it. Sometimes it is so true that I cut it out to show it to my wife when I go home. Sometimes it tells me I won't lose even if I try; sometimes it cautions me to be careful in what I say either at work or at home.

I can rarely solve the bridge problem but I learn how to bid from it. I learn how I can bid my hand to give the most information about it to my partner, with the least amount of risk. This is why when René and Allison come to play with Mitra and me, they often lose. Allison jokes when she pays the five or six dollars by saying, "This is Elizabeth's milk money," their youngest daughter. I remember the day she was born in the maternity ward at Victoria General Hospital. Now she is about ten years old and paints. I bought her first drawing, when she was six, for five dollars. Now, a few years later, she has painted a large angel for me, "with love" and mixed media, free. I shall keep it. I have put it for now beside the book about Sohravardi by Henry Corbin, the cover of which features an angel under a willow tree not unlike my angel. The love of a ten-year-old girl must be among the purest sorts of love.

The horoscope always begins with my sign, Aries. I read mine first, then Virgo, my wife's sign. And sometimes I phone her about it. She is not into these things. She plays solitaire with real cards in front of the television, sometimes till late at night, when I am writing. She is not too happy about my writing, mainly because she worries that it might damage my job. She liked my mother but does not see the point of writing a book to her, and I don't blame her. Maybe when my book is finished I will dedicate it to her and thank her for "putting up with my unpredictable moods all this time." One of the books about writing says, "Never discuss your book with your spouse." That is why I don't take it personally when she does not appreciate what I am doing.

She has a computer too but does not use it much except for tracking the stock market. She does not use the Internet very often. She does not need it. She can navigate her way around the world with her cordless telephone.

I don't like the telephone, cordless or not. My mother did not like it either. I called her long distance only once from here. She said, after replying to my *Salaam* with a simple *Salaam*, "Put the receiver down. Don't waste your money. Whatever you want to say, write it in a letter."

Some other doctors read their horoscopes too, but Gordon is not one of them. He is against it. He is a kind and Catholic family physician with short grey hair. He has told me before that his ten-year-old daughter once told her friends at a birthday party in their own house, "My father is not as old as he looks." He knows that I am spiritual but irreligious. One day, when I told him that I was waiting for a personal miracle to believe in God, he gave me a book about a Christian woman, a saint who was so convinced in her belief that she bled from the healed scar on the palm of her hand every Friday night.

Gordon begins to fold the page of newspaper in which he was doing the crossword puzzle and looks at me with disbelief. He is horrified to see that I am reading my horoscope. He is also against smoking. Once I told him that the danger of smoking is exaggerated. While it is true that it shortens the smoker's life, it cuts off years from the end of it, the part that is usually associated with diseases and disabilities. "It is not just a quick death by a massive heart attack that cigarette smoking can cause; you could lose a leg due to gangrene and live on with one leg for years," he said.

David is here today too. He is a young-looking physician who spends half of his time in family practise and half of his time assisting surgeons in open-heart surgery, mainly with coronary artery bypass grafts, CABG for short, pronounced *cabbage*. His job during the operation is to remove long segments of veins from a leg, cut them to the required lengths without crushing them or touching their delicate endothelial lining. The surgeon makes a single hole or up to four or five holes in the root of the aorta as soon it comes out of the heart and connects one end of the vein to the hole, and the other end to the side of the coronary artery a little beyond the blockage. Maybe the surgeon lets him do other things too, like closing the chest after the critical part of the operation is over. I don't know how much of the sewing he does, but I am sure he does at least some because sometimes he comes to the lounge long after the surgeon he was helping.

We have known each other for a long time. For years he has been after me, asking me, semi-sarcastically I thought, "When are you going to write the Great Canadian Novel?" I hope he will ask me the same question again, because I have a different answer for him today.

He has not talked to me much since he became preoccupied with the Internet and his handheld electronic device. He is now reading a book he has saved in it. He says he can download up to five books in it and read any one of them while waiting in the doctors' lounge or anywhere else. He shows me his electronic version of Pharmacopoeia that tells him the correct dose of any drug for his patients, and whether the new drug he is prescribing for his patients is compatible with the previously prescribed medications or not. He can even tell if the results of the tests he has ordered are within normal range or not because he has all the normal values in the same device as well as the list of his patients with their history and their main complaints.

Today he says that he has found a site on the Internet with good scientific information. From that site he has learned that the endothelial cells that line the inside of the veins, even though they are morphologically similar, are functionally different from vein to vein.

After I put the newspaper on the coffee table, David asks me about my book.

"I am writing it."

"Hurry up, please, we are waiting."

"Don't push me, David, I want to do a good job."

"Put a lot of sex in it, if you want it to sell."

"David! It is a letter to my dead mother in Iran."

He blushes. His pink skin becomes red and remains red for a long time after his laughter dies; then he looks with downcast eyelids at the palm of his hand, reading his e-book.

The cool cardiac surgeon who never loses his temper comes out of the back door wearing a short-sleeved green gown and white cloth booties over his shoes. His gown never has a drop of blood on it, unlike the general surgeons who are often stained with bile and blood, even on the soles of their booties. Not only that, they insist on putting their feet on the coffee table or the nearest chair. Dr. Penner, my old boss in Winnipeg, never let any of the residents, or even the pathologist, put their feet on the table. Dick is well-mannered. He never puts his feet on the coffee table even when he is tired, like today.

Dick always has something interesting to say to the person sitting next to him. Today he tells me that he has found special shoes in Seattle. After wearing them for three consecutive days, his heels do not hurt anymore.

"Why don't you wear them during the operation as well, so that you can stand longer hours on your feet?" I ask. He says that walking on the hard tiled floor of the long corridors causes or aggravates the problem, not standing still. I tell him that our new house on Arbutus Road has large square tiles on the floors the colour of an arbutus tree, but they have not caused me any pain yet.

Dick likes travelling and likes to write about it. He goes to Egypt very often, but he happened to be in Germany when the Berlin Wall came down. He showed me several pictures of that historic event. In one of the pictures he is in a black shiny raincoat among the crowd on the west side of the wall. I could tell it was its west side because it was decorated with overlapping, convoluted graffiti.

As soon as he had his first sip of coffee, I asked him why Dr. T, the Iranian dean of engineering, did not survive his open-heart surgery.

As we talk about him, we can see his magnified photo in the middle section of the *Globe and Mail* on the coffee table. His head looks like the head of Socrates, with a goatee and large skull. They say he had an appropriate philosophical phrase posted above the door of his office, but I have forgotten it now. I did not know he was so important that this prestigious newspaper would dedicate a full page to his obituary.

Dick begins to explain why his patient did not survive. This was the second operation on his heart.

I remember the first one. He had an aneurysm of the left ventricle of his heart due to an old and major myocardial infarction. I remember that because I heard his Iranian name on the loudspeaker in the hospital one day and went to see him in the recovery room. That was the first time I saw him.

Dick rips opens the envelope of a thank-you card from a grateful nurse whose father had been saved by him, which had been lying unread beside a box of chocolates on the coffee table. He looks around for a pen to draw the diagram to explain to me what kind of operation he had performed on the heart of my countryman.

I offer him my red pen. He proceeds to discuss and dissect my friend's heart on the back of that envelope. I understand it at the beginning, but by the end the diagram gets so confused that I cannot make head nor tail of it. I wondered how he managed to work on that tangle of confusion particularly when it is flooded by blood.

"I am going to his funeral in a day or two. Can I have the diagram to show to his wife if she asks?"

"I'd rather explain to her myself, in my office."

There was no autopsy performed on my friend because his death was not unexpected, but I am going to his funeral because it is my turn to visit him. Ten years ago when he was released from the hospital, before he went home, he came to my office to thank me for visiting him in the ICU and also to give me the unsaid message that, unlike most Iranians, he did not have the time or intention of paying back my visit at home. He was not an atypical or an unfriendly Iranian or Canadian; he simply did not have time for new friends. Later, however, he told an Iranian student from the Islamic Republic of Iran, Ahmad, who was on sabbatical leave in his department, that he knew me and liked me.

Ahmad was writing his thesis on how to dry wood scientifically and went back to Iran to make use of his specialty and pay back his debt to the government that had sent him.

While Ahmad was here, one day Ernie, the medical director of the hospital, came to my office and after joking about my wife's bright smile in the photo and asking whether he could borrow it to brighten his office, he told me what he had come to say, "There is an engineering student sent from Iran to study at UVic. He has a wife with a newborn baby. She is very bored staying in their apartment all day. She is a fourth-year pathology resident in Tehran University. Can she come sometimes to your office and watch you work?"

I agreed and she came a few days later. She was smartly dressed with a striped navy blue jacket, long matching skirt and a head scarf with a pale flowery pattern. I extended my hand to her after exchanging *Salaam*. She hesitated for a moment but shook it. I immediately realized that I shouldn't have offered my hand and put her in such an embarrassing position, because shaking hands with strange men is not allowed in Iran for women nowadays.

She sat beside me on a separate chair and listened to my dictation as I was looking at the slides. Sometimes I would move my head away from my microscope to let her see what I was seeing. As soon as I found out she was not a spy and just a normal student, I asked her about education in Iran and particularly about women. When I was in medical school in Tehran in the early 1950s there were 13 girls among the more than 300 students in our class. I wondered what the ratio was today, 15 years after the Islamic Revolution.

She said she had done her medicine in Esfahan, but her cousin who had done it in Tehran told her that the ratio of women to men was about 45:55, almost like the medical school in Vancouver. Then she said if I wanted more accurate information I could ask her husband.

I did, when they invited us, me and my wife, to their small apartment for dinner. He had some booklets full of statistics about the number of students in Iran as well as the number of teachers and the ratio of men to women, all of which took me by surprise. Surprised because of the large numbers of students and teachers. There were many more than the pre-revolutionary time when Iran was a Constitutional monarchy.

I take one chocolate from the box of chocolates on the coffee table as I get up to go back to my office.

2

THREE LOOSE DRAWERS

NOTHING HAS HAPPENED SINCE I LEFT MY OFFICE less than half an hour ago except for being flooded with more light. As I push open the door of my office, a bright orange triangle rushes out to lay half a welcome mat under my feet, brightening the corridor at the same time. By reflex, my hand goes towards the light switch on the wall next to the door to turn it off. Nothing of course happens when I turn it off, because it was already turned off.

The inside of my office is similar to the other offices: an off-white L-shaped bench hugging two of the walls, a brown desk pressing against a bare wall, a wheeled chair at the desk indenting the linoleum floor, and an aluminium cabinet the same colour as the bench. I don't know about other cabinets, but mine includes a disturbing album made of many Polaroid pictures of an unsolved murder. The pictures show a young white woman in her late twenties, beside a pine tree, off a logging road. One picture shows a branch of the tree about two meters above the ground is freshly broken, as if the body has fallen from the sky. The skin of the fingers is superficially chewed away by rodents. Her golden necklace, a fine chain with a small cross, is around her neck, lying on the superficial scratches on the front of her neck. One picture shows the wheel marks of the car that has brought her to that spot, the distance between the two lines shows it was a small car.

The windowless wall is covered with shelves, and the shelves are stuffed with books and boxes of 35 millimetre slides and bundles of glass slides wrapped together with disrupted elastic bands that have lost their elasticity. The books are all shut tight except for a few which have medical journals inserted in them. The glass slides have lost their stain over time, but a bleached foot of a foetus is still discernible with the naked eye on one of them.

On the bench there is a binocular microscope, a dusty dictating machine, a black telephone and the bleached picture of my wife with a radiating smile and raisin-coloured hair. Her hair always glows red in the sunshine.

There is no group photograph on the wall of my office, but my next-door neighbour, Doug, has one. Because he came from Winnipeg a few years after I did, whenever I go to his office to show him a problem slide, I look at his group picture while he is looking at my slide. It shows, in the back row, pathology residents in white coats and pleomorphic faces from the four corners of the world. I don't recognize any of them, but I know all the professors and my teachers sitting in the front row.

Dr. Penner, my first teacher, has not changed or aged. He always looked old, older than his age. The cause of his premature aging was obvious: his excessive exercise outdoors in the sunny Manitoba, and his diet. He jogged in the streets long before anyone else in Canada. He had a car but commuted by bicycle. Not that he rode on it; he ran beside it for the purpose of spending more energy. This is why once a policeman, on a cold Manitoba morning, over a bridge, mistook him for a bicycle thief and arrested him. When he said that he was the head of the Pathology Department at Winnipeg General Hospital, the policeman thought he was bluffing and replied, "Oh, yeah? And I am the Shah of Iran!" Those were the days, of course, when the Shah of Iran was so important that being him was like being the luckiest and the best-dressed man in the world.

Soon after I came from Winnipeg to Victoria, I wrote Dr. Penner a letter to apologize for thinking that he was a bad boss.

His reply reached my hand within a week. He had written it with his familiar but barely legible handwriting on an orange colour sheet of paper: "Dear Nasser, the choice of this paper is not accidental; your letter brought sunshine to my office."

With nothing better to do, I sit at my desk, looking at the objects accumulated over decades in my loose drawers. To compensate for the windows, my drawers open easily, perhaps too easily. They slide out so easily that I am sure they have four little wheels under them. They open with the gentlest pull of a hand, or from the vibrations of the floor if someone walks on it heavily.

In the top drawer I find layers of things, like in an archaeology dig; the sedimented things. At the bottom, there are metallic things like pins, disposable blades and paper clips. A disrupted plastic box of thumbtacks has spilled its pointy contents everywhere, making the search dangerous. I find a chain for holding the bifocal glasses that I did not really need. A round blue souvenir button with the logo of the new General Hospital on it saying, *I was here*, dated 1985, when we moved from the old St. Joseph's to the newly built cement-and-glass hospital out in the countryside among the pine trees.

There are other things that I have collected along the way from other places, mainly hospitals, particularly the Winnipeg General Hospital, like the large glass slide on which the cross-section of both cerebral hemispheres is mounted like a butterfly, and an oval gallstone which looked like a jewel before it dried. Among lighter stuff, I see an English dictionary the size of a matchbox that, like its French counterpart, *Le petit Larousse*, has never helped me with a single word.

Lighter and larger things are on the top, like letters, some from Iran, sent by my mother, some from the rest of the world, sent by friends. They are all old letters. I don't know why I have kept them. Some of the envelopes from Iran are stamped with the head of the Shah, some with the heads of revolutionary clergymen.

The post-revolutionary stamps are more varied and colourful than those of the time of the Shah. One of the more recent stamps depicts a large red eye with the head of a revolutionary woman in Islamic *hejab* replacing its iris, carrying a rifle over one shoulder. I pick it up to see what was so important in it that has made me keep it in this drawer. I don't have to read it all to find out. The reason for it being kept is most likely due to the following phrase from my mother, which I have underlined with a red pen:

Yesterday, three women from the red-light district were executed by revolutionary guards. If you had exchanged any Salam-o-Aleik with any of them, it is time to ask for their forgiveness.

My mother, of course, is speaking tongue in cheek here. By *Salaam-o-Aleik* she means exchanging the words of greetings, literally, saying *Salaam* and receiving the reply of one's *Salaam*. But, since the three victims here are accused of running a prostitution house, it shows that my mother expects men, even her sons, especially if they are not married, to frequent that infamous district.

There are some letters from Moose Jaw, from Dr. Ian. He is the childless colleague who did his residency in pathology in Winnipeg two years after me, even though he was three years older than me. When he finished his training he went to Moose Jaw to work until he could find a better place, but he liked it so much that he stayed there until he retired and died there.

This pale, rigid thank-you card is from Sam, Victor's wife. Victor was the Scottish pathologist who couldn't take it any more, went mad and lost his job. Or perhaps first lost his job and then went mad. I don't know why I have kept this card either.

I don't know what my mother's letters are doing here, in the hospital. It is true that most of the letters I have written to her or my friends were written from hospitals where time, paper and pen are always available, but I always wrote our home address on the envelope. I don't know where the rest of her letters are. Some are at home, I know, in the shoebox where other old letters are, but there should be more. We have moved so many times since we came here, in midsummer 1965, that no matter how organized we were, we were bound to lose something. Maybe these letters that have survived contain specific replies to some specific questions that I had asked my mother about our dead father.

In the middle drawer I find larger things like the multi-use envelope in which I have put the receipts and expenses incurred during an educational trip, for tax purposes. A larger English-to-Farsi dictionary is here that I have brought from Iran. Another Farsi-to-English dictionary is here too. This was given to me when I left my work in the treatment centre for insured workers in Shemiran, Iran. There are also a few burnt-out light bulbs and a small pocket-sized gilded crucifix.

I know why this gilded crucifix is here, though. It used to be on the wall of my office in St. Joseph's Hospital, the one run by nuns, and the one that I ran to, like a refugee, when I left this secular hospital shortly after Victor was fired. My room was not built as a pathology office. It must have been the bedroom or private chapel for a nun. It was located in the dark corridor on the fifth floor attached to the lab. It was long and looked longer when it was bare. It had only one window at one end, opposite this crucifix. The crucifix was nailed so high on the wall that it could have been forgotten when the movers moved everything out. The window opened toward a tall brick chimney with a serrated edge resembling a ruler, rising from the powerhouse adjacent to the parking lot. Once I asked a nun who had changed her black robe for the white uniform of a nurse, why the chimney of their hospital looked like a carpenter's ruler. She said because St. Joseph was a working saint, "That is why the International Day of the Proletariat used to be known as St. Joseph's Day."

When they furnished the room for me, I asked the movers to leave the crucifix where it was. And after five years of working there, when we had to move to the new hospital, I took it with me to hang on the wall of my new office to continue the good times I had while it was on my wall. It remained there for the seven years that I worked there. When the two hospitals became one by amalgamation, I brought it here as a good omen.

Here, first I nailed it to the wall above the door, and soon after that the boss from whom I had run away made up with me and made me his vice-chief. Since I never intended to go higher than being the vice-chief of the lab, and the place was a comparatively secular hospital, I brought it down and kept it in this drawer to take home one day. It is a collector's item now. Soon after the amalgamation, St. Joseph imploded upon itself with a puffing sound like a beached whale, leaving this crucifix behind as its only souvenir.

Our newly hired, energetic colleague steps on the triangular patch of sunshine and enters without knocking. He comes in with a glass slide in his hand, the one I had given to him for consultation. He is good at lymph node pathology. Lymph nodes are difficult for me. They are like bean bags, filled with monotonous, patternless purple dots, each representing a lymphocyte. I can guess what a cell is up to if it has enough cytoplasm, for cytoplasm is what makes cells differ from each other. The nuclei of the cells are all the same, whether from brain, bowel or muscle.

He plays hockey in his spare time. He has spent his childhood in the snowy fields of Quebec playing hockey outdoors. Light hurts his eyes. "Gee! Nasser, you have more light in your room than the tanning salon in the Oak Bay Recreation Centre," he comments while shading his eyes with his free hand. "Can I have your office when you retire?" he asks, semi-seriously.

He can't. I am the last occupant of this office. The hospital is going to build a new Diagnostic and Treatment centre in the parking lot and the whole lab will move there in a few years.

I push the middle drawer back to where it was. I do not want to give him a chance to make fun of me.

My tall learned colleague tells me that the slide I have given to him represents a typical example of cat scratch disease. I tell him that I did not see the pathognomonic stellate abscess in it. He says that was because it was not an acute case. I say that the history did not indicate that the patient owns a cat. He says that it does not matter, because any scratch by any sharp object contaminated with the right virus can cause the same disease.

As he attempts to leave the room, the vibration of the floor causes the middle drawer to slide open, blocking his way. He steps over it with the agility one expects from young hockey players, but immediately turns back to stare at the crucifix sparkling in the drawer.

"Gee! Nasser, what is this? Whose leg are you pulling now?" he exclaims, knowing that I am not a Christian.

"Good omen," I say, "It changed my life as of the day I left this hospital in February of 1978."

"Then why is it here in this dark drawer?"

"Where would you like it to be?"

"Why not put it on the wall, above this doorway, for example?"

"I can't reach it." I said, "You do it for me. You are taller."

He bends down, picks the crucifix up, stands up, and places it on the existing nail high above the door. The gilded pocket-sized crucifix matches its pre-existing negative imprint on the wall like a hand inside a glove.

3

GEORGE THE BIBLIOPHILE

EARLY IN THE MORNING, the L-shaped corridor of the amalgamated lab is dark because the doors of the offices from which it gets its light are closed. Were it not for that inviting band of orange light under the door of my office at the bend of the corridor, this place would be even darker in the mornings. The office doors are wooden and opaque, all painted off-white and each marked with the name of the pathologist who occupies it. We have lost only one room in the lab after the amalgamation. This is why the signs for male and female washrooms are both on the same door. The other washroom is converted to an office for one of the four pathologists who came from the other hospital. The washroom signs are diagrammatic, depicting two simplified human beings standing beside each other as in a wedding picture, one wearing a skirt, the other a pair of pants.

Every time that I pass this door to reach my office, the bitter-sweet notion of amalgamation comes to my mind, and with it comes the sad thought of the loss of George.

George was the librarian of the other hospital and my learned friend. He lost his job due to amalgamation of the two main hospitals of this city. When he was leaving, I was among the few who attended his small goodbye party and said a few words about him. The cake served with the refreshment in the party was no larger than a large muffin, and not many people had attended his party in the lecture room. Even those who came did not stay for long because they too were worried about their jobs. And I do not blame them. There was a lot of duplication of staff before amalgamation. From any two identical positions, one had to go. My speech was very short too and I terminated it by saying, "After George, I might be able to continue working as a pathologist in this hospital; what I am not sure of is whether I can stand this hospital without George."

The door of my office opens inward, and when it does it hides the clipboard on which the roster and many other papers are attached. Several of the pages of the glossy calendar inserted between the wavy plaster of the wall and the wooden frame of the clipboard are hanging over some of the notes and memos. The precarious location of the calendar was supposed to be temporary—just for the first few confusing days of January—but already more than half of its pages are turned over. I might as well leave it there for the rest of this year. The overlapping memos are prematurely sun damaged because of excessive light in the room. The only thing that has not lost its colour to the sunshine is the rectangular cardboard with golden margins. I have deliberately inserted it at that corner of the clipboard so that it would require the minimum number of thumbtacks. It is a handmade souvenir. It is a gift from George to me when he left.

Within the gilded rectangle George has copied a quotation from someone—someone I do not know—with his fine fountain pen and his obsessively regular and contracted handwriting. It reads:

You have three relationships: the one to the body which surrounds you;

the second to the divine cause from which all things come to all;

and the third to those you live with you.

Marcus Aurelius (To himself)

I'm not sure I understand this quotation, but I know it must be important, otherwise George would not have gone through the trouble of framing it for me. George knows a lot but he rarely shows it. I have learned a lot from him, but he does not know it, perhaps because whatever I have learned from him, I have learned it by osmosis. His library was not as frequented as he wished, so he gave a cup of Italian coffee to anybody who went there to borrow a book. He liked to give away books, any book, medical or otherwise. He was nicknamed "Bibliophile" by his intellectual friends, because he not only read a lot of books, he repaired them, and collected them. His wife was a librarian too, but she lived in another city, Vancouver. They would see each other only on weekends when George went there by ferry. I never actually saw George in the act of reading, but I could tell how much he had read by how much he knew. In addition to books, George knew about wine, cheese, art, and had the past experience of managing a hotel. I heard him once arguing with his counterpart in the other hospital, who was also a well-read man, that art was not a mirror to be held in front of nature, but a hammer with which to shape nature.

Whenever George bought a hardcover copy of his favourite philosophy books, he gave me his old paperback with underlined pages and notes on the margins. Most of the times we met in the cafeteria at coffee break, but, before he left, he invited me to his apartment one night.

He was cooking, and his brother-in-law, the husband of his twin sister whom I had never seen, had come from Vancouver and was there too. His brother-in-law did not seem to be sad enough about George losing his job. I asked him why. He said because the job he was losing was not good enough for him. "What is wrong with his job?" I asked, somewhat dismayed by his negative attitude, "I thought being the librarian of a prestigious place like our hospital is the best possible position that he can have. Where do you think he should apply for a job after this?"

"The Library of Congress of the United States of America," said the brother-in-law. I thought he was pulling our legs, but when George got a job in a medical school in Alberta and then was invited to China to computerize their ancient libraries, I realized that the brother-in-law knew George better than I did.

His apartment had a long living room with a table for six at one end to make a dining corner. The long windowless wall that stretched the entire length of the room was covered from floor to the ceiling with leather-bound books that smelled like a shoe shop. The kitchen counter was cluttered with cooking utensils resembling the tools of an alchemist. His kitchen was too orderly for a man who lived by himself. Like a professional, he wore an apron in his kitchen. The air of the kitchen was laced with the smell of French cuisine, wine and garlic.

George sipped a glass of white wine while cooking and talking. He sliced the vegetables much thinner than I thought, even thinner than the professionals on television. He cooked eggplant, familiar to me and all Iranians—that dark purple vegetable that all Iranian children hate before puberty and love afterwards. He sliced them like a bread loaf, rather than longitudinally; the way we were used to. But when George took them out of the frying pan, they were the right golden shade, and when he sprinkled them with some green herbs, I have to confess, they looked and tasted much better than all the seedy eggplants we were force fed as children.

That was just the appetizer. George was in no hurry to get to the end of the dinner. He paid more attention to what he said than what he cooked, but he lost neither the train of his thoughts nor the recipe for his cooking. Occasionally, as I said, he stopped both activities to have a sip of his wine. He had brought the wine by himself from Lyon, France—his dream city and country.

One had to listen carefully when George talked. His voice was low and his lips were almost covered by his overhanging moustache, but whatever he said was loaded with meaning.

George's room had at least twenty times as many books as mine. All my books put together would not occupy a space larger than a normal closet, and most of them, if not all, are given to me by friends, either in Iran or in Canada. Most of the philosophical ones in

English are from George. Those in Farsi are from my learned Iranian friend, Ezzat.

"Why don't you write something, George?" I asked, after dinner, as we sat around the table, "You know so much!"

Either he is too humble, or has been paralyzed by reading too many good books. To encourage him to write, I read my recently published essay, "In Praise of the Middle," in which I had expanded the theme of moderation and avoidance of the extremes by defending the middleness and mediocrity.

George knew about that article, but his brother-in-law did not. George had even helped with typing it and fixing it by adding a few more proper words, and replacing the wrong prepositions with the correct ones. He used his newly acquired IBM computer in the library to do that. He made it look easy, except that he had to type a long string of unfamiliar letters and symbols before he could begin typing. I was sitting beside him, dictating, almost sure that it would win something. For George, however, it was a distraction from the worries of amalgamation.

Maybe without George's contribution, I would have not received the second literary award among the Canadian doctors who had participated in the contest, the number of which I don't know. It was offered by the now folded *MD* magazine. Maybe without that award I would not be writing this book. It did not prove that I had talent, but proved that if I tried my hardest, it would look as if I was talented.

When George and his quiet brother-in-law said that they liked the essay, I was encouraged and told them that I might expand it to make a book out of it. The brother-in-law said that I had already done it. That article was no more than two pages. Was this all in my life that was worth telling? Then I realized that I had to borrow a lot of wisdom and understanding from others, if I were to write a book of at least 250 pages—250 pages because M&S, also known as *The Canadian Publishers*, the only publishing house to which I am planning to send my manuscript, will not even look at a manuscript less than 250 pages. I thought because I was going to talk about cross-cultural things, they would be inclined to publish it.

My intellectual exchange with George, I am ashamed to confess, has always been one-sided. He knows so much that I can never add to his knowledge. Only about Iran, I might be able to help him a little. So, one day, during a coffee break, I told him a half-truth—even though George was the person who had told me for the first time that Nietzsche has said, "A half-truth is twice a lie."

I had said that half-truth several months earlier to George. I told him that I had read in the introduction of the *Alchemy of Happiness* by a Persian theologian, Ghazali, that he had said something very similar to that of Descartes regarding the proof of one's existence. His book was published, I thought, only about seventy years before Descartes. Ghazali too, apparently had thought about how he could prove that he existed, and after much meditation he came up with this saying, *"I am that from which I have news,"* which is the same as saying, "I am the one who is aware that he is." I thought this saying was not unlike Descartes' saying, when he, after a period of meditation and systemic doubt suddenly became aware that he could doubt anything that he wished, but there was no doubt that he was in the process of doubting, and concluded, "I doubt, therefore I am."

"This, of course, does not mean that one has to begin to doubt to prove one's existence." George interjected hurriedly to prevent me from misunderstanding his favourite philosopher. I reassured him that I had not misunderstood Descartes. *Doubting* here is interchangeable with any other human activity that can have *...ing* at the end; like think*ing*, walk*ing*, eat*ing* or writ*ing*.

Two weeks later, after George had done some research he came to me to let me know that Ghazali, whatever he had said, must have said it about five hundred years before Descartes, not seventy years as I had misinformed him.

"It does not matter, George," I interrupted. "The important thing is that if *Ghazali* has said it, he must have said it before Descartes, and not after."

George got a return ticket to Milan in Italy, to check the library which he knew Descartes frequented. He thought if the library had that book, he could find out if Descartes had ever borrowed it, and if so, exactly how many times and on what dates.

Two weeks later, when I ran into George in the cafeteria, he was not as friendly as before the trip, but he was not too unfriendly either. He had not found the book, but on his way back he had stopped in Paris and had seen something that had compensated for his expensive disappointment, something which he called, "the ultimate irony."

We never talked about Descartes after that unfortunate mistake of mine until tonight. Tonight, George suddenly interrupted the conversation and went to his room to come back with the black-and-white photograph of a skull to put it in the middle of the table.

"What is this George?" I asked. "Is the table going to move, next?"

The famous phrase of Descartes was inscribed in black ink on the skull. George explained that when he was walking along the Seine River in Paris he ventured into the Museum of Strange Coincidences.

George already knew that the last twenty years of Descartes' life was spent in Sweden, as the teacher and consultant to the court of the king. As long as Descartes was alive, there was no problem. He was welcomed and was treated almost like a member of the royal family. But, when he died, since he was not a member of the royal family, legally and traditionally he could not be buried in the royal cemetery. So he was buried in a public cemetery.

What George perhaps did not know was the fact that the French were always unhappy with the place Descartes was buried, and were negotiating with the Swedes to bring his remains to France. When the Swedish government finally agreed, the French sent a truck and a wooden box like the ones used for transporting fruits, for Descartes' bones. There was enough room in the box for all the ribs and long bones except for the skull. There was room for the skull, too, but the lid of the box would not close if the skull was put in it. The best the French truck driver could do was to put the skull in another box and begin moving back to France.

Once in France, the truck driver got distracted because he had to attend a union meeting and when he went to the cemetery to deliver the bones, he forgot about the little box containing the skull. The officials looked for it for a long time and when they could not find it, they buried the remaining bones, hoping to add the skull to them if it was ever found.

Several weeks later when the little box containing the skull was found, it was decided that rather than adding it to the rest of the skeleton, they should make a better use of it and phoned the museum on the other side of the river to ask if they were interested in having it. They, of course, were delighted to have it.

I see the strange coincidence, I told George, but I fail to see the irony in it.

"The irony is that the head and the body of the philosopher who is responsible for separation of the body and mind are buried separately," George explained with a smile wide enough to be visible from under his overhanging moustache.

4

THE REST OF THE RESTLESS

I GET UP FROM MY WHEELED CHAIR to go to the doctors' lounge for another cup of coffee. As I get up, a folded sheet of paper towel falls on the floor. It is a note from me to me, written yesterday. It reads, "Don't forget Mars's funeral tomorrow at McCall's Chapel, at 10 A.M."

I phone Donna, the morgue attendant, to see if I have any cases, and, whether I have or not, to let her know that I was going to Mars's funeral and would be back before noon.

"You have three autopsies to do," she tells me, sadly.

The sadness in her voice is for one of the three bodies, that of Mars. She knew Mars very well. Not only was he her boss, he was the one who had hired her and trained her for that job. It was not the job she always wanted to do when she was a little girl, or even when she was a young woman working at the Bay, but she did it so well—as if she was born to become a morgue attendant.

Mars was also the man who hired me right away as soon as I resigned from the lab at the Royal Jubilee Hospital.

"Are they hospital or coroner cases?" I ask Donna, hoping that she would not say hospital cases.

"All three are coroner cases, sent by the new coroner."

Hospital cases are more complicated than coroner cases. They are more complicated, not because of the tangle of plastic tubes and nylon lines trailing in and out of the natural or man-made orifices, but because they are often accompanied by voluminous charts with illegible handwriting. Also, hospital cases often have multiple causes for death in contrast to the coroner cases that always have a single cause or none at all.

Mars was the chief who gave me that long bare room in the old St. Joseph's Hospital, with a small crucifix left on its wall. The first day I went to that hospital, happy as a boy going back to school after a long, boring summer vacation, he saw me from the window of his office on the fifth floor and came down to the parking lot to welcome me. He too must have been spending a good portion of his time looking through the windows of his office. When we reached the lab, he told me that I was hired not only as a pathologist but also as his S.I.C.

Thank you, but what do those letters stand for? I asked, wondering if I had to do some extra thing for him, like spying.

"Second in command," he explained to my relief.

The last time I saw Mars he was in a bed as a patient on the sixth floor of the new General Hospital, the hospital of which he was still the head of its lab and was resisting its amalgamation with the other lab in the other hospital.

I went to visit him. His beefy, hairy legs were sticking out from under the inadequate hospital gown and hanging over the hard edge of the bed. Donna was visiting too. When I arrived she was standing behind him, on the edge of the bed, trying to pull him up and to keep her own balance with his weight. I gave his calf a heave and we laid him horizontally on the bed. As soon as he was horizontal he commented, "You don't know how heavy your legs are until you lose their function."

Mars had lost the function of his legs the previous weekend. He had many daughters, one wife, and no sons. He liked his wife and his daughters equally, but he seemed to like his last daughter the most. Mars, like most men, did not discuss personal matters with his colleagues or friends. He missed coming to work only one day in his twenty-seven years of uninterrupted service, and, somewhat ironically, the next day he was brought to his work place in an ambulance.

I know legs are heavy, I commented. This is perhaps why those who have one artificial leg can run faster and longer than expected. They don't have to carry the weight of one leg.

Mars laughed a short laugh at my pathetic attempt to inject some humour into a tragedy.

While his eyes were looking at the ceiling, Mars stopped laughing to show me with his finger the headline of the daily newspaper. It read, "Missing Chief Coroner. Abduction Feared."

"What do you want me to do about it?" I asked, somewhat perplexed.

If the coroner was found dead, and I happened to be the pathologist who performed the autopsy on him, Mars wanted me to represent the medical staff of the hospital and go to his funeral and say a few words about him. Before I could decline, however, Mars died a sudden death in front of our eyes, most likely due to pulmonary embolism. Our pushing and pulling might have hastened his death by mobilizing a blood clot from his leg to travel to his lungs.

I did not like his request a bit and right away I wished that Mars had died a day or two earlier so that he wouldn't have time to ask me for such a big favour.

Fear of public speaking, they say, is worse than fear of death for many. I had lost most of my fear when I joined the speakers' group of the Victoria Medical Society. My problem was, and still is, that I could not make a good speech when I did not know the subject very well.

All I knew about the missing coroner was that he was a lonely man, with no wife, children, friends or relatives. More than once, while he was waiting by the locked door of the morgue early in the morning, he had told me that his great-grandfather had been a drummer at the battle of Waterloo for the British troops. I also knew that he had a habit of moving his dentures with his tongue when he talked.

I am late for Mars's funeral. I did not know he had so many friends, none of whom I knew. The inside must be full; otherwise so many people would not be standing outside. I recognize most of the doctors and some of their spouses among them.

Everybody is in a sombre mood. They are listening to the loudspeaker protruding from the upper edge of the white wall like a gigantic morning glory. Some smile a little when their eyes meet mine, but I don't smile back. Do they miss him or do they merely think they ought to be here? I am glad that I came.

I move closer to the entrance door. In contrast with Tehran where crowds were so dense that if you threw a needle up in the air it would not reach the ground, there is always room to move within a crowd here. I crane my neck to look inside the hall. An invisible piano is playing somewhere behind the curtain. Mars's wife is dressed in black, accentuating the ivory whiteness of her arms and her long delicate neck. Her wide brimmed black hat makes her look like her black-and-white picture that Mars always had on his desk. She is sitting in the front row along with her daughters. No one is talking. The stained glass window above the drawn curtain depicts a man with a lit lantern in one hand and a searching look in his eyes. Perhaps Rumi was referring to this man when he said in one of his *Ghazals*—the one in which each line ends with "I am longing for" or "I am looking for."

Yesterday, in the broad daylight

Our Master, tired of the beasts and ghouls

Was looking for a human, with a lantern in hand.

"There is no such a thing in this place."

"We've looked for it before," he was told.

"That which cannot be found is what I am looking for."

Said the Master.

The filtered sunlight through the stained glass window falls on the heads and shoulders of the seated mourners like rainbow fragments. The irreverent dust particles dance along the slanted monochromic columns of light. A high-ranking police officer is among the mourners, wearing a navy blue uniform and six suns on his shoulders. I did not know Mars had such a high-ranking police friend or relative.

The soft-spoken speaker is praising Mars for his hard work. And I agree with him. He was a working kind of chief. He was different. He made the monthly roster himself rather than asking his secretary to do so. Whenever he was not sure whose name to put under certain duties, he would put his own initials. When the speaker said that Mars worked so hard that his colleagues often referred to him as a workaholic, however, I conclude that he did not know Mars as well as I did. The speaker, however, is a good speaker. He must be used to it. He is in no hurry. He doesn't change colour when he talks—or if he does, he is lucky that the place is dim. His hands do not shake. Even the sheet of paper in his hand that is well known to accentuate the slightest tremor of a hand, does not tremble.

One of the first things that I learned about public speaking was not to talk with a note in hand. It diminishes the sincerity of the speaker, especially if the speaker wishes to introduce someone he claims to know. You should have notes, of course, but not visible notes. Notes should be written but should also be hidden in a handy pocket or in the fold of a sleeve, just for reassurance, or in case you have to quote something where accuracy counts.

I try to listen carefully to see if I could learn more about Mars, but my thoughts keep drifting.

How am I going to talk about the coroner if he is found dead today?

As I said, I don't mind public speaking, provided it is about something I know or at least about something that I think I know. During the weeks before the Iranian revolution, for example, when I was excited about it and wishing for its success, the Victoria Medical Society asked me to talk about it and predict what was going to happen if the revolution succeeded. They were worried that Iran, by getting rid of the Shah, might jump from the frying pan into the fire. I reassured them that this would not happen and that most likely the reverse would occur. My prediction, of course, did not come true, but the speech went quite well because I thought I knew what I was talking about.

I began to leave before the service was over because I had three autopsies to do. I whispered this along with repeated apologies as I made my way through the dense pack of surgeons. Most of the younger ones understood and moved back to give me more room to pass, but some of the older ones blocked my way to whisper their tired joke in my ear, "Bodies can wait."

As I leave the chapel, I wonder if all my friends and relatives who might care to come to my funeral could fill at least the first two rows of this chapel.

5

MORGUES DO NOT HAVE WINDOWS

THE ONLY PLACE WHERE I CAN WORK IN PEACE and without distraction is in the morgue because morgues do not have windows.

"You have three autopsies to do," Donna's voice replicates in my mind as I go down to the ground by a reluctant elevator. I have to walk in the sunshine on the ground for a short distance before I descend to the morgue by stairs. I help Donna undress the body of the first case which is that of the former coroner. He was found dead on the concrete floor of the spiral stairs of a parkade downtown. The cause of death is obvious, a fall, but since he was well known and his death was not witnessed, the new coroner has ordered an autopsy, mainly for documentation.

The former coroner never ordered an unnecessary autopsy, but any autopsy that he did order had to be followed by an inquest. He had conducted so many of these hearings that some of the citizens of this small city had served twice as jury members.

I feel somewhat responsible for the death of this man. I always do. I feel somewhat responsible for any death that happens in my vicinity, whether I know the deceased or not. But I feel a little more responsible for the death of this man. Even if he had suicidal tendencies to begin with, the method he chose to kill himself might have had something to do with what I had told him about two weeks ago, as an expert witness, in an inquest in the court-house.

That night in the courthouse the coroner had arranged for two inquests. The first was a case of a drunken pedestrian run over by a car driven by a sober driver. It could have been finished in five minutes or less, had he not prolonged it by unnecessary questions.

To prolong the session, as he was sitting comfortably in his high chair under the large picture of the Queen and the two flags, he looked carefully through the file in front of him and asked me, "Doctor! In addition to the high level of alcohol in the blood of this unfortunate pedestrian, I see another test result in this file showing a high level of alcohol in the urine as well. What is the significance of this test Doctor?"

"No significance, Your Honour," I said, and quickly explained that the impairment generated by consumption of alcohol was due to its effect on the brain cells. Since it is the blood that circulates in brain, it is only the blood alcohol level that counts. The stenographer, who was sitting alone in the well of the almost vacant theatre, chuckled, inappropriately I thought, as she was typing every word that came out of anybody's mouth.

To make the coroner feel that his question was not too irrelevant, I added, "Of course, if urine were to irrigate the brain, your point would have been well taken, Your Honour."

The stenographer laughed louder and her laughter made the matter worse. The six members of the jury smiled like school children behind their desks.

The coroner did not laugh. Nor did he ask why I had ordered the urine test if its result was going to be irrelevant. Instead, the coroner bent down and pulled out another folder, looked at it for a while as if hesitating to introduce it that night or another night, and finally said: "You are excused, Doctor, but stick around. Time permitting; we might get to the second case tonight."

Time permitting? This is the worst kind of waiting, worse than waiting for the ferry. One does not know how long one has to wait; half an hour, one hour, or two?

I waited for two dark hours in that well-lit hall, either pacing the length of the marble floor or sitting on the slippery wooden benches. God knows how many times I looked at the plaques and pillars displaying the serious portraits of men with much facial hair. There were notes on the walls with warnings about things one should not do in the courthouse. I had two Styrofoam cups of burning coffee dispensed by a singing vending machine, before I was called back.

The commissioner of the court came out and called me by my name, no title, and the first name of my father, as if I were an inmate in a prison.

The coroner was in the same seat and I was led to the same box, even though I knew where I had to go.

The commissioner presented the Holy Bible again for me to swear by and I did. I swore that I would tell the truth, the whole truth, and nothing but the truth, in the same way that I had always done with no questions asked.

"Do you believe, Doctor, in the book you are swearing by?" asked the coroner.

"Yes, Your Honour."

"Do you believe in Our Lord?"

"Yes of course, Your Honour."

"Do you believe in God?"

"No, Your Honour, I mean not yet."

"No?!" the coroner exclaimed, trying to look surprised.

"Not yet, Your Honour, but I have not given up looking for God. I am one of those atheists who wishes there were a God." I uttered the last word with the intensity of a believer.

He went silent. His silence superimposed on the pre-existing silence of the vacant hall of the court worried me. I am not proud of what I said, but I had to tell the truth. I don't know if it is a sin or it is illegal to swear by the Bible if one does not believe in God. All I wanted to do was to save taxpayers' money by shortening the duration of the inquest. I have been swearing on the Bible since my first court case in Cranbrook, BC, in 1969. I had gone there from Winnipeg as soon as I finished my training to become their first and only pathologist.

Only in my first appearance as an expert witness was I asked about my religion before being presented with the Bible. I told them that I was an ex-Muslim. They missed the ex and began looking for a Koran for me to swear by. After they looked in vain for a long time, the judge asked me if I wished to *affirm*.

I agreed to affirm without knowing what exactly it entailed, and the case began. Never again, after that first case, had I been questioned about the sincerity of my oath until that night.

I am sure the coroner was hurt by my abrupt replies on the first case and was trying to take revenge by opening the door for the jury to ask the questions they always wanted to ask an Iranian atheist, but had never had the chance.

The first jury member raised her arm. The coroner allowed her to speak.

"How can I be sure that a non-believer in God is telling the truth?"

"But I believe in all the prophets and saints, and I am always looking for God."

"What do you think would happen to you if you lied?"

"I would suffer its bad consequences."

"What are its bad consequences for you?"

"All sorts of discomfort. Telling the truth is easier than telling lies, at least for me. Once you lie you have to keep remembering what you have said, and keep lying to match your first statement, but truth is said once."

"Do you ever lie?"

"Occasionally."

"On what occasions?"

"On the occasions where I feel that the questioner wants to abuse my truthfulness."

"Is it fair to ask, Sir, how could you believe in the twenty-four thousand prophets and saints, as you said, but not in the God who sent them?"

"This is a fair question Madam. I have been asking this question of myself, every day, maybe more than five hundred times a day. I don't have a good answer for it yet, but I have reached the conclusion that looking for God is perhaps superior to finding Him. Because a thing found is a limited thing, and God, I am told, is unlimited. One has to make God small to fit in one's brain."

A middle-age motherly looking woman raised her hand to be excused. Permission denied, rather than retracting her arm to its initial position, she used it to ask a question.

"What about your mother? Does she believe in God? Does she have a religion? And if she does what in the world is the name of her religion, if you don't mind?"

"I don't know Madam. She was a pious woman, but never mentioned either the name of the God or that of her religion."

"Didn't she teach her religion to her children?"

"No. How could she?"

"Do you know why?"

"I am not sure Madam. Perhaps she hoped that her children would find God by themselves when they grew up. It could also be that she knew children in general are prone to do the reverse of what they are told to do. Who knows? Maybe she was afraid that one of her children might rebel and say *no* to her; the word she never wanted to hear from her children. Or, maybe my mother was not sure that her own religion was the right one because whenever I heard her talking to God at her praying mat she was asking God, '*Show me the straight way*' in Arabic."

What I did not say in the court was that I did have a God, as a child, but I lost my God in Sharaf High School in Tehran during recess time after the Chemistry class in grade nine, when we learned about the Law of Lavoisier. By mixing two chemicals, probably iron and oxygen, Lavoisier proved that nothing comes out of nothing, and nothing disappears into nothingness. Right away, half of the class began to develop doubt by asking each other, "Then, where did God come from?" And by the end of the next year half of the doubters had lost their doubt and were sure that there was no God.

"How about your father, was he a religious person or an atheist?"

"I cannot tell you much about my father. I never saw him pray during the first six years of my life, and after that he died."

The only male jury member, the one with spiky hair, asked for permission to speak. His face was familiar but I did not know where I had met him. He could be one of the repeat jurors.

"Did I hear you correctly that your mother did not marry again after the death of your father?"

"Correct."

"Is it fair to ask about the belief of your siblings?"

"It is unfair, but I will tell you anyway. I don't know about my two sisters, but as long as I can remember, when we were young, at least the seven brothers believed as I did. Some of my brothers were even worse than me as far as belief in God was concerned. When I lost my God, for example, I was sad about it, and I envied those who believed in God as much as I envied the rich. But one of my older brothers, after losing his belief in God, began arguing against God in the school and made several of his friends lose their God."

"Did your mother say anything to him when he spoke against God?"

She did not know about it. He was doing it, as I said, in the school. But a few years earlier, when he was forcing us to pray at home because one of his teachers in the elementary school had convinced him that praying is good, I told my mother about it and she said that he was doing too much and too soon. Despite all that, I don't know what good thing he had done that one day I heard my mother telling him, "You are the most religious among my children."

The hall went silent for a while; nothing could be heard for a few seconds, not even the distracting sound of the stenographer, because she had stopped typing.

"Would you like to *confirm*, then, doctor?" The coroner finally broke the silence.

I was not sure if he said *affirm* or *confirm*; but whatever it was, I knew it was a good way out, so I said, "Yes, I would like to do that, Your Honour."

"Had you done that in the beginning, you could have saved yourself and the court and the taxpayers of this country a lot of time and money," the coroner scolded with a conciliatory tune before turning to the second case.

The second case concerned a young, overweight woman who had thrown herself from her apartment on the thirteenth floor of a high-rise building to the underlying gravel parking ramp.

"The police investigation revealed that there was a party on the second floor of the same building, to which she was not invited," the coroner informed the jury while looking at me.

"Yes, Your Honour, it could be true, but I don't see the connection."

"Is it possible, Doctor, that she went there anyway, uninvited, and jumped or was pushed from its balcony?"

"It is not possible, Your Honour."

"What makes you so sure, Doctor?"

"It was the depth of the imprint of the pebbles of the parking ramp on her skin that makes me sure, Your Honour, that she fell from a much higher level than the second floor."

The coroner sank into deep sad thought.

To soften the impact of my testimony, I said, "But I am sure that she did not feel any pain when she hit the ground."

"How so?" The coroner woke up.

"Because pain is for the living, Your Honour. It is not for the dead. By the time she hit the ground she was not alive anymore. It takes time for the pain to travel from the site of injury to reach the brain, and time was what she did not have any longer.

"The court is adjourned," the coroner announced.

That was the last time I saw this man alive, and those were the last words I heard from him.

Now I see him dead and silent. His whale-shaped body in its wrinkled grey suit is heavier than he seemed when he was alive. I don't know why human beings become heavier after death. Maybe the soul has a lightening effect on the body. Maybe it is the Anti-Matter that scientists are looking for all the time.

I go through the routine of describing the outer aspects of the body before I get to the inside: The hair is grey. The irises are blue. The pupils are regular but unequal, the left measuring 0.3 cm in diameter, the right 0.5. He appears older than the 64 printed on the toe tag. The external ear canals are plugged by blood clots. A superficial scrape is present immediately above the right Achilles tendon. One shoe is missing.

Donna has to invert the pockets before undressing any corpse or cutting away the clothes with scissors. A few coins drop on the painted cement floor of the morgue, amounting to thirteen cents. No wedding ring. No ring mark. No watch, no wallet, and no keys.

Donna puts the coins in a plastic bag and marks it with the name, number and the date. It will be sent to the safe later in the day, when I am gone.

Bundles of grey hair, similar to his scalp hair are attached to the sole of his socks. He must have been pacing his room without slippers the night before.

A young policeman brings the missing shoe to the door of the morgue, hesitant to approach the stainless steel table.

"Where did you find it?" I ask to make the policeman feel more at ease, and to let him know that he had found an important clue.

"It was located at the bottom of the well of the parkade, at Johnson."

"You mean the shoe?"

"No, Sir, the body."

"Where was the shoe? It is an important clue."

"It was on the roof of the antique shop, next to the parkade."

"Thank you," Donna says to the constable as she accepts the shoe and places it in the green plastic bag next to his other shoe and the rest of his belongings.

"How high is that parkade?" I ask the policeman, before he hurries to go.

"It is a five-storey building, Sir!" He holds up five fingers as he says this.

"Did you find his car on the top floor?"

"There is no car registered under his name."

I leave Donna in the morgue to sew up the body cavities and get ready for the next case, while I go to my office to dictate my findings. I always record my findings right after I finish a case. I don't want to mix the weight, shape, colour and consistency of the internal organs of one body with those of another in my brain.

6

A CLUSTER OF CUMULUS CLOUDS

As IT IS, it takes Donna longer to straighten things up than it takes me to go upstairs and record my findings. Normally, I dictate them, but this time I want to do the summary of my findings in longhand. I have to be careful. I have to try to tabulate my postmortem findings in such a way that they appear to be related, preferably each item resembling the result of the preceding item, or the preceding item appears as the cause of the next finding, without my having said it. I gather any information that I have, whether it is supplied by the coroner or by the dead coroner while we waited behind the door of the morgue. The ante mortem fact that the coroner had told me that his grandfather was a drummer in the battle of Waterloo becomes part of my postmortem findings. I just put the ante mortem findings and those extracted from the history in brackets.

Provisional Autopsy Summary:

1—(History of drumming in the family)
2—Fall, unwittnessed
3— Hairline fracture at the base of skull
4—Blood clot in external ear canal—bilateral
5—(Absence of friends, family and relatives)
Provisional cause of death: Brain damage secondary to a fall.
Final diagnosis: Pending microscopic examination.
Note: No toxicology ordered.

I make a photocopy of the provisional summary for myself before taking it along with the tape to the office of the secretaries to be typed. I might need it as a prompt when I eulogize him in the courthouse where he sat and listened for forty years.

The day the coroner threw himself from the roof of the parkade, according to the information supplied by the new coroner, coincided with the sunny day that my wife came to my office to take me out for a lunch together.

It was a grade A, perfect Victoria autumn day. Mitra was on time. Her face, as always, was as immaculate as the glowing face of a girl on the cover of a glossy magazine for women and dressed better than a model. She drove and I sat, as always, on the passenger side in her unroofed, two-seater, two-tone dream car.

I watched as she drove, sometimes looking at her perfect profile, sometimes at the passing trees that rose as we approached and sat as we passed. Sometimes I turned towards her to say something to make her laugh. Her raisin-coloured hair was held in place by a navy blue baseball cap, matching the iridescent blue of her car. Her ponytail flowed horizontally in the air like the mane of the Mustang that she just overtook.

She drives fast. The happier I am the more worried I get when she drives so fast. She drives fast even when we are not late for anything. I am not afraid of speed. I sometimes go fast myself, but when I am a passenger in her car her fast driving deprives me of watching the people on the sidewalks. The sky above the street, high above the angulated skyline, was clear and blue, studded with cottony clusters of cumulus clouds, partially on fire.

We pass the tourists with grey hair and yellow sunglasses. The women wearing straw hats with red ribbons, the men baseball hats, some with a name, some without. The men had short khaki pants and hairy legs. Old men and women bite into their ice cream cones with their insensitive dentures and the enthusiasm of children. None of them looks at the endless baskets of flowers hanging from the blue lamp poles, the flowers that I always thought were earmarked for tourists.

It was then that I commented to my wife, out of the blue, that anybody who commits suicide on such a perfect day should have his brain examined.

She did not laugh. She does not laugh these days so much as she used to. She suggested we share a lottery ticket. I agreed, but, not finding a convenient parking spot, we forgot about it.

I don't know how to begin my eulogy for the coroner. I might begin with the drum, and end with a dream, or begin with a dream and end with a drum. I should not forget to emphasize his plugged ear canals. Maybe I should terminate my eulogy by saying, "whoever kills himself on a glorious and grade A Victoria Day must have a cloudy interior."

Maybe I would use the blood clots in his ear canals to conclude that he was perhaps listening to another drummer with another ear when he fell to his death. Or maybe I should make use of his plugged ear canals and conclude that he was listening to the mystic Rumi who said, "Your external ears are like cotton balls in your internal ear. Put a cotton ball in each of your ears so that you can hear the secret with your internal ear."

7

A ROUND-BURNING KEROSENE LAMP

MY SECOND BODY IS THAT OF A SEVENTY-FOUR YEAR OLD RETIRED MAN who has spent the last twenty years of his life playing golf, twice a week. The accompanying coroner's note contains the summary of what went on between the dead man and his wife the night before.

"I don't feel very well," he had said to his wife the day before. "I think I will skip playing golf tomorrow." The wife did not think that it was anything serious, but when night came and they went to bed together, she could not sleep. In the silence of the early hours of the morning, the wife noted that her husband had stopped breathing. She touched his pulse; she could not feel it. She touched his chest to feel his heartbeat; he did not have one. She jumped on his abdomen and began vigorous artificial respiration. After two or three minutes, the husband sat up, bewildered to find his wife sitting on him, and he asked for an explanation. The wife, both happy that her husband had come back to life and ashamed that she was sitting on him, said that he had been dead and she had brought him back to life.

"No such luck," the husband playfully told his wife, "I was in a deep sleep."

The wife believed him, but before they went back to sleep, she made him promise that he would get an appointment with their family physician in the morning to have a general check-up with particular attention to his heart.

The next day the husband spent a good part of the morning making an appointment with his physician for one o'clock in the afternoon. After lunch, when the man bent down to tie his shoelaces, he fell over. This time neither the wife nor the ambulance crew or the doctors in the emergency department could bring him back to life.

In summary, the coroner wants me to differentiate between death and sleep. I don't think I will be able to tell the difference, but I get to work anyway, hoping to prove that sleep is a reversible death.

The body is that of a lean, well-built man who appears slightly younger than the stated age of seventy-four. Judging by the ease with which Donna can move the body single-handedly from the stretcher to the steel table, rigor mortis seems to be fully established.

His heart is enlarged, heavy and flabby. The heart muscle is marbled with white fibrous scars secondary to previous heart attacks. The coronary arteries are narrowed due to athero-sclerosis, but there is no evidence of total occlusion and no sign of a blood clot in the lumen. It is one of those hearts that can go either way at any moment. The wife is right. The heart must have stopped the night before and then restarted due to her effort. It is hard to be sure, though.

When old couples are in one bed together and one dies, the other always knows. Some-times, the other is afraid to know or to touch with a toe to make sure. Some pretend to be asleep and wake up late the next morning. Some are braver and try to bring the dead back to life.

Some damaged hearts do not start by themselves, some do. Some start and stop a few times before the terminal arrest, not unlike the round-burning kerosene lamp on our *korsi* on winter nights. When our mother turned it off, it would spout a flame, once or twice, with a spit-like sound, before finally blacking out.

Did he dream anything during his interrupted sleep? I can't tell and I can't even guess. I don't know what the dreams of a golfer would be like. I don't play golf. Golf balls are among the few balls I did not get a chance to play with in the grassless land of my child-hood.

The new coroner is wasting my time. As far as I can tell, nothing suspicious ever hap-pens in this town. These old couples are playing peek-a-boo with each other and want to make a referee out of me. They blunt the sharp line of demarcation between life and death. They go to sleep as if they are dead. They die to appear as if they are asleep.

I try to phone the coroner before tabulating my findings. She is not in her office. Her answering machine is saying that the office is closed between noon and 1 p.m., asking me to leave a message after the beep.

I leave my message and add that our cut-off time for forensic cases is one o'clock, too, and, since I have not heard from her about the third case, the one for which she had sent a Polaroid picture of the deceased the night before, it cannot be done today. Then, I soften my refusal by adding, "Maybe it can be done on Monday morning, either by me or one of my colleagues." The answering machine politely ends the recording after it hears my last word.

In one of her last letters, my mother wrote: "These days, when I open my eyes in the morning, I am surprised that I still see the world."

I told her, "Dear Mother, stay on a little longer; the world is just getting interesting."

She stayed on for a short while to prove to me that she could move the time of her death back and forth at will.

Then, one night, she died without warning. No autopsy was ordered on her because her death was as natural as a natural death can get. Nevertheless, I feel I should perform an autopsy on her despite my reluctance to do a third autopsy in one day.

Perhaps my mother is my third obligatory case. I have to do it because every adult body could be the mother or the father of somebody. If I begin to make exceptions, I might lose my job. Besides, I don't want to find the cause of her death. I want to find out what was going on in her mind when she did not teach us her religion. I don't have her body at hand. The only things I have from her are her letters in my drawer and what is left in my memory.

8

HAVING A HAIRCUT

I TOLD MY EDITOR THAT I WAS GOING TO TAKE IT EASY this long weekend and not write anything or think about the book.

I began by spending a good part of the Saturday morning with my wife, putting old photos from my disrupted album along with some she had recently borrowed from my sister-in-law, Pari, in the new album. Pari is younger than me, but she has collected more family photos. She is the archivist of the family. Among the borrowed pictures are two group-photos from late 1940s, when Agha Khan, the father of Prince Ali Khan who married the movie star, Rita Hayworth, had come to Tehran to visit the homeland of his dead ancestors and his living relatives. In one, Aunt Seddigheh, in respectful black, is standing in front of Agha Khan to introduce others. Agha Khan is seated in a luxurious wheel-chair next to a European-looking lady who is sitting like a queen on a low chair. She could be his wife. I have forgotten her name, but Dr. Naz, the Ismaili pharmacist in our neighbourhood, knows her by name and he added the respectful prefix *Bibi* to her name when he mentioned it to me. In the other group picture, Ali Gholi Khan, my civilian brother-in-law with sparkling, raven black hair, has replaced Aunt Seddigheh. Agha Khan seems to be more amused listening to him than to our aunt.

Among the people standing behind and beside Agha Khan are my mother, General Javadi, the man who lent money to my mother during the Second World War; Sohrab and Chehry, the two sons of Colonel Sharabi; and Ninish, short for Nosratollah, the blond European-looking young man who is my age and is the cousin of Sia. No one in the family ever explained to me why he has turned out to be so enviously good looking. There are about twenty more people in the picture, including the first three of my siblings. The rest of us — the six brothers from Mehdi down to Mahmood — are not here, not because we were not invited but because we did not consider the occasion important enough to attend. It was the time that we were beginning to lose our respect for the authorities, be it the Prime Minister, the Shah, or Agha Khan, relative or not.

Here is another group picture that looks like the negative image of the previous group picture because it shows only the six missing boys: Mehdi, Hossein, Nasser, Hamid, Majid and Mahmood. We are standing in line in the living room of our voluminous cousin, Shazdeh Fatollah Mirza in Torbat. We are his guests from Tehran, but he also has another guest from Tehran and wants to show off the sons of his dead uncle to him. His guest is a tall lean man in a grey suit with a tie and a short grey beard, carrying a cane. He is shaking hands with us, one by one, from Mehdi downward. His name is Bahar, but is known by his Arabic nickname Malek-ol-sho'ara, meaning "The king of the poets," bestowed upon him by the last Shah, if not by his father. Besides being a poet, he is truly a learned man. He is the one who, in addition to composing old-style Persian poetry, had written a book in two volumes about recognition of style in classic Persian poetry. In its introduction he says that in the same way that an expert in Persian carpets can tell if a carpet is woven, say, in Kerman or Kashan, one can tell if a poem is composed by Sa'di or Ferdowsi, because each has a distinct style. He is also the one who, near the end of his life, perhaps under the influence of the left-wing activists, made the long *Ghassideh* for peace; *The Owl of War*, that begins with this line:

Cut the throat of the owl of war

Open the cage of the pigeon of peace.

Yazdan Mirza, the leaner and the younger brother of our host, was there too, but he is not in the picture. He too was an established poet in old-style Persian poetry. In addition to being the brother of the host, he was there because soon he was going to marry the daughter of Bahar, Maah-malek.

When Bahar was reading his *Owl of War* to him before publication, Yazdan Mirza extemporaneously, said the following line that rhymed seamlessly with the *Ghassideh* while making use of a well-known Persian proverb:

Suppose the lid of the pot was off

Where was the shame of the cat?

Bahar liked it so much that he inserted it in his *Ghassideh* without referring to its composer, but gave his daughter to him. Every Iranian knows, of course, that the line is a modified Persian proverb, but the cat in the context of the poem is also an oblique reference to the American policy in Iran in those days.

Those days were the days that the Cold War had just started and the communists had begun their "peace attack" against the West, particularly the United States of America. The Tudeh party, as well as their sympathizers, who imitated the Russian policies like a monkey, was collecting signatures for peace, not only from the mass of ignorant young, but also from some elderly intellectuals like Colonel Sharabi, the author of *SOS*, and Bahar. Pari, I remember, was one of the young students who went door to door to collect signatures for peace.

When Bahar was reading his *Ghassideh* in the public hall where many genuine peace-loving people sat in the front row, including Colonel Sharabi in a civilian suit, a dog was heard barking in the street. A quick-witted person in the audience cried, "This is the Voice of America!" a parody of the announcer for Radio America in Tehran. Needless to say, everybody in the hall, except for the front row, laughed and applauded the comment.

Here is another group photograph. I am the only one among my siblings who is present in this photo. And Sia, short for Siavosh, one of the two brothers of Pari, is the only member of our extended family who is there with me. This was taken in the courtyard of the Ghasr Prison in Tehran, in the summer of 1954, a year after the military branch of the Tudeh Party was discovered. The total number of the officers caught was about 323. Twenty-three of them were executed, the rest imprisoned. We were divided among the four sections of the prison. Sia and I were in the section 4 which contained about seventy prisoners. They are all young men in military uniform without epaulets, stars or suns. Mitra does not know any of them, except for Sia and me. This last group picture makes me want to leave the house and go for a walk.

I look for my walking stick. I have not gone for a walk since I began this book. I used to go to walk on the sands of the Cadboro Bay beach, the beach that was so close to our old house that I used to refer to it as my backyard. I find my walking stick and pick it up, but put it back, having changed my mind about going for a walk. Walking on that sand would take me back to my book, and my book is what I don't want to think about this weekend. I go to have a haircut, instead.

I haven't been to a barber shop or a hair stylist, as they call themselves nowadays, for a long time. My last haircut was done at home by a recently arrived Iranian named Bahman. He was a friend and relative of Ali, my new atypical Iranian friend. Atypical, because he does not look or behave like any of my other Iranian or Canadian friends. To begin with he is the champion at wrestling, with a black belt from Iran and brown belt from Canada. He is young but is already a veteran of the Iran-Iraq war. He was not in the army but fought as a civilian volunteer. He did not have a gun but a Jeep. He said those were the best days of his life. He knew the exact moment that Iran was invaded by Iraq: at one-thirty in the afternoon of Tuesday, thirty-first of Shahriar, Persian Calendar 1359—equal to 1980 AD.

It was dark when we picked up Bahman from the ferry coming from Vancouver. From his Farsi accent, and not from his blond moustache, pale skin and wavy blond hair, it was obvious that he was from the city of Rasht in north of Iran.

As we were coming back to Victoria, Ali, driving in his small low-powered car compared to his musclebound body, turned his neck with difficulty towards me to tell me that Bahman, sitting beside him, was a barber in Vancouver. To have acknowledged the receipt of this information, I commented that in my experience Iranian barbers have done a much better job on my hair than their Canadian counterparts.

"And no one among the Iranian barbers," Bahman acknowledged my comment, in Farsi, deliberately exaggerating his Rashti accent to show his sense of humour as well, "does a better job than the Rashtis."

Bahman was not a barber in Iran. Cutting hair was the last of the six or seven various temporary jobs he had found to survive after he had come to Vancouver with little money in his pockets. "On my first morning in Vancouver," Bahman explained, "I saw a parking lot covered with snow, and the cars had trouble coming in and out." So he bought a shovel with his last dollars and without negotiating with the parking attendant cleared the lot from the snow and slush. The parking attendant liked his work and gave him enough money to survive for a week.

Ali said that Bahman had brought the tools of his trade with him and, if I wanted, he could give me a good haircut. I wanted one, but I had to accompany them to Ali's house first so that they could break their daylong fast, by doing their *Eftar*. I did not know that it was the fasting month of Ramadan. Nor did I know that Ali and his friend were fasting. Ali had not told me that he was fasting. No wonder his short temper was even shorter that evening.

Ali's house was cluttered with scattered stacks of videotapes of his matches. His son, Omid—meaning hope in Farsi—was watching a video in which a wrestler broke the bones of his opponent's forearm. In another, by the sound of it, I thought Ali's ribs broke when he fell over his opponent whose head he had held under his arm like a watermelon. But when Dr. David, the attending physician whom I happened to know and had many good conversations with in the doctors' lounge, stopped the match to check the bones, he saw that it was his opponent's neck that was almost broken.

One of the videos showed Omid kicking a girl in the shin during a match. The girl cried and Omid won, but he did not seem to be proud of it. In another video, where Ali was badly immobilized by his opponent, I asked him how he managed to finally untangle himself. He said that he was almost ready to lie on his back and give up, when he heard Omid's voice, "Baba! Try your own way, the one you've taught me." And that was enough to give him the badly needed extra power to free himself.

Ali volunteered to tell me that fasting was hard for him. Knowing how much he liked to eat, I told him that I was not surprised. But he surprised me by saying that it was not the abstinence from food or water that bothered him, but the avoidance of using bad words or thinking bad thoughts during fasting.

When Ali was working as a bouncer in a bar in the Italian district in Toronto, frequented by bikers with leather jackets and metallic accessories, he had to incapacitate one of them without killing him. He volunteered to teach me his method. I thought about it for a second, and then declined with thanks. I thought it would be less painful to avoid going to those places than successfully incapacitating a dangerous man.

Ali's rented house looks ordinary from the outside, but extraordinary from the inside. There are more things on the walls than on the floor. A fanned peacock tail greets you on the wall, upstairs, in front of the stairs. A curved saber is suspended from the ceiling in a corner. The skin of a spotted tiger is splashed on the ground. A lone large poster of a lion occupies another wall. Most of the objects show his intense love for Imam Ali, the son-in-law and the nephew of the Prophet Mohammad (Salute), as well as the favourite imam of the Persians or Shi'eh Moslems. A framed hand written Ali in calligraphic Farsi is on the wall in front of me at the dining table. Ali tells me that it was recently written by a devoted Persian dervish who lives in Vancouver. One can see the devotion of the artist to Imam Ali by noting the undulation that his pulse has imparted on the last, extended letter of Ali.

When we arrived, the coffee table was already covered with Persian pastries: baghlava, pistachios, fluffy pashmak—the Iranian version of cotton candy—and *zoolbia,* the brilliant hallmark of the month of Ramadan. There was no room left on the table for the boxes of pastry and cookies that Bahman had brought from a Persian pastry shop in North Vancouver. When Ali apologized for the smallness of his table, I told him that it was of normal size, but looked small in comparison with his generosity. The dining table too quickly became covered with round and oval Persian dishes, mainly the specialties from Rasht, among which I spotted *baghala-ghatogh,* made of fava beans, eggs, garlic and some unknown herbs.

After dinner, we drove to my house so that Bahman could cut my hair. Once in my room, Bahman spread his few tools on the desk and sent me to get a bed sheet and an empty squeezable, plastic bottle to spray water on my hair, if he needed to. When he put the white sheet around my neck to begin his work, I reminded him not to flatten the back of my head like the head of a Rashti. He laughed and said that he did not blame me for saying that. He had had the same request when his partner in Vancouver was cutting his hair. He even drew on the mirror with a red lipstick the profile of a head with flat back to make sure his partner understood what he did not want. Yet his partner did exactly the opposite. I asked him if he knew the reason for the flattening of the back of the head of children from Rasht. He thought it was due to the use of wooden pillows in their wooden cradles in that wooded city.

While cutting my gun-grey hair, Bahman told us the story of how he was a draft dodger at the beginning of the Iran-Iraq war, because he was the only son of his parents, and how he was caught and was sent to the front. He said, without boasting, how he had saved the lives of seventy Iranian soldiers by disobeying his superior and not surrendering his men and their weapons prematurely to the advancing Iraqi troops and tanks.

He was telling the truth, but his appearance did not match his heroic accomplishments. He was so different from Ali that I wondered, besides being in a war together, what else had brought them together, so faraway from home. It turned out that they were relatives. They liked each other, but they did not agree with everything that the other said, particularly about the war. When I asked them who fought better, the civilian volunteers or the Iranian army, Ali said the civilians, Bahman, the army. I believed both of them and both agreed that the Iranian sustained progress in the war began when the professional officers and soldiers of the Iranian army joined the war. Ali said that in the beginning more people died of thirst due to fasting than from bullets. When Bahman finished, he sent me to the nearby wash-room to look in the mirror.

What I saw then in our small mirror was much better than what I see now in the wall-to-wall mirrors of the barber shop.

Reg finally sees me waiting on one of the chairs along the row of chairs. He spreads the fingers of his left hand to indicate that he would be ready in five minutes. Then he changes his mind and looks at his schedule and asks me, "Half an hour?" I accept the delay, provided he will give me a cup of coffee while waiting.

It takes him so long to get the coffee from a dark closet at the end of the shop that I have to apologize to the man who was left unattended in his chair in front of me. The man, however, says that he did not mind the inconvenience, provided he gets a coffee too.

When the coffee finally comes, it is too hot, since Reg added a whitening powder to it instead of milk. It burns my tongue. My tongue was already sore, ever since I began writing this book, I don't know why. This coffee makes it worse. I thank Reg nonetheless and sit among the row of inverted domes of dryers where ladies watch the television in front of me above the mirrors.

From the television I learn that today is the annual Victoria Day Parade in downtown. No wonder I did not see many people walking or driving on my way here. They must have gone downtown to watch the parade.

The last time I watched one of these parades was five years ago. I caught the tail end of the procession in front of the vine-covered facade of the Empress Hotel, the proud centre of the city. The harbor looked particularly beautiful and crowded; many boats were stationed in the water and many pedestrians walked along the sidewalks. An adolescent boy with a backward baseball cap left his gang to climb over the stone wall of the causeway, made a trumpet out of his hands and shouted as loud as he could, "Super!" The crowd and the crews became silent and waited to hear what the boy had to say next. The boy repeated the same gesture and the same word once again, "Super!" But this time, when the entire downtown transformed to a single ear, the boy completed his sentence, "Super-fucking boring!"

Rather than waiting inside the hair salon, I went to sit on the bench in front of the corner store at the crossroad near the barbershop. The corner store used to be run by a Chinese family, and most of the neighbourhood children, including two of ours, worked there in the summer holidays to earn some pocket money.

The intersection has four stop signs and no traffic. Except for a young man, or perhaps an old boy, no one is walking along the sidewalks. His profile looks like Hamid at puberty, but his back looks like the back of the shouting boy on the causeway. He walks slowly and aimlessly. He goes to the corner store and soon lumbers out without having bought anything. He stands at the crossroad, confused, then seeing me on the bench, comes to sit beside me, not too close. He has a green army coat over his collapsed knapsack, making one wonder if he is dealing in street drugs.

He searches his pocket as he sits. I wonder if he wants a match or a lighter to light up the cigarette that he has fished out of the pocket of his pants with much difficulty.

"George knows me," the boy says as he sits. "He knows me well," pointing with his chin towards the corner store.

"Who is George?" I ask, even though I understand by the motion of his head that he means the new owner of the store.

"George, the owner of the corner store," he says. "The whole city knows me, at least those who read the newspaper. My picture was in it."

"Why? What had you done to deserve such an honour?" I ask more out of politeness than curiosity.

"I was beaten up by fifteen cops at the same time downtown."

I believe him, not because I believe in police brutality, but because he did look like a kid who could be asking for it.

"Did it hurt a lot?" I asked sympathetically.

"No, not then," he said. "But the next day and the days after, it was bad and was getting worse." Then he re-enacted the sequence of the events, "The first punch went whoop! Like this." He moves his head sharply to one side to show the effect and the intensity of the blow. "Then I fell. The more they beat me, the louder I shouted that they were pigs."

"What had you done to begin with," I asked, "to deserve such a severe punishment?" feeling sorry for him mainly because of his similarity to one of my younger brothers, Hamid.

"I had shoved my face into the face of the first cop I met that evening, and told him that he was a pig, and said it to the next one and the next one, up to fifteen times."

After sitting on the bench for a while, he shrugs his bony shoulders and gets up to go. His wrinkled knapsack appears even emptier than when he sat, as I watch him go. He crosses the deserted street without looking in any particular direction. He does not seem to have a home or an appointment. He walks over the crosswalk at the crossroad, moving in the direction of Killarney Road, where our old house used to be. I put my coffee down on the bench to cup my hands and call after him to ask his name. He turns and says, "Shane," while walking backward.

"Your family name?" I ask, while looking in vain for a pen or a pencil to write it down.

The boy ignores my last question and continues going away from me. I go back to Reg to have my hair cut.

"What do you want me to do with it?" Reg asks, with a smile at the corner of his lips, knowing that sometimes I come up with unexpected suggestions.

"Just cut it the way my new Iranian friend has done the last time."

"How was that?" Reg asks, amused.

"He made my head look like the head of the Shah of Iran."

Reg smiles an understanding smile and begins working on my head.

9

THE TELESCOPE THEORY OF TIME

AFTER GOD, FOR ME, TIME IS THE MOST DIFFICULT CONCEPT TO CONCEIVE OF, especially when I compare it with space. Space is easy to conceive; all I have to do is to imagine a three-dimensional thing like a watermelon or a house, and I know right away that space is the place which things occupy. But I don't know what I have to imagine to conceive time. This is not my problem alone; great thinkers like St. Augustine have had similar problems. When he was asked, "What is time?" he simply replied, "I knew it just before you asked." The irony with time is that we can easily measure it—if we translate it to a moving three dimensional thing, like the hands of a clock—but we cannot imagine it.

Even Einstein—the scientist who said God does not play dice with the world, meaning that God does not leave anything to chance—cannot help me in this regard when he considers time and space as a continuum and separates them only by a forward slash. Not only does his theory not help me, it makes time even more difficult for me to conceive.

Common sense imagines time as being a linear thing, like an endless string. Fair enough. Nature, by bringing about the repetitious cycle of seasons, tries to tell us that time is linear all right, but circular in nature, like the lines on a disc of gramophone or the cut surface of a tree. Children too think it is a circular thing, but a spiral form, like the comings and goings of their birthdays, since each time that they arrive they become a little taller. All of these analogies point to only one aspect of time, but none of them explains what time is. In my everyday life, especially where I work, things happen simultaneously, as if within each other, like the collapsible tube of a telescope.

In the following paragraphs and pages I want to demonstrate the effect of the telescope theory of time on my work, and if it works, I would like to add my theory to the above theories regarding the anatomy of time.

***

Every now and then the loudspeakers in the hospital corridors warn the patients and the staff about an explosion which is going to occur in the parking lot north of the hospital, within three minutes, and every time that it says so, it happens. I keep hearing about the explosion, but have never seen it. I wish my office was where it used to be so that I could watch the construction while working. That office had only one window, but it looked towards the north. This is why it never had the sun, and I was in a melancholic mood when I was there.

At the same moment I am called to perform a rapid, intra-operative diagnosis on a segment of liver containing a spherical nodule, within the same three minutes. The patient is under general anesthesia, and the surgeon has stopped working, waiting for my call. When I cannot make the diagnosis in the first few seconds, I take the wet slide made of the tumour to Bruce who occupies that office now. He is good in diagnosing lesions of the gastro intestinal track that includes the liver. Seamus, my Irish colleague, is also good at G.I. lesions, and has written a colourful book about them, but his office does not look over the construction site.

I knock and enter without waiting for Bruce to say "Come in." His voice is so low and his reaction is sometimes so delayed that I am sure he doesn't mind if I go like that. Besides, we can't function fast enough if each time that we need to consult with a colleague, we have to knock and wait for an invitation.

Bruce's office is small and cluttered with stacks of books and layers of slides. It is much more crowded than when it was mine. Bruce is not sloppy, not at all. The reason his office is not tidy is because he is a keeper. He keeps the old slides, for example, either because they represent a good example of a bad disease, or a bad example of a good disease, all for teaching purposes.

Bruce is one of the few pathologists who still wears his white coat at work. Through the narrow gap between his wide white back and the edge of his desk, I squeeze myself in the direction of the window. The blind black monitor behind his back on the desk seems to be waiting to project pathological slides on the screen of his back. I leave the wet slide on his gun-grey microscope and stand at the window, ready to reply to any question he might have regarding the patient or the tumour.

Grapevine—the green newsletter of the hospital—is loosely resting on the top of one of the many books on the desk. It is the same free newsletter that he picked up yesterday, on his way back from lunch in the cafeteria. On the front page, it shows the disrupted parking lot and the partially demolished brick building of the Harmony Room, the old cafeteria. The next page is about a contest. The hospital is looking for the best suggestions about things to put in the time capsule that is going to be left under the foundation of the new building. Bruce is not going to participate in this contest. He reads many books, thinks many ideas, and collects many things, but he is not the type to get involved in sentimental things.

I see that there is a short course in the newsletter that I might take. It is about learning to navigate the Internet. The registration fee is only forty dollars for hospital staff. My navigation is very bad. I think I suffer from a sort of cyber phobia. I might take this course.

Bruce is quiet and thinking. I am glad. The more he thinks, the more he must be sharing my ignorance. He must be wondering whether the tumour has a capsule around it or not. Having a capsule is a good sign. It often means the lesion is benign. Bruce does not seem to hurry when time is short. He does not change the gears. He is taking his time, my time, the surgeon's time, and the precious time of the patient. But I don't rush him. One cannot rush Bruce. The more you push him, the slower he moves. His only concern is to reach the right diagnosis, no matter how much time it takes.

I turn to face the window and let him look and think as much as he wants. I am not like Bruce. I either recognize the pattern or I don't. If I don't, no matter how much I think, the diagnosis does not come to my mind, and I have learned that rather than wasting everybody's time, I should take the slide to someone who knows. When Bruce brings his skin problems to me, within two seconds I tell him if he is right or wrong, and most of the time he is right.

A crow flies from a window ledge to land on the horizontal trunk of a fallen tree. It walks along the trunk towards its rooted end, and caws. Rather than saying "Nevermore" like the raven of Edgar Allen Poe, however, it says only "More," four times.

The place that was once a flat parking lot has been transformed to piles of blasted rocks and deep rectangular dugouts. Rainwater has made shallow pools out of the dugouts and three ducks are already swimming in one of them. If they want to put a time capsule under this building, they would have to make it waterproof. The newsletter also suggests examples of what the readers can suggest for the time capsule, most of which begin with *bio* and end with *gene*.

No one is working at the construction site, but it is coming along nicely. Things, it seems, always happen when I am not looking. The cement columns, fortified by iron bars, have grown out of the dugouts like the ruins of Persepolis. Two motionless cranes have extended their skeletal necks towards the sky like a pair of extinct dinosaurs. No sound of hammering is coming from the construction site, and no hissing of a saw.

I see a few nurses watching the construction through their own open windows. Some have rested their chins on the back of their overlapping hands on the window sill. One of them is pointing to her breast with one hand while pointing with the other to the almost finished building of the new cancer clinic.

I don't want to sound negative or unappreciative, but neither a new cancer clinic nor a new laboratory was urgently needed. We already had a new cancer clinic. I remember its opening day. We went there with my old boss, and he introduced me to the previous CEO as his vice-chief, to show him that despite the past troubles, we were friends again. I remember some refreshments were served, too, like triangular clubhouse sandwiches on pigmented napkins and coffee-coloured soft drinks in Styrofoam cups, as well as a large pink bowl containing alcohol-free refreshment.

The hospice, that humble, bungalow building next to the old cancer clinic, does sometime a better job for the dying than the heroic actions occurring in the operating rooms. I did work in the hospice for a short time. I thought with my familiarity with death I could handle its victims better than the nurses or other doctors in the hospice. I was wrong. I found out that it was harder to deal with the dying than the dead.

With the demolition of our parking lot, there is now confusion as to where to park the car in the mornings. Every day I find a different, unfamiliar spot and meet different doctors, different from the ones I used to encounter when the parking lot was intact.

I see Basil, the political pediatrician who has been working here longer than most other pediatricians and was here before I came to this city. He bends to pick up a brick from the rubbles representing the residue of the Harmony Room. I know what he is going to do with it. After many years of opposing the policies of every CEO and medical director, and the heads of some departments, he has become the president of the medical staff for two years. He wants to make a point with this brick in his inauguration speech.

Basil is interested in the history of people and places. He regrets that he does not have time to make use of the notes of his long dead grandfather. His grandfather, General Bolton, was as important, perhaps, as his opponent, Louis Riel, in Canadian history. Since he was on the English side and did not die in action, or was not hanged after, his name is not remembered as well as that of Louis Riel. I asked him why he thought he was obliged to write about him. He said, "If I don't, there is no one else to do it. Besides, my children have never seen their great-grandfather and want to know about him."

Many people are walking on the temporary gravel paths, some diverging to find their cars, some converging towards the small rear door of the hospital. Some of them I do not know. I used to know more of them in the past. The ones I knew have either retired or died. Some of the dead were my friends. The new doctors are mostly young. Neither do I know their names nor do they know mine. The few younger doctors that I know were classmates of my sons, Kamran or Nima, in medical school at the University of British Columbia.

All of a sudden the two cranes begin to move, slowly and reluctantly, in unison, each having a rigid rope hanging from its beak, like a worm. I ask Bruce if he knows whether the water in the trenches was seeping from the sea or was just accumulated rainwater. He does not reply. His mind must be focused like his eyes on the slide.

"How about the ducks?" I ask Bruce to remind him that I am waiting for his expert opinion, "How did they find out about these man-made lagoons, so soon?"

Bruce murmurs something to the effect that birds are small versions of the departed dinosaurs, but he does not explain why they have found the pooled waters. Instead, he says that he is worried that one of these days a child will fall in these dugouts and the hospital and the contractors will have a big lawsuit on their hand.

One has to arrive either very early in the morning these days to find a decent parking place, or learn to live with the unforeseen consequences of coming late to work.

Today I was late. I was late because of a fallen tree on my way due to the storm of last night. Its roots were flat and fan-shaped, like those of an artificial Christmas tree. The reason the trees here fall so easily after a minor storm is because, except for the thin layer of topsoil, this island is made of rocks. Roots, no matter how strong, cannot penetrate rocks, no matter how soft.

The crow jumps to perch on a boulder the size of a car. A man, my size, walking an unhurried sort of walk like me, is approaching the chicken-wire fence that separates the cranes from the cars. He seems to be looking for his car. He has his keys ready in his hand. He resembles Naz, the family physician who refers his occasional psychiatric patients who speak only Farsi, to me. And I usually make the diagnosis of reactive depression secondary to forced emigration or premature retirement. Some are in the middle of a messy divorce. Despite being a busy doctor, Naz stops to look at the rock and the crow.

The first time we met, Naz recognized right away that I was an Iranian and quoted for me the short but famous poem from the atypical Persian poet who had a lot to do with establishing Ismailis in Iran, Nasser Khosrow, about the eagle and the rock. Every Iranian school boy or girl knows that poem because it was in our textbook in the elementary schools:

Once a proud eagle flew off a rock

When it reached the highest point in the sky

It said, "Today the whole world is under the span of our wings"

As soon as it said that, an arrow pierced one of his wings

When it looked at the arrow and saw an eagle feather at its end

It lamented, "Who can we blame, but ourselves

Since it is from us, that comes towards us?"

Nasser Khosrow was one of the most serious Persian poets. He was not only a poet, but also a statesman. He differs from all other Persian poets. He never drank wine and never laughed. Against wine he has said this:

The learned does not drink.

The wise does not get drunk.

Why should one drink something that

Makes a cypress tree appear like a reed

And a reed like cypress tree?

If you become generous and give to charities (while drunk)

They would say, "The drink did it; not he."

But if you yelled and blared, they would say, "He did it; not the drink."

He was a political poet, a philosopher, a traveler and a visionary. He was both a revolutionary and a spiritual man. Naz tells me that Nasser Khosrow was instrumental in reviving the *Esmailieh* sect in Iran and elevating Agha Khan from Mahallat, a small city in Iran, to big cities in India. Naz knows a lot about Agha Khan and Qajar dynasty in Iran. In the small book that he has given to me to keep as long as I wish, it is written that the first person that coined the title of Agha Khan was Fatali Shah of Qajar. It means the chief of the chiefs, or the Lord of the Lords. He gave it to the first Agha Khan whose father was assassinated by a fanatic Muslin.

Naz too does not laugh very often. He is polite and considerate. He smiles when he greets, but that is all. He never tells jokes. He writes many of the editorials of the newsletter of the Victoria Medical Society, some of them containing dry humour, but he avoids saying ridiculous things.

"Are you talking about the same Agha Khan whose followers weighed him with diamonds annually?" I asked.

"Yes," he said, "but that was for the first Agha Khan; the subsequent ones were weighed with gold."

"Was that because diamonds were becoming scarce and the Agha Khans were putting on weight?" I asked to see how much he knew about the man he was talking about with such reverence.

"And also because gold is much denser than diamonds," he said.

"If you know so much, could you tell me how Agha Khan is connected to Islam? I have never understood this connection very well."

"If Shi'eh is a small branch of the main trunk of Sunni Islam, Ismaili is a twig of Shi'eh. The split occurred after the death of the sixth Imam of the Shi'eh. The Shi'ehs, as you know, have twelve imams."

"I know that. And I know that the twelfth imam has become invisible and will reappear one day as the master of time to make the world peaceful and just."

Imam Ja'far Sadegh, the sixth Imam, Naz tells me, had two sons: Kazem and Ghaher. They were both good and ambitious, both wanting to replace the father after his death. After much debate, Kazem became the seventh Imam and became Imam Moussa Kazem, and Ghaher, disappointed, left Iran, went to Egypt, opened schools and centres for higher education. He helped that city with science so much that the inhabitants of that city named their city, *Ghahereh*, Farsi for *Cairo*, after him.

Naz, like me, took his medical training in Tehran, but not all of it, maybe the second half of it. He started his training in Uganda, where he was born, but he had to interrupt his training to go to Iran at the time when Idi Amin foolishly came to power and made many good people leave Uganda. I asked him why he chose Tehran, among so many other universities, because none of the graduates of Tehran University has ever won a Nobel Prize in science. He said his grandparents were Iranian from Kerman. Due to persecution, they had to emigrate from Iran during the reign of Agha Mohammad Khan, the eunuch founder of Qajar dynasty.

After graduation from Tehran Medical School, Naz spent several years in general practise in Tehran and continued practising for several years following the Islamic revolution of 1979. Then, for some reason, he moved to Vancouver and took a few more years of training in order to become a family physician.

He is an early riser. When I arrived at the hospital today, he was already returning from visiting his patients in the hospital to go to his office where his predominantly ethnic patients are patiently waiting for him.

Naz has never said anything bad about Agha Mohammad Khan, even though he was responsible for his parents emigrating from Kerman to the other side of the Send River, east of Iran, but he has said a lot of good things about the Agha Khan Foundation.

Naz's knowledge of history is as inaccurate as mine, but his spirituality is much greater. He says the followers of Agha Khan take both science and religion seriously, with equal importance.

Once Naz told me that the Agha Khan Foundation, wanting to know the ameliorating effect of architecture on religious belief, asked the modern architects to build a new mosque, regardless of cost, in one of the middle eastern countries, in a new style but without losing its traditional meaning. One of the innovations in that mosque is the wall of *Ghebleh*—the direction towards which the Muslims pray. The wall is transparent, made of a special crystal that let the light in but filters out the shapes and images.

"Do men and women still sit separately in that mosque?"

"Yes, but instead of being separated by a curtain, they are separated by levels."

"Who sits on the higher level, who on the lower?"

Naz did not know, since he had not seen that mosque.

Naz knows history, at least as much as it relates to the exodus of his people from Iran. He knows about Richard Burton— not the movie star—the British explorer who went to find the source of the Nile, and wrote many books. He needed eleven desks in his house, after his return to England, to write eleven books, simultaneously. Perhaps he too knew that things happen at the same time, but when you want to write about them they seem to follow each other. When he saw a brave and armed group of Ismaili refugees, he sent a message to his government that it was possible to help the refugees to return to Iran and replace the Qajar dynasty with them, but, for some reason, the British did not take his message seriously.

I told him that my grandfather—the father of my mother—when he was a twelve-year-old boy, was given to the court of Nasseredin Shah of Qajar as a gift and a symbol of everlasting peace between the Qajar and Agha Khanies.

Naz was in hurry to go. At the last minute he shook my hand and said, "If your mother is that close to the holy Agha Khan, then you are semi-holy."

"If your other first name, as you said, is Mehr-Ali, you are as close to me as my half brother." I returned the compliment as I shook his hand.

I see Bill, the internist leaving the hospital to go to his office. I saw him this morning too, when I was coming to the hospital. He has two specialties, the other is neurology. Many of his patients have Alzheimer's disease. When I saw him this morning, I happened to be listening to a CBC radio program in my car, talking about new findings in Alzheimer's disease.

Bill is a serious physician with a deeply hidden sense of humour. The mild curvature of his upper back is due to the heavy weight of his briefcase. Like doctors in the past, when effective drugs were rare and they always blamed their patients if their treatment failed, Bill scolds his patients when they do things that he considers to be stupid, such as smoking cigarettes. Reading his mind is sometimes easier than reading his face. He always appears determined. No one can guess that his hobby is ballroom dancing. No one even suspects that one of his dancing partners is an Iranian woman from whom he learns some words of greeting to use on me. He is exceptional in this regard, because most of the other doctors who have or have had an Iranian friend have learned only the bad words. There was an anesthesiologist from England who every time that he saw me in the hospital shouted in front of everybody, "K…k…," meaning, "Oh, you who have a promiscuous sister," before disappearing in the bowels of the operating suites. Too bad he died in a car accident. I wish he was alive to read my book to see how wrong he was.

The curvature of Bill's back has lessened these days. It was worse two years ago when I saw him at the Cadboro Bay beach in the middle of a working day. He was wearing a casual summer shirt and a straw hat, biting into an ice cream cone, while reading a thin soft book. I asked him what he was doing there in the middle of a working day and what was he reading. He did not reply right away, but the cover of the book showed that it was about workaholics. Then he book-marked his book with his index finger and explained that he had decided to change his lifestyle. He had accidently discovered that he had been doing too much mental work at the expense of his body. One day, he said, he was sitting in his office at home, dictating the histories of the patients he had seen that day. His wife was getting ready to go for her evening walk. As she was putting on her runners, she asked him if he wanted to join her. He did, and he enjoyed walking with her, but he also noticed that he kept falling behind. It was then that he realized that he had lost much of his leg muscles due to lack of activity.

Every time I meet Bill I learn something new from him and about him. He is not a talkative man and does not stop to talk to people, whether in the parking lot or in the corridors or the cafeterias. But when he sees me at coffee breaks, he always joins me if I am alone.

Usually it is he who asks me questions, but once I decided to ask questions first.

"What do you think about sex when children are still at school?"

"I have advised my children that the longer they postpone sex, the better they will study."

"I agree with you. It did work for me. But in my case it was not my choice. Our schools had boys only. I can't even imagine how an adolescent boy can study in the presence of girls. I bet if coeducation had been available when I was growing up, I would have never made it to medical school. Then I modified my opinion and I told him, "But in this country, education is so good that even those who don't postpone sex while in school can become somebody, and many of them become good educators."

When Bill asked me why I had become interested in this matter so late in my life, I told him that I was writing a book in which I talk about the method my mother had chosen to raise her nine fatherless children, and I wanted to compare it with the way they do it here.

"A man, they say," he quoted someone, "is not complete until he has begotten a son, planted a tree, and has written a book," Bill said when he heard that I was writing a book.

"Have you thought of putting some of your sayings in the time-capsule under the foundation of the new building?" I asked.

"Apoptosis," he said readily, as if he had been thinking about it all this time. Luckily I knew what he meant by that unfamiliar word. It means programmed death. A cell is destined to die after certain time or after undergoing a predetermined number of mitotic divisions. There is no gene for death in human genome, but the other genes can make life so difficult for a cell that it commits suicide. One can make therapeutic use of this and make cancer cells commit suicide. Apoptosis is as important in the production of tumourous masses as is mitotis.

"Do you have any advice for me, something to make me happier than I am?" I asked Bill before letting him go.

"You would be committed to a psychiatric ward if you were any happier," Bill diagnosed.

If he were George, he would have said something more meaningful, something from Nietzsche, such as, "Happiness is a woman, if you follow it, it moves away from you; if you don't, it might follow you."

When Bill saw that I did not laugh, he said, "I have no advice for you, but I can tell you what I do to prevent unhappiness."

"What do you do? Tell me."

"I follow the rule of five F's."

"What are they?"

"They are my faith, my family, my friends, my fun, and my firm." By "firm" Bill explains that he means his office and his practice of medicine that generated the funds required for the other four.

The radio in my car said that Alzheimer's patients, in their retrograde voyage, pass through all the stages of life that they have passed, but in reverse order. When they feel like a three-year-old, for example, they should also be treated like a three-year-old. You should not leave them in the dark, for example, because a three-year-old is afraid of darkness. So, when his car tried to pass my car as soon as he pulled out, I stopped and let my window down to ask him if he knew about this new finding.

Bill too stopped with his window down, and I heard that he was listening to the same radio station. I could tell it was the same station because it was beeping to tell the exact time of the day, "The beginning of the long dash following a series of beeps, indicates ten o'clock."

"Do you know who bothers the Alzheimer's patients the most?" Bill asked.

"No," I said. "Not the caregiver, I hope."

"It is the other patients with Alzheimer's disease in the next bed or in the same room." He gave me this disturbing news before he pressed gently on the gas pedal. I heard the radio of our cars began simultaneously sounding the long expected dash, the beginning of which indicated 10 o'clock.

I turn towards Bruce, "Bruce! If you cannot make up your mind, let me know so that I can take it to Seamus. The patient is running out of blood and the surgeon out of patience."

"What is the hurry, Nasser? You just gave me the slide ten seconds ago. Let me at least go through the differential diagnosis in my mind."

"Forget about the differential diagnosis. Just tell me if the patient is going to live or not."

"Is she on contraceptive pills?"

"I don't know. Her age indicates that she could be. Why?"

"Because there are benign nodules in liver, just like this, which happen, rarely, in women who are on these pills.

"Thanks."

I came back to my own office to phone the surgeon to get more clinical information and gave him the good news. The surgeon had already closed the wound.

"Then why did you send it for rapid section diagnosis?"

"To keep you on your toes, but thanks for your timeliness anyway." said the surgeon. Right after the surgeon said that, the explosion that we were warned about occurred in the parking lot, and I missed it again.

10

BLUE THOUGHTS IN BLACK WATERS

Fed up with the outside world?

Begin to look inward.

Looking inward, I see the image of the beloved,

Looking outward, I see my own imagination.

Rumi

I MURMUR THE ABOVE LINES, as I drive from hospital to home. I go home rather early today because it is Friday and it is sunny. Also because I have done almost all my work and I am happy. And when I am happy I like to be with my wife. I often murmur something in my mind when I am alone or driving, be it a Persian poem, left over in my mind from the days we had to memorize things, or a wistful Canadian song I heard many years ago in Winnipeg, like "When I need you, I close my eyes and I am with you." I particularly elongate my way so that I see more of this garden-like city. What I murmur or sing might be relevant or irrelevant to the situation at hand. When a line gets hold of my mind, I have to repeat it. And since they say never discard a recurrent thing or thought, I have to bring my thoughts here.

The road is crackless and the car runs effortlessly. The trees along the road are beginning to know and respect me. They rise as I approach and sit as I pass. The sun always makes me happy, whether it is only one in the middle of a cloudless sky, like a coin fallen in a deserted street, or it is multiple, running behind the tree trunks, the way Ebi, my Persian friend, has painted them. The multiplied sun reminds me of my uncle colonel in Tehran, who, regularly, on sunny Fridays, would come to our house to pay pocket money to the fatherless children of his sister.

Oops! I must have changed lanes without signalling, because the driver of the car that just passed made a vulgar gesture with his hand.

In Tehran they say never drive behind an empty taxi because it might stop unpredictably. Here, in Victoria they say never drive behind a poet. I hope the startled driver has taken me for a poet rather than an uncivilized person who does not respect lines. I know lines are important in this country, especially the solid ones that function like a wall.

At the intersection, when our cars stopped, side by side, for the red light, rather than waiting for the green light to go home, I turned to my right to go to the nearby recreation centre to sit in the lukewarm water of its baby pool.

I know how to swim but not very well, just enough so that if I fell into the deep end of the adult pool, I could hold my breath long enough to thrash around to eventually get to the edge of the pool.

Like any other house in Iran we had a pool in our yard in Torbat and Tehran. The one in Torbat was square and contained colourless water. The one in Tehran was oval and contained green water. We were not allowed to swim in the pool in Torbat because we were small and we were told that if we approached the pool, *Maadar-aab*—the water-monster or the mother of the water—would pull us under. And when we were older and did not believe in the water monster anymore, there was not enough room in the oval pool for all of us to swim. Occasionally, however, we did swim in the oval pool and the last time we did our mother ordered us to come out because despite having fun and blue thoughts when we came out the water was turned to black.

I jam my clothes into the small metallic locker and put a quarter in the slot that releases the key. I hang the key carefully by its safety pin to the elastic waistband of my swimming trunks and tiptoe across the wet but not slippery ceramic floor to shower before going to the pool area.

Three naked men are showering at the four-headed shower. They must be coming out because for going in everybody wears swimming trunks. One is singing while shampooing his hair. I am the only one with swimming trunks on and I am glad that I am because as soon as I start to shower a confused elderly lady, who I know is the mother of one of the talking men in the baby pool, walks by mistake into the male change room and I am the only one who can take her back to her son.

The adult pool is oblong and blue. I have never used it because I don't know how to swim and its water is not warm enough. The baby pool is square and colourless. With its checkerboard tiles on the floor, it resembles a sunken chessboard. Were it not for the flight of light glinting off its surface tension, one could not tell it contained water. Six or seven men, middle-age and above, are sitting in the pool, some talk, some listen.

Before I get into conversation, I sit by myself for a while, to think about the events of the passing day. The first thing that comes to my mind is the last thing that happened, the driver of the car and his insulting gesture. I don't know why I have taken it so personally this time. I always believe that it is not the drivers who insult each other; it is the cars.

I would rather be praised than blamed. It is true that I spent part of my childhood in Torbat Heidarieh where the tomb of the Master of the Malamati dervishes, *Ghotbeh din Heidar,* is located, but I was born in the capital city of Tehran.

I don't like to be blamed. To blame, in Farsi, is to *Malaamat*, and those who like to be blamed are called *Malamati*.

There were also a group of Moslem dervishes, who, to avoid being praised—because a good Moslem should not seek praise—deliberately committed distasteful acts and shouted blasphemous-sounding words, so that they got blame. For the same reason, they made their appearance unattractive, by shaving all their hair, including their eyebrows, and they dressed scantily with a minimal amount of dirty-looking, but clean canvas. Actually, because the dusty tomb of the master of Malamaties is located in Torbat, Torbat has become Torbat-e-Heidariyeh. It also distinguishes it from the other Torbat in Iran, Torbat-e-Jam, where the poet Jami comes from.

Very often the wishes of the Malamati would be fulfilled and many, especially the followers of another sect of dervishes—the followers of Shah Ne'matollah Vali in Kerman—were ready to beat them with stones and sticks. This happened so often in Iran that whenever there was a quarrel between two groups and one asked someone coming from the quarrel scene, "What is going on over there?" if the disturbance did not have a good reason as its cause, the man would reply, "Nothing, just another Heidari/Ne'mati encounter."

I am not a Malamati. Maybe my siblings are, but not me. I was born in the asphalted city of Tehran, while they were born either in Mashad or in the dusty city of Torbat Heidariyeh.

The invisible advantage that my birthplace bestowed upon me, however, was overshadowed by the darker colour of my skin, as compared to the skin of my siblings. I don't know if it is my colour which is abnormal for an Iranian, or theirs. In our Farsi textbook in the elementary school in Tehran, we read, "The colour of the Iranian race is the same as the colour of a grain of wheat." Anytime, however, that I looked at the grains of roasted wheat mixed with kingseeds that our Aunt Seddigheh poured into our pockets when we visited her, I would see, to my chagrin, that my colour was closer to the greenish hue of the kingseeds, than the colour of wheat.

The man sitting near the far end of the pool is a retired French teacher. He is Canadian but not from Quebec. He is Armenian but looks so Iranian that the first time I talked to him, I foolishly made that silly French joke that we used to tease our Armenian classmates with, in Tehran, "Why do all the Armenian names end with *an*, except for *Gharapet* that ends with *pet*?" He did not laugh. This is perhaps why he is sitting so far away from me and the rest of the adults in the baby pool.

On the ceramic wall, there is a small square green board on which a different quotation is written every day. Today's quotation is this: "The enemy of clarity is insincerity," by George Orwell. This is perhaps not exactly what Orwell said, but it is what I understood from it. Sometimes the French teacher objects to the quotations, not because of what they mean, but because of mistakes in grammar. He says that only those whose native tongue is not English notice those errors.

Another man, about my age, sitting near the shallow steps at the proximal end of the pool with only his bottom immersed in water, seems about to talk to me as soon as he can catch my eye. He has developed slightly darker skin and a mildly larger abdomen since I last saw him. The last time that I saw him, we talked about Hawaii. I have not gone to Hawaii yet and I am not planning to go there.

"But why, why won't you go?" he asked, somewhat disappointed.

"First of all, I am not retired yet. Secondly, I don't want to exchange my house and my car and my keys with strangers, no matter how good their houses, or their cars. Besides, I don't like to travel anymore. I think I have already travelled far enough."

"Far enough from where?"

"From where I come from, Iran."

"I-ran?"

"No Sir, Iran. It is pronounced *ee-raan*; not I-run. You make it sound as if I've run away from my country like a fugitive, if not a refugee."

In the adult pool, men and women much older than me are swimming, some more than forty lengths. They swim in parallel lanes demarcated by ropes, studded with Styrofoam beads like stretched rosaries.

A mature, middle-aged woman in a one-piece swimsuit has just finished teaching a younger woman in a two-piece swimming suit how to swim and is on her way to the change room for women.

I get out of the baby pool in time to intercept her and ask her if she could teach me too.

"I know the basics," I tell her to make her think that teaching me would not take much of her time.

"Let's first see how much you know."

I show her that I could swim on my back better than on my front. She teaches me how to crawl, and then takes me to the deep end, away from the ropes and the long-distance swimmers, to teach me how to float. First, she jumps in and stayed afloat, her neck and shoulders sticking out of water as if made of wax. When my turn comes, rather than jumping, I go in gently from the hard edge of the pool, so as not to give the force of gravity an extra excuse to pull me down. My carefulness, however, does not help much and I begin to sink right away. I close my eyes when the level of water passed my nostrils.

To come up for air, I kick my heels against the cemented curve of the pool where the bottom meets the side wall. The mosaic floor of the doctors' lounge and the operating rooms of our hospital are similarly curved. Fungi and bacterial colonies do not get a chance to grow on them, and even if they did, it would be easy to clean.

I come up, obliquely, far away from the edge of the pool, gasping for air, disoriented. "What happened?" I ask my teacher with the first gush of air escaping from my lungs.

"You are a sinker."

"Thinker?" I ask, misunderstanding her, wondering how clear the water must be to enable her to see even my thoughts through it.

"Sinker, sinker!" she repeats, "With an *s*." Slightly irritated, she sticks her index finger into the water, twice, to make sure I understood.

"Should I try again?" I manage to ask, having lost part of my fear of drowning.

"Try again, but relax and don't panic. And come up soon, please. I have to go to work. I work at the cancer clinic."

I try to relax and float, but right away I begin to sink again. As I close my eyes, our oval pool in Tehran comes to my mind and the summer day our mother had given us permission to go in it but had quickly changed her mind.

I hear Hamid, the brother a year younger than me, laughing and running down the stairs towards the pool, while throwing off his shoes and pulling out his shirt over the top of his head. "Did Modar-jun give permission that we could go in the pool, Hamid?" I asked, because whenever our mother gave permission to one of us, it meant for all of us. He jumped in the pool in his shorts and paddled by himself for a few seconds before answering my question with a laughing "yes."

We all—from Mehdi down to Mahmood—jumped in as soon as Hamid said "yes," except for Mahmood, the youngest, who had to get the spade from the flowerbed to measure his height against the depth of the pool with its handle. The wet part of the handle came to his upper lip, just below his nostrils, so he too jumped in.

Only a minute or two seemed to have passed before I heard, through the sound of hands smacking the water, splashing it into my eyes, that our mother was shouting—so uncharacteristic of her—something from the balcony.

I made everybody stay quiet to hear what she was saying.

"Come out! Come out! All of you," she was saying, disappointed with all of us.

"What for, Modar-jun?" I said. "Didn't you give permission to Hamid?"

Never before had she changed her mind about anything as fast as she did in that midsummer day in Tehran.

We obeyed and came out and stood, shivering, on the hot bricks of the pavement, heads up, looking at her for explanation.

She was standing at the edge of the balcony next to the central pillar towards which we never saw a Parastoo fly in or fly out.

"We are out, Modar-jun," I volunteered again to speak for all of my swimming siblings, "but why?"

"Look at the water you are swimming in," she said, instead of explanation.

We all turned our head towards the pool. The restless water was not green anymore. It was black like China ink. It was more like diluted *lajan*—the black sediment at the bottom of stagnant waters—than water. Our joy and jumping must have brought up the black sediment to the surface. Then, we looked at ourselves. We looked ridiculous. Each one of us, even Mahmood, had developed a black line above our upper lips, like precocious moustaches.

I kick my heels to the bottom and come up to the surface of the blue waters of the adult pool, exclaiming with laughter, "It happened again!"

"You are definitely a sinker," she diagnoses.

"What do you mean?"

"There are two kinds of people, those who float and those who sink. You are among the sinkers."

"Will I ever learn to swim properly?"

"You will, but you have to work harder."

Finding it unfair, I lost my enthusiasm for learning to swim.

As my teacher moves towards the women's change room, she asks one of the long distance swimmers—an elderly looking gentleman with greying hair—to watch out for me.

She does not know who this man is, but I sort of know. He is a priest.

11

THE ROBELESS PRIEST

THE PRIEST AND I WALK FROM THE DEEP END of the adult pool to the shallow end of the baby pool. He is English and Anglican. We are about the same age, both looking a little younger than our age, and both a little short of breath—the priest for having swum forty lengths of the adult pool, and I, for having sunk twice to the bottom of the same pool. Like the emphysematous or asthmatic patients who talk more when they are short of breath, the priest talks more after his swimming, something that makes me wonder if he is truly English, because most of the Englishmen I have met are hard to engage in long conversations.

The first time we met was when I walked in the shallow pool and saw him sitting alone but ready to talk to anybody within two feet of him. He had been in Iran during the Second World War as a young officer in the British Navy and as part of the Allied forces. He says that he stayed most of his war time in the historical city of Ghazvin, far away from any lake or ocean. After the war, he left Iran and the Navy to go to a seminary to become a priest. I have never seen him in his clerical robe, but, even without it, he looks spiritual enough to suit priesthood. Sometimes the less one wears the more one reveals spiritually, the obvious example of it being the scantily dressed Mahatma Gandhi of India.

On our way towards the baby pool, I asked the priest if he had a cure for my hypersensitivity towards being blamed. He said I could not get rid of that as long as I was overjoyed when being praised.

The other adults who usually sit in the shallow pool have gone, leaving us the entire lukewarm pool to ourselves. We sit with our backs to the adult pool, facing the solid ceramic wall marked by a pair of ceramic footprints to indicate that the walkway that leads to the exercise room should be traversed with bare feet. There are two rectangular doorless openings in the wall, one for men, and one for women.

"This is a nice *Feeroozeh*," the priest comments as we sit, while looking at the turquoise ring on the little finger of my right hand. "Is the stone from Mashad or Afghanistan? It has the shape and the colour of the dome of the mosques in Mashad, but has the colour of a genuine *feeroozeh* from Afghanistan."

"It could be from either," I reply with confidence "since Feerooz-Kooh, or Turquoise Mountain, from which good turquoise comes, is located near both Afghanistan and Mashad."

"I thought Feerooz-Kooh was a small town rather than a mountain," the priest politely corrects.

Surprised that he knows so much about the eastern part of Iran despite having been stationed mainly in Ghazvin, I say, "I stand corrected. You are right. I have been away from Iran for so long that I am beginning to mix the names of the mountains and places."

"You *sit* corrected!" The priest corrects my correction with a gentle smile, revealing at the same time his sophisticated British sense of humour and his familiarity with the parliamentary rules.

I remember now. Feerooz-Kooh was not even a little town, but a small village or just a swelling of the gravel road that connected Tehran to Mashad. In the summer holidays, when we went from Tehran to Mashad or Torbat, the bus always stopped there for gas and water, or for repairing its punctured tires or broken springs. As soon as the bus would stop, craftsmen swarmed the bus to offer their handicrafts made of a soft stone with a greenish hue, to the sitting passengers through the windows, begging them to buy something. They mainly sold rosaries, bulky containers and mortars. Since the Farsi name of turquoise is *feeroozeh*, and those soft stones had a greenish hue, I don't blame my subconscious for mixing them up to create a plausible but false story regarding the origin of turquoise.

After I turned my ring to straighten it for the thousandth time, I thank the priest for noticing such a small semiprecious stone. And to compensate for the misinformation I have just supplied to him, I feel that I should give him some genuine information. So I ask the priest, "Do you know why it is called turquoise?"

"Haven't got the faintest idea."

"The word turquoise is derived from Turkey, the country. The Europeans have named it such, and for two reasons. The first, because it was imported to Europe through Turkey, and the second, because the concave ceiling of some of Turkey's majestic mosques are covered with this colour tiles."

"Most of the domes of the mosques in Persia have the same colour as well," the priest recalls his old observation. "But the Europeans have not called it Persian stone. Do you have any explanation for that?"

"First of all, the Europeans often misname things. Persian lamb, for example, comes from Afghanistan," I replied. "Secondly, the blueness of the Persian domes is on the outer or the convex aspect of the domes. And thirdly, as I said a moment ago, since it was imported to Europe through Turkey, it acquired the name of that country, even though it was exported from Iran or Afghanistan."

"What is so special about this semiprecious stone that most Iranians carry it with them-selves, especially those who come out of their country?" the priest continues.

"I wasn't aware that most Iranians carry a ring like this," I tell the priest. "I thought mine was unique. My mother gave it to me when I went back to Iran for a short visit after being away from her for twelve years."

"Does it have any other significance?" The priest asks.

"When I was in San Francisco, recently," I say, "my cousin whose name is Rezvan, said that carrying any blue thing—not necessarily a turquoise—is a good omen; it wards off bad things and keeps one out of harm's way."

"When was the last time you saw your mother or your country?"

"The last time was the summer of 1977, two years before the revolution of 1979," I say, and before he can ask his second question, I volunteer to reply, "And I didn't see it coming. Not only me, but no one else saw it, not even the CIA."

I went to see my mother after twelve years of being in Canada. She had moved, or rather her house had changed. She was not living in her own house near the south end of Tehran anymore. She was living in a house that belonged to our Auntie Pouran, near the Jaleh Square at the northeast end of Tehran. The familiar oval brass that showed the family name of our mother on the door had changed from *Shojania* to *Agha Khani* on a rectangular plaque.

Early in the morning, I rang the doorbell and waited, having a hard time containing my emotions. My mother, of course, was not expecting me since I had not written to her that I was coming. I wanted to surprise her. I could hear the muffled sound of footsteps getting close to the door. I thought a servant would open the door. But when the door opened, I saw it was my mother. She appeared shorter than her image in my mind. There was a new brown patch on one of her cheeks, resembling the map of an unknown country. For a moment I thought it was me who had grown taller. We embraced in a clumsy hug. Neither of us knew how to hug properly. Apart from her religion, proper hugging was the other thing that she had not taught us. I squeezed too hard, believing that the harder one pressed the more affection one has shown. Her breast pressed against my liver. Before I could even say *Sa-laam*, she removed her ring from her little finger to give it to me.

"No, Modar-jun," I refused to accept it, "not your last ring." She had no other rings on her hands, "*Beh-Khoda* no," I swore to God that I wouldn't take it.

"Take it," she ordered. "*Beh-vallaaheh* I don't need it anymore." She pleaded, swearing to God in Arabic that she would rather let me have it. How could I refuse?

I believed her and took the ring, perhaps without sufficient thanks, as if it were the ticket I needed to have in order to enter her house. But even then she did not let me in. Once before she had said that getting into the chest of women is dangerous, because weeping, like yawning, might be contagious.

"What good timing!" my mother exclaimed. "Today is the third day after the death of the mother of your cousin, Farhad Mirza. All of your friends and relatives whom you are so anxious to see are there, in the Majd Mosque. Be a good boy and before you take off your shoes, tiptoe to that mosque and come back soon. You will see all the people you haven't seen all these years in one visit."

"I didn't know the mother of Farhad Mirza, Modar-jun," I said, slightly irritated. "I have never seen her, let alone known her," I added, disappointed that my mother was not excited enough by my unexpected presence at her door after twelve years of absence.

"It does not matter," she said. "Going to a funeral is not for the dead. It is for the living."

I went and saw, as my mother said, all the people I wanted to see and more. There were several that I did not know at all. Since Farhad Mirza was elected as a member of parliament after his return to Iran from America, he had many highly placed new friends that we did not know. Because of his specialty, my cousin was active in the favourite project of the Shah, the Land-Division project that was supposed to prevent a revolution by the landless peasants, but worked in reverse. The reason for this paradoxical effect was the unforeseen phenomenon that the peasants mostly sold their share of land and bought either a bicycle with the money or a motorcycle and went to live on the periphery of Tehran. When the jobless number reached the critical mass required for a revolution, the revolution happened.

Farhad Mirza was smartly dressed, as usual, but with a black tie rather than his usual matching one, standing at the top of the red carpet that bisected the tiled floor. Everybody was sitting on chairs. No one was crying. All the men wore black or dark ties. Some women wore ceremonial scarves out of respect. No woman wore a veil.

I saw many friends and relatives, but I did not talk to any of them. It was not a place to talk. I only exchanged smiles with those who recognized me as I walked softly along the carpeted walkway. Even after the somber ceremony ended, I did not talk to anyone. I had to go to my mother's house.

Going back however, I was not as anxious to reach the house of my mother as I was in the morning. The surprise effect of my arrival was gone and we had nothing to say to each other. Our communication was through letters, and through letters we had already said whatever was worth saying.

The only couple I talked to was Amir Teymourtash, my cousin who is about ten years older than me and about three times darker, and his wife Rezvan, another cousin whose skin is as white as her brother's, Farhad Mirza. Her brother's skin is so white that many years later, when he came to Canada and had open heart surgery in Vancouver, the nurse who pulled down his pants for a few pre-operative injections exclaimed that she had "never seen such a white ass." As far as skin colour is concerned the Iranian race is very heterogeneous; particularly when compared with, say, the Chinese or Japanese. This should perhaps be expected from people who have lived along the busy Silk Road for more than five millennia.

My consanguineous, married cousins, wanted to ask me about Canada because they were thinking of emigrating. This surprised me because Amir was doing well and was friends with one of the Shah's brothers that would guarantee him to continue to do well. And Rezvan had just won the largest lottery to that date, 25,000 *Tuman*, the first winner ever in our family. She did not need it though. I don't know why she even bothered to buy the ticket. She said her picture was used as propaganda on lottery posters by the lottery company. Even though she was not the best looking woman among the women of our extended families, I am sure she was the best looking among the previous winners whose pictures always looked like losers.

Like his sister, Farhad Mirza was lucky. Even though he was born and raised in the religious city of Mashad, he was not very religious. Something happened to him, however, during his final exam in high school in Mashad, that if it had happened to me, I would have definitely believed in God and all the miracles attributed to Him.

"What was that?" the priest suddenly becomes interested.

It happened during a written exam on physics and the question was, "Describe and discuss the image of a candle reflected in *mohaddab* (convex) and *mogha'ar* (concave) mirrors." An easy question as far as he was concerned. He wrote the reply quickly and went out of the class among the first few students. In the school yard, when the other students came out and began to discuss the exam question, my cousin realized that he had answered both questions wrongly and would get zero out of the maximum of twenty. He thought it would take a miracle to prevent him from failing. The only thing that he could do was to go to the shrine of Imam Reza in Mashad—which was very close to their house, so close that he had seen only the inside of it once as a child, when he was taken there by their maid—and pray for a good mark. And if he did get a good mark, he promised to Imam Reza, he would believe in him and God and all the miracles attributed to Him.

About two weeks later, when he got his report card, he saw to his amazement that he had received 20 out of 20 in physics.

"So miracles do happen," says the priest.

"This is exactly what I said to my cousin, but he said that it was not a miracle at all."

"Then what happened that instead of zero he got twenty?" the priest asks disappointed.

"I asked my cousin the same question, but he said that it was no miracle because he had found the reason why he had received such a good mark despite having answered both questions wrongly."

"And what was his reason?"

The reason was that my cousin had learned the curved mirrors backward from the beginning. This was partly due to their confusing Arabic names, and partly because he had rarely seen the outside of the most famous dome in Mashad due to the proximity of their house to the shrine. This is why when their teacher had said that *Mohaddab* (Arabic for convex) meant dome-shaped, my cousin had imagined the interior of a dome which is hollow or cup-shaped. And when the teacher had said that *Mogha'ar* (Arabic for concave) was like a bowl, he had imagined the outside of a bowl which is dome-shaped. With this kind of reverse learning, when, at the time of the examination he had answered the questions wrongly, the result had turned out to be right. In other words, in the case of my cousin, two wrongs did become one right.

"Too bad" says the priest sadly, "that the moment we find an explanation for the physical phenomena, we forget about their metaphysical dimensions."

"I know," I agree with the priest, "and this is despite the fact that in Arabic classes in high schools in Iran all of us are taught that Imam Ali has said, 'There are two kinds of sciences; the science of *Abdan*—Arabic plural for bodies or physics—and the science of *Adyan*—Arabic plural for faith, religion or metaphysics.'"

12

A TURQUOISE BRIDGE

THE NEXT WEEK, as soon as the priest and I sat on the checkerboard floor of the shallow pool, he uttered "A turquoise bridge" with a nostalgic sigh. I did not know what he was referring to. His mind, like the motion of a knight on a chessboard, works unpredictably. I was not sure if he was referring to my turquoise ring that he knew was given to me by my mother on my last trip to Iran, or to something spiritual. Spiritual, because I knew there was something sacred about bridges. This is why, when they want to talk about popes on the radio or other media, they use the respectful adjective *Pontiff*, derived from the French word *Pont* for a bridge.

Omid, the contemporary poet from Khorassan, who is also a friend of my poet cousin Mohammad Mirza Ghahreman from Torbat, also uses the word *poll*, Farsi for bridge, in one of his blasphemous poems, named *Mord-aab*, meaning swamp; literally dead water:

I am squatting at the shore of this motionless water

Letting a river of insults run out of my mouth

Towards "Khoda" and whoever has

Built a "Poleh Peyghaam"—a bridge of message

From anywhere to anywhere.

I changed the subject to talk about my uncle colonel who wrote a book by the name of *SOS* during the Second Word War, advocating international peace. "Did you know Colonel Abdollah Khalvati when you were in Iran?" I ask the priest, "He was a colourful character known to many Iranians, especially in Tehran, as Sarhang Sharabi, meaning the Wine-stricken Colonel."

"I was, as I said, stationed mostly in Ghazvin, but on one of my trips to the port of Abadan I met a courageous Iranian Cavalry officer with the family name of Khalvati. He was a lieutenant then. He was in charge of seeing that troops and trucks went safely by train from the tip of the Persian Gulf to the north of Iran, destined for the Russian front."

"No, that must have been Sohrab, one of his two sons," I said, disappointed that he did not know the father.

"The father is dead now, but has two living sons, both colonels. Sohrab, the younger, is a Cavalry colonel, Manuchehr, a year older, an Infantry colonel."

The priest did not seem to be interested in continuing this subject, so I changed it and asked, "By the way, did you know that Iran had declared neutrality before it was invaded by the Allied forces?"

"No, I'm sorry, I did not know," said the priest genuinely feeling sorry.

Yes, the Parliament of Iran had done so, when Foroughi was the prime minister. I don't know what the religion of the prime minister was. Most likely he was a Moslem, but Shah-rokh, the Farsi-speaking announcer of Radio Berlin for Iranians got so mad at this decision by Iran that he called the prime minister a Jew. The Germans expected Iran to join the Axis and fight against the Allied forces.

Colonel Sharabi seemed to know by intuition that invasion of Iran would happen, whether Iran declared neutrality or not. This is why he kept saying, "The Allied forces would not pay any attention to a torn piece of paper, and since they badly need to send troops and ammunition to Russia through Iran, let us give them a corridor so that they can accomplish their purpose with minimal damage to our country and no bloodshed."

He kept saying this so often and so loudly that, to get rid of him, the government created the Department of Civil Defense and made him its chief. Immediately, the father and the son, like the legendary Rostam and Sohrab in the *Book of the Kings*—if not Don Quixote and his assistant Sancho—sat on their horses and went to check all the borders of Iran, the watery ones as well as the mountainous ones. Three months later they were back in Tehran. The father wrote his report, the summary of which was this: If we want to defend Iran against the invasion of the Allied forces for six months, we need so many cannons and so much ammunition that the budget for it would be equal to fifty years of the budget of the country. He gave his report to General Hedayat who was a colonel at that time and was in charge of the correspondences with the court of the king of the time, Reza Shah. Hedayat knew Sharabi very well, not only because of his earnest patriotic sentiments, but also because Sharabi was the husband of his aunt. He accepted the report and promised that he would give it to Reza Shah, but he was afraid that Reza Shah might get mad and kill the Colonel somehow, if he did not like it. This is why as he was accepting the report he said to Sharabi, "Sarhang, I will show this to His Royal Highness at an opportune moment, but make sure you don't make a premature widow out of my aunt."

Sohrab, even when he was a boy, when he needed to go to a public bath house, never went to the one near their street, the Little Bazaar of Asheikh Hadi. Instead he would go to the one in Pahlavi Avenue, often with his father. Once when he had come back from Abadan, he went to the same bath house as an adult, alone. The master of the bath house recognized him and asked, "Is your father dead?"

"No," Sohrab said, somewhat annoyed. "Why do you ask?"

"Because," the man who was waiting for that question replied, "if he was alive, these foreign soldiers would not be marching in our streets today."

"What did your mother say?" The priest resumed questioning.

"About what?"

"About the cause or causes of the Iranian revolution."

"If you are asking about the revolution that Reza Shah began—which began with unveiling of women in Iran, purification of Persian language from Arabic words, prohibition of mendacity in the streets and closing of any public bathhouses that used pools of re-usable waters rather than *douche* (French for shower)—my mother said nothing about them. Actually, my mother did not talk very much. Our meaningful conversations began only when I left her and began writing to her.

"I am asking about that latest revolution," the priest brought me back to the topic he was most interested in, "the Islamic one, the one which caused re-veiling of women in Iran."

"She did not say anything about that either, but when I asked her in one of my letters why the revolution succeeded so easily, compared to the time of our youth when we tried and couldn't do it, she replied, 'It was not the revolution that succeeded; it was the government that fell.'"

And when the semi-secular Bazargan, who was educated as an engineer, and was chosen by Ayatollah Khomeini to be his first post-revolutionary president, failed to help the country, my mother wrote to me what Ayatollah Khomeini had said about that failure. "Some think that the only way to turn the wheels of a country is to imitate the West. We, too, have had great thinkers like Razi, Ebneh Sina and Sohravardi."

"But wasn't Sohravardi the one who was strangled for his anti-Islamic blasphemies?" A cleric in the religious city of Ghom objected to Ayatollah Khomeini's reference to Sohravardi, the next day.

"Ending 2500 years of monarchy in Iran and bringing down its last shah," Ayatollah Khomeini countered the objection on the national radio, "were easier than the struggle we have ahead of us against these few dry-minded, die-hard individuals."

"What was at the root of the success of the Islamic revolution?" the robeless priest asked.

"Underestimation of the intelligence of the clergy men by the intellectuals," I said without giving some examples. And then, to change the sensitive subject, I asked the priest, "Who coined the phrase you uttered as soon we sat down today?"

"I am not sure," said the priest, "but I know who coined the phrase 'the Iron Curtain,' right after the end of the Second World War."

"Who?"

"Mr. Churchill," said the priest, "referring to the impermeable wall surrounding the secretive Soviet Union."

"Then I think it must be the French who coined the phrase, "A turquoise Bridge" referring to Iran." I concluded so because I remembered when I went to Expo 67 to Montreal with my wife, we could not get inside the Persian pavilion because one of the Shah's brothers, we were told, was to visit the pavilion on that day. So we stood outside and we heard the Quebec minister of culture talking about Iran, its miniatures, and its contribution to the success of the Allied forces. And, now that I am thinking about it, I remember that he mentioned the "Bridge of Turquoise" in his speech as a nickname for Iran during the Second World War.

The French are more romantic and more familiar with Persian culture. They captured Iranian culture with their Victor Hugo and Montesquieu, but never with their soldiers, even when they were part of the Allied forces. They did it with their language. The father of Farhad Mirza, the one who was the mayor of Mashad for a short time during the reign of the last Shah, often said, "The voice box of Iranians is better adapted to speaking French, than to Arabic or English."

Colonel Abdollah Khalvati, the father, could have been the architect of that bridge.

"What was the number of casualties suffered by the Iranian army and how soon were they defeated?" asked the priest, opening a chronic wound in our family.

"Iran was defeated in less than 48 hours. The Russians invaded Iran from the north, and the British from the south. I don't know about the Army, but half of the Persian navy—composed of two battle ships: *Palang* (Leopard) and *Babr* (Tiger)—was damaged, and the commander of the Battleship Palang, Na-Khoda Milanian, the son-in-law of Colonel Abdollah Khalvati, was killed."

"Didn't you say that your uncle had only two sons and no daughter?"

"Yes I did, but she was his adopted daughter. Her name was Rakhshi Khanum. Actually, she was one of the several orphaned nieces and nephews of Sharabi." The other children were adopted by our other aunts and uncles. When they were dividing the children, my mother said, "I have enough children of my own, give me the mother." This is why Auntie Pouran lived in our house all her life, soon after she lost her aging husband to consumption.

"How was the manner of death of Milanian?"

The British Oil Company in Abadan had thrown a big party the night before the attack. For the first time they had invited all Iranian navy officers as well. Milanian was invited too, but he did not drink because he was worried about his ship and left the party early. Early in the morning the British bombarded the ship and wounded him. He was thrown to the shore, bleeding. He was brought to Tehran half the way by an Iranian truck driver and the second half by train. Colonel Sharabi went to the railroad station to take him to a hospital. When Milanian saw his father-in-law, he said, "Sarhang, I defended our land on the ship, at the shore, and in the streets, but I bled so much that I fainted, I am sorry." When Sharabi tried to cool him down by beginning to praise his courage, Milanian died. Before he died, however, he managed to say his last words for which he had kept himself alive all the way, "I leave my two sons, Hormoz and Houman, in your capable hands, Sarhang."

"What was the first name of Na-Khoda Milanian?" asked the priest.

"Hassan," I said, having no idea why the priest was always interested in trivia, "Why?"

"Because," said the priest with sadness, "I was the navy officer who first found him bleeding beside a creek and offered to take him to the British Hospital in Abadan, but he refused."

13

WASHING OFF THE BLASPHEMOUS SONGS
OF MALAMATIES

CAUTIOUSLY STEPPING ON THE WET CERAMIC FLOOR, I make my way to the men's change room. I don't want to fall again. Once I fell as a child in the slippery public bath house for women in Mashad and promised myself never to fall again nor go to women's bath houses.

There are three new naked men under the four-headed shower, all unconscious of their genitals, one pissing like the boy in Brussels.

I take off my swim trunks and throw them onto the plastic chair standing at the farthest corner of the shower room. They hit the intended target and I take my place under the vacant showerhead.

As the warm droplets of water hit my head I feel so happy, it's as if granular sugar were dissolving over my solar plexus. The cause of my happiness is the fact that I have found a name for my book. I will call it *Persian Letters* so that it includes all the letters I have written to or received from my mother or friends. But my happiness quickly changes to sadness when I remember a French writer and sociologist by the name of Montesquieu, a contemporary of Jean Jacque Rousseau, used that name for his French book, *Les Letters Persans*, almost 200 years ago. So, I change it to *A Persian Letter*, and my happiness returns to its initial level, indicating that I have made the right decision.

I did not have enough time to explain to the priest the importance of the shower in Iran, and why I included it as one of the revolutionary acts of Reza Shah. Like any revolutionary act, of course, there was much resistance towards the drastic change from *Khazeeneh* (Arabic for reservoir of water, especially hot water in public bathhouses) to a *Douche* (French for a perforated metallic device with no Persian equivalent, resembling the expanded head of a watering can for flowers, also known as a shower-head in English).

The children did not mind the change at all, but some of the old and most of the owners of the bathhouses resisted the change. The former resisted the change due to the fact that one could not *Ghosl*, meaning ablution and ceremonial bathing, with a shower, and the latter for an economical reason, considering it a waste of hot water if it was going to be used only once and for one person only.

All these changes were happening so close to our moving from Mashad to Tehran that I was wondering if Reza Shah was trying to fulfill my childhood wishes, or perhaps I was trying to accommodate my wishes with the revolutionary acts of Reza Shah.

I am so happy that I wish to do something wrong. I begin to sing blasphemous songs like the two-liners attributed to the Malamaties in Torbat. These are not among the two-liners my poet cousin, Mohammad Mirza has collected and published under the *Feryad-haayeh Torbati*, meaning *The Cries of Torbat*. Not many people know these lines. These are made by those who wish to be blamed. They attack the national treasures like Arash the Archer who put his life in the arrow to determine the border of Iran-land after a humiliating defeat. Or worse, they attack the book of Shah-nameh by Ferdowsi, the Persian poet who tried his hardest not to use any Arabic word in his voluminous *Book of the Kings* that he considered to be "A stony castle that would last forever and would not get damaged by the elements; whether wind or rain." His book is one of the reasons that the Persian language is still alive.

I murmur them under the shower without the fear of being detected or attacked by the anti-Malaamaties. The other three are singing their own undecipherable songs.

Arash the Archer was nobody

But a Torbati kid with a Palakhmoo (slingshot) in hand

Shooting sparrows in the trees.

      ***

The stony castle of Ferdowsi

Will grind down to nothing

By the corrosive effect of the sandpaper of time.

The dusty tomb of the Master of Malaamaties

Will remain for ever

Like the grains of sand in an hourglass.

      ***

This semiprecious stone of mine is superior

To the ring of Suleiman.

It is not the master of wind

But is a peerless whole.

***

The rosary of Malamaties in Torbat

Is made of turquoise.

The rosary of the Ne'mati in Kerman

Is made of donkey beads.

The hot droplets of water burn my head and shoulders before I shut off the shower and leave the recreation centre.

14

MUCUS-SECRETING BRONCHIOALVEOLAR ADENOCARCINOMA

THE SUN DOES NOT BOTHER MY EYES when I come out of the recreation centre because the inside was almost as bright as the outside. The slender body of a white woman in black, moving towards the building for the elderly, attracts my attention. She looks like the wife of my colleague, Victor, who lost his job due to unconfirmed insanity. I wonder if her hair has gone rapidly grey in the last few years that I have not seen her, or it is her black dress that makes her hair appear greyer than it actually is. She used to wear a white nursing uniform; now she wears black like a nun. I wonder if Victor is still alive.

It is still too early for me to go home. Maybe I should go and see how Victor is doing. The sun is still above the ground, running behind the tree trunks, blinking in approval of any decision I might make.

My wife does not like me to be at home too early anyway. She has things to do. I am not the only interest in her life. Even if she has nothing to do, she and her mirror have a lot to do with each other.

The last time Victor came to my office was several months ago. He said he had come to make use of my microscope to look for the cancer cells in his sputum. I moved away from my chair and found the slide he was looking for and let him look at his own tumour cells. He did not spend too much time behind the microscope, though. His chest pocket was bulging with a bundle of letters. I thought he was going to show me a new letter he had written about the person who had fired him. But I was wrong. He had stopped doing that. Instead, he showed me a certificate of sanity obtained from a psychiatrist in Ontario. As I was reading it, he was asking me how was it possible to be considered sane in one Canadian province, but insane in another.

"Why did you come back, then?" I asked Victor, upset that he might soon become permanently unemployed.

He said he had been working happily for three months as an anatomical pathologist in Ontario until he misdiagnosed a needle biopsy of a prostate gland, but instead of sending a short amended report, he wrote a long apologetic letter. That made the head of the lab change his mind about doing him a favour and terminated his employment while Victor was still on probation.

I believed in the certificate of sanity that Victor produced and I shared his enthusiasm in obtaining it. I know how hard it would be to prove one's sanity after one is labelled with insanity.

I never believed that Victor was insane, anyway. I always thought he was a normal and colourful man from Scotland, with perhaps accentuated characteristics. He wore a colourful kilt, for example, instead of a black tie or tuxedo, whenever he attended formal parties arranged by the Victoria Medical Society. I could be wrong, though. I could have let my friendship with him colour my medical impression. That was another reason why I switched from psychiatry to pathology when I came to Canada. It was unwise to diagnose insanity in a culture so different from mine.

I was practising part-time psychiatry while I was doing general practise in Iran, before coming here, but I was not good at it there either. The problem with me is always the same: using my own psyche as the norm, and comparing my psychotic patients to myself. Once, I remember, I let an in-patient, who was the chief of one of the rebellious tribes in Iran—the tribe whose men were known for keeping their word—go home and spend the weekend with his wife and family. Instead, he went to the justice department in Tehran and raised hell for being hospitalized without sufficient reason.

I benefited from my patients more than they benefited from me, when I was doing part-time psychiatry with my friend, Dr. Massoud. I still remember a middle-aged woman with unkempt, frizzy grey hair, in Rooz-beh Mental Hospital in Tehran. Massoud was showing me her peculiar multiple obsessions. Usually, if an Iranian woman developed obsessive behaviour, it was about excessive washing and cleaning, but she was not like that. This was why she had to be hospitalized despite a severe shortage of psychiatric beds.

She was smart but her smartness was overshadowed by her obsessions. One of her obsessions was in having problems passing through a door, whether in or out. She would walk normally and with normal speed up to the moment that she reached the threshold of the door. Then she would stop there like a nail to make several hesitating and oscillating motions, as if she was trying to gather all her courage to jump over a high bar, before passing through the door. I shifted my attention from her to the yard to diminish her embarrassment. *"Regardez la malade!"* Massoud said to me, not knowing that the patient knew French. She got upset with Massoud and said, "What is so interesting to look at? I am sick.

Can't you see?"

Several months later when she came back to the same hospital to get a certificate of sanity to resume her teaching job in a high school, carrying only a book and her purse, I asked her what finally had cured her. She said, "The only thing that worked, among all the things they had tried on me, including electroshock therapy, was a frontal lobotomy."

That was many years before the appearance of the movie, *One Flew over the Cuckoo's Nest*, the movie that made the useful electroshock and lobotomy as the last resort, look like the worst things a doctor could do to a patient.

Victor had to quit smoking his pipe several years before the diagnosis of his lung cancer. He did not know he was going to get cancer. He quit smoking just because it gave him cold feet at nights. And to make things worse, he had to quit his occasional drink of Scotch whisky because it made him want to smoke.

During the boring years of his unemployment, Victor did not suffer much financially. Money or lack of it was not his problem. If anything, he was over-insured. His insurance, and the medical associations with which he was associated, paid him enough to eat steak, drink Scotch, play golf and take French lessons. Yet, he said, he was bored. He spent most of his time walking alone, talking to himself, and sometimes moving his arms more vigorously than his legs. He must have read many newspapers, judging by the number of letters he wrote to the editors trying to correct what he thought was a mistaken view about Quebec and her constant threat of separation from Canada. Sometimes he wrote about Robert Burns whose annual gathering in Victoria he never missed. He was at his most eloquent self on those nights.

I turned left towards the new address that Victor had given me on his last visit to my office.

Their home was at the end of a short cul-de-sac. It had a brown door and grey interior. Victor was in bed on their double bed, alone in their bedroom. He looked better and rosier than I expected, almost cheerful. The only other time I had seen him so cheerful was when he heard that he had lung cancer. He said at least now something was wrong with his body, not his mind. Something real and palpable to justify the benefits he was getting from the insurance companies. With his greying curly brown beard and glowing cheeks he looked as cheerful as a commercial Santa Claus.

"You used to come to my office to look for the malignant cells in your sputum under my microscope. What made you stop coming?" was the first thing I asked.

"Wastage of muscles," he said. "The tumour is suddenly acting up. In two weeks, it has robbed me of most of the bulk of my muscles."

He talked about his body as if it belonged to someone else. I could not verify the wastage of his muscles because his hairy legs and his bulky calves that were always exposed when he wore his kilt, were now hidden under layers of sheets and blankets. His left arm, he said, had become paralyzed the night before. He could move it but only by using his right hand.

"Why don't you go to the hospice, Victor?" I asked. "They do a good job at this stage of your disease. They make one die painlessly and with dignity."

"My wife is a nurse." he said. "She knows how to take care of me. Why should I burden the purse of the public with my unnecessary expenses?"

"You did not have a primary brain tumour, Victor, and metastatic tumours of the brain, as you know, do not come so suddenly as to cause such a sudden paralysis like yours. What is the connection, in your opinion, between your lung cancer and your paralyzed arm?"

"Hyperviscosity," Victor said readily, as if answering a medical question at examination time. "My tumour is now secreting its viscous mucus secretion directly into my blood stream, causing hyper-coagulability. I think some of the vessels in my right hemisphere are plugged by a blood clot as the result of it."

"But your faculty of reason seems to be intact," I said. And then, I told him the story of Dr. Stuart, our psychiatrist neighbour whom Victor knew, too, and did not live far from his house. Stuart had a primary brain tumour but it manifested itself suddenly, not unlike Victor's brain infarction.

Like Victor, who had diagnosed his lung cancer himself by hearing continual sibilant sounds in his chest at nights, Stuart had made the diagnosis of his brain tumour himself, one morning. On that morning, as he was going through the wide open door of his office, rather than going through the doorway, he was arrested by the hard edge of the door frame. The side bar of the door frame hit him right in the middle of his forehead. Right away he diagnosed himself as having an advanced brain tumour, a tumour capable of obscuring exactly half of his visual field. Visual field is amazing; one does not know one has lost part of it until one hits something.

Mitra and I went to see Stuart at his house a few weeks before he died. I remember his wife's first name because Stuart had made an extra effort to make me remember it. He knew that I, coming from a different culture, could not remember names for very long, so when he introduced his wife to me, he said, "Carina, like the bifurcation of bronchi behind the sternal bone," pointing to a specific point in the middle of his chest as he said that.

His wife was not a nurse but she took good care of him, partly because she loved him and partly because the hospice doctors and nurses had shown her what to do.

When we saw Stuart that morning, he was still in bed on the left side of a double bed on the floor in the middle of their living room. After the exchange of greetings, he said, "Last night, Nasser, I kissed my right hand good-bye!" I thought he was joking, but he was not. "Every night, when Carina comes to bed," he continued, "I search for her hand under the blanket to bring it up to my lips to kiss it as a sign of my appreciation for her taking care of me. Last night I did the same but the hand I brought up to my lips was my own paralyzed hand."

Carina confirmed his story, laughing with sadness, "Yes! Last night I was waiting for my nightly kiss that never came."

Carina had black hair and white skin. She did not speak Arabic but she liked the look of Arabic script and was practising writing it with a broad-tipped reed pen. She showed me her work for my comment and to ask me if any of the words she had written made any sense. None of them, of course, made any sense. The chance of making a meaningful word out of a random assembly of letters is very small, especially if they are put together according to their shape. But since I did not want to disappoint her or discourage her from practising, I told her that some of them did make sense, but such a bad sense that I was ashamed to say it in the presence of mixed company.

Stuart was a wise and truthful man. I liked him from the first day that we met. He always asked relevant questions. For example, he asked me if childhood was invented when I was growing up in Iran. I told him that it was just beginning as I was finishing my childhood.

When Stuart told us about the loss of function of his arm, I thought it was a good time to play the Persian game called "Bring-bread-and-take-out-kabob" with him. We played it in our boring, toyless home when we were children. It required two people to play it. Two people facing each other, preferably in standing position, with bent arms. The palms of the hands of the person who "wants the kabob" are facing down, touching the palms of the hands of the opponent who will rapidly pull his hand away from the superimposed hand and try to slap the back of it, before it could be pulled away. If the person "wanting the kabob" managed to evade the slap, it becomes his turn to try to slap his opponent's hand which should go on the top. The slapping often started mildly but got rougher as the game went on. Our mother always prevented us from playing this game because, "You begin with jokes and laughter, but one of you, I am sure, will end up crying."

After I explained the rules of the game, Stuart was anxious to play, not only with me, but with Mitra and Carina as well. He soon learned to cheat and to make use of the sympathy we all had for the loss of the function of his arm, and began disobeying the rules of the game and hitting our hands, freely, with his good hand, laughing like a baby, as if he had discovered the use of his arm for the first time.

I asked Victor what he thought about the imminent Quebec referendum for separation or sovereignty, and how he was going to vote.

"As a Canadian Scot, I like to remain neutral regarding the internal affairs of my chosen country," he said and abruptly terminated further discussion on that topic.

His reply surprised me, though. This was one of the topics he always brought up in most of the letters that he used to send around the world regarding the injustice he had suffered at work. He must be close to dying, I thought.

He gave me a thin book of words to keep. It contained all the words common to French and English.

I told him that I liked French, too. My foreign language in high school in Tehran was French. I always wished Victor Hugo was my grandfather or that my grandfather at least looked like Victor Hugo whose picture I had seen in our French text book. I even translated one of his poems in grade eight to Farsi—the one in which Victor Hugo takes a bottle of jam to the dark closet in which his grandson was unjustifiably, he thought, imprisoned for having committed a certain childish crime. When I read it to my uncle colonel, he liked it, but advised me not to neglect my Arabic. "If you want to write good Farsi," he said, "you must know Arabic well."

Maybe it was at the time when he was trying to write his *SOS* and had found out how much Farsi had been enriched by Arabic. Because he was a busy man and was in the army, he did not have sufficient time to read his Koran and learn French. This is why he would read the French translation of the Koran while riding on a horseback in pursuit of armed highway robbers.

"Are you religious, Nasser?" Victor asked abruptly. He had never asked personal questions like this before.

"Yes Victor. If not religious, I am at least spiritual," I told him.

"Is your saviour the same as mine?"

"I don't know Victor. As far as saving is concerned, I consider you as my saviour."

"How so?" Victor asked, amused and surprised. "And in what sense?"

"In the sense that by going insane first and showing me its bad consequences, you have saved me from insanity," I said.

He laughed what I thought was his last laughter.

I told him that I might write a book and I might talk about him, if I had nothing better to say.

"Don't write about me," Victor said. "Write about him."

"About who?" I asked.

"About the man who fired me," Victor said, without any rancour, revenge or any sign of malignancy in his voice. He seemed to have completely forgiven his enemy like a good Christian. "What a mighty fighter he is," Victor praised the resiliency of his forgiven enemy since he had withstood all his toxic letters.

"I think your letters did hurt him, though," I reminded Victor. "He just underwent a quadruple coronary bypass on his heart at the same time that you were undergoing an operation on your lung."

"I don't draw any satisfaction from that."

"What cured you Victor, finally, and when, if I may ask?"

"It happened on a Sunday in our church. It suddenly occurred to me that the whole thing was just medical politics and nothing personal."

"What started it all?"

"It started at the welcome party that he threw for you at his house when you arrived from Winnipeg. I was happy. I had a few drinks and told him, as he was standing beside his newly renovated copper-plated fire place in his living room, that he was running a mill."

"Is that a bad thing to say to a man?" I asked, not knowing the significance of "running a mill."

"He knew very well what it meant, because he was from a mining town in England."

"Does it mean a kind of sweat shop or something like that?"

"Sort of" he said, and then his mind went somewhere else and when it came back he quoted William Blake, "dark, satanic mills."

"What has Robert Burns said about mills?"

"He didn't say anything about them, but scribbled a few words on the wall of a mill that he visited once.

> *We come not here to view your works*
>
> *In hopes to be more wise*
>
> *But only lest we go to hell*
>
> *It will be no surprise.*

"Why don't you start smoking again, Victor? You liked your pipe so much! It was your pacifier. It was part of you. It suited your beard and personality." I prescribed.

"I don't enjoy it anymore. I've lost my sense of taste. My mucus-secreting, bronchioalveolar adenocarcinoma is drowning me in mucus. Even my taste buds are coated with it."

"How about a spicy-hot chicken curry to cut through that tenacious membrane that has covered your taste buds?" I suggested. "Do you think you would be able to taste that? It comes with steaming Persian saffron rice. Persian rice or any other rice that is made the way Persians make, you should know, beats any other rice whether Chinese or from India."

Victor began to cough, almost choking, as he tried to tell me that he has never tried curry before.

I told him that Mitra knows how to make a good chicken curry. She has learned how from an English lady in Winnipeg, Joan, who was married to a psychiatrist friend of ours from India, Guibinda.

I waited for his cough to subside before saying my last goodbye to Victor. I said I would bring the curry tomorrow but would not come upstairs. I would leave it with Sam, downstairs around dinnertime, in the evening.

He smiled his last smile when I shook his functioning hand and coughed again when he wanted to say, "Chicken curry would be fine."

As I drove towards home, I shut off the radio of my car to do some original thinking. I am amazed by the plasticity of the human brain that is capable of working normally despite missing a big chunk to an infarction or a brain tumour, and the vulnerability of the human mind that can get confused by a single pill or a bad news.

15

MIKE THE STONE MASON

EFFORTLESSLY MY CAR TAKES ME UP THE LOW HILL that leads to the circular driveway of the University of Victoria. But before reaching there, I turn sharply to my left into our own driveway. The front of our house looks southwards, away from the street to look at the narrow band of blue water beyond the trees. This is why its less attractive side, with exteriorized stairs, faces the street.

I turn off the engine and remove the key to get out, but the engine keeps going. It keeps going like my old car in the asphalt-melting heat of summer days in Tehran. I pull the lever to release the hood to see what is stuck to what in the engine of my so far problem-free car. As soon as I step out I realize that the car is innocent and the noise is coming from our house. My wife must be running the vacuum inside.

Our house, being built in 1975, is typical of the houses built in the 70s, with a built-in vacuum cleaner, shaggy carpets, and an intercom near the main entrance. Everywhere, including the interior stairs is wall-to-wall carpet except for the hall which is covered by a Persian carpet from Kerman with a navy blue background. I have repeatedly pleaded with my wife not to use a vacuum on Persian carpets because it shortens their life, but she does not seem to be listening. The proper way to clean a Persian carpet is either with a smooth brush, or by a handbroom, made in the city of Ghazvin.

I have three ways to enter my house: the little blind door under the balcony, the sliding door of the renovated kitchen on the balcony, and, of course, the front door. Today I choose the front door because of its new stone deck that Mike the stone mason built in front of it. It used to have a wooden deck, with parallel lines of dark-brown two-by-fours. I would rather step on this solid monochromic quilt, than on those rotting parallel bars. They always look wet, even when it is not raining. They shine with the iridescence of the cracked ice on the surface of a pool.

One of the reasons I like this deck so much is because I helped Mike build it. I happened to be on vacation when Mike was building it. First, I came out of the house and began talking to him and gradually I got involved. Initially, when he was noisily cutting the slabs of stone, thicker than two inches, with the rented diamond saw, my job was to spray water at the cutting edge of the blade with the hose.

Mike does not consider himself a stone mason. It is I who has given him that nickname. He consider himself a landscaper, but he is basically a gardener. "When I came out of the ferry and saw Victoria had so many gardens," Mike said, "I knew I would not be without a job for too long in this city." Mike is the man who turned our small front yard and the narrow trickle of water in front of it into a small Japanese garden. I also helped him move the stone slabs from his beat-up truck to the driveway. Cutting the stone with the saw made so much noise that the neighbours thought we were topping the trees of our downhill neighbour to expand our sea view. It also created so much dust—fine volcanic dust like the sand dust that fell in our neighbourhood a few days after the eruption of Mount St. Helens—that our neighbours had to shut their windows for days and dust their furniture for weeks afterwards.

The first time that I met Mike was when he was hired to work in our front yard. He was standing, naked from waist up, exposing his lean, well-built sweaty body to the sunshine. Like the Greek statue named Atlas, he carried large rocks with his bare hands that no ordinary handyman or a manual labourer or anybody who did not work for himself would care to carry. They were so heavy that even Mike with all his rippling muscles would lose his balance sometimes and step with his rough boots on the recently pruned rosebushes in the flowerbed next to the Japanese garden. Despite his perfect body, Mike had two scars on one side of his head, each the size of a penny, both the same age. They were the result of being attacked from behind by a mob when he was hitchhiking in Florida, the first time he had run away from his home in Toronto. He said he has become street-smart, since.

"Why don't you use gloves?" I asked. "Your hands are your only tools. You should protect them, like a boxer."

"I'm more likely to hurt them if I wear gloves," Mike explained. "Gloves give you a false sense of security and make you take risks and do stupid things." As he said that, he stabbed his finger with the thorn of the nearby rose-bush. Disgusted with himself, he pulled the thorn out with his teeth, without uttering a vulgar word. To introduce himself better, he pulled a Polaroid picture out of his back pocket. It showed him in boxing gloves and a helmet. It was taken after the final match in Toronto in which he had lost to become the second in his weight class, which was 64 kilograms.

More than to his body and his hands, Mike paid attention to his expensive mountain bike. Even when he was talking to me he would look beyond my shoulders to see if the bike was still lying in his rusty truck. His truck was so dysfunctional that I could not believe it had brought him all the way from Toronto to Victoria. It is too bad that those who need a dependable car often have the most undependable one.

Mike took another Polaroid picture out of his pants pocket to show an example of his workmanship. It is the same picture that he had shown to Mitra on the first day. It shows the stones he has laid on a wide garden path in Toronto with proportionally wide gaps between the stones. It looked good enough to get him hired for his first job in Victoria. Mitra, however, wanted as little gap between the stones as possible, so that children and the dog did not bring sand and gravel with their feet into the house. He had agreed to do it her way only because he badly needed the job.

When I wanted to give him a hand moving the largest rock that he wanted to leave standing upright like an incomplete sculpture, he refused. He said certain loads, no matter how heavy, should be moved by one person only. When I told him that he was abusing his body, he said, "This is nothing. After I finish here, I'll go biking for an hour and then I'll run. This work is just a warm-up before my daily exercise."

"Why not jogging, instead of running?" I asked, "Everybody jogs in Victoria."

"No. I don't jog. I run. I run as if wild dogs are after me. I won't allow anybody to jump me ever again."

Some of the rocks he had brought for landscaping were smooth river rocks, incorporating the element of time in them. Some were sharply angulated, indicating they were freshly blasted rocks. He had no objection when I gave him a hand in carrying the angulated ones. We carried them from beside the road beyond the new Victoria General Hospital.

Mike was a rock hunter. Once he told me that he had spotted a rock that was perfect for the single step the patio required to connect to the sunken walkway going towards the backyard. It was not among the blasted rocks at the roadside, nor was it a river rock. It was located near the General Hospital at the foot of a hill behind a chicken-wire fence displaying a "Keep out" sign. He used the removable back gate of his truck as a lever to move the rock closer to the truck, and then he heaved it up himself.

The diamond saw was to cut slabs of stone no thicker than one inch, but most of the slabs were thicker than that. When we returned it, we had to pay for the damage, too. Since Mike had no money, he had to give our credit card that he had obtained from Mitra.

The last stone that Mike cut with that saw was L-shaped. That was his signature. He has been doing it wherever he has worked. That stone is now hugging seamlessly one of the corners of the single step that leads to the front door. It is not easily visible because no one pays attention to it. If you had seen it being cut, you would never miss it.

"Why L-shaped," I asked, "rather than the shape of any other letter of the alphabet?" I wondered if there was any spiritual significance to it, such as L for Lord, indicating Jesus Christ.

"It is the easiest letter of the alphabet to cut with a straight cutting saw," Mike said, while he moved his hand in the air as if drawing half a crucifix. As soon as he did that I saw that he had a fine golden chain around his neck from which a small gold crucifix was hanging.

"When did you change from being a runaway street-kid to a normal working man?"

"As of October 15, 1985," he remembered precisely. "It happened in a church."

His relationship with stone was more than the relationship of a stone mason or an artist with his raw material. When I asked for an explanation he said because stones were "forever and permanent."

"Is that why they make castles out of stone?" I asked, thinking about what Ferdowsi had said about his book.

"Correct."

When Mike asked me for a trowel, I had to ask him to repeat his request several times because I did not know what he was referring to. Finally, he spelled out the word, but I still did not know what kind of tool he was after. He was surprised that I had never heard of such a thing. When I asked him what he wanted it for, anyway, he said he wanted to fill the gaps between the slabs with crushed rocks. I picked up a wedge-shaped stone chip that looked like the first tool used by a human, to do the job. It worked even better than a trowel. He liked it and remarked that I was a good improviser. I told him that it was the result of never having the proper tool in our house when I was a child. We had to improvise, pulling nails out of wood, for example, with the pair of scissors, and using the handle of the mortar in the kitchen as a hammer.

"Do you know how long eternity is?" Mike asked.

I told him that in Winnipeg, there was a rock near the road leading to Birds Hill Park—perhaps left behind by a glaciers, because there was no other rock like it within miles around it—on which someone had written, "Eternal! So what?"

"Eternity" he estimated, "is more than the amount of time it would take to eliminate a rocky mountain from the face of the earth by the pecking of a single humming bird."

"Even then I don't think one gets any closer to the end of eternity," I said, as I shook his delicate hand for providing our house with the most permanent deck in Victoria.

16

To Be or to Have

I ASKED MY FRENCH TEACHER at the University of Victoria to teach me a formula to remember when to use the auxiliary verb *être* (to be) and when to use the auxiliary verb *avoir* (to have) when I want to make *passé composé* (present perfect tense.) She said that all French verbs should be conjugated with the verb *avoir* except for those that have something to do with a house. Then she showed me the diagram of an ordinary two-storey house with exteriorized stairs and said, " Imagine this house is *la maison d'être* (the house of being); whatever you *do* to it, like going into it or coming out of it, or climbing its stairs or falling from its roof, is to be conjugated with the auxiliary verb *être*, like *je suis descendu*, meaning I've climbed down the stairs. I admired her example because not only did the diagram she showed me look a lot like our own two-storey stucco house with exteriorized stairs, it also made sense, since a house, more than being a property *to have*, is a place *to be*.

I ring the doorbell before going in, even though the front door is unlocked. I don't want to startle my wife. I know one gets easily startled when there is a continuous, especially self-made noise like when one is under a shower or running a vacuum. The noise of the vacuum cleaner prevents my wife from hearing the doorbell. I gently open the door and step in to utter a relatively loud *Salaam*. She is badly startled and jumps up from her kneeling position, almost hitting her turbaned head on the oblique beam of the stairs in the hallway. She must have taken a shower and wrapped her head in a brown bath towel to dry her hair while vacuuming. The vacuum hose was left idly on the ground while she was investigating an early thread showing spot on the blue background of the Kerman carpet with the red tip of her already manicured fingers. The pink soles of her pedicured feet were supported by the wedge of her high-heeled slippers. When she wears these slippers upstairs I think she wants to see a little more of our sea view, but I cannot guess the reason for wearing them downstairs. She is so surprised by my unexpected entrance that she leaves my *Salaam* without a reply.

"Do you think we could have curry for dinner tonight?" I ask, pretending not to have noticed anything out of the ordinary.

She unwinds the towel from her head with disgust and says, "First of all, curry is not a Persian dish, and secondly, why are you suddenly interested in dinner so early in the afternoon?"

"It is not for me," I tell her. "It is for Victor. He is dying. He has lost most of the bulk of his muscles. He has not lost his taste buds but they are covered by tenacious mucus. I told him about your chicken curry and mentioned that you had learned it from an English lady in Winnipeg."

She knows Victor and his wife. She knows how close I was to becoming like Victor, and she likes his wife. Also, she does not say so right away, but I know she will make the curry. To change the subject, I ask her to guess who I saw in the elevator of the hospital today. She is in no mood for guessing.

"Mike," I volunteer.

"Which Mike?" she asks, uninterested, ready to dismiss whoever it might be since she has had some arguments with several of the many Mikes that we know.

"Mike the stone mason," I say, "the landscaper, the one with the L-shaped signature. He is sick."

I usually don't stare at the faces of patients when they are transferred from ward to ward in the elevator. It is uncomfortable enough for a sick man or woman to be in a horizontal position, next to the healthy individuals in vertical position. There is no need to accentuate the contrast by looking them in the eye.

As I was trying to avoid the face of the young man with light brown curly hair, I caught the shadow of his smile aimed at me. When I looked, I saw it was Mike, looking much better than when he was working in our yard. His face glowed with a yellow-orange hue, and his golden hair had covered his twin scars. By the time I asked what was wrong with him the orderly pushed him out and away from the elevator. I followed them as he was being wheeled down the corridor. I learned that he was going for a liver biopsy. I assured him that most likely he won't need the biopsy and reassured him that even if he had to have it, it would not hurt. I said so because I knew he did not like needles. He is one of those fearless people who paradoxically are afraid of needles. He had told me that himself. He had confessed that he could take punches to his chin in boxing matches and lead pipes on his head in the street, but when he is approached by someone with a needle in hand, "My fists will fly."

She interrupts me to tell me that she is not interested in the Mike who used her Visa like a blank cheque to pay for the rented diamond saw that he had damaged.

When I told Mike that I had been thinking about him often in the last few days, his smile got wider and, as he was being wheeled away, he craned his neck backward to ask me why. I said because I was writing a book. Writing a book is like entering a house. Even though it is the same house, it would look different depending on which door one uses to enter it. And since I was going through the front door that Mike had made the nice stony deck in front of it, he had come to my mind.

I take off my shoes to go to my room upstairs. My room used to belong to Nima before he went to Vancouver to continue his education. Most of the heavy things in the room, like the boxes of books and the large container of copper pennies, are Nima's.

I pin the square Polaroid picture of the dead man I was carrying in my chest pocket to the wall, next to the miniature bouquet of fragile wild flowers, made by Ethel, the wife of our neighbour on the other side of street and brought by her husband, Bob. Instead of glass, the flattened flowers are covered by a wavy transparent paper.

I can't even guess how many dollars the pennies in the brass basin amount to. Once I thought of doing a good deed and donating them to the cashier in our cafeteria so that people who are short of pennies could help themselves to them and by doing so, shorten the line-ups at lunchtime, but I could not carry the brass basin to my car. When Nima found out about my good intentions, he was glad that I was not able to carry it out. He said he needed them, but did not tell me what for. He can't buy things with them. He cannot make a sculpture out of them, either.

I pin the photo on the wall so as not to forget to take it back to the hospital on Monday morning, in case I change my jacket.

The picture shows an elderly white man, with hands the size of a small rake, lying in the supine position in the middle of the shady lawn of a well-kept backyard. His bamboo rake rests flat on his sunken abdomen to make an asymmetrical multiplication sign with his body. It is obvious that he has expired in the middle of gardening, even though he is not dressed like a gardener. He is wearing an old grey suit that was probably meant for semi-formal occasions, but with time it has lost its rigid lines and is now more suitable for gardening. Rather than shoes, he is wearing heavy brown army boots, making him look like a retired general from a country with too much sunshine. His forehead is paler than the lower part of his face. His skin shows evidence of sun damage represented by solar elastosis and pre-malignant actinic keratosis.

It is a peaceful picture. There is no evidence of violence, such as blood or bullet holes, and no sign of struggle before death. The door of the house, the coroner said, was open, and nothing was stolen from the interior, which had Persian carpets and was decorated with artifacts, such as elephants from India. A freshly cut stump of a small tree is sticking out of the grass a few feet away from the body, surrounded by a perfect disk made of freshly fallen wrinkled dry leaves. Away from the man and the lawn, leaning against the stucco wall of his Tudor-style house, a hand-saw is standing on its tip to give away the cause of death as sudden death due to fatal cardiac arrhythmia secondary to violent physical exertion in a man with a bad heart and a sedentary lifestyle.

In Winnipeg old men with cardiac problems die from shovelling snow on a winter morning. In Victoria they die from excessive gardening which, according to my learned friend Doug, has an unusual name, *godwottery*.

On closer examination of the Polaroid picture, I can see two birds perching on the naked branch of an alder tree right above the head of the dead man. The back of the man's right hand is resting on his forehead, partially covering his eyes, as if he does not wish to see the world he has left behind. His orbits are sunken like those of a skeleton, indicating either severe postmortem dehydration, or the eyes have been removed by the birds. According to the coroner's note, the last time he had been seen alive and walking was a week earlier. He could have been dead ever since.

I take off my jacket and go to view our backyard from our newly built balcony.

Our balcony is low. It does not make things on the ground look smaller than they are. If anything, it magnifies them a little. The single magnolia tree that Nima once asked me to paint when it had no leaves and was full of flowers is still there, now full of leaves and no flowers. Its trunk is as thick as the stump of the freshly cut tree in the Polaroid picture, but instead of being surrounded by a disc of fallen dry leaves it is surrounded by a round glass. When our smoky glass tabletop, with a hole in the centre for the stem of a parasol, broke in two halves one windy night, instead of throwing it away I placed the broken halves, like brackets, under the tree to make it look as if the stem was growing out of a frozen pool. I must have done a good job since it has fooled a few ducks. When Keyvan, our second son, saw the chalky duck droppings on the glass, he remarked, "Dad, the ducks have made a rude comment on your art work."

The green shadow of the magnolia tree at the corner of the yard extends to reach my shadow in the middle of the lawn. My shadow and its central location resemble the body of the dead man. The shadow of the bars of the balcony makes me look like an infant standing in a crib.

As I wonder why the coroner insists on a postmortem examination on an old man who obviously died of a natural cause, Mitra comes to the balcony with the cordless phone in hand, saying, "For you. It is the coroner."

I duck to protect my eye from the short antenna of the phone as I take it from her hand.

"Thanks for the photo of the scene, Coroner," I say before saying hello, to dissuade her from ordering an autopsy. "It is self-evident, isn't it?" I also tell her that my son, Nima, who is in medical school in Vancouver, has just come to spend the week-end with us and as soon as he saw that picture exclaimed that he had never seen in any medical book a picture of such a perfect natural death as in the photo she had taken from the scene.

"I wonder if the cause of death is a wasp sting?" the coroner said. "I was stung by one when I visited the scene. There is a wasp nest hanging from a tree in his residence."

I ask her to hold on so that I could go and have a closer look at the photo.

There is no scrotum of a wasp nest hanging from the trees in the picture. The scene is as calm as the surface of a sea with no wind. Besides, an old man would not die of a wasp sting even if he was allergic to it; because if he was, he would not have survived that long. Also, judging by his pink skin which is devoid of any pigmented spots, it is very unlikely that the man was suffering from the rare condition known as Mastocytosis which can make one lethally vulnerable to a wasp sting.

"How about postponing this issue for an indefinite period of time?" I suggest. To my surprise, the coroner appears to agree with me, at least for the duration of the week-end. I hand the phone back to Mitra, carefully, as one would hand someone a knife at a dinner table. She asks what the coroner wanted. I explain that it was about an autopsy that I refused to do.

"What?" she objected violently. "You refused to perform a forensic autopsy?"

"The Queen has forgiven, the commoner has not," I say to her, somewhat sarcastically, instead of explaining why I did not want to do that autopsy.

"What do you mean?" she asked. I was pretty sure that she knew what I meant.

"I mean the coroner who is representative of the Queen in this country has forgiven me for disobeying her order, but you have not. That is what I mean."

"Is your forgiving Queen also going to pay the dollars that you did not make by not doing the autopsy?"

I know she is right. I know it looks like too much of a loss, especially when children like to buy the newly invented Atari machine that costs about 300 dollars.

I want to say, "Compared to my ridiculously high income from the hospital, as Keyvan once said, this is not a great loss. Besides, I came home early to be with you. Do you prefer me to stay in the morgue all the time?"

Rather than getting bogged down in details of income and outcome, I take her to my room to show her the photo of the man she wants me to perform an autopsy on.

"Is he dead?" she exclaims as she moves her trembling body away from the wall.

"Yes, of course. Natural death, as natural as it can get."

"How do you know it is natural?"

"It looks like it."

"What do you think the poor man died of?"

"I think he died of excessive gardening."

"Oh, by the way, if you write to your mother, say my *Salaam* too and thank her for the five hundred dollars that she sent for the children."

I could not see the connection between not performing a postmortem examination on an old man and writing a letter to my mother, yet I do not ask for an explanation and say that I will convey her regards to my mother. I am glad that she is not concerned anymore about my refusal to perform that autopsy.

She leaves the room, fearfully, followed by the convoluted tube of the vacuum cleaner. When she reaches the middle of the corridor, she stops to tell me as an afterthought, "By the way, why don't you become a good husband for a change and water the grass in the backyard? Someone is coming to see our house. They might be interested in buying it. They have seen many houses with wider sea view than ours, but they want to see this one, too."

"What is so special about this house that they want to see?" I ask with sadness.

"Because it is near the university and they have three young boys."

"Any better reason?" I ask for no apparent reason.

"They come from Winnipeg. They know Majid and Moti." she says as an additional reason in favour of selling our house to them.

Selling this house, in which we have lived for more than twenty years and have raised three sons, makes me sad. As I descend the stairs in the hall to go to the backyard to water the grass, I tell my wife with increasing loudness, "Our French teacher says a house is a place to be, and not a property to have."

"Your French teacher does not know what she is talking about," my wife said as she went towards the mirror to dry her hair. And then, through the noise of her blow dryer she said, "When it comes to one's house, having and being are the same."

"I did not know that," I confess.

"Another thing that you don't know is that it is not a question of having or being; it is rather the question of doing or not doing. And it seems that it is me who always does the doing and you the talking."

17

WATERING THE GRASS IN THE SUNSHINE

THIS HEAVY-DUTY RUBBER HOSE SNAKING IN THE FRONT YARD and that light aluminum ladder in the backyard, have followed us almost against our will from Winnipeg to Victoria. When we told the professional movers in Winnipeg that we wanted to take everything to Victoria, they thought we really meant *everything*, and wrapped and packed everything to bring them here.

The hose is now crossing the oil-stained driveway to drip into the waterless creek in front of our house. I grab it by the neck, like picking up a poisonous snake, and pull it towards the backyard to water our neglected lawn. It is reluctant. It resists my pulling. It gives a little, then stops, and then begins pulling me backward like the elastic rope of nostalgia. It catches on the slightest protuberance of the ground or gets caught in the narrowest gap at every bend of the building. When I lose patience and pull it as hard as I can, it yields eventually, but with such a desperate sound that makes me wonder if I have broken something beyond repair. When I give up pulling and go back to estimate the damage, I see that it is stuck at the mossy corner of the stony step that Mike has made for the front door of our house. Mike had specially chosen this slab with moss at the edge to make it look as if it has been there since the beginning of time.

I think the hose knows that we are going to leave this house.

The sprinkling tip of the garden hose has long been lost and its metallic end has been crushed to a fish mouth by recurrently being run over by cars. I have to use my thumb if I want to create spray. As the water escapes from under my thumb multiple holograms of little rainbows appear and disappear in the sunshine.

This backyard has been kinder to me than I have been towards it. This round shallow hole in the centre of the lawn, with a small leafless fig tree in the centre, was made by me. I wanted to show to Christos—the Greek father-in-law of our first son, Kamran—how much I valued this gift from his fruitful garden in Vancouver to our fruitless backyard in Victoria. It needs a lot of water, though, and I made a passionate speech about it at their wedding and made reference to the old Persian-Greek conflicts. And once again I thanked Alexander the Great for destroying our only Greek-like castle by a fire ignited by the handkerchief of a Persian girl, because, by so doing, Alexander the Great sterilized the stones of that unique stony castle postponing its decay to become known as the permanent ruins of Persepolis.

This leafy magnolia tree is the model for my best acrylic painting. Nima asked me to paint it, when it was full of flowers and no leaves. When it is full of flowers it brightens my days for a month or two every year, and at nights it glows with white phosphorescence like an unlit chandelier. I cannot count how many years I have wasted my days and nights pacing this backyard, thinking about Victor's destiny, worrying about my own future, trying to figure out the meaning of a "go-getter," the nickname given to the man who had terminated his employment. Memories beget memories. When Keyvan was seven years old, or eight, he would say fingering out, instead of figuring out. I never corrected him because his way of saying made more sense to me than the correct way of saying it. Too bad that he grew and learned the right way by himself.

These three pine trees are now taller than our roof, except for the one that is pressing against the overhang beside our bedroom. They were smaller than the smallest of our three sons when I planted them more than twenty years ago when we moved to Victoria from Winnipeg.

This bald patch of grass in front of the stony step coming up from the sunken pathway to the backyard will never grow anything. I know this because I once grafted this site with a square-foot of green grass from the shady side of the lawn. It did not take.

Nima was watching me when I was doing that. He was in grade one, so he must have been seven years old. He immediately used my method on the green shaggy carpet of his room after he had spilled a blue inkbottle on it. No one knew about it until Mitra found out about it a few months later when she was vacuuming his room as part of the ritual spring cleaning which coincided with Persian New Year. When Mitra discovered it she screamed so badly that I rushed to see if she had mistakenly picked up again a curled-up live spider, pretending to be dead, while running the vacuum. But, when I reached the room I saw to my relief that she was standing near Nima's desk staring at a square foot of green carpet stuck to the sucking end of the vacuum tube, held upright in her manicured hands.

When Nima came back from school that day—with his navy blue knapsack and his little yellow bicycle—he confessed that he had cut out the stained part of his carpet with the kitchen knife, and replaced it with a patch of similar carpet from the spare roll left in the spider-infested closet that also housed the electric control panel for the house. While Mitra was quite upset about Nima's mischievous act and his dangerous reparative action, I was glad that he had learned the right lesson by watching his father.

The sharp end of the garden hose hurts my thumb. I have to interrupt this hissing fan of water if I want to save my hand. Auntie Pouran, who was in charge of gardening in our house in Tehran, had many harsh and impractical rules, but not watering the plants in the sunshine was not one of them. Remembering her, I stop watering the lawn and leave the hose running beside the foot of the taller trees that no one has watered since they have grown.

I take away nothing from this fruitless garden but my sunny memories. I leave nothing behind but the L-shaped signature of Mike the stone mason, embedded forever in front of the front door.

18

WALLS AND SHADES

Good fences make good neighbours.

Robert Frost

IN TEHRAN, WHERE I GREW UP, or in any other city in Iran where houses are surrounded by walls, the adjacent neighbours are called *ham-saayeh* meaning shade-mates. They are called shade-mates because they share the shade of the wall that separates them. The sharing is of course a kind of time-sharing in the sense that if one neighbour has the shade in the morning, the other has it in the afternoon. In Victoria, on the other hand, or in any other city in Canada, where there are no walls around the houses and therefore no shade, the shade-mates are called neighbours. Neighbour, of course, is not a combined English word and has no other meaning than shade-mate, but if it is translated to Farsi the way it sounds to an Iranian ear, it would mean a reed-cutter, since *nay* means reed and *bor* means cut in Farsi. It is also useful to mention that in Farsi both shade and shadow are known by the same word, *Saayeh*.

With the above linguistic background in the back of my mind, when I saw the shadow of my adjacent neighbour extending from his cool-green lawn into my pistachio-green grass, without being arrested by the opacity of a wall or filtered through a fenestrated fence, I knew by intuition that he was going to equip me with the most important tool that I have ever borrowed from him.

The moving shadow of the rake in his hand was trying in vain to rake away the fallen yellow leaves from our lawn. His forearm resembled the strong forearm of a heavy-duty mechanic, but he has the face of a white-collar man. He is a man of books, pens and rulers. He had just retired as the principal of the largest high school in this town. His high school has the tallest students in this city, if not the smartest. Many of the high-ranking government officials in Victoria claim that they are graduates of his high school. As his shadow gets closer to me, he exchanges the rake with a longer tool that belongs to me. He wants to return it to me. It is the long-handled clipper that is good only to cut the tip of the branches of the trees that diminish our common sea view. This is the only tool that he borrows from me, no more than once a year; otherwise it is always I who borrows tools from him. He has all the tools necessary for a household, and then some. I have seen them hanging neatly on the dotted board on the wall of his tool room or neatly arranged in his red metallic toolbox. Whenever I borrow one of his tools I make sure to return it quickly so that the next time I need a tool he would not hesitate to lend it.

Once he phoned to borrow our idle aluminum ladder. Instead of waiting for him to come and get it, I volunteered to carry it to their house. When I took it to his house he was not in their yard, so I put it down on the ground, horizontally, along the wall of their house. When he saw the ladder the next day he phoned me that I should not have done so. When I asked him why, he said his small boy might have used it to climb to the roof and fall. I realized that I had done a foolish thing and apologized for it and promised that I would never do it again.

I raised my face and turned my gaze from the ground to look at the face of my fenceless neighbour. As soon as our eyes met, my neighbour began to apologize for having planted a short row of reed along the junction of our lawn, last summer, without letting me know in advance.

I responded by thanking him profusely for having done so because not only do "Good fences make good neighbours," as Robert Frost, an American poet said, but like any Iranian boy who has grown up in Iran, I had grown up with reeds. Not only did our well known poet, Rumi, begin his famous book of *Mathnavi* with the sound of a reed, but we have used it as a calligraphic pen in the elementary schools in Tehran.

As I said that, his wife called him from the window of their kitchen to let him know that dinner was ready.

As he turned to leave, I asked him if I could use the dried stem of one of his reeds to make pens to write a letter to my mother.

"Go ahead, please," my fair-minded neighbour said as he was going to have dinner. "They are at least half yours."

19

WHERE IS MY SWISS ARMY KNIFE?

NOT THAT ONE. Not the one that I bought for twenty dollars in 1968 at a souvenir shop in Banff where I had gone as a fourth-year pathology resident from Winnipeg to participate in the annual convention of the Canadian Association of Pathologists. I gave that as a gift to the young American couple who were there as tourists and who played bridge with us on the checkerboard tiles of its long and majestic hall. Gail, the wife, was visibly pregnant at that time. We invited them to come to our house the next year when we were going to be in Cranbrook for my first job as a pathologist. They were kind enough to accept our invitation and came with a carton of canned California almonds and some seeds but no baby. In a hurry we put away Keyvan's old crib that we had set up for their baby. They did not say what had happened to their baby, but it was obvious that they had lost the baby to SIDS— Sudden Infant Death Syndrome. In that convention we were taught that when a newborn infant dies suddenly and unexpectedly without ever being sick, it makes the parents sick and sad for the rest of their lives, but our guests were kind enough not to show their sadness to protect their hosts. Not that knife that I gave away without ever having used any of its multiple blades.

I am not looking for the one that I found on the rocky shore of Cattle Point in Victoria either, when I was walking with my guest, Dr. Dikran Horoupian. Dikran was my Armenian friend from Egypt who left Winnipeg in the early 70s for Detroit to specialize in the super-specialty of neuropathology and left me in charge of the brain-cutting session to demonstrate the pathology of the brain to pathology and neurosurgery residents. The latter came to watch the session with their opinionated head of department, Dr. Parkinson. At the very first session, before slicing the first pickled brain, when I expressed the opinion that the brain was heavy because it was removed from a heavy man, Dr. Parkinson almost violently objected to my saying so and said that there was no correlation between the size of brain—or the globe of the eyes for that matter—and the size of the subject from whom the brain is removed. I had no statistical data to support my remark. I had said that only because I thought in nature, especially in the human body, things were proportional at least as far as size and weight were concerned, but I accepted his objection and stood corrected so that I could begin slicing the five brains which were waiting for me like clusters of fresh wallnuts on the marble table of the morgue. The next week, however, during the second brain-cutting session, the medical student who was present at the previous session whispered in my ear that I was right. He had gone to the library of the hospital and had found an article that said, not in every individual case but statistically, there is a positive correlation between the size of the brain and the size of the human body.

I gave that knife to Dikran since he and his wife, Hermin, had come a long way from Stanford University near San Francisco to our house in Victoria just to spend a week with us.

The knife I am looking for is the one that Dr. John, the family physician whose family name I can never remember, had given to me.

John didn't come to the doctors' lounge very often, but each time that he did, I asked him for his family name, only to forget it when he appeared the next time. In one of our conversations he told me that he was going to Winnipeg in the summer to build a cairn in memory of his two brothers who were killed in the Second Word War. The summer came and went and the next time I saw him I asked him if he had done it or not. He said that he could not go that summer for a reason that I've forgotten now. The next summer came and went without seeing John to ask him if he had done it or not. But after that summer, near Christmastime, he came to my office for the first time with the familiar sound of "Ho, ho, ho," that did not suit his melancholic personality. He was wearing a red Santa Claus toque, and carrying a thick envelope containing paper, pictures and a Swiss Army knife. Luckily, I was in my office. I invited him to sit down on the spare chair so that we could chat. Without sitting, he took the papers out of the envelope and handed them to me. There were aerial photographs of swamps, maps of Manitoba dotted with blue patches, and a typed letter from him to his sister, Pat.

John had gone to Winnipeg with his grown son and a friend, and from there they had rented a small yellow airplane to go to the uninhabited Stratton Island in the middle of Stratton Lake—both recently named Stratton fifty years after the end of the Second World War, by the federal government of Canada, in honour of John's two brothers. John had told his father that he wanted to go to war, too, but his father had changed his mind and suggested that he should go to medical school instead.

The map was white, with many pale blue patches, representing some of the 100,000 lakes of Manitoba, making it look like the map of Finland. There were two Canadian flags with their small red maple leaves, indicating the sites of the island and the lake near the upper edge of the paper.

John had built the cairn that he had promised to do, two years earlier. One of the photographs showed the cairn to be about waist high, built with river rocks, each the size of a human skull. The river from which they had carried the rocks was not visible in any of the pictures, not even in the aerial photographs. The commemorative plaque on top of the rocky column was made of brass and set at a slant so that it did not look like a sundial. The letters were in relief. I could read the surname *Stratton* on the plaque glowing in the sunshine on that green swampy island with no human in sight.

"How did the land feel under your feet on that island?" I asked as I finished reading the letter he had written to his sister. John is a good writer. He has published a few articles in *Stitch Magazine* that is dedicated to doctors' writing.

"Springy," he said laconically, and when he saw me waiting for more words he added, "Bouncy." I told him that only in my dreams did the land under my feet feel springy. That is why I never get hurt when I fall in my dreams.

In the letter to his sister John had said every interesting thing that had happened to him on that trip, the most interesting of which was the fact that as they were carrying the rocks, he had found a Swiss Army knife on that uninhabited island in the middle of nothing. So, after finishing his letter I asked him what he was going to do with the knife. He said, "It is your Christmas gift, because you were the only person who kept asking about my trip."

Now I find the knife in the top drawer of my wooden desk at home, where I looked for it numerous times without seeing it. I use its saw to cut the dry stem of reed from the short row of bamboos along the junction of our yard with that of our neighbour. I break the stem through its gouty joints into nine pen sized segments and with one of the blades of the knife I shape all of them into calligraphic pens the way Mr. Meer Hosseinee, our calligraphy teacher in the elementary school of Kherad, used to do for us in Tehran. I keep two of the smaller ones from the tip of the stem for the two small boys of my neighbour in case they wanted to see how a reed pen writes. Then I rehydrate the black ink that I painstakingly brought from Tehran to Winnipeg in the summer of 1965. Finally, with one of the thickest pens I begin writing a letter to my aging mother in Iran.

20

MOVING

The moving shadow of the bamboo sweeps the stairs; making no dust

The shaft of the moonlight plunges in the pool; making no waves

Lao-tzu

I AM MOVING, moving things and boxes full of things, some of which I wish I did not possess. I carry things that everybody has and nobody wants. Things that cannot be left behind nor given away. Some are so little used that they look almost brand new, like these containers with long handles, named fondue, designed for the entire family, parents and children, to sit around and have fun in the fashion of the 70s. One is for boiling liquid cheese, the other for boiling oil, both for having fun with morsels of bread or meatballs. We stopped using them because the little fun that they generated was not worth the anxiety of accidental burns. Heavy things, like this brass basin full of copper pennies, or these boxes of books, left behind by departed children, every page of them underlined by colourful markers. Weightless things, like the pale rectangular imprints of the pictures now removed from the walls. Things that I did not know I possessed, like this book *SOS* by my uncle colonel that says everything on the cover with one colourful picture, and this leatherbound book by my grandfather that says nothing, not even the name, on the cover. Things that I am glad to possess but cannot carry with me because they have roots in the ground, like this magnolia tree or this little fig tree in the centre of the yard, the gift of Christos, the Greek-born father-in-law of our first son, Kamran. It is just beginning to grow leaves.

That was the little fig tree about which I made a passionate speech at the wedding of Kamran after Justin, my Irish colleague, had made fun of it along with ridiculing the smallness of our yard when he heard that we were using the help of a gardener for that "postage stamp-sized garden" as he put it.

I specifically invited him to the wedding to hear my passionate speech about his comment, ending my speech like this: My garden could be small, Justin, but it makes me feel I own the entire vastness of this country. To formalize a deed of land, one does not need more than an official stamp at the lower corner of the document. My postage-stamp sized garden, located at the left lower corner of this white vastness, formalizes the deed, perfectly.

One of the things that I am glad to leave behind is this burnt brown patch on the yellow kitchen counter next to the stove, the permanent mark of my momentary stupidity when my wife was not home and I tried to cook dinner.

These empty baskets of flowers, made of twisted branches of trees, catch on the pocket of my pants as I try to take them away. That green disposable vase that looks like a flower on its own was sent from Moose Jaw by Dr. Ian Farquhar for our wedding anniversary along with two white napkins rolled up to fit within their silver napkin rings for us to go and dine in a restaurant for that occasion. I can't imagine how Ian could remember the date of our anniversary that we sometimes forget.

Ian, too, had done his residency training in pathology in Winnipeg, but two years after me. Once he had difficulty differentiating between normal and malignant cells in the peripheral sinus of a lymph node. I taught him the rule of thumb that I had discovered by myself, "When in doubt, it is benign."

"Are you sure?" he asked.

"How can one be sure when one is in doubt?" I replied a Cartesian reply to make him stop asking and find the answer by himself.

Mitra came home in a hurry, highly excited, to tell me with utmost urgency that she had seen a large house with expanded sea views on Arbutus Road and wants to have it because it was her dream house.

"But everybody among our colleagues is downsizing their houses. Our children have grown up and gone. We have already three empty bedrooms in our house. Do you think it is wise to sell this and go to a bigger one?" I asked my wife to dissuade her from leaving this house.

"You come and see it. I bet you'll fall in love with it too."

"How far is it from here?"

"About five minutes' drive from here."

"Can I walk from there to the same beach at Cadboro Bay?"

"I am sure you can," she said eagerly. "You come and see," she repeated. "If you don't like it we won't put an offer on it."

I look at our backyard for the last time before I leave the house in which I have lived longer than any other house, whether here or in Iran. The grass is soaking wet and there is water damage around the roots of the larger trees where I left the hose running.

The surface of the street in front of our house is wet with water coming from the backyard. A gentle breeze moves the row of reeds, their shadow sweeping the driveway, making no dust, as we depart. I ask Mitra to stop her car so that I could go back and check my room for the last time to see if I had collected everything and forgotten nothing.

I see the Polaroid picture of the dead gentleman gardener on the wall, and scattered segments of a fractured stem of reed on the window sill. I put them all together into a bundle to put them in my chest pocket along with the Polaroid picture before returning to the car.

As the car moves up the steep segment of the hill to go to our new house, it changes to lower gears, with the augmenting sound of the sobbing of a Persian boy. The naked arms of the arbutus trees embrace me like the arms of a new wet nurse as we enter our new neighbourhood. I think I will never grow up.

I keep changing places, but I feel I am living in the same place all the time. The only difference being that I see the old place better from the point of view of my new place.

21

"MAN'S MANNERS ARE SUPERIOR TO HIS WEALTH"

DEAR MODAR-JUN, *SALAAM.* A long and a loud *Salaam* so that you could hear me better, and a circular *Salaam,* so that you can share it with the concentric layers of friends and relatives who surround you and share this letter with you. I hesitate to mention their names, fearing that some names might fall off the pen and cause more harm than good.

Modar-jun, this is not the letter that you are waiting for. This is an extra. The one you are waiting for will come in September. This is an urgent letter and does not contain the usual meagre inclusion that you do not like. You always said that you preferred those letters of mine that did not contain any inclusion. "Because it shows that you truly wanted to talk to your mother, rather than merely fulfilling the duty of a son towards his aging mother," was your comment about my previous empty letters. Not only is this letter free of any inclusions, it even requests something from you.

You won't believe it, Modar-jun. I have two coffee mugs full of pens and fountain pens, yet I am writing this letter with this primitive, rustic reed pen. I do so partly because this is a tongue-in-cheek letter and partly because this is a special pen. It is from the garden of our shade-mate. Our shade-mate, Modar-jun, unlike the shade-mates in Iran, is shade-less. Not that he is unkind or graceless; not at all. The reason he does not have shade is because he does not have any walls around his house to cast a shadow.

Shade here is neither as important as in Iran, nor as meaningful. I remember when we were in Iran and living with you in your house, whenever at the end of the night the guests, whether important or not, were leaving our house, you and Auntie Pouran would follow them into the courtyard and up to the exit door to thank them profusely for their visit by saying, "May your shade never retract from our head." Even though the houses here are not enclosed within walls, some of them seem to feel naked and try to substitute the missing walls with elaborate fences or ornamental plants. This is, I think, why our neighbour had planted a row of bamboo along the junction of our yards, somewhere between their bedroom and where we leave our garbage cans outside. He said the land here was too wet and the feet of his wild berries were soaked in water and therefore did not give them much fruit last year. The bamboos were supposed to suck out moisture from his flowerbed like a bent straw does from a glass of soft drink. He, of course, was quite apologetic about it, but I pretended to be ignorant of his intention and thanked him for having planted the reeds because as you know we are quite familiar with reed. To prove to him that I was not hurt by his segregating action, I cut a dried stem of it with his permission and made a few calligraphy pens from it and told him that I was going to write a letter with them to you.

This is why I am writing this letter with this inappropriate pen. I hope you won't mind. I know this pen is for homework, if not a pen of punishment for those who have not done their homework. Interestingly, the moment the tip of the pen touched the paper, like an exteriorized heart that remembers how to beat after being dormant for an undetermined amount of time when it is transplanted into another chest, the broad-tipped reed pen remembered the first Persian maxim that our calligraphy teacher had written on the blackboard for the students to copy:

Man's Manners Are Superior to His Wealth

We were to copy a full page by repeating the same line from the top of the page to the bottom, and our calligraphy teacher, Mr. Meer Hosseini, always insisted that the students write each line completely before starting the next line. The students, however, rarely complied with his wish and columnized the line beginning with the last word. Of course when you do that, some of the columns would end up being slanted and for that reason the teacher would know that the student had done what he was not supposed to do. I never understood why Mr. Meer Hosseini insisted that we do our homework line by line rather than doing *Raj*—to columnize or make a vertical row out of a single word, chosen from the end of the line before making another column out of the next and so on and so on until the page is full. I never understood why, until today when my pen, out of habit, began to columnize. Our teacher wanted us to understand the meaning of the line. He particularly chose meaningful lines as examples for our calligraphy exercise to improve our morals. Calligraphy was just an excuse. He did not consider himself merely a teacher of calligraphy. He rather considered himself to be a teacher of morality first, and then a teacher of calligraphy. Unlike our math teacher, Mr. Jowhari (meaning *blue* or any other colour ink except for black ink) our calligraphy teacher never resorted to bodily punishment, no matter how bad a student behaved in his class. If a student, for example, complained that his classmate sitting next to him was dipping his pen into his inkpot because he had not brought his own, Mr. Meer Hosseini, rather than hitting the palm of the hands of the forgetful student with a green stick, would merely say, "He is like a mason who has gone to work without taking his *Teesheh* (a chip-axe) and *Maaleh* (a trowel) with him."

The son of our calligraphy teacher was in the same class as I and their house was in the same street—As-You-Wish Street—as ours. His name was Hossein. His handwriting was naturally better than mine, but his mathematics was worse. On the nights that we had math the next day, he would come to our house and would write down the math problem with his nice handwriting on two separate pages, one for himself and one for me, while I would work on solving the problem. At the end of the night he would add my solution to the bottom of the pages, and would write his name on the top of one and my name on the top of the other. This went on for several months until one day Mr. Jowhari discovered that our homework was so identical that it must have been written by one and the same hand. So, we each received several painful blows to the palms of our hands.

After elementary school, I did not see Hossein until I heard he had become a doctor in pharmacology and had opened a pharmacy at Thirty-meter Avenue, not too far from the bottom end of As-You-Wish Street.

In your last letter, Modar-jun, you said, "Dear Dr. Nasser, these days, when I wake up in the morning, I am surprised that I still can see the world." I thought you were fed up with the world and were ready to die when the world was getting more and more interesting since the cold war was ending. Please stay a little longer. I need you. I need important things from you, actually two things: One is the diary of my adolescent times in Tehran that I have forgotten in my mattress, and the other is your permission to let me talk about you as an example of a good Moslem on the occasion of the World Religions Day at the University of Victoria, for the public.

The reason that I have suddenly become interested in my childhood diary is because I have begun writing a book which is composed mainly of the things I remember. Paradoxically, once you put words on paper they get deleted from memory. I happen to remember everything except for the things that I have made note of in that booklet. And the reason that I have to talk about you as an example of a good Moslem is the fact that out of the six major religions of the world, five of them have already chosen their representative to talk about their religions, except for Islam. And why I have volunteered to undertake such a grave mission is a long story, but the short version of it is this.

As I was writing this letter to you the phone rang and a man who, judging by his accent appeared to be Iranian, asked me in English if I did not mind to come and talk about Islam on the occasion of World Religions Day—On the 9th or 19th of January, 1997, which, judging by the excess of number 9s in it, sounded very much like a date chosen by a Baha'i.

"Why me?" I asked with utmost surprise. "I am an atheist." And when I heard deep disappointment in his voice I added that there were many knowledgeable Moslems and theologians in this city, "Why don't you ask one of them?" The man whose name was Shah-rokh said that he had gone to the only mosque in Victoria at Quadra Street and had asked them, but they had told him that they did not have time to do it on that particular day. After this disappointment he had gone to the pharmacy that is run by an Iranian pharmacist by the name of Dr. Bahr Hosseini to see if he knew anyone who could represent Islam on that date and he was told, "The only person I know that might be able to do this job is Dr. Shojania." Since I knew Dr. Hosseini very well and he is a good friend of mine, I knew he was not the type that would cause me trouble. I told him that even though I was not a religious person, I was born to a pious Shi'eh Moslem and, if he did not have any objection, I could go and talk about my mother as a good Moslem. He seemed to be so desperate to fill that chair that he immediately accepted my offer with no further questions or suggestions. Now it is up to you Modar-jun; if you want me to talk about you, you have to give me your written permission.

About my diary, since you told me in your last letter that you had lost your memory so severely that among your children you only remembered my name; I can direct you from here to help you find it.

It is, as I said, inside my mattress. And my mattress is in the children's room, flat on the floor like a Moslem tomb stone, between the mattress of Hamid and that of Hossein. Hamid, to refresh your memory, is one of your seven sons who was a year younger than me and after becoming a doctor in Tehran went to America and returned to Iran after five years as a cardiologist and worked in the oil company at Abadan for a year or two, got separated from his wife and was living the last days of his life with you in the house of your younger daughter, Monavar. He is the son that when you saw in his eyes something unusual, you immediately diagnosed him as being addicted to narcotics.

So, without telling him anything, the next night, after you finished your routine nightly *Namaaz*, you did not get up from your praying mat. Instead, you continued sitting there and prayed to your God, "Either cure him or take him away from me while he is still as good as the first day that You gave him to me." And God—often choosing the easier way when He is given options—made Hamid come to you late the next night. You had made his dinner, composed of a plate of rice topped with eggplant stew, ready for him at the corner of the large dining table. Hamid came in, tired after having worked all day, and said *Salaam* to you and sat at the table to have his dinner. After two or three spoonfuls, he said to you, "Modar-jun, I feel uncomfortable keeping you awake and waiting while I am eating. I will take my plate to the room where I will be sleeping, and finish my food there." You had no objection and agreed with his reasonable request. The next morning he was found dead and the autopsy showed that he had aspirated the seedy eggplant you had cooked for him into his lungs.

And Hossein—sometimes I think that God wanted to kill me but missed me twice — is the brother who was a year older than me. He too, after having worked in a bank for many years and was living by himself, had returned to live with you when you were living in the house of Auntie Pouran. He had been diagnosed with chronic schizophrenia. You were getting old and wanted to die, but did not wish to leave a schizophrenic son behind. So, one day when Hossein, having cut his wrists with his shaving blade, came down to your room, bleeding on the carpet and the quilt that you and Auntie Pouran were making for me, saying, "It is over, Modar-jun." You scolded him by saying, "This is not the right way! Anything you do in life, Hossein, has to be done the right way, even if it is suicide." So, Hossein ran back upstairs and threw himself off the balcony onto the pavement of the yard in front of the window of your room and died. Of course you cried a lot and pulled a lot of hair out of your head, but you also scolded him further for the way he had bloodied his good face which looked better than the faces of any of your other sons.

I know, Modar-jun, that you loved your children, but you seem to have loved manners, morality and sanity more than your children. You knew addiction would inevitably lead to immoral behaviour, no matter how moral one was at the beginning. You also knew that grown men or women, when afflicted by mental illness, could become the subject of ridicule by children in the streets and you wanted to spare Hossein from that unfair and unjust embarrassment in your absence. You are one of those few Iranians who do not subscribe to the famous Persian saying, "After me, I don't care if the world is a sea or a mirage."

By the way, Modar-jun, if you find my mattress, you don't have to tear it apart to find my booklet in it. All you have to do is to palpate it very gently and carefully, like the way doctors palpate the abdomen of a patient afflicted with malaria in search of a palpable spleen. My diary has a soft leather cover; this is why it is not easy to distinguish from the consistency of the compacted cotton in my mattress.

Were you to ask about our *haal* and health, I have to say that we are all healthy and happy, with no problems except for being away from you for so long. I am still working in the same hospital, full-time, doing pathology during the day and writing my book during the nights. Oops! The phone is ringing.

I have to go, Modar-jun, because the phone keeps ringing. It could be the coroner. She wants me to do an autopsy that I am reluctant to do. I would rather spend my spare time thinking about you in preparation of my speech while waiting for your reply. I omit the *Salaams* because I am in a hurry, but I cannot omit thanking Auntie Pouran for the hundred pairs of underwear she made for us when we were growing under your watchful eyes.

Mitra sends her regards and wants me to thank you again for the 500 dollars that you sent for the children. The children all remember you. Nima was seven when he saw you in 1977.

He remembers you gave him an empty brown Coca Cola glass that had a large eye on the outer surface and blinked when the glass was shaken. With part of the money you sent them, the children bought a badly needed Atari to play computer games with the help of its two joy-sticks. Where did you find so much money to spare, by the way? If I knew you could afford to give away so much money I would have never insulted you by sending you those meagre amounts in my routine letters. The amount was so meagre that I did not even declare it in my income tax return for a refund.

Your middle son,

Nasser

22

THE BORING DANCE OF THE AADAMS

In 1934, when I was four, I was so ignorant and innocent that I thought human beings, rather than being male or female, were divided into grown-ups or children. The grown-ups in my classification were further subdivided into masters consisting of *Agha* and *Khanum* depending on whether they wore pants or skirt, and servants consisting of *Nowkar* or *Kolfat,* depending on the presence or absence of facial hair. Our mother, however, always corrected us whenever we referred to the servants as *Nowkar* or *Kolfat* by saying that they were collectively called *Aadams* since they were *Bandeh-ye-Khoda*, meaning slaves of God, "like you and me."

At that time, we were still living in the religious city of Mashad where dance and music were not only discouraged, they were absolutely prohibited. Nevertheless, the *Aadams,* who had no good reason to dance, always jumped on their feet at the slightest opportunity to begin their boring and momentous dance.

One of those opportunities was when I was sitting on the L-shaped balcony of our house on a grey winter evening, observing the masters come and go. The strange thing that I noted on that day was the masters who normally wore a veil over their skirts when they were planning to go out, came out of their rooms in new colourful dresses without a covering veil. While they were waiting at the bend of the balcony for our father to join them, the *Aadams,* noticing that they were unusually good looking and well dressed, went and brought a dish of fire to burn the black seeds of *esfand* to spare them from the bad effect of jealous eyes in the streets and, of course, received their expected coins from my mother. A few minutes later my father came out of his room; followed by a whiff of opium smoke, walking with his black shiny shoes that made a rude sound with each step that he took as he passed by me, and they all went out, leaving the children at the mercy of the *Aadams.*

As soon as the grown-ups left the house, one of the *Aadams,* who always appeared so polite and caring in front of the masters, scared Hamid—who was crying in one of the unlit rooms, missing his recently dead grandmother—to sleep. Her action—which consisted of making the sound of a baby-eating monster while hiding her head inside a black pot— awoke Majid with inconsolable cries in another room. After the wet nurse of Majid silenced him with a hurried lullaby, they all disappeared into the kitchen to reappear a moment later with pots and pants and anything that could make a percussive sound. They sat in a circle on the pavement of the balcony and began clapping. Needless to say I was scared too, but since I knew who the woman who pretended to be a baby-eater was, I managed to hide my fear, and remained where I was without having to go to bed. When they saw me sitting alone, they invited me to join their circle and I, having nothing better to do, reluctantly accepted their invitation and joined them by moving towards them in sitting position. The reason I was moving in that position even though I could walk at that age, was because the balcony was not child-proof and our grandmother had forbidden the younger children to walk on it. Even though she was dead, I still respected her instructions because she was a wise woman. Ironically, when two men were carrying her coffin down the steep stairs at the end of the short limb of the L-shaped balcony, they lost their balance and she almost fell off the coffin, making the onlooking *Aadams* gasp with fright.

A few moments later, the young daughter of our oldest nanny, who was about eighteen years old, stood up in the centre of the circle to begin the purposeless motions of her arms while others either clapped with their dry bony hands or struck the back of the pots and pans.

My face must have unknowingly shown my displeasure with the purposeless motions of the dancer's arms because she immediately added some purpose to them by trying, sneak-ily, to undo the knot of the cord that held up her long black pants under the skirt of her flowery dress. The pants collapsed over her ankles like a pair of compressed accordions to cause an explosion of scandalized laughter in her surrounding circle. Everybody seemed to enjoy the attraction except for me. For me, who had recently seen the naked body of a woman in the public bath house including her black pubic triangle, seeing a little skin of her legs above the ankles did not appear to be a big deal. When the maids looked at me with their questioning eyes, wondering why I was not enjoying the attraction, I explained, "I am not interested in watching the naked body of women anymore. I have seen it all, including your dool, and I didn't like it."

With that remark the dance stopped as well as the cacophonic sound of banging on the back of the pots and pans to be replaced by an explosion of laughter. When the maids finished their inappropriate laughter they all turned towards me to ask what my impression of their genitals was and what, if any, was the difference with that of the boys.

"Yours has hair while a boy's dool is hairless," I naively differentiated for them without realizing that I was referring to women's genitals by the same name as that for a little boy's. That innocent remark made them explode with a second wave of laughter, but rather than thanking me for it, they sent me to my bed for being rude and fresh with women.

23

THE NEXT MORNING

THE NEXT DAY, I WOKE UP AFTER THE SUNRISE and went to sit on the same spot on the balcony to have my usual morning cry. I sat with my back to the wall and my face towards the luke-warm sunshine.

The grown-ups kept passing in front of me, asking questions, as they went on with their chores, some covering their mouths to hide their laughter, some holding their noses. The last person who passed in front of me was Afsar-jun. She was the nubile daughter of Aunt Seddigheh who was send to Mashad to live with us while waiting for our stepbrother to come back from France to marry her. She stopped right in front of me, blocking the sunshine, to ask the same question that everybody else had asked, "What did you say last night about the difference between boys and women?"

"It wasn't about boys and women," I corrected her. "It was about children and grown-ups."

"Whatever! What was your comment?"

"Hair," I said, laconically at first, and then I objected with anger, "Why? Can't I even mention the word *hair* in this house? Remember children are *Aadam* too."

She held her laughter to ask more questions, but I stopped her by saying, "Please move a little aside. Your shadow is depriving me from the sunshine. I am cold and I have not had my breakfast yet, and I am not in a conversational mood."

She picked me up by the arm and took me through the doors to reach the door of my mother's room, and left me there and disappeared.

Modar-jun was sitting, cross-legged, on one of the two blue springy beds with blue metallic bars capped by cone-shaped brass knobs (the beds that would become our trampolines a few years later when we move to Tehran). She did not appear pregnant at that time, but the belly of the bed she was sitting on was sinking like the belly of a pregnant cow. Hamid was sitting under the bed, his favourite spot, and sulking, missing his grandmother's lap.

Modar-jun was thankfully oblivious to my presence, as if her mind was somewhere else. She was writing a letter on her knee, using a French pen with a sharp metallic tip, spindle-shaped wooden handle, and purple ink. When she reached the bottom of the paper she did not turn the page over; instead she rotated the page and began to write obliquely on the wide white margins of the same page, as if framing her letter with words.

On the floor, a fluffy blue dress was caught in the hollow of her Singer sewing machine, covering the machine's colourful picture of someone like a Russian general, maybe Peter the Great with a red coat covered with medals.

I sat on the lid of the sewing machine that was left beside the door, straddling it like a legless little donkey. Rather than waiting for her to question me about what I had done the night before, I began asking questions about her last evening.

"Did you bring any candy from wherever you went last night?"

"No, I am sorry. It wasn't a party."

"Where did you go then?"

"It was a practice run. Your great aunt, Princess Banuan, your father's aunt, the one who opened the first private school for girls in Mashad, had invited all of her lady relatives to see what kind of dress they should wear after the prohibition of the chador. There were no cookies or candies."

That great aunt was like a man, both physically as well as the way she behaved. She was one of the rare women who smoked a pipe, a long-handled one, sharing it with her sister, Princess Forough. Khosrow Mirza, our cousin, said that once, at a meeting in Mashad, the minister of education was listing the schools in Mashad and forgot to mention the name of her school for girls. Dressed in a long blue satin gown, with a long scarf loosely covering her head and falling over her shoulders, she rose to her full height in the middle of the crowded salon, stretched her long arm towards the minister to object, "Why? Why, Mr. Minister, why you did not mention the only school for girls among so many schools for boys in the province of Khorassan? Why?"

The minister had to apologize profusely and attributed his omission to forgetfulness which made the matter even worse. How could he forget the only school for women?

"Why are you sewing this dress again?" I continued with my questions, "Isn't this the same you wore last evening?"

"It needs alteration. Princess Banuan said its sleeves had to be shortened a little."

"Last night, when you were not here, the maids were whispering among each other that a girl in our neighbourhood had written a love letter to her teacher and her father found the note in her book and strangled her with the help of his brother for doing that. Is it true?"

"They are not maids. They are *Aadams*, like you and me." My mother skillfully changed the subject.

"The *Aadams* said that they had seen our father weep for the first time. Is that true Modar-jun? Did our father really cry? Why? Is it because of the death of your mother?"

"Your father does miss my mother, but his tears were for Mansur."

"Did Mansur-jun die too?"

"No! Bite your tongue!" she said, while biting her lower lip. "Your father misses Mansur because we have sent him to Tehran where they have better schools."

"Don't they have schools in Mashad?"

"They do, but Mansur likes Tehran very much and thinks that the schools over there are better than those in Mashad. He could be right. This is why Monir, Monavar and Mehdi have been sent to Tehran too."

No wonder our house looked so sad and gloomy in recent weeks.

"Why don't you send me to Tehran?"

"You are too young to go to school. When your time comes, God willing, you too might begin your education in Tehran."

"How come you never cry, Modar-jun?"

"I am not able to. I would if I could."

"What are you writing, Modar-jun?"

"I am writing a letter to Pouran Dokht Agha Khani, my niece."

"If she is your niece and not your sister, then why you said we should call her Khaaleh-jan, as if she were our aunt?"

"Because she is like my sister, and we are almost the same age. She is perhaps one year older than I, like you are one year older than Hamid."

"Why are you writing to her? Why not to Auntie Seddigheh who is your real sister?"

"I send my regards to her in the same letter."

"Does Auntie Pouran give my brothers and sisters everything free?"

"No, of course not; I send her money every two weeks. That is why, if you let me, I have to finish this letter soon so that it can get mailed today and hopefully it will be in Tehran in two weeks."

"Does Auntie Pouran have any children, herself?"

"Yes, she has one daughter of her own, named Maheen, but you should call her Maheen Khanum. She is a few years older than your sisters."

"What does 'of her own' mean?"

"I mean Maheen is not her stepchild. Auntie Pouran has four grown stepchildren who do not live with her since her husband passed away, recently."

"What happened to her husband?"

"Her husband was an old gentleman who had married first one of my sisters, Maymanat Khanum. After their four children were almost grown, she passed away. At that time your Auntie Pouran was very young and very beautiful, with golden hair and honey-coloured eyes. After Zoka-ol-mamalek became a widower he married your Auntie Pouran and passed away soon after they had their first daughter.

"What did her husband do for living?"

"He was taking care of several villages belonging to Prince Farman-Farma in Mesraghan."

"How come with such an important nickname he was almost like a Nowkar to Prince Farman-Farma?"

"Because Farman-Farma was one of the important princes of Qajar, so important that Reza Shah was one of the men working for him before he became Shah."

"What did he die of? In other words what was the cause of death of the husband of Auntie Pouran? I thought it was the woman who died after giving birth to a child, not the husband."

"He passed away due to consumption, or tuberculosis, if you prefer."

At this moment I dismounted the lid of the sewing machine and went over to the bed to see what she was writing, even though I was not able to read. My mother stopped writing and turned her face backward toward me and said, "It is impolite to look over the shoulder of a person who is writing anything, particularly a private letter."

"I know, Modar-jun, but I can't read yet."

"That is worse. Go play with Hamid. He misses his grandmother."

As I was going, glad that she had not brought up the messy topic of the last night, she said, "And put your pants on. It is not nice to move about in a houseful of women with your bad place showing."

The polite name for the genitals in our house was "bad-place" and I always referred to them by that name in front of the grown ups. I remember once when Hossein was running with a ladle in his hand, fell and hurt his genitals and began crying. I ran to my mother, before she thought that I was responsible for it, and told her, "Modar-jun, Modar-jun, Hossein was running with the ladle in his hand and fell and hurt his bad place." Even in that state of utter excitement, I did not forget to call it by its polite name. I called it by its real name only in front of the *Aadams*, thinking that they did not know its politer version.

"My shorts are drying on the clothesline on the balcony, and I don't have any others. Why don't you sew some shorts for me?"

As my mother was trying to hide her smile she said, "They are dry now. Go and put them on like a good boy."

"I can't do that, Modar-jun."

"Why?"

"Have you forgotten that our grandmother has told us not to walk on the balcony?"

"Now you can …" she said, without finishing her sentence.

"Is it because your mother is dead now?" I finished her sentence for her as I began running towards the balcony.

I got my shorts from the clothesline and put them on by myself. I sat at my usual place on the balcony, against the wall, to pass the time. A fly came and sat on me. I moved my hand in front of my face to make it fly away, but it got caught between my fingers. I did not let it go. It was my first fly. I made a little donkey out of it and made it walk the full length of the L-shaped balcony with the help of a broken broom straw, following it in a sitting position.

Hamid was not on the balcony. My mother had forgotten that he was under her bed, crying. Suddenly, I heard Hamid's crying changed to laughter. I left the wingless fly on the balcony and ran to my mother's room to see what was happening.

She had put away the sewing machine and the writing equipment to replace them with a bomb-shaped sugar cone that she had taken out of its purple paper wrappings and was breaking it into much smaller pieces with her special chip axe on a smooth clean piece of rock in the middle of a purple mat the size of her prayer mat.

Sugar flakes were flying with every strike of her axe to land in all directions and Hamid and I were allowed to pick them up and put them in our mouths. We could not stop laughing.

24

GOING HOME

Remember, the day your father passed away

I had nine children, from three to thirteen.

From a letter by my mother

I DO REMEMBER THE DAY MY MOTHER IS TALKING ABOUT. It was a snowy day. It might have been a sorrowful day for her, but for me it was one of the best days of my life. I am always happy when it snows. Sometimes so happy as if granular sugar is dissolving over my solar plexus. My only worry was to reach home before the day was over so that I could throw snowball with my younger brother, Hamid.

I was six, in grade one, going home with my sister from the Namoos Elementary School for girls. She was twelve, in grade five, carrying my single book with her books in one hand, holding my hand with the other, letting my left arm swing in the air at will. There was already a thick layer of snow on the ground, up to my knees, and it was still falling. Falling with large parallel particles that turned into turbulent eddies behind the passing cars like feathers exploding from ruptured pillows in a friendly pillow fight. The snow on the ground had muffled the metallic sound of the horses' hooves, while accentuating the nagging sound of their wobbly wheels. It was still daytime, but the streetlights were on, giving off not much light, but shortening the already short winter evening. It would be night, I thought, by the time we reached home. Hamid was probably getting bored at home, waiting for me.

"Monir jun," I asked my sister, "do you know why the lights have come on so early today?"

"Because today Tehran is celebrating."

"What is the occasion?"

"Today is the second anniversary of the unveiling of women in Iran."

It was then and only then that I saw with pride the tricolour flags of our country, bleached behind the falling curtain of snow, hanging from the lampposts and the taller buildings. I was somewhat ashamed that I had not noticed them by myself. Some of the flags had a laughing lion in the middle with a sabre in one hand, moving it in the wind.

One had to be careful crossing the busy Amirieh Avenue at the intersection with the Monirieh Avenue, where Kherad Elementary School for Boys was located and my older brothers, Mansur, Mehdi and Hossein went there. Hossein, like me, was in grade one. The reason for both of us being in the same grade was not because Hossein had failed a year, but because I was sent a year earlier than the legal age of seven to school. And to make the matter worse, I was sent to a school for girls, while I was neither unusually smart nor particularly pretty.

Maybe I was too much trouble at home. Or maybe it was the frugality of my mother who did not know what to do with the old uniforms of her two daughters and waited until I became old enough to wear them. I don't know. If saving were an art, my mother would have been its Michelangelo, if not its Picasso. Saving had nothing to do with having or not having money. A good house wife would throw away nothing, not even the skin of fruits. The skin of watermelon for example which was the favourite snack for the donkeys, was sometimes saved to make jam out of it.

It was not a very cold day, but I was cold. The reason for that was because my hair was cut short like a boy's, and I was wearing a girl's uniform because I went to a girls' school. Monavar, my younger of the two sisters, was going to the same school too, in the same class as my older sister. The reason for that, again, was not because my older sister had failed a year, but because Monavar was truly smart, not only for her age, but absolutely, since she became the first in their class at the end of that year as well as for many more years after that. She was going home by herself. She could be either ahead of us or behind.

My sister and I both had dresses made of iridescent, pigeon grey *ormac* with removable white collars. Hers was marginated with a delicate ribbon of lace; mine—thanks to God—was devoid of extra decorations. Nonetheless, I looked quite ugly and ridiculous in comparison with my good-looking sister with her pale, angelic face, framed by her straight, parted black hair. I felt like the hairless doll that my younger sister had given to the daughter of her nanny. Had I known that a girl's dress has no pockets, I would have never let my mother put it on me.

I was beginning to read, not fluently, but I could read the name of the shops that I had passed by hundreds of times. Most of the names of the shops along Amirieh Avenue had changed from Arabic to Farsi during that year, some sounding better, some sounding worse.

The carpentry shop was changed from *Najjari* to *Dorood-gary* and the barber shop from *Salmaani* to *Aaraayesh-gah.*

"This is not right," I said to my sister, pointing to the barber shop.

"What is wrong with it?" my sister said, slightly irritated. "And who said so?"

"Sohrab said so. He said *Aaraayesh* is for women. It is *Peeraayesh* for men. They should have called it *Peeraayesh-gah*"

"What did he mean by that nonsense?"

"*Aaraayesh*, he said, involves decorating, or beautifying by adding something to something, like the way women do when they add jewelry to themselves. *Peeraayesh*, on the other hand, means beautifying by removing something from something, the way men do when they go for a haircut. He even quoted half a line from a poet who advises, 'Man's *Aaraayesh* is accomplished through *Peeraayesh*.'"

My sister was not an arguing type of person, but even if she was, she could not argue with Sohrab's convincing explanation.

After crossing the Amirieh Avenue we had to go through the Little Bazaar of Asheikh Hadi to reach the Shapoor Avenue beyond which there was Sanguelaj District where our house was located. The Little Bazaar was called little but it was not so little for the legs of little children.

The Shapoor and Amirieh Avenues were parallel to each other, and together formed a long ladder that stretched from the south of Tehran up to the north, and the Little Bazaar was only one of its many rungs stretching from west to east, or visa versa, depending on whether one was going home from school or from school to home. It was a bisected street, both longitudinally and crosswise. Longitudinally, it was narrowed down to one sidewalk for pedestrians and one narrow band studded with horse dropping for vehicles. The sidewalk allowed no more than two or three adults to walk side by side. And the street part barely allowed two cars or two *Doroshkehs* to pass by each other, often requiring exchange of greetings or insults by the drivers at the moment of squeezing by each other.

Crosswise, the bazaar was divided almost equally into two halves: the eastern half was covered like any other real bazaar with a perforated roof and slanted columns of lights. The western half was open with no roof, like any other street in Tehran, or in the Western world, for that matter. The Little Bazaar was also bisected along political lines in the sense that the eastern half was generally against modernization while the western half was either neutral or highly in favour of it. The shops were mainly in the covered section. The open section was mostly composed of bare cracked walls with occasional doors that rarely opened. It was mainly residential, but at the junction with Amirieh Avenue there was a large gate that was always open, guarded by a soldier at all times.

On that particular day, however, the guarding soldier was replaced by a high-ranking police officer with a grey uniform, a detective type of hat, and a long grey moustache. His uniform looked Swedish. He was standing, almost at attention, too rigid for his high rank. When we crossed the Amirieh Avenue, my sister said *Salaam* to him, and the man, to my surprise, replied to her *Salaam* with a barely detectable smile, as if he knew my sister.

"Who was that man you just said *Salaam* to?" I asked. "He looks a little like Reza Shah."

"He is Colonel Niayesh, the father of Zohreh Khanum."

"Why does he have a Swedish uniform?" I asked. "And why has Reza Shah who is changing everything to Persian or Iranian, not changed their uniform?"

"Because the first Iranian police officers were trained by the Swedes, and to answer your second question, I have to say that perhaps Reza Shah has not had the time to do it yet."

"Was it Reza Shah, by the way, who changed the nice-sounding name of Persia to Iran?"

"He did not change it. Both names are more than a thousand years old. Reza Shah only emphasized Iran perhaps to show its connection with Aryan race."

The daughter of that fatherly man, Zohreh Khanum, was a small woman, but everybody in our extended family was scared of her. She was obsessively clean and relentlessly progressive. When she visited any house, the hostess would worry that she might notice some unmade beds or uncollected dust at the corner of a carpet. "Unluckily, she always visits at the worst time of the year, like when we are in the middle of spring cleaning," the housewives often expressed their frustration. She was about half a century ahead of her time. Her lipstick was the brightest red in our family and she owned an electric refrigerator long before anybody knew such a thing existed. When we came from Mashad to Tehran and she came to welcome us, she chose me as her son, I don't know out of pity or out of genuine affection. I thought because the good ones, like Hamid and Majid, were already spoken for by our late grandmother and Auntie Pouran, she had chosen me as the only one who was left over. I think she understood my doubt about her benevolence, because one day she took me, alone, to her house and sat me on a chair beside a shining dining table in her empty guest room, opened her refrigerator door and took something red and trembling out of it and put it in front of me in a glass bowl with a small spoon.

"What is this?" I asked, having never seen such a cold and trembling delicacy, and so much of it!

"This is what I have named *larzoonak*, meaning, trembling," she said. Many years later I learned that it was made of dissolved gelatin mixed with the juice of black cherry, commercially known as Jell-O. I especially thanked her for giving it only to me and not to anybody else. To please her more, I thanked her in French, the way Auntie Pouran had taught us, by saying *merci*, instead of Arabic *Mamnoon* or *Moteshakker* that would make me sound like a little beggar. Nor did I say it in pure Persian form, *Sepaas gozaaram*, that would make me sound like a solider in the Persian army. My thanking her in French pleased her so much that she gave me a firm kiss on the cheek, so firm that the imprint of her lipstick remained on my face for days. I especially did not wipe it off until I made sure that everybody in the house, especially Hamid and Majid, had noticed it.

"Is he the chief of police?"

"No, but he is a high-ranking police officer. There are not many colonels in the police, compared to the army."

"Why, if he is so important, is he standing so fearfully?" I asked. "Even privates don't stand at attention like that and for so long."

"Because Reza Shah might visit this military establishment at any moment today, unannounced"

"Why unannounced?"

"Because he knows that if he announced the site he was going to visit, they would fix the place up temporarily. He wants to see the things as they are, so that he can fix them, permanently, if he did not like them."

The junction of the two parts of the Little Bazaar was not sharply demarcated. Sporadic stores appeared as one got closer to the covered section. The covered section was always more crowded than the open section because two or three narrow tributary lanes joined the Little Bazaar, right at the mid section. It just happened that the houses of our Aunt Seddigheh and Uncle Colonel were located near that junction, but we would never knock at their doors on our way to home or to school.

One of the sporadic shops was right in front of the sun-coloured door of our uncle's rented house. It was a nameless carpentry shop with a single, glassless window, run by a bearded man with a black robe and a long white beard. The workshop contained a hammer, a saw, and a chisel, with a few long boards and a pair of broken legs from an absent chair. When he wanted to pray at the nearby mosque, he would arrange two of the boards like a multiplication sign within his glassless window and left his shop without having the fear that it might get broken into.

The Little Bazaar was also an elastic street. It would get longer when it was cold, shorter when it was sunny. It was long in the morning and short in the evening. Before reaching the carpentry shop, a nameless grocery shop would appear that sold dried berries. My mood always changed for the better whenever I passed that store which was open in the evenings.

It was a small dark windowless outlet with a straw overhang extending from its roof to protect the underlying inverted gunny sacks on the public sidewalk that always stood there like circumcised genitals in front of a primitive temple to celebrate human fertility. I never looked inside that shop to see the face of its owner. All I knew was that the sack containing dried white berries was in front of the other sacks. I was not interested in his dry tasteless chickpeas or his sack of split peas.

Except for these last two, some of the shops were lit by silent electric bulbs, some with a hissing gas lamp. The latter warned the pedestrians that the road was slippery and wet. One was to be extra careful crossing the streets. I felt as if I was walking in the silent scene of a black-and-white movie, a Charlie Chaplin movie, expecting at any moment a grown-up fall and make me laugh.

The tallest flag was hanging from the roof of the house of our Uncle colonel. Unfortunately it fell to the ground due to the excessive wind as we got close to it.

I looked around to see the effect of the unveiling of women in the streets, blaming myself for not having noticed any dramatic changes in women, while consoling myself at the same time that it was not easy for a child to notice the absence of things, no matter how important.

As we passed the berry shop, my swinging left arm scooped a handful of berries. Had I had a pocket I would have put them in it to eat them slowly and secretly until we reached home, without my sister noticing anything. But since I did not have a pocket I was forced to chew them two or three at a time, as we continued walking towards home. With the renewed energy obtained from the sweet berries, I began to look around to see the effect of the unveiling.

I did not see any woman wearing a veil or a head kerchief, but because it was winter and everybody, whether woman or man, was covered with thick and woolen garments, one could not see any dramatic difference. No woman was weeping out of sorrow or jumping out of joy. Only a boy, my age, was crying bitterly in the crowded section of the bazaar, having lost his mother. That scene saddened me because I thought the only purpose of unveiling of women was for the children so that they did not lose track of their mothers when they were shopping in the crowded bazaars. I approached the boy, sympathetically, to ask, "Have you lost your mother?"

"No, no, no..." the child interrupted his cry to prove me wrong. "I've lost my father."

The grown-ups were mainly men, walking within their long and rigid overcoats, their chins disappearing in the opening of their collars, the steam of their breath obscuring their faces. No one appeared in a festive mood. One man's chin was invisible, covered by his beard. Some men were wearing hats with a shallow groove in middle, as if run over by a bicycle. Most of the adults were wearing nothing on their heads, whether man or woman. As soon as I made that observation, a woman passed by me wearing a blue hat with a red feather on one side. One side of her powdered face was covered by a black lace with large holes. Her lips were reddened with dark red lipstick. The black mole beneath her lower lip reminded me of the letter *Beh*, the second letter of the alphabet that was fresh in my mind. She walked with the swinging motion of a partridge. She did not seem to be going anywhere, but moving away, with protest, from something she did not like. A moment later, another woman passed, as if pursuing the woman with the hat. She had a dead brown fox around her neck with eyes that looked alive.

"How come Reza Shah unveiled the women in wintertime?" I asked my sister.

"I don't know. The principal in the school said that they wanted to do it in the summer, but it was postponed because of the protest by many men. A mosqueful of men went *Shaheed* in Mashad to prevent the unveiling from taking place."

"What does *Shaheed* mean?"

"Shaheed is Arabic for martyrdom," said my sister and continued with the same breath to ask me, "what are you chewing on, by the way?"

"Berries"

"Where did you get them?"

"From a friend at the school," I lied. "Why?"

"And you did not begin to eat them until now?"

I gave her one to keep her mouth busy. She ate it and became quiet and did not talk about it anymore, but I was not convinced that she really believed me. We continued for a few slippery steps in silence until we reached the main shops.

To break the uneasy silence, I asked, "Why did the men get themselves killed, so many good fathers and uncles and cousins and husbands?"

"For their *namoos*."

I got confused again since the name of our school was also Namoos, and I was sure they did not get themselves killed just for that. So I asked for further explanation. She explained that *namoos* meant *chastity*, and many men referred to their mother, sister or wife, as their *namoos*. And they believed that it was their duty to protect them.

"To protect them from what?" I kept asking questions to distract her from thinking about the berries.

"From the eyes of strange men."

"Why can't women wear a head kerchief at least?" I said. "It is cold."

"Wearing a head scarf is prohibited, too." My sister informed me. "The government thinks that if they allow a headscarf it might soon grow to become a chador."

"How about boys?" I asked. "Can they wear a head scarf when they are cold?"

"Don't be ridiculous!" said my sister, obviously irritated, judging by increased paleness of her face. "Boys never wear head kerchiefs, no matter how cold it gets. Think of what an Ajan would say if he saw you covering your head on the day that Tehran is celebrating the disappearance of the chador?"

All the shopkeepers were men whether in the covered or uncovered section of the Little Bazaar. Most of the shopkeepers had short beards and no hats, but some had caps on their heads, and some had neither a beard nor a cap. Some seemed to be shy, trying not to look at the face of the women who was buying things from them. Some were not shy at all, watching the female customers long before and after they had left their stores. One shopkeeper, who sold only birdcages and wooden rat traps, called after a woman who was not interested in his merchandise, saying that he would sell her both for the price of the cage alone, but she did not even look back. Then, when the man became certain that she was not going to come back, he began to be rude, laughing loudly while looking around to find another man to share his rude laughter with.

My right hand was still in my sister's as we stood at the creek to cross the Shapoor Avenue. The creek was overflowing with light brown water as the result of melted snow. As I watched the foaming water I saw in the middle of a large boot print, probably that of a soldier, judging by the imprint of many hobnails in it, a ten-*shahi* coin glittering like a jewel inside an open jewel box. I looked at it in disbelief for a second or two, before taking my hand out of the hand of my sister to jump on it. It was the largest current Persian coin that one could find. It had an unusual golden colour. On one side of the coin was the number 50, indicating its value in *Dinar*, equal to ten *Shahi*, on the other side, the laughing lion, the crown, the sun, and the sabre, all in relief. It was minted in solar year 1315 by the Persian calendar, and there was a rumour in the school that by mistake the bank had put more gold in it than its face value. It could be sold for at least twelve *shahi* in the bazaars, but I was not going to sell it. I could buy at least ten separate things with it.

At the gate of the Sanguelaj District my sister let go of my hand because from there until our house it was safe. No car or carts could go into the district because it was narrow. It was made of a maze of narrow and tortuous mud made lanes. It was the oldest part of Tehran, soon to be demolished to become known as the Ruins of Sanguelaj for several years before it became the city park. It was enclosed by mudmade walls eroded by the sandpaper of time, resembling the nest of gigantic termites. As of the moment that my sister let go of my hand, I began running and tumbling in the snow with the coin in my hand and joy in my heart.

Finding money is great, but finding it when there are no more shops to spend it is no fun. There were no shops in our district up to our house, unless I managed to miss the turn into our cul-de-sac and went far beyond our house to reach its dilapidated shopping centre located in the middle of our district like a large dental cavity in a molar tooth.

One day Hamid and I went to that forbidden place with his one or two *shahi*. We followed the appetizing smell of the smoke of burning liver kebab and found it beside a dilapidated wall, being fanned by a scantily dressed, unclean-looking man. We were not allowed to buy cooked food from street merchants, but this time we bought one shish and shared it. I was surprised by the fearlessness of Hamid regarding disobedience. The only condition he imposed on me before sharing it with me was that I did not tell Auntie Pouran. I promised that I would not, but I did threaten him several times afterwards, for several days, that I would tell if he disobeyed me. I abused that threat so much that finally Hamid got fed up and said, "Go ahead and tell it to anybody you wish." So I told it to Auntie Pouran, but to my surprise, Auntie Pouran did not punish him. Instead, she said,

"What did you eat? Besides, you were the older. Why did you let him buy such a filthy food?"

"I am not my brother's keeper."

"Did you eat any yourself?"

"Yes, I did," I confessed, "but I did it to make sure that it was not poisonous. Hamid has a delicate constitution. And I don't think you should drag this matter any longer especially when neither Hamid nor I got sick," I continued while running away from her, ending the conversation by saying, "and excuse me, I have to run to the washroom."

"And if it was poisonous?" She shouted as I was running away from her.

"I wish it was," I said. "Then I would be dead and would not have to listen to your impractical instructions anymore," I continued talking until I disappeared into the restroom at the farthest corner of the yard.

The snow kept falling, undisturbed, in loose parallel flakes. The snow on the ground was thicker than the snow on the sidewalk in front of our school. It was now up to my waist. The only thing that disturbed its smooth monotony was the imprint of my body and the occasional large footprint. If I could not spend the money at least I could show it to my mother. Money always made my mother happy, or at least lack of it made her unhappy.

I stopped once for my sister to catch up with me so that we could enter our house together as we were told. I was also worried that if I let her think for too long, she might reach the right conclusion regarding the origin of the dried berries. When she did not appear, I began to run again. The closer to our house I got, the more footprints I saw, all converging towards our nameless cul-de-sac at the end of which our house was located. There were only two other doors opening into our dead-end lane; one was always closed and the other was closed on that day. I was very glad that the latter was closed because whenever it was open there was a *Masdar* (soldier/servant) sitting beside it and a small white fluffy dog running in front of it that attacked nobody but me.

Out of the plethora of the footprints, I concluded with joy that we were having company. Whenever we had guests, everybody was politer than usual, and there were more things to eat without the objection of the grown-ups, particularly Auntie Pouran.

The door of our house was wide open. Even the panel on my left that was always closed was open, framing our courtyard like a colourless winter landscape. The farthest spot visible beyond the snow-covered square outer yard was the dark opening of the kitchen at the end of the sunken rectangular inner yard. I stopped like a nail at the threshold of the door to wait for my sister.

I thought something good and big must have entered our house in my absence. Good things always happened when I was not home. Maybe that is why my mother had sent me to school a year earlier. Once, coming back from school, I saw a mountain of coal dust in the courtyard. Our nanny was squatting beside it with a copper pot full of black water making coal balls for under the *korsi*, to prepare for the coming winter. Another time when I came home from school I found half of the courtyard was filled with a cloud of beaten cotton, the other half occupied by stacks of compacted cotton from eviscerated mattresses. In the middle was the cotton-beater, squatting to transform the pile of compacted cotton into the cloud of fluffy cotton with his gigantic guitar-shaped instrument, shaking his scrotum with every beat that he inflicted on its single string.

As I was looking toward the end of the yard, wondering if such an absolute silence was compatible with having so many guests, my mother exploded into the yard from one of the windows on my left, breaking its glass panes, running in the snow in her pink stockings and no shoes, chasing after four strange bearded men who were carrying a long box on their shoulders, covered by layers of expensive fabric, shouting at them "Don't take him! Don't take him!" while pulling her hair and scratching her face as she ran. Her pleading, rather than making the men stop, made them move faster and chant louder.

La elaaha ella Allah

La elaaha ella Allah

La elaaha ella Allah

La elaaha ella Allah

The men were four but they sounded as if they were sixteen. Several women, among whom I recognized Aunt Seddigheh, were trying to pull my mother back to the room, but she managed to overcome all of them and free herself to go after the men. She could have caught the men if she had not fallen several times on the slippery ground. The men were in such a hurry that one of them almost stepped on my toes as they went through the door with their stolen cargo. I could smell the arresting smell of mothballs coming from the expensive fabric as they passed through the door. I made use of the chaotic moment and broke the rule of not going into the house alone and ran toward the kitchen to ask our nanny what was going on, almost falling over the frozen pool as I passed the struggling women.

Night had begun, starting from the kitchen. It was hard to see what was going on. Our kitchen was always the first place to go dark and the last to get light. The only light in the kitchen was coming from the climbing flames rising to lick the lips of the gigantic copper pots and highlight the wet cheeks of our nanny. She was in her black dress, and weeping while boiling water. She always wore black and her eyes were always wet, either from the smoke in the kitchen or due to her inverted lashes. I pulled at her skirt to ask what was happening. I was worried. I had never seen my mother so desperate to throw a tantrum. Nanny wiped her eyes with her sleeve and said: "They are taking Shazdeh to a hospital." She called our father Shazdeh.

Was that all? I thought someone had died the way my mother was crying and the cook weeping. Nanny's reassurance relieved me, but only partly. I was still saddened that my mother should be so ignorant that she would equate going to a hospital with going out of this world. True, hospitals were few and the sick were many and only the terminally ill were admitted, and naturally few would return, but still some would come back home alive. Besides, our father was not terminally ill at all. He only coughed occasionally. All men coughed in our house. Some coughed when they were approaching a restroom, some when approaching a room in which women were sitting, mainly to announce their coming so that if the women wanted to cover themselves they could do so in time.

The kitchen was more crowded than usual. I could make out the moving shadows of strange men and the presence of unfamiliar samovars in the dark. Some of them I recognized as the servants of our close or distant relatives. Because they were not used to our kitchen, they ran into each other in the dark when they were looking for things. They were more trouble than help, just as there was more smoke in the kitchen than fire. Two young male servants whom I did not recognize were outside, standing on the drifted snow on the shady side of the yard—the south side where the snow never melted away, but shrank insidiously and slowly to a sad grey mound, to disappear long after the arrival of spring. They were preparing coal fires for the internal chimneys of the samovars, and perhaps for the top of a water pipe. Auntie Seddigheh was the only one I knew who smoked one, both at weddings and in funerals. I could never tell if she was smoking it out of joy or sadness. The men did not seem sad at all. They were playing with the fire. The fire was glowing with red and blue flames, but the men continued turning the wiry baskets in the air, making two interlocking circles of fire, like an incomplete Olympic logo. They seemed to be celebrating with homemade fireworks on the gloomy side of our yard. We were told playing with fire at night had bad consequences, the least of which was wetting one's bed during sleep.

In the darkness of the kitchen, one of the male servants who seemed to know the guests better than our nanny did, was pouring tea into the little transparent tea glasses with silver holders on an oval silver tray. One of the twelve glasses did not seem to have tea in it. As the man stood up to take them out, our nanny, who always complained that she could not see very well and always asked one of us to thread her sewing needle, reminded him that he had forgotten to add tea to one of the glasses. The man smiled a knowing smile and said that it was full, but full of hot water. Then he explained that one of my father's brothers from Mashad drank only hot water instead of tea or coffee.

In the guest room

It was time for me to break the rules of the house for the second time in one day and venture into the guest room where we, the children, were forbidden to go when we had guests. Also, since our father slept in the middle of that room during the last few days, we were not allowed to go in that room even when we did not have guests. But my father was not there anymore according to what our nanny had said. Besides, I was going to give my mother the good news about the money I had found. It would surely cheer her up and make her forgive my intrusion.

As I stepped down from the single step of the kitchen into the yard, I heard the chanting of the men coming from the lanes of Sanguelaj District with diminishing intensity. It sounded better from the distance: *"La elaaha ella Allah, La elaaha ella Allah, La elaaha ella Allah,*

151

La elaaha ella Allah." Now I could remember that I had heard my mother saying it several times at home when she was at her praying mat, or when one of the children had done something wrong and instead of punishing the child she would mouth that Arabic phrase. Once I asked my mother what it meant, but she said it was too big for my head. I insisted she tell me anyway. She said, "There are no little gods, but only the one God." What was its connection to my father being taken to a hospital? God only knows. I had also heard my mother saying the same phrase, when the children inadvertently entered her room in which she was doing her *Namaaz*, to express her disapproval.

Once it happened when I was playing hide-and-seek with my brothers. I had run out of places to hide. Mehdi was the wolf and was supposed to find me. It was in the middle of the day and I thought it was empty, but when I went there I saw my mother was there, covered from head to toe with her spotted chador, whispering to an invisible person, sometimes in erect position, as if talking to an equal, like a man to a man, sometimes bending like a servant, and finally touching her forehead to the ground in the most humiliating position. First, she said nothing to me, as if she was paralyzed as far as talking was concerned. Then her lips began moving faster and when I circled around her a few more times, she uttered those words in a manner that seemed to contain a threat of severe punishment. I went out faster than I had come in and gave myself up to Mehdi who was laughing behind the door like a hyena.

I ran towards the broken window to go to the guest room. There were too many shoes and boots and galoshes in the corridor between the guest room and the children's room, some of them covered by an extra layer of rubber. I took off my long, loose, leaky rubber boots that were handed down to me from one of my sisters and put them at the bottom of the row of shoes of the children and tried to go into the guest room. A rigid rug was nailed to the door to keep the cold air out and the warm air in. It resisted my entrance, but I pushed it aside and opened the door and went in, armed with my money.

Our father's bed was removed from the centre of the room. Quilt covered canopies were laid along the walls against the cushions with rabbit ears covered by rugs. Mourning women without veils or scarves were sitting on the canopies, some leaning against the cylindrical pillows to make it difficult for me to differentiate their voluminous thighs from the bulky pillows. Untouched brown plates of bitter-sweet halva were put on small tables, here and there. The sound of a man with a good voice was coming from an invisible corner reading the Koran. The air smelled of rose water laced with tea, Turkish coffee, and tobacco smoke. The latter was coming from the noisy water pipe of Aunt Seddigheh. The blue-framed windows looking to the yard were tightly shut and their gaps were blocked from inside by raveled cotton, making it look as if snow was trying to push itself into the room. The door to the other room where men were sitting was open into the room where women were sitting.

A high, insurmountable step separated the two rooms. The entrance of that room was from the square outer yard. That was the room where my father entertained his guests when he was not sick. Men were sitting on chairs against the walls around that room, some smoking cigarettes, some having Turkish coffee, some tea. I looked for the uncle who drank only hot water but could not see him. Some had not taken their overcoats off, as if they wanted to get up and go at any moment. A few had military uniforms on. The male servant with the oval silver tray was making rounds with exaggerated politeness, looking sadder than when he was in the kitchen. No one was crying. They were talking about our father's parcel of land and whether it was more profitable to rent it out to a stranger or let one of our cousins cultivate it and give the money to our mother.

I did not recognize most of the women in the room, but I could feel the pitiful weight of their gaze on my back. I recognized Aunt Seddigheh near the fireplace, sitting beside my mother. The other sound in the room, beside the soothing sound of the declamation of the Koran, was the gargling sound of the water-pipe of Aunt Seddigheh. Synchronous with the gargling sound, pink petals of Mohammadi roses were dancing in the glass bottom of that elaborate pipe to accentuate the smell of rose water already in the air. My mother was sitting, cross-legged, calm and quiet, next to Aunt Seddigheh. She was so calm that I thought her tantrum in the yard a minute ago was just a show. Had I began to cry like that, I would have never stopped. And to anybody who wanted to console me I would have recited this line from an unknown Persian poet.

Why?

Why not cry my benevolent adviser?

The heart is mine

The eye is mine

The tear is mine

And the sleeves of my shirt are mine.

Or maybe her calm was due to the fact that she had given up. The root of Islam is *Tasleem*, and *Tasleem* means to surrender, to put one's will power in the hands of God.

I stepped foreword for a closer look. Aunt Seddigheh put the tip of the pipe on the dimple of her cheek and smiled in silence as she saw me approaching. She was the woman who had started the premature widowhood in our families and knew how to deal with my mother and her children. Her reassuring smile indicated to me that things were not as bad as I thought, and my mother's behaviour in the yard was nothing but an overreaction. I held my coin in front of the face of my mother, the way one holds a magnifying lens, between the index finger and the thumb of my right hand and said, "Modar-jun, I found this money in the street today."

"Good for you," she said, "now go the children's room."

I went, but I was highly disappointed. My mother's reaction to the money was much less enthusiastic than I had expected; much less than my money's worth.

In the children's room

The children's room was colder than the guest room, unless one went directly and up to the neck under the *korsi*. A kerosene lamp with a round burning wick was burning on top of the *korsi*, projecting larger-than-life shadows of Hossein and Mehdi on the wall, doing their homework. I passed them silently and went directly to the attached small chest room that was also my sisters' private room. Monir-jun was home now, still in her uniform, pulling the silver cutlery out of the velvet boxes to take them to the guest room. "What kept you?" I asked my sister with controlled anger.

"Nothing, I was just behind you," she said sheepishly. "As I turned the last bend of the road to come home, I saw four men were carrying a coffin. I moved aside until they passed. Then, out of respect for what was inside the coffin, I followed it for seven steps. Then, as I was about to return, I thought I should take seven more short steps for you too. Each time I wanted to return I thought of one of the people I liked and I took seven steps for each of them until I ended in Shapoor Avenue where they put the coffin in a black windowless car to take it to the shrine of Prince Abdol-Azeem at the City of Ray." She kept going until I interrupted her.

"You seem to like too many people," I said grudgingly as I took my girl's uniform off and, rather than giving it to her, threw it, with protest, on the ground and demanded my home shirt that had a pocket. She was responsible for my clothes and Monavar was responsible for Hamid's. They kept our washed underwear and socks in their small identical chests which were only slightly bigger than a doll's chest.

She gave it to me, washed, folded, but not ironed. I took it without saying *merci*, and put it on by myself. My sister did not think that I could do it by myself. She had seen me several times putting it on backwards. She did not know that a few days earlier I had found out the secret of putting it on the right way so that its front fell on my front and its back on my back. I had learned by myself that I had to face its back at the beginning if I wanted its front to fall on my front. I came out of the chest room without talking to her anymore. I thought she knew all the time what was going on in our house without telling me, and all the discussion about the berries and unveiling of women were just for my distraction.

Nothing in the children's room seemed to have changed since the disappearance of our father. Hossein, as usual, was carefully and diligently doing his homework. He had to write extra pages as a penalty for something bad he had done in school, but rather than writing them with large, loose letters and on every other line to finish it faster, he wrote them with the finest pen and on every line. He never learned to cheat. Once, when my mother saw him writing penalty pages as carefully as routine homework, she was tempted to teach him to cheat but changed her mind to let him learn by himself. He never told anybody what bad thing he had done in the school to deserve such a harsh punishment.

Mansur, our oldest brother, was in the room too, pretending to be doing something with pen and paper. He was never interested in what I did, but that night, unexpectedly, he asked me if I had any homework to do. I gave him a negative reply. He did not believe me. I explained that I had some work to do, but it did not include writing.

"What does it include then?"

"Erasing"

"Editing?"

"No," I said "E R A S I N G," emphasizing every letter of the word to make him feel more ignorant than he was.

"What do you mean?" he said. "I don't understand."

"I am not responsible for your lack of understanding," I said. "Have you ever seen those red lines that teachers draw on the homework of the students?"

"Yes, I have seen them," he said, getting increasingly more irritated. "What about them?"

"Well, my homework is to erase those lines from my last night's homework."

He smiled, thinking that I was joking. I told him that I was dead serious and was not like Hamid who joked all the time, and without continuing the fruitless discussion, I began to erase the line from my previous homework. Something had happened to him that night that had made him assume the role of a big brother for the first time. Something that I thought had to do with the absence of our father. We both wanted to teach each other a lesson. He wanted to show me who was the boss in the children's room, and I was determined to show him that I could not be bossed around. As soon as I finished erasing the line, he drew a new one. The more I erased the harder he drew. We repeated the same maneuver back and forth several times until he finally used both ends of his fat red-and-blue marker to make several deep and inerasable red and blue lines on my homework, wrinkling the page and almost tearing it. That was when I gave up and cried. In my cry, I wished his father would die because in our class the students were saying that if one sharpened both ends of one's pencil one's father would die.

I don't remember when I fell asleep that night, or what I ate for supper. I must have fallen asleep early without supper, because I always slept well after a good cry.

I woke up in the middle of the night. The first thing I did was to touch my pocket to see if the money was still there. It was there; therefore it could not be a dream. I was surprised that I had fallen asleep while I had money in my pocket. Ordinarily, I could not fall asleep until I had spent my money to the last *Shahi*. Tomorrow did not exist for me. What if I never woke up? What if tomorrow the stores did not accept my money? I liked money not because of its shape but for its potential to be transformed to anything I wished.

It was still night, but light was coming through the windows. The only sure sign of the presence of night in the room was the breathing sound of my sleeping siblings.

I could clearly see the profile of Hossein who was sleeping next to me along the longer side of our rectangular *korsi*. Hamid was on the short side of the *korsi*, sleeping beside Majid. I urgently needed to go to the nearest shopping centre to spend my money. I could buy hard candies to either chew on or suck on them to last longer. I could spend some of it on a candy rooster on a stick and suck on it until it became semi-transparent when held against the light, like the back lights of a car. I could buy brown stretchable chocolate and keep stretching it until it became white, and then eat it.

The shopping centre was not too far from our house and I knew how to get there, but I was afraid of the dog of our neighbour. First, I wanted to wake up Hamid to go with me. I looked at his profile on the pillow. It did look as perfect as a tableau, as my mother had described it in one of her post-partum letters to Auntie Pouran. There was nothing wrong with it, nothing that I could improve on was I to draw it in my booklet. My mother once had confessed, "I cannot tell my sons apart when they are asleep. I'm afraid that one morning I might wake up the wrong one." After that, I pretended, several times, to be asleep in her vicinity, hoping that she would wake me up by mistake, instead of Hamid.

I stood up, looked around in the darkness before moving towards the window. There was neither sun nor moon in the sky. The light was coming from the ground. The snow was soundlessly falling to cover the footprints in the yard. The only thing that had escaped the healing action of snow was a loose ball made of the black hair of my mother, bouncing against the walls. The interlocking branches of the leafless trees, frozen over the pool re-sembled a herd of caribou standing still in a polar winter to conserve energy for the coming spring. I turned my gaze towards the room to wake up the first brother that moved. No one moved. I coughed a fake cough. No one heard it. I concluded that they were all pretending to be asleep because I always could wake up anybody who was really asleep, but never managed to wake up anybody who pretended to be asleep.

Hamid was younger than me, yet he was not afraid of the dog. I could wake him up, but I was reluctant to show my cowardice to him. So I let Hamid sleep with a piece of bread still stuck to his lips. He must have been eating bread while lying down. We were told never to eat anything in reclining position. It was a sin. "It would get into your pharynx and kill you," Auntie Pouran always warned us, backed by our mother. Hamid always did what he liked, regardless of the rules and regulations of the house.

I looked at Hossein. His profile on the pillow did look like Hamid's. I could not tell if he was Hamid or Hossein either, had I not been sleeping beside him. He was so fast asleep that I knew he wouldn't appreciate it if he was disturbed, but I thought if I promised him that I would buy something for him, too, he wouldn't mind and would likely agree to go along with me. First, I touched his head once, before calling his name; thinking that he might wake up without knowing who had caused it. His hair was short and sharp like a baby porcupine. He did not move. I whispered near his ear, "Hossein?" He did not reply. I repeated his name once more, and slightly louder, but not so loud as to wake up the others. He raised his head slightly above the pillow, opened half of one of his eyes to look at me with utter disgust and fell back to sleep without saying a word. I put the money in my pocket and went back to the window.

The snow was falling in straight, mesmerizing dotted lines. I stared at it for so long that it appeared that it was not the snow that was coming down, but the planet Earth rising, carrying me with it as its only living inhabitant. I felt I was that little prince who lived on that little planet, the drawings of which I had seen in a French book titled *Le Petit Prince*.

Breakfast in the Sunshine

I woke up in the morning after the sunrise, with the golden money still in my possession, glad—as always—that I had not given in to the sinful temptation of the previous night. I sat on the sun-bleached segment of the carpet next to the windows. My sweetened tea was put in front of me beside my warm *Taftoon* bread the centre of which was marked by a white morsel of cheese. Hossein did not remember anything of the past night, or if he did, he was noble enough not to say anything about it. I sat, cross-legged, on the carpet to break my nocturnal fast.

The snow had stopped. The sky was as clear as a blue crystal. The rays of the sun passing through my glass of tea had projected a long gold fish on the Nile blue ground of the carpet and resurrected its dead flowers at the periphery. The cool fragrance of the ice-flower—the only shrub in our house that flowered in the winter, with yellow humble petals the shape of bumble bees, and Monavar sometimes took a branch of it for her teacher—was coming through the closed windows. The arched imprint of the windows on the carpet had decorated the room like the interior of a mosque. A prayer was in order, a short prayer, no, a child's prayer, if not the truncated prayer of a traveller.

Many thanks to Khoda:

Thanks for the glorious mornings

Thanks for the gloomy evenings

Thanks for the dog of my neighbour

Thanks for the reluctance of Hossein

Many thanks; as much as the number of snowflakes in one day, because:

Unlike the fall of snow

Unlike the fall of the lion from the Persian flag

Unlike the fall of Hossein from the balcony

Falling asleep is still reversible.

No more sorrow and no more Siah

Exactly one year after that gloomy evening, we, the children, were sitting around the same warm *korsi* in the same cold room; doing our homework. There was no sound in the room except for Mehdi's broad-tipped reed pen making cricket sounds on the paper as he stretched the long letters of alphabet even longer. I was still in grade one, but now in the boys' school, doing my homework, seriously. There was neither sadness nor sorrow in the room. The same round-burning lamp in the middle of the room projected shadows on the wall bigger than us, like incomplete statues of baby bears. Our father was not there, but his absence was not felt. The only absence that was felt was the absence of our mother. No one had seen her since we had come home from school. And no one knew were she was. No one was worried about her either, and if they were, they were doing a good job of not showing it. I was worried. I was not used to coming home and not seeing my mother. I tried not to think about her by concentrating on my work. My feet were warm because they were under the *korsi*, but my back was cold because it was towards the entrance door that never could be shut tightly enough.

As soon as I turned my head to see how incompletely the door was shut, it opened widely and our mother burst into the room with laughter and a boxful of large cream-puffs in her hand: one for everybody, regardless of age, size, sex or grade, and one extra for whoever finished first and wanted more. When she saw me looking more at her new dress than the box of our favourite pastry, she said: "I am not wearing *Siah* anymore because tonight is the first anniversary of your father's passing away."

"Why?" I asked to the dismay of everybody else who were more interested in having the share of their pastry.

"Because exactly one year has passed since your father passed away."

Still, not knowing what passing away meant I continued, "Then how come you never celebrate the anniversary of any of your children's birthday?"

"Not every anniversary is a happy occasion," someone corrected me from behind.

"What is it then?" I said, as I turned back to see who had corrected me.

"Can't you understand a hint?" Mehdi said impatiently.

"No I can't," I confessed. "Let me know exactly what has happened a year ago."

"Our father died. He died exactly a year ago, tonight," Mehdi put it bluntly.

"Thank you, but how come no one told me?"

"Couldn't you see for yourself?"

"How could I see something which is not there? Besides, Nanny said our father was taken to a hospital when I asked."

No one offered any explanation. Everybody just waited until I shut up. No wonder when I went back to school three days after, my sisters' classmates kept asking me what had happened to my father and when I told them that he was taken to a hospital, they quickly turned away while holding their mouth so that I did not see they were laughing.

Auntie Pouran broke the silence to gain at least part of her lack of status among the children, by asking me, "What could you do, if you were told the truth?"

"I would have cried."

"Well, why don't you cry now while the others are having their cream puffs?"

I did not glorify her question with an answer. Instead, I looked at my mother's dress to detect any drastic changes. There were not many. She was still in black. What she was wearing was not much different from what she wore all her life. She had a tight black woolen top and a shiny black skirt. Her black hair was cut short, almost like that of men with long hair. The only colourful thing on her dress were a few vermicular ribbons of ravelled cotton in green or white, sewed to her skirt, in relief, like the beginning of snow fall on a green lawn at night. It was only when I saw my mother's pathetic attempts to appear cheerful that I began to cry. I was not sure if my crying was for my dead father or my living mother.

I had begun my delayed mourning with my cries as the rest of my siblings had begun to break theirs with their cream puffs.

"Don't eat sorrow," my mother came to my rescue. "Eat your cream puff, instead."

A short prayer for a long life

The last day in grade one was easier than any other day in our school. Not only was it just for half a day, we did not have to carry any books with us either. It was just for getting our report cards. My sister carried my report card with hers in one hand, pulling me along with the other. It was warm and I was happy. There was an extra spring in my steps. Perpendicular rays of the midsummer sun bounced off my shaven head like rays of rain bouncing off an umbrella. Just the fact that as of that day I did not have to wear that ridiculous dress anymore, was enough to make me happy, let alone not having to go to school for two-and-a-half months as of that day.

The wind in the Little Bazaar was laced with the inoffensive smell of fresh horse droppings. Before reaching the berry shop I tried to change hands, so that I was on the left side of my sister as we walked, but she, without saying anything, did not let go of my hand. Did she know the truth about the origin of the dried berries? I wondered as we continued in silence our march towards our home through the Little Bazaar.

"I am thirsty," I said to my sister as we got close to the house of our Uncle Colonel.

She thought I wanted to go to our uncle's house for drinking water.

"No," I said. "I am not going to knock at his door and ask for water like a beggar," as I pointed to the entrance of the public *Aab-anbaar* (underground cistern of drinkable water for the public) underneath his house. "I want to drink from that public reservoir." She reluctantly agreed to take me down its forty slippery stairs. Was it not for the worn-out edges of its stairs, one would have thought that no one had ever descended so deep into the belly of mother earth to get water. Everything was cool, damp and dark down there. Occasional copper-coloured earth worms, matching the colour of the brick stairs, were moving sluggishly at the deep wet end near the fractured fragments of *Koozeh* and other broken earthenware. A sparkling brass faucet was dripping into a dark cubic hollow at the very end. I could not reach it with my cupped hands. So, I asked my sister if she had brought her collapsible aluminum cup that she always took with herself to the school.

"No. I thought we would not need it today, because we were going home soon," she replied.

"How am I supposed to drink water then?"

She looked around in desperation and finally picked up a concave fragment of a broken *Koozeh* from the ground to give me to drink out of. But my thirst suddenly disappeared when I saw, underneath that fragment, a one-*Shahi* copper coin beside a coiled worm, jealously guarding it like a treasure. It was the smallest coin that one could find, but its effect on my mood at that moment and the rest of my life was no less than a treasure. My thirst disappeared. I ran up the stairs faster than I had descended. I stopped at the cavernous opening of the staircase to wait for my sister. There was no sidewalk to separate the opening of the public cistern from the passing carts and horses. One had to be doubly careful crossing that narrow street. The light outside was too much for our eyes, as if we had spent weeks in a cave, but there was no spider web across its opening. I looked, nevertheless, at my coin in the sunshine to see if it was still a current coin. We let pass the occasional *Doroshkehs* and a few man-drawn carts before crossing to reach the sidewalk.

"Would you like we go back a few steps to buy some dried berries with your money?" My sister asked, deliberately I thought, to remind me of my bad intention on that day and my recurrent bad actions during that year.

"No thank you. I don't like berries anymore, fresh or dried."

"Good. Do whatever you want with your money."

I wanted to use it differently, different from the ways I had spent my money in the past. I did not want to use it for something to eat. I wanted to give it to someone else to eat so that God would forgive me for the free berries I was having every day thanks to that blind berry store. So, I told my sister that I wanted to give it to a beggar.

"There are no beggars anymore in Tehran, or in Iran for that matter," said my sister.

"Why? What happened to them?" I asked with total amazement. I always thought the most constant thing one would see in the streets was a beggar, if not two or three. "Don't tell me again that they are removed by Reza Shah, please; it is getting boring." I said.

"Exactly," said my sister, "Reza Shah has prohibited mendacity in the streets."

"But what if someone wants to do something good?" I said. "Something for others."

She said I could throw it away and make the lucky finder as happy as me.

I wanted to see the person who finds it. As I was wondering how to part with it and still see where it was going I saw the bearded man who always sat outside of his carpentry shop in front of my uncle's house. He had not stretched his hand out, but when I gave him my money, after a moment of hesitation he looked me in the face and took the money and said, "*Peer shee*!" which I knew was not Arabic since it had the letter *p* in it, and therefore it could not be a prayer.

I ran back to my sister to ask her what the man meant by those two short words. "May you become old" was my sister's translation.

"Is that a good thing to become old?" I asked my sister, "I heard old age is associated with wrinkles and tragedies."

"It is still better than dying young," said my sister, "and to buy a long life with the smallest amount of money, is a bargain."

Whether she was right or wrong, I said no more. I said no more because I was happy. Whenever I am happy I know what I have done or whatever decision I've made anterior to that moment of happiness must have been the right one.

Money, I concluded, is like a flower; it is more fun when it is given away.

Presenting our report cards to our mother

My sister and I were a little late. By the time we reached home my other siblings were standing in a line in front of my mother in her room, each holding his or her report card in hand. Everybody had received their report card on the same day; the difference in the time of arrival at home was due to the variation in the distance between our home and their respective schools. My mother was sitting, cross-legged, on the quilt-covered canopy bed, beside the artificially smiling Auntie Pouran.

I went to my place at the end of the line, while Monir-jun filled the gap between Mansur and Monavar. Mansur must have been in high school, probably grade seven, because he had long pants on, making his long legs looking even longer. Mehdi and Hossein had short pants because they were in elementary school. And I was wearing my sister's old uniform that as of that day was of no use to anybody but for Nanny to clean the kitchen with.

It looked like a small military ceremony— boring, tiring, and long-lasting. One by one, from the top of the line, each child approached my mother and presented their cards, saying, *"Ghabool."* She smiled for each and said something nice as she searched her purse for money to give to them for having done well in school. Why didn't she have the money ready beforehand to save time? Don't ask me.

I kept shifting my weight from one leg to the other. Auntie Pouran asked if I needed to go to the washroom. I did not even answer her improper question.

"Ghabool," the monotonous word that my siblings were repeating at the time of presentation of their report card was Arabic for passed or graduated. I was glad that mine, which was *Rad*, Farsi for passed, was refreshingly different. I did not know at that time that it also meant rejected or failed. For failure we used the French word which in the Persian spelling was *Rofoozeh* and my teacher had reassured me that I was not *Rofoozeh* when she gave me my report card. I was therefore quite surprised when my mother did not display any sign of satisfaction when I told her that I was *Rad*. She took the card from my hand and put it on her draped lap and kept looking at it for a long time. I stepped closer to her to look at it together. Maybe I could help her solve the problem, if any. My head was so close to hers that her hair was tickling my nose. It smelled of Darjeeling tea, laced with the sunny smell of turmeric, mixed with the sweet fragrance of rose water. My only two-digit mark was 10, for arithmetic. The rest were lower. Our arithmetic consisted of counting numbers. I could count up to ten, so our math teacher had given me 10 out of maximum of 20. My Farsi was bad and I had got a single digit mark for it, with dashes on each side like wings. The wings were there so that I could not add any number beside it, as if I would ever think of doing such a thing.

The sports teacher liked me and I liked her a lot. Unfortunately, she had not given me a mark. Just a good written comment: "Nasser is a gentleman. He never stepped on the toes of his partner during the dance class."

"What kind of sports did your sports teacher teach you?" my mother asked as she let go of her lip. Whenever she did not want to laugh, she would bite the corner of her lips.

Our school was small and had no gymnasium. As far as sports equipment was concerned we had only a single volleyball and that was always in the hands of grade six students. Our teacher therefore had substituted dancing for sports because it did not require any additional equipment. We danced the western type of dancing, Tango, two by two, one hairy girl with one hairless boy on the brick pavement of the yard— two bricks to the right, one brick to the left, or visa versa. She made the music with her tongue, throat, and lips. She had a wide mouth with a pink interior outlined by carefully drawn lipstick the colour of cherry. More than hearing her "la-la-la-la," I kept looking into her mouth to see a glimpse of her vibrating little-tongue.

I did not like to dance, whether alone or as a couple, but I did participate in it to support the enthusiastic attempt of my teacher for speedy modernization. I did not enjoy it though. The only good thing about it was the fact that for the first and the last time in my life the number of girls exceeded that of the boys, and the girls had to wait their turn by sitting at the edge of the pool.

My mother did not seem to believe me. She had never heard of that kind of a teacher, nor had any of my brothers. Most of the female members of our extended family were graduates of the same school, too, but none of them had ever seen or heard of such a super-modern female teacher that I was lucky enough to have on my first year in Chastity School.

My mother put my report card on the stack of the other report cards and sent all the others to their rooms, including Auntie Pouran, to talk to me in private. When there was no one else left in the room, my mother began talking to me grown-up to grown-up.

"Do you know why I sent the others out before talking to you?"

"No, Modar-jun. I have no idea," I said. "Could it be, by any chance, that you want to give me advice but since you believe, 'to advise in public is to scorn,' you have sent the others away so that I wouldn't get humiliated?"

"I have no advice for you," my mother said. "I am not worried about you. The one I am worried about is Hossein."

"Why, Modar-jun?" I objected. "Hossein is doing fine. Why not worry about me? I don't even know the difference between success and failure at this age."

"You will learn the difference. You are just a little slow. Slow students can become good if they decide to do their homework," my mother reasoned, "but good students — God forbid — if they become bad, they will have a hard time to become good again."

"What school did you go to, Modar-jun, that has made you so good and wise?" I asked, wondering if she too had begun her education at the same school as I.

"It takes good children to make good mothers." My mother countered my compliment with a better one.

"*Merci*, but do I get any money, for being so good?" I made use of the opportunity of her momentary softening.

She unclasped her bulging black leather purse and took out two ten-*Shahi* coins, one of them slightly brighter than the other. I knew it had more gold in it than its face value. I could sell it for twelve or thirteen *shahi* in the main Bazaar. But I did not sell it. I spend both of them on the same day, but I don't remember what I bought.

The last walk through the Little Bazaar

I cannot leave this chapter and the Little Bazaar without paying my final respects to Colonel Sharabi.

The last time that I was walking along the covered section of the Little Bazaar without anybody holding my hand was for the purpose of following the coffin that contained the body of Colonel Sharabi. I was twenty years old then and in the second year of medicine, wearing my colourful military uniform with layers of golden ribbons and rows of shiny buttons. I was only one of the more than two hundred who had come to pay their respects to Colonel Abdollah Khalvati by following his coffin on foot.

Sharabi had died quietly and peacefully in his rented house. Death did not approach him like a cat on silent paws but like a wounded soldier with a black tongue. He had seen enough dying soldiers in wars and battles to recognize that a black tongue was the pathognomonic sign of approaching death. His death was witnessed only by one person and that person was his daughter-in law, my sister, Monir. I asked my sister to tell me what she had noticed in the last minutes of his life. She said that a minute after experiencing an unusual chest pain and a few minutes before dying, the colonel had asked her to bring her hand-held mirror for him so that he could look at his tongue in it. The moment he saw that it had turned black he threw the mirror away, lay down and died.

"Did the mirror break when he threw it away?" I asked my sister.

"No. Why?" my sister said, slightly surprised of my apparent lack of sympathy.

"Your uncle is dead and you are worried about a little mirror?" she scolded me.

The reason I asked that question was because I was always interested to know the last words or the last action of dying people, especially Colonel Sharabi. I wanted to see if he kept his promise of breaking nothing and live peacefully and for peace after he had broken his sword, like a true chevalier, in front of the last Shah, for, unlike his father Reza Shah, the son did not chose the right people for the right job.

"No," my sister said, "he just let the mirror slide softly from his hand on the bed, next to where he lay down to die."

Sharabi had no last words and had said nothing regarding what to do with his body after his death. In his book, however, he had said that he wished to be buried under the steps of the United Nations building, if such an institution had become a reality rather than being just a wish. He had even thought of other contingencies. For example, if he was killed in a battle and the flesh of his body was eaten by wolves or dogs, he was satisfied if his bones were carried to be buried under one of the stairs of the said building. He wanted to be remembered as the colonel who told only the truth. His book was actually written because one of the guests in the house of one of his friends had accused him of confabulation, if not lying, when he was telling a story —which was actually the simplified version of part of his book— for the young daughter of his host.

On the day on which the funeral procession of Sharabi was taking place, I was supposed to be in the university-affiliated Vazeeri Hospital which was located not too far from the Little Bazaar, as a second-year medical student. Dr. Mazaher was the clinical professor of internal medicine in that hospital and was teaching us bedside medicine, using the patients in his ward, the first one of whom happened to be a young man in perfect shape dying of renal failure. Renal dialysis and renal transplant were not yet part of the armament of medicine, so we, a dozen medical students, stood around the bed of the comatose man, incontinent of urine, dripping short streams of urine from his exposed penis, as the professor talked about the signs of deepening coma before his eventual death. The professor knew our uncle and was aware of his death because he was remotely related to him through the influential Hedayat family to which our uncle was also connected through marriage. I had therefore no problem obtaining his permission to attend my uncle's funeral. In fact he was going to attend it, too, but later, after he finished teaching. He was going to go straight to the cemetery in his own car.

We followed the coffin of the colonel on foot through the Little Bazaar up to the intersection with Shapoor Avenue. From there the body was to be put in the hearse that was waiting there, to be followed by cars to the cemetery near the City of Ray a few kilometres beyond the southern limit of Tehran.

The procession went quietly and uneventfully up to the intersection with Shapoor Avenue where it was abruptly stopped by a bearded and muscular man known as Sha'ban Ja'fary, nicknamed Sha'ban the Brainless by those who did not like him. Those who did not like him included those who did not like the Shah, all the left-wing students and their sympathizers. He was pro-Shah and anti-Tudeh Party. He had built an elaborate sports club next to the City Park known as Bash-gaheh Ja'fary in which he demonstrated ancient Persian wrestling and traditional Persian sports. Not many ordinary people used his club but it had become a tourist attraction and whenever high-powered dignitaries visited Iran, they were taken to his Bash-gah to show off his place as a pure Persian place. He did not seem to be highly educated but somehow knew that education was a good thing and educated people should have good manners. That is why when he was taken to the emergency department of Sina hospital for some reason and some interns who had spotted him from the windows of their pavilion on the second floor had laughed at him, he had exclaimed, "Those assholes are so impolite!"

The propaganda against Mr. Ja'fary was so extensive and far-reaching that even Sohrab, who liked the Shah and was not a members of the Tudeh Party, disliked that man so much that once he confided in me that he had been ready to shoot him with his revolver, if his father had not advised him otherwise. Sohrab, of course, later regretted having such a mistaken impression about Mr. Ja'fary, especially after the revolution when he realized that the man nicknamed Brainless had more brains in his head than the sum of the brains of all the university intellectuals put together.

On this particular day, Sha'ban Ja'fary had stopped the procession with good intentions. He considered every resident of the Little Bazaar as a "child of his district," as he put it, and it was his duty to eulogize them as they passed one last time through the gates of his domain. So he climbed on a high stool and began to sing such a sad mourning song that, except for the Shojania brothers who rarely cried, everybody else began to weep. He did not let the coffin go until he finished his eulogy.

Out of respect for Colonel Sharabi the army had manned the road from Tehran down to the cemetery by soldiers. I was watching the trees and the soldiers pass as I was sitting in the back seat of the car of the grown son of Aunt Seddigheh, Dr. Shab-gueer, whom we called Mozaffar Khan. He was older than me by at least ten years. Since I had no car he had offered to take me in his car. And I, not having learned yet the etiquette of cars and where one should sit when there are only two people in a car, out of respect for him, had sat in the back seat rather than beside him. We did not talk much as he was driving and I was looking out of the window. After he drove for about a kilometre or two my cousin, wearing his usual one-sided smile that was the hallmark of the decedents of Aunt Seddigheh, turned his head towards me to say, "Nasser, the soldiers are saluting you!"

"Me?" I asked with surprise. "Why?"

"Yes, you," my cousin said, somewhat amused, "because you are sitting in the back seat alone with all your shiny buttons and golden ribbons, and the soldiers think you are an army general and I am your civilian driver!"

I immediately apologized for having misled the soldiers and asked my cousin to stop the car so that I could get out and go to sit beside him.

He did not listen and drove on.

After my cousin denied me the opportunity to correct my mistake, I thought the least I could do was to do something for the Iranian soldiers to justify their mistaken salutation for me. To achieve this goal, all I had to do was to tell the whole world what Colonel Abdollah Khalvati has said about Iranian soldiers in his *SOS*. He had seen the Iranian soldiers both in action and at rest and had reached the sincere conclusion that they were among the bravest and the least demanding soldiers in the world, and were ready to lose their heads for their country if they had an understanding commander.

No wonder the Persian word for soldier is *Sar-baz*; meaning the one who is ready to lose his head (for his country). And no wonder Sharabi considered himself, above anything else, a simple *Sar-baz*; and how much he regretted the fact that he had to change his military uniform for a civilian suit in the last few years of his life. Only God knows how much he must have regretted his dying in bed rather than on a battlefield, during the last few seconds of his life, between the moment when he saw his cyanotic tongue in the mirror and the moment he expired.

25

AS-YOU-WISH STREET

SOON AFTER OUR FATHER PASSED AWAY we moved from the nameless cul-de-sac in Sanguelaj District to an open ended, well-known street in Tehran, named Koucheh-ye Del-Bekhah, meaning *As-You-Wish Street*. It was located near the southern limits of Tehran, just before the intersection of Amirieh Avenue with Mokhtari Avenue. It connected the prestigious Amirieh Avenue to its dusty parallel, See-metree Avenue. The Mokhtari Avenue was named after the brutal chief of police during the time of Reza Shah, who was tried and sentenced to a few years in prison after Reza Shah was replaced by his son during the Second World War. For those who were familiar with words, like Captain Vokhshur, the word *Mokhtari* was an Arabic word derived from *Ekhtiar*, meaning "to have a choice" or "to have an option," which is not much different from having a wish. And Vokhshur would make use of this similarity to make the bus stop where he wanted.

Apart from its funny name, As-You-Wish Street was like any other residential street in Tehran: encased by two parallel walls, narrow enough to prevent any car to go in, but wide enough to be longitudinally bisected by a dry groove, decorated by a few *arr-arr* trees to attract donkeys. No one knew why those die-hard trees were named by the same name as the braying of a donkey. I thought it was due to the fact the donkeys of the men who brought ice or watermelon to that street, chewed on their bark while the donkey man was talking to a housewife. Its grumpy residents, however, believed that it was due to the fact that whenever they wanted to have a short sleep in the hot summer afternoons, their sleep was interrupted by a few *arr-arru*, or crying children who climbed the branches of those trees.

Regardless of the origin of the name of those trees, it was refreshing to have a capricious name like As-You-Wish Street in a city where the name of its main avenues and important streets were borrowed from the names of its royal family or its high ranking military officers. It generated a visible smile across the lips of anybody who mentioned that name, or heard it.

It was a contagious name, so much so that the bus stop at Amirieh Avenue in front of that street, had gradually acquired the same name. The assistant bus drivers had all sorts of fun shouting that name into their bus to make the passengers ready to get out.

The assistant drivers were famous for their lack of manners, so much so that whenever we used a slang word such as *"Zekee!"*—for the occasions when something went unexpectedly wrong — Auntie Pouran would scold us, "Why are you talking like a *Shaguerd chauffer?*" (She did not know that we had learned it from Captain Vokhshur.) They were particularly rude towards anybody who moved slowly like the elderly and the sick. When a slow-moving old woman, for example, took her last step through the narrow opening of the bus, partly occupied by the assistant driver, he would increasingly narrow his eyes during her last few steps to suddenly open them widely with a fake sigh of relief when both feet of the woman touched the ground, saying, "Aah, my eyes finally got opened!" No one of course would laugh or understand their joke except for those who suffered from chronic constipation. The lack of manners was so prevalent that when a military man became the chief of traffic police, he ordered that every bus should have this phrase written on its windshield: "Adab is the greatest capital."

The other occasions when the rudeness of assistant bus drivers would fully manifest itself was during the hot summer afternoons when not many people were walking in the streets and the bus was almost devoid of passengers. In those occasions, God forbid if the assistant driver spotted a pedestrian walking along the As-You-Wish Street towards his bus. He would keep the driver from moving the bus by telling him that a coin worth one *Rial* was rolling towards the bus. Nothing would happen if the walking person got into his bus, but if by any chance he or she turned away from his bus towards the grocery store at the corner of As-You-Wish Street, the driver would floor the gas pedal so harshly that the bus would make rude noises as it took off, while the assistant driver showered the poor pedestrian with cat calls and rude comments.

At the beginning, As-You-Wish Street was not an official bus stop. Sometimes the bus would stop in front of it, sometimes it would not. It would bypass it, no matter how much we screamed, to stop at the next official bus stop at Mokhtari Crossroads.

It was only when Captain Vokhshur was in the bus that they would stop right in front of As-You-Wish Street. The first time that Vokhshur ordered the driver to stop there, the driver refused and kept going. When the assistant driver informed Vokhshur that the street in front of which he wanted the bus to stop was not an official bus station, Vokhshur said that it was. "What is the name of it," the assistant driver asked with unaccustomed politeness, "if it is an official bus station?"

"Its name is As-You-Wish Street, not much different from the next bus station," said Vokhshur. The bus driver did not wait for further explanation. He grudgingly stopped the bus and backed up to stop in front of the street where Vokhshur wanted to get out.

After that incident Vokhshur decided to make that name official. Now everybody in Tehran knows the name of As-You-Wish Street, but unfortunately nobody knows that I was present at its naming ceremony and, to a small measure, contributed to making its name official.

It happened in a hot summer afternoon when I was about eight years old. The streets were deserted and I was preparing to play hopscotch on the sidewalk in front our street with my friend Shambool. Shambool had brought his smooth pet rock, and I, a piece of coal from home. I was in the middle of drawing the diagram on the ground—resembling the blue-print of the two-storey houses that Vokhshur liked to build. When Captain Vokhshur, the father of my friend, came out of the street and asked me if he could have the charcoal for a moment. I, of course, after looking with bewilderment at my friend, realized that I had no choice but to give it to him.

Even though Vokhshur was already a tall man, he went to the corner store and brought out a chair with one hand, put it down beside the wall at the head of the street, stood on it and wrote in Farsi with large letters *Koucheh-ye-Del-Bekhah* at the highest point that he could reach. He came down, took the chair back to the store, gave my charcoal back to me and left. I don't remember if he thanked me for it or not, most likely not.

26

GOD IS NOT A MATHEMATICIAN, BUT KNOWS 16 = 9 + 7

IF THE SORROW AND THE SIAH OF MY MOTHER ended exactly after a year, mine began exactly a year after hers ended. It began when I met Captain Vokhshur, the father of my first friend.

After the death of our father, God the merciful sent Auntie Pouran to help our mother with her daily chores as well as playing the role of a father figure for her nine fatherless children. I, of course, thanked God for that great gift for our mother, but remained silent regarding her role as a father figure for us. God must have heard both my thanks and my silence, since, without taking Auntie Pouran out of our lives, He made Captain Vokhshur our second father figure, and his seven children, our seven extra siblings, made a total of 16. Number sixteen, because God remembers that if my mother was not sterile during the first seven years of her marriage, the number of my sibling would have been 16, rather than nine.

On the first day of our arrival on that street, as the caravan of cars, carts and porters stopped behind a stationary bus at the head of As-You-Wish Street to unload us, Nadereh Khanum, the fair-skinned, almost blonde wife of Vokhshur who had come to Sanguelaj District to bring us to our new neighbourhood, pulled me towards the window and pointed to a running boy, about my age and my size, with a darker colour of skin, and said, "That boy is my son. His name is Shambool. You and he will become friends as of today up to the end of your lives." The boy was wearing unattractive homemade shorts and a shirt. The back of his shirt was billowing in the wind as he was trying to keep his kite in the air. "Why?" I objected, "Just because he too is *Siah*?"

No one heard my objection let alone provided me with an explanation because, at that moment I and everyone else, as well as whatever stuff was compressed in the car, poured out along the waterless creek, into it, and onto the sidewalk beyond it.

Shambool's colour was darker than mine, for sure, but I was not sure if it was due to excessive running in the summer sunshine or whether it was just a visual illusion on my part, a contrast with his spotless white shorts and shirt. It did not take me long, however, to conclude with pleasure that he was born like that, and the sun and the shirt had nothing to do with it.

More than the colour of his skin, it was his name that bothered me on the first day that I met Shambool. It sounded ridiculous, especially for me who was already sensitized to any word that rhymed with the forbidden name, *dool*. I knew that his mother had nothing to do with naming of their children, because it was Vokhshur who was always playing with words. He must have become so excited when his second child turned out to be a boy that as soon as he saw his genitals, he combined it with his previously chosen name, Shamseddin—the Sunshine of the Faith—to become Shambool. He never thought of what would become of that name when the poor boy grew up. Some of his classmates in the school were already calling him Sham-dool.

Before he married Nadereh Khanum, no one in our family knew who Vokhshur was except for Colonel Sharabi. The wedding of Vokhshur and Nadereh Khanum was one of the twenty free weddings that Sharabi had arranged for his friends and relatives. As far as looks were concerned, Captain Vokhshur was not considered a handsome man, but he must have had some hidden qualities that had convinced the good-looking Nadereh Khanum to consent to marry him. In fact, there was a kind of pleasant asymmetry in his features that was better expressed in some of his children, particularly Shambool, which consisted of narrowing one eye in bright light, a habit that I tried to duplicate but my mother caught me one time and stopped me before it became a bad habit. The military uniform improved his appearance a bit, but that was only when he was in the streets. When he came home from work, the first thing that he did was to remove his military uniform and his long military boots. He had a special wooden device for removing his boots, named *Chakmeh-Kesh*. That device, however, was often unavailable because it was also the toy of the children. Vokhshur not only did not mind its absence, he seemed to enjoy it, too, because he would make use of his wife, instead, to remove his boots. His wife did not seem to mind it much either. She would straddle his stretched legs, one by one, facing his foot, grabbing the back of its heel with both hands, leaning forward to pull it out with the help of her weight while Vokhshur would press with the soles of his feet, one by one, on the cheeks of her bottom, until both of his sweaty feet and smelly socks were out.

He was an honest and shrewd business man. He had seven houses on that street and was still building. His seven children were composed of alternating girls and boys. The girls beginning with Farangueece, and the boys with Shambool.

The house we had rented was one of his seven houses. It was located near the bend of his private L-shaped cul-de-sac, in the middle of As-You-Wish Street, hugging his own house. His own house was so big that many years later when they moved permanently to Shemiran, it became an elementary school for girls by the name of *Parvaneh*, meaning butterfly. His first two daughters married two of my brothers, Mansur and Hamid.

Vokhshur and his family were smart and most of them had a good sense of humour, but we claimed that they were neither as smart nor as funny as the Shojanias. In fact, our lasting relationship was based more on that friendly rivalry than multiple intermarriages between the two families.

Vokhshur, like any other builder in Iran, had to be a good improviser as well since there was always a shortage of proper tools for construction and precision instruments for measurement. To make our oval pool, for example, when he was supervising the construction of our house after a few years of renting one of his houses, he used only two wooden pegs and a loose rope. For another example, when I showed him the crack appearing on the plaster of the ceiling in one of the rooms of that house, when it became finished, Vokhshur, without saying a word, took a cigarette out of his wrinkled Oshnou package, cut it up longitudinally with his thumbnail, carelessly emptied its tobacco on the carpet, stood on a chair, wetted the flimsy paper with his saliva and stuck it over the crack of the ceiling like a band-aid.

"Do you think that flimsy paper is strong enough to keep the crack from expanding?" I cracked a joke while he was still standing on the chair.

"No, this is just a test, dummy!" he said while looking down at me. "Tomorrow or the day after I will come to check."

"To check what?" I followed up with my joke. "To see how many of us are dead under a fallen roof built under your supervision?" giving him more rope to hang himself with.

"I will come to see what has happened to this paper," he was forced to explain. "If the paper is torn apart, it will indicate that you are right and the crack is widening. But if the paper remains intact, it will mean that the crack is nothing to worry about. Houses settle for a while after they are built. These little things are part of the settling of any new house; just like you who are new in this neighbourhood and cracking these tasteless jokes."

"What if the crack is trying to expand but is unable to do so because of the application of your testing device?" I continued to see what crazy reply he had for that.

For a few seconds, he remained speechless, moving his tightly pressed lips back and forth in quick succession, as if a speck of tobacco was stuck to one of his lips, and when finally he talked he had to fall back on the banal, default Persian proverb as a reply, "The best reply to idiots is silence."

His duties in the Army were vague and ill-defined as far as the children were concerned. He seemed to have something to do with the kitchens of the army and that of Reza Shah. He was supplying the produce and vegetable and other perishable things for the kitchen. He would buy them himself in bulk from the market that he called *Maydoon,* located at the periphery of Tehran where a chaotic mixture of camels, peasants, truck drivers and donkeys present their fresh merchandise. Some of whom, especially the truck drivers, used foul language during transactions. Even though that market was close to As-You-Wish Street, near the Customs crossroads to be exact, we never went to it. We could tell, however, whenever Vokhshur was coming back from there because of the way he talked and the smell coming from his boots.

He was fond of Reza Shah and his great achievements. When we asked him why the right arm of the statue of Reza Shah in front of the German-built building of the railroad station was stretched like a German salute, he said that it was not a German Salute, but was Reza Shah's way of saying, "I have cut through the Alborz Mountains in front of me to make tunnels for the Trans-Iran Railroad."

Even though he was not Reza Shah's cook or his gardener, Vokhshur must have been working very close to the residence of the Shah because he observed that every morning before going to work, that Reza Shah, fully dressed in his military uniform and his long black boots, would smoke three puffs of opium in standing position from the *vafoor* that his cook would hold to his lips. "Only three puffs," Vokhshur always repeated whenever he revealed that top secret to us, for some unknown reason. As far as eating habits were concerned, Reza Shah ate modestly and monotonously according to Vokhshur, always rice and chicken, carefully prepared by his special cook.

Vokhshur was not a political person, nor was he a severely patriotic one, but he was informed. He was one of the few on our street who regularly bought the daily newspaper *Ettela'at.* Also, he was one of the first who obtained a radio on our street and every Friday morning all of the children would join his children to listen to the children's program, beginning with stories told by mystic Mr. Sobhi. Many of his stories were the simplified version of stories from the magic book of Mathnavi. His story of Moses and the shepherd, in which God scolds Moses for scolding the simple-minded shepherd for attributing limbs and head to God, was particularly refreshing, and its conclusion, "Let anybody worship me in his own words and ways," was quite liberating.

Vokhshur's play and problems with names did not end with naming his street or his children. He had problems with his own first and second names too. His own given name was Roohollah, probably given to him by a pair of either severely Muslim or Baha'i parents. The reason I thought so was because that name is a deeply Arabic name, meaning the Spirit of Allah. Apparently attributing a spirit or a soul to God is not as bad as attributing limbs or a head. Since the Baha'i faith originated in Iran and many of its initial converts were Islamic theologians, particularly the Shi'eh mullahs, they carried their given names with them when they branched off from Islam. Roohollah happens to be the given name of Ayatollah Khomeini as well. This is why *The Spirit of Allah* became the title of the book about Ayatollah Khomeini, written by Amir Taheri, the editor-in-chief of Keyhan, Iran's largest selling daily newspaper, between 1973 and 1979—subtitled, Khomeini and the Islamic Revolution.

I happened to have that book in my meagre library. I recognize it quickly by its red jacket and pick it off the shelf of my religious books to check if the spelling I have chosen for Roohollah is the common one or if there is a better one. To my chagrin, I see that there is a better one; Taheri has spelled it *Ruhollah*. I don't know if I should change mine or leave it as it is.

As I attempt to put the book back on the shelf, however, a few quotations from Ayatollah Khomeini on the back cover of the book attract my attention. I read them once again to refresh my memory, since I have not read them for more than twenty years.

Perdition begins with but a small step, a tiny step that can be dismissed as insignificant.

Man moves towards Hell step by step.

All those who were lost did not become corrupt all of a sudden, with a giant leap as it were. They began with tiny insignificant steps and were soon beyond salvation...

There is a devil in every man, corrupting him little by little.

Those who oppose the mullahs oppose Islam itself; eliminate the mullahs and Islam shall disappear in fifty years. It is only the mullahs who can bring the people into the streets and make them die for Islam—begging to have their blood shed for Islam.

America cannot do a damn thing.

Jews and their foreign backers are those who are opposed to the very foundation of Islam and want to establish an international Jewish government, and, since they are a crafty and active lot, my fear is that, may Allah forbid it, they may one day succeed.

The heritage of Satan is none other than egoism. All the corruption the world has suffered from results from this: every corruption caused by individuals or governments in every society... Satan is everywhere, even alongside those who sit at home and pray ...

Every path can lead to Hell; at times even monotheism can lead Man to Hell;

Mysticism can lead Man to Hell; Technology can lead Man to Hell; Ethics can lead Man to Hell....

End of quotations.

Vokhshur's given name, despite its highly religious significance, does not provide much insight into his soul, simply because it was given to him. In other words, he did not choose it himself. It was his family name that he chose by himself, but even that does not open any window towards his soul. For his last name he chose the most unfamiliar name from a Zoroastrian book, Vokhshur, which is apparently a very spiritual name in that religion, but Vokhshur was not a Zoroastrian or Zartoshti either.

After studying Vokhshur's obsession and hesitation regarding names, one cannot help but conclude that his faith was always in a state of devolution. He had began his life normally and religiously, then lost his religion to become a spiritual person and lost his spirituality at the moment of the birth of his first son and became an atheist when his son was about ten years old.

Even though as a child I did not like my name, I knew that at least it was in line with the names of the rest of our family. There was a rhyme and reason among our names. To begin with, they were all in Arabic and each had a good meaning, such as giving off light, to praise or to be praised, to help or to be helped, with only harmonious variations in the quantity or the quality connoted by those names.

Such harmony did not exist among the children of Vokhshur. Let us do a brief study of their names, from top to the bottom:

Farangueece, shortened to *Feri*, was probably meant to remind us that she was pale and blond like a *Faranguee*; the general name given to French people or Europeans in general who have blue eyes and blond hair. Even though she was my age, Mansur married her because Mansur had the most affinity among us towards the Western world. He was the first, for example, who left Iran to go to America during the Second World War, at a time that few Iranians knew where America was.

The second child, a boy, was Shambool whose name was discussed before.

The third was a girl, *Parivash*, Farsi for *Pari*-like or fairy-like. And *Pari* is that ethereal and imaginary being who is the opposite of a *Jen* or *Jinni*. We called her *Pari of Hamid* after she married Hamid, to differentiate her from *Pari of Mehdi*, who was the granddaughter of Aunt Seddigheh and married to Mehdi.

The fourth child was a boy, named Kuros, a very Persian name, given usually to the boys from well-to-do and at least semi-educated families, a name that I preferred to my own. The day we were moving with our stuff to our new house in As-You-Wish Street and everybody was helping, Kuros had just begun to walk. Everybody was amused to see him helping by carrying a little sieve, almost the size of his little round face, from the car to our house. His cheeks were trembling like jelly with every little step that he took.

Their fifth child, a girl, was named Mahvash, meaning moon-like, but her face, even though as bright and pale as the moon, was not as round as the full moon. She was delicately built but her will power was much stronger than her physical attributes. When once she took something of mine and kept it in her fist and told me that I could have it if I could open her fist, I tried a little, but soon gave up, fearing that her will power might be stronger than the resistance of her bones, and I would break her wrist before she gave up and opened her fist.

Their sixth child, a boy, was named Jamshid, another very Persian name. He was blond and tall with normal features and abnormal sense of humour. When he reached the age of eighteen he did not behave like his predecessors; rather, he behaved like the teenagers of the new generation and those in the Hollywood movies. He did not study seriously in high school. He made his father buy a second-hand Italian sports car for him and roamed the streets of Shemiran with it, skipping school. Every summer he had to repeat several exams to be able to go to the next class. That car made him a good mechanic, so much so that when the car of his botany teacher in grade twelve stalled and Jamshid happened to be passing by, he fixed it for him and the teacher, rather than paying him money, asked if he knew the name of the tree along the creek beside which the car had stopped. "A *Chenar*," Jamshid replied and the teacher told him that he should consider himself passed and not to worry about repeating his botany exam after the summer.

After grade twelve he did not go to a university. He tried various businesses, and ended up in the business of supplying the kitchen of big institutions with his chickens and selling them either fresh or barbecued out of multiple outlets in Shemiran and Tehran. After the revolution, when lamb and beef became scarce or expensive, people discovered that chicken did not have to be consumed exclusively for wedding or funeral ceremonies and began rushing to his store. When he would spot his friends among the clients in front of his store, he would say, loudly, to his vendor behind the scales, "Mr. So-and-So is my friend, clip the claws of the chicken before weighing it for him." His business had become so successful that once he commented, "It seems that it was Mohammad Reza Shah who was interfering with my business, since I do so much better after he is gone!" Similarly, a few years later, when his long-widowed mother died and all of his siblings, who rarely could be seen all in one place, were gathered in their guest room in Shemiran for her memorial, Jamshid, after looking around and, seeing that all of his brothers and sisters were present, commented, "It must have been our mother who always kept us apart; now that she is gone, we are all together!"

Jamshid never left Iran but watched his older siblings leave for Santiago or La Jolla. When he saw that most of them had gone and he was left with only Shambool and Nasrin—

his younger sister whose complexion was closer to that of Shambool than to her other sisters—he complained that, "All the good ones are gone and have left the shitty ones for me!"

The name of his seventh child, a girl, was borrowed from a flower named *Nasrin*. She was the last child and was born when the Vokhshurs had permanently moved to the resort city of Shemiran. Her mother jokingly explained that the reason her skin turned a little darker was due to the fact that during her pregnancy she had consumed too many fresh walnuts—the specialty of Shemiran, the green outer skin of which is known to impart a light brown discolouration to the hands of whoever touched it without a glove. She married one of her cousins—one of the many sons of one of the brothers of her father by the name of Habibollah, meaning "the friend of God." Her husband, like Jamshid, had a shocking sense of humour. At a friendly party, when he saw his wife was sitting rather carelessly on a chair, exposing part of her brown thighs studded with mosquito bites, he shouted at her from the opposite corner of the room, "Nasrin! Sit properly; otherwise everybody will know that I've married you just for your money!"

Vokhshur's children called their father simply Baba, without adding a Jan or Jun to it. Their family relationship was much more liberal than ours. I had a lot to learn from them.

Vokhshur's mother was alive and lived with them in a separate room. I never heard her talk and if I did, I do not remember what she said so that I could quote her here. All I remember of her is that she was a woman with grey hair who never wore a scarf and never went out of the house and was Baha'i, but Vokhshur was not. At the age of eighteen, when he had to choose his faith, he must have declined. Actually, he was the only adult who had said to his children, "There is no God."

When Shambool told me that his Baba had told him that there was no God, I was shocked. "How could this be true, when my wise mother talks to Him five times a day?" I asked Shambool, putting him in a difficult position of choosing between his father and my mother. It made me wonder if Shambool's occasional bursts of stupidity were inherited from his father. His father's opinion, of course, did not shake the foundation of my belief in God, at that time. It took me a few more years before I lost my faith in God.

The brother of Vokhshur's mother, Mr. Nazeefi, meaning the clean one, was so quiet that no one knew if he had chosen to become a Baha'i or not. He was a very handsome man with a full head of silver hair and iron-grey striped suit. He was a businessman and his business was a luxury tailor shop for men in the best shopping district of Tehran at that time, Lalehzar Avenue, far away from As-You-Wish Street. I had my first good suit made in that store as soon as we grew old enough not to depend on Auntie Pouran for choosing either the material or the tailor for our annual suit.

That handsome quiet man lived two streets further down our street towards south, on Mokhtari Avenue, with his wife and seven children, six daughters and one son. The only one among them who was the same age as me was his well-dressed son. He always wore well-groomed long hair and long, wrinkle-free trousers, even when he was in elementary school. He became my second-best friend as we grew up in that district and went to Sharaf High School together, where we both chose French as our foreign language. He was so well dressed that everybody in school thought that he must be a Baha'i even without knowing his parents. He was born to a Baha'i family but before he had reached the age of eighteen, the age when he had to choose his faith, he had lost his faith in God, like me, in the chemistry class. And, just like a typical non-Baha'i, in grade twelve he entered into politics, participating in some of the demonstrations of the Tudeh Party and landing in jail for a few days. When he came out they had shaven his nice shiny long black hair. His older sisters were friends with my top three siblings and his younger sisters were friends with my bottom three siblings. Sometime, when I grew older, I wished he were a girl, too. His name was Houshang, shortened to Houshi. Compared to him I was so badly dressed that the first day that we were to go to visit them, my oldest brother, who was always as well dressed as Houshi, gave me twenty *Shahi* not to go with them. I accepted the money not because I was not interested in girls, but because I wanted to be equal with Shambool, for a change, as far as having pocket money was concerned.

Despite all the friendly rivalries and childlike competitions between the Vokhshur and the Shojania families, the two families became so intimately interwoven that I felt I was one of the sixteen siblings rather than nine.

Judging by the average number of 200 million spermatozoa that God sends to meet only one ovum each time that He wants to make a new human being, I had reached the conclusion that God was not a mathematician because for Him one and many were the same. Be that as it may, as far as the Shojania family is concerned, God surely knows that the sum of nine plus seven is sixteen.

27

CONSTELLATION OF DISASTERS FOR AUNTIE POURAN IN THE HOUSE WITH STELLATE POOL

THE SEVEN RENTAL HOUSES ON CAPTAIN VOKHSHUR'S PRIVATE CUL-DE-SAC were all similarly constructed with variation only in size. They were composed of a square courtyard housing two-storey brick buildings with four large rooms, two on the first floor, separated by a short walkway, and two upstairs, separated by a small extra room covering the underlying walkway. Each courtyard had a pool, and the pool was either square or rectangular except for ours.

Ours was star-shaped and I had taken it as a good omen because if it was otherwise the army would not have put six of them on the shoulders of its captains and God would not sprinkle the night sky with billions of them. Also, shortly after our arrival to that house the wedding of Maheen Khanum, the only daughter of Auntie Pouran, took place, and she was showered by numerous small silver coins and snow coloured candies, indicating that good things had began to happen.

There was, however, a sad willow tree in one of the two symmetrical flower beds that imparted an air of melancholy to that house. Every year, a few weeks before the Persian New Year, Auntie Pouran would order a few loads of horse manure for the flower beds to plant yellow and purple pansies. The umbrella-shaped willow tree had an inviting look to it but one could not make a house under it because it was always infested with small insects camouflaged by the same colour as its leaves. Auntie Pouran had forbidden us to urinate at nights on the flower beds even when they were devoid of flowers. And if you told her that a boy's urine was not much worse than loads of horse manure that she had ordered to unload on them, she would not change her mind and would say, "Just don't do it; and this is an order," as if we were living in a military camp.

The stellate pool looked great, but was not much use to us because no one could swim in it either due to its sharp indentations or its obtuse extensions. Only once did I jump in it with my clothes on, and that was to save Mahmood from drowning.

It was noontime and everybody else was inside having lunch, but Mahmood had sneaked out to have a swim without permission and without knowing the depth of the pool. When I came home I saw the water level was just below his nostrils. He must have been standing on the tip of his toes. If he had an instinct for survival, he could have jumped up and down to bring his mouth out of the water and yell for help, but he was not doing that. Instead, he was weeping silently, shedding silent tears into the water. Perhaps he did not want our mother to know that he had gone into the pool without her permission. I was glad that it happened right at the time that I was coming home. Modar-jun appreciated the importance of my deed and mentioned it several times to several of her companions. "Nasser did a boy scout thing today!" she would say to her guests and when some of them asked for explanation she would tell them how I saved Mahmood from drowning. And I mentioned it in my composition in which we had to describe one of the best things we had ever done for someone else in our life.

We did not swim in that pool but kept running around it frequently and jumping over its pointy corners. Hossein was once running after me around the pool with a short stick in his hand and a mask of an old man on his face. Even though the mask was not scary it matched the slight bend of the back of Hossein, and that matching was the main source of my fright. So, when I had enough money after the next New Year's, I went and bought three scary masks, one of them depicting a devil with horns and a goatee beard. I could not scare anybody with any of them. Modar-jun got upset that I had wasted all my money on three useless masks and sent me back with our Masdar to return them. With the shamefully obtained refunded money I bought a pocket watch on my way home. The hands and its numbers on its white dial glowed at night, and during the day if one took it under a blanket. I learned to tell time from it, but the motion of its hands was so slow that soon I got fed up watching them and gave the watch to Mansur-jun to turn it to a *Vige-vigeh*—a term invented and used only in our house, applied to a clock or a watch from which its dancer is removed. Then I would wind it tightly to its full capacity and let go of it so that its hands could circulate rapidly while making a *vigey* sound.

Except for being bored occasionally, we all had a good time in that house with stellate pool except for Auntie Pouran. She had the worst of her times in that house. In one year she lost her job as a secretary, her newly wed daughter, her newly born grandson and her only son-in-law. She had quit her job herself before the marriage of her only daughter so that the family of the future son-in-law—a medical doctor by the name of Dr. Parsa—did not think that the bride was so poor that her mother had to work outside for her living.

She lost her son-in-law after losing the daughter and the grandson that she had named Ali Reza. The last time that we saw Dr. Parsa was when we were playing with a yellow tennis ball under the extra room in which Maheen Khanum had died due to typhoid fever soon after delivering her boy. Dr. Parsa had seen Maheen Khanum only once before asking the approval of her mother to marry her, and that was when she was on her way home from the Superior House of Knowledge, which was a teachers' college. Within two months he married her. On the night of the wedding, however, when the bride saw her fully made-up face in the mirror and noted, perhaps for the first time, that how beautiful she looked, she told her mother that she did not want to marry Dr. Parsa after all. Auntie Pouran shamefully took the message to her would be son-in-law along with much apologies. Dr. Parsa, who was a large man with balding scalp, promised that he would not consumate the marriage and they would sleep in separate rooms until she decided by herself to sleep in the same bed with him. That made her daughter change her mind.

After giving birth to her son Maheen Khanum developed an unrelenting fever that the doctors failed to diagnose at the beginning as typhoid fever. They thought she had meningitis. It was not until my mother suggested bringing Dr. Kowsari, who was a pious Moslem and a good diagnostician, and his office was near Custom Crossroad, not too far from As-You-Wish Street. He was the one who had diagnosed my pain in the back and one leg due to an abscess in my deep-seated psoas muscle and cured it by an application of burning mustard plaster on my back. He came to our house and diagnosed her illness as typhoid fever complicated by encephalitis.

A few weeks later Mehdi recovered from the same disease without developing its cerebral complications. And Auntie Pouran, who did not like Mehdi to begin with, began to resent him all the more after the death of her daughter. She was probably thinking that her daughter had contracted that contagious illness from Mehdi.

The newborn boy survived for two-and-a-half months to keep Auntie Pouran busy and away from mourning continuously, then he developed progressive jaundice and died.

After the death of Ali Reza there was no reason for Dr. Parsa to come to our house anymore. And that last time that we saw him was after he had come to say his last good-bye to his mother-in-law. We saw him coming down the stairs at the end of the short walkway. When he reached the children who were playing with the yellow ball, he caught the ball high in the air as it bounced off the pavement, turned himself around, doing a pirouette, threw the ball hard on the ground, and went out of the door.

The forearms of Auntie Pouran that were never cleansed by water of ablution, after freedom from washing the yellow diapers of her short-lived grandson, were once again ready to serve our mother, her childhood friend and her only refuge.

28

THE WATER OF SHAH VERSUS PUBLIC WATER

OUR MOTHER DID NOT SEEM TO WORRY MUCH about the premature loss of her husband as much as she worried about the effect of that loss on her children. This is why she had put most of her efforts on minimizing the negative effects of that loss on her children. As far as I was concerned she almost succeeded in her efforts because I did not suffer much from not having a father. I thought it was normal to live in a single parent family. That feeling of normality, however, lasted only until I met Captain Vokhshur. He was the first man to prove that not having a father could be a great loss.

I was particularly impressed with his attitude towards money and the pocket money of his children. At home, he always hung his trousers on some visible spot, such as a nail on the wall or the top of the door of a closet. Even though he had already given the weekly allowance to his children, as soon as they ran out of money, they would help themselves almost freely with the money from the pocket of his hanging trousers. Many times I saw Shambool standing on a chair, pulling down the trousers, pulling the wallet of his father out of its back pocket, taking a small bill from the folded bundle of bills, and putting the rest back in the wallet and the wallet in the pocket and hanging the trousers on the same place that he had gotten them from. His father seemed to know about this and Shambool knew that his father knew, but both seemed to pretend that they did not. His daughters did it, too, but less often than his sons, and that was because Vokhshur would give more pocket money to his daughters than to his sons. When I asked him for the reason for this discrimination he replied, "Too much money can spoil a boy while a girl can go bad by not having enough money."

The boys were taking money out of his pocket so frequently that sometimes they would deplete his pocket of any money and Vokhshur would discover it too late, often when he had to pay the *Doroshkeh-Chee* who had taken him from home to work. After this happened several times, rather than punishing his children and forbidding them from taking money from his pockets without his permission, Vokhshur bought a *Doroshkeh* with two horses and became the first man on our street to own a private *Doroshkeh*. And later he became the first to buy a car, a black Ford, operated by his *Doroshkeh-Chee*, turned driver.

On the thirteenth day of the Persian New Year known as *Sizdah-beh-dar*—when it is customary and almost compulsory for everybody to spend the day outdoors, preferably away from the city—if Vokhshur was not with us, we could never make it to the door of the bus, let alone getting out of the city and going to Karaj to sit along its foaming river or run in the fields with new grass and blue flowers. Even if miraculously we managed to go, I'm sure we could never have been able to come back all together in one bus, if Vokhshur was not there. This was because we were at least ten families, many of whom with many children, not counting the bundles of provisions and numerous samovars, some of which were so large it was as if they were pregnant.

Going out of Tehran was easy if Vokhshur had arranged for a bus to come and take us there, but he never planned for our return, or if he did, the bus did not honour the arrangement. On these occasions, Captain Vokhshur, in his golden summer uniform that outshone the sparkle of the stars on his shoulders, would run to the door of the bus that had stopped at an unmarked bus stop away from the waiting crowd, jump on its single step and bar the entrance with his outstretched arm. He would face the crowd, letting first the children in, then the grown-ups of his families, before letting go of the door so that others could get in. Usually, though, there was no more room in the bus for anybody else, even if they did not mind standing.

The other times that Captain Vokhshur abused his authority and his military uniform was on the nights of public water coming to As-You-Wish Street. On those nights, which happened every two weeks, he did not dress fully in his military uniform, but used only the top part of it and the hat, as well as carrying his sword. Water would come along the creek at Amirieh Avenue towards the south end of the city. From there it had to be diverted into the side-streets by a temporary dams built by the children and some of the grown men. And the dam often required protection and constant supervision; otherwise, the children of the lower streets would come to ruin it so that the water could run towards their street and into their houses.

Sometimes more than one grown up was needed to ensure continuous flow of water to our street. Most of the time our Masdar would do the job, but sometimes that was not enough and Vokhshur's presence was needed.

Ironically, Vokhshur, who was a captain in the army and could have at least one *Masdar* if not two, did not have any, and we, who had no father, let alone a military one, did have a military servant thanks to our uncle colonel, Yahya Khan.

So, on one of those nights that we were standing at the head of As-You-Wish Street to guard our dam, Vokhshur, half in military uniform, half in striped pajamas, and I in my usual daytime uniform, composed of shorts and a shirt, I asked Vokhshur why he did not have a *Masdar*.

"Because I have daughters," he replied quickly so that I did not continue the interrogation.

"So what?" I continued. "My mother has daughters too, but we have a *Masdar*."

"Your mother's daughters are not as good-looking as mine."

I did not fully understand the connection between having beautiful daughters and not having a *Masdar*, but just to hear his reaction, I said, "They say a virgin girl, if she is innately *Najeeb* and trusts herself, can go naked in a military camp among hundreds of hungry soldiers and return still a virgin."

He did not have time to counter that because at that very moment a child from Saghafi Street had managed to make a hole in the dam and run away. Vokhshur neither made use of his sword, nor did he run after the child. Instead, he asked me to repair the dam while mouthing a *pedassag*—the contracted form of *Pedar-sag*, meaning father-dog, indicating that one's father must have been a dog—at the running boy. He sometimes used that insult for his own children too, but it did not sound as bad when he used it on them.

Many years later, when two of Vokhshur's daughters had already married two of the Shojania brothers, and the third one was thinking about it, Feri, their first daughter, to prevent further marriage between the two families, had said to her unmarried sisters, "Enough marrying the Shojanias! Is there a drought of men in Tehran? People would wonder why only the Shojanias marry us." Had I heard Feri's comment a few years earlier, I am sure I could have made good use of it on that night just to hear Vokhshur's reaction to it.

Captain Vokhshur never punished his children and because of that his children did not seem to respect him as much as I thought they should. They were not scared of him. They did not add any prefix or suffix to their parents' names, calling their mother a simple Maman, and their father a simple Baba.

Even though Vokhshur was a friendly man, he did not have many friends. Maybe he had friends when he was younger and a bachelor, but we never saw any friend frequent his house. The only one I once saw a few times was Mr. Khazaei who was a civilian but looked and talked more like a military man than Vokhshur. I saw him once in As-You-Wish Street walking towards Vokhshur's house, smoking a cigarette. Before reaching the house of Vokhshur, he became surrounded by a group of men, objecting to his smoking in public because it was the month of fasting, *Ramezan*. He extinguished his cigarette with disgust and a mild apology, but the men did not leave him alone. As the circle of men grew larger and denser, he drew his concealed revolver and fired a shot in the air. The crowd dispersed faster than it had gathered, and he continued walking towards Vokhshur's house. If I knew Mr. Khazaei was going to become my future father-in-law, I would have had followed him to Vokhshur's house to get to know him better.

Regarding not associating with friends at home, perhaps Vokhshur had learned his lesson from his brother-in-law, Captain Bozorg Omid, who lost his wife to his best friend, Captain Foomani. The latter was frequenting Bozorg Omid's house so frequently that he fell in love with his wife, Iran Khanum, the prettier and the younger sister of Nadereh Khanum, the one with a contagious laughter.

Of course Bozorg Omid did not know anything about it. The friend wanted Iran Khanum to get divorced from her husband and marry him. Numerous times his request had been rejected, but the man was so madly in love that would not take no for an answer. The elders of the family, who were influential in the army and knew about this developing tragedy, had made the army send Bozorg Omid away from Tehran to the city of Kerman-shah, so that the lover left them alone. A few weeks after their departure, however, Foomani found out about their location, grew a black beard for camouflage and put civilian clothes on, and went to Kerman-shah to wait at the head of their street, hoping to see Iran Khanum alone if she came out of their house. No one knows how long he waited there, but eventually Iran Khanum came out, holding the hand of their five-year-old daughter, Mehri, who was walking beside her, followed by their *Masdar,* who was carrying Ali, their few months old son. Apparently the man renewed his request once again and threatened that if he heard another negative reply he would kill her and himself. He must have heard a negative reply because he first shot and killed Iran Khanum, then shot one bullet towards Ali, whom he missed, and then killed himself with one shot to the head.

When the news reached As-You-Wish Street it made such an explosive sound that it made the revolver of Mr. Khazaei sound like a fire cracker. Shambool was so full of anger and revenge that for weeks he tried to imagine what kind of torture he would have inflicted on the assassin of his aunt had he not killed himself. "How about plucking his hair, one by one?" I suggested, to help my friend find the most painful torture.

Despite all our efforts, the coffee-coloured water that eventually found its way to the house was not drinkable. Even though the water that went for filling the underground reservoir to be used for drinking was coming late at night and was less polluted, those who could afford to buy better water did not drink it.

The better water was named "the Water of Shah" and came from the spring of Shah located in the centre of Tehran, near Canon Square. It was brought to all parts of Tehran by horse-drawn carts in empty oil barrels. The price of that water was twenty *Shahi* per pail, and our house used two large pails, made of empty BP tincans, each day.

Auntie Pouran, our female father figure who did all the outdoor chores of our house to spare our mother the humiliation of bargaining with the vendors, once tried to bargain with the waterman to lower the price of the Water of Shah. "Because," she was reasoning, "it is just water" and water was supposed to be free. The man became so angry with her that, after a moment of speechlessness, he wetted the tip of his index finger with his tongue and drew an oblique line on our door and said, "*Khanum!* Never mind water and forget about my double hernias. Had you asked me to come to your house every day from Canon Square just to draw a single line on your door for this price, I wouldn't have come."

The face of Auntie Pouran went as red as the henna-stained portion of her hair as she stopped bargaining with the man, and went inside to take care of her newborn grandson, Ali-Reza, whose mother had been running a fever for two weeks, probably from typhoid fever, due to the polluted public water brought to our house under the supervision of Captain Vokhshur with my assistance.

29

CHEATED TO UNDERGO CIRCUMCISION

TO UNDERGO CIRCUMCISION IS EMBARRASSING, but to be cheated into it is painful. This is why I still remember it. It was not our mother who cheated us into it. It was Captain Vokhshur. And he did it through the play of words. He had a peculiar affinity for words. Maybe because he was the only one in As-You-Wish Street who subscribed to the daily newspaper and did its crossword puzzle every day.

Vokhshur knew—and we knew—that the word *khat* in Farsi meant a line. So he made use of our partial knowledge and related the word *Khatneh,* which means circumcision, to *Khat* and subjected four of the boys of As-You-Wish Street, namely, Shambool, Hamid, Nasser and Holaaku, to circumcision.

The summer before, he had told us that *Khatneh* is performed in two stages, a year apart. "The first year they draw a line around the prepuce or the tip of the penis, and the next year, if the tip does not fall off by itself, they might cut it with a small knife." In short, it was not going to be a painful or bloody procedure. With this false reassurance, the next summer, when I was playing in the yard, minding my own business, Modar-jun came out of the children's room and asked our *Masdar* to take me to the grocery store at the corner of our street, "And buy him whatever he wants."

Armed with this blank cheque and followed by our obedient servant, I ran out of the house, pulling the obedient but reluctant *Masdar* after me. I don't know if I was moving too fast or he was unusually slow on that day. It was not very often that our mother was so generous towards me, but our *Masdar* did not seem to share my enthusiasm. He was walking at least ten metres behind me and slowly like a wounded soldier in retreat.

When he finally reached the store he had a hard time finding his money in one of his numerous pockets. And when I finally chose the things I wanted, he was reluctant to pay the owner of the store, whom we called Moussio because of his European look.

"I thought Modar-jun told you to pay for whatever I wanted," I reminded our *Masdar.*

"Yes, but..." Inappropriate laughter came out of his mouth before he could finish his sentence. For a moment I thought my mother had said something different to him in my absence, but that thought was quickly dismissed when I remembered that my mother never said one thing in front of me and a different thing behind me. I wished I were an army officer right then and there to show him the terrible consequences of slowness and disobedience.

All I managed to buy was a bottle of Sinalco—which tasted just like lemonade but had a cherry colour and was a little more expensive—15 *Shahi* instead of 10—and one *tongue*. Tongue was the name of a flat cookie the shape of a tongue, with a caramelized glazed upper surface, sprinkled with granular sugar, like the tastebuds on the coated surface of a real tongue. I finished my soft drink on the way home and was about to bite the tip of my tongue when I reached our house.

At home, our *Masdar* went straight to his room near the kitchen, sheepishly, still carrying his mischievous smile, and I went to our room, downstairs with my truncated tongue in hand.

The scene in the children's room had changed drastically, so much so that at first I thought I had entered the wrong room. It had become much cleaner and more orderly and smelled like a pharmacy. A bearded barber was squatting in one corner, burning some alcohol-soaked cotton to sterilize his blade over the flame. Captain Vokhshur was standing beside the barber. Modar-jun was standing on the other side of the room beside Hamid's bed. Hamid's knees were drawn up and apart, making a taut tent out of the covering white sheet. He was quiet, but it looked like he had cried a lot while I was out. His face was turned towards the ceiling looking into the pink skirt of the lamp shade with scalloped border. Two colourless shiny lines, like traces of a departed slug, were connecting his eyes to his ears.

Modar-jun, who was wearing an apologetic smile that meant "It is not my fault. I am just following the tradition," asked me to lie down on the empty bed beside Hamid's.

I concluded that my mother had sent me out so that I would not hear Hamid's crying. And I did not appreciate it at all. But what bothered me more was Vokhshur's presence in the room.

The blade did not hurt as much as the initial, unnecessary pinch that the barber applied to my prepuce. I don't know why he did that. Maybe that too was part of the tradition. And both together, the pinch and the blade, did not hurt as much as Vokhshur's smile when I uttered a muffled *aakh*.

I was not a crying kind of boy; even if I did cry, I would not do it loudly. Hamid was the one who cried loudly whenever he cried. Shambool was at his own house having his own post-circumcision depression. And Holaaku, God knows if he cried or not. Perhaps he did not, because he was used to lies and injustices from grown-ups, whether from his own relatives or the strangers. He looked more like a street kid than a well-loved house boy. Even though they had a house in As-You-Wish Street, Shambool and I never went into it. No wonder when he grew up he tried to set a fire in the battleship *Palang* and had to run to some Arabic Island in the Persian Gulf to escape execution.

After the circumcision, however, we collected a lot of money. Vokhshur, Modar-jun, and whoever came to visit, gave us some money instead of toys or other useless presents. It took weeks, however, before we could go out and spend it. For three weeks we walked around with colourful checkered bath towels around our waist, running only indoors or in our L-shaped private cul-de-sac.

It took a long time for our wounds to heal. In the meantime they looked very ugly. The barber had put burnt cotton on them to stop the bleeding, making them look like the nipple of Mahmood's wet nurse when she wanted to wean him off her breast. Mahmood, however, cried more for his missing *mameh* than I for my missing prepuce.

One of the better side benefits of being circumcised, luckily, was that we were not taken to the women's bathhouse anymore. The only woman who took me there, once, after our circumcision, was Shambool's mother, Nadereh Khanum. We were washed and cleaned, and everything went fine and uneventfully but coming out, the woman at the counter glanced at my *dool* and that of Shambool and said, sarcastically, to Nadereh Khanum, "Why didn't you bring their father as well?"

I am not so vengeful as my brother Mehdi, but when the occasion for revenge arises, I don't pass it easily.

The occasion arrived about 15 years later, not in Tehran but in Shemiran. I had become a second lieutenant in the army with one bright star on each of my epaulets when I had reached the fifth year of medicine while Colonel Vokhshur had lost all his artificial suns to retirement. Shambool had gone to Montpelier in France to study medicine. It was a snowy Friday and I had nothing to do. So, even though Shambool was not there anymore, I went to Shemiran to visit whatever was left of the Vokhshur's family.

It snows more in Shemiran than in Tehran. So, before I entered their heated living room, I had to bang my snow-covered boots on the ground several times to shake off the snow. That alerted Vokhshur to my arrival and gave him time to ask me the question he was asking himself on that morning. He was in the middle of solving a crossword puzzle. Before I could say *Salaam*, he exclaimed with a sense of relief, "Oh good, a doctor came. What is the name of the organ in the human body which is composed of three letters and has cartilage in it?"

"In Farsi?"

"Of course!"

"*Kir*?" I said impulsively, but added a question mark to the end of it so that it did not appear like an insult. That word is the name of circumcised male genitals, when it is used in the streets as an insult to the opponent. It is used almost like a weapon.

Vokhshur understandably got upset, threw the little pencil and the folded newspaper on the carpet and pointed to his daughter, Mahvash, who was sitting on a chair on the other side of the fireplace, her legs glowing pinker than the cherry coloured cheeks of the fireplace, and exclaimed: "Ba'ah! A girl is sitting here! Where are you manners?"

I looked and saw that Mahvash was laughing uncontrollably, trying to hold her laughter with her hand. She did not seem to mind my manners at all. Nevertheless I quickly corrected myself by touching my ear to say, "Oh, I am sorry. It could be *gush*, because it too is made of three Farsi letters and has cartilage in it."

Mahvash let go of her mouth and laughed even louder. She laughed so much that Vokhshur had to leave the room, his hands looking for a cigarette, his lips moving nervously as if a speck of tobacco was stuck to one of them.

30

SENT TO BUY SILO BREAD

Looking down at Tehran from the eye of a Zeppelin

WERE YOU TO LOOK AT TEHRAN, in the middle of the Second World War, from the bomb-shaped eye of the single zeppelin that was suspended over our house, you would have seen a sea of flat mud-straw roofs, studded with diamond shaped metallic roofs, broken up into irregular blocks by intersecting lanes and lines like a meshwork of fractured swastikas. The only straight line that you could have seen was the asphalted Amirieh Avenue that stretched, like the column of mercury of a gigantic thermometer, from the oval square in front of the German-built railroad station at the southern limit of the city, up to the snow-streaked Mountains of Alborz in the north.

The side streets extending away from the Amirieh Avenue constituted the gradation lines of that awkward thermometer. Rather than measuring the heat, however, it indicated the political temperature of the city. The Little Bazaar of Asheikh Hadi, for example, where our moderate aunt and uncle were living, constituted its 37 degrees centigrade which is the normal body temperature. The Pahlavi Crossroad where the castles of the Shah were located constituted its feverish 40 degrees. In this sense, the Saghafi Street in which our new house was located and the As-You-Wish Street constituted, respectively, its levels two and three.

If you turned your eyes towards the east on your right you saw the Ruins of Sanguelaj at the east end of the Little Bazaar, not yet transformed to the city park. If you looked to your left you could see the bronze statue of a man trying to kill a contorted dragon with a lance through its throat in the middle of the lozenge-shaped Ferdowsi Square that sharply defined the west end of Tehran. You could not have discerned the exact eastern limits of Tehran because they were dusty and ill-defined. All you saw would have been the newly built houses that merged imperceptively with the treeless hills of *Lashgarak* where the young Shah skied in the wintertime if he did not go to the Alps in Switzerland for that purpose.

Despite the smell of roses in the air, you did not see many flowers nor greenery on the ground. Close up, however, a curious eye could have detected some green dots along the wider roads, representing trees, or a set of dotted lines, representing the holes in the dome-shaped roofs of the main bazaars, converging towards a semicircular square which was not green but was named *Sabzeh Maydan*, meaning the Green Square, located a few blocks south of the Ruins of Sanguelaj.

The smell of roses was coming from the two rows of pink Mohammadi roses planted along the upper part of Amirieh Avenue which had changed its name to Pahlavi Road and stretched from the northern end of Tehran up to Shemiran. The number of those roses rapidly diminished as those who could afford to buy a car kept going to Shemiran to come back with bouquets of flowers in their hands. Every weekend that the Vokhshurs went to see their newly bought garden in Shemiran, for example, Shambool came back with a handful of flowers for me, and his younger sister, Pari, came with a lapful of the same for Hamid.

The reason I know the Amirieh Avenue and its extension so well is because I walked and rode along it longer than any other road in the world. Not only were our houses located along it, my entire education was accomplished along the same road and its major tributaries. The high school of Sharaf, for example, to which I went the next year, was in Mehdiyeh Avenue which was just beyond the Monirieh Avenue, equal to 37.5 degrees. While Namoos Elementary School was one street north of it at the level of 38. At Pahlavi Avenue, in addition to the castles of the Shah, the Officers' Academy was located in which I spent three years of my life, day and night, to become an army officer while going to medical school. At Shah Reza Avenue, a few streets beyond that, marking the northern limit of Tehran, I did my medical training for six years. Exceptionally, no statue of Reza Shah marked the northern limit of Tehran, but the south, which was marked with the building of the railroad station, had the statue of Reza Shah in the middle of its oval square. My final apartment, which was combined with my medical office, was located at the end of the same avenue too, but at the lap of Alborz Mountain in Shemiran.

Having lived all the time that I was in Tehran along that straight road makes me conclude that the Straight Way that my mother was always looking for was shown to me by the bronze arm of Reza Shah that pointed along that horizontal column of mercury.

Trying to cheat our uncle

Finding the straight way is no guarantee that one will remain honest and straight for ever. In my experience, as long as one is endowed with will power and has the choice of making a decision, there is always a chance to deviate from the straight way. Hamid and I are good examples to demonstrate this deviation.

A Persian Letter

If one looked down at the sidewalks of Amirieh Avenue on the day that Hamid and I were walking southwards with our report cards in hand, one saw that instead of going straight southward towards our home, we turned left as we came out of Monirieh Avenue to go to the Little Bazaar, where the house of Colonel Sharabi, our *Daii*, was located. We had successfully passed our exams and were quite happy—walking towards our house, sometimes running and sometimes jumping with one leg trying to avoid the parallel shadow of tree trunks stretched on the sidewalk. The next year Hamid was going into grade six in the same elementary school of Kherad, and I was going to go into grade seven which is the first year of high school. The only thing that diminished our happiness was the chronic lack of money in our pockets.

Our *Daii* had promised us that he would pay us money if we got good marks on our final report cards according to the following formula: two *Tuman* or twenty *Rials* for every 20; fifteen *Rials* for every 19, ten *Rials* for every 18 and five *Rials* for every 17 or 16.

None of us had any 20s, but Hamid had a few 19s and 18s, and I had only one 16. I had, however, several 11 or 12 written with blue ink on my report card that could be easily transformed to 19 and 18 by the same colour ink which I happened to have with me. When we reached the intersection of the Little Bazaar with Amirieh Avenue, it was about ten o'clock in the morning and I concluded that our uncle must be awake. So, I suggested to Hamid that we could go to our uncle's house to get our money when we needed it the most. Hamid agreed and we crossed the street to go to his house. As we were walking in the Little Bazaar, I suggested to Hamid that we could change our 11 and other modifiable marks to 19 or other money-generating numbers and, after we got our money, we would erase the changes with the tip of the Gillette razor blade that I always carried in the upper pocket of my school uniform. Hamid reluctantly agreed with me and we changed as many numbers as we could, more, of course, on my report card than his.

We knocked at our uncle colonel's familiar orange door next to the black doorless opening of the public cistern. His *Masdar* opened the door and led us to the end of their long paved yard, to the mosquito net in which our uncle was asleep. His trousers were hanging from one of the four poles that held the net upright over a weather-beaten wooden bed. We managed to find the blind opening of the mosquito net that was deceptively tucked under the mattress on his side and through it we handed him our report cards while saying our *Salaams*. We thought since he was still in the twilight zone between sleep and wakefulness he would have a quick look at our report cards and ask us to hand him his trousers to give us our money and would fall back to sleep. But no, we were badly mistaken. Instead of his trousers, he asked us to give him his glasses which were on the edge of the wooden bed, and he stayed inside for a long time looking sometimes at my card, sometimes at Hamid's, more at mine. Eventually, he came out and asked us to follow him upstairs to his room. Once upstairs, he left us behind the door, went to his room and sat behind his desk without closing the door and began calculating line by line, horizontally and vertically. When he finished calculating, he wrote a letter, put it in an envelope, wrote the name of his sister on it, and gave it to us without sealing it to give it to our mother. He also gave us our money: five *Rials* to me and a few *Tuman* to Hamid, exactly the amount that was due to us before the alteration of our marks.

We went away, ashamed and silent for long time. After a while, Hamid suggested that we take the letter out of the unsealed envelop to see what our uncle had said about us before giving it to our mother. I disagreed. I told Hamid that the reason our uncle had not sealed the envelope was not because he wanted us to read it. On the contrary, he wanted to teach us that as far as the etiquette of carrying a letter to a third person is concerned, sealing it would be an insult to the honesty of the one who carries the message. Hamid laughed at my reasoning and insisted that we read it. We read it. Hamid kept laughing as he was reading it but I failed to see the humour in it. Luckily, our uncle had not taken our action too seriously. In the letter he was trying to tell the truth about what we had done, but in a jocular way, like, "… It appears that the blue ink of the teacher on Nasser's report card had run a little on the cardboard and had made, among other things, his 11 resembling 19." When we gave it to our mother, she did not take it too seriously either, judging by the smile she was wearing as she read it. Perhaps she thought it was partly her fault for keeping us so poor as far as pocket money was concerned that we were forced to cheat. Or maybe she thought we had already learned our lesson of never trying to outsmart the grown-ups, no matter how stupid we thought they were.

My embarrassment increased in time rather than decreasing after I learned that the night before that morning our *Daii* had stayed up late to finish his book. His book ended with this phrase. "Tonight I will sleep late, but comfortably, since I have written the last page of my book."

Waking up on the rooftop

If you looked straight down from the zeppelin you would see our flat roof at Saghafi Street on which I and my brothers were asleep. I woke up early on that early summer morning. I could not tell if my early rising was due to the rude cries of two crows on the radio antenna of our adjacent neighbour, or the joy of not having to go to school as of that day for the entire summer. A dust-free cool breeze was passing over the moist mud-straw roof. The night before, it had rained a little, not severe enough to force us to drag our bed and ourselves into the extra room that Vokhshur had added to our house to make it look like a three-story house in a neighbourhood made of two-storey houses. It rained just enough to bring the aroma of rose water out of the mud-straw roof mixed with the smell of farm animals, making me wish to go to our summer trip sooner rather than later. There was no sun or moon in the sky. The moving shaft of light that was scanning the sky all night in search of German airplanes had cleared the sky of stardust, leaving behind only the metallic zeppelin. The constellation of Seven Brothers had disappeared from the heavens to reveal the terrestrial cluster of seven brothers on the roof of our house.

I stood up on my mattress to bend over the elevated edge of the roof to see who was awake in the yard. The courtyard was darker than the roof. Our samovar was the only bright spot standing on a colourful rug, next to our sitting mother. An oval tray with twelve saucers and tea glasses was waiting in front of her. She must have finished her before-the-sunrise *Namaaz* as well as her breakfast, and was waiting to serve the others as they woke up. I could not see her lips moving, but I could tell she was whispering her after-*Namaaz* prayers because her finely beaded rosary was moving in her hand.

I walked, barefooted, over the springy roof towards the small slanted room that covered the stairs. The air in the stairway was warm and still. At the bend of the stairs, where the steps became a little wider, I saw my notebook and that of Majid for copying our school text books of Farsi. Our uncle colonel had made a deal with us: "Copy your book of Farsi, page by page, and get five *Shahi* per page." Pages with mainly pictures and little writing were also counted as one page, as if there was no picture.

Midway down the stairs, where Vokhshur had provided us with some elbow room, there was a small square hallway with four doors opening towards it. On my right, in the children's room, I saw that Majid had not put away the chess set after he had finished playing with me. Several times I had told him that the younger brother should collect the pieces after the game, but, because he always won, he thought that it was the job of the loser, regardless of the age. Actually, I didn't mind the mess if Majid had not substituted one of its missing black bishops with that dangerous metallic object. I had told him more than a hundred times to find a softer substitute because someone might fall on it while wrestling beside the chessboard and lacerate a kidney. He always said that he was looking for something better, "But for now this will do because it is made of heavy metal, so it sits well on the board, and, because of its pointy tip it is easy to remember that it is substituting a bishop." I was so preoccupied with Majid and his bishop that I had a bad dream about them.

Majid and I were playing chess on the rooftop of the Kherad Elementary School. The chessboard was almost the size of the entire roof on which green and brown pine needles were scattered as well as pine cones. I was losing and was ready to give up, but Majid—so unbecoming of him—was not ready to quit. He was laughing an unfamiliar laughter and was demanding that my pieces, which had fought a hard battle before they were captured should be executed right then and there. I was pleading with him not to do so and leave the final decision to the vice-principal of the school. He refused and ordered his men to shoot. His men all had guns even though there were no military men among them. Some wore ordinary civilian suits, some wore fine, semi-translucent cloaks that were specific to educated clergy. A second before they began to shoot, however, his *Vazeer* stopped the firing squad to look into the blue eyes of my *Vazeer* and said, "Don't shoot him because he could be a foreign consultant, maybe an American." Before I could thank him for his good deed, my white *Vazeer* stepped forward and said, "No. Kill me too. I am Iranian. It is you who are foreigners, perhaps Arab, judging by the way you are dressed." Unfortunately, I did not wake up until they shot all of my best men, including my courageous blue-eyed *Vazeer*.

The door of the room in which Auntie Pouran and my mother slept on summer nights was wide open to create an air current coming from the three open windows to the balcony. Their beds were on the floor, side by side. That of my mother was empty but Auntie Pouran was still asleep in hers. Because she did not do *Namaaz* she could sleep as much as she wished. Her bared voluminous thighs were showing. We never saw our mother in bed, let alone sleeping so carelessly and so exposed.

I continued my descent down the last flights of the stairs without kicking the *Koozeh* of water that always sat on the last step like a beggar beside the door of a mosque.

Without having washed my face, I said my *Salaam* to my mother and sat in front of her, facing her and the tall wall of our western neighbour behind her. Modar-jun did not mind if we forgot to wash in the mornings and would never send us back to do so after we sat. It was Auntie Pouran who always insisted on that and would send us back, but she was not there on that morning. We did have running water, but for some reason I never thought that my face would become so dirty during sleep that it would require washing in the morning.

Cold tap water for washing was available in our house. Vokhshur had included a sink for washing up in the building. To make our yard square, he had cut off the crooked end that was near the street and had used that part to build the wet part of the house. He had jammed a row of small cubicles on that narrow trapezoid segment, diminishing further its size from west to east. The first cubicle consisted of the incomplete shower room and the wet stairway that led to the faucet of the underground cistern. Next to it was the kitchen in which a manual pump was installed to pump water from the underground cistern up to the empty oil barrel on the roof of the kitchen. The barrel did not have a lid and once we saw from the roof of the main building that a dead cat was floating in it, discouraging us from using its water for either drinking or washing. The next cubicle was the short hallway leading to the front door. Next to it was the room for servants. The last cubicle was divided in two equal halves to house the sink and the toilet. The sink was white, made of china, and had a horizontal S-shaped faucet with two open ends, both giving cold water, but one running straight downward, the other going up first, like a fountain, before coming down.

The other reason for my reluctance to wash my face in the mornings was my good intention of not wanting to waste the water that our old cook was pumping up to the tank with her failing heart. Despite all my efforts, however, she did develop acute pulmonary edema secondary to the failure of the left ventricle of her heart. She was lucky that it happened in front of me when I was in the fourth year of medical school and knew how to treat it. I diagnosed it right away by the appearance of white foam at the corners of her mouth and her sudden shortness of breath. It was a medical, rather than a surgical emergency and I knew how to treat it. Its treatment consisted of doing three important things: 1—bleeding her to reduce the volume of blood and therefore the work of her heart. 2—an injection of ouabain to increase the force of her heart muscle, and 3—injecting morphine, to reduce the anxiety and the feeling of approaching death that was part of the syndrome, as well as other, less known beneficial effect on pulmonary edema. I did not have the facility for cutting her veins to bleed her, but I used several teacups as suction cups and applied them to the back of her chest; then, with my razor blade I made numerous superficial cuts on the congested parts of her skin after removal of the cups to bleed her and injected my last ampoule of morphine that I had kept for an emergency occasion just like that. I had no ampoule of ouabain, but she got better even without it. She rapidly improved and went to work without a word of thanks to me or a smile of appreciation. Either she did not know how serious her condition was or if she knew she considered it my duty to cure her.

She never smiled during the twenty years or so that she lived in our house and worked in the kitchen. She was not made to be a cook or a maid. Her white face framed with her silky grey hair was more ladylike than that of our mother. She had come from Rasht, a city located on the northern side of the Alborz Mountains near the shores of the Caspian Sea. I remember the first day that she came to our house, looking for a job. She came with her son and her daughter-in-law. They had come to Tehran to work as servants because they could not afford to live like masters as they used to, due to the rising cost of living as the result of the war. The first day, my mother asked her by what name she would like to be called in her new role. She didn't know what to say at first, then, after a while she said, "My daughter-in-law calls me Khaleh, you can call me by the same name." So we called her Khaleh, even though we knew it meant aunt and that she was not our aunt.

Mehdi used to lift the heavy water tank that Vokhshur had not installed for the shower, as a weight to improve his muscles, and Auntie Pouran would sometimes shout at him from the balcony that, instead of lifting the tank why did he not pump water for poor Khaleh. And Mehdi would listen sometimes and do as she said, and within minutes the barrel would get filled and water would come out of its overflow pipe into the kitchen. But he did not do it regularly, and Khaleh never thanked him even for his occasional bursts of energy.

My mother replied to my *Salaam* with a smile and a *Salaam* as well as adding, "Good boy! What an early riser!" And to indicate that my early rising was a very unusual phenomenon, she added, "One wonders from which side of the sky has the sun come up today." She was not of course expecting any reply, but I was tempted to be equally sarcastic and say, "From the west side, across from the east."

Before pouring my tea, my mother looked under the folded towel covering the basket for bread, then, as her hand went up towards the head of the samovar to hold the handle of the tea pot, I stopped her arm in the air to exclaim, "Oh, Modar-jun! A *hezar-pa* is crawling behind you along the junction of the wall with the edge of the rug."

She did not even turn her head to look, but I knew that she believed me. Once before, I had saved her life by warning her of an approaching scorpion. It had happened a few years earlier, at night, on the roof of a barn in one of the twin villages of our Colonel Sharabi; Tokhteh and Mansur-aabad. She did not believe me at first until Monavar asked her, "Even though it might be just an illusion, why don't you, Modar-jun, get up and shake your chador to make sure that there is nothing on it, so that Nasser's mind can rest?" She stood up and, as soon as she took her spotty chador away from her lap, even before shaking it, a long and segmented scorpion fell from it. It was longer than the length of the index finger of a grown man and made the sound of a small rattlesnake when Sohrab stepped on it with his military boot.

This time she believed me and without looking, said, "Centipedes and most crawling insects always move along the interface of the walls and floors. This is why I have told you not to lay your mattress tightly against any wall. If you give them room to pass, they won't go out of their way to come and sting you."

I knew that. She had also told us that whenever we wanted to put our shoes on after a few days of walking barefoot, it was a good practise to look inside them first, or shake them, so that if a cockroach had nested in them, it could get away.

The reason I pointed to the *Hezar-pa* was firstly due to the fact that I could not help it, and secondly, I was looking for some topic of conversation that could delay my having breakfast. It was not the sweet tea that had brought me down to the yard. It was the various snacks that came with it to compensate for the scarcity of sugar during the war.

After the war began, one of the things that immediately became scarce was lump sugar used by the grown-ups for having what they called bitter tea. So every house provided various substitutes for it. Granular sugar was still available though, but that was for sweet tea. And sweet tea was the one that was served with bread and cheese for breakfast. To have a bitter tea, the grown ups would put a lump of sugar in their mouth and without chewing on it they would let the hot unsweetened tea pass over it on its way towards their throat.

I helped myself to dried berries from the cup next to the raisins. There was also a cup of dates and a saucer containing coin-shaped caramelized candies, made of melted granular sugar, often stuck together as well as to the saucer, difficult to pick up with one hand.

"I never saw a cockroach or scorpion jump out of my shoes. Why do you tell us to shake them before putting them on, Modar-jun?"

"That was when we were in Tajrood. Here, it is asphalted everywhere and there are fewer insects around."

My arm moved toward the coin-shaped candies, then made a detour towards the dates and picked one up and put it in my mouth as I reminded her of the night I had saved her life. She remembered it and said, "I am still thankful to you for that night."

"Why, Modar-jun, do some people call Daii-jan Colonel Sarhang Sharabi? He is not always drunk with wine, is he?" I asked my mother while putting a few raisins in my mouth.

Modar-jun did not want to tell me the real story behind that nickname because it would have damaged her brother's reputation. So she substituted it with another true but less damaging real story about her brother related to bringing water from Karaj to Tehran. When Reza Shah had told him, "Tehran is suffering badly from water shortage. Go and bring water." And Sarhang, instead of going to the snow-streaked mountains of Alborz, went to the city of Karaj near Tehran with dynamite and increased the flow of Aab-Karaj, from forty stone to close to two hundred stone. And because the word city in Farsi is *Shahr*—as in *Shahr-zad* meaning city-girl—and the word for water is *aab*, if one put them together one would get the combined word *Sharabi*, meaning "the one who brought water to the Shahr of Tehran."

"But, Modar-jun," I objected, "you know better than I that you can't just put two words together and make a meaningful new word out of them. What happened to the *h* in the *Shahr* in your combined word?"

Then she told me the other story for the origin of that nickname. Even though this second story was a true story too, it was not the true basis for that nickname: "When my brother was a generous young lieutenant in the army, one night, they say, he invited the whole division, officers and soldiers alike, to free wine. Since then they call him Sharabi, meaning the one who gave free wine to an army."

My hand went towards the cup of raisins while I told her the true story behind it. It was written in *SOS*, but since it had not been published yet, my mother pretended that she did not know it. Hamid and I had read it the day we were waiting behind his door while our *Daii* was sitting behind his desk writing that embarrassing letter to our mother. They were five square booklets in which he had written his manuscript. In one of them he said, "When I was young and ignorant, I did many extraordinary things, some heroic, some foolish. My countrymen attributed my deeds to being intoxicated with wine. I resented that accusation while I was still young, but now I accept it with pride. It is true; I am intoxicated. I am drunk with unconditional love for humanity."

My mother put half a piece of *Taftoon* bread in front of me with a relatively small morsel of white cheese in the centre and began to pour my tea.

In the basket of bread there were two kinds of bread, *Taftoon* and *Barbary*. The latter was given by the army to any household that had a military servant.

Every colonel in the Army could have two *Masdars*, but rarely did they use both of them. Instead, they accepted one and received the money equivalent of the other, or gave the other to one of their relatives. Ours was given to us by the twin brother of my mother whom we called Daii Jan Yahya Khan. So, to elongate the conversation with my mother I asked her, "Why, Modar-jun, does our Daii-jan Yahya Khan provide us with our *Masdar*, instead of Daii-jan Sarhang?" My mother did not want to tell me the real reason because it would involve saying a bad thing about her sister-in-law. So I said it myself, "Because, your sister-in-law is too frugal and she would rather receive the cash equivalent of the second *Masdar* than giving the second one to us?"

She neither confirmed nor denied my assumption; instead she looked again under the towel and into the basket of bread and moved about the two thick pieces of *Barbary* bread in the basket.

The yard was still cool and grey, but a barely detectable reddish hue was beginning to appear in the air. Shortly after, like a thief, the sun climbed above the low wall of the yard on the east side and transformed the tall plastered wall of the western neighbour into a red screen. At that very moment the black shadow of a cat passed across the screen, as if a sinister movie was about to begin. Simultaneously, a series of hollow sounds came from the corridor on my right, followed by our *Masdar* carrying two empty oil cans. He stood at semi-attention in front of my mother, next to the oval pool, and asked, "*Khanum*, I am going to get *Naft*, if I can. Would you like me to get anything else while I am out?" Modar-jun looked under the towel, then looked at me, and then said, "No, thank you."

As he went out of the door, a temporary silence settled in the yard. Modar-jun continued moving her lips without making any sound, with her shoulders raised to touch her ears; she kept looking at the door, hoping that the mailman would show up and bring the always delayed letter from Torbat that contained the money order from our rented village.

"Do you pay interest to General Javadi for the money you keep borrowing from him?"

She had never told us how much she borrowed or how much she already owed, but that morning she told me, "Yes, of course, compounded." I did not understand what compounded meant. I thought she meant something bad, something complicated by shame. "Is not getting interest on lent money forbidden in Islam?"

"Giving it is not forbidden. Besides, if Timsar Javadi did not lend money to us, who else would? What would you eat if no one lent us money?"

"What are we having for lunch, Modar-jun, today?"

"*Ab-gusht*"

"Does it have *Ghalam* in it?"

"Of course"

"Why, Modar-jun, do they call that bone in *Ab-gusht Ghalam*? Does not *Ghalam* mean a pen?" I asked while trying some more of the dried berries.

"What did I tell you from the balcony the day you were running in the yard to climb up that wall?" said my mother while pointing to the wall above which the sun had just come up.

"You said, 'Be careful; you might fall and *Ghalam* your leg.'" As soon as I said that I understood by myself why that bone in *Ab-gusht* is called pen: When long bones, like the femoral bone—whether a lamb's or a human's—breaks, the broken end of it is never straight but slanted like the tip of a badly made reed-pen.

My mother looked again under the towel into the basket of bread, and then looked at me to say, "Would you like to be the man of the household today and go to the bakery to buy bread?"

"Me! Why? Why you always ask me when it comes to doing the dirty and the donkey works? You have so many children."

"No one else is awake, but you."

"Our *Masdar* just asked you if you wanted anything from outside and you said *no*."

"He was going to get *Naft*. Bread and *Naft* should not be carried by the same hand. Didn't you see he was carrying two empty cans for *Naft*?"

Of course I saw. I even saw that each can had letters BP on one side and the same letters in Farsi on the opposite side.

"By the way," I asked my mother, "our *Masdar* does not have much hope of finding enough *Naft* to fill one can, why did he carry two cans with him?"

"He likes to hear the sound of drums when he walks. He had only two weeks of training in the camp before coming to our house. He does not want to forget marching with the big drum under his left foot. Besides, even if he were carrying only one BP can, it would still be inappropriate to carry bread and *Naft* together. The bread would acquire the smell of *Naft*. But if you don't want to go, don't go. Mehdi is going to wake up soon."

She did not mention Hossein or Hamid. And that bothered me again. Whenever it came to donkeywork she called on either Mehdi or me.

"Are you going to get the bread or not?" My mother finally ran out of patience.

Yes, I was going. Did I know where the bakery was? Yes, of course.

Bakeries were not the best places to shop. They were crowded and had no rules or regulations. They were bad before the war and had become worse during the war. War, for some reason, had increased people's appetite for bread. I had seen one such bakery near the Mokhtari crossroad, when we went to the railroad station to see the statue of Reza Shah. Even if I did not know, I could find it easily. Bakeries did not have names, but one could find them easily just by the smell of fresh bread. I had seen the chaotic crowd on the sidewalk in front of it. The master baker did not follow the rule of "first come, first served." If a man, for example, wanted twenty and a child came much later and wanted only one, he would give the bread to the child first. That was, of course, after the child had made his presence known by screaming his head off, or going through the legs of men and between the women in chadors to stand in front of the baker. If the child said that he was an orphan, he could have his bread first even if he wanted ten. Once I saw a child standing away from the crowd for so long that his mother had to come to get him and fight with the baker. Out of his religious conviction or due to respect for women, the baker never looked at the face of the women, or if he did, he would do it in such a way that no man would notice. He would sometimes listen for the sound of hunger coming from the abdomen of pregnant women, or detect the imprint of starvation in the concavity of the cheeks of men and give them their bread regardless of when they had come or how many they wanted.

"Is it the bakery near the Mokhtari Crossroad?" I asked my mother to make sure.

"No, no. I need Silo bread from the bakery near As-You-Wish Street," Modar-jun corrected my wrong impression.

I exhaled a sigh of relief. That was easy. That was not a bakery, though. It was a government outlet. I had seen it everyday going to school or coming back. They had converted the empty shop next to the Moussio's into a distribution outlet. In the evenings it was either empty or had only a few damaged leftover loaves of bread the shape of broken bricks, and bread crumbs on its wooden shelves. No brass scale. No shouting crowd in front of it and no discretion. Instead of a crowd, it had a silent line in front of it composed of a single file of waiting men and women.

My mother gave me two coupons and I jumped to my feet and over the narrower end of the oval pool, and darted through the door that was left ajar by our *Masdar*.

Outside, it was still morning and cool; not many people were walking along the sidewalks and not many cars were passing. Every now and then a truck with new tires, belonging to Allied forces, camouflaged with the colouration of a frog, went effortlessly uphill, making the sound of the wheel of a roulette in a casino. Much less frequently a colourful but dented bus, half full, began to move downhill, changing gears with the escalating sound of a child's cry, as if carrying the weight of an army on its worn-out tires.

I turned to my left to run the rest of the way up to As-You-Wish Street, but I did not have to run very far. A silent line of *Aadams* stretched from the outlet down to Saghafi Street. An *Ajan* was walking back and forth along the line so that no one jumped the line.

I joined the end of the line. As far as I could see I was the only child in the line. I did not mind, though. When there is a line, I reassured myself, age, sex and size did not matter.

Before I joined the line it appeared to be moving. It stopped moving as soon as I joined. I did not dare to step out of the line to see what was stopping it. Nor did I crane my neck too long to see what was going on so that the *Ajan* did not think that I was uncomfortable staying in line. Lines were new in Tehran, so new that I thought they were introduced by the Allied forces along with their Silo bread, typhus and recurrent fever.

The sun was not yet visible but one could tell its presence by its reflection on the wall above our heads. The opposite sidewalk was always shaded in the morning due to the row of two-storey apartments that blocked the sun. Mostly Armenians lived in those apartments. Perhaps due to their reduced dependence on water, Armenians were more comfortable living in apartments than the Moslems. Some of those apartments were now occupied by the Russian and Polish soldiers. The American and the British had better accommodations on the northern part of Tehran.

A sleepy Russian or Polish soldier came out of his room to the small balcony protruding over the shady sidewalk with a tin bucket of water in hand to wash his face. He had a pair of green woolen military pants, a white sleeveless undershirt and a pair of very pink arms. He moved the metallic container to his mouth to fill it with water, but did not swallow it. He put the container down, and then made a cup with his hands, emptied the water from his mouth into his hands and splashed his face with it. He repeated the same series of motions three times, and then went in.

I felt less guilty for not having washed my face that morning.

Our line must have moved a little, since I had reached the wall and the low window of the house of the German-looking, Germanophilic, Iranian engineer who worked in the railroad station. He might have had something to do with its building too because the ceiling of the main hall of the station was tessellated with white squares in relief on a blue background, with alternating thin and thick segments that, if one looked at it for a long time, one could see that it was made of interconnected thin and thick swastikas.

A war poster was stuck to the wall beside his window, displaying the stretched, fisted arm of the Allied forces, the sleeve of which was made of the flags of America, Great Britain, Russia, France and a few lesser known countries, striking a cracked three-dimensional black swastika in a red background. The Iranian engineer did not know that we knew he was a German sympathizer. We knew it since the day he came to our house to take home his little cute daughter. Mansur had brought her to show us how closely she resembled the envy of all the children of the world, Shirley Temple. When he arrived, we were playing with date pits and a rock on the ground of the L-shaped cul-de-sac that hugged our house along its eastern and northern sides. We knew that it was the first time that he had come to our house because he did not know that the main entrance to our house was the door that opened towards Saghafi Street and not the one that was always closed and could open towards the cul-de-sac. When he reached the middle of the long limb of that semi-private walkway he stopped to look at something drawn on the plaster of the wall of our house. We said *Salaam* to him but rather than replying to our *Salaam* he asked us with a controlled smile, "Did you draw this?" while pointing to a drawing on the wall. We went closer to see what he was pointing to. We saw a circle about fifty centimetres in diameter drawn with an ordinary pencil encompassing multiple small swastikas drawn with the same pencil, captioned, "A drop of Iranian blood under a microscope."

"No, we did not," we all said together.

He did not seem to believe us since he said, "Naughty boys!" somewhat approvingly, as he went back towards the proper entrance door of our house.

The line moved again, slowly and imperceptibly, as if synchronized with the slow motion of the descending sunshine on the wall above our head.

The *Ajan* suddenly broke its routine and changed the direction of his pacing to walk towards me. When he reached me he asked how much bread I was going to buy. "Two," I said. "Get three for me, too," he said as he was trying to put a bunch of coins and a badly folded bill in my hand.

"No," I said, as I pulled my hand away so quickly as if it was bitten by a wasp.

"No?!" the policeman repeated my word.

"No," I repeated my refusal.

He pulled me out of the line and pushed me towards the creek.

I was so shocked by his reaction to my refusal to commit an illegal act that I did not know whether to flee or fight. I stopped, luckily, like a nail, at the very edge of the dry creek. I had learned to stop like a nail while I was repeating my grade one in the Kherad Elementary School. The end of the ten-minute recess in that school was always announced by two sets of bells; the first was composed of a single stroke of a hammer in the vice-principal's hand, after which all the boys in the yard had to stop running and shouting, followed by a series of bangs to indicate that all should go to their respective classes. The grade one students had only two hours of class in the morning because they were small and full of energy and could not tolerate sitting still for three long hours behind their desks. So, on one of the mornings, as I was running towards the gate to go home, near the end of the second morning recess, and my right foot was almost out of the gate when I heard the single stroke went off and I froze right where I was only because my left foot was still in the school. Mr. Jowhari, well-known for his tough stance, must have been watching me because he made use of the silence that ensued after that initial stroke to ask all the students to say together, "Bravo Shojania," three times, for observing the rules and regulations of the school at the time that I could easily ignore them.

It was too bad that Mr. Jowhari did not know my first name. He knew only my family name and that was because of my similarity to my older brothers who went to the same school, particularly Mehdi who always made us known by his naughty or notorious actions in that school. Three years later, when we were six in that school, one in each class, the vice-principal expressed his amazement regarding our many-ness by using a Persian proverb that is used when something is too abundant, "If you hit a dog with a stick, it would rain Shojanias." Hitting a dog on the head I suppose, had formed the proverb to indicate the commonest and the most trivial thing that one could do in the streets of Tehran in those days.

I stood at the creek, facing the street exposing my back to the silent line for Silo bread. No one either objected to or applauded the action of the *Ajan*. Thanks to God, no one knew me in that line; otherwise shame would have been added to my complex and confused feelings at that moment. For a moment I thought I was in a foreign country. I was particularly glad that Shambool was not around; otherwise he would have laughed at me for the rest of his life.

I don't remember where Shambool was. His family did not usually leave Tehran during summer holiday. Maybe he had gone to Mahallat with his family as they did a year ago before the arrival of the Russians to Tehran.

Even though everyday at school we were hearing that the Germans were advancing up to Ghazvin to reach Tehran within forty eight hours to liberate us from the tyranny of the British, the Russians and the teachers, it turned out that it was the Russians who had advanced up to Ghazvin and were about to attack Tehran. The day before they reached Tehran, Captain Vokhshur came to our house—in a civilian suit the sleeves of which were too short for his arms because he had borrowed it from his shorter brother who lived at the end of As-You-Wish Street—to ask our mother, "Ammeh-jan, let us all go to Mahallat. The Russians are coming, and my car is waiting for you at the head of your street."

Modar-jun politely refused to go, saying, "Thank you for your offer. Please go ahead because you are in the military. I would rather not come, since it is the beginning of the school year for children. Beside, what would the Russians do to a mother with nine fatherless children?"

"Forgive him this time," said a woman in the line to the *Ajan*. "His parents could be waiting for him."

Two or three years before, when I was in grade four or five, I stood almost at the same spot, facing the street, but on the other side of the creek, with a bouquet of flowers in my hand. It was for the wedding of Mohammad Reza Shah with Fowzieh, the sister of King Farouk of Egypt. Reza Shah in his military uniform and grey moustache was sitting in front of an open car with large, protruding, exophthalmic headlights. The king of Egypt and someone else were in the back seat. The next car carried the crown prince who was well shaven and looked no more and no less than his age of eighteen. But I was not the only student welcoming them on that day. All the students of Kherad School as well as all the rest of the elementary schools in Tehran were there, in two parallel lines standing along the two creeks, extending from the railroad station up to castle of the Shah, each student holding a purple bouquet of flower. I was glad that my spot happened to be close enough to our house that the moment the cars of the dignitaries passed, I could be in our house within two minutes, rather than the usual tiring walk of about an hour.

"Forgive him, Mr. Ajan," a man's voice came from the line, sucking up to the *Ajan*.

"They don't teach them manners in schools anymore."

A *Doroshkeh* passed by, going uphill, pulled by a single, malnourished horse with noble face. Before the war each *Doroshkeh* used to be pulled by two well-fed horses. Colonel Sharabi objected to this unfair practise and considered it as yet another bad side effect of the war in the countries far away from the battlefields. "One horse-drawn *Doroshkeh*," Colonel kept saying, "is okay only for the cities along the shore of the Caspian Sea where the land is flat; but not for Tehran which has a rather steep slope from north to south." Due to the increasing price of straw and alfalfa for the horses, and lack of requisite increase in the fare for riding a *Doroshkeh*, the *Doroshkeh Chees* first reduced the number of their horses to one and then lost their single horse to starvation. One of the favourite horses of Sharabi, named Chehri-Zaghi, also died due to lack of feed. Sharabi liked that horse so much that he printed its picture in his *SOS* among his family pictures.

A boy, about my age, was hanging precariously on the bar at the back of the *Doroshkeh*. The *Doroshkeh Chee*, without looking, became aware of the presence of the boy and tried to hit him with the backward motion of his long whip. The boy let go of the bar and followed the cart for a few steps before he stopped to run backward. When he was a safe distance from the man, he made a horn out of his hands and shouted at the *Doroshkeh Chee*, "*Ali-Shah!*" The *Doroshkeh Chee* stopped his horse to run after the boy. When he realized that he could not catch him, he returned to his vehicle and rode on. The boy, reassured that the *Doroshkeh Chee* had given up the pursuit, shouted the second part of the rhyming insult, "*poshteh Baagheh Shah,*" meaning, behind the Garden of the Shah. The latter being a less well-known military institution located at Thirty Metre Avenue, a block or two beyond the Rooz-beh Mental Hospital. The boy was referring to a rumour that an incident had taken place behind the wall of that garden between a drunken General and a good-looking *Doroshkeh Chee* by the name of Ali-shah.

If I jumped over the creek and stepped ahead a few steps and stood in the middle of the road, I could see the statue of Reza Shah, and the marble building behind it. Even though it looked German-built, with tall square white columns, it had the tricolour Persian flag on its forehead, made of narrow tubes of neon lights, visible only at nights. These were the first tubular lights that I had seen in my life, until I saw a lot more of them on the wedding night of the Shah.

The other dignitaries that I had seen passing in their cars on that road were Mr. Roosevelt, Mr. Churchill and Stalin who had come for the Conference of Tehran to discuss the fate of Adolph Hitler and Europe in general after their victory. Although nobody could come out of their houses on that historical day because of the curfew, I managed to get a glimpse of them from the window of the single room on the rooftop of our house, as they passed in front of the opening of Saghafi Street. To catch that historical moment, however, I had to crane my neck for such a long time that I had to rub it for days afterwards.

Is it worth enduring so much humiliation for two loaves of Silo bread? I asked myself. Should I stay or go home? Go home and return the coupons to my mother and say that I could not do it? Or should I stay and see what would happen at the end? Should I kick the *Ajan* in the rear and run away or should I beg him to put me back in the line?

I did none of the above.

Silo bread was the only bread among many kinds of bread that we did not like. It looked deceptively like a cake, as far as the size and the shape were concerned, but it did not taste like a cake at all. To make it even less appetizing, its cross sections showed shiny black insects the size of small ants.

"You have no right to pull that boy out of the line," a man with serious Turkish accent objected to the *Ajan*'s action.

I did not have to turn to see who said that. His voice was familiar. He was the man with *kepi* hat who always sat on the sidewalk with his back to the wall, selling oranges from a basket. I never saw anybody buying his oranges. Maybe that was why he changed his job to become the janitor of the Mokhtari branch of the left-wing Tudeh Party.

As I was standing at the creek, I heard the familiar sound of two empty tin cans hitting each other, coming from the street beyond As-You-Wish Street. Our *Masdar* was approaching the scene. One of his epaulets hung from his shoulder. As he got closer I could see his belt was loose and all of his buttons were undone, some were missing. He must have had a fight with the oil man.

The police and the army did not like each other to begin with, and if our *Masdar* saw me in that situation, I was sure an embarrassing fight would break out. As he got closer, I looked for a tree trunk or a cement pole to hide behind until he passed. The cement poles were far apart and none was close enough to hide behind. There were no big trees on the southern end of Amirieh Avenue. That part was newly populated. Were it not for the presence of the railroad station it would have been like the south end of Shapoor Avenue that was so poor that some of its houses were made of cane and straw; nicknamed *Hasseer-Aabad.*

I moved—imperceptibly I thought—closer to the *Ajan* to make a shield out of him for myself. Thankfully, our *Masdar* came and went uneventfully. With each step that he took I could hear the sound of the letter *B* alternating with the sound of letter *P*. Vokhshur had misinformed us that the *B* stood for *Benzene* and *P* for Pars or Persia and the two meant "Benzineh Pars." It would take me years to learn, to my chagrin, that the two letters were the initials of British Petroleum. The street kid, who had bothered the *Doroshkeh Chee*, was back in time to utter loud catcalls as our *Masdar* was passing along the length of the bread line like a general seeing his troops.

A woman volunteered to buy the bread for the *Ajan* but he seemed to have changed his mind about making money on the black market with Silo bread. He expertly put the money in his pocket and turned towards me to ask where my place in the line was before he had pulled me out. I looked along the line, but could not tell where my original place was. My place in the line had healed over like a wound. I showed him a random spot near the middle, near the liquor store that kept opening and closing for the few who were more interested in a morning drink than in Silo bread. He put me there. As soon as I got there I realized that it was not my original place. It smelled of musty wine laced with sunny turmeric, while my original spot smelled of tea and tobacco.

The line began to move relatively rapidly as I rejoined it. I got the two loaves of bread and started back towards our house, marching along the same dolorous way that our *Masdar* had taken a few minutes earlier. Even though I did not like Silo bread, I took a big bite from the end of one of the loaves as soon as I passed the last man in the line. I managed to chew on it, but my mouth was too dry to swallow it.

As I turned into our street I saw Mehdi coming out of our house, running towards me. I wiped my tears with my sleeve before he saw me. "What kept you?" he asked, as he came within a shouting distance, "Modar-jun was worried about you."

"The line was too long," was all that I cared to tell him.

As I began to run to keep our mother from worrying, Mehdi, out of habit rather than meanness, put his foot in front of mine and tripped me. I fell and the loaves of bread fell out of my hands and landed inside the central creek in which a few new bricks had fallen from the pile of bricks waiting to be used for the Mosque of Haji Lotfollah. The good man, who had sold part of his large garden to us to build a house on it, had later donated another, but smaller part of it for building a mosque. Modar-jun became much happier when she heard a mosque was being built in our street than when she saw a liquor store was opening at the head of it.

I got up, picked up the two loaves of Silo bread, kissed them and dusted my shirt and continued running towards our house. Bread was bread, whether Silo bread or any other kind. It should be respected, picked up and kissed. We were told that if we saw even a bread crumb fallen on our way as we were going to school we had to pick it up, kiss it and put it at the edge of a wall so that a poor man or a beggar could use it.

The door of our yard was ajar. No one was in the yard except my mother, sitting on the same location and in the same position, beside the steam-less samovar. The sunshine had carpeted the entire yard and bleached the colour of the flowers of the rug. I sat in front of my mother before giving her the bread so that it did not appear as if I was giving bread to a sitting beggar. I did not repeat my *Salaam* because once it was said in the morning it was good for the rest of the day.

After removing the tea pot from the head of samovar, Modar-jun folded the towel of the breadbasket to hit the neck of its internal chimney to rekindle it. She hit it so hard that ashes issued from the holes at its bottom to spill over the tray and the saucers. As the samovar began to resume its sibilant sound a pair of wispy vapours snaked out of the two holes on its shoulders, before disappearing in the sunshine.

Projecting her own anxiety to the samovar, Modar-jun said, "You came so late that the poor samovar fainted." Then, she put half of the oval bread that was the size of the brass tray, in front of me with a small morsel of white cheese in the middle and said, "Have your bread and cheese until the water get warmer, and I can give you your tea."

"No, Modar-jun," I said as I pushed the bread and the cheese away from me.

"Why?" asked my mother, surprised to see me refusing food for the first time.

"I am going to have bitter tea today."

"Have some berries, then, while you are waiting," said my mother; realizing that I was in a very bitter mood.

At that moment, I exploded like a pomegranate to begin sobbing inconsolably. Modar-jun did not try to stop me. She knew that I could not be stopped easily whenever I began to cry. Soon after I began to cry, the door of the yard flew open with a big bang to reveal our uncle colonel, followed by his son, Sohrab, both in their sunny military uniforms.

Sharabi had finished his book and was going to Sangueh-Sar, where he used to catch armed robbers, to buy lamb for the army in Tehran. He had been granted the contract to supply the meat for the army in Tehran. They had come to take Mehdi with them to watch over the meat so that the butchers or others did not steal it. He had also hired the jobless father of Holaaku to help with the transportation to Tehran.

Like a rekindled samovar in the sunshine, my tears evaporated as I saw Sharabi and his son in our doorway. The *hegh-hegh* of my cry—like that of the drunken man in one of the poems of Omid—got transformed to the *ghah-ghah* of laughter, as my right arm extended towards the cup of dry berries to sweeten my bitter tea with.

31

MY MONT BLANC FOUNTAIN PEN

I ALWAYS LIKED PENS AND PENCILS, especially the good ones. It is true that there were not many toys or tools in the land of my childhood, but pens and pencils were always available. I discovered the magical power of a pencil the moment I touched the tip of it to a paper, pulled it, and it left a mark along the place it had been pulled. That was the first tool that could reveal the path it travelled, so accurately, without a millimetre less or more. Not only that, you could change the shape of the line and show it to someone else and he would know what you were thinking. And you could leave the paper in the room and come back the next day and you could tell what had happened in that room the day before.

The first thing that I wanted to do with the first short pencil that I had found in our yard in Mashad, when I was about three, probably after seeing my mother always writing, was to write with it, rather than drawing a picture. I did not know any words and did not know that words are made of letters. But I knew that I should make interrupted wavy lines on the paper and make sure that they were not all the same length. I showed it to my mother as soon as I finished the page. She liked it so much that she went to show it to my father. She never came back to tell me what my father said about it.

As I grew older I acquired better and more expensive pens, especially fountain pens, the best among them was my Mont Blanc fountain pen. I carried it always with me, whether I was in civilian suit or in my military uniform. I don't remember having written any important thing with it, but I remember the day it made me ashamed of myself.

It was a hot Friday afternoon and I had nothing to do. I put on my green military uniform and put my Mont Blanc fountain pen in one of its pants pockets and went to play cards with Houshi at their house. I always carried my pen in my pants pocket whenever I wore my military uniform because if I put it in one of the pockets of its jacket its lid would not close properly.

The oldest of Houshi's three younger sisters was sitting on the top of the short flight of stairs in the courtyard, wearing a loose semi-transparent summer dress. Rather than running up those stairs as usual, I stopped at the bottom of the stairs to ask her if Houshi was home. Before saying "yes" or "no" she looked at my pants, smiled and said, "The tip of your Mont Blanc is showing." Either by a reflex or due to a Freudian mistake, rather than looking at my pants pocket I looked at the zipper of my pants. That mistake changed her smile to a hysterical laughter. As she was laughing her Mont de Venus became visible for a fraction of a second, but I did not say anything about it. I just wished that to my question about the presence or absence of her brother she would reply negatively. Unfortunately, after she finished her laughter, she said, "Yes, he is in his room, upstairs."

Rather than going immediately upstairs, I remained standing at the bottom of the stairs and even though it was summer and the schools were closed I asked her if she had a composition to do so that I could help her with my pen.

"Yes, please," she said. "I have to write an essay, comparing the pen with the sword."

I knew she was joking; nevertheless I told her that pen was better because our uncle colonel—the father of Sohrab who was in love with one of her older sisters—used to have both of them but he broke his sword in front of the Shah to pick up his pen to write a book.

Among the six pretty sisters of Houshi only one of them married one of the seven Shojania brothers, and that was the same girl who was sitting on the top of the stairs. She married Mahmood, our last brother. I asked her how come she, being so good-looking, married our Mahmood who was not our best-looking brother at that time, even though later on he became the best-looking among us. She said he was the best among us. Soon, however, before having a child, they were divorced. Both their marriage and divorce happened when I was in prison. When I came out I wanted to ask her the reason for their divorce but I did not. I thought it was none of my business to begin with. Besides, I reasoned, there are always two sides to any divorce story and I might not get the correct answer if I asked only one side.

Her younger sister Beheen— Farsi for the best—fell in love with our best-looking brother, Hossein, but since many other girls were in love with Hossein, her love did not end in marriage. She was a small woman who coloured her hair purple and her lips sour cherry. She had a mature and manly voice and sang meaningful love songs in our outing on the *Sizdah-beh-dar* occasions. One of the songs that she sang still rings in my ear:

With the black arrows of your lashes

You have perforated my faith a thousand times

Come and let me remove a thousand pains

From the illness of your eyes.

The last girl who confessed that she was in love with Hossein was the daughter of the neighbour of our mother when she was living in the house of Auntie Pouran. She did not say it to Hossein though. She said it to our mother from the same window of her house through which she had been watching Hossein, when he was alive and when he was dead. When they were taking his blood-stained corpse out of the house, she told our mother, "I was in love with your son."

Hossein enjoyed women and women enjoyed him while he was alive without ever marrying him. This is why the word *Naa-kam* is not written on his tomb. *Naa-kam* means without pleasure in Farsi. It is a negative word often carved on the gravestones of young Persian boys. Even though girls too died without ever having experienced sexual pleasure, this word was never carved on their tombs.

Houshi's last sister became infatuated with me, but it was too late. It happened when I had to postpone love for the sake of my revolutionary thoughts. One of my favourite revolutionary poets by the name of Houshang Ebtehaj—pen name H. A. Saayeh, meaning shade or shadow—might have had something to do with my unfortunate postponement. I never saw the lips of Saayeh because it was always covered by a thick black moustache like that of my favourite Russian writer in those days, Maxim Gorky. But I remember the poem he was reading in one of our dance parties regarding postponement of love. He had made that poem for the Armenian girl who danced Persian folk dance like a professional dancer. Her name was Alma but in the poem it was changed to Gaalia.

It is late Gaalia

Love

Between you and me

Can make an interesting story

To be told over and over again

But

At this time that many go to bed

Without a morsel of bread

There is no room for love.

Siavosh Kasraei, my other favourite revolutionary poet, pen name Kowli, was also present when Alma was dancing. He was so impressed with her dance that he made a long poem and titled it "An Iranian Dance."

Later, Saayeh made the following short poem about his loneliness at night:

My bed is a hollow shell

And you hang on the neck of others

Like a pearl.

Saayeh married that girl, more out of jealousy than love, as is often the case. Perhaps he thought if he did not marry her, Kowli would have done so. Kowli and Sayeh were often together. One day, Kowli took me to Saayeh's house. He was the first artist I met who had framed the pictures on his wall with ropes. He was also one of the first people who possessed a movie camera. With that camera he had made a short movie of their little girl, but showed it backward to us, fast, to make her look tidier than she actually was. In that movie, his three-year-old daughter was collecting fallen books from the carpet and putting them back on their shelves. Then immediately without resting she picked up a fallen lamp from the floor to put it on the coffee table, and miraculously returned the spilled milk back into her bottle. Saayeh, however, was not as happy as I thought he would be despite having married his ideal woman and having the cutest daughter.

In fact he was very sad and did not try to hide the cause of his sadness from me because I was almost a medical doctor. Their daughter had been diagnosed having a tumour in the back of one eye for which she was to undergo enucleation. I tried to console him that one could live a normal life with one eye, but he said that his worry was for the time that she would go to school and her cruel classmates would make fun of her by calling her *Ghasem Koori*, referring to the mythical one-eyed boy who closed one eye whenever he lied.

When Saayeh found out that I was in my last year of medical school, he asked me a nagging question that must have been bothering him, but was not important enough to go to a doctor for it.

"Why, Doctor," he asked, "when I am in the middle of composing a poem do I keep going to the washroom?"

"Do you drink many glasses of tea when you compose?"

"No."

"Beer?"

"No."

"Water?"

"No."

Had he answered any of the above questions positively, especially alcohol, I would have made use of the inhibitory effect of alcohol on the anti-diuretic hormone secreted by the posterior lobe of the pituitary gland, and had explained why he would urinate more when he made poems, but since he said no, I had to resort to the axis that connects brain cortex, where mental activity occurs, to the hypothalamus and anterior pituitary gland, and try to justify it somehow. So, I told him that he must be under severe emotional distress and deeply in thought when he was composing poems and that could affect his kidneys.

My lack of cooperation with the infatuation of the youngest sister of Houshi, however, beside the poem of Saayeh, had another and simpler reason. And that reason was not the lack of beauty on her part. She was pretty enough. She looked like the female version of her handsome brother, but she had developed some sympathy towards the Tudeh Party and since I had recently and secretly joined that party while in the army, I had to be extra careful and not get too close to the Tudeh Party sympathizers. It was okay to associate with those who were actual members of that party since the actual members pretended that they did not belong to that party. It is always the sympathizers who are careless and with their carelessness reveal, not only their own tendencies, but those with whom they associate. And if my tendency was revealed I could have gone straight to prison, if not executed in front of a firing squad.

Defeated in love, she went to America and married an American and did not return to Iran as far as I know. When she was leaving, I went to see her off in the airport. In the airport she quoted the following line from Baba-Taaher whose two-liners were as simple as the words of a peasant.

I wish loving was bilateral

Since one-sided love is nothing but a headache.

When she saw me not responding even to her love poem, she recited another line from the same poet.

The heart of lovers is like a wet log in a fireplace

While one end burns, the other end weeps.

I finally got the message and wept a little when I kissed her goodbye.

32

A WALK WITH HOUSHI, MY SECOND BEST FRIEND

WHEN WE WERE YOUNGER, my best friend Shambool and I had an arrangement with each other that he had named a *Shart*. It meant that, except for the three main meals of the day, whatever edible things we had were to be shared with each other. This *shart* was only between us and nobody else, including Houshi who, after Shambool, was my best friend.

Having *Shart* was new to me and like anything new I was pleased to embrace it, especially when Shambool's daily allowance was ten *Shahi*, while my weekly allowance was six *Shahi*. This inequality, rather than being the cause of envy for me, was a source of irony because Captain Vokhshur was supposed to give less money to his boys to prevent them from going bad.

Despite the above arrangement, since Shambool was a year younger than me and went to a different school both for the elementary school and high school, it was Houshi with whom I did most of my walking and talking. He was the same age as I and went to the same schools. Houshi, of course, was aware of our *Shart* but he did not mind not having such an arrangement with me, because, being the only boy among six girls, he had free access to money and snacks and always had a hard candy hidden inside one of his cheeks, or under his tongue, when he talked. So often was this the case that our classmates thought he either had some kind of speech problem or was trying to talk like the American soldiers who sounded as if they had a hot potato in the their mouth when they talked.

Houshi must have been doing this in our class too because one day in the chemistry class in grade seven at Sharaf High School, when the class was so quiet that you could hear the flies circulating above our heads, we heard a loud sound and when we looked we saw the red face of Houshi as the result of the slap by the teacher. The teacher, who was walking back and forth along the gap between the two rows of desks, had slapped him on his right cheek that was exposed to the walkway. Nobody knew what he had done to deserve such a severe punishment without warning, except me.

Only I knew why the teacher had committed such a shameful and illegal act. It is true that eating in class was forbidden, but that was not sufficient reason for the teacher to resort to bodily punishment. Corporal punishment was forbidden in schools, especially in high schools. Even in the elementary school the teachers and the vice-principal always hid their sticks under a desk or behind a tree, whenever the inspector from the Ministry of Education visited the school. The real reason was that the teacher, judging by the nice way that Houshi always dressed and his family name that meant clean, had suspected that he must be Baha'i, and was looking for an opportunity to punish him for that. Eating in class was an excuse and the opportunity that the teacher was looking for.

But the teacher was wrong, because Houshi, even though he was born to a Baha'i family, was not a religious boy at all, and, like me, he was going to lose his God within the next two years, before reaching the age of 18 when he had to decide whether to become a Baha'i or not.

When Houshi and I were both eighteen, we went for a walk in the streets of Tehran. We both had lost our God and our religions without discussing it with each other. My loss was not as obvious as Houshi's because he deliberately did the things that Baha'is were not supposed to do. For example, he had already participated in political demonstrations and had gone to jail for it, a thing that Baha'is were not supposed to do. Also, he was looking for a way to do the other thing that was forbidden by the Baha'i religion, namely drinking alcoholic beverages.

Neither of us liked the taste of alcohol but it was Friday night and we were bored. So we decided to buy a dozen chocolates that contained liquor from the Café Ferdowsi at Estambol Avenue.

The Armenian owner of the café had the longest and the best-known moustache in Tehran. It was more recognizable through the window of his café than the mannequins in the display windows of fashion stores for ladies. His café was the gathering place for the poets and intellectuals. It was there that I once met Nosrat Rahmani. Even though it was our first encounter, he asked me to pay for his table and when I did, he signed his newly published thin book of poetry for me, "To my new-found friend, Nasser." When he was signing his book for me I noted that the third finger of his right hand had a blister near the tip. I asked him for the cause of it. He said he had burnt it with a cigarette while he had fallen asleep under the influence of heroin. As he was talking, I realized that the brown stuff that he was chewing on was not a piece of chocolate, but a chickpea sized fragment of opium. He was also writing his life story in a weekly magazine under the title, "The Man Who Disappeared in Dust." I thought, the way he was abusing his body he would be dead in a few short years, but, to my surprise, he survived long enough to die almost at the time that Shamloo, the most important "new" poet of Iran, who died when he was in his early seventies.

Uneventfully, Houshi and I bought the liquor-containing chocolates and ate them as we walked along Shah Reza Avenue towards Tehran University. We both had passed the difficult entrance exam and were eligible to go to medicine, pharmacology or dentistry, in that order, and were going to register ourselves in that university after that summer. Even though Houshi's marks were good enough to register for medicine, he chose pharmacology to open a pharmacy after graduation. I thought perhaps his unusual choice was due to the dominant gene for commerce that runs through Baha'i families, whether believers or not.

I did not think either of us had become drunk on those sweet nectars, but when my foot hit the back of the leg of a little girl that was walking beside her mother and the mother told her child, "Don't worry, he is just learning to walk," I realized that I had become a little impaired and began walking along the straight edge of the creek to make sure that I was walking straight.

When we reached the gates of the university, we could not go in because it was surrounded by soldiers. When we asked for the reason, we were told that the Shah and his entourage were there to open the Faculty of Law. Shortly after, we heard two shots from inside of the university and right after that we saw two street kids running and yelling with pleasure, "The Shah is shot. The Shah is shot."

We thought the Shah had been shot dead and concluded that the Tudeh Party must be celebrating. With this sinister thought in our head we decided to go back to Ferdowsi Avenue and see the reaction to the shots in the headquarters of that Party.

The gates of the headquarters were made of black wrought iron and lance-like bars with golden tips. It was located in front of the Hotel Ferdowsi where Hossein used to go and drink excessively with his high-class friends. The doors and the windows of that hotel were always closed and its curtains drawn. I had never gone inside that hotel and I did not think that I would ever need to go there. About five years later, however, when I was working as a volunteer intern in the private psychiatric hospital of Dr. Reza'ei in Niavaran and I wanted to take its head nurse to a decent place, the Hotel Ferdowsi was the only place that came to my mind and I took her there. During our uneasy conversation I found out that she knew my sisters and was a classmate of them in Namoos elementary school. That information dampened any sexual desire in me so rapidly that I took her back to Niavaran after spending all of my seventy *Tuman* on that dark place, and a taxi. I kissed her only once on one of the cheeks, like kissing a sister when we reached the gates of that garden turned into a private mental institute.

I thought that was the end of her, but no, I was wrong again. A few years later, when she went mad and occupied one of the beds at Rooz-beh Mental Hospital, she became one of the patients of Massoud, my psychiatrist friend. At that time I was not in Tehran. I was working at the cement factory of Dorood, doing my compulsory two years of medical practice out of the capital city. While in that little city, I was in touch with Massoud through letters. In one of his letters, Massoud had written, as a funny coincidence he thought, that his patient had mentioned my name as one her lovers. "You didn't, I am sure, write that in her chart," I wrote in my reply to Massoud's letter. He replied that he had to because she was hospitalized for having megalomaniac ideas, and that was the only proof for it.

The gates of the headquarters were half open and the young doorman, who often stood on his hands when he had nothing to do, was standing on his feet beside the gates. I always thought that the doorman had either some Russian blood in him or was an ex-acrobat from a Russian circus. He seemed totally unaware of the assassination attempt at the university. We stepped into its brick-paved corridor without going deep into the courtyard. Wrinkled newspapers were stuck to the walls of the corridor, one of them reporting the successful strike of the workers in a factory in Germany. They had demanded fewer hours of work per day or fewer days of work per week, whichever was shorter. Houshi and I were the only ones in the headquarter except for another ordinary looking man with a big head and a *Kepi* hat, standing on his feet, reading the papers on the wall.

Highly disappointed, we turned back and left that deserted place.

We were very lucky to have come out at that moment, because, as soon as we left, truck loads of armed police and soldiers, followed by jubilant mobs, arrived, captured the doorman while standing on his hands, rushed into the place and took everything out, including boxes of files and the man with big head.

Rather than good luck, it could be that it was the God that we thought we had lost who was responsible for saving us from the trap that we had walked into with our own feet. God the benevolent must have been watching us when we were buying those liqueur containing chocolates, and had concluded that any eighteen-year-old man who was having his first drink at that age must be innocent.

On our way back towards our homes, I asked Houshi why he had chosen pharmacology rather than medicine that would make him a real doctor. "First of all," Houshi said, "a pharmacist is a doctor, too, and secondly, to tell you the truth, I like neither of them, whether pharmacology or medicine.

"Why did you participate in such a difficult entrance exam, then?"

"That was for my parents. I thought I would fulfill at least one of their wishes."

"What was the wish that you failed to fulfill?"

He murmured something that I could not understand, as if he had a candy under his tongue.

33

THE SHAH AFTER THE ATTEMPTED
ASSASSINATION

THE SHAH SURVIVED THE ATTEMPTED ASSASSINATION with only a minor scratch on his upper lip which he covered by a temporary moustache, but the assailant was killed right then and there in front of the Faculty of Law by the Chief of Police who was in attendance. The assailant's name was Nasser Fakhraraei. He had entered the university on that day by pretending to be a reporter and had hidden his revolver inside his cubic shaped camera. In his pocket they found his membership card of Tudeh Party. Because of that, the Tudeh Party was declared illegal the next day, and it went underground as of that day. The man who had introduced Fakhraraei to the Party was the same man with big head and *Kepi* hat who was reading the newspapers on the walls in the corridor of the headquarter of the Party the night we went to see what was happening there. His family name was Arkani.

The pictures of the incident were in the newspaper the next day. The Shah was alive with a band-aid on his upper lip. Fakhraraei was dead and naked with two bullet holes on his chest. Arkani was in civilian suit with no wound. From his picture and his family name I recognized him as the older brother of Dr. Arkani who was doing his Internship in Rooz-beh Mental Hospital with Massoud and me.

As of that day the Shah did not change much as far as appearance was concerned, but he became a tougher man. After getting rid of the Tudeh Party he began his White Revolution. He introduced the law of "Where have you got it from" to catch the people who had gotten rich by illegal means. His new power did not seem to be due to his moustache because he later shaved it yet managed to imprison Dr. Mossaddegh, his prime minister, who had nationalized the oil. He took a firm stance against the Mojahedin who were born underground and were Red and Black by being both Marxist and Islamist.

I got to know Iraj, the brother of Arkani, during the year of my voluntary internship in the Rooz-beh mental hospital. I was in the fifth year of medical school, which is not the official year for internship. Because of my interest in the diseases of the mind—or perhaps my lack of interest in the diseases of the body—I had volunteered to work at that hospital a year earlier than my time. I was doing it at night though, so that during the day I could do the things that other students were doing during the fifth year of medicine. And what a good thing I did by doing it prematurely; otherwise I would have not been able to do it had I postponed it for the next year. Because the next year, I had to go to prison and when I came out, my two friends were not in that hospital anymore.

Curiously, I've heard that Iraj, after quitting politics, left Iran to go to America to become a pathologist, never to return.

The leaders of the Tudeh Party were captured, tried and imprisoned from three to fifteen years, according to their importance. Colonel Bozorg Omid, as I have said before, was the only judge that had voted not guilty, but he was in the minority. It would take about three years before Khosrow Pouria, our revolutionary relative who was in the air force, could free them from prison and send them out of Iran, mainly to the Eastern European countries.

Arkani was sentenced to life in prison and was sent to the almost uninhabited Khark Island in the Persian Gulf where there were a few donkeys and fewer donkey men, and occasional sheep. He was pardoned after about ten years because even if it were true that he had introduced the assailant to the Tudeh Party, he had not asked him to assassinate the Shah. When he came out, Massoud invited him to his house to tell us how he had spent his time on that island. He had passed most of his time by trying to translate the *Encyclopedia Britannica* into Farsi. He was not bitter about what had happened to him.

Being miraculously saved from death, the Shah's religious conviction strengthened and, to show his appreciation, he ordered changed the old covering of the shrine of Hazrateh Reza in Mashad to expensive green velvet and went to Mashad as a pilgrim to express his thanks.

When the Shah felt that he had brought his country to its fullest potential and his enemies to their weakest level, he threw a big party at the ruins of Persepolis and invited the dignitaries of the world and housed them in the luxurious tents that he had ordered from France and fed them food that was made by French chefs. The location of that party was deliberately chosen to remind the world of the first king of Persia that had established the Persian Empire 2500 years earlier. And since he was not officially crowned during the tumultuous time when he became a Shah after his father was exiled from Iran by the Allied forces, he made use of that party to crown himself. And, like Napoleon, rather than waiting for the top religious man of the country to crown him, he put the heavy Kiani crown on his head with his own hands.

Because of his big projects, many Iranians had accused the Shah of becoming megalo-maniac. Even if this accusation were true, his throwing a big party could not be counted as a symptom of that malady, because throwing large parties, disproportional to the income of the host, is an innate habit of any genuine, guest-loving Iranian, whether rich as a Shah or poor as a Gueda. This is why when the party was over and the criticisms regarding his over spending had begun, the Shah had replied, "What did you expect me to feed my guests? Bread and radishes?"

In 1964, when a short-lived rebellion took place in Tehran, led by some religious leaders, including one by the name of Khomeini who was not yet an ayatollah, the Shah crushed the rebellion and imprisoned its leaders. Immediately after his imprisonment, to save the life of Mr. Khomeini, the top religious men of the country elevated him to the high level of ayatollah, because it would be an enormous sin to kill an ayatollah. The Shah went to prison to ask him personally why he, being a *Seyyed*, meaning from the decadents of the peace-loving Prophet Mohammad (Salutation), was such a non-compromising warrior. Ayatollah Khomeini, while remaining in sitting position, in his cell, replied, "Because I am a Hassani *Seyyed*, rather than a Hosseini one." Apparently between the two grandsons of the Prophet, Imam Hassan and Imam Hossein, the former was a warrior and the latter a more peace-loving person. This is why, when Imam Hossein was martyred with his family, in Karbela, his death made the Shi'eh Moslems of Iran and the rest of the world, weep for him for centuries. So, the Shah, rather than making a martyr out of Ayatollah Khomeini, ordered him to be exiled to neighbouring Iraq.

Around 1978, when the followers of Mossaddegh and the remnant of the Tudeh party as well as most of the religious mass of Iran rebelled against the Shah and monarchy, the Shah asked Saddam Hossein to send Ayatollah Khomeini out of Najaf to somewhere farther away from Iran so that he could not influence the evolving revolution any further. Only two countries were ready to accept Ayatollah Khomeini; one was perhaps Kuwait; the other was France, for sure. Once in France, the media discovered the charismatic leader and from that moment onward Ayatollah Khomeini gained every drop of prestige that the Shah was losing.

And the rest, as they say, is history.

Everything that the Shah did was, of course, approved by the two parliaments the members of which were either chosen by him or elected by fraud elections. The Shah was supposed to be a non-interfering and non responsible figure head, but he did not behave like that. And since, whether rightly or wrongly, he took credit for every positive event that happened in the country during his time, he should not have been upset when the negative events were also attributed to him.

That is perhaps why the last time I saw the Shah, he was not too upset. He was just a little sarcastic. I saw him on television. He was in a comfortable civilian suit composed of a white striped shirt and a pair of nicely ironed trousers, wearing thick-framed spectacles. He was sitting beside a small aquarium in his luxurious living room, in an apartment in New York. Farah, his wife, looking as good and as simple as in her pictures, had made their dinner ready in the dining room, was calling him to come for dinner. When her husband did not leave the fish and kept feeding them, Farah repeated her calling and added, "Don't feed them so much; they have been fed before. They are satiated."

"No, they are not," said the Shah, with more sadness in his voice than firmness. "If they were, they would have shouted, 'Death to the Shah,'" referring to the fact that the Iranian revolution, unlike any other revolution in the world, happened at the time when the country was in good economic shape, and there were fewer hungry people there than ever before, and the slogan of the revolutionaries was "Death to the Shah."

34

UNDER THE KORSI OF SIAVOSH KASRAEI, PEN NAME KOWLI

Years passed until the bird of love

Sang on the twigs of my fingers

Kowli

HAVING SEEN SEVERAL LEATHER-BOUND DIVANS of the ancient Persian poets that belonged to our father, some of which were partially eroded by rodents, I asked my mother if our father was a poet too. She said, no, but he mixed with them.

I must have inherited some of the mixing genes of my father, because one day, as I was walking with Massoud in the vacant streets of Tehran, I suggested to him that rather than walking aimlessly in the streets, we should go to Kowli's house, even though neither of us was close enough to him to go to his house without an invitation.

Massoud did not like my suggestion. He thought Kowli was not poetic enough to appreciate our presence. Massoud differentiated between a poet and a poetic person. "No, let us go to a tavern instead," he said. "Besides, one always has to have an intelligent remark or a deep literary comment ready in one's pocket, when one goes there, neither of which I possess today."

At the fork of the road we separated. I went to Kowli's house and he went to a nameless underground tavern. Massoud was the reverse of Kowli, in the sense that he was not a poet but behaved poetically and drank uncontrollably, while Kowli was a poet but never drank in excess. In fact, Massoud had noted that Kowli was more interested in taking vitamin C regularly than alcohol.

Massoud had many excuses to drink; one of them was the following lines from Hafez.

Why drink the elixir of sorrow?

Out of the wrinkled hands of this old mean Saaghi

Why not wine?

It is a pity to disturb the tranquility of a knowing heart

By the recurrent waves of anxiety generating thoughts.

As I was walking towards Kowli's house, I was thinking of more reasons why Massoud considered him non-poetic. Perhaps it was due to the fact that Kowli was always well-dressed and well-shaven and wore a well-trimmed moustache, instead of dressing carelessly and keeping his hair unkempt as was the hallmark of the poetic people.

I knocked, using the crescent-shaped knocker at their old-fashion wooden door that was studded with two rows of gigantic hobnails, waiting for it to open. It was a sunken door. It looked like the door of a tavern or a rustic mosque. In a minute, a well-instructed young maid opened the door. I asked if Siavosh was home. She acknowledged that he was but did not invite me in right away. She went in to announce my arrival, then came back and invited me in. I concluded that she had been instructed not to let anybody in before making sure who the person was. The brother of Kowli, Iraj, who was in prison with us, was not yet pardoned, and police were perhaps watching their house for more hidden members of the outlawed Tudeh Party. And Kowli, even though he was never a registered member of the Tudeh Party, was constantly under the watchful eye of SAVAK because of his revolutionary poems.

The weather was not too cold. It was not winter yet. It was probably the autumn season judging by the occasional fallen yellow leaves that had problems sliding on the cobblestone floor of their street, but Kowli had put their *Korsi* in the middle of the room, already. Their *Korsi*, like any other *Korsi* that I had seen in my life, was much smaller than our rectangular *Korsi* in the children's room in my mother's house. Four men in their street suits had occupied each side of the square *Korsi*. Kowli was sitting on the side of the *Korsi* farthest away from the entrance door. Opposite him was a mature man with soothing voice and thick lips who was introduced to me as Ezzat Rastegar. The left side was occupied by an older man who was Ezzat's father. The right side of the *Korsi* was occupied by a well-built thin man who was introduced to me as the one who had translated many literary books with political overtone, under the pen name, Beh Azeen. I recognized the name because he was lately publishing a semi political semi-literary monthly magazine by the name of *The Book of the*

Month, and, to my chagrin, it was closed by the secret service that carried the well-known acronym of SAVAK. In the last issue of that magazine Beh Azin had given the reason for its closure as this, "The tenderness of the heart (of SAVAK) is such that one cannot (even) whisper a prayer."

There appeared to be more room beside him than any of the other three who had offered to share their side with me. So I sat beside him. He was not a talkative man. As he was listening to others discussion, he was busy peeling an orange very carefully and cleanly, expertly removing even those tasteless cottony strands from its exposed surface using only one hand and a dull fruit knife. When he finished peeling, he offered a piece of the orange to everybody around, before having some himself. When my turn came and I attempted to take a wedge, a large chunk came to my hand, but rather than manipulating it to take out only one piece, I put the whole piece in my mouth. My piece was bigger than the share of everybody else including that of the peeler. I did not think much of it and did not feel ashamed about it either until later when he was gone and I learned that he had only one arm.

"What happened to his other arm?" I asked with shame.

"Lost it when he was in the air force."

"In a war?"

"No, during a practice run."

After that incident he had to leave the air force and, because his French was good, he had begun translation from French to Farsi for a living. When I expressed my regrets for having thanklessly consumed what he had so painstakingly prepared, I was told that I had inadvertently done the right thing and he probably had appreciated it more than if I had done otherwise, since he did not wish to be regarded with pity.

When Ezzat heard my family name during the introductions, he immediately asked if I knew a Dr. Shojania whose wife was named Afsar and had a village beyond Karaj.

"He is my oldest brother," I said in a neutral tone, not knowing whether I would get credit for that close relation or blame, because, even though my step-brother had many political friends, none of them had any sympathy or connection with the left-wing parties.

"He is a *maître* in bridge." Ezzat used the French equivalent of master about my step-brother. They had been playing bridge with each other for years.

I was relieved.

Siavosh was in the middle of composing his version of *Arash the Archer* and the samples he was reading sounded better and more professional than the one composed by my childhood friend, Arsalan Pouria. When Arsalan joined the Youth Organization of the Tudeh Party he was the youngest revolutionary in Iran, and, when he got shot in the liver during one of their early confrontations with the police, he was the first atheist whose blood was shed for his belief among the people I knew.

Arsalan was neither a poet nor poetic. His thin book, *Arash the Archer,* was his first or second book and was written near the end of his revolutionary life. His favourite Persian poet was Ferdowsi and his favourite non-Persian poet was Shakespeare. He had written it partly in prose and partly in verses. Despite being a communist most of his life, near the end he wanted to show his deep-seated patriotic feelings by reviving a forgotten mythical Persian story.

It is a short story. It goes like this. The Iranian army was defeated by the Aniranian army. To humiliate the Iranians further, they were told that the new border of their country would be determined by the place where the arrow of their best archer could land. The Iranians looked around for a long time and finally chose a young man by the name of Arash as their best archer. Arash went to the top of the highest mountain with his bow and arrow and pulled as hard as he could before releasing the arrow. The arrow was found, three days and two nights later, by two men on their galloping horses, having pierced the trunk of an oak tree near the Turkistan border, far beyond the original border of Iran-land. When the jubilant crowd climbed the mountain to thank Arash, neither he nor his dead body could be found. They found only his bow on the spot he was standing. They concluded that Arash must have put everything that he had, including his life, behind that arrow to make it go as far as it did.

Ezzat's father was not one of the princes of Qajar dynasty, but he had been the speechwriter for the last Shah of Qajar. Maybe the passionate speech made in London by the last Shah of Qajar about the Persian oil and why he was reluctant to sign it over to the British Companies was written by him. He too made occasional poems, but did not read any of them that day. Instead, he said something about the cleanliness of the pen of a poet. He said that not only one should avoid using vulgar words in one's writing; one should be careful not to put two good words too close to each other so that when they are read aloud they could sound like a single bad word. And he gave a convincing example of it which would not make sense if I translated it here because it was based on a play on Farsi words. He left before everybody else did, perhaps due to his advanced age. When he was leaving, rather than saying the usual goodbye, he murmured a line from divan of Hafez, "Get out of the tavern, Hafez, when comes the old age."

When I was leaving, I shook hands with everybody including Ezzat. Ezzat shook my hand with special firmness and invited me to a party at their house the next day.

I accepted the invitation with pleasure, but when I looked at the face of Kowli to see his tacit approval, I saw that he was not very happy about the invitation. I concluded that Kowli was going to be there too and was considering me as a potential rival as far as meeting girls was concerned. That was the time that he had not yet found his ideal woman and had not composed his "Bird of Love" that began with this line:

"Years passed before the bird of love sang on the twigs of my fingers."

"I don't know the address of your house, Mr. Rastegar." I called him by his family name without knowing that as of the next day, I would be calling him by his first name for the rest of his or my life.

"Please call me Ezzat," he said, "and my home is right in front of the house of Siavosh. If you recognize his door, you won't be missing mine."

35

DANCING IN THE HOUSE OF EZZAT

EZZAT WAS RIGHT. His house was on the same tortuous street, located in the older part of Tehran, near the Parliament buildings right in front of the sunken door of Siavosh. When I passed by the iron gates of the Parliament, once again I read the circular logo stuck to its front. The logo is made of two words, set in a blue background: *Adleh Mozaffar,* meaning victorious justice. Justice, because the constitutional revolution in Iran had began with a demand for justice. They did not know about the other advantages that could come with having a parliament elected by the people. And *Mozaffar*, meaning victorious, was added to it because the constitutional revolution was victorious. The logo, they say, has other cryptic meanings as well. Numerically, for example, according to the *Abjad* alphabet in which each letter represents a number, these two words translate to denote the date of the success of the constitutional revolution in Iran.

The house of Ezzat was more modern that that of Kowli. It was a one-storey building with flat roof and brick-paved yard. The yard was crowded. I could not tell if the house was small or if he had too many guests. I estimated that there were about forty people there, mostly couples except for Kowli, me and the youngest sister of Ezzat. Taped music was playing in a room with the window wide-open to the courtyard. The yard was warm. I don't know why Kowli had lit the *Korsi* so early in the year. The moon was full and friendly.

Most of Ezzat's friends were more important than I, and each was expert in something that I did not know anything about. And those who were not there were even more important. For example his older brother-in-law, the husband of his oldest sister, the famous Khosrow Rooz-beh, was not there because he was in hiding. He was an ex-captain in the army and an ex-prisoner and one of the more militant members of the central committee of the outlawed Tudeh Party. Also, Ehsan Tabari, the great orator and strategist of the party, was not there because he was outside of Iran, probably in East Germany.

Khosrow Rooz-beh had been outside of Iran, too, but had returned to continue his covert political activities. When Ezzat had asked his militant brother-in-law why he had returned to Iran during those dangerous years, he had replied, "Our party has behaved so awkwardly and cowardly that until the blood of one or two of its leaders does not drip on this land, Iranians will never trust us again."

In the Kasraei house Ezzat was saying that even though Rooz-beh was a communist, he was a man of principle and was not like the Bolsheviks who, for the advancement of their goal were ready to ignore any principle. When he was asked to give an example, Ezzat said that when General Razmara became the prime minister and was thinking about toppling the Shah and becoming a president, he had asked Rooz-beh through a third person to cooperate with him and share the benefits with him after the Shah was no more. Rooz-beh had declined because, not withstanding their common dislike of the Shah, his ideas and that of Razmara were not totally compatible. If he was a Bolshevik type of communist he would have agreed with Razmara and then, after the success of their combined efforts, he would plot against Razmara to become president himself.

When Rooz-beh was a lieutenant in the army, even before becoming involved in politics, he wrote a book titled *Blind Obedience*, criticizing the army that demanded total obedience from the subordinates, and never asking "Why?"

I never read that book but I read his second book that was about the game of chess. I learned more from that book than from my bother Mehdi who had taught us incorrectly from the beginning by transposing the site of the knights and the bishops on the board, right from the start.

A few years after the secret return of Rooz-beh to Iran, a detective—whose picture in the newspaper made him appear like an unassuming and unintelligent opium addict—outsmarted him, discovered his hiding place, captured him, and delivered him to a military court to be tried and quickly executed.

In his defense, Rooz-beh told the military court that he knew he was going to be executed no matter how well he defended himself, but he did not mind it. He looked at his death unemotionally and statistically, reasoning that every year in Tehran hundreds of innocent people die in car accidents. "So, it would be no big tragedy if one more death is added to those accidental deaths," he said. Despite that easy attitude toward death, he took life and any details in it quite seriously. During the last weeks of his life in prison, for example, he had asked his wife to bring him a Parker no. 21 fountain pen. When his wife brought a different kind of fountain pen, probably a better one, like Parker number 51, he sent it back and demanded the pen he had asked for.

Ezzat's other brother-in-law, who was not there for some obscure reason, was no less courageous than Rooz-beh. His father was not there either, but for the obvious reason of advanced age.

Kowli was standing beside me. Just to reassure him that I was not going to be a serious rival to him, I told him that I would never be brave enough to become another brother-in-law for Ezzat. He took comfort in it.

Some men were gathered around a small round table having pistachios with beer and talking about music and poetry. Some were dancing with their wives and occasionally with the wives of the others. Ezzat's wife, Fari, short for Farzaneh, was nervous, running around to see who needed what and what needed cleaning. She danced only once with her husband, and sang a Persian folk song with a well-trained voice. She had been the soloist of the chorus in the Franco-Persane Institute.

A thin, ethereal young woman in a flimsy dress approached me and asked me for the first dance, and danced with me continuously for what seemed to be a long time. She introduced herself as the youngest and the dearest sister of Ezzat. But I, rather than enjoying myself, was worried all the time that I might be upsetting my favourite poet who seemed to be more interested in her than I. She was not weak, but delicate and light. So delicate that I was afraid that if I pressed a little tighter, her bones would break. So light, that I could move her around with the ease of moving a mannequin made of straw. She danced so tightly as if the skeleton of death would appear at any moment to insert itself between us. She was so oblivious of her surrounding as if we were alone in the world and would remain so forever. She was not political or opinionated and was not going to sacrifice her life for freedom, but she talked freely and did not mind if her tastes were different than those of the others. Her idea of beauty, for example, unlike most Iranians who preferred the European kind with blond hair and blue eyes, was the brown beauty of the East Indian women, like that of the female character in the *Blind Owl* by Sadegh Hedayat, who always put the tip of her index finger at the corner of her mouth when she talked.

The music, taped by Ezzat, was coming from the room with the wide-open window. After dancing a few steps together on the square bricks of the pavement in the yard, she led me to the room where the music was coming from. We went, with short dancing steps; no one following us but the moon.

When I bent my head to pass under the clothesline that was stretched across the corner of the yard, she told me that the clothesline always reminded her of the day that she made her mother cry.

"What did you do to your mother?" I asked with surprise. "How can you look so angelic and be so cruel at the same time?"

"I was about six," she began, "sitting beside my mother. She was sewing a dress for me, when it began to rain outside."

"You don't have to add the word outside" I interrupted, "when you are talking about the rain. It is obvious that when it rains it does it on the outside."

She ignored my sarcasm and continued, "My mother sent me to the yard to bring the clothes from the clothesline. I ran to the yard and brought back only my own dress. When she saw me bringing in my own dress only, she became so disappointed with my selfishness that she began to cry."

"Our clothesline, too, once made me ashamed in front of my mother."

"What had you done?"

"Nothing. My mother was pacing the yard as usual and I was playing with a ball. When she saw my underwear on the clothesline, she stopped, looked at it and then looked at me to say, "It is time for you to go to the bathhouse more frequently, once a week rather than every two weeks from now on."

She laughed and pressed her chest to mine tighter than before.

The moon had made use of the large blue bowl of ice water on the window sill to launch itself into the room. When she saw the reflection of the moon in the bowl, she remembered that the night before she had dreamt that the moon had fallen on her lap "like a *Tootak.*"

"What is a *Tootak*?" I asked. "Is it a sort of berry?" She laughed at my ignorance with a tinkling laughter and said, "It is a small bread the shape of the moon when it is neither crescent shape nor perfectly round. It is usually made for peasant children when they are waiting beside the oven while their mother is baking."

"The moon was our servant when we were children in Torbat, playing in our yard."

"How come?" she asked, disappointed.

"Because, wherever we went, it followed us from a respectable distance."

"We too played with the moon," she remembered. "It followed us when we ran away from it. It stopped when we stopped. And it moved away when we walked towards it."

"Maybe the moon is a woman," I said, pretending to have had experience in these matters.

"My friends say that you have already torn the bottom of the world, like the famous womanizer, Don Juan." She told me as her last comment, waiting for my reaction. Ezzat, I concluded, must have told her about my coming to their party and she must have already discussed me with her friends.

"Your friends are wrong," I said. "They must have done it themselves; now they want to hang the torn bottom of the world around my neck."

She laughed with relief.

Ezzat's tape broke and the music stopped. I seized the moment and thanked her for choosing me for the first dance as I pulled her towards the courtyard. She wanted to dance more. I thought it was embarrassing enough to have had the first long dance, and I did not want Siavosh to think that I was stealing his girl.

As I was leading her through the crowd, still talking about art, music and anything else but love, I planted her like a queen on the square bricks of the pavement, somewhere in the vicinity of Siavosh who was standing alone and bored, cracking too many pistachios.

36

HAVING A BAD DAY IN THE ROOZ-BEH MENTAL HOSPITAL

ROOZ-BEH MEANS BETTER-DAY, in Farsi. I had numerous good nights and only one bad day when I was doing my premature internship in that hospital.

That hospital was located at the western side of the See-metri Avenue, opposite of the western end of Monirieh Avenue. It consisted of a rectangular garden with a single row of rooms on the street side for patients and staff. The offices and the wards were separated through the middle by a wide gate and its walkway. The walkway narrowed to continue perpendicular to the rooms until it hit the western wall of the garden. A narrow creek with wrinkled clear water always passed through the midline of the narrowed walkway, emarginated by a ribbon of perennial flowers on each side. The patients' ward was located on the left side of the gate as one entered the hospital, the offices on the right. The interns' room was the first room on the left side where the patients and the wards were located.

The teaching staff consisted of Dr. Reza'ei who was a full professor and had a petite French wife, Dr. Meer Sepassi, an associate professor, with a colourful personality waiting to become a full professor, and Dr. Davidian, an assistant professor, a normal-looking man, difficult to characterize. He was one of the few Armenian doctors among the teaching faculty of the medical school at Tehran University. The other was a professor of chemistry whose Farsi was okay, but sometimes when he was talking about fecal analysis, would mistake feces with fart, saying, for example, "You drip two drops of fart in a test tube, shake it well, then add your reagent to it; it should change colour, if there is occult blood in it."

There were two official interns, Massoud Meer Baha and Iraj Arkani; both were members of the outlawed Tudeh Party. And I was an unofficial intern in military uniform and a covert sympathizer with both of them and their political opinion.

Dr. Reza'ei, having noticed the discrepancies between the humble building of the hospital and the high caliber of the teaching staff, once gave a fund-raising party to collect money to build a new building on the northern side of the garden. The Farsi word for a party is *Mehmaani* because *Mehman* means a guest, but he called his gathering neither a party nor a *Mehmaani*. He coined the new Farsi word of *Shab-chereh* for it, which can be translated to grazing at night. He called it by this name because the party was taking place at night and there was a lot to eat and drink. He collected just enough money to build the foundation of the new building. The concrete foundation was built immediately after that night but it lay there for years like the foundation of an excavated ancient ruin, until it became a decent, multi-layered modern white building. Before the building was erected I once asked him what was the use of the foundation when one could not admit patients to it. He said it was the foundation that was essential; once it was there on the ground and everybody saw it, it would be easy to eventually convince the faculty to finance its completion.

The interns' room was minimally furnished with two springy beds, a wooden table and two chairs. Its floor was tiled. The centre of the floor was a little sunken and it collected water after being cleaned. The interns used the wet patch on the floor as an ash tray when they smoked at nights in their beds.

Unlike the other two professors who were always somewhere else, Dr. Davidian was always in his office. This is why I went to him to ask him to let me work there as an unpaid intern at nights, which he approved without asking too many questions. He asked the orderly to add a plate for my food when he set the table for the interns, and an extra chair. He did not say many interesting things, either medically or non-medically, but he was interested in the unconscious of Iranian people and was looking for an intern to choose it for the title of his or her final thesis that was required before being granted the title of doctor. He was expecting Massoud to do it but Massoud, after thinking about it for a while, decided not to do it due to the extensive research that it required, and wrote his thesis on the interpretation of dreams, instead.

Actually, Massoud wanted to write his thesis on yet another topic, laughter and crying, but he rejected that topic, too, because, "The more I think about it, the more difficult it becomes." I asked if I could have it if he really did not want it. He said, "By all means, go ahead, but there is more to the causes of laughter and crying than a funny joke or the death of a beloved."

At nights I interviewed patients who had recovered or were recovering from their delusions to see how they interpreted their delusional ideas in retrospect. Some nights I played chess with an engineering student who, like me, was in the army, but, unlike me, had two stars on his shoulders instead of one. He was there because of acute schizophrenia. His hand sometimes would stay in the air, above the chessboard, for five minutes or more until I reminded him that it was his turn to move. He would move it as soon as I reminded him, but only to freeze again in another spot. Where would his mind and his thoughts go in those moments of absent-mindedness? God only knows. I can't even tell where the flame of a candle goes when one blows it out, let alone guessing where the mind of a human goes when he appears to be thinking. He did not talk during those moments of immobility, making him look as if he were in deep thoughts. Only once did he say something after a long period of silence, "Give your watch to me," which sounded more like the expression of a trivial wish than the outcome of deep thoughts.

Among the forty or so male patients, there was only one Armenian. I asked Massoud if he knew why he was so quiet. He said because he suffered from chronic schizophrenia. His voluminous body in his tight grey hospital gown, accentuated by his slow motion and lack of emotions, had made him look like a baby elephant, demanding to be touched. When I once touched him on the back of his vast shoulders, to ask for his name, he smiled without telling me his name. It was Massoud who told me that his name was Aram. What a fitting name, I said to Massoud, because Aram meant quiet or slow in Farsi.

Aram is also a common Armenian name, at least in Iran. Even those Armenians whose name was not Aram, somehow managed to use it in their everyday conversation or bring it into their life. A good example of this is my Armenian friend whose name was Edmond. He graduated from the same medical school in Tehran as I did, but a year after me, so he must have been a classmate of Hamid. After graduation he went to Winnipeg, became a professor of physiology, and retired at the age of 65 to write a science fiction book by the name of *Arax* under the pseudonym Aram. I have bought his book but unfortunately have not had time to read it yet. The reason for my reluctance to read his book is the fact that I don't like science fiction books, be they written by friends or strangers. I like either science or fiction, not the combination of the two. To encourage me to read it, he told me the secret that the four letters of the name of the book and the four letters in his pseudonym were reflection of the four basic amino acids that constitute the building blocks of the twisted ladder of a DNA molecule. I might read it after my own book is finished.

Beyond Aram and that military man, I don't remember the faces of the other forty or so patients in the ward. I can roughly estimate there were about six or seven schizophrenics among them, a dozen of what used to be called neurasthenic, perhaps equivalent to what we might call today a nervous breakdown, one or two maniacs, a dozen depressives, and several with no definite diagnosis. Among the latter was a young man who believed he had worms in his head. For treatment there were no effective drugs. The effective psychoactive drugs were not invented yet, or if they were they had not reached that hospital at that time which was the early years of 1950s. For the schizophrenic, the treatment of choice was insulin shock which consisted of injecting insulin subcutaneously with an increasing dose for about a week or ten days until the patient went into a hypoglycemic coma. Once in coma, the patient would sweat a lot. A few minutes after sweating the patient was brought out of coma by slowly injecting a hyperglycemic solution into a vein. The other useful tool available for the depressed and some schizophrenics was electroshock therapy, better known as ECT rather than EST because shock in French is written with C. The ECT was used without anesthetizing the patients. It therefore required at least three people: the doctor to apply the electric shock to the head, and two strong orderlies to hold the patient firmly to the bed so that the violent contraction of the muscles did not break their bones or dislocate their joints.

Having seen the occasional dramatic and beneficial effect of ECT, I asked Massoud why he did not use it for the young man who thought he had worms in his head and one of his ears. "It is easy," I said. "We could give him the shock and when he is coming out of it, I would show him a few mercurochrome stained worms that I will dig out from the garden and stain his ear with the same red stain, and will tell him that he was right, there were worms in his head, but we took them out by surgical incision through his ear." Massoud said that it wouldn't work, but I could go ahead if I was convinced that it would. I went ahead and did it. When the patient came out of confusion induced by ECT, I showed him the worms and told him that he was right all the time, and it was our fault not to have believed him many months earlier when he was hospitalized for it. "Didn't I tell you?" he said triumphantly, "Now, believe me, there are more of them, deep in my brain."

Frontal lobotomy was also available, but it was rarely used.

The women had a similar distribution of mental illness among them as the men, with the addition of post-puerperal depression. I remember the face of one of the female patients, a forty-year-old woman with uncombed hair and several cigarette holders in her hand. She suffered from two severe obsessions: one, when she had to pass through an open door, the other when someone passed in front of her when she was outside. That was why she had to have several half-burnt cigarettes and several cigarette holders ready in her hand because sometimes two or three people passed in front of her and she had to light up several cigarettes in a short time. Her obsessive behaviour regarding passing through an open door was demonstrated by her visible hesitation and multiple unsuccessful attempts, like when normal people prepare themselves to jump over a fire or into an icy cold pool of water, before she could step over the threshold of the door. She was an intelligent and educated woman but it did not show. Her obsessions had paralyzed her. That is why she could not take care of her appearance. Once, when Massoud was showing me her obsession regarding going through doors, to diminish her embarrassment, I turned my gaze away from her. To bring my attention back to the patient, Massoud said, "Regardez!" assuming that the patient did not know any French. The patient however, understood the word, was hurt, and said to Massoud,

"What is there to look at? I am sick, can't you see?" As I have said before, two or three months later, I saw the same patient having come to the office of the same hospital, well dressed with a purse in her hand, requesting a certificate of sanity so that she could go back to her job as a teacher in a high school. When I asked her what had cured her, finally, she said, "a frontal lobotomy." She had no cigarette holders in her hands, and went out of the door of the office and through the gates of the hospital with no hesitation.

Attached to the northern part of the garden was another mental institution for the chronic and incurable cases. That institution was not called *a Beemarestan,* Farsi for hospital, meaning the place to cure the sick. It was called *a Teemarestan*, Farsi for the place to care and manage the insane. For the public it was known as *Divaneh Khaneh*, meaning the house for the fools and the crazy. That institution was connected to the Rooz-beh hospital through a locked door.

Once, when Iraj and I were walking along the ribbon of flower bed along the central creek, he deviated towards that door and, with the key that he had somehow obtained, he opened the door and went in, followed by me. Once there, away from the group of scantily dressed inmates, he spotted a middle-aged man who was walking alone along a gravel path with no flower beds. To my surprise, Iraj asked for his name. The inmate stood at attention like a subordinate military person and said his first and second names in quick succession. I have forgotten his first name but not his second name, because his second name was the same as the second name of Iraj. When he saw my small, hard-cover black booklet in the pocket of my white gown, he asked if he could have a few pages of it to write something because he had not talked to anybody for years, and he thought he might at least write a few words on them. I cut out the few pages on which I had made note of a few pearls of wisdom that I had learned in that hospital and gave him my entire booklet. He appreciated it a lot and thanked me profusely for it.

Coming out, I asked Iraj if it was just a coincidence that he and the patient had the same family name. He said it was no coincidence. The patient was his cousin.

Years later, after I had come out of prison and had done my two years of out-of-the-capital practise, a friend of mine whom I had met in Dorood asked me if I could use my influence to admit his younger brother who was suffering from chronic schizophrenia to the Rooz-beh hospital. I did and they admitted him, but in the adjacent *Teemarestan* rather than in the *Beemarestan*. Two weeks after the admission, when the older brother went to visit his younger brother, he was told that his brother had died. Two months later, when he happened to see me again, he thanked me for my help, but he was sad because of what had happened to his brother. I went to that institution through its formal gates to investigate. There was only one doctor there and one orderly for the fifty inmates. I could not get a straight answer as to the cause of death of that young man who did not have any history of physical illness. As I was going out of the gate to go to police, the cousin of Arkani saw me, recognized me and showed me his booklet in which he had made note of a "tragic death" with no dates, "Last night, a young and well dressed man was added to our group. The inmates asked him for his name, he said, 'Tehrani.' Since none of the inmates were from Tehran, they thought he was an informer and strangled him."

Iraj was not handsome and his head resembled the head of Socrates who was not known for being a handsome man. He was not a smoker or mentally ill, but, like the inmates of the Teemarestan, never refused a cigarette when he was offered one. The first night that I slept in the interns' room, he was talking about everything except psychology or psychiatry. I kept offering him cigarettes to make him talk more. He smoked almost half of the package of my flattened Homa cigarettes, while lying on his bed, throwing the cigarette butts on the wet sunken patch in the middle of the floor. That night he talked about philosophy. All I can now remember from that night is that Aristotle has said that those who craft plays should consider the unity in three spheres: time, place and action.

"Is it true that your brother was a member of Tudeh Party and he was the one who introduced Nasser Fakhraraei to the party to assassinate the Shah?" I asked him on the first possible occasion. He replied to the first part of my question affirmatively, but he denied the second part.

"How does he spend his time on Khark Island?" I asked.

"He is translating an English encyclopedia into Farsi."

"Won't it take a long time to finish?"

"He has time. He is sentenced to life in prison."

Dr. Davidian did not usually socialize with the interns. Nor did he do it with the professors. Only once did he accept Massoud's invitation to go together to Café Naderi, the place of intellectuals and defeated political people. When the next day I asked Massoud how sociable Davidian was, he said that he was normal.

"Did he drink?"

"Yes, but only one glass of wine with dinner."

"Why don't you invite him more often?"

"He seems to have barbed wire around him. You can't get close enough to him to see what is going on behind his mask."

Going for a drink with Massoud was no fun. He drank to get drunk and would never stop by himself. It was always one of his friends who had to make him stop and take him out of the tavern. In the tavern he behaved like Omid, if not the shadow of Omid on the wall of a tavern.

I kept pouring, he kept drinking

He kept pouring, I kept drinking

Until I reached that blissful moment of emptiness

And nothingness

....

And I saw a drunkard repeating and repeating

A famous line of a bad poem

Then he began to cry

The "hegh-hegh" of his cry

Indistinguishable from the "ghah-ghah" of laughter

As far as the purpose of drinking was concerned, however, Massoud followed the old Persian poets, like Hafez or Sa'di, who always asked the Saaghi in their *Ghazals*, "Bring me a large bowl of your brain-removing, thought effacing wine."

The reason those poets advocated wine was not for its taste or its look. It was rather for the following two reasons:

1—Because it was forbidden by the clergies and the religious authorities.

2—Because wine was supposed to diminish or eliminate reason. And reason, they thought, was not a thing that the events of the world were based upon.

Massoud did not like the taste of alcoholic drinks either. His facial features always contracted when he gulped his drink. He used the drink as a drug to escape from his agonizing thoughts, in the same way that he used insulin to induce coma in some of his mental patients.

One day near the end of the year of internship, when all the hospital staff had gone home and the patients were in their rooms, Iraj and I were walking together along the central walkway between the creek and the row of pondering pansies. When he ran out of topics and was about to talk about political matters that I was trying to avoid, I saw a frog jumped from the flower bed into the creek and began to swim against the current. There is a method of swimming in Iran that is named frog-swim due to its resemblance to swimming of frogs. "No human can swim a frog-swim as good as a frog," I commented. Iraj, who was not prone to laughter, burst into hysterical laughter, but when he stopped laughing, rather than telling me how funny I was, he told me, "How ridiculous you are!" as if hurt by not being able to control his emotion.

Massoud was not with us that day, and this was unusual. I did not think much about his absence but Iraj was visibly worried. He knew that Massoud had been arrested for his political views and was in jail, but he did not know how to tell me this secret because I was in the military and could be an informer. Even if I was not an informer, being in the military was enough for him to conclude that I could not be a member of Tudeh Party and therefore could not be trusted to tell me why Massoud was not there. All he told me was that Massoud was caught by police and was in jail. Massoud could have been tried and imprisoned for up to fifteen years, if he did not sign the "repentance letter" in which he was to denounce the Tudeh party. But, again, Iraj kept all this to himself.

Had I known that freedom of Massoud depended on signing that shameful letter, I would have sworn that he would never sign it and would remain in prison until he died. Not only was he an exemplary revolutionary among the medical students, he was always the flag bearer in front of all the marches and demonstrations by the university students of all the faculties in the university campus. Also, he was a Turk, and Turks, whether from Zanjan, Tabriz or from Turkey, were famous for their one-track minds and keeping their word up to their death.

When we reached the western wall of the garden, we turned back. As we did, we saw Massoud entering the gates of the hospital, walking towards us with an unsteady gate. We met where the frog had jumped in the creek a minute ago. We stopped in front him and without us asking any questions he confessed, "Think whatever you wish and laugh as much as you want. I could not play the role of a hero. I am a coward. I signed the damned paper and came out."

"Why did you sign?" I asked as a sort of reflex, despite Iraj's whisper when we were walking towards Massoud that I should not say anything that could make him feel worse.

Massoud simply replied with a disarming phrase that sounded as true as any word coming from the bottom of the heart of any Turk, "To be with you." And by "you" he meant the plural "you," meaning both of us, Iraj and me, rather than just me or Iraj.

He sounded so disappointed with himself that Iraj thought he might commit suicide that night. So we began to console him by saying that it was okay and anybody else in his shoes would have done the same thing.

Again, without us asking, Massoud said that right after coming out of the police station he had bought two half-bottles of vodka and had gone to the washroom of the Mosque of Shah to drink them.

"Why did you buy two halves, instead of one full bottle?" I asked, just to test if he was telling the truth.

"Because it is easier to hide two half bottles in the inner pockets of one's jacket than a single full bottle."

"Fair enough, but why did you go to a sacred place to do such a stupid thing?" I asked. "Why didn't you go to a corner in a public park or at least drink them in the same taxi that brought you here?"

"I wanted to, but the taxi driver wouldn't let me. By that time the taxi happened to be passing in front of the main bazaars not far from the Mosque of Shah. I knew the washrooms of that mosque were famous for their bad smell because they were used as public toilets as well. So, I asked the driver to stop there and wait for me until I came back. I went there, drank the two bottles in standing position, and quickly came back. Do you have any problem with that? You are lucky that you are in the military and don't have to make these destructive decisions."

"I am sorry, Massoud," I said, while pointing to a spot deep in my chest cavity. "You are all right. You are no coward. The coward is me who is hiding a full bottle of wine here without sharing it with my friends."

Massoud fainted and did not hear my confession. Iraj and I carried his unconscious body to the interns' room. Like the schizophrenic in an insulin coma, his unconscious body was heavier than when he was conscious.

"Is consciousness made of anti-matter?" I was asking Arkani as I was helping him carry Massoud's body, "that makes one heavier when one loses it?"

Iraj did not reply to my question. I don't know where his mind had gone.

37

DEATH OF MASSOUD MEER-BAHA: A SHORTCUT TO *FANA*

ONE FRIDAY EVENING I PHONED MASSOUD to tell him that if he was not doing anything I could go to his house to spend the evening together. He said that he had a guest but I was welcome to join them. I asked who his guest was. He said he was a man who works in the National Library in Tehran, helping master Deh-Khoda to finish his Persian encyclopedia.

I went. His rented house was on Safi-Ali-Shah Street where the *Khaneh-Ghah*, meaning the House of Sufis, or the place where the mystics gather. That street was not far from the Parliament where Ezzat lived. Even though it was I who had introduced them, they could see each other more often than I could because of the proximity of their houses. In addition to Ezzat, Massoud was associating with most of his family. In fact, once, after I had married, when I went to see Massoud, I saw the younger sister of Ezzat was there, but I was not sure if she was waiting as a patient or as a friend, or both. It was a small house with five small rooms. In fact, it was the guesthouse of a larger house. Their landlord lived in the main part of the house. Massoud lived with his wife, Ghodsi, and his newborn baby girl, Afsaneh, meaning story or legend, in the living room downstairs, which was also the dining room and guest room. The bedroom and his office, and the waiting room for his office, were upstairs. They could not use the yard, but they could use the porch that extended over the yard from the second floor. Television had recently come to Iran and his landlord had bought a set. Massoud could hear the sound of it but not see its pictures. He considered it a form of torture to hear a television without seeing its picture.

When I arrived, Massoud and his guest were sitting on the porch around a table. There were wedges of cantaloupes, bottles of beer and a bowl of pistachio nuts on the table. His guest, to my surprise, did not look like any of the people he usually associated with, neither in appearance nor regarding the topics he was talking about. He was a slender, quiet young man with small black moustache without a beard, in clergy attire composed of a narrow white turban and a black see-through cloak. He was neither drinking nor eating, but did not mind if Massoud or I drank. He was a soft-spoken, unassuming man. Right after me one of the relatives of Massoud dropped in and talked all the time before he left. Massoud apologized to his guest on behalf of his relative, for his excessive talk. His guest did not seem to have minded it. When Massoud repeated his apology to extract some reaction from his guest, his guest proved to be very understanding and fault-covering, rather than the fault-seeking type. He just said, "Some are lucky to have a good memory," attributing his excessive talk to his ability to remember.

After the relative of Massoud left, they resumed the topic they were discussing before the interruption. They were talking about the following lines from the book of Mathnavi.

If you know the whereabouts of my beloved

Let me know

If you have the slightest information regarding where she could be

Let me know

Death, I know, but if you know any shorter way

Let me know

Massoud asked his guest—Mr. Ha'eri—to clarify the poem, especially what Rumi meant by seeing his beloved after death. His guest reluctantly explained that perhaps death in this poem refers to death of self which is apparently the last stage of enlightenment known as *Fana* in the vocabulary of Sufis. It is a kind of nothingness or annihilation, not unlike the Nirvana of Buddha.

"How could there be any shorter way than dying then," Massoud asked, "as there is no shorter way than a straight way between two points?"

"Rumi knows that," Mr. Ha'eri explained, "With his question, Rumi wants to teach the reader that indeed there is no other way than getting rid of the self, if one wants to reach the blissful state of *Fana*."

In those days, Massoud's life was relatively organized. It is true that in the next summer when his landlord left his house for a summer vacation and let Massoud use his basement, Massoud would take his mattress to that cool basement and spent the entire weekend there, drinking with minimal eating. But on the first day of the next working week he would take a cleansing shower and would go to the university to teach psychiatry to the undergraduates in the university and see patients in Rooz-beh Hospital and see his private patients in his office. For teaching, unlike some professors, he never used the same notes, every year. He always kept up to date regarding his teaching. He never missed a day of work because of his binge drinking. Then his younger brother, who was also a Tudehi and was a dentist, developed schizophrenia and committed suicide. His suicide did not bother him as much as when he was diagnosed with that devastating disease. To use his own words from one of his letters, "To a psychiatrist such as me, the worst thing that could happen is to hear that his beloved brother has come down with paranoid schizophrenia, and suspect me as being a covert member of SAVAK, about to reveal his political tendencies."

And for me, the worst thing that could happen was to see Massoud, my mentor and my best friend, to come down with such a behavioural problem that had no name in the textbooks of psychiatry, but terminated with his death.

Let me review some of his abnormal behaviours in the hope of finding a posthumous name for his malady.

His habit of binge drinking we know, so let us go into his relation with women, because not only Freud has said one should look for repressed sexual desires to find the cause of neurosis, Napoleon has said "look for a woman" if you want to solve a crime.

His relations with women were paradoxical. He respected women firstly due to his upbringing in a house with a wise mother and two wiser sisters, and secondly, due to the teaching of the Tudeh Party, that women were equal to men, but he was against wives and marriage. He was the first among his friends to get married. He had married the sister of one of his friends in the medical school before graduation. Once, when sober, he told me, "Nasser, don't marry anybody, even if she happened to be my sister." Perhaps this was due to the fact that he had married too early, before having enough experience with women. His anti-marriage comments were always associated with a sense of humour. Some nights, for example, when the tavern in which he was drinking was about to close and the waiters were preparing for closing by putting the chairs upside down on the tables, and his friends were pleading with him to go home, he would say, "Don't take me home, I confess whatever you want to hear," as if going home to his wife was a kind of torture. Yet, he missed his wife if he did not see her for two or three days.

Once, when he had come to the little city of Dorood where I was doing my two years of compulsory out-of-capital medical practise, to stay with me for a few days, on the second night, as we were sitting in the guest room, having finished all we had to say to each other, as he was looking at the entrance door of the room, he said, "I don't mind if that door suddenly opened and Ghodsi came in." And Ghodsi was an educated woman with a PhD in education. Once, when his wife attempted suicide with sleeping pills in one of the rooms upstairs in their house, after seeing her semi-comatose body, Massoud carried her downstairs to ask for help. In the middle of the stairs his knees buckled under her weight. His wife recovered but Massoud never forgot the shock that was severe enough to bend his knee.

"There is only one thing good about marriage," Massoud once confessed.

"What is that?"

"When, in winter nights, she hugs one's back in bed."

Massoud's views on marriage were probably responsible for postponing the marriage of his friends, collectively, for at least fifty years.

He was not a womanizer and unlike many Iranian husbands, did not have any extra marital affairs. Some nights, however, near the end, when he was very drunk, he would glance romantically at one particular bar girl who had an angelic face. Based on this, once, while his wife was in France, some of his suspicious friends who thought he was playing the role of unhappy rather than being truly unhappy, just to see if he would ever confess to having had a good time, decided to make his dream come true and housed him and the bar girl in the vacated house of one of our friends, Kamal, to sleep there over night.

The next Friday night we asked him if that night had fulfilled his dream.

"Not at all," he said.

"Why Massoud?" we all asked, disappointed. "What was lacking?"

"When she took her dress off, her body was studded with numerous healed scars of old stab wounds."

"Did you do anything for the incision that was not healed?" one of the surgically oriented friends asked.

"Her naked figure," Massoud replied sadly, "was more pathetic than the nude women in the paintings of Vincent Van Gogh."

Massoud's condition deteriorated through the years that I was there, requiring hospitalization either in ordinary hospitals due to aspiration of his gastric contents into his lungs secondary to mixing his drinks with sleeping pills, or in mental hospitals among the agitated patients. While I was there, with the help of my most normal friend, Dr. Azeem Vahab Zadeh, we did our best to bring him out of what could be a manifestation of depression. The last thing we did to him after obtaining his oral consent was subjecting him to electroshock. He was not hopeful though that it would work. He said first of all it would not be indicated in his condition and secondly, if it were to work, it would be after a course of seven or eight sessions, not just one. We insisted to try it once and continue if it had the slightest benefit. He reluctantly agreed.

We did not do it in the Hospital for Insured Workers where we three worked—Massoud being the head of its Psychiatric Department. We took the ECT machine to my apartment on the roof of the Zahabian building in Shemiran and did it there. Beside the patient, as I have said before, the minimum number of men required to apply electroshock is three, two for holding the patient tightly on the bed so that the violent contractions of muscles did not dislocate a joint or fracture a bone, and the third to apply the shock by pressing the button on the machine while holding the two wet electrodes to the sides of the patient's head. A minute or less after the shock, Massoud woke up to complain that his spine was hurting because we had not held him tightly enough. No change in his mental status.

Then I left Iran and went to Winnipeg and was in touch with Massoud through letters. Two to three years later, in 1967 to be exact, the letters stopped and a few months later I received a book about psychology by Jung, translated by Massoud, sent by his wife. The handwritten dedication on the upper corner of its first blank page read like this:

Dear Dr. Shojania,

Here is the last souvenir of Massoud. I am sending it to you who were his most precious and dearest friend. I hope you will value his memory and his souvenir.

Ghodsi Sadeghi
Summer of 1967

The book is translated with such an obsessive accuracy and fidelity that it interferes with reading and understanding. The only paragraph that is not a translation and therefore is easy to understand is the following disclaimer on the first page by Massoud.

Turning this book into Farsi is by no means an indication of its uncritical acceptance or a sign of some sectarian tendencies by the translator. Also, in this ever-changing world, I believe that tenacious adherence to any opinion is far from a sane mind.

M. M.

On the next page, there is an introduction by his friend and psychiatrist colleague, Dr. Sa'edi, who is also a well-known writer and has intransigent leftist political tendencies. The introduction is preceded by the following quotation form Attar. (Attar was the mystic poet in Neyshaboor who saw Rumi at that age of 12—when he and his father and 300 followers of his father were running away from the advancing troops of Changeez khan towards Baghdad to go to Anatolia or today's Turkey—and told his father that the fame of his son would one day spread to the entire world.) This is the poem:

Those who, in Fana, live through each other

Die and live a thousand times per day:

They die at every moment with a new pain

They come back to life with every breath.

Attar

After the above quotation, Sa'edi writes:

"This book is being published at the time that the face of its translator, along with similar victims like him—victims of a crime that only his close friends knew—is covered by a mask of *Khaak*."

"The short life of Dr. Massoud Meer Baha can be divided into two different periods separated by the day, fifteen years ago, when he put his signature at the bottom of a page containing his repentance for belonging to the Tudeh Party. A signature that resulted in an accusation of treason from castrated intellectuals who did the same thing only a few years later, and became involved in running the wheels of the government they were fighting against."

"The first period of his life, witnessed by those who were close to him, was accompanied by enthusiasm and excitement and writing poetry and prose. At this time he was devoid of the hopelessness and empty feelings that were the main components of his second period. It was in the beginning of this second period that he had found his refuge in psychology and was pursuing it with much interest and obsession."

"But Dr. Meer Baha was not a man to be satisfied with life of "doctoring." He needed something else. He detested the uselessness which had caught up with him and many like him. There was no way he could get on with the anemic environment that surrounded him and it was this very "not getting along" that made him more and more isolated."

"In the last few days of his life he was totally alone, without the ineffective advice of his friends or the useless prescription of his colleagues. Dr. Meer Baha had reached the point that nothing could interest him in life anymore. He had lost everything and had reached the bottom of that dark emptiness that made him end his life by swallowing two vials of Tuinal sleeping capsules. Insomnia had made his days and nights alike: falling, rising and taking refuge in more sleeping pills. Nevertheless, even in these days, he did not feel free. His job alone did not satisfy him. He never put his books aside, even for a minute. Even in the worst hours of his life he talked about what he had read. It was this contrast in his behaviour that made some of his friends accuse him of mimicry and imitation: imitation of hopelessness, imitation of nihilism. But if everything in him was an imitation, it cannot be denied that his suicide was authentic."

"This book is the last of his works as well as the first to open the works of Jung to Farsi readers. More important works were expected from him, had he lived a few years longer. Like thousands of others in the last ten to twenty years, he became the victim of aimlessness and uselessness."

Signed, Gholam Hossein Sa'edi

To further introduce Massoud, in addition to the above, Sa'edi quotes him from the personal letters exchanged between them. Though not a suicide note, the following is written close to the time of his death.

"I, with the rather deep insight that I have towards my past, present and future, have no apology to make to anyone....I, like any human being, have limited patience. For this reason I am not able to continue living in an environment in which its thinking majority considers me insane. It is true that I am extremely sensitive and sometimes affective imbalance gets hold of my collar, but I am still in possession of sufficient amount of intelligence and insight to be able to manage the unchallenging life of a civil servant....I am rebelling against no one but myself. I have neither the right nor the power to do so. I have no extra or outside power, nor do I have the patience to tolerate. And if—assuming the impossible—I were to be tried for what I have done, I am sure, due to the events of my past, the jury's verdict would not be in my favour....At this moment in my life, I believe that at least *Mohebbat* (love) is the *Shah-fanar* (the main shock absorber) of life, especially living."

"Therefore, for someone such as me, and for the continuation of "tilt-but-don't-spill" type of work in the hospitals, university titles are not necessary. It has been years since I have put those ambitions aside."

I'm now sorry that I have thrown out Massoud's letters to me. I had kept them for the ten years that I was in Winnipeg, and for a few years here in Victoria, but one day, when I was in a positive mood and the pathological thoughts carried over from Iran were leaving me, I discarded them. Now I regret my action. I want to compare them with the letters he had written to Sa'di. Even though I have destroyed those letters I have not forgotten the salient features of them, particularly a line in one of his last letters when he had been released from his last mental hospital, the one near the city of Ray, which is for the very agitated and hard to handle patients. He wrote, "Despite all the humiliations and sufferings that I have gone through, I am not ready to exchange myself with anybody, including you."

Once, when I had come back from Dorood, I told Massoud that I had enjoyed his confessional letters and the truth that they contained. He said, "Ignore the written words. As far as confession is concerned, only the spoken words are true." I was shocked to here that, but when I thought about it for a few seconds I realized that he was right. Not only in his case, but in anybody else's, the spoken words are truer than the written ones. This is perhaps because spoken words are ephemeral and are often told confidentially to a friend, but written words, especially the printed words, can be read by anybody and at any time; therefore a lot of thoughts get into them before being committed to paper. And to the extent that thought gets into them, their sincerity diminishes. These confessions of Massoud can also help reconcile the discrepancies between his letters to me and those to Dr. Sa'edi. Either Sa'edi chose those letters in his introduction that fitted his own political views, or Massoud wrote to him about the topics he knew Sa'edi was interested in reading.

What is even truer than his oral words are the actions of Massoud. Except for himself, he did not harm anybody with his actions. His last action, I think, was not a suicide. It was his book which was the translation of the book of a psychologist who was one step above Freud on the ladder of human ascent. Freud was not wrong, but his psychology was limited, reducing mankind to a predominantly a sexual being. Jung does not deny the sexual nature of man, but he thinks man is more than that. He brings in the collective unconscious of human being and the concept of archetype. When Massoud says his translation of that book should not be considered as his total acceptance of Jung, it is because he knows that when a newer theory comes to explain better the complexity of human mind, he would be leaving Jung for the newer one. He does not want to be labeled as a believer in anything, be it political or scientific. His death I believe, like the death of a man climbing a ladder, happened accidentally and on the way up, rather than being intentional or a suicide. Of course he was not afraid of dying because he knew the flowing lines from Rumi.

I died from being an inert matter

I became a plant

I died from being a plant

I became animated like an animal

I died from being an animal

I became human

Then why should I be afraid

That I would diminish if I died again?

But knowing the above does not mean that he committed suicide.

Massoud had never lost his insight. In one of his destroyed letters he wrote to me, "I would have been dead like my younger brother at least ten years earlier if I had not chosen psychiatry as my specialty in medicine."

When I wrote to Ghodsi to thank her for the book I also mentioned that I was sure that Massoud's death was an accidental death, rather than a suicide. She wrote back to thank me for my thanks and particularly for my comment about Massoud's manner of death, "I will keep your letter to show to Afsaneh for when she grows up, in case she wanted to know what happened to her father."

Many years later, in 1998 to be exact, my best friend from Sharaf High School, Abolhassan Khakzad, came to Victoria to see his son, Pirouz, and saw me as well. He had become a petrochemical doctor. In grade nine, as soon as we lost our God, he bought the Farsi translation of the theory of relativity by Einstein. During his stay here, we had more to talk about than he and his son. I read the article about Silo bread for him and he liked it a lot and said that I should write it in Farsi too because Iran has changed so much that most of the things I was talking about in that article do not exist there anymore. He was still interested in the universe and appreciated the little book I had sent to him, *The Tao of Physics*, the name of its author I do not remember now, but I remember he had PhD in physics. Like Massoud, he was on his way up and had put Einstein behind, without refuting him, to reach a more comprehensive theory to unite the universe and its 225 billion galaxies. When I asked if he had seen Massoud near the end of his life he said, "No, but I saw Ezzat." He was reluctant to tell me the rest of his story until I insisted. Then he told me that Ezzat had told him that it was he who had told Massoud that the best way out of the trap he had put himself in was to die.

When Ezzat told him that his best option at that stage of life and at that state of mind was to die, Massoud borrowed 250 *Tuman* from him and went to rent the backroom of a teahouse and drank tea and vodka and ate whatever food the owner of the tea house could give him. He stayed there for about two weeks or until he finished the borrowed money. During that time he finished the translation of *An Introduction to the Psychology of Jung* , by Frida Fordham, and gave it to the owner of the teahouse to give it to Ezzat for publication. Ezzat was to take his money from the sale of the book, and pay the owner of the teahouse what he was owed, and the balance, if any, was to go to his wife.

38

WHAT IS ERFAN?

"MY DEAR NASSER, I am glad that you still remember your Farsi and are interested in matters that have nothing to do with your profession. In your last letter you asked, "What is *Erfan?*" *Erfan*, being a mystical issue, foggy and ill-defined, is a difficult metaphysical matter that is hard to grasp. My reply would be long and vague, the two things that I am sure you won't like. It just happened that I have already, at least partially, replied to your question in my essay "A Look at the Foundations of Persian *Erfan*," in *Sahand Magazine*, volume I, number 4, pages 211-276, published in the summer of 1986 in Paris, of course in Farsi."

I get up from behind the word processor to look through the row of *Sahand Magazines* on the shelf beside the desk. This is a magazine in Farsi the size of an average soft cover book, on the back cover of which is written in English: *A Persian Journal of Political and Literary Study*. Ezzat has been sending them to me as they were being published, free of charge without me even asking for them. Ezzat is one of the main founders. That symbolic mythic bird on the summit of the mountain on the cover of Sahand is designed by him. Many articles in them are written by Ezzat, none of them showing his real name. I recognize many of his pseudonyms; like "Salman" or "Pouria." It is easy to recognize him. He makes sense.

Knowing his style and familiarity with his thoughts, however, do not aid understanding all of his sayings. "Most of the things in that article are said in silence, i.e., between the lines," he says in his explanatory private letter. "They're so hidden that even an intelligent person like you might not see them," emphasizing the convoluted nature of the topic rather than the flatness of the grey matter of my brain.

One of the thinnest *Sahand* jumps into my hand. It is not the one I was looking for. It is number 14, December 1997, or the month of Azar of 1376 by the Iranian calendar. It opens by itself to a page showing a 6x4 centimetre photograph of Ezzat with a wide forehead, thick lips, striped tie and spotty blazer. There is a poem by one of his sisters beside the picture—the sister I have never seen, or perhaps just once. The poem is about the death of her brother. In her eulogy, among the many adjectives that jump out of the page are words like "luminous" and "boiling" or plain "source *of Kherad*." *Kherad* being that rare human quality that is more than knowledge and wisdom put together. She raises Ezzat to the level of *Arefeh Khamoosh*, meaning a silent *Aref*. And *Aref*, of course, is the one who knows *Erfan*, as far as the word is concerned. Or she could be the wife of his other brother-in-law, the engineer—or maybe the doctor, Rahim Sharifi. Dr. Sharifi, too, has written something about Ezzat in this special issue. His eulogy is accurate, but it is more like a documentary or curriculum vitae. It does not open a window or even a key hole into the soul of Ezzat.

Also present in this issue is a short segment by Mohammad Mosheeri about loss of his new friend, Ezzat. On the top of the page he quotes a familiar line from a two-liner.

Ey, deer be-dust-aamadeh! Bass zood berafti!

Meaning: Oh, late-comer! How soon you departed!

This is the same half line that my mother quoted in her first letter after I returned from my three weeks of vacation in Tehran, in the summer of 1977, after being away from her for twelve years.

Since then I've often wanted to remember the other half of it, and I've asked a few of my learned friends, but neither I nor any of them could remember it. I look for it frantically through the article, and I see to my chagrin that Mosheeri, too, has omitted it. Maybe he thinks everybody knows it. I knew it and kept repeating it to myself whenever a friend of mine died here.

After that line Mosheeri begins his eulogy by saying, "The only regret that I have from my past is that I did not get to know Ezzat a little earlier. I got to know him in Paris. I was lucky that, for the last few years of his life, I got to see and hear him almost every day," most likely in the office of *Sahand*. The more I read about the shortness of their acquaintance, the happier I get, not out of jealousy, but out of the realization that I had been with Ezzat more than him. Also, I don't feel I have lost Ezzat forever, because I have kept his letters and he lives in them.

I finally find the issue I was looking for, but I forgot the reason I was looking for it. The underlined paragraphs in another, thicker issue of *Sahand*, however, help me remember the purpose of my search.

Some of them make sense.

"What is *Erfan*? You ask. It is easier to say what is not *Erfan* than what *Erfan* is.

Some say it is the same as *Elm*, Arabic for knowing or being aware of what is happening around you, including what is going on within you and with time and all of its three human dimensions: past, present, and future. But this is not a complete definition."

"Some say it is the same as philosophy, or its Arabic parallel *Hekmat*. When one graduates from science, particularly the science of the body, one gains the title of *Hakeem*. And, after acquiring that title, practitioners can express their opinion in the form of a *Hokm*, meaning a verdict. However, *Hakeem* is restricted to medical specialists who deal with the pains and problems of body, but *Arefs* deal with both the mind and the body, not only those of himself, but also those of others around him. Calling someone a *Hakeem* is equal to calling someone a doctor."

But some say *Erfan* is a *Ravesh,* Farsi for "method" or a way, or "the manner of living one's life." In this sense, it is not something that lends itself to be studied through reading books, particularly books about methodology. Rather, it is a method of *training*, not training oneself, but the method the knower chooses to *train* his disciples. One can try to learn what *Erfan* is by oneself without the guidance of a peer, but the chances of getting lost are great. A guide is recommended, at least at the beginning.

I pick up again the thinner *Sahand* in which Ezzat dies. I see with surprise that Sa'edi too is dead in it. There is an article in this issue under the title of "In Memory of Sa'edi" on page 209. He too was one of its prolific writers. I feel I owe him an apology. I don't know why. Only once did he come up to our house on the rooftop in Shemiran with Massoud. He did not leave an impression that he was pleased to meet me. Maybe he thought I was responsible for Massoud's deterioration. I served him and Massoud vodka and left over cold green Persian stew. I don't know if he drank his drink too quickly or his drink did not go well with the *Ghormeh-sabzi* stew. He got sick and vomited on the terrace. His vomit did not look much different than the swampy stew I had fed them, so I did not expect any apology from him. Nor did I think that I had to apologize to him. Besides, when one is dead one is forgiven regardless of what one has done.

According to the article, Sa'edi died at the age of fifty, outside his native land, in Paris. He never stopped writing and he knew it. He had told his friends, "I bet I will be buried with a blue ballpoint pen in my hand." Many Iranians attended his funeral in Paris. Some felt he was still leaning too much towards the left and some, mainly those on the extreme left, accused him of being too accommodating to the right. "In reality his political views did not define him," the article concludes. "Before anything else, Sa'edi was the servant of literature and culture."

I put down the *Sahand* to look at the letter of Ezzat.

"Perhaps," an underlined sentence in the letter reads, "one can extract the definition of *Erfan* from the following statement.

"Ordinary human beings live in the world so seamlessly as if they are made of the world, but an *Aref* has the ability to be in the world without being made of it. He can pull himself up by his bootstraps and look down to examine the world he is living in."

I interrupt the paragraph to think. No wonder our mother kept shouting from the balcony in our house with the oval pool, "Come out! Come out! And see what you are bathing in." We could not see the turbid waters we were immersed in. Only she could see, and that was mainly because she was standing on a higher level.

"…Man is the only creature that can detach himself or herself from the chain of causality and look at the world in which he resides, and go back to it at will. Man is the only animal who is *Shaa'er* to his world."

For a moment I thought Ezzat had made a mistake by calling every human being a *Shaa'er*, because *Shaa'er* meant a poet and not everybody is a poet. Then I remembered that *Shaa'er* is an Arabic word derived from *Sho'ur*, meaning consciousness, particularly reflective consciousness. This is why every human being can be considered a *Shaa'er* because man can reflect on any thing including his own thoughts. It is not sufficient to define man as a thinking animal because dogs, monkeys and most other animals think, too. What they are incapable of doing is reflecting on their thoughts. No monkey, for example, says to himself, "I wonder why I am so sad today." Similarly, no monkey reflects on the fact that not only he, but all his family, will be dead in the future.

"According to the doctrine of *Noor* (light) there are two kinds of *Aref*," Ezzat repeats himself, forgetting that he had written me this a few letters ago. "Those on the side of brightness who believe one should not abuse the power obtained by knowing (the secret) and those who are on the side of *Zolmat* (darkness) and use the knowledge for their personal gain."

Back to *Sahand*

"Persian *Erfan*, in addition to the philosophy of Plato, has its roots in the ancient, pre-Persian Persia and the Indian *Erfan*. The basic principles of *Erfan* are borrowed from the ancient pre-Persian belief under the name of *Mehr*. *Mehr* is one of the names of the sun and means light. *Mehr* could also mean love or friendship because to be *Mehr-ban* is to be the guardian of friendship created between two human beings. In the tradition of *Mehr* one has to control and guide one's senses. Wishing for too much and suffering its subsequent disappointment is often the result of bad thoughts by those who have not been good guardians of their senses, particularly their sense of vision."

On page 222, I have put a question mark in the margin. I read the paragraph beside it to see if I had questioned the meaning or I had not understood the meaning. It seems to say what a pious *Aref* does or should do.

"Persistence in piety is this: The traveller does not hurt animals and has *Mehr* and sympathy with all living beings. He shuns the things he is not given. He is clean-hearted. He abstains from telling lies and is always at the service of truth. He has his feet on the ground and is trustworthy. He eats once a day. He does not eat at nights. He avoids dancing, shows and plays. He does not accept a flower for his head nor fragrance for his body. He avoids ornaments and the instruments of A*araayesh*. He does not sleep on a high or soft bed and does not accept gold and silver as gifts, nor does he buy them. He avoids tortuous ways, competition, deceit and bribery. He restrains himself from getting into a fight, robbing and thieving. *Aref* does not force his opinion on the others. This is the definition of persistence in piety."

The more I read, the less I understand *Erfan*, particularly less and less about Sufism. There is no mention of Sufis or Sufism in this article. Now I know what Ezzat meant when he said that even smart people like me could not get it at first or even by the tenth reading. I look between the lines to read the things this silent *Aref* has not said. I discover that he has avoided mentioning the word Sufi or Sufism in an article about the roots of Persian *Erfan*. Maybe he does not want to perpetuate the confusion.

I look for one of his private letters, where he is not silent about these matters, letters he has written with his highly readable handwriting, firmly pressed on the legal-sized paper pad with his black ballpoint pen. He must be sitting at the small square table inside his one-room apartment in Paris, while Farzaneh is asleep; the television is on, the tape recorder off. "This universal silence about the difference between Persian *Erfan* versus Islamic Sufism is of the same nature as the silence of the Judeo-Christian thinkers regarding the lumping together of the Persian arts and literature with Arabic art and literature, under the title of Islamic art."

"Even Henry Corbin," Ezzat continues, talking about his most painful problem that chews on his bones worse than his cancer cells that are replacing his marrow, "who is the most independent and the deepest thinker in this matter, and has studied this matter intensely and written a book about the philosophy of light and beliefs of Sohravardi, ignores, or does not sufficiently emphasize this distinction between Persian *Erfan* and Islamic Sufism."

I look at Henry Corbin's book in French about the works and philosophy of the martyred Sohravardi that Dr. Hamedani—my old friend from France, ex-prisoner, and friend of Azeem –has brought for me when he and his wife and their ophthalmologist son came to Victoria to stay with us for a few short nights. In his introduction, Corbin says, "Some people have in their mind that there existed and ancient, pre-Islamic Persians in Persia, and a relatively recent, post-Islamic country named Iran. The fact of the matter is that one can hardly extract Islam out of Persia, nor Persia out of Islam in Iran"—or something close to it. My French being as it is, I do not guarantee that the translation is exactly what Corbin said. All he was trying to say was that all those distinctions between *Erfan* and Sufism are trivial, from the point of view of an outsider.

***

Ezzat stops trying to crack the hard pit of *Erfan* and starts a new paragraph, separated from the previous one by the above triple stars.

"You said you have began reading Plato, and since I have not let go of the skirt of love, I am going to imitate a Platonic symposium for you—and invite Timeh and Fedoras, as well as invoke the memories of Jalaleddin, Hafez, Mansur Hallaj, Sohravardi, and whoever is or was a traveller on the path to love—and if you promise to tear it up and throw it in the trash as soon as you finish it, I will write it down for you on the next page. It is not finished yet. It is not the final version, but I don't think I have enough time to finish it. The stupid spleen is beginning to act up, as you said, after fifteen years. It is growing faster than the spleens of the malaria-stricken patients I used to palpate for my statistical analysis on progression or regression of malaria in Iran. You will make me happy if you did not propagate these hallucinations."

"By the way, I enjoyed your drawing in the middle of your last letter in which you were describing the construction of your house in Saghafi Street, that snaking interlocking line representing the rows of mud bricks, standing upright to get dried in the sunshine. I also enjoyed the poem by the man whose pen-name was Khesht-mal (the one who makes mud-bricks by pressing a chunk of mud with consistency of dough, into a square wooden frame) but his real name you did not remember.

The clay of my body does not fit into this frame

The flames of my rebellious soul extend beyond the limits of this universe.

Since I do not read the *Keyhan* newspaper, I did not see the name of the poet of that line either, otherwise I would have given it to you.

Now get ready to hear my private and confidential version of the delicate phenomenon of love. I hope you keep it to yourself."

The axle of the wheel of time is love and love

The essence of the universe is love and love

Ezzat had put the above line at the top of his letter with regrets that he does not know either the name of the poet nor his pen name. Then he fills two or three legal-sized pages with his poem summarizing what he knows about love from what he had read in books. He annotates his definition by an increasing number of stars, footnotes and endnotes. But since I am not planning to give its Farsi version, and by doing so destroy the poetic thought that it might contain, I might as well incorporate those annotations in my translation, in brackets, or out of brackets, or omit them all together. Once a poem is ruined, it can't get ruined any further.

"These are not poetry. These are the convulsions of a fish fallen on dry land." Ezzat emphasizes once more the unimportance of his poem before beginning

After many days of hesitation I decide to publish the unfinished poem of my friend despite his insistence that I not do so. It is better than the best chapters of my book. Besides, it is not a poem. It is the condensed summary of what his masters and his father have said about love.

Ey Eshgh!

(Oh Love!)

Ey Eshgh! Oh, *sweet ancient legend*

Born to the Prime Wisdom

Of the strangulated Sohravardi

Oh love, the *antidote of Reason!*

Sitting in the heart like a guest

But not any heart!

In vain am I asking what or who you are, oh love.

You are beyond the what-and-how

You are on the outside of the frame of

Space, Time and Nayestan

You are the mysterious core of The Eternal Secret.

In the beginning

Oh, superior song of that limited Universe!

Your name was declared

In Sokhan, (spoken words)

Then the circular world appeared and began to turn.

Now

From the time that this world began to turn till this moment

And in the future

The echo of that initial word

Will resonate in this world

Like the words of Hafez

That repeat themselves

Under the echogenic hollow of this rotating dome

Forever.

From the very first day of Azal onward

Ey Eshgh!

Neither the sky nor the earth

And not even the angels

Could bear your burden

Until

As luck had it

The lot fell on Adam

Oh, yes: The angels are incapable of laughter and tears.

In the horrible hole of darkness

In the ancient fireplace

You are the light and the fire of Zaratushtra

In the cathedral and the church

In the seclusion of contentment and surrender

You are the secret of patience and the mystery of the Cross.

In the fields of irretrievable creed and credence

You are the monastery

The synagogue

The mosque

And the temple of the ornate idols.

In the hidden circle of the friends of Hafez

That Rendeh aafiat-sooz

You are the Shoor, *the* Shaahed, *and the* Sharaab *of the tavern.*

And for the love-stricken

You are a poem

You are the tears of a candle

You are the ashes of the burnt wings of a moth.

Nasser Shojania

In the moisture of spring

You are the fragrance of earth

The arresting smell of rain-sprinkled plains

That brings about the memory of the bygone friends

And the bygone lands

And the bygone days

Singing along the garden alleys

Nocturnal songs

You are the fragrance of the hanging clusters of acacia.

Oh, Love

Hanging from the web of moonlight

Spinning the loose meshwork of sorrow

Within the chest of a fearful, lonely passer-by

You are the complaining cry of a reed,

Plucked from the Nayestan

You are the bubbly fermentation of wine in the khom.

You are the silent song of the inebriated at nights

The telling-silence of rends, Ey Eshgh.

For the free men

Deep in the valleys of poverty

You are the crest of the mountain of Needlessness

Ey Eshgh.

You gave us many cups

Filled with heart's blood

You gave us one Paymaaneh, *filled with wine*

You made me break my Payman: *My promise*

My words

Do not break, for God's sake

Neither our Paymaaneh *nor our* Payman.

"Ey, soul-burning love"

"May your house be in order!"

"Welcome to the ruins of my heart."

As said my own father.

      ***

"With my best regards and wishes for your health and that of your family. By the way, my greetings of *Now-Rooz* to you and your good Mitra and your children who, I am sure, have forgotten the Persian New Year, as well as your parents-in-law, Mr. and Mrs. Khazaei.

Ghorbanat, Ezzat

P. S.

"With the hope that when I receive your next letter, I will still be alive and not kicked out of my room. You won't believe it, Nasser; despite my eagerness to receive a letter from you, I am afraid of the mailman. Anytime he brings me a printed letter or a form to be filled, I think it is a letter from the landlord to evacuate my room, or from the government to leave the country.

Paris, December, 1987"

Ezzat did not know that ten years later he would still be in that room and after that he would be able to remain in France, but in a famous public cemetery.

I warned him once, "Ezzat! Be careful and take care of yourself. Don't let them spill your diluted, hypo-chromic blood on the wine-stained sidewalks of Paris." He listened. No one shot him in the street as he was walking between his rented apartment and *Sahand's* office. He died a natural death beside his only *Parastar* in exile, Farzaneh, his wife and his nurse.

Farzaneh took care of Ezzat the way a rainy night took care of Omid:

Night

This night is one of those rainy nights

One of those sympathetic, doubt-generating and Mehr-*bounding nights*

One of those cooperative weeping nights

Hidden from me

Making me wonder if the tears are for my tonight

Or my tomorrow morning

Waiting beside my bed

Malool *and melancholic*

Weeps the night

I say these things and the tale of the night grows longer.

Silent and Mehr-ban *like a nurse*

Wearing black in advance

Seated beside me, shedding tears

Continues the night ...

As I say these things

M. A. Omid

Tehran; 1341 (1962)

39

TO SURVIVE IS MORE PRODUCTIVE
THAN TO LIVE

"Nasser-jan, your letter written with the broad-tipped reed pen with which you had written your last letter to your mother has reached my hand. I envy the ease with which you write. You don't seem to follow any particular rule or regulation and say whatever your heart desires. My fear of saying the wrong thing prevents me from doing that. This bad habit has been with me since childhood and I think my father had something to do with it."

"I have so much to say and have so little time. This stupid cancer, to compensate for shortening the length of my life, seems to have increased the width and the depth of it. Even my heart beats faster than the time I was free of cancer."

"About my article in *Sahand*, regarding Shah-Nameh of Ferdowsi and Rostam, I did not say that Rostam was a dervish. Rostam was not a dervish, but he passed through the *Haft-khan* (the seven houses) which points, obliquely, to the seven gates or the seven stages of *Mehr*. The graduates of the last stage of *Mehr* are sometimes referred to as *Peer*. The latter is the word that later became one of the chosen words of Hafez. Also, remember the proverbial "seven pairs of iron shoes" and the "seven pairs of iron canes" in Persian stories that the traveller needs if he wants to undertake the long and dangerous road to freedom. The journey is of course internal, but it is externalized so that it can be talked about in the stories. The intended destination of this journey is named Maghsood."

"And *Peer* is what you see frequently in *Divaneh Hafez*; particularly in the form of *Peereh Moghan. Moghan* is the plural of *Mogh*, the elder of the Magi, synonymous with fire-worshippers. Similarly, *Moghaneh* is an adverb derived from *Moghan,* for Magian conduct or manners. Ancient manners, even pre-Islamic, and perhaps before the formation of Persian Empire. This word and a few others like *Rend* and *Kharaabat* (the contracted form of *Kharab-aabad*, a demolished place or ruins in the process of being rebuilt) are the words that differentiate the *Ghazals* of Hafez from those of Sa'di."

The Cambridge scholar A.J. Arberry who has translated (interpreted) the Koran, and knows Hafez, has said that when Hafez, the perfectionist who came about seventy years after Sa'di, matured and began his *Ghazals*, he realized that Sa'di had already elevated the *Ghazals* to its highest level. The only way he could distinguish himself from Sa'di was to invent his own words. Not new words, but old words with new significance. *Rend*, for example, the adjective that Hafez keeps for himself, does not mean the usual meaning of tricky in his *Ghazals*. It means free. Free of everything, including family, religion, *Erfan*, Sufism and "Anything that can acquire the stain of possession" as he says in this line:

I am proud to be the salve of the person who is free

From anything that can acquire the colour of possession.

"By the way, I don't know why I have to tell you this: The other day, as we were sitting and talking in the office of *Sahand*, Hossein Malek made a point about the great treasure of child-like stories that make up the backbone of our cultural memory and how they are ignored by the children of today. 'Today's schools' he says 'are places for training modern slaves to produce homogeneous raw material to be consumed in a global market.'"

"Remind me to once more talk about the *Erfanic* interpretation of Shah Nameh by Shahabeddin Sohravardi. Suffice it to say here that the two arrows that blinded Afraciab, he interprets as not made of the branches of a *Gaz* tree, but from the feathers of the wings of that mythical bird that resides in the Mountain of Ghaaf: *Seemorgh*."

"To talk about the roots of Persian *Erfan*, one has to begin with the *Fereshteh Shenassi* (Angelology) of Mazda and the books of Yasht, as well as several other ancient documents. I have not finished my research yet, but I think it will become something heartwarming for you and whoever is interested in these matters, when I am done."

"Oh, just remembered to give you another piece of good news, Nasser. The last issue of *Sahand* has found its way to Iran and is quickly moving from hand to hand in Tehran."

"Nasser-jan, your *Ruba'ei* or 'prayer' as you named it, about love and hate surprised me."

"You pray:

Oh God, I'm going to make it easy for you

By not asking for too much.

All I am asking for is this:

Instead of giving me the ability to love

Why not removing this hatred out of my chest?"

"I am surprised that a heart like yours which is filled with the purity of *Safa* is contaminated with the leprosy of hatred. Hatred is not good, I agree with you. I once asked my revolutionary brother-in-law, Khosrow Rooz-beh, "This 'sacred hatred' that one hears in "The International Anthem," sounds like the wrong word. If the anthem is about celebration of humanity there should be no room for hatred in it. It should be replaced with 'sacred love.' I do not remember his reply, but I am telling you now that hatred does not suit you."

I did not tell Ezzat that I was not totally sincere in my prayer. What I really wanted was love, but I was too shy to ask for it directly. I asked for lack of hatred. Because I knew that when hatred disappears love would immediately fill its place. I know this because I know nature hates a vacuum.

"I believe completely in your comments and interpretation of the events in Iran. Like you, and unlike many Iranian, I do not interpret the Iranian revolution through conspiracy theory. I think we did it ourselves. An intelligent person like you, even though being in *Ghorbat* (exile), and for a long time, cannot guess wrongly. And believe me, this is my sincere belief, with no *Ta'arof*. As you said, things should be looked at with a pair of reversed binoculars to put them in perspective."

"Your letters are the cure for my cancer. Whether this ridiculous cancer is going to kill me or let me live for a while is immaterial at this moment. I am too busy to think about it."

"Thank you for using your newly acquired skills in palliative care on me. I know death and I know dying is painless, and the reason we tolerate life is because we know it is temporary. But at this moment, I am afraid to say, unlike what you thought; the only two things that I do not think about are old age and death. I do not feel old at all and I do not wish to die now. I have work to do. If you encourage me, if you tell me that I still have some times ahead of me, you would make me happy and I would hang onto my remaining days like a child to the skirts of his mother."

"Nasser, some nights, when I go to bed, late, my heart, like the engine of a car in advance mode, beats so fast and so loud that keeps me awake. What you have asked me to write about requires a stronger man than me. My weight is now down to fifty-five kilograms."

"By the way quote the following lines from Jalaleddin (Rumi) about love to the speaker on your television who diminished love to merely an addiction."

Love is not for the tenderhearted

Or the weak-minded

Love is for the strong

Don't ask anybody about love, but love itself

Love is the cloud that rains pearls

Love, like the nature, the sunset or the sunrise

Is not translatable to a better image

Love is its own translator.

Or this:

The nation of lovers is different than any other nation

The religion and the nation of love is God.

Or to quote Omid who thought love is green in colour:

How high did you take me last night?

To the plain of God and beyond

I don't say that it was fantastic

Or it rained droplets of gold

Or made me swim, wing in wing, with the angels

But tell me really, Oh! shade-grown fragrance

Where did you take me last night?

"You wrote that you think about me and all your other friends, dead or alive, whenever you walk on the pistachio green grass of your backyard and you feel cheated because you are sure that none of your friends think so much about you. Don't be so sure of that."

"I envied you once again when you said you have too much free time and wished that you could give some of it to me. Thank you. I think you have already given it to me by telling me that my cancer is a good one and will let me live at least for fifteen years. Time elongates itself when I talk to you or when I am with you. You said that you have reduced your alcohol consumption to one cup of red wine every Leap Year, and have given up tobacco. Good for you. But the last time you came to Paris, you looked a little too healthy and your cheeks were too shiny. Your face was swollen like Massoud's after a weekend of binge drinking. When I imagine you ten kilograms lighter, I see you more handsome. If you have quit writing because writing makes you crave for cigarettes, I suggest you go back to writing. And if the craving for smoking came back, let it come. Whatever you do, don't quit writing just because you want to live a few years longer. It is better to die a few years earlier than to leave this world without leaving anything behind."

"The last thing that I have to say, Nasser-jan, is that I do not deserve so much praise from you. Of course I feel happy and lucky that I have been able to occupy a little corner in your heart and your memory. Keep that corner for me. I am tired of renting."

Ghorbanat,

Ezzat

Ezzat has filled five legal-sized pages with his words and the words of those he liked, leaving no room for *Salaams*. He had to turn his writing pad sideways to write on its narrow margin the only person he could not omit: "I cannot kiss Mitra from this long distance; so I leave this job to you."

The second and the last time I saw Ezzat was when I went to Paris to see Hormoz Milanian—the son of the late commander of the battleship *Palang* killed by allied forces in World War II in the Persian Gulf—who was teaching linguistics in Paris and driving a taxi. I made use of that visit to meet Ezzat as well. We met in the city rather than his apartment. It was night but there was light all over the intersection except for the pubic-shaped grassless boulevard at one of its four corners. Except for a few yellowing poplar trees and several green wrought-iron benches on one of which a man was drinking wine out of a bottle hidden in a brown bag, there was no one in the boulevard. We sat on one of the benches under the shadow of a tree, looking towards the opening of the Metro on the opposite corner of the intersection.

We spent only a few minutes together, but it seemed like hours. We had nothing more to say to each other. Everything we wanted to say had already been said in our letters. We sat in silence for a while on the bench under the shadow of a tree. Then Ezzat stood up to go home. Right at that moment it began to rain. I wanted to ask him to stay a little longer under the trees until the rain stopped, but I did not. I offered to walk with him to get a taxi together and drop him off at his place, on my way to visit Hormoz. He said I did not need to do that because he was used to the Metro. "France," he said, "has a good underground transportation system."

I watched him crossing the hazardous street. When he reached the black opening of the Metro, he turned to bid me a last good-bye with the wave of his hand. I reciprocated with the wave of my hand but I don't think he saw me under the shade of the trees. He just moved his arm in the air as if saying farewell to the world he was leaving behind before being swallowed by the black opening for the underground. As soon as Ezzat disappeared the following line from Sa'di or perhaps Hafez came to my mind and kept repeating itself, like a broken record, until I reached the tight corridor leading to Hormoz' apartment.

Oh, love-stricken nightingale

You just ask for a little more time

Then the garden shall grow green again

And the red rose will re-appear.

40

LOVE AND SILENCE

——————————————————————

···

···

Last night, I went mad; love saw me and said,

"Here I come; don't yell anymore, don't tear up your shirt,

Don't say a thing."

I am still afraid; afraid of something else, I said

"That 'something else'" he said, "is no more. Don't say a thing."

"From now on," he said, "it will be me who would do the talking; "Whispering the secret in your ears."

"But even then, if you wished to agree,

Except by moving your head up and down, don't say a thing."

"The trip towards the heart is delicate and dangerous

"Only dimly lit by the moon."

"On such a dimly-lit and dangerous road, don't say a thing."

It is incredible! I said, are you an angel or a human?

"Neither an angel nor a human," he said, "Don't say a thing."

Tell me! I said, I am getting upside-down, if not inside-out.

"Be so upside-down or inside-out," he said, "yet don't say a thing."

I am getting confused, I said, whoever you are, tell me.

"Be so confused," he said, "but don't say a thing."

My heart! I said—for the lack of a better term—

Be compassionate, be merciful, be fatherly!

Aren't these the attributes of a fatherly God?

"Oh soul of the father!" he said, "They are so, but don't say a thing."

Jalaleddin (Rumi)

"NASSER JAN, your letter of January 28 reached my hand ten days after you had mailed it. The reason it has taken a hundred days for my letter to reach your hand is that I was looking for the proper time and the right mood to write, as you asked, about the difficult topic of love. Socrates the Great, whenever his discourse went off the track of philosophy and went to the slippery road of love, always asked for forgiveness from love itself. He never knowingly subjected the topic of love to dissection or discussions."

"The poem of Jalaleddin, with which I have begun my letter, is one of the numerous *Ghazals* in his divan that he has named Shams-e-Tabrizi who is his beloved, his master and his everything. Of course a *Ghazal,* whether composed by Rumi or Hafez, does not have a name or a title. I've taken the liberty of giving it a name to emphasize why one cannot talk about love. As you can see it is about the connection between love and silence, but what you probably don't see is that Jalaleddin has composed it to break the silence of Shams. Elsewhere in that divan, Jalaleddin puts the hints aside and frankly pleads with Shams to talk."

Oh King of the men, say something, say something.

Radiating being, say something, say something.

Dispenser of the wine, say something, say something.

Secret of the rose-garden, say something, say something.

You are good at Robaab*; play something, play something.*

You are the sanctuary of my faith; say something, say something.

"I don't know if I have told you this or not. The first time that I read the *Ghazal* about love and silence for Dr. Mahmood Human, he liked it so much that he invited me to their weekly gatherings where they read the *Ghazals* of Rumi with diluted wine and a muted background of sitar music. Dr. Human believed that the atmosphere in which the *Ghazals* of Jalaleddin are read is almost as important as the *Ghazals* themselves."

I know Dr. Human. Ezzat has given his book about Hafez, and his two volumes of the history of philosophy to me when our first son, Kamran, was born.

"I don't know why when anybody whom I know dies, I feel somehow responsible for it. I knew Sohrab, your cousin, distantly, but I did not know Kay, his wife. Nevertheless, when I read the news of her death in your letter, I felt responsible for it."

The letter of Ezzat reached my hand at a very opportune time, when I was pacing our backyard, preparing my speech for the occasion of the death of my mother. Our mailman saw me and instead of putting the letter in our mail box, handed it to me.

I opened my speech with that poem and connected it to my mother, not through love but through her silence. Silence was her most distinguishing sound, if not her signature. I read, of course, the simultaneous translation of it in English, while holding the heavy *Divan of Shams* in my hands rather than from the letter of Ezzat. I did so mainly to show the gravity of the subject. The only thing I read in Farsi was the recurrent words of *Heech Magou*, at the end of each line that meant, "don't say a thing."

After the ceremony, Carina, the living widow of my psychiatrist friend who died of a brain tumour, was chanting the recurrent words in Farsi, as she was climbing the stairs in the hall to reach the dining room where the rest of the guests were already present: *"Heech Magou! Heech Magou! Heech Magou!"* once for each step that she took.

The poem survived the death of my mother and Ezzat. When the good husband of my sister, Monavar, died a few years later, I decorated my condolences with that poem.

Among many friends and relatives who had read that letter, Khosrow Pouria was the one who had replied to it in a letter longer than Ezzat's letter.

I did not know that Khosrow, the first atheist and most tenacious communist in our extended family, if not in Iran, had learned Arabic and was reading the Koran and had become an *Aref* in my absence. His *Erfan*, however, was different than that of Ezzat. In his long enlightening letter Khosrow wrote the whole poem, including the first four lines of it that Ezzat had omitted due its apparent irrelevancy as far as definition of love was concerned.

Unlike Ezzat, Khosrow believes that the poem was addressed to Hessameddin, the man who wrote down the verses of *Mathnavi* as they poured out of the tired throat of Jalaleddin, intoxicated with love. And when Jalaleddin says "I am afraid of something else," that "something else" according to Khosrow's interpretation is the departed Shams. Jalaleddin feels that by channeling his love and attention from Shams to Hessameddin, he is betraying his old love. This is why he is afraid. But, Hessameddin is reassuring him that Shams is gone for good and would never come back and therefore there is no reason to be afraid.

Khosrow wrote that letter about forty years after I had seen him for the last time. And the last time that I saw him, he did not see me because it was through the small window of my prison cell. Even then I could not view him sufficiently because I did not want to bother further the person I was standing on in order to be able to see Khosrow. I was standing on the wide shoulders and the balding head of my co-prisoner, Soheil, an ex-police officer, in prison for the same reason as I.

It was the beginning of our imprisonment and we were two or three in each cell. Soheil and I happened to be occupying one cell. In the two weeks that we were in that room we had already exchanged our short past histories and had nothing more to say to each other. He had recently been married to a university student who was political and pretty at the same time, something that was relatively rare in those days. As we were sitting in our cell I heard loud laughter coming out of the courtyard of the prison. Soheil recognized the laughter and said that it was the laughter of Marzban. I knew Marzban was a friend of Khosrow and the two, along with a third one whose name was probably Ahmadi, were sentenced to be executed in front of a firing squad. They were brought from Khark Island to be with the rest of the military network of the Tudeh party and get executed along with the first series. The three were air force officers and were always together like a tierce in the game of belott. This is why when Soheil said that the laughter belonged to Marzban, I knew Khosrow would be with him. I told Soheil that Khosrow was a relative of mine and I would like to see him. He hooked his hands and offered his shoulders to me to stand on and look through the square window of our cell that was near the ceiling. When I stood on his shoulders, however, I saw to my surprise that Khosrow was not with Marzban. He was walking separately along another wall of the courtyard, far away from Marzban. Later I will learn that Khosrow had *Ghahred* with his friend because unbeknown to him and without prior discussion with him, Marzban had asked the youngest sister of Khosrow to marry him when she reached the legal age of marriage. Marzban and Ahmadi were executed a few weeks after I saw them. Khosrow would have been executed, too, if it was not for the tears of the wife of his Daii and the mediation by General Hedayat.

No, I am wrong. I am sorry. I saw Khosrow once more during the past forty years. It was in the summer of 1977 when I went to Iran for a short vacation for the last time to Mahmood's apartment. Khosrow was pardoned and was freed after being in prison for fifteen years. Mahmood, knowing who among my friends I liked the best, and knowing that I did not have enough time to meet all of them, had invited Khosrow along with Ezzat, Arsalan and Sia.

That day gave me the opportunity to compare and contrast these two *Arefs*, but, as always, I did not make use of that precious moment. The poem of Rumi has provided me with a second opportunity. It would be bad more than twice, if I missed this second opportunity.

41

A LOVE LETTER FOR TWO

2-Ordibehesht -1377

(April 23, 1998)

Tehran, Iran

Dear Nasser, I am writing this letter for two men. I had promised Ezzat to write him a forty-page letter. I had written twelve pages of it—from the years of my childhood as far back as I could remember up to the Shahrivar of 1342 (September of 1963) the year of your marriage—when I heard the news of his death in Paris. Now I owe him 38 [her miscalculation] more pages. I was preparing to go and see him for the last time, but the permission for a visa to France arrived too late and he died. And this year, on the ninth of Farvardin, Farzaneh gave me your address.

The last time I was in Paris with Ezzat, when we reached his home, your letter, opened, was on the table and Ezzat said I could read it if I wanted to and I did. You had written about your son's wedding in Vancouver and the death of your brother, Hamid, in Iran, and that Ezzat should not write the number 1 of the address of your house like number 7 so that the mailman could read your address faster and would not further delay the delivery of his letters to your house. Now that I look at your address I see it has neither number 1 nor number 7. Perhaps your address has changed. I hope this is the right address. Farzaneh said on the phone that after the death of Ezzat you had written her a letter, and sent a copy of some of Ezzat's letters to you, to her and to his daughters, Mahta and Beeta. She now is in possession of things that she does not wish to share with others. But you are not a thing. For me, you and Ezzat are so inseparably combined in my mind that makes me wonder how and when this amalgamation happened. I know your moods and your occasional *Kaj-taabee* (non-cooperation) that prevented one from getting close enough to you. And I know him and his silence, as well as his forgiving and his *Mehr-varzi* and his fascination with love.

What a vast capacity he had in establishing connections between *Ensans* (humans), and how much he loved you! This habit of him always reminded me of *Morteza Keyvan*. And how much he wished to make all the *Aadams* friends with each other! He was a catalyst or a conduit for *Eshgh* to flow in both directions. His heart was like a vast ocean, yet letting the smallest stream to join it. How lucky I am for having had a brother and teacher like him, and how fortunate I am that he had a friend like you.

The month of Ordibehesht of each year reminds me of that very year that I returned from Italy (and met you three years after the night of dancing with you in our house). The Aghaaghi trees (false acacia) were full of yellow flowers and the moon and clouds were in the evening sky. And the yellow canary that I always waited for every afternoon came regularly except for that day in the middle of the Shahrivar when you stopped coming.

Some nights I have nightmares. Did you know that when I heard the news, my only wish was that there were hands that would hold my hands so that I could share my sorrow with someone? My roommate is an uncommunicative *Khodavandegar* (master) and my son, confused, was pacing the room, not knowing what to do. And my hands were alone. They have been alone for years, but they were alone differently on that day. I longed to see … [here a short word is missing due to a droplet of water or tear. I cannot make out if the missing word is him or you. Nor can I tell for sure if she is talking about the death of her brother or the news of my wedding. But having a grown son indicates that the news is a recent one and therefore ought to be about the death of her brother.] But words could not found their way to our lips. Perhaps they would have created more distance if they did. I needed to share feelings the way hands share warmth.

A few nights ago I had a dream in which I was pressing my hands against a glass door to reach a hand behind it. The glass did not break but began to melt over my hand like a glove, preventing me from touching anything directly on the other side with my bare hand. But a light appeared and I thought it must be Ezzat transformed into a shooting star and my brain began to turn inside my head. Then I felt I was in a room the walls of which were made of ice. I could see from below the legs, boots and sticks, as if people were playing hockey on its rooftop. I was frozen stiff. In the morning I could not get up from the bed. All the muscles in my arms, neck and back were stiff.

Sometimes when Sohrab hugs me, it calms me a little.

I asked Farzaneh to send me some of Ezzat's shirts. I used to wear them sometimes. They hug me when I wear them and I warm myself with the smell of love that they contained.

When I was acting the role of the sister in the Greek play named *Antigone*, I often wondered which of my brothers I loved as much as I pretended to love the brother in the play. It was always Ezzat that came to my mind. It is too bad that I did not see him one more time.

I do not see him when I am asleep either. He is in nowhere. He is light. He is flame. He is heat. He burns me from head to toes, yet I cannot see him. Are you sure you have not hidden him somewhere inside you? Tell me the truth. Why is he not even in his pictures?

Nasser, wherever he is, he must be very close to you. I have not seen you either, neither in my dreams nor in my waking hours. When I wake up, I sometimes hear his voice from our last telephone conversation, when he was so weak that he could barely talk.

What can I do? There is drought of love in the world. Thousands of good people die everyday, but no one took love with himself or herself as did Ezzat.

How crude I have become! Where can I find a rain that can wash me, cleanse me, kill me, and bring me back with a new breath? Maybe I am dead. Maybe I am breathing in vain.

I move about in search of him, but do not find him anywhere. He is nowhere, neither in nor out or around me. I am ready to unravel the twisted fabric of the world and whatever there is in it to once again find myself with him the way he had found me. I want to give myself away, *Eessar* myself and die again and again.

His last picture that Farzaneh showed me was that of an *Ensan* who had more love to give than he could afford.

I am talking too much. I am giving you a headache after so many years. Forgive me. I hope you will write to me. Perhaps it will calm me down. There was always something unknowable about you—and still is.

Is it too much if I asked you to send me a copy of some of Ezzat's letters to you?

Signed.

Her signature is illegible, composed of a few long, loose disoriented lines with no polarity. But I am almost certain that it is from Ezzat's youngest sister. The reason I think so is twofold: one is the fact that the sincerity contained in it is similar to the one she was using in her short letters to me during the short time we saw each other. The other reason is the fact that men who were against literacy for women in Iran were predicting that as soon as women learned writing, they would write love letters to strange men. Ezzat's youngest sister fulfills perfectly their prediction. She was very literate and no one but her could write such a love letter for one, let alone for two.

42

FIVE PERSIAN CHARACTERISTICS

SOON AFTER I BEGAN MY FRIENDSHIP WITH FRED KASRAVI—a Canadian man of Iranian origin—this Persian proverb came to my mind, "Either avoid friendship with the elephant-men or build a house to accommodate an elephant."

Like always, I met Fred without looking for him. Mitra was becoming active in politics and was throwing a fund-raising party in our house for the Liberal Party and rheumatology, when the phone rang and a woman from Toronto was asking why the famous friend of the Liberals, Fred Kasravi, who has recently moved from Toronto to Victoria, was not invited. The name sounded half-Persian, so my wife, as she covered the mouth piece of the receiver, asked me if I knew an Iranian by that name.

I said I knew an Ahmad Kasravi in Iran when I was about fifteen years old. He was assassinated by one of the members of Moslem Brotherhood in Tehran while he was de-fending himself in the courthouse. He was a judge himself, but the day he was assassinated he was a defendant. He was being tried for his negative books and comments regarding the Arabic language, religions, and old Persian poets, particularly Hafez. His books and speeches were so blasphemous that even though it was during the secular times of the Shah, he was put on trial to explain.

As Mitra was listening, with one ear stuck to the phone and the other to my irrelevant comments, she pointed with her chin to the computer in the kitchen and said in a whispering voice, "He has a web site that explains everything about him."

Luckily, Anna, the "head-hunter" wife of our first son, Kamran, who is used to seeing the applications of the high power CEOs who want to go to bigger firms, was there and quickly went to Mitra's computer and brought up the page. "Wow, how impressive!" she exclaimed when she saw his picture standing beside gigantic officials, and repeated the same exclamatory remark after she read the summary of his elephantine achievements.

The rest was easy. Mitra phoned and invited him and I met him in the luxurious hotel where the party was taking place and Allen Rock, the health minister, was speaking about the importance of medicine, particularly rheumatology.

Fred looked just the way I had imagined. Only his teeth were slightly whiter and his smile a little wider than I had imagined. Within five minutes we got to know each other as if we had known each other for fifty years. Before Allen Rock finished his speech, Fred suggested that we leave the party and go in his car to see his unfinished garden. His garden was not far from the famous Butchart Gardens and turned out to be no less impressive.

Among the many things that we learned from each other in that twenty-minute drive, I learned that he was the nephew of Ahmad Kasravi. Perhaps no one knew this fact about Fred in Victoria. Those who thought they knew Fred knew him only as a fundraiser. After talking to him, I learned that Fred was much more than that. Nor was he a social climber. If anything, he was a ladder for others to climb up.

The walls of the rooms in his home are covered by framed pictures, showing him with famous people like prime ministers of Canada, the son of the emperor of Japan, or alone, throwing out the first pitch at a Blue Jay's game in Toronto. There are so many pictures that there is no more room on the walls of the rooms in the main part of the building. The picture showing him being knighted by the medal-studded representative of the Queen is on the wall of his garage, low, lower than the eye level, at the level of the headlights of his car. In the same garage, there are posters depicting nostalgic scenes from Iran and significant locations around the world. His library contains collectable books. Among his Farsi books I recognized the thin book of his uncle with his picture on the cover, the same stern, non-smiling pale face with abundant grey hair wearing black tie, white collar, and black jacket. Looking at this picture, it makes the black hole of his assassination re-open in my heart after more than fifty years. How sad and surprised we became when we heard he was assassinated by a man from a group we had never heard before.

Fred's picture with Prime Minister Trudeau is telling. It tells a story that reveals a bad Persian habit. The photograph depicts them face to face, their jackets almost touching. Fred is smiling and pointing with his right index figure to the chest of Mr. Trudeau. Mr. Trudeau's mouth is opened towards the left ear of Fred.

When Fred noticed that I stopped in front of that picture a few seconds longer, he asked if I knew what Mr. Trudeau was telling him at that moment. When I gave up guessing, he said that Mr. Trudeau was telling him, "Fred, let me give you a friendly advice. Never point, particularly with your fingers at anything, especially at another person. In this culture, it will be interpreted as if you are accusing the person you are pointing to of having done something wrong."

His library has twenty times more books than mine, most of which are much more precious. He also has collectable Persian arts and paintings.

Over the mantlepiece there is a large coloured drawing, maybe a water colour painting, of a dervish with *Kashkool* and other paraphernalia of dervish-hood emarginated by slanted lines of Persian poetry, signed by a well-known artist in Toronto. The paucity of colours and the poverty of the background did not match the central position of the painting in his room. I stopped in front of it to find out why it occupied such a central position. Then, I noticed that the face of the dervish was the face of Fred. This discovery, however, did not surprise me. Having learned that the atheist Khosrow Pouria had become an *Aref* and the warrior Rostam of Ferdowsi was on his way to become a dervish, these discoveries did not surprise me anymore. I had learned that dervishs or Sufis do not have a special uniform. It is true that the ancient Sufis had to wear a woolen robe because *Suf* meant wool, but not anymore. One can wear a military uniform and be a dervish. General de Gaulle of France, I've heard, was a Dervish inside, as far as his attitude towards the world was concerned.

Canada has acknowledged the philanthropic qualities of Fred and has shown it by ordering a special coat of arms for him. And Fred seems to appreciate it very much because he uses it everywhere. The large version of it is on the white flag in his garden next to the flag of Canada. The coloured version of it is sewn with golden threads on the upper pocket of his formal jacket. The smaller versions of it, either in multicolour or in pure golden colour, are printed on his visiting cards. He gives the coloured ones to anybody he meets, but the golden one to those who are somehow special. I have not yet printed my own visiting card, but I carry both of Fred's in my wallet among my plastic credit cards.

His coat of arms has two symmetrical maple leaves symbolizing Canada and a comma-shaped peacock feather in the middle as a Persian symbol. The whole thing is set within a shield-like background with a crown on the top and a winged lion with a torch in one hand. Underneath all these there is a wavy white ribbon on which five Persian words are written in Farsi.

When they were making that coat of arms for him, the prime minister of Canada asked Fred to chose five qualities that he thinks best characterize a typical Persian or an Iranian. And those five Farsi words are the ones that Fred has chosen. I had to get my magnifying glass that is also armed with light— another useful gift by Khosrow Mirza, from Mashad— to be able to read those words. They are as follows:

1—*Nezaakat*; meaning good manners. I asked Fred why he didn't choose the better word *Adab* which is shorter and every Iranian schoolboy or girl is familiar with it. He said because *Adab* was Arabic and not a pure Persian word. I was surprised to hear that because we had used that word in our calligraphy classes in Iran so frequently that I thought it was a Farsi word. And *Nezaakat*, on the other hand, sounded quite Arabic because it rhymed with *Sheraafat*, meaning nobility, derived from the Arabic adjective *Sharif*, meaning noble.

I looked it up in my Farsi to English dictionary and I saw that we were both right. *Nezaakat* is an Arabic-looking noun that is derived from the Persian adjective *Naazok*, meaning thin, delicate, or fine. Now that I know the root of *Nezakat* is *Naazok*, the best English rendition of it could be finesse, like the finesse that one uses in the game of bridge.

2—*Forou-tani*, meaning humbleness, a good but rare Persian characteristic. Many Iranians lose their humbleness when they leave their county or when comparing the Arabic and Farsi languages.

3—V*afa-daari*, meaning loyalty, especially towards friends. Fred has this characteristic in the extreme, so much so that if he was forced to choose between truth and a true friend, he would side with the friend even if the friend happened to be on the wrong side of the truth.

4—*Nekou-kaari*, meaning doing good. Fred has been doing good for a long time. In addition to saving the lives of thousands of children in the remote parts of the world through his Christian charity organization, he has saved the life of, maybe, a million horses in France. This is the reason that the Queen Elizabeth II, who also loves children and horses, has made him a knight. This is why in England he can carry the title of Sir, but not in Canada. Canada has eliminated some of the British titles that are reminiscent of colonialism.

When I got to know Fred a little better and found out that he was a knight, I asked him for the explanation and he told me the story of the horses in France. He said, "Many years ago, when I had so much money that money was as valuable to me as paper, I heard that a disease had come to France that was killing many horses and could spread to the rest of the world if it was not stopped. I hired seventy-five veterinary doctors and sent them to France and asked them not to come out until they have found the cause of that disease and the cure for it. They went there and did exactly as I had asked them to do. Most of them did not know who had asked them to do so. Only one of them knew that a Canadian person by the name of Kasravi was paying for the entire project." When the prime minister at that time or the president of France, found out who was behind this gigantic deed, he invited Fred to France to offer him French citizenship. Fred—so uncharacteristic of him—declined it by saying, "Thank you, but I don't think I need this because France has been already receiving me with utmost kindness whenever I have entered it from no matter which entrance door or port." It was after this refusal, perhaps, that the Queen of Great Britain heard about his generosity towards the horses and invited him to England to make him a knight.

I told Fred that he should have accepted the French citizenship, too, because refusing a favour is a very bad thing especially among Iranians, particularly towards the French. They are even more patriotic than Iranians. He agreed and said, "But it happened so many years ago, and I did not want to make it look as if I had done that for my personal gain. Besides,

I had already accepted Canadian citizenship and I thought if I accepted the citizenship of another country, I would have had diluted the importance of my Canadian citizenship."

5—*Shookh-tab'ei*, meaning to have a good sense of humour.

True, Iranians don't take things as seriously as most people of other nations, especially their Arab neighbours. Humour is part of Iranian life. It is needed for their survival. Sometimes it is used as a weapon. During the Islamic revolution, those who did not believe their eyes used humour as a self-defense, albeit ineffectively.

After I saw Fred's pictures beside most important people and the five Farsi words he had chosen on a Canadian coat of arms, I told him, "I don't think you are going to get any more famous than you already are." He laughed and said, "What makes you think so?"

I said, "Because you have already reached the summit of the mountain of fame."

Less than a year after I told him that, the prime minister of Canada, Mr. Jean Chrétien, appointed him the chairman of the Canadian Museum of Nature—perhaps Man and Nature—in Ottawa. Also a few months ago, Royal Roads University in Victoria made him an honourary doctor of laws. Regarding the latter, Fred said, "This title is more important to me than the sum of all my other titles and pictures."

Just two weeks after I met Fred, he came to our house with a famous musician from San Francisco to plan to send tickets for the Philharmonic Orchestra of Moscow, which is composed of one hundred musicians, which was to play in his garden to raise money for charity. That was the time that I translated that Persian proverb regarding friendship with elephant-man for his guest.

Nowadays if you happened to be visiting the garden of Kasravi, please first help yourself to the free refreshments that he has put outside on the walkways but don't ask him who has put them there because if you do, he would point to the sky with his eyes and would say, "I don't know, maybe someone up there." After refreshments, go in the rooms and look at the door of his refrigerator in the kitchen. On that door, among the many overlapping photographs, he has one with me. In that picture we are both in formal black tie; it was taken at the first official party that happened right after we had met each other. I have a glass of red wine in one hand, while Fred, a broad white smile.

I have made the enlarged version of the same picture the wallpaper of my office computer, bragging about him as soon as my colleagues ask for an explanation. I say to them that he is my new friend and if they want to know more about him they should go to his web site.

The only question about Fred that I do not refer to his web site for an answer is the story of his generosity towards the horses in France. I have repeated it so many times that I cannot even guess how many. Many who have listened to it have invariably asked me the same question at the end, "How much did the hiring of those seventy five veterinary doctors and the related expenses add up to in dollars, for your friend?"

This is the same question that I had asked Fred when he first told me the story. "I really don't remember," he answered. "That happened so many years ago when money was like paper to me."

"Is there a Farsi word for what you have done, Fred?" I asked.

"I don't know what you mean," Fred said, somewhat perplexed. "What do you want it for, anyway?"

"For a special coat of arms for you," I said. "I think France owes you a coat of arms too, under which there should be written six Persian characteristics rather than five, thanks to you."

"What would the sixth be?" Fred asked.

"It would be not remembering the cost of one's generosity," I said. "I still remember with bitterness the four thousand dollars we paid to a veterinary doctor in Vancouver to operate on the dislocated back of our dog, Max, a long-haired, long-backed dachshund."

43

AHMAD KASRAVI, A NAY-SAYING PROPHET

UNLIKE THE KNIGHTED FRED KASRAVI, who is the most positive man and whenever you ask him how he is doing, he would invariably reply "never better," his assassinated uncle, Ahmad Kasravi, was the most negative man. He was a literate man, but never wrote any poem. In fact, he was against poetry, especially *Ghazals*, particularly those of Hafez. He wrote several thin books about religion, but he was not a religious man. In fact he was against religion, particularly the organized ones. He was a judge, but was forced to retire early because he was incorruptible. He was a philosopher, but he was against philosophy. The only non-judgmental book he wrote was his thick book, *The History of Constitutional Revolution in Iran.*

Like his nephew, however, Ahmad Kasravi tried hard to avoid Arabic words in his speeches and writings. Because he knew Persian language very well, he knew how to find the Farsi equivalents of Arabic words. *Hezb*, for example, meaning a political party, was discovered by him and was quickly used by Tudeh Party to become *Hezbeh Tudeh*. Many years later, during the Islamic revolution in Iran, it was used by those who believed that there is only one legitimate party in the world and that is the party of Allah, and called their party Hezbollah. He was not a member of the Tudeh Party, but the Tudeh party benefited from his activity against religion and his negative view of the government. His assassination made many high school students sad in Tehran. He was shot from behind while he was defending himself in court. He believed in God and perhaps in some of the prophets including Hazrateh Mohammad (S), but he did not believe in miracles, mysticism and extra-terrestrial things. He seemed spiritual enough, but his God seemed to dwell on the earth rather than in the heavens.

When Reza Shah came to power by force and forced many to do what he wanted them to do, regardless of legality or illegality, he asked Ahmad Kasravi to do something that was apparently illegal. Anybody who refused Reza Shah's order would either go to jail, or be exiled or died in prison. And if he was an important civil servant he would be asked to retire early. When Ahmad Kasravi refused Reza Shah's order, he was told by Reza Shah to become "waiting for service" which is like early retirement but with the possibility of coming back to work in the future if one repented. "Service should be waiting for me," said the courageous, Tabriz-born Ahmad Kasravi to Reza Shah as he turned his back to him to go home.

His opposition to *Ghazals* and love poetries and dervish-hood was based on the belief that they were important factors in the backwardness and lack of progress in Iran. He would burn those books. He had designated one special day per year for book-burning in which the divans of Hafez and many good poets like him were burnt in public. To make fun of love, in one of his books, he made a caricature of the ideal woman or the beloved, according to the wishes of Hafez and the old Persian poets, by showing a woman whose body is made of a tall and sad cypress tree, her face a full moon, her eyebrows two symmetrical bows, her lips a rose bud, and her eyes made of two symmetrically located narcissus flowers.

On one of the days that I was in Fred's house to play backgammon, I saw a thin book by his uncle about philosophy. Since I had not seen it when I was in Iran, I opened it to see why and how seriously he was against philosophy. Quickly I learned that he believes everybody, including the ordinary man and woman in the street already knows enough philosophy to be able to conduct a reasonable life, and knowing more about it is not necessary. To certain extent he was like Socrates who believed that everybody, including the slaves, already knows everything; it just requires someone to extract the knowledge out of them the way a midwife extracts a baby from the abdomen of a pregnant woman. To show the ridiculous nature of philosophy Kasravi brings the following amusing story from the philosophical books he had read in the remote past, "An old Greek philosopher possessed a single tree. He lived under it, but others could use it too if they wanted to hang themselves from it. Near the end of his life he asked the people of his city to gather in the central square because he wanted to make an important announcement. When people gathered, he stood on a stool and told them, 'I am getting too old and tired of living under a tree. I want to cut it down and build a room in its place. I am going to do this after three days. Anybody who wishes to hang himself from it should do so within this time limit.'"

There are two more thin books by Ahmad Kasravi in Fred's library. One is named *Baha'i-guary* in which, by giving the history of the birth of this new religion in Iran, he diminishes its mystery and its significance. The other is named *Shi'eh-guary* in which he diminishes the importance of Shi'eh branch of Islam by bringing its historical roots and the political reasons for its existence.

Colonel Sharabi, our uncle, also knew Ahmad Kasravi and to a certain extent agreed with some of his objections to Persian poetry. But the colonel's objections were not as severe as that of Ahmad Kasravi. The colonel believed that one of the bad Iranian habits was exaggeration, and he thought the root of this exaggeration was embedded in some of the famous Persian poems. But the colonel did not agree with the anti-religion attitude of Kasravi. One day, to my surprise, I heard that our uncle was saying, "Ahmad Kasravi claims to be a prophet." I said, "Daii-jan, this is impossible. How can a person who is against religion claim to be a prophet?"

"Exactly," Sharabi said, "when one denies all the prophets, one is saying 'I am the prophet,' without saying it."

Maybe Sharabi was right. Ahmad Kasravi had already many serious followers, mainly outside of Iran, some as far as Vienna. Who knows how many followers he would have by now, had he not been assassinated?

44

GOING TO A GREEN GRAVEYARD
IN A YELLOW CADILLAC

I CAN'T RECALL IF IT WAS A YEAR BEFORE OR AFTER THE LAST EARTHQUAKE when I went to a pathology conference in San Francisco as part of my continuing medical education. While I was there I broke the rule of not mixing business with pleasure and went to see several of my cousins on my father's side—those whose male names have the suffix Mirza—in San Francisco, and the only cousin on my mother side, Sohrab, who lives alone in Oakland, not too far from San Francisco.

The cousins who were in San Francisco included Amir and Rezvan Teymourtash, and Khosrow Mirza who had come from Mashad to see his two sons, Vahid and Hamed. Vahid is the brainy one and lives in San Francisco. Hamed is the body-builder and lives in Phoenix, Arizona. Vahid is responsible for the computer system that runs the water for the entire city of San Francisco. He was chosen among the five hundred or more who had applied for the job. There were 150 Iranians among the applicants. Their number was proportionally so high that the one who was interviewing them asked Vahid if all Iranians were specializing in computer sciences. Hamed, in addition to body-building, builds big, white houses in Phoenix for himself and for sale. He is also employed in the municipality of Phoenix to supervise the construction of smaller houses on the cactus-studded lands at the periphery of the city where mainly the American Indians live.

I spent my first free day and night with Sohrab because his last wife, the fourth, had recently died. Also present there was Farhad Mirza, the youngest bother of Khosrow Mirza and the older brother of Rezvan, who had come from Vancouver to see his oldest brother.

No, I am wrong again. Vahid, too, was living in Oakland on that year. It was during my previous trip to San Francisco that Vahid was in San Francisco. His apartment was in front of Amir and Rezvan's, and he was in a bad mood because he had some trouble with the real estate agent who had sold him the apartment. He was angry mainly because the agent had brought up the ugly matter of American hostages in Tehran that had happened three years or so earlier, when she thought the deal was not going to go through. She had pulled herself away, as if scared, saying, "Oh no, I don't want to become a hostage."

Finding Sohrab was easy and uneventful. Once I reached Oakland, I began walking through the town to reach the residential part. Once in the sleepy residential part, I began looking for Sohrab's house while holding the paper on which I had drawn his address, in one hand. All the landmarks that Sohrab had mentioned on the phone, including the pine tree and the flowering tropical trees, appeared and disappeared at the right time and the right turn. I was beginning to enjoy the aroma in the air that reminded me of the warm days in Shemiran. Not many people were walking on the sidewalks. Actually I did not see any-one until I saw Sohrab. He was standing on his familiar bowlegs, in his nice grey suit with matching burgundy tie beside an unfamiliar yellow Cadillac that made him look smaller than he actually was. Was it not for his bowlegs—secondary to a life of riding horses—I could not recognize him from so far away. He was waiting for me in front of his house. As he saw me approaching, he bent his head downward and sideway to light up his half-burnt, extinguished, fat French cigarette. He was careful not to burn his Clark Gable-like mous-tache. As he was narrowing one of his eyes to protect them from the rising smoke, he resembled the actor more than ever. As I got closer, his grimace changed, imperceptively, to a slanted smile. Right at that moment I noticed how much his prominent cheeks resembled those of his father as well as those of the skeleton standing beside the imaginary building of the future United Nations. His fat cigarette was probably the residue of the cigarettes he had brought from France. He had recently gone there to visit his daughter Zoli.

Zoli is short for Zoleikha. She was as pretty as Shirley Temple when she was a little girl and became even prettier as she grew older, without losing her dimples. Her beauty was one of the two reasons why General Nassiri, the head of SAVAK, chose her as his wife. The other reason was because the general knew her father and grandfather and knew them as a good family. The general was a widower and was much older than Zoli, but Zoli loved him nevertheless. At home her husband was no general. He was more like a dervish than a military man. The reason Zoli lives in France is because the general had sent her there along with their two sons. He did it just a few months before the revolution. He was executed by the revolutionary guards a few days after the revolution.

When General Nassiri was executed, he was not the head of SAVAK anymore. He had been demoted. About three or four months earlier, the Shah, to show the revolutionaries that he was listening to their demands, had removed him from his post and sent him to Pakistan as the Ambassador of Iran. And when that demotion did not satisfy the revolutionaries, the Shah called him back and jailed him to await trial. When the revolution took place, therefore, Nassiri was already in jail. He actually managed to escape, along with many other prisoners, when the revolutionaries broke the prison gates, but a fourteen-year-old boy, who used to serve him Coca Cola at his private parties, recognized him. They say Nassiri offered the boy one million *Tuman*, if he remained quiet and went with him in a taxi away from the crowd. The boy, however, refused and screamed and made everybody recognize his catch. Once recognized, he was taken back to his cell to await a quick trial.

No one in our extended family, nor in the family of General Nassiri for that matter, dared to claim his bullet-ridden body after the execution, even though the government kept asking for someone, anyone who can prove to be even remotely related to the general, to come and claim his body for burial. No one, except for Ebi, short for Ebrahim Khalvati, Zoli's cousin. He is also the first son of my sister Monir Shojania and Manuchehr Khalvati, the nephew of Sohrab, the grandson of Sharabi and the first grandson of our mother. Ebi perhaps thought this was the least he could do for the general. The general had been kind to him. He had given him a job that, if he wanted, he could accumulate millions of *Tumans* by just accepting the gifts. Many people in Iran of course thought that Ebi did accept the gifts, but since Ebi never became rich, and had nothing when he went to France, it proves those people wrong. Had he accumulated money, he would have bought a house in Paris rather than staying with Zoli.

All of the above thoughts rushed to my mind as the details of Sohrab's face were shaping up. I was walking towards him in no rush. I was not about to run and give him a big hug even though I knew he deserved one. I thought he had lost so many bigger things like his country, his Shah and his powerful son-in-law that he had gotten used to loss, such as the death of his fourth wife. When I finally reached him, after a single kiss and a short and firm embrace, instead of taking me to his house, Sohrab asked me to get into the car to go to the cemetery where his last wife was buried.

I had seen his fourth wife during one of my previous trips. She was a middle-aged American widow of German origin. After a year or two of living with each other, she separated first from her bedroom then from her house and finally threw herself from a high-rise hotel in San Francisco in which she was living alone, visited on regular hours by a private nurse. During the last few months of her life, she had developed a vague connective tissue disease with lupus-like symptoms and a suicidal tendency. When she was alive, she managed her own store at the edge of the city, selling unattractive things, like brushes with long handles and buckets of chlorine and anything else related to the maintenance of swimming pools. Sohrab used to help her in the store by doing the heavy work. He would carry heavy buckets of powdery stuff to the clients' cars. He would do it with style and without shame. He would do it while dressed as immaculately as today. He carried them with the exaggerated politeness of waiters in luxurious restaurants, but without the expectation of a tip. Even though all his life, since grade one to be exact, he had been riding horses and in fast-moving cars. He did not mind carrying loads like a donkey, if that became his duty. He always said, "If I am kicked out of the army, I would do any other job, be it manual work or working in a restaurant, but I would do it with style."

When I sat in the car next to Sohrab in the front seat and stretched my legs as far as I could, I asked him to explain about the Cadillac, because the last time I had visited him he had a lowly Volkswagon, and was complaining of not having enough money. He said the Cadillac was not his. His neighbour, who is a developer, had run out of cash and had borrowed his last ten thousand dollars. The deal was for two months only and during that time, in addition to paying ten-percent interest, the neighbour had let Sohrab drive his car while he was driving Sohrab's.

"Are you sure he is not going to eat your money, Sohrab?" I asked, worried.

"Yes I am. Besides, no one has ever eaten my money whether here or in Iran," Sohrab reassured me to my surprise. Surprise, because until that moment I had not seen any Iranians who had not lost money by lending it to a friend.

"Not even to Mansur?" I asked. I asked, not because Mansur was a known money-eater, but because Sohrab had confided to me once, when we were in Iran, that Mansur never counted him among his friends and never invited him to his parties, until the day he had sold his property and had cash in his pocket. He did not remember he had told me that, but after I refreshed his memory, he said, "It is true, he did invite me to his parties after that, but he never asked for money and I never lent it to him."

"What did you say to friends or strangers if they wanted to borrow money from you, and you didn't want to lend it?" I asked Sohrab to learn what to say to such a person, in case, in the future, when the children have grown up and have left the house and we accumulated some money, and someone wanted to borrow it from me.

"Who said I don't lend money?" Sohrab surprised me again. "I would do if I had it, but would make double-sure to get it back."

That wasn't very helpful. How can one make sure that one gets one's money back, let alone double-sure? It does not make sense. The numbers don't add up. At the time that a person asks for money, he has zero amount of money in his possession; otherwise he would not ask for money. After borrowing money, his capital becomes negative. Not only he has no money in his possession, he owes someone some money. It was a common practise in Iran among our families and friends as well as the strangers to borrow money from each other and lose both the money and the friend, as Shakespeare had predicted so long ago. So many friends in Iran have become mortal enemies, just because of lending and borrowing.

I could not figure out how the gentle Sohrab had managed to lend money and not lose it.

"Can one refuse money to a friend and still remain friends?"

"Depends on the friend," Sohrab said.

"Maybe the only way not to lose money in Iran is to avoid friendship in the first place," I said, painfully remembering the friend I had lost due to lending money, and the friends whose request I had denied.

The cemetery was a long away from Sohrab's house, but I did not mind. Why should I have minded being driven in the countryside on a sunny day in a yellow Cadillac towards an unfamiliar cemetery in which I knew none of the dead deeply? The warm wind was pulling on my hair and playing with my ear lobe on the right side of my face. The straw-coloured fields of nothingness, studded with sporadic semi-tropical trees, were whirling beside the yellow Cadillac like a gigantic gramophone disk to remind me of the nostalgic songs and the dried fields of wheat passing by our bus during our summer holidays in Iran.

"Nasser!" Sohrab's call brought me back to the car. I turned my head, like the broken neck of the dead bird we just passed, towards him and said, "Yes?"

"You be the judge of this. I don't want to tell you how I feel. I'll tell you the story; you be the judge."

"Okay, no problem," I said. "I am ready to judge. This is what I always do when I am not doing something else. What is it? Does it fall into the category of family problems or is it a political one?"

"Family problem," Sohrab said laconically.

"It is hard to be an impartial judge in this matter because I consider myself as part of the family," I said to Sohrab, "but, since I have been away from family problems for such a long time, tell me anyway. I might be able to look at it objectively and judge it properly."

"I am not happy with the way Ebi has behaved in Zoli's house, in France. As you might know, when Ebi and his children left Iran, they stayed for the first few months in Zoli's house. She did everything for them to make them comfortable, even sending her own sons to a boarding school for a few months so that even the quarrel of children did not become an excuse for disagreement between the parents. And Ebi, of course, did not ignore her liquor cabinet and used it as freely as he would if he was still in his own house in the pre-revolutionary times in Iran."

"This sounds like gossip," I interrupted, "and I have lost my tolerance for listening to it after being away from Iran for such a long time. Please, Sohrab, fast-forward your story to where my judgment is required. So far I haven't heard anything out of ordinary. Zoli was always kind to Ebi, and Ebi always felt at home in her house."

"Listen, Nasser, I will tell you if you listen."

I let him talk as long as he wished. Maybe he hadn't had the opportunity to talk about these matters for a long time. Or maybe he had nobody in this town to talk to about these matters.

"Ebi has explained," Sohrab finally said the main reason why he needed my judgment, "that the reason he has behaved like that was because he carried more Shojania blood in his veins than Khalvati. What do you think about that, Nasser Shojania?"

"I cannot be a good judge here because I too carry the same Khalvati and Shojania genes. Maybe I should excuse myself and decline judgments, but since I have promised you that I would make a judgment, I would say that Ebi is right because there are some Malamati genes among the Shojanias that come from our Torbati father."

"Seriously, Nasser," Sohrab objected with a serious tone. "Is this fair?"

"No, Sohrab. I don't think so," I became serious for a change. "It does not sound fair, but it is hard to compare good deeds with good deeds. How much weight would you put, for example, on Ebi's good deed when he dared to claim the bullet-ridden body of Zoli's husband, and how much weight on Zoli's continual sacrifices to make Ebi and his family feel at home? They are cousins, after all. Aren't they? I don't think anybody is at fault here. These are friction-burns that come as the result of living too close to each other and for an extended period of time. Even if the famous pairs of lovers like Romeo and Juliet or their Persian counter parts, Yousef and Zoleikha, had lived so close to each other, whether married or not, I bet they would have had similar problems after a few weeks."

Sohrab was not fully satisfied, but by this time we had reached the rolling green hills of Oakland Public Cemetery, and cemeteries are well known for making one's problems look small. He stopped the car and we came out to walk on the grass towards the graves. The wind died as soon as Sohrab stopped the car, but the sound of the engine of the car continued to disturb the tranquility of the graveyard. "Why didn't you turn off the engine?" I asked. "A cemetery is no place to show off one's car."

"It is okay," Sohrab said with a smile. "My neighbour pays for the gas too. It is part of the deal."

"But the silence and serenity of this place is out of this world; it is a pity to disturb it. Besides, I cannot enjoy myself if a car is running idly, regardless of who pays for the gas."

Sohrab returned to the circular driveway to turn off the engine and came back. We moved towards one of the uniform brass plates that showed only the name and two dates that indicated the age of the deceased. Almost each plate had a bouquet of artificial flowers in the waterless hole next to it. I asked Sohrab why artificial, instead of natural, flowers in a city where even its trees had decorated themselves with exotic natural flowers.

"They used to have natural flowers, but the deer kept eating them."

"That makes sense," I told him. "We too have deer in our neighbourhood in Victoria. They too keep eating Mitra's flowers, especially the roses." Then, I told him about the various dubious ways that one can discourage the deer from eating the flowers, including the use of that white, semi-translucent material that absorbs static electricity in the dryer. He was not interested in hearing about them, perhaps because he was looking for the grave of his wife. Suddenly he accelerated his steps and stopped beside two adjacent graves and pointed to one of them and said, "This is it."

"Whose?" I asked, "Your wife's?"

"Of course," Sohrab replied abruptly, while tears were rolling down his bony cheeks.

His tears surprised me. I thought Sohrab wanted a wife only to satisfy his insatiable sexual desire.

"Who is in the grave next to her?" I asked to bring him out of his sorrow.

"Her ex-husband," Sohrab said. "He died about ten years ago. He had long-standing diabetes and one of his legs had been amputated many years earlier. Then his other leg became gangrenous and he died following the amputation of his second leg. They think he died of too much blood loss." Sohrab explained the pathological mechanism of his death to a pathologist.

"On the contrary," I jumped on the opportunity. "He might have died of too much blood, because when both legs are amputated the body does not need as much blood as a complete body, but sometimes a busy surgeon might forget this fact and overcompensate for the blood loss during the operation and the patient dies of congestive heart failure."

Sohrab was not paying any attention to my explanation. Silent tears were rolling down his waxy cheeks like water droplets down a duck's wings. To interrupt the flow of his tears, I asked him why he had buried his wife beside her previous husband. He sniffed and said, "Because it was written in her will."

Then, as I was looking at the two graves side by side, an idea came to my mind to save Sohrab some money. "Had she thought of any place for your grave if, God forbid, one day you died?"

"No, but why?"

"No reason," I said, "I was just thinking, since there is room at the lower half of her ex-husband's grave, maybe you could save money by using that vacancy for yourself. This is of course in case you didn't mind being buried in a squatting position, like the genuflexed skeletons buried under the ruins of Persepolis."

Sohrab smiled a Clark Gable-type of smile and pointed with his neck toward the yellow Cadillac that was waiting for us in the circular driveway of the cemetery.

45

IN THE WIFELESS HOUSE OF SOHRAB

COMING BACK FROM THE CEMETERY TO SOHRAB'S HOUSE was more somber than going to the cemetery. Sohrab was quiet and the car was moving noiselessly. My mind had departed to faraway places and the distant past. I was thinking of the historical ruins in Iran from which the archeologists had concluded that not just the Aryan race but several other races had passed through the land that later became known as Persia. The only sign by which they could reach such a conclusion was the various ways by which they had buried their dead. The archeologists know that two things never change in a culture: the wedding and burial ceremonies. Having this clue in hand, when they saw that the position of the skeletons suddenly changed from a fetal to a supine position, they knew a new people must have replaced the previous one. With this macabre background, I wondered, with a mischievous smile, what the archeologists of the distant future would conclude if they saw Sohrab sitting up in fetal position, sharing a grave with a legless skeleton in the supine position.

"You know, Nasser," Sohrab broke his silence and interrupted my thoughts, "no matter how painful the death of one's wife is, that of one's son is hundred times more painful." I did not argue with him. I believed him and at the same time felt an extra beat in my heart, wondering if any of his two sons had attempted suicide.

Sohrab lives with his two sons, Abdi and Yousef. Abdi, short for Abdollah, the name of Sohrab's father, is the older one, and Yousef, Farsi for Joseph, is the younger. Abdi's mother is Estephan, the first or the Polish wife of Sohrab. Yousef's mother was Kay, the third or the American wife of Sohrab, who had lived much longer in Iran than in America. I wanted to ask if Abdi or Yousef had attempted suicide, but did not dare. He let me guess that perhaps Abdi had tried it, but, fortunately, unsuccessfully.

When we reached his home, Abdi was there, but Yousef was not. Yousef was working as an apprentice with a builder who was a specialist in tiling kitchen counters and floors. After a warm and sincere hug, the first thing that Abdi said to me was about the death of my mother. "Sorry about your mother. She was the only woman in our family that would give us money whenever we went to your house." Sohrab agreed with Abdi and improved on it by contrasting the generosity of our mother with lack of it in his own mother. "What Abdi said is very true. My mother was the opposite of your mother in this regard. She was *Khasseece*—Farsi for being stingy, or beyond frugal. She never gave money to children, not even to her own." "But she gave ten *Tuman* to that carpenter in front of your house in the Little Bazaar of Asheikh Hadi, didn't she?" I reminded Sohrab from what I had read in the book of *SOS*.

Not only in matters of largess and stinginess but in everything else, Sohrab's mother and mine were the polar opposites of each other. Not that they were personal enemies, nor that one was bad and the other good. Not at all. They were both good and the few good adjectives that exist in the Persian language were equally applicable to both of them, but as far as adverbs go, they behaved much differently. For example, since our mother had divided a dish of rice among her numerous children for numerous years, she knew how much each child would eat and was able to divide a dish of rice among all of her children and the grown-ups without leaving any of her children hungry or leaving any extra rice in the dish. Her sister-in-law had noticed this and had attributed it to the fact that our mother's hands had *Barekat*. Barekat is an Arabic word for blessing, abundance, or plenty. She believed that our mother's hand could augment the amount of food merely by touching it and she would make use of it when once in a blue moon, she invited us to their house for lunch. Her invitation, of course, was most likely due to the insistence of her husband to at least partially compensate for the numerous lunches that my mother was giving to their sons who every Thursday noon came directly from their military high school to our house in As-You-Wish Street. Even though our mother was a guest in their house and guests are not supposed to work, she would put the obviously inadequate dish of rice in front of her, asking her to divide it for everybody around the table.

Abdi was about twenty-seven years old and almost unemployed, worrying more about his father than himself. When Sohrab's friends were becoming impatient with having to repeatedly listen to the poem that Sohrab had made about Kay's death, Abdi was the one who would let them know that their reaction was not appropriate. He was not lazy and was ready to do any job, but was reluctant to ask his father to ask his friends for a job. Sohrab had many Iranian acquaintances and friends who had become successful businessmen, and could easily employ Abdi if only Sohrab asked. Abdi finally found a job by himself in an ice cream factory located about sixty miles away from Oakland. Every day he had to travel 120 miles for that job in his secondhand oil-leaking car that always threatened to stop running. The only fringe benefit of his job was that he could have as much ice cream as he wanted. This is why every other day he would bring home a small bucketful of ice cream.

The reason Abdi was not working on that day was because it was a holiday. He was in his room, on the floor, smoking cigarettes that he rolled himself, and was watching an educational program on television, occasionally scooping hard vanilla ice cream out of a bucket with a bent spoon. He was self-educating, trying to find his true self. When I asked him what he had found out about himself he said, "I have found out that I would have fewer problems in dealing with others if I treated them like an *Aadam*." Despite having suffered such a big drop in his social status—from being the brother-in-law of the head of SAVAK in Iran to a semi-employed ice cream man—he was in much better shape both physically and mentally than I expected. We sat and talked about everything for awhile, including body, mind, and the magical effects of the two on each other. I did not find him suicidal. Nor did I see any evidence of self-pity in him.

"Daii Nasser," Abdi called me as I was getting out of his room, "you mesmerize me." I did not know what exactly he meant, but there was some evidence of appreciation in his voice. I left him to his television and went to see what his father was doing.

Sohrab's house was a one-level, old-fashioned bungalow building with bay windows looking towards the streets. An L-shaped corridor ran through the house to provide access to bedrooms and the washroom. Sohrab was in the kitchen, cooking. He had protected his immaculate suit with a white apron. He was frying chopped celery to make celery stew. "I like it a little fried, but Abdi and Yousef don't like it that way. How do you like it, Nasser?"

"I like it a little fried, too," I said, and asked, "Where is Yousef?"

"He is out, working."

"Tiling business?"

He did not reply. Sohrab wore a hearing aid in one of his ears and he would shut it off whenever he wished.

"The streets in your neighbourhood are as nice and safe—if not nicer and safer—as the ones in Victoria. How come you told me to be careful when I go for a walk?" I shouted.

"Once a man had come out of his house to go for a walk in the morning, just a block from here, and he was robbed," Sohrab replied.

I went out of the kitchen for a tour of his house by myself.

Yousef's room had a disproportionably large double bed and numerous military airplanes hanging from its ceiling on nylon strings. He was about seventeen years old at the time, too old to play with toy planes. Then I found out that they were his model airplanes when he was living in Iran and that he had brought them with him when they came to America.

His double bed was empty. Sometimes Yousef and his 15-year-old girlfriend lay on it, looking at the planes and talking about Iran, the army and the revolution. Neither Sohrab nor his last wife liked Yousef's girlfriend, each for a different reason. Sohrab did not like her because the first day that Yousef brought her to their house, she did not say *Salaam* or hello to him.

"What were you doing when he brought the girl here?" I asked to see if I could find a logical explanation for her apparent lack of manners.

"I was in the kitchen, right here, doing the same thing that I am doing now," Sohrab said.

"That is it. She must have thought that you were Yousef's cook, or his servant," I said. "Besides, young people today, particularly in this culture, are not like the young people of our time. They are not impolite, but they have not been taught the etiquette of dealing with grown-ups. Some of our sons' friends are like that, too. When occasionally our sons bring them to our car to be taken to their home or to an ice cream shop, they get in without any salutation, as if they are entering a bus, and get out without any thank you or saying good-bye. My explanation did not change the girl's image in Sohrab's eyes. Sohrab is a man of etiquette and no explanation about the lack of it satisfies him.

"What is the reason for your wife's dislike of the girl?" I asked. "Is she jealous?"

"It is not a matter of jealousy," Sohrab said. "The first time that she saw her in Yousef's bedroom, she became so hysterical that she left the house and promised that she would never step here as long as the girl was frequenting this house. Because the girl was under legal age, she thought that if the police found out about it, every adult in this house, including her, would be prosecuted."

"Where did she live, then?"

"In her own house, the one that I think you saw the last time you came here."

That is right. The other time that I came to see Sohrab he took me to his last wife's house. Even though she was married to Sohrab, she was living there by herself. It was a modern bungalow house with white walls and white crushed rocks around a blue swimming pool. She was stretched beside the pool on a blue lawn chair in her bikini. She seemed to be having a good time and was happy with her life. After her death, that house went to her only brother. The only significant thing that went to Sohrab was her health insurance. Her health insurance covered both of them. Thanks to that insurance, a few years later, Sohrab would have a triple coronary bypass in one of the most expensive American hospitals without having to pay a cent.

The guest room was dark and empty of guests, occupied by bulky brown furniture and dusty glass tables. The heavy burgundy curtains were fully drawn, letting only a flickering blade of sunlight into the room, shedding light on the pictures on the walls and the spider web around the light fixture on the ceiling. The photographs on the walls depicted Sohrab on horseback jumping over a high hurdle and General Nassiri in his military uniform decorated with all of his medals. Several black-and-white pictures depicted the last Shah of Iran, either talking to Nassiri or shaking hands with Sohrab. There were pictures of horses, some with and some without a saddle. There were also framed photographs of Zoli and Kay. The only colourful thing on the glass table was the tricolour flag of pre-revolutionary Iran. It was made of silk, emarginated with golden thread. The laughing lion in the centre, the crown and the sabre were also made of the same golden thread. His own bedroom had a large, king-sized bed and half drawn yellow curtains.

Sohrab caught me in his bedroom, looking at an opaque vase on the mantlepiece.

"What is this unattractive vase doing here?" I asked as soon as he saw me. "There is not even an artificial flower in it."

He said that was not a vase, but an urn containing Kay's ashes, his wife who died about three years ago from cancer of one of her fallopian tubes—the conduit through which her ovum and his sperm had once met to produce Yousef.

A beam of yellow light was coming in the room through the gap between the two repelling halves of the curtain. Sohrab showed me the left side of the bed where Kay slept at nights and died one morning.

"How did you found out that she was dead on that morning?" I asked without knowing why.

"I touched her skin, it was *Sard* (cold)," Sohrab said as if reciting a line of poetry. "I pulled the curtain aside; she was *Zard* (yellow)." "Then I kissed her on the pubic area and went to my desk to write a poem about her death. The first line of that poem is what I just told you."

Then Sohrab continued reciting the rest of that long poem that he remembered by heart.

"Why did you kiss her on that particular spot rather than her face or her forehead?" I asked, somewhat dismayed. "Because it was from there that she gave me my dear Yousef," Sohrab replied. His reply made me ashamed of thinking of him unfairly, but just as I began to change my mind about him, he took me to a closet in Yousef's bedroom to make an unnecessary confession. He opened a suitcase containing a deflated doll with smooth rosy cheeks and said, "Remember the last time you and Mitra came here and slept in our bedroom, after Kay's death, before I married my last wife?"

"Yes, I do remember," I said. "But we didn't come here just to sleep in your bedroom; we came to express our condolences for Kay's death, and you kindly offered us your private bedroom and we accepted it."

"Whatever. It does not matter," Sohrab said. "What I want to say is that, after Kay, this used to be in my bedroom, but the night you and Mitra came to sleep there, out of respect for Mitra, I brought it to this closet and it has been here since then."

I bent to touch its hairy triangle to see how real it felt. Sohrab caught my wrist in the air.

"Are you jealous?"

"No. It is dirty. Your hand will get dirty."

"Why you don't marry again?" I asked, "if you cannot live alone or without sex."

"A fifth marriage is out of question," Sohrab said with determination. His reply was so unequivocal that I concluded that he had considered my question at least a hundred times already.

"Then why don't you, at least, live with a widow who is your age or even older?" I advised. "Most of the names on the nameplates in the cemetery were masculine names; there must be a lot of lonely widows in this city."

"These days, in this country, if you stay or sleep with a woman for two weeks in a row, they consider it co-habitation, and on the third week, as they go out of the door, they claim half of what you have, and the court often agrees with them."

"But you don't have much to share except for this house on the ground and ten thousand dollars up in the air."

Sohrab laughed and began to tell me how he picked up a middle-aged woman selling liquor in a liquor store and had spent a full night with her in his house, and in the morning, instead of $70 that was her agreed upon price, he had signed a check for $69, and the woman had accepted it with an understanding smile.

When he finished laughing at his own joke he said, seriously, "I am going to sell this house and give some of it to Yousef and a little to Abdi and spend the rest of it until I die. Or maybe I will go to San Diego and rent a room near Mansur's house."

"Don't give it to your children, Sohrab. They will make their own money. Keep all of it for yourself."

"But I feel I owe them something," Sohrab said. "Because it was me who brought them out of their country and separated them from their friends and relatives."

"I know it is good to give a lump sum of money, like seed money, to children, particularly when they don't have a stable job," I told Sohrab. "But, as far as you are concerned, the beneficial effect of your benevolence will last no more than two weeks. After that, their appreciation towards their father will revert to the same level as it was before you gave them the money. The only difference would be that their father would become poorer and therefore more prone to get hurt."

Sohrab did not listen to my advice. He sold his house. He gave a little to each of his sons and took the rest to San Diego to buy a small apartment near Mansur's house.

46

SOHRAB AND HIS LIGHTWEIGHT SUITCASE

WITH OUR INSISTENCE AND THE HELP OF HIS FRIENDS in the United States, Sohrab managed to come to Canada and stay with us for three days in Victoria. On his way to Victoria he slept one night in Iraj and Layli's house in Vancouver. I don't know what Iraj and Layli had done for him such that when he came to Victoria he said, "Last night I had one of the best nights of my life since I have been away from Iran."

Sohrab traveled lightly, carrying only one black suitcase containing his pajamas, a pair of slippers, one Yardley eau de cologne for me, and two hardcover books. He cherished those books. One of them was written by François Mitterrand when he was the President of France, autographed to Kay, Sohrab's wife, near the time of her death. The other was written by G.H.W. Bush, the ex-president of the United States of America, dedicated to Sohrab in his own handwriting, also asking in his dedication, "How is Abdi doing?" indicating that he remembers not only Sohrab but also some of the members of his family.

The reason Mitterrand has signed his book to Kay was because Sohrab had asked him to do so. Mitterrand and Sohrab had three things in common: love of horses, interest in women and belief in socialism. They had met each other at horse races in Europe where Sohrab was an international judge.

The reason the ex-president Bush had signed his book to Sohrab is because they knew each other in Iran many years ago when Mr. Bush was a lieutenant or a captain in the U. S. army. He was a guest in the house of Sharabi on the Little Bazaar of Asheikh Hadi where Sohrab also lived. At that time Abdi was a cute little boy, just beginning to walk. Whether at that time Mr. Bush was also a CIA agent, is immaterial. Being a CIA agent is bad if one is anti-American, and is good if one is pro-American. The reason President Bush was in Sharabi's house was not related to his mission in Iran. He was there only as a guest and the reason he was a guest in that house was because both Sharabi and Sohrab knew how to treat foreign dignitaries. This is why at the time of the first wedding of the last Shah with Fowzieh, the sister of King Forough of Egypt, Reza Shah had asked Sharabi to be in charge of the foreign guests. In addition to his Persian hospitality, Sharabi liked America almost as much as his own country and he loved his country very much. This is why he had asked the Armenian caricaturist who designed the cover of his *SOS* to put the American flag on the most prominent place among the flags of other nations on the indented rooftop of the imaginary building of the future United Nations. Sharabi respected the flag of the other nations, too. When he saw that the caricaturist had omitted or forgotten to include the flag of postwar Federal Germany, he became very upset and apologized for this omission in a printed page and inserted it inside the remaining copies of his book—which were almost all of its 1500 copies, minus a few copies which were sent to the heads of nations and the one that he had to sent to the Library of the Congress in America where all the books of the world are apparently registered, as well as a few copies that were given to his close relatives and Iranian scholars.

During the few days that Sohrab stayed with us he did not have as much fun as he had in Vancouver. At the end of the third day, I took him through downtown Victoria to go by ferry to Port Angeles. From there he had to go to Seattle by a bus and from Seattle he would fly to San Francisco with the return ticket that he had in his pocket. As we were walking towards U.S. Customs, Sohrab stopped near a beautiful girl who was giving rides to visitors in her horse-drawn carriage. I pulled him back and warned him that this was not Tehran and he could not flirt with any strange woman he saw on the streets.

"What did you say to her?" I asked, somewhat annoyed.

"I just said, 'You are the black beauty,'" Sohrab replied. "What is wrong with that?"

I let out a sigh of relief. "Black Beauty" was the name of her carriage and Sohrab wanted to make a pun out of the carriage, the horse and the beauty of the woman. The rest of our walk in downtown was uneventful. We got the ticket, and I paid for it. The reason I paid for it was because, firstly, it was not expensive, and secondly, I knew Sohrab had no income, and, thirdly, because I live so far away from my friends that I feel I have to pay at least partially for anybody who goes through the trouble of coming to see me.

Sohrab is not poor. He has a big house in Tehran, located in the good part of the city, but, like his father, he never lived in it. Before the last details of his house were completed, he went to Europe, once again as an international judge, and as soon as he left Iran the Iranian revolution occurred and he decided not go back. He lived out of Iran with the help of his daughter, Zoli, and whatever he had taken with him on that short trip. Monir, my sister and Sohrab's sister-in-law, has been living in Sohrab's house for all these post-revolutionary years without paying a penny for it. God knows what Monir and Manuchehr would do if Sohrab decided to sell his house. Sohrab is such a gentleman that I am sure he would not sell his house as long as his brother and my sister are alive.

There were only three people in the small, one-room customs office: Sohrab, me and the American customs officer. Sohrab sat on the single slippery wooden bench. I paced the floor with the lightweight suitcase of Sohrab in hand, and the customs officer stood behind the wooden counter, bored, looking for a friendly conversation.

I don't know if it was Sohrab's gangster appearance—with his chapeau, mustache, tight triangular necktie, and smoldering half-burnt cigar—or the unusually lightweight appearance of the suitcase in my hand that made the officer want to see what it contained.

I thought nothing of it and gladly put the suitcase on the counter in front of the officer, hoping that in addition to opening the suitcase he would open the books and notice the name of their authors. I thought the moment he saw those names he would feel ashamed of thinking of Sohrab as a member of Mafia and me as his body guard. I looked at Sohrab to see if he was as anxious as me for the officer to open the books. He was not. His face was pale with anger. He had lifted his bony buttock off the slippery bench like a jockey off a saddle, ready to pounce like a pebble through a tense slingshot. The next moment he was standing at the counter beside me, objecting to the officer who had attempted to open one of the books. "You can open the suitcase, but you have no right to open the books to see what kind of books I read," Sohrab said, to my chagrin, to the friendly customs officer.

I did not know Sohrab, with all his problems, had become so legal-minded and interested in rights and wrongs. I had to apologize on his behalf. The officer politely put the books back in the suitcase without knowing who had written them and to whom they were dedicated.

The loud whistle of the ship announced its arrival. In the five minutes interval between the whistle and Sohrab's departure, I told him, "You should have let the officer open the books because they could be fake books encasing a knife or a revolver."

Sohrab had nothing to say regarding my last comment. He just hugged me and left the room and walked towards the ship. I think he had shut off his hearing aid in anticipation of another ear-piercing whistle by the big boat.

Years later—actually in the year 2000—when the custom officer of Port Angeles, or perhaps another small port, caught the man who was going from Victoria to explode a bomb in Los Angles Airport on the occasion of Y2K, I wished Sohrab was back in Victoria so that I could tell him, "Didn't I tell you that you should have let the officer check the contents of your suitcase?"

47

Captain Kalali:
The Revolutionary Guest of Sohrab

IN THE OFFICERS' ACADEMY, when they were not riding on horses, Sohrab and Captain Kalali always walked together. They were the same size and shape and had similar bowlegs. They both were teachers in the officers' academy when we were students. Unlike Sohrab, however, Kalali never smiled and looked too serious. He had nothing to do with women and his moustache did not look like that of Clark Gable. He wore thick brown trapezoid moustache that stopped sharply below his upper lip. No one suspected that he was a member of the military network of Tudeh Party, not even Sohrab.

It was only when the military network of the underground Tudeh Party was discovered and all of its 323 members were captured that Kalali had to confess to Sohrab that he was one of them and asked if he could hide in Sohrab's house in the Little Bazaar of Asheikh Hadi for a few days to see how serious the matter was. Sohrab, even though he was not a member of any party, agreed with his friend's request and gave him a room in that house—perhaps the same room that was occupied by the ex-president G.H.W. Bush for a few weeks.

After a few days, when Kalali saw that the matter was very serious and would create a big problem for Sohrab if they found him there, he left Sohrab's house and gave himself up to the military authorities. We, of course, knew nothing about these matters until a few weeks following our imprisonment.

We were sitting in the room with 13 other prisoners, including Sia, in the fourth section, when the iron door of our room opened and Kalali came in. He was in his military uniform, but without his hat, epaulets or stars. He was closely followed, almost like a shadow, by an armed soldier. Without any introduction, he said, "This is not a trial. This is a waiting room to be butchered. Twelve of our friends have already been executed, and it is going to continue this way. We have to escape. Think about it and let me know. I have a plan. Ten per cent of us might get killed, a few more will get injured, but the rest will be free." As soon as the word *free* came out of his mouth the soldier pulled him away.

I don't know about the others in the room, but Sia and I were triply surprised by the sudden appearance of Kalali in our cell. Firstly, we did not know that he too was a member of the same network as we. Secondly, we could not figure out how he had managed to get into our corridor and our cell because the gate of the corridor was always locked and guarded by an armed soldier. And thirdly, what kind of plan he had in mind that would cut through so many locked gates and double layers of walls? Double layer, because the military section of the prison was located inside the Ghasr Prison. We knew very little about Kalali, but some of the other prisoners in our cell knew more about him. They told us that Kalali was an expert in karate as well as judo, and was an avid mountain climber and knew about guerrilla warfare.

To escape or not to escape? I asked this question of myself. After a few seconds of thinking about it, I rejected the idea of escape. Even if I were lucky enough not to be among the initial casualties, I thought, I would have to keep running and hiding for the rest of my life. The other prisoners in our room reached the same conclusion, but some of them after a longer period of thought.

We never saw Captain Kalali again. He was tried among the third group composed of six officers, some of whom as brave as he. In his defense—we later heard—he had quoted a saying of Imam Ali, "When there is a riot or rebellion in an army, the head of that army is not exempt from the blame." In other words, if he was wrong, the Shah ought to be wrong, too. All the six were sentenced to death, regardless of what they or their lawyers had said in their defense. They were to be executed in front of a firing squad the next day. When the six were being marched towards the execution yard, Kalali managed to disarm one of the guarding soldiers, grabbed his rifle and marched the group and the guards towards General Azmoodeh, the chief military prosecutor who had come to watch the execution, personally. He made a short speech, letting the general know that he could kill him with the rifle in his hand if he wanted to. He also told him that they would not be able to kill all of the 323 captured members. "But I will not kill you," were his last chivalrous words "provided you do not punish this soldier who has lost his rifle to me. He did his best to defend it." After Azmoodeh promised not to punish the soldier, Kalali gave his rifle back. Then the six officers were tied to six poles and killed in a hail of bullets.

Some of them did not want their eyes to be closed. Some of them shouted a few courageous slogans before their death. One of them, probably Captain Shafa, a police captain, did not die right away. When the soldier who was to deliver the shot of relief to his head was approaching him, he pointed to his chest with his chin and told him, "Oh, la mazhab!" meaning irreligious, "The heart is here!"

During the interrogations, the army badly wanted to know where Kalali was during the three or four days before giving himself up, and particularly what he had done with his revolver. But Kalali never told them where he was in those few days and where his gun was. He lied. He said that he had slept for three nights in a cave in the Mountain of Damavand and had put his revolver on the summit of the same mountain.

Many years later, I asked Sohrab what he had done with Kalali's revolver. He said that on the third day after Kalali had left his house, he took it to the officers' academy and threw it on the pile of horseshit in the dugout that they called *Manage*. It was a square dugout like a large pool without water, about two metres deep. Sohrab and Kalali often rode their horses in it. Once, Sohrab managed to jump out of it on his horse, into the grassy soccer field next to it.

48

KAVEH, KALALI AND MOUNT DAMAVAND IN IRAN

MOUNT DAMAVAND IS A WHITE, CONE-SHAPED MOUNTAIN, visible from Tehran, on a clear day. From the distance, it might look like one of the mountains of the snow-streaked chain of Alborz Mountains, but it is not. It is a volcanic mountain that happened to erupt near those mountains. It is as well-known in Iran as Mount Fuji is in Japan. I don't know about Japan, but in Iran more people know Damavand through poetry and history than by climbing it. Kalali was an exception. Since it was visible from the rooftop of any house in Tehran, it made everybody think about it, or say something about it.

The first time that I saw it from our rooftop on Saghafi Street, it made me wonder why the volcanic eruptions puncture the crust of the earth through its thickest spot like the summit of a mountain, rather than through its weakest spot such as the depth of the deepest valley. It took me many summers and days of mediation until I figured out that the mountain was the result of the eruption rather than the cause of it. Once I learned that rule, whenever I saw an isolated cone-shaped mountain I knew that it was the site of a volcanic eruption and had nothing to do with the other mountains in its vicinity, no matter how close.

Bahar, nicknamed "the king of poets" of Iran, known particularly for the strength and the length of his *Ghassideh,* has addressed that mountain in a long poem that begins with, "*Ey deeveh sepeedeh pie dar band! Ey gonbadeh gueeti; ey Damavand!*" Meaning, O gigantic whiteness, feet in chain! O dome of the universe, O Damavand!

Although the translation is relatively accurate compared to my other translations, something has been lost that I cannot put my finger on. It does not have the same strength as its Farsi version. Bahar was old and made old-fashioned poetry, but Kowli was young and made new Persian poetry. He said the following lines about Mount Damavand or perhaps about another snow-covered mountain in Iran.

What a white mountain!
What a black moonlight!
There is no sound
But the moaning cries of an eagle.

Kowli wrote this in the days of political suffocation in Iran, at the time of the reign of the last Shah. He was glad when the Shah was ousted by the Islamic revolution. He was so glad that, even though he was not a religious person, he went to see the leader along with another of his poet friends, who was perhaps a lady poet by the name of Beh-Bahaani. Coming back from that visit, Kowli was silent for a while. When his companion asked what he was thinking about, they say Kowli has replied, "I hope we are coming back from kissing the hand of Freidoon rather than Zohhak."

Freidoon was the first legendary king of early Persia, when it was not yet called Persia. He could have been the first king in the world, but I am not sure of this. I have to check this with Pari. She knows. Some of the things in this chapter I learned from her, but not all of them. "Freidoon had two sons," for example, was in our textbook in elementary school, *"Kambeez and Kamboojiyeh."*

When Freidoon was dying, he made a peculiar will regarding which of his two sons should succeed him: the one whose horse neighed first in a certain parcel of land. Kambeez, the smarter one, took a mare to the place of contest the night before and stayed there until the mare urinated on the ground. The next morning, when the two sons went there with their horses, Kambeez led his horse towards the site of urination and his horse neighed immediately when it reached there. He became the king and his brother, disappointed, left that land and went towards the East. He went as far as the land that today is called Cambodia, perhaps because of him. I am not sure about the names of the sons.

Names sometimes change so much with time or from language to language that it becomes hard to believe that they are referring to the same person or the same thing. I am told by Layli's friend; Mrs. Mo'tamedi, who knows so much about the history of ancient Persia and Ferdowsi, that Zohhak, for example, is the same as Ejdeha, and *Ejdeha* means dragon in Farsi.

Legend has it that Zohhak lived on Mount Damavand. Some say he was chained to it. Some say he was ruling like a king. Our textbook of Farsi in elementary school said that he was the cruelest man and was imprisoned forever in a cave in Damavand Mountain. He was nicknamed "Zohhak with snakes on the shoulders" because he had grown two snakes on his shoulders, one on each side.

History says that Zohhak was a good ruler in the beginning, and then turned bad. Not only he did not hunt, he did not even eat any food that contained meat. He was, perhaps, the first vegetarian in the world. And he remained so until one day Satan, disguised as a cook, came to ask him to make him his cook. When Zohhak gave him the job, Satan kissed him on the shoulders as the sign of his appreciation, and one snake grew out of each spot that he kissed.

Satan began cooking from the first day and from the first day he began mixing meat and other animal products, including brain, with his vegetarian food. When Zohhak ate it, he did not notice any meat in it. All he noticed was the fact that he liked it. Not only Zohhak but the snakes liked it too. Satan stayed there for a few weeks and during that period gradually trained the snakes to eat nothing but human brain. When the snakes became completely dependent on human brain, Satan said to Zohhak that he had to go back to the village he had come from because he missed his family and friends. Zohhak let him go and hired an ordinary cook to continue with the same diet for him and the snakes.

For a long while the new cook did as he was told, using the brains of two men who were delivered to his kitchen every day. After a few years, when the number of the people around the Mount Damavand diminished, the cook began to economize by not killing both men. He used one and saved the other. But to compensate for the shortage he killed and used a lamb. He fed the mixture to the snakes and the snakes ate it without noticing any change. After this success, the cook continued this practice and kept feeding the brain mixture to the snakes and fed Zohhak the meat of the lamb. In addition to all this, the men whose lives were saved in this way were sent to be hidden somewhere behind the Mount Damavand, and were told not to show themselves in the villages so that people thought that they were dead.

Meanwhile there was a blacksmith by the name of Kaveh who had lost all of his sons to the kitchen of Zohhak except for one. When Zohhak's men came to take his last son he decided to resist. He hung his leather apron on the end of a long pole and marched towards Zohhak's place and gathered people behind him as he went.

Meanwhile a woman in the vicinity of that mountain was pregnant. She carried her pregnancy away from the eyes of the public so that when she delivered her child the child would not become meat for the kitchen of Zohhak. She named that child Freidoon. As Freidoon was growing up, he learned about Zohhak and his cruelty and decided to replace him with someone more just and less cruel. That was when Kaveh had rebelled against Zohhak. The men whose lives had been saved and were hiding behind the Mount Damavand followed Kaveh and defeated Zohhak. And they made Freidoon their Shah.

After the victory of Kaveh the Blacksmith his leather flag evolved to become the proud *Drafsh-e-Kavian* and the Drafsh of Kavian, in turn, became the precursor of the Persian or Iranian flag with its laughing lion, and the laughing lion was replaced by stylized name of Allah after the revolution of 1979 that terminated 2500 years of *Shahan-shahy* in Iran.

When Kalali said to the interrogator that he had left his gun on the summit of Mount Damavand, I am sure, he was thinking of Kaveh the Blacksmith. He was brave enough to be a second Kaveh. Too bad we did not follow him when he asked.

49

LOOK INSIDE MY NARROWED MATTRESS

DEAR MODAR-JUN, *SALAAM*. I am still waiting for your reply. What happened? You never delayed your replies more than two weeks. How come this time it is taking more than two years? Is it because I said your reply is urgently required this time? Your long silence is so unusual that the only explanation I can imagine for it is to assume that, God forbid, you are dead.

Forget about your permission regarding me talking about you as a good Moslem on the occasion of World Religions Day. I did that without your permission. I know it is bad to do something so important without a permit, but it would have been worse if I did not do it. The chair of Islam would have remained vacant on the panel of six, if I had not done it. And it went quite all right. I told them that you had direct line to God and God listened to you when you gave Him a choice of either curing Hamid or killing him. You received more applause than the sum of all the other five religions. What I badly need is my diary. If it was not inside the mattress of my adolescence—the one that was always on the floor of the children's room, like a tombstone, between the mattresses of Hossein and Hamid—maybe it is inside the striped mattress that I brought back from prison. The blue striped mattress that you blamed me so much for having ruined it by narrowing it, and no matter how much I explained that it was because we were fourteen men in one room smaller than the children's room in our house, you were not satisfied and showed your dissatisfaction by telling me, "Why don't you leave and go to a place where they have enough room for the shoulders of my sons?" Please have a look inside that mattress and palpate it carefully and send it to me if you find it. I hope you haven't sent the mattress to the cotton-beater. What is the average life span of a mattress in Iran anyway? I know the life span of an ordinary grave is twenty-five years. I hope a mattress lives longer than that. It is more than 35 years that I have not used it, since I have been away from Iran.

My book is almost finished. It is looking like a pilgrimage. I began as an atheist, now I am an agnostic. After my speech about you I almost became a believer, but something bad happened and I lost Him again.

Please convey my *Salaams* and regards to those who read my letters. Sorry for the shortness of this letter. I have to go. I am still working. I have not retired yet. Working every day and writing every night has consumed all my free time. No more time for long letters. The nice son who entertained you with his long letters is no more.

Khoda Hafez.

Your middle son,

Nasser

P. S. Two nights ago there was a fund-raising concert for the benefit of the victims of the Bam earthquake in Iran. Dr. Meralli had asked me to recite a Persian poem at the beginning. He was arranging it. He was participating in the Persian music as well. He said I should try to connect the poem to the catastrophic event if I could. I chose the poem that I have named "Love and Silence," by Rumi. Many of the audience knew Rumi, but I reintroduced him by his own words, translated by R. A. Nicholson.

What is to be done, O Moslems? For I do not recognize myself.

   I am neither Christian, nor Jew, nor Gabr, nor Moslem.

I am not of the East, nor of the West, nor of the land, nor of the sea;

   I am not of Nature's mint, nor of the circling heavens.

I am not of this world, nor of the next, nor of Heaven, nor Hell;

   I am not of Adam, nor of Eve, nor of Eden and Paradise.

My place is the placeless, my trace is the traceless;

It is neither body nor soul, for I belong to the soul of the beloved.

I read it from the magazine *Sufi*, issue 45, Spring 2000, published in London, England. Then I told them that his beloved was Shamseh Tabrizi and opened the thick *Divan* of *Ghazals* by Rumi that he has named Shamseh Tabrizi and read that poem. I read it first in Farsi, then I read its translation from this book.

I could not firmly connect it to the earthquake. The only connection, I said, was that I had read the same poem for the funeral of my mother. And I told them that its connection with your death was your silence even when you were alive. I did not tell them that it was the fault of your silence that I never learned any religion. The audience liked the poem very much and many asked where they could get my book. Everybody, Modar-jun, including me, is waiting for this book and you are still looking for my diary. Please, Modar-jun! Have another look around the house. It is narrowed, remember, it could be anywhere.

50

A TELEPHONE CONVERSATION WITH SOHRAB

I PHONED SOHRAB TO TALK, but his phone number had changed. I phoned Mansur in La Jolla to see if he had Sohrab's new phone number. To my surprise, Sohrab picked up the phone, and like a well-instructed soldier-servant said, "Shojania's residence; they are not home at this time. Any message I can convey to them? I am Colonel Sohrab Khalvati."

"Sohrab!" I exclaimed, "What are you doing there?"

"Nasser!" he exclaimed bitterly. "My … in your …! How inconsiderate of you!" He lost all his manners as soon as he realized it was me.

"Why?" I asked, "What have I done?"

"They opened my chest and cut through my heart. Not only did you not send a card to wish me well, you did not even phone to see if I was alive or dead."

I could have said that that was exactly why I was calling, or I did not have his phone number, but since I did not want to lie, I said, "I am sorry, Sohrab. I was busy. I am glad that you survived the operation. Actually the reason I am calling was to get your phone number from Mansur to let you know that I was writing a book in which your father plays a major role. Now that I got you instead of your phone number, could you tell me any interesting story about your father? Something, of course, that I don't know."

"I do not have a phone number of my own anymore," Sohrab said with a bitter voice. "Nor do I have a fixed address. I have sold my house in Oakland, gave a little to my sons, and with the rest I came here to see if I could buy or lease something close to Mansur. Unfortunately we could not find anything. I will go back to San Francisco and live in one of the rooms in Yousef's house. You can phone me there in a few days. I don't feel sufficiently at home here to talk about the intimate aspects of my life. I don't want to talk about my private matters, even though there is no one in this house but me."

"Where are Mansur and Feri now?"

"They were invited to their friend's house."

"Why didn't you go with them?"

Sohrab did not reply to my last question.

Many months later, after I finally found his new phone number through Amir Teymourtash, I phoned Sohrab again. Yousef picked up the phone. After *Salaam*, I asked him to ask his father to turn on his hearing aid and come to the phone because I wanted to talk to him. When he came to the phone I repeated my request regarding my book and interesting stories about his father.

He was glad to hear that and praised my intention by saying he was proud of me to have undertaken such a project, especially for doing it while still working as a pathologist. He was watching a movie on television and my phone call had caught him off guard, so much so that he could not remember any story about his father. Then he said, "Why don't you write about me? My life is adventurous, too, and is more connected to recent history of Iran. It could become a movie."

"So said your father in his *SOS*," I said. "Do you know, by the way, the name of the Armenian artist who drew the caricature of the cover of his book?" Sohrab thought about it for a while, and then gave up. "His name is written on the lower corner of the cover," I tried to boost his memory, "but it is in small letters and the corner of my copy is worn out a little. It looks like Avanecian." "It could very well be," Sohrab said, and then he remembered to tell me the following story.

"Once when I was in Abadan, doing my first out-of-Tehran duty, my father came as the guest of the British contingency during the years of occupation. The British respected my father so much that they allocated a whole luxury car of the train to him and supplied him with a cook and everything he needed. One night they went to his place and played bridge with him. At the end he was the only winner."

"Did they provide him with any woman?" I asked just to help him remember more interesting things.

"Oh yes. They did not, but I did. One of those nights he came and stayed with me in my bachelor apartment. I did not have Estephan at that time, as you know."

Of course I knew. I remembered the exact day and date that Sohrab brought Estephan from Abadan to Tehran. I remember it like the memorable scenes of a good movie like "Gone with the Wind."

"You looked more like a gentleman in the railroad station in Tehran than Clark Gable in that movie, though he wore a civilian suit and you were in a military uniform. Unlike him who said to Scarlett, 'Frankly my dear, I don't give a damn,' you did give a damn. You brought Estephan from Abadan to Tehran to ask for your father's permission to marry her. We were waiting for you on the marbled floor of the German-built railroad station in Tehran, decorated with framed photographs of Reza Shah and his son, either together or separate. The one that showed them together through the window of a train resembled a doubly framed photograph."

"The train stopped with a protracted sigh of relief. You and Estephan and a blond little girl about four years old, were the first people to step out of the train. Estephan was carrying the girl a few steps behind you. Your face was pale and serious, paler than the little girl's hair that was the palest hair we had ever seen up to that day. You walked a few steps ahead of them, looking for your father. The moment you saw him standing erect and alone, you went back and made Estephan and her daughter stay where they were, and turned back to march towards your father. You stopped in front of your father like a nail and made a firm military salute as if he were not your father, and said, 'Forgive me, *Pedar*! I have promised this woman to marry her and take care of her daughter, only if I could have your permission.'"

"A few uneasy moments passed, and then you said, 'God be my witness, I will send them back to Abadan on the same train if you did not approve of this marriage.' Estephan—paler than a white wall, like the anxious face of women in Charlie Chaplin movies—was watching the drama unfold with her already dilated, Betty Davis eyes. Even though she was a soldier in the victorious Polish army, and you were an officer of a defeated army, your body languages told a different, almost the reverse story. Then your father clicked his heels together as sharply as yours, and saluted you as firmly and said, 'Permission granted, Sohrab!' and moved on to embrace you first, then to shake hands with Estephan and kiss her once on one cheek, and finally he knelt like a true chevalier to kiss the cheeks of the little girl. As soon as the little girl was kissed she said in Farsi that her name was Marisha."

"Tell me more, Nasser. You remember it better than I do," Sohrab said.

"No, you tell your story, Sohrab. Sorry for interrupting you," I said. "What happened when your father came to your bachelor apartment in Abadan?"

"Oh yes," Sohrab continued his story, "the night I invited my father to Abadan, I had prepared for him everything that he liked: wine, kabob, fire for opium, and women. I had invited two high-class prostitutes, one of them, the prettier one, was my own, and the other was her friend. I asked my father to choose any one he wished, expecting him to choose the one that was not mine. Unfortunately, he chose my friend, but I let him have her. As they were going to the next room together, my woman looked back to see if it was okay with me, and I showed her my approval with a wink."

"Don't you have a better story?" I said. "Something more representative of your father and more presentable in a book? This book, if it ever gets published, might be read by many respectable people. Your story says more about you and your generosity than your father. "

"I have no objection to whatever you say about me."

"Thanks for giving me this permission, Sohrab. You don't know how often I have been thinking to delete the deflated secret in your closet. Now, before I go, may I abuse your trust in me and ask you one more personal, but final question?"

"Go ahead, Nasser."

"Do you think having extramarital sex is good, or bad?"

"It is good."

"Why?"

"Because, after it, one appreciates one's wife more."

"But how come Chehry did it but never appreciated my sister?"

"Manuchehr and I are brothers, but we are very different."

"I know. You and your brother never had a normal conversation with each other. Anytime you began talking to each other, you ended up fighting like cats and dogs."

51

A PACKAGE FROM SOHRAB

A WEEK OR SO AFTER OUR LAST TELEPHONE CONVERSATION, I received a large brown envelope from Sohrab containing a handwritten short note and long pages of typed paper constituting his writings and some of his poetry.

The note begins:

Dear Nasser, my *Azeez* and *Mehr-ban* cousin,

First, I have to apologize for the badness of my handwriting. Writing is difficult for me, because of my visual problems. My eyes have given half of their life to you, and my doctor has told me that my left eye is going to be totally blind soon. But don't let that worry you; consider both of my eyes as a sacrifice for your left testicle.

You asked about the poems exchanged between my father and Sadegh Hedayat. I don't remember all of it, but a few weeks ago, some of its lines came back to me in a dream. First, my father wrote the following invitation in the form of a poem to Sadegh Hedayat.

Ey Saadegheh Hedayat, ey mountain of noor (light)

Why should you and I, from each other, be always so door (far away)*?*

The following four horses are carrying me towards the grave:

The wind of sorrow (goiter)

The malady of sugar (diabetes)

The aches of heart (coronary artery disease)

The pains of stomach (gastric ulcer)

May all the four, from you, be door.

To which Hedayat replies with a tongue-in-cheek poem, the end of each line of it rhyming with the same-sounding words that ended the lines in Sharabi's verse.

Sarhang Khalvati that I hope

Any gazand (injury) *from you to be* door

Your letter made my room full of noor. (light)

I devoured it like a hungry man having a plate of jaghoor/baghoor.

(A spicy fried liver and onion dish made only at street corners, at noon.)

You said four horses are pulling you towards the goor (grave)

Rest assured that none of the horses will survive the trip

They will die too, but without the pleasure of having a goor.

Vafoor (the mace-like pipe for smoking opium) was the only word that rhymed with the row of...*oors*, but they had both deliberately avoided it. It was also the main reason that Hedayat had accepted the invitation. Even though Hedayat was a relative of Colonel Sharabi through Sharabi's wife, the two did not see each other very often due to their different lifestyles. Hedayat had written several thin but famous books, including *The Blind Owl*, *Three Droplets of Blood*, and *The Doll Behind the Curtain*. But the colonel had finished only one book, and was beginning to write his second one, *Dorr Dar Guel*, meaning pearl in mud. Since *Guel* in Farsi can be read as *Gol* as well, and *Gol* means rose or flower, the book's name is meant to bring to one's mind the *Golestan* of Sa'di. Like the book of *Golestan*, the second book of Sharabi was written with good prose, infiltrated by timely poems.

Sohrab says in his letter that he had written both of those poems on the back of his copy of *Dorr dar Guel*, and that Hossein Kalali had borrowed it and had taken it to his house. That book, along with the other papers of Kalali, was confiscated by the army when they went to his house in search of him and his gun.

In all his life, Sohrab smoked nothing but cigars and cigarettes. He has promised to himself to never smoke opium and never touch its *Vafoor* to his lips, and he has kept his promise. Even when he was much younger and much hungrier for women, when a famous female singer, at a private smoking party, asked him to smoke first if he wanted to have sex with her, Sohrab did not do it. Perhaps he thought that his father's continual use of opium was the reason that the Shah and a few influential people in Iran, did not take him seriously.

Perhaps Sohrab is right, but I think opium saved the life of his father. It did it the way insulin saves the life of a diabetic patient. It made him manage his anger. It more than just calmed him down. When he was a young officer and did not smoke opium, he was so short-tempered that he shot one of his friends to death at a drinking party just because the man had accused him of having a few morsels of kabob without having contributed any food to that picnic. He was so irritable in those early days that when he was sitting in a *Doroshkeh*, he would sit on his own hands to prevent them from impulsively slapping the *Doroshkeh Chee* from behind, if the poor man happened to utter the wrong word or treated his horses unkindly.

Sohrab has also included some of his own poems in the package. They are about the Shah, the revolution, his childhood, his wives, as well as many other things, even though I had asked him not to send me these things because I did not have time to go through them.

His first poem was written in 1934, when he was a young boy of perhaps ten or eleven. In that poem he congratulates Reza Shah after the parliament has passed a law to bestow upon him the highest title that a shah could have in Iran, namely *Kabeer*, meaning great.

Reza Shaha! Now that you are Kabeer

You are unique and bee-nazeer (peerless)

With your power,

You have made the mountains saaf (flat)

With your tunnels,

You have made in the montains, many deep-seated shekaafs! (splits)

Sohrab mailed that poem to his father who was probably chasing armed robbers along the borders of Iran. His father's reply was unexpectedly discouraging. The reply was in the form of verse, but discouraging Sohrab from doing it.

Sohrabeh azeezeh del-pazeeram (My dear and heart-pleasing Sohrab)

She'ri zeh to man nemi-pazee-ram (I don't accept any poem from you)

I don't accept any poem from you,

My dear Sohrab, at this age.

Leave poems and poetry to the old age

Or until you reach the age of earning wage.

So far, you have been very dear to me

But make sure you keep it that way

By not spilling "the water-of-the-face" of your father in the school.

If you don't keep studying every night,

You might fail in grade five.

And the light of my eyes will be extinguished

And I might not see you anymore.

Listen to what Iraj the poet said to his son:

>   *"I have your happiness in my mind,"*

>   *"My sweetheart"*

>   *"When I say these bitter words to you."*

There are several other long poems in the package that I am not going to translate. I translate only the first line of the one he had made after the death of the last Shah, the son of Reza Shah. It must have been a year or two after the revolution of 1979. I cannot make out the exact date of it. He has dated it like this: the next day after the passing of Shahanshah the Aria-Mehr, Concord, Oakland.

Oh Shah! You died and Iran is ruined

The only sound one can hear is that of the owl.

Sohrab, a believer in conspiracy theories, goes on to describe in what shape Iran would have been if his son-in-law, General Nassiri, was the Shah of Iran at the time of revolution:

If Nassiri was ruling Iran

Carter and Vance would have regretted their plan

General Hauser would have been among the captures

And Sullivan among the refugees.

Nassiri was not a false friend like Gharah Baaghi or Fardoost

Except for his Shah, he was nobody else's doost. (friend)

His fekr *(thought) was Shah and Pahlavi*

His Zekr *(mantra) was Khoda and Ali.*

Sohrab is emotional and makes occasional poems, but he does not exaggerate. When he says that Nassiri's mantra was Khoda and Ali, I believe him and have to conclude that Nassiri too must have been a kind of dervish; because dervish's only mantra is *Khoda* and Ali. Real dervishs, of course, don't say *Khoda* in their mantra. They say *Hoo* instead, which is another name among the one thousand-and-one names of *Khoda* (God).

In his footnote, Sohrab explains that since this poem was written too soon after the death of the Shah, he had been too emotional about it and had said things that he did not believe in anymore. He had forgotten that he was no longer in favour of monarchy in Iran nor anywhere else. "Like always," he says, "I am a socialist and I have been this way for 34 years, since I met François Mitterrand for the first time."

I did not know Sohrab had known François Mitterrand for such a long time. I thought they had met rather recently during horse racing. How wrong I was! Mitterrand must have been the model and the teacher of Sohrab. When Mitterrand died, I watched his funeral procession in France on television. In front of all those who were following his flag-draped coffin were two women, his wife and his mistress. No one, including any of the onlookers from the windows was surprised, as if it was normal in France to have a wife and a mistress. The mistress had a young daughter by Mitterrand. I thought the last message of Mitterrand to the world was this: The chariot of life is too heavy to be drawn by only two; it takes at least three horses to move it towards the grave. At the end of his letter, Sohrab had written the following short story about his father.

Dear Nasser,

The night you asked me to remember anything interesting about my father's life, I could not remember many things. Right after I put down the receiver numerous significant incidents came to my mind. The following is one of them.

Even though our father lived in the Little Bazaar of Asheikh-Hadi, all his life, and there was a good public bath-house near our house, we never used that bath-house and our father always took us to the one in Pahlavi Avenue. He knew the master *Dallak* there (the master of the men who wash the clients) and the master *Dallak* knew us. During the war, when the

Allied forces where in Iran, I came back from Abadan to Tehran for a short visit. I was quite dusty and dirty and was supposed to go to a party on the first night. To clean myself, out of habit, I went to the same public bath-house that we used to go as children. The same master *Dallak* was still there, standing behind the counter. He immediately recognized me and asked, "Is your father dead?"

"No," I said, "Why do you ask?"

"Because foreign soldiers would not be marching in our streets today, if he was alive."

This story about Sharabi says more about him than the entire book of *SOS*. And I thank Sohrab for sending it to me and myself for asking for it. When a *Dallak*, who knew his naked body due to washing it a hundred times, and his brave soul due to watching him in the battlefields, considers him patriot enough to ward off the entire allied forces, one has to believe it.

Sharabi was no Don Quixote. He was under no illusions. He believed and behaved like a true chevalier.

He was not Rostam. He was real. Not only Iran-land, he wanted to make the entire world a safer place in which one can have fun for a while.

52

THE POSTPARTUM LETTERS

I DID NOT RECEIVE ANY REPLY TO MY LAST TWO LETTERS TO MY MOTHER for the obvious reason that she was dead. Instead, I received a package from my two sisters, containing copies of my mother's letters from Mashad to Auntie Pouran in Tehran, during the years 1933 to 1935, when my mother was 33 to 35 years old, and I was three to five.

These letters are much more significant that the diary of my adolescent time. If there is any typical or true Persian letter, it would be among these. Even though her age at the time of writing these letters was about half of my present age at the time of writing this book, the level of her maturity is twice that of mine. She has not written anything in them that would make her regret if it fell into the hands of the wrong person, or read in public. Her handwriting is better than mine and her knowledge of Persian literature is deeper than that of any of her children. The topic she is talking about is more important than what I am talking about here.

They are about 30 letters, all dateless, but I can date them out of the datable events contained in them. For example, when she talks about *Paltow* (overcoat) I can guess that it was near winter, or when she talks about whether to buy new dress from Tehran or Mashad, I know it must be the landmark year of 1934 in which prohibition of chador (veil) occurred. Since her ten children were born almost one year apart, one can use them as a ruler and guess the year in which the letter was written when she talks about any one of them. The reason I have called these letters collectively postpartum letters is because many of them seem to have been written in bed after delivering a child.

She had sent her first four children to the house of Auntie Pouran in Tehran so that they could attend better schools, compared to those in Mashad. She wrote regularly, almost twice a month, once to send money and give news about her five children who still live with her, the other for receiving news about those who are away from her.

These letters are uniform as far as the shape is concerned. She used special paper for writing letters, which is slightly larger than a single standard sheet when it is unfolded. She never covered both side of the paper, always leaving half a page blank at the end. They all have wide margins at the top and at the right side, to be filled with short oblique lines when her pen reached the left lower corner of paper. In this way, the completed page resembles a half framed picture.

Sewing occupies a good portion of many letters. The nagging fever of unknown origin of our father, whom she refers to as Shazdeh, is mentioned very rarely, but is never forgotten.

There is no gossip or secrets in any of the letters. This is why I can translate them, randomly, and publish them for the whole world to see, without worrying about having violated her privacy. I might even photocopy one of them for those Iranians who cannot read English so that they could see what a true Persian letter looks like.

I should also add that my sisters had sent these letters after long hours of discussion and hesitation. They thought—wrongly, of course—that I might be offended by the part in which my mother has described my face, as a newborn infant, when I am perhaps about half-an-hour old, as *Torob-siah*, Farsi for the ugliest root vegetable, known here as horseradish.

How did these letters come into the hands of my sisters in the first place? They were among Auntie Pouran's personal belongings. After her death, which was about a year after the death of our mother, all her belongings, including her house, according to her will, went to the daughter of her youngest stepbrother, Ali Khan, with whom she was living during the last three years of her life. These letters, as well as a few very personal things like the decorated booklet which contained the marriage contract between our father and mother, and a black-and-white photograph of our mother, went to Monir. Monir gave the gilded marriage contract to Shirin, her daughter. The photograph of Modar-jun—the one in which she is dressed in black, with grey hair, sitting as a single guest in the house of Navab-poor, with half a large crystal plate showing on the coffee table containing one last apple—is sent to me along the letters. I framed that picture temporarily—for the last ten years or so—in a cheap frame, until I find a better frame for it. It sits on the mantlepiece above the fire-place, along the row of black and brown pictures. The brown picture is that of the father of my mother, taken by a French professional photographer. It depicts him on a royal chair with an open book in his hand. It has its original frame made of wood inlaid with ivory. When I wrote, tongue in cheek, to my mother that I was so appreciative of her sending me that framed picture that I resisted the temptation to sell its expensive frame, she sent me, as the reward for my resistance, a couple of boxes with delicate woodwork, made of similar material as the frame. I think the art work employed on the frame and the boxes is referred to as *Khaatam-kaary* in Iran.

I could never figure out why my mother, who began her widowhood by possessing a large village and several houses in Torbat and a home in Tehran, ended up homeless (though she lived happily in her daughters' homes, half a year with each one) but Auntie Pouran, who was homeless in the beginning, ended up with a house. Was this due to the difference in their attitudes towards money? Perhaps.

Maybe it was because my mother was always busy paying compound interest, while Auntie Pouran collected compound interest. Even though near the end of her life Auntie Pouran was saying her prayers and doing her *Namaaz* as often as my mother, the fact that she continued receiving interest for her money makes her less of a good Muslim than my mother. But, I could be wrong. We, the children, never let my mother have extra money to see what she would do with it. Maybe we are the cause of her piety. Maybe it is good children that make good mothers, rather than the other way round.

We were never told about the financial arrangement between these two friends. I know that Auntie Pouran had a meagre monthly revenue from the Agha Khan Foundation that was earmarked for his close relatives in Iran—the same money that my mother's father had refused to accept because he did not want to be "the servant of two masters." She also must have had a non-growing meagre pension as the widow of someone with the title of *Zoka ol Mamaalek*, meaning, I guess, the intelligent of many countries. But I could be wrong. My Arabic is bad. Our uncle colonel kept telling us, "Learn Arabic." We didn't listen; now I have to suffer the consequences.

"Sarhang, you have told the truth and nothing but the truth," I sometimes say out loud when I am alone in my room because this is what he wanted to be said about him after his death. He says in his book that all he wants people to say after he is gone, if they care to say anything, is this short phrase, "Sarhang, you told the truth."

The name of Sharabi (Sarhang) too appears in some of the postpartum letters. My mother seems to be waiting for his arrival to Mashad as eagerly as someone waiting for a saviour, even though I do not detect any unhappiness in her life in Mashad to be saved from.

I will write a long letter to Monavar, copy to Monir, to thank them for sending me these precious letters.

Monavar's own note in the package is written with a large loose script on every other line of the page. This is because she has pain in her hands. Both her thumbs are painful, so much so that she cannot hold the pen firmly enough to write. I am going to invite her here so that my two rheumatologist sons can examine her hands and either cure her or close their offices if they can't.

Previously, after she insisted that she would like to see some of the chapters of my book, I had sent her the chapter "Going Home," in which our father dies and our mother throws a tantrum in the yard. I had asked her to tell me if she remembered that gloomy evening and if she did what her reaction to it was. In her note she says that she remembers it clearly, "As if it was yesterday." She was thinking that our mother would die as the result of her sorrow. "I kept asking Auntie Pouran if Modar-jun did the same things in Mashad when her mother died," Monavar writes, "hoping that she would say 'yes' so that I could reassure myself that it was possible to survive such sorrow."

53

TRANSLATION OF ONE OF THE
POSTPARTUM LETTERS

HERE IS THE TRANSLATION OF ONE OF THOSE THIRTY LETTERS, probably written during the winter, most likely near the time of unveiling of women in Iran.

Estimated date: Winter of 1934

Mashad, Iran.

Tassadoghat, [an Arabic salutation, with a complex meaning] your precious letter is at hand. While I was reading it, Shazdeh unexpectedly returned from Torbat and I let him read it. I did not think he would be back so soon. Now, with my listlessness and heaviness with my tenth child, and his recurring fever, I don't know what I am going to do. Thanks to God, the fever has ceased for now.

The thought of purchasing a *Paltow* [an overcoat for winter] has become an obsession for me. It does not leave me alone even for a minute. You can't imagine how crowded the seamstress shops are in Mashad. So many people want to make new dresses at once. Not only are they crowded, they all have long waiting lists too. I am sure Tehran is like this too but since the Tehranis knew about it a few months earlier, they did not have to rush to the tailors all at once, as women are doing here.

A few days ago, I went to the bazaar with Afsar. We saw several Khanums buying hats. Not to remain hatless [a Persian pun; also meaning to be a pushover] Afsar and I went in to try a few. In the store I found out that the size of my head is not 53. A number 53 hat does not exist at all. When I wrote to you to buy a number 53 hat, it was because I had tried Alieh Khanum's hat, when she came to our house for a short visit, and Afsar said that it suited me, and its number was 53. Either she made a mistake in reading the number or perhaps the numbering system differs from hat to hat. If you decide to buy a hat for me, buy one that fits your own head. And if you have not bought it yet, let me know the price of the hat as well as the price of material for my *Paltow*. I will see if it is better to get them from Tehran or here in Mashad.

Tonight, to my surprise, Shazdeh said that the material for a *Paltow* is less expensive in Mashad than in Tehran, and of much better quality. Also, Shazdeh was wondering how is it possible that a dress made for me in Tehran, in my absence, would fit me. I think he is right and I agreed with him to buy it here, because one *Paltow* is not enough for anybody anyway. If you have already bought the material for it, it is okay, but if not, don't bother. I too don't think that if one adds the price of the material to the high cost of labour in Tehran, it would be less than what it is in Mashad. Write to me about the price of *Mahout* [broadcloth] and *Fastooni* anyway.

Since the beginning of the month, I have written more letters to you so that you won't worry about me. I hope I will be postpartum soon [delivering Homa] so that I might be free of worry, like you. Because you are praying for me I am a little reassured. I know that your prayers for me are effective. Hazrateh Sarhang [Colonel Sharabi] has not arrived yet and his delay has sewed my eyes to the entrance door. He will come, I know, but I am afraid that he will come at a time when I won't be able to see enough of him.

If you can, buy two more hairpins for me—like the two you have already sent me—and give them to Sarhang to bring when he comes. I am sorry that I lost the hairpins that I liked so much in the change room of the bathhouse. I promise you that I will be careful not to lose the ones I hope you are going to send me.

Convey my *Salaams* to your daughter, Sar-kaareh Maheen Khanum. Also, give my eager *Salaam* to Mansur-jun, Monir-jun, Monavar-jun and Mehdi-jun. [This is the only time Mehdi receives the suffix *jun*, most likely due to his being away.] *Ensha-Allah*, they are all healthy and happy. The children here are all fine and kiss the hand of their Auntie Pouran. As well, Hazrateh Ellieh, my mother, sends her regards to you.

At this time everyone in the entire world seems to be preoccupied with hat and *Paltow*. You too must have become a hat-wearing lady by now! My mother is going on a pilgrimage to Atabat [religious cities for Shi'eh Muslims in Iraq, mainly Karbela and Najaf] or Ghom.

Maman-jun, tell me, what do I do? Everybody has a *Paltow* except me! And now that Shazdeh wants me to have it made here, how am I going to go for measurements and fittings every hour with this distended abdomen of mine? You don't know how ashamed I am to let a male tailor measure me so late in my pregnancy. It would not be so embarrassing if it were you who were measuring me.

I end this letter to stop bothering you any further.

I *Ghorban* myself for you,

Nayyereh

54

A Scolding Letter to Auntie Pouran

Tassadoghat, TWO OF YOUR LETTERS, the one in which you had helped the children regarding their pocket money and your regular letter, arrived together today, two weeks after you had mailed your second letter; and I thank you for both of them.

Also, reading between the lines, I see that you are again upset with me for some unknown reason. This astonishes me. I don't understand you. Why? Never do I deliberately do anything to annoy you, especially now that my heart is so constricted for having not seen its Maman-jun, which is you. Every hour of the day I tell myself the story of the coming summer and your arrival here. Yesterday, I cut shorts and an undershirt to sew for myself so that when you come you won't say that I am still wearing what you sewed for me the last summer, but I don't have the patience to sew them. All I do is think about you and the summer.

Actually, on second thought, I don't want you to sew dresses for me anymore. Ignore my request about the overcoat in my last letter, too. I really don't need a new dress. What I have is already too much for Mashad. I will wait until the summer, when you are here.

No. I don't want that either. I don't want you to do any sewing for me during the summer either, so that you won't think that I need you only for sewing. You shouldn't sew anything for me anymore.

In Torbat one gets bored sometimes, and sewing is a good antidote for it. But in Mashad, I don't want you to waste your time on sewing, especially now that you have become a woman with children. I don't want you to spend your precious time on anything but me.

You said the children wake up every morning and tell you their dreams and you try to fulfill their dreams so that they will develop will power. I too would have had a dream every hour had I had someone like you to reward me for them.

You said that you wanted to help develop the children's will power. I thank you for that and I hope that the children won't abuse your compliance and kindness. Do you remember this line "Those whose words are the deeds of kings should say that which is worthy of the ear of kings"? Please don't spoil my children. I won't be able to continue your kindness with them when they come back to me.

Maheen Khanum, of course, has good taste, and Monir and Monavar look at her during the day and have beautiful dreams at nights. The reason I bought their last dresses here in the same colour and the same material was not because I wanted to dress them similarly. Actually, I had let them choose the colour and the material by themselves. Unbeknownst to each other, each chose the same material and the same colour, after one thousand times of hesitations and *Ta'arof* of course. I would become spoiled, too, had I had a person like you beside me.

I had to do some sewing for the *Aadams* the day before yesterday. It is ironic, I thought. When you are here, I don't even sew back the fallen button of my pants. When you are not here I become the seamstress of the *Aadams*! Whose fault is this? Tell me; you or me? Of course it is your fault.

Despite your morbid prediction, my Mahmood-jun has recovered from his measles and today he has been to bathhouse and now he is sitting beside me, healthy, clean and alive. God forbid, he did not go the other way; otherwise you would have attributed his demise to my incompetence as a mother. How do you know that I have been inattentive to him or any other of my children? Or, do you want to say that I should have prevented him from catching them in the first place? How come all your four children caught the black-cough [whooping cough] despite all your hygienic measures and preventive methods. No, I don't rinse our lettuce head with permanganates solution before serving. Unlike you, I believe that when one has many small children, when one of them comes down with one of these contagious diseases of infancy, one should expose the rest to it so that they too catch it and get it over with all together. And if, God forbid, they are destined to go the other way [die] the sooner they let me know the better.

If you want to get credit for taking the children to the doctor as soon as they cough, go ahead and collect the credit. I don't mind. But be reasonable and give me some credit, too. Be fair. Thanks to God, all of my remaining children here are healthy for the moment and are sitting around me and talking to me and to each other.

I wish you were here and could listen to the conversation between Nasser and Hamid. They are not aware that I am listening. Hamid is saying to Nasser, "Yesterday, when I said to you, 'I don't like you,' I was joking." And Nasser—you can't imagine with what an officious and manly voice—is telling Hamid, "What do you mean by joking? Jokes are for women. Have you ever seen two men joke with each other in this house?"

The point is that, for now at least, all my children are alive and healthy and they kiss the hand of their Khaleh-jan from this long distance. Despite all my inattention and carelessness, there seems to be someone higher up and kinder than you and me in this world that is taking care of them. And I am confident that *Khoda* will continue to do so until their time is up. Therefore, don't worry about these matters anymore. You have not grown your wisdom teeth yet. I know my job. I don't know if I am doing the right thing or the wrong thing, but this is the only way I know. I am sorry for having said these things in this letter, but it is you who make me say them.

Ensha-Allah, try to teach me when you are here next summer. Whatever you say to me from faraway, I will scold you. Please convey my *Salaams*, once again, to your good daughter, Sar-kaareh Maheen Jun.

Ghorbanat,

Nayyereh

55

EXCERPTS FROM THE REST OF THE POSTPARTUM LETTERS

I CAN NEITHER IGNORE THE REST OF THE POSTPARTUM LETTERS, nor do I wish to translate all of them here. The best I can do is to translate the occasional paragraphs that catch my eye as I go through them.

Here is something about the two sisters, Monir and Monavar that seems to be written before they were sent to Tehran.

…Today Monir, from the early morning that she has gotten out of bed, has been wanting to write a letter to her Auntie Pouran, and Monavar, of course, says, "Then I have to write too." And I, always impatient with the rivalry among my children, dampened their enthusiasm by telling them that no one in Tehran is anxiously waiting to receive a letter from either of them. Nevertheless, both are now sitting down to write their letters.

…Also included in this letter is what you cannot see. The rest of the children have included their kisses for their Auntie Pouran's hands for what she is going to do for their mother.

…I hope once again *Khoda* will facilitate my coming to see you and to bother you.

…I seem to have nothing to give to them [the children?] but the heavy burden of my weight on their little shoulders. The children are always thinking or talking about Tehran, and I don't blame them. I hope God will provide me with the opportunity of meeting you again, and the rest of the family in Tehran. Of course, Fatmeh Khanum must have already arrived there, and I am sure she has talked about Hamid's *Jamaal* [beauty] and *kamaal* [perfection], so I don't have to brag about him in this letter. Despite your always making fun of Nasser's looks and calling him ugly and *Siah*, he is good at music. My mother has nicknamed him Sheikh Sheypoor [master of the trumpet.]

In defense of myself (the translator) I have to say that I don't remember playing any musical instrument as a child. Having no musical instrument in that house also makes it very unlikely that I played the trumpet. The only instrument that I played for a short while was accordion and that was when I was about twenty-one and was a medical student. I particularly never played the trumpet because I did not like its sound. To me, it sounded like a children's fart mixed with those of grown-ups.

…Yesterday, the Princess and several other chic ladies were here, visiting. Unfortunately Hamid was not home so that I could show off his face. Only Nasser was home. I am afraid by the summer when you will be here Hamid will lose his charm and good nature because it will be his teething time.

…But don't laugh too loudly about Nasser. Be patient. Wait just a few more years till Nasser become a man. Then, he will show you what he can do to you.

… My *Salaam* to Afsar Khanum, and please tell her that her departure from our house has left a larger hole than the departure of my own children.

…Yes I have become a chicken factory as you said. That is my *Ghesmat* [Kismet; share or destiny]. God willing, I will share them with you. I know God's hands work in mysterious ways. You can have the first four of my children forever.

… Write to me more about Sarhang's problem so that I can put my mind at rest. Include how much his salary has been reduced to while being *Montazer-Khedmat* [waiting to re-enter the work force for the government].

I think my mother is referring to the demotion of Colonel Sharabi after he shot to death one of his colleagues in a drinking party beside a pool in a garden.

…Is Sarhang hoping to go back to work soon or is that it? No? Tell me more about him, please. What kind of letter writing is this? Either don't give me any news, or, if you do, tell it completely. You start to tell me news and then forget about it and go on to tell me something else. Remember, from a long distance, one tends to interpret any bad news much worse than it actually is.

…Don't "share the information and keep the secrets." This bad habit is the motto of some of the ladies in our vicinity in Torbat, who want to sow the seeds of *Nefaagh* [discord] among friends.

… If you find Tayyebeh Khanum's identification booklet, please sent it to her. She might need it for her marriage. These days, whatever one has to do, they ask for one's Sejel [identification booklet].

… My best regards to Fatmeh-Khanum. Her absence is very noticeable here, especially for Hamid and his mother.

…Shazdeh Khanum Afsar-Saltaneh [the Tehranian wife of Shazdeh Mohammad Sadegh Mirza], my best friend in Torbat, is running an intermittent fever and might go back to Tehran for treatment. I hope it is not consumption.

We never saw that beautiful princess, but judging by the appearance of her first daughter, Anvar, whose long and delicate neck, large black eyes and upward tilted nose made her resemble the romantic and dramatic Hollywood star, Hedi Lamar, we could tell how beautiful she must have been. We never saw the agonizing letters exchanged between my mother and the princess, but those who have seen them say that, compared to these postpartum letters, they were ten times better. The two women had similar destinies and loved each other very much. And our father was aware of their intense friendship. This is why whenever our father wanted to reward my mother for having done something good, he would send for a *Doroshkeh* to come and take my mother to her friend or bring her to our house. Sometimes, when neither of them could get out due to illness, the *Doroshkeh chee* would carry only their letters from one house to the other.

…I don't know why consumption makes one's eyelashes so long and emotions so tender. I hope she is not *Maslool*. They have small children.

Afsar-Saltaneh did die of consumption and left Mohammad Sadegh Mirza with many motherless children. It was worse to be motherless than fatherless. One of the daughters, Maheen, was the one who was sent to Mashad for her incurable illness and died in the room where I burst my red balloon for her.

… My heart burns more for Maheen than if she were one of my own daughters.

The other son of her friend, Mohammad Mirza, now a great poet living in Iran, spent the time of his higher education in our house in Tehran and educated us in traditional Persian poetry. And I have told the story of Gholam Hossein Mirza and his failure in grade nine when he was living with us in our house in Sanguelaj district.

But soon after the death of his wife, Mohammad Sadegh Mirza went to Tehran and married Ghodsi Khanum, a woman who looked a lot like our mother, with rounded and elegant features as well as visible nobility in her movement. She too became the best friend of my mother.

… Yesterday was the day of practice for the day of unveiling again. Luckily, there was not enough room for all the families to attend, so Ghodsi Khanum [the new sister-in-law] was among the ones who had to go, and I was the lucky one who got to stay home with my children. Tell her mother, Khanum Modeer, that her daughter (without a chador) did not look as chaste as she claimed to be in Tehran!

Khosrow Mirza, our cousin who is old enough to have known our father and Mohammad Sadegh Mirza, has told me that they were both very smart but Mohammad Sadegh Mirza had an additional skill that many, including our father, lacked. "He knew the times table," Khosrow Mirza said, "and that put him ahead of his rivals when they had to quickly calculate the profits or losses of their transactions."

I can understand that. It is like someone knowing about computers today among those who know nothing about them.

Ghodsi Khanum's mother, like my mother's mother, was wise, and, unlike my mother, she was very argumentative. They both argued with unreasonable preaching mullahs. Once, they say, my mother's mother, objected to an uneducated preacher when he said of a woman saint that she was so busy at home that she had to throw her breasts backwards over her shoulders so that her two children could help themselves to milk, while she was doing her daily chores, by saying, "Why don't you give us a better example of her sainthood, rather than saying these incredible and ridiculous things?"

Khanum Modeer was called by this name because she was the principal of a high school for girls in Tehran. For this reason, she was more prone to teaching and scolding than our grandmother. Once, an overzealous neighbour scolded his daughter for wanting to wear high-heeled shoes and a satin chador like Khanum Modeer's, because "it would lead to her losing her virginity before getting married." When the news reached Khanum Modeer's ears, she put a pair of polished black high-heeled shoes and a shimmering satin chador together and sent them to the house of the zealous neighbour, with this message: "Keep these things in your house next to your daughter's shoes and chador for a few days and let me know if any bad thing happens to the virginity of your daughter."

… Shazdeh, *Behamdollah* [thanks to God] is better. I hope it is not consumption; otherwise, with so many small children, I don't know how to prevent any contagious contact. Thanks to God that Shazdeh is not the kissing or hugging type. They [he] have just gone to rent a car to go back to Torbat. And I am taking this opportunity to write these few lines so that you won't worry about me. As I said, my health these days is not very good. I know it is because of this temporary heaviness near the end of my pregnancy. Also I know it is going to get worse before it gets better. I have to be patient until the next month, which is the month of Bahman. I hope that this time, too, with your prayer, I will survive.

… You always ask why I do not come to Tehran instead of you coming here—as if I don't want to be in Tehran. On the contrary, I swear to the uniqueness of *Khoda* that this is my only wish. The reason I don't keep saying it is because I do not want to include the impossible among my wishes.

…The schoolgirls are now going to school without *hejab*. Their parents will do the same in a month or two when it becomes compulsory. I have not found either a hat or *Paltow* yet, and I don't think I will be getting them until after the New Year—which would suit better the height of a minaret than me [a Persian proverb: A dress after the New Year is good only for a minaret].

… Don't worry about me. Your worries won't help me, but would make you sick. Whatever is the will of God will happen.

…. The letters of Malek Mansur, Monir, Monavar and Mehdi have arrived. I am satisfied with them and their progress. I hope I will soon have money to make them satisfied with me, too.

… Hossein has written a letter to Mansur, and I, out of laziness, am writing a few words in his letter to be counted as one of mine. Today is the ninth [postpartum] day. *Ensha-Allah* I will go to *the Hammam* [bathhouse] tomorrow. Even though it is the ninth day, I have not gotten out of bed yet. I am so worried about my *Haal* [condition], especially today, because it is snowing a little too. All this winter the weather has been good, but today it is cold and snowy, and I do not dare to get out of the bed even if I had the energy. I have become very small. Yesterday, I tried on the ready-made *Paltow* that I bought. It was a little too large for me. Afsar-jun and the children are all healthy. The name of the newborn might be Homa. We have not decided on that yet. I don't like her yet. She bothered me too much before coming out.

… I am sitting in the children's room. They are doing their homework, I am writing mine. Mehdi is doing so well in the first year of school that it surprises me, even though until the middle of the month of Sha'ban his seventh year won't be complete. I did not insist that he should start going to school early, but he wanted to, mostly because the older ones were going to school and they seem to enjoy it. I was always worried that Mehdi was a little *Kam-Zehn* [low intelligence] but so far he has proved me wrong and I am very glad about it. I hope he will be like this all his life. Hossein's head is now all right. Nasser is also free of problems. He plays his trumpet and is busy with his own thoughts. It is because you have asked me to write about all and each one of my children that I am writing these trivial things; otherwise I have so much to do that you wouldn't believe.

…life is passing uneventfully for now.

… I have not heard about Bozorg Omid for a long time.

In her triple letter written to her first three children, she talks to each of them individually. She first thanks Mansur for doing well in school and reminds him that he should continue to do well and even better because he is the first son and will be an example for the rest. And by attributing Mehdi's success to his leadership, my mother is indicating that Mansur is already an example for his younger brother.

She thanks Monir and reminds her to improve on her handwriting because one is often judged by one's handwriting. She thanks Monavar for doing so well and writing so sensibly. She says that Hossein is becoming naughty and *Sheitoon* [like a little Satan] and so far has received many threats and warnings that he would receive bodily punishments if he continued to be like that. "I will see when I am going to actualize my threats."

… I am surprised at the slowness of education in schools in Mashad. Hossein is doing so well in school because I have taught him a little at home. The things Hossein learned in one day, the school teaches in six days. Hossein is bored, that is perhaps why he has become so *Sheitoon.*

…From the very hour that you departed, my heart has become tight and constricted. I hope you have reached Tehran with complete health and that your letter will reach me soon. In the last two days wrong thoughts have occupied my brain again. I have been crying for you, too, as you had requested.

… Hamid is sleeping in my mother's mosquito net. And I have erected another mosquito net for Nasser and the rest of the children in my room. Nasser does not cry anymore in the morning. Last night, when Hamid's nanny came, I did not give him to her to be taken to her house because at nights he is not a problem to me when he is asleep, and in the mornings, I am awake anyway. Why shouldn't he sleep with me? He knows how to make room in one's heart for himself. He keeps hanging from my neck to tell me, "I like you."

…The children, as soon as they saw I was writing a letter to you, have begun ordering the things they want you to send them. It is the story of the *Bazargan* [businessman] and the Parrot. Hossein is ordering a bicycle, Monavar, a sewing machine. Nasser wants all the things that the others want, and Hamid whatever Nasser wants. Mehdi is at school. I am getting dizzy just by listening to their demands.

…By the way, let me tell you about Shazdeh. He sheds so many tears over Mansur's absence that I don't know where he had hidden them before. He cried continuously for two days and two nights after Mansur left. He did not eat his supper the first night.

…. Majid has become so good and obedient. After I told him once that one should not keep asking for candies, and should ask for some good words instead, now, when he wants candies, he says, "I want good words, Modar-jun."

56

THE ONLY LETTER FROM HOSSEIN

AMONG THE POSTPARTUM LETTERS OF MY MOTHER there is a short one from Hossein to Mansur. He must have written it when he was in grade one in Mashad. This is the same letter that my mother has added a few lines at the bottom of it to be counted as one of her letters to Auntie Pouran as well.

"Mansur-jun, we have reached up to the head of *Aab-paash* [The watering can with a head like a shower-head, used predominantly for watering the flowers in the outdoor gardens]. Last week we had examination. Mr. teacher said that I will receive an award. By the time you come back I will be going to grade two."

Signed

Hossein Shojania

The following lines are what my mother has added to Hossein's letter:

… Hossein's handwriting is usually better than this. He has tried too hard to write this letter; that is why it is not as good.

Hossein is doing well, almost too well. I am more worried about Hossein than Nasser or Mehdi. I am afraid that if one day he becomes lazy he won't revert to studying again. Lazy children have a good chance to study seriously, but when serious students become lazy, it would take a miracle to become good again.

Nayyereh

57

THE ONLY LETTER FROM OUR FATHER

AMONG THE THIRTY POSTPARTUM LETTERS, there is one from our father to Auntie Pouran. It is a short one and it has a date. His handwriting is better and more mature than that of our mother. The string of superlative adjectives and salutation at the head of the letter, without mentioning the name of the receiver, makes it difficult to know if it was addressed to Auntie Pouran or the mother of Modar-jun, but since it has been in possession of Auntie Pouran, I have assumed that it has been addressed to her.

It is not surprising that my father's handwriting is better than my mother's because our father was the teacher of our mother in this matter. During the first seven years of their marriage, because they had no children, practising handwriting was one of the better things my mother was doing.

25-10-1314

(Winter of 1935)

Torbat

Hazrateh Ellieh, Sar-kar Khanum …

Ensha-Allah [God willing], your *Haal* and *Ahvaal*, as well as those of the light-of-the-eyes [the children], are fine. Were you to ask about my health; it is about a week since I have gone to Torbat from Mashad. Of course, you do remember that for a while—that would be about forty days—I was running a fever in Mashad. The treatments were not effective at all. Finally, the professor and our own doctor prescribed travelling to a better climate. The climate of Torbat seems to suit my constitution better. For the first time, my fever has come down today, which is the second day of my arrival to Torbat, by two *Oshr* [Arabic for a tenth] but it has not ceased completely. I feel weak and powerless. I am disappointed with

343

my health and my constitution. I think this last recurrence is due to the fact that I went to the notary for some land transaction; the office was chilly and the floor was bare. I think I caught a cold through my feet by putting the soles of my shoes on the cold floor.

Of course, when the weakness is complicated by the lack of a private *Parastar* [nurse], it is always the cause of worry, whether one is at home or on the road. If the fever does not cease today I will return to Mashad—and will see what the *Khaajeh* of destiny [God] has preserved for me.

I don't feel good. Inquire about the health of the light-of-the-eyes for me. Of course "veil-ripping" by the police has not totally stopped here and it is the news of the day in Torbat. Today, the officials with their wives are invited to the Culture and Education Building. The officials, their wives and their friends visit each other every night. Hopefully this [prohibition of the chador] will spread to the entire country so that the progress of *Khanum-ha* [ladies] in Iran can begin.

A bank note for the amount of fifty *Tuman* is enclosed, for now. Please convey my *Salaam* to Seddigheh Khanum and all the other Khanum-ha and *Aghaayan* [ladies and gentlemen] of the family.

I feel so weak that the pen weighs heavy in my hand. I apologize for my weakness.

Offering my respects to all; I say *Khoda-hafez* for now.

Mojtaba

58

ALCOHOL: THE MOTHER OF ALL VICES

Estimated date: Early 1970's

Tehran

Azeez Doctor Nasser, my own good son,

In an interval of three days I have received two letters from you. Believe me, the one that did not have an attachment made me happier than the one that did. It indicated that you were truly thinking about me and wanted to talk to your mother from the bottom of your heart. I enjoyed it a lot. Anybody who reads your letters enjoys them tremendously, as if reading the best writing. This is I think due to the sincerity which is embedded in them. When words arise from the heart, they have no choice but to sit on the heart.

About three weeks ago I wrote three letters, through you, for your three children. I hope they have arrived by now. The attachment in it was for your three sons. It was not for the feast of Janvier. It was what I owed them. It was the money accumulated for the numbers of chewing gum they did not receive from me because they were away all these years. It was not for the New Year. New Years will come and go, every year, but where would I be in the future New Years? God only knows. *Ensha Allah*, my good boys, remain good forever, and you'll be satisfied with them.

Offer my many *Salaams* to Mitra Khanum. I don't know where Mr. and Mrs. Khazaei are now. When they were here we would occasionally hear from them by telephone, but now, nothing.

I have already written to you about the passing of Mr. Neek-Eteghad [Sia's father] but you have forgotten it. It is now four months since his passing. Too bad you did not write any letter to Pari and Sia to express your condolences, but now it is too late. You also wanted Shambool's address, which I have given to you, but I am sure you have lost it.

By the way, I am very glad that you have eliminated alcohol from your everyday life, because when one ages, the side effects of bad things become worse and last longer. It becomes a vicious cycle. First, it [alcohol] diminishes one's wisdom a little bit—as little as the tip of a sewing needle—and then, with that diminished wisdom, one begins to treat oneself through self-medication by taking pills to become the way one was before the drink. But, unfortunately, when wisdom is lacking no ruins ever becomes *Aabad* with these measures. How is it possible that an essence which is devoid of existence, could impart existence to the non-existent?" Who can guide a *Divaneh* [fool] who considers himself to have the *Aghleh Koll* [total wisdom]?

Talking about *Koll*, it is not a coincidence that this word appears in the word alcohol as well. Alcohol is an Arabic word, meaning the whole or the totality, but a Persian scientist by the name of Razi discovered it. He chose an Arabic name for it because that was the language of science in those days—Farsi was for the ordinary people and poets. He named it such because he thought he had discovered the most important and the most encompassing chemical.

Let us read the rest of my mother's letter.

A while ago, *Jesue* [Shambool's divorced French wife] came back from France with Shambool's approval to see her children. Apparently, she did not have Shambool's permission to come back sooner. She has remarried. Shambool too came to see her, but during the month that she was here, Shambool slept all the time, taking ten to twenty pills a day. Because he is a doctor and is wise (!) No one can tell him anything. Poor Naadereh Khanum is eating her heart out for him. She does not feel well these days. No one asked Shambool, "Why did you come, if you didn't want to pay attention to anybody?"

Here, there is a lot of news about divorce in many families. Khosrow's nerves [Monir's second son who committed suicide with sleeping pills a year or so later] are very weak. Now he wants to divorce his wife. Soraya, Tayyebeh Khanum's daughter, and Layli, Dr. Shojania's daughter, want to divorce. We will see which one succeeds.

Hossein's *Haal* is very good. As of the beginning of the month of Ramezan, when everybody in this house was busy with *Ebaadat* [slavery to, or worship of God] he too became *Abed* and decided by himself to put alcohol aside and do *Namaaz* for a few days. This abstinence from alcohol was really good for him. Alcohol definitely accentuates the states of mind that one is in. At the moment he is very good. He does not get out of the house at all. He is sitting beside me and Pouran-*dokht* and of course reads your letters, too.

Auntie Pouran always has some nagging problems, such as pains in the lumbar region, legs or other places. She goes to doctor and takes medicine but is surprised that why she does not recover as fast as she used to. No matter how many times I tell her, "*Khanum*, we are not the same people we used to be, anymore" it won't make any difference to her.

Ghorban you all,

Mother

PS: Regarding our relation to Agha Khan, I have said it twice before. I say it now for the third and last time. Write it down somewhere that you can find it again, when you need it.

Both my father and mother are closely related to Agha Khan, but each differently. The mother of Sultan Mohammad Shah [the Grand Agha Khan] was my father's aunt.

My mother is the daughter of Sardar Abol Hassan Khan who was the brother of the grand Agha Khan. He lived in Iran. When Agha Khan became powerful outside of Iran, they put his brother in prison, to prevent him from becoming king and replacing the Qajar Dynasty. While in prison in Tehran he copied the sacred book of Koran, seven times in his good handwriting that was indistinguishable from print. After seven years he was pardoned and released from prison. As a sign of friendship and lasting peace, Abdollah Mirza, one of the sons of Fatali Shah, gave his daughter to him as his wife. My mother and my Daii Sahaam Nezam [Bozorg Omid's father] are their two offspring.

Mother

59

AN OLD LETTER FROM MONIR, DATED SPRING OF 2537

THE DATE OF THE LETTER OF MONIR IS MORE SIGNIFICANT than its contents. The year must be a year or two before the Islamic revolution in Iran that occurred near the end of 1979.

A year or two before the Islamic revolution, the Shah of Iran with the approval of the Parliament decided to change the Persian calendar from *Hejri*—the year that Hazrateh Mohammad moved from Mecca to Medina, which is the year 622 AD—to the Shahan-shahi calendar which begins with the year of coronation of the first Shah of Iran, about 2500 years ago. This abrupt change, rather than fortifying the position of the Shah, backfired and weakened it, so much so that soon, after a year or so, under the pressure of the clergies and the advice of some experienced political figures, he reverted to the previous calendar. Only a few collectable golden coins and stamps remain from that period, as well as this letter:

I *Ghorban* myself for my very dear Nasser,

I hope that your *Haal*, like always, is good and better than ours. I have delayed my reply to your letter for a ridiculous reason. Knowing that you did not like air letters [the ones that fold to become a stamped envelope, ready to mail] because of their limited space, I had decided to write my letter on proper writing paper. Would you believe me if I told you that no stationery shop or any supermarket carried those papers? It made me really mad. They had only those old postal papers (the ones our mother always used before the advent of air letters) and I did not like those. I waited for a while, and then I thought I should at least reply to Mitra and tell her that her letter had made me very glad. I wrote it, and I thought for a few more days, then I saw that, no, there is no benefit in waiting, and I finally mailed that letter. That is what happened up to yesterday.

I don't know if you remember Iraj Jahan-shahi*, the son-in-law of Mr. Niayesh. He is one of the best *Aadams* of the world, and I like both him and his *Khanum* very much.

I go to their house almost twice a month and stay about two hours each time. His house is the only place in which I really have a good time. His passtime, unlike that of most of our friends, is not playing cards. As he says, he drinks occasional glass of *May*. He is a learned man, writes good pieces and speaks well. His wife is also a good housewife. She does not gossip and laughs well. In short, the matter of letter-writing came up in our conversation and I told him what trouble I had regarding finding proper paper to write to you. He said he had some and brought these very thin pages on which I am now writing.

Meanwhile, you came into our conversation and I told him how much joy your letters bring to my life, and how well you write. And I recited your poem, "Forty Parrots for the Forty-Piece Quilt of Modar-jun," for him, as much as I could remember from memory; which was almost all of it. He liked it very much and made me promise to bring him a copy of it next time. In summary, as much as it was possible I bragged about my dear brother, and made Jahan-shahi feel sorry that he has not seen you for a long time. He frequently travels to your side of the world, especially now that his heart has suffered an infarction. He goes there for annual check-ups and follow-ups.

So far my letter is all about Jahan-shahi. My own *Haal*—deaf be the ear of *Sheitoon*—is not bad. My jaundice, luckily without contaminating anybody else, has disappeared, and my convalescence is finished. The visits and paying back visits of the New Year are over. Hossein Gholi Khan (Bozorg Omid) is still alive. Ali, his son, after divorcing his Italian wife, Anna, married the youngest daughter of Norolhoda Khanum (mother of Holaaku) named Zohreh.

Modar-jun and Khaleh-jan are average, not good and not bad. Today they were at our house for lunch, with Hossein. Hossein did not seem in good shape because he reported many bad news. (By the way, Nasser-jun, Modar-jun asked me to tell you that Hossein reads your letters too. So remember not to refer to his mental status in your letter.) Also let me tell you that Homa Khanum Mazaher, the sister of General Hedayat's wife, passed away this morning.

Monavar-jun and her family are well, and we are planning—God willing—to go to Mashad together for four days to see our cousins, as well as to make a pilgrimage to the shrine of Hazrateh Reza. By the way, Mehri Khanum Poorpak, who had gone to America to stay for good, came back after two years. Last week was the wedding of the daughter of Mehri Ghahreman, Shapoor Mirza's wife. Even we who are living here can't believe that children grow so fast, let alone you who are not here.

By the way, how are Kami and Keyvan and Nima? I write so much nonsense that I have to apologize. I like, when I am writing to you, to keep writing and writing, but I don't have your pen to make my letters sweet and readable. So I have to fill them with junk, but it is okay. Ebi and Khosrow and Shirin send their *Salaam*. Ebi was saying that he had not done anything to be worthy of his Daii Nasser to deserve so many thanks that you had sent to him in your letter.

By the way, I don't know how much of Ali Reza and Mehdi—the two sons of Ebi—you have seen. The younger one, Mehdi, looks very much like you, both in appearance and intelligence. His sharp mind and incisive comments always remind me of you. Shirin's daughter is also reaching the age of cuteness. At the end of Ordibehesht she finishes her second year of life, and makes a lot of *Shirin-zabani* [sweet talking] all day, and this takes all the tiredness out of my body.

Well, dear Nasser, I have to think of you, too, and stop this nonsense here. Kiss Mitra for me and thank her again for her letter. Meanwhile I hope my letter has reached her hands.

Raastee [truthfully], Touran Khanum, the widow of General Hedayat, always asks about you when I see her.

Your sister,

Monir

P.S.

Nasser-jun, *Salaam* again. The poem I have included in my letter is from Mohammad Mirza, made for his deaf and mute son. For years, his wife's pregnancies ended in spontaneous abortions. Finally, after a lot of *Nazr-o-neeyaz* [vows and promises of charity], she delivered a beautiful boy, but unfortunately, he turned out to be deaf and mute. It is in its original Mashadi or Torbati dialect. I don't know if you remember anything of our father's language. And I can't guess whether you will like this poem or not. But I send it anyway to compensate for the emptiness of my own letter.

Monir

I cannot find that poem now. Maybe I have referred to it in one of the previous chapters. Anything that I have talked about before has disappeared from my mind. The only thing that has stayed in my mind is its title because it was made of three words, each beginning with the harsh sound of 'Kh': *Kheday* [for] *Khodaayeh* [the God of] *Khodom* [myself], in Torbati dialect.

And I remember its first line:

What is the use of telling or not telling my story?

When my own son cannot hear it, what is the use?

I know why the wife of General Hedayat talks about me whenever she sees my sister. After she became a widow, she began writing poems about her husband's goodness, so many that those who were close to her thought that she had gone mad. Only I, from distance, diagnosed her poetic reaction to the death of her husband, as a normal phenomenon and had encouraged her to say more about her noble husband. Was it not for her husband, maybe Sia and I would still be in prison and Khosrow Pouria dead—even though I know Monavar's tears had a lot to do with our release.

*Mr. Jahan-shahi: An educated educator

Of course I remember him. He is the one who undertook to take care of the proof-reading and publishing of *SOS*. And apparently his relationship with our *Daii* was not as good at the end of the book as it was at the beginning—typical of the relationship of any author with any editor, whether related to each other or not.

I know him as a born teacher. Among my unique books, filed beside the books of my grandfather and other Persian heritage books, there is one published by Iraj Jahan-shahi and Abbas Sayyahi.

This book is published by the Ministry of Education, expenses paid by the Shahan-shahy Foundation for Social Services, headed by the twin sister of the Shah, Princess Ashraf Pahlavi.

It is titled *A Guide for Teaching Farsi in Grade One*. Had it been available when I was in grade one, it would have made a better person out of me. This book and three others were to be distributed, free of charge, to all the students across Iran from grade one to grade four.

The cover of the book looks like any other textbook for elementary school with its ever-present logo "Knowledge is Power" stamped at the left upper corner.

The first few pages of the book are covered by the pictures of the royal family:

1—The Shah in a civilian suit.

2—Farah Diba, with straight, combed black hair, black eyebrows, black eyes, smiling lips, and triple strings of pearls as necklace.

3—Reza Pahlavi, at the age of seven, but as good-looking and well dressed as Houshi when he was a child.

4—Ashraf Pahlavi, the twin sister of the Shah, standing with hair down to her lower neck, dressed in a thick overcoat like those worn by models in winter fashion shows, downcast eyes, and well-delineated closed black lips, reading something from an open white book in her hand.

The book is well illustrated with drawings over-painted with watercolours. In the first chapter which is titled, "From Home to School," it shows the things a little girl in grade one should do from the moment she wakes up: the yawn, the washing in front of a sink equipped with mirror, putting on her overcoat over her shirt, one arm at a time (no picture of lost socks, no crying, no hint of reluctance in the face of the girl about going to school).

Among the things that teachers should not do is this: "If a child is left-handed, do not force him or her to become right-handed. Teach him or her how to write well with the left hand. Remember that they would need to put the left lower corner of paper on the desk slightly higher than the right-handed students."

Among the things that the authors remind the teacher to do is this: "Have lines on the blackboard, and introduce punctuation in writing." "Literacy," it says in the introduction, "is a means to reach a better life; not an end by itself." About teaching language, "Language is built on four pillars: two auditory, hearing and speaking, and two visual, reading and writing. Before teaching the latter two, make sure the child has learned the former two at home."

The last time I met Mr. Jahan-shahi was in the summer of 1958, when I was working as the doctor of the cement factory in Dorood, doing my compulsory two years of medical practice outside of Tehran. He came with a group of high school students as part of their scientific excursion. He recognized me as one of my mother's children and asked if I would be kind enough to do two things: to be the judge in the students' literary contest, and to give a talk about a medical topic to the students.

I still have a picture of him dressed like a Boy Scout, wearing a baseball hat, sitting beside me on a desk, our feet on the bench. I am doing the talking, he is listening attentively. The students are not visible because the camera is looking at us. The whole thing is happening in the open air beside one of the two rivers that had made that city and given it its name: Two-River. If it did not have two rivers, perhaps the cement factory would not have been built there to begin with, because stone, the main ingredient for making cement, could be found anywhere in Iran; it is water that is scarce.

The students were apprehensive because the day before some of them had cut off a few branches of the nearby poplar trees to make walking sticks, and the night before the men of Kad-Khodda of Dorood—who owned those trees unbeknownst to the students—had gone to their dormitory with lights and lanterns in their hands, appearing more numerous than they really were, wanting revenge for the broken branches.

Looking at this picture helps me remember what topic I had chosen for those two dozen adolescent boys: "The Harms and Benefits of Masturbation."

The benefits apparently far outweighed the harm in the students' minds, since several of them came to me after the speech to ask, "Up to how many times per day it is not harmful?"

I told them that I did not know, "But less seems better."

In the declamation contest there were two finalists: one of them recited a drama, the other a comedy. Even though the audience was more impressed with the dramatic one, I gave the award to the comedian. And I told the student the reason why I did that. "It is easier to make people cry than laugh."

60

A POST-REVOLUTIONARY LETTER
FROM MY MOTHER

25 August 1981

Shemiran, Iran

In the name of *Khoda*

Dear Dr. Nasser, *Salaam.* Your letter was on its way for exactly one month. It reached my hand on the twenty-fourth of August. Even though it had become old and stale, it still brought joy to everybody's heart, because everybody in the house [Monavar's house] reads your letters. Now it is early in the morning and I am writing this letter to you. Ali Gholi Khan said, "Who are you writing to, so early in the morning?" I said, "To my writing son, Nasser." He said, "Nasser is now asleep; don't wake him up." I said, "He is used to my noise."

Before I forget I should remind you that our postal code is 1939. The mailman said it has to be written on every envelope; otherwise your letters might not reach my hand. Therefore, before you forget, write it on the back of two blank envelopes along with my address, for your future letters.

About news, I am sure you know more about it over there than we here. Whatever I write, you know; therefore I shall write about the things you don't know. You have asked me to tell you things about myself that you don't know. Here they are.

I sneaked into this world on the fifteenth of *Shavval* (an Arabic month) which is equal to the sixteenth of August 1900. Every year, Sarhang Yahya Khan [her twin brother] reveals this secret by coming here with a cake, and accompanies me one step further along the years. This year I stepped beyond the age of eighty-one. He also believes that our mother made a mistake and dated our identification booklets one year younger than our real age. Maybe our mother wanted to have a younger daughter. Anyway, it does not matter. I came into the world on that date, give or take one or two years. And beside myself, I pulled another human being along as a spare. I opened my eyes, and what a dark and mixed up world I saw! Much worse than the convoluted and chaotic hair of an African from Zangebar. [She begins her life story with the moment of her birth, but forgets to continue due to the more important news of the present time.]

The war [Iran-Iraq] is busy with its carnage, but these terror attacks in Tehran and bombings have disturbed the minds of people much more than the war. It is not clear what the aim of the terrorists is. When they assassinate one of the heads of the post-revolutionary government, the government seeks revenge by executing twenty of them, mainly those already in prison.

I am certain that you won't believe my words about what I am going to say.

A few days ago, Khalil Khan—the brother of Abdol Hassan Khan Agha Khani—passed away and was taken to the cemetery of Beheshteh Zahra to be buried. In the cemetery we found out that things have changed. Nowadays the cemetery's employees place the dead in the grave, but it is the job of the relatives to fill it with *Khaak*. I think it is because the workers don't have time.

As for the news from here, except for these things, I have nothing further to tell you. They moved Dr. Shojania from Evin Prison to the Fortress of Hessar, which was built on a parcel of land bought from him in his village near Karaj. As Hafez has said, "How can a bird know that the branch of the bush under its feet will become the bar of its cage?" His house and his village are confiscated now. Of course, he was not the only one who was transferred to that prison. He went there with many others, some of them his close friends. It was because the Evin Prison was full. Since they put a bomb in the headquarters of the Party of Islamic Republic and one hundred people were killed, visiting the prisoners is temporarily forbidden. But yesterday some of the members of his family managed to visit him, after insisting for a long time, only to talk to him by an internal phone inside the prison. Meenu was happy that she had seen her father from behind a window.

Monir-jun, Monavar-jun and Mahmood are all healthy. Ali Gholi Khan, wakes up every morning, puts on his street clothes and says that he has to go to the "front." The front for him, of course, is the lines for bread or other things. There is a long line for buying anything. Many things are replaced by cheap substitutes. The other day Ali Gholi Khan went to a pharmacy to buy a toothbrush. When the pharmacist said, "We don't have any." Ali Gholi

Khan asked, "Don't you have its substitute either?" and made everybody in the pharmacy laugh. The poor man works a lot without ever losing his sense of humour.

Send, on my part, many *Salaams* to everybody, especially to Mitra Khanum. Also tell her that I know the shoulder covering that I knitted was not good enough for her and I have in mind to knit another one for her. I am anxious for Kami, Keyvan and Nima. And because all three have passed their exams "without any *Tajdeedi* [having to repeat an exam after the summer holidays]," congratulate them on my behalf, and kiss their faces for me. God willing, these empty kisses will bear some fruits in my future letters. For now, *Al sabro meftaah ol faraj* [Arabic proverb: Patience is the key to opening any door].

I *Ghorban* myself for you,

Mother

61

A LETTER FROM DR. AZEEM VAHAB-ZADEH

Azeem is an Arabic name meaning great.

MY BEST FRIEND, DR. AZEEM VAHAB ZADEH, was a great human being, too, but he was not an Arab. Nor did he have anything against the Arabs. He was an Iranian from the Turkish-speaking city of Ardebil in the northern province of Iran, named Azerbaijan. It is adjacent to the Russian Azerbaijan. The two are separated from each other by the undulating Aras River and several layers of barbed wires.

He was good-looking, but his good looks were overshadowed by his other better qualities. With his pellucid complexion and Caucasian features, had he told me that he was from Russia or any other European country, I would have definitely believed him on the first day that we met. He was about my height and in the Officers' Academy we often stood in the same row. There were no anomalies in his behaviour, nor habits nor sayings. He never lied, whether as a joke or seriously. He did not even exaggerate. For example, I never heard him say, "I don't have money." Instead, if he had to declare the amount of money in his pocket, he would say, "I don't have enough money."

We met each other in the first year of medical school. We were both military students. Out of the 320 students in our class, about forty of us were military students. The civilian students saw each other only during the day, but the military ones lived together day and night. This is why the military ones were either very intimate friends with each other, or serious enemies. Even though he did not study more than the others, Azeem came first in the final exam in the third year of medical school.

I did not know that he too was a member of the Tudeh Party, until I met him in prison. It turned out that he was two levels above me in the military network of the party. This is why he was sentenced to 15 years while I got only ten. Also, this is why, when I was released from prison, he was still there. He is the one who started translating *The Fisherman of Iceland* by Pierre Loti, from French, but when he came out he gave it to me to finish. He also gave me a painting when he was released three years after me. That painting was given to him in prison, painted by one of the prisoners. It was an oil painting with "too much green in it," as he said when he gave it to me. He brought it to me the day I opened my private office in Shemiran. I hung it in the waiting room. After coming out, he too was employed by Massoud and worked as a psychiatrist, but unlike me, he registered in a residency program at the university and did four more years of official training to become a certified psychiatrist.

Psychiatry did not suit him because he was too normal. He never drank or gambled, and never used a pill to sleep or a drug for pleasure. He was not a womanizer and remained a virgin perhaps until the end of his life. He never married. Only late in his short life he became friends with a psychiatrist nurse who was a friend of Mimi, the wife of Sia. She was a psychiatric nurse. They did not live with each other, but she spent all her time sitting beside his bed during the six months that he was dying of terminal cancer of his prostate.

Dr. Daoud Hamedani, who came to Victoria in the summer 1997 and brought me the book about Sohravardi by Henry Corbin, said that he too saw Azeem frequently during those six months and said that I was often the subject of their conversation. He also said that even though Azeem experienced severe pain, he did not use morphine or other narcotics to diminish his pain. He only took ordinary pain killers, like Tylenol when the pain became intolerable. His refusal to take narcotics was definitely not due to the fear of addiction or phobia about use of narcotics. He wanted to observe the remaining days of his life in a lucid state.

One of the last few times that we managed to meet was when I went to the treatment centre in Vanak, halfway between Tehran and Shemiran—during the summer of 1977— when he was the director of the methadone program to help addicts quit.

Azeem was the one who first told me about this important truth: "True addicts are patients who have found their medicine, like diabetics who have found their insulin. They function better with their drug than without," he explained. "They function almost normally as long as they have the drug in their system. You take it away from them; they become miserable and dysfunctional."

"Is this your discovery?" I asked, expecting to hear yes.

"No, I read it in a book. I don't remember if it was *The Ceremonial Chemistry* by Thomas Szasz, or his *The Myth of Psychotherapy, Mental Healing as Religion, Rhetoric and Repression*, but I have also observed it in my practice here."

I bought the first book right after I returned to Canada and discussed it with Ez Ford. He said he had heard of Thomas Szasz. He knew him as a maverick among psychiatrists.

Azeem did not know Massoud until he began working with him in the mental hospital. That hospital had become a sort of halfway house between prison and normal life for me and many of my friends who were released after me.

When Massoud was switching between being normal and abnormal, he asked Azeem for a diagnosis during one of his normal intervals.

"The key to your problem is in your hands. You behave like a spoiled child," Azeem said to Massoud.

His diagnosis, even though it was not very flattering to Massoud, made him think. Later on, I heard Massoud comment on Azeem's diagnosis of him. "His diagnosis is correct, but so firm and unexpected that one feels one's head has hit a solid wall."

I have only one letter from Azeem, and this is a reply to my letter. It is dated according to the short-lived *Shahan-shahy* calendar.

30-Azar-2536

Tehran, Iran.

Nassereh *Azeez*,

I received your letter of November the eighth, 1978. Truly, it made me as glad as the unexpected sight of you on your last visit to Iran. Even though I was determined not to let the delay in this reply reach the level of months, it seems that your prediction has come true and it is already more than a month.

Our few meetings in Tehran that took place during that anxious time, and our hurried conversations about various topics, were extraordinarily interesting for me. I regret that we did not set aside more time for them. Your enthusiasm, or more precisely, your need for discovering the truth, was extraordinarily interesting and at the same time astonishing to me.

Your saying that you have too much time on your hands made me jealous. Believe me, today is Wednesday, the fifth day of the week and a holiday because of *Aashura* [the tenth day of the mourning month of *Moharram* for Shi'eh Muslims during which Imam Hossein has been martyred, with up to seventy-two of his family members and followers] but it seems that the four days of the beginning of the week have passed like a single long and exhausting day! Even though to stretch time, I wake up very early in the mornings, it does not make any difference. I remember in the past, whenever I was nursing a desire in my heart, I would make myself glad-hearted by postponing it to the future *Forsat* [free time or opportunity] but I am now gradually beginning to believe that there is no such a thing as future *Forsat*. And the dragon of the present time devours everything.

You wrote about being forty-seven and its effect on your mind. Me too, even though I was unaware of you and your feeling. I am re-reading the *Sa'di's Golestan*. I think he had the same mental experience when he reached the age of fifty when he addresses the fifty-year-olds:

O you who were asleep and the fifty came and went.

Wake up! You have no more than a few days to catch up

But for him, "catching the last few days" was easier than for us. He thought perhaps that with the help of *Aghl* [wisdom] and the hope of *rasteguary* [freedom, deliverance, and salvation] one could catch the slippery fish of time. Maybe he, too, like Sisyphus, should be considered among the lucky ones. You know who I mean, don't you? [No I don't, but it does not matter.] I am grumbling behind the back of Mosleheddin and his famous piece that begins, "At every moment, my life diminishes by the length of a single breath...." Really, this man has preached too much and given too much advice, so much so that one begins to doubt his sincerity and purity a little. Let us postpone this topic for later.

A while ago, I began Alan Watt's book. [I think it was his *Psychotherapy: East and West* that I had given to him or had recommended to him. No, he must have obtained it himself because the Alan Watts book that I took with me to Iran on that trip was named The *Two Hands of God*.] I am in the middle of it. It is very interesting for me, especially as these days the press discussions about East and West in the radio and television are hot. What was unexpected, and made me want to read more of it, was that from the very first page of the book I thought I had known the author for a long time. Perhaps this is because I had reached the conclusion, a few years ago, that religious beliefs, along with other social norms, have psychotherapeutic—with its precise modern meaning—value.

The last segment of your letter is very Fromm-like. Erick Fromm's explanation about alienation is very much like our own Mowlavi [Rumi]. Also, your view about the source of suffering was not unlike that of Fromm. If you have not read his *Escape from Freedom* and *The Art of Loving*, read them. They are interesting books, and I think they will suit your taste. Fromm, in the first book, discusses the phenomenon of individuality as a historical determinant specific to capitalism. In the second book he discusses the phenomenon of *Joda'i*—distance—the irreducible gap between man and everything.

My situation is as you saw. Unfortunately, I have not been able to change it. Gradually, I am losing the hope of finding any kind of right way—and this is very bad.

Raastee, I forgot to write at the beginning of this letter that seeing your good children was very interesting for me, and to some extent incredible. Incredible, not because they are good children, which is perfectly natural, but their mere existence. This is because I always remember you as you were, without children, in the years of university.

I saw very little of Mitra, and I am very sorry for that. I wish there had been more opportunity to talk to her too. Please convey my *Salaam* and regrets to her.

I frequently see Marandi [Dr. Marandi completed and published the book of *Medical Emergencies* that I had translated in prison], and Sadeghi [Dr. Parviz Sadeghi, Massoud's brother-in-law, an internist]. I talked about your letter with them, but I have not seen Khalil. [Dr. Khalil Sa'adat, to whom I gave my job, when I moved from the cement factory of Dorood to Tehran. He was released from prison a few years after me and, without going through Massoud's mental hospital, went straight to Dorood. He was, however, so honest that the new chief of the factory made him quit medicine to become chief of the factory's storehouse in charge of dispatching cement bags to contractors to prevent profiteering.]

I have not seen Neek-Eteghad [Sia] either. I finish my letter here, the rest for later.

Eradat-mand [Sincerely],

Azeem

62

A Letter from Khosrow, My Living Hero

KHOSROW, MY HERO, was a difficult example to follow. It was partly by following him that I landed in prison. He was more than just a close, good-looking relative, good in everything from sport to intellectual matters. He is one of the eight children of Sartip (a general in the army) Pouria and Turan Khanum. He has been rebellious all his life and most of his childhood, yet has been changing all the time. He was a champion of weight-lifting, boxing, and was an ace pilot in the Iranian Air Force. He is the ex-pilot, the ex-prisoner, and the eternal freedom fighter. He is five years older than me and has always been several steps ahead of me. When I entered Sharaf High School, he was leaving to go to the army. When I went to the army, he had gone to the air force, and from there to prison. And when I went to prison in Tehran, he was moved to Khark Island in the Persian Gulf, the tropical island that was home to a few palm trees, three or four donkeys and seven or eight dangerous prisoners mixed with a few political ones. He was ahead of me also regarding political activities and spiritual evolution. He was the first atheist in our family, if not in Tehran.

Even though he was leaving that high school when I was entering it, he came back one day to prove to the grade eleven and twelve students that there was no God. I remember that day. It was noontime. There were no classes, but we had remained in school because we took our lunch to school. By we I mean me and Arsalan, the younger brother of Khosrow, who was my age and colour and my friend, in grade seven. He was in the English class, I in the French, as far as foreign languages were concerned. Arsalan knew about his brother's lecture and it was he who told me to go and watch it through the window at the back of the class. We did not go in but saw Khosrow and the short physics teacher, Mr. Ahghari (Arabic for the smallest) were standing at the blackboard and about twelve students from grade twelve and eleven were sitting behind the desks, asking questions. No one in the family had seen or heard of him for five years when the news came that he and his two pilot friends, Marzban and Ahmadi (?) had been caught for being covert members of Tudeh Party while in the army.

The letter that I am going to translate is a reply to my questions I had asked in my letters to my sister, Monavar. And those questions were based upon the news Pari had brought from Tehran in her last visit. Her last visit had coincided with the death of Arsalan and absence of Khosrow in his funeral. "Daryush Froohar, the founder of the Pan-Iranist Party in Iran," Pari said, "was there but Khosrow was not." The Pan-Iranist Party was the opposite of the Tudeh Party and their members were the enemy of the members of the Tudeh party. The Pan-Iranist Party, however, did not last very long and most of its members grew out of it. When Froohar participated in Arsalan's funeral, for example, he was a member of parliament in the Islamic Republic of Iran. Also Pari said that she saw Iran, the wife of Khosrow, in the mosque, alone, anxiously looking around with her markedly pale and anemic face to see if Khosrow was there. This is why my other question was whether Khosrow and his good wife were separated, and if so, why.

It happened that Khosrow was visiting my sister in her house when my letter arrived. My sister gave the letter to Khosrow to read, but Khosrow told her that he would rather take it to his own house to read it carefully and give it a complete reply. The letter I am going to translate is that complete reply.

No, I don't think I can translate all of it. Not only it is long, it has a unique style that can easily get lost in translation the way a good poem loses its charm in translation. Almost every phrase in it is pregnant with multiple meanings. Many lines are either underlined with ordinary pen or coloured with variously coloured crayons. The length of it, I thought at the beginning, was not a problem since I could compress its 22 legal size pages into a normal-sized article of seven or eight short pages. When I read it again, however, I saw that it was already condensed. There is not a single extra word in it. Many sentences are followed by explanatory notes in brackets of various forms, sometimes in double brackets. He has used so many of these segregating symbols that I don't know what symbol I should use if I want to insert some explanatory notes in his letter. I might use the square bracket that looks like this, [...]. To complicate matters further, some of the quotations are in Arabic without their Farsi translation. Khosrow must be assuming that I know enough Arabic to understand them. I wonder when Khosrow has learned so much Arabic. Even those common Arabic phrases that I thought I knew, like the famous *Besmellaheh Rahmaneh Raheem* that I had understood to mean, to the name of God, the Forgiving and Merciful turns out to mean a totally different thing when Khosrow translates it. Khosrow says that this significant Arabic phrase was translated to Farsi not from its original Arabic but through its European transla-tion. Then Khosrow translates it once more to selected pure Persian words, like *Parvardegar*, and *Aafaridegar*, the Creator, the Generator, and the Degenerator and somehow he con-cludes that the world is based on the trinity of creation, construction, and destruction. The following is part of his reasoning.

…And this is the most obvious truth that every one sees in everyday life; everything is in the process of changing. Things are made out of things, like the formula E=MC², which expresses how matter is changed into energy. But *nothing* never changes to *something*. Therefore the world is old. It has no beginning. Allah, *Khoda* or *Zaateh Vojood* [the essence of existence?] are names for a *thing*, an existing thing which is not the product of the human imagination or the invention of a religion. This is also believed in Islam and is reflected in the Koran; verse *al Hadeed*, often referred to by the Esmailis. And it is expanded in the second lesson of *Nahj ol Belaagheh* [a book about ethics and morality attributed to Imam Ali]. Molla Sadra refers to this [paradoxical] phenomenon as "*Zaateh vajeb- ol-Vojood*" or "the tiniest and the last [subatomic] possible particle."

But any existence requires space, no matter how small. The last particle or the last indivisible thing, therefore, must be in what is called in Arabic *la-makan* [no-where]. And because it has no place, it does not require the preposition *in* either. And that *thing*, therefore, is the distance between two infinitely small things. And so far, we are far away from knowing it.

Therefore, Allah—being equal to *Kolleh Shei'* [the totality of *things*]—exists with everything. (Since there is no symmetry in the last particle), therefore that very last particle of existence [that essence?] is Allah, or *Khodavand*, or better, the essence of existence. It is not a vague or imaginary thing at all. This is why, when you begin to talk about these things with people who have a mixture of objective knowledge and superstition, hallucination and semi-scientific experiences, unpleasant arguments begin to develop….

To prevent unpleasant arguments I interrupt this difficult translation and get to the more pleasant and easier parts of Khosrow's letter. Besides, Khosrow begins his letter with a poem by Hafez about the importance of keeping secrets secret. The following is the translation of the poem that appears on the top of his letter before the greetings begin.

Years passed without putting down a single word on paper

Where is a trusting friend to carry a few messages?

I know your sunny place is beyond my reach

Unless the shadow of your grace extend a few steps forward.

Now that the wine is poured from the barrel into the bottle

And from the bottle into the cups

And the flowers have unveiled their faces

Make use of the occasion and have a few sips.

The sweet syrup and rose water are not sufficient for my lips

Add a few kisses to the insults that come from your lips.

O Pious! (Nasser) *Avoid talking to a few notorious*

If you want to pass safely through the street of a few rends like me (Khosrow).

O preacher! You enumerated all the vices of the wine

Don't deny its virtues just for the sake of a few.

O beggars of Kharaabat (Kharab/aabad or re-constructed ruins) *(Iranians)!*

The popular Khoda *[turn of events] is on your side*

Don't expect any favours from a few unpopular.

The old man of the tavern said it so well to his last dreg-drinking client,

"Don't tell the tale of a burnt heart to a few raw-minded.

Hafez (Khosrow) *was incinerated in the light reflected from the face of your* Mehr

O kaam-kar! [pleasure fulfilled] (you)

Cast a glance towards a few Na-kaams [without pleasure] (us).

Now the letter.

Thursday, 23-Teer-1379

[13-July-2000]

Tehran, Iran

Nasser-jan!

My very dear, very precious, the absolute good and the servant of all people and their *jans*! I don't know what part of your brain has been so stimulated that after 35 years of no communication you have mentioned my name 37 times in someone else's letter.

You said, by following me, you ended in prison. If I tell you that how close our genetic make-ups are, you might correctly conclude that whatever happened to you was determined more by our inherited common genes than by following me.

Let me tell you where you come from by showing you your genealogy, but, out of respect for the innocence and deprivation of women, let me begin with women. Not only women supply us with 23 of our 46 chromosomes, they feed us with their blood for 280 days in the womb, and for two years outside of the womb. We are the continuation of their lives. They live in us and they are as happy with our good deeds as we are with theirs.

In your case it goes like this:

Fatali Shah, Abdollah Mirza Dara, Mehr-jan Khanum Bibi Shazdeh, Bibi Gashasb Banu Khanum Bozorg [I remember her. She was the one who almost fell out of her coffin off the stairs in Mashad], Nayyereh Ashraf Khanum, Nasser Shojania.

The second branch in your case:

Shah Khalilollah the Imam of Esmailieh, Abolhassan Khan Sardar Ghowmi, Bibi Gashasb Banu or Khanum Bozorg, Nayyereh Ashraf Khanum, Nasser Shojania.

In my case:

Fatali Shah, Abdollah Mirza Dara, Mehr-jan Khanum Bibi Shazdeh, Mohammad Ali Khan Agha Khani Sahaam-Nezam Saramad, Touran Khanum Agha Khani Pouria, Khosrow Pouria.

The second branch in my case:

Shah Khalilollah Imam of Esmailieh, Abolhassan Khan Sardar Ghowmi, Mohammad Ali Khan Agha Khani Sahaam-Nezam Saramad, Touran Khanum Agha Khani Pouria, Khosrow Pouria.

Mehr-jan Khanum, as the wife of Sardar Abolhassan Khan, and Khanum Bozorg, as the sister of Sahaam Nezam, make your mother and mine double cousins, both from the father's side and the mother's side.

Your mother and mine liked each other very much. As children, one of the games we played with each other was the game of *Nayyereh Ashraf*. Your mother, always pregnant, having come to Tehran to visit our mother, pregnant, would try to hug and kiss each other, but their distended abdomens prevented them from doing so. Our game was to imitate this impossible encounter by putting pillows and sheets under our shirts and walking towards each other, rubbing our tummies against each other, trying to imitate their impossible kisses. Our mother was always amused watching us playing this game.

From your father's side:

Fatali Shah of Qajar, Hassan Ali Mirza Shoja-ol-saltaneh, Ghahreman Mirza, Mohammad Mirza, Mojtaba Mirza, Nasser Shojania.

In my case:

Zeinolabedin (Ben Haj-ma'sum), Mirza Kuchek Khan Naayeb-ol-sadr Rahmat Ali Shah, Mirza Ali-Reza Agha Khani Mahallati, Mirza Morteza Khan Agha Khani (also known as Sarhang Ghazzagh), Mohammad Ali Khan Agha Khani, Sartip [General] Pouria, Khosrow Pouria.

Our relations, generally, are those of the families of Esmailieh.

Also, Mirza Ahmad, (the envoy of Agha Khan from India who came to Iran soon after the coronation of Nasseredin Shah with elephants and jewels to congratulate the Shah), the son-in-law of Shah Khalilollah, or Bibi Gowhar Beigum's husband, had two sons by Bibi Gowhar. The first son was Mirza Ebrahim Khan Seddigh Khalvat (your mother's father) and the second was Mirza Mehdi Khan. After Bibi Gowhar Beigum's death, he married Anvar Mahallati's sister who was one of the descendents of Ismaiily imams. The result of that marriage was two sons, Mirza Kazem Chimi (father of the mother of General Pouria, my father) and Mirza Nassir known as Nassir-ol-Atebba.

You and I have a common soul in Mirza Ahmad as well, the nearest vital and genetic connections being Sardar Abol Hassan Khan and Mehr-jan Khanum. They both live in us. Our letters and our written conversations are as much an expression of the secrets of those two great souls, as the *Nay* of *Mowlana* [Rumi] was the tool of the expression of his internal secret: distance.

Whatever kindness you have expressed towards me, God be my witness, *Alhagh*, are reflections of yourself in a mirror.

That was about our genetic connections. Now let us go to other topics you had raised in your letter to Monavar.

Before Khosrow goes on, I have to interrupt him to mention another similarity between us, namely, our hatred of dance. I have heard from Touran Khanum, Khosrow's mother, when she was visiting our mother that Khosrow as a child hated dancing so much, particularly if it was his mother, that whenever she wanted him to do a chore that Khosrow was reluctant to do, she would threaten him that if he did not do it she would begin to dance and Khosrow would immediately do it.

It is a pity, dear Nasser, to waste your time with the past, but you have asked and I have to oblige.

You have cast your gaze to this earthquake-prone land with its whirlpool of calamities and want to know about this "eternal warrior of the battlefield of *Ahoor-Mazda* and *Anguereh-Meenu*." What can I do except to obey?

In general, the lands located in the northern parts of the Earth are places of joy, freedom, abundance, and eternal paradise as far as the connection of the souls of humans is concerned; while the lands located in the south are the site of dry deserts (place of death and decay), hell, fire (and not-being of humans). This uneven playing field has given rise to two contradictory sets of religious beliefs. The northern religions talk about abundance, happiness and freedom, while the southern religions talk about deficiencies, depression and slavery.

The history of religions is almost the same as the history of human ascent.

Our land [Iran] which is itself a mixture of greenery and dryness, hell and paradise, joy and sorrow, abundance and shortcomings, as well as the passage of the tribes from north and south (that made them neither northern nor southern, but both northern and southern, rich with both kind of life, and rich with both kinds of beliefs and thoughts) and (contradictory sayings) the leaf of leaflessness, the sound of soundlessness, the death of deathlessness, in short the principle of no principle; bewildered and bewildering, wandering in this place of *howl and haul* [terror and power].

People of the northern lands are more active because of the cold weather, and more powerful because of the abundance of food and nutrients, and therefore ready for human proliferation and matriarchal rule, but in the south, because of the scarcity of plants and shortage of water, any running water or any little river was guarded by a sword-bearing man, leading to patriarchy and the slavery of women.

In the north, women are free and friends with men; in the south women are slaves, if not buried alive. This is the root cause of all the contradictions in our land.

Our land has been the unavoidable passage to and from the East and West as well as from North and South of the Old World (touching the three continents of Asia, Europe, and Africa) and has been enriched by the imported culture and literature from the four sides, as well as being the site of earthquakes and the damage caused by the invaders. A few years of cold in the north sent its tribes moving towards the sun in the south; and a few years of draught caused those whose back was towards the sun to move towards the north. [It must have been a hard life and a hard trip.]

Those who left their land for a better life—or at least survival—had to accept death on their way, which they called martyrdom. [But] after they became conquerors, they imposed their draconian rules with respect to their superiority and the slavish inferiority of the tribes that had given up resisting under the name of *Din* [faith, something more basic than religion. Religion can be regarded as a branch, a way, or a manner of practising a *Din*].

(Islam is derived from *Tasleem*, meaning to give up and to stop resisting. *Kofr* means the contrary. *Ebaadat* means slavery. *Abd* means slave. *Aabed* and *Ma'bood* mean slave-owner and his slave.) Judaism, Christianity, and Islam, these three *Dins*, are known as *Adyaneh Elaahi* [the Godly *Dins*] and they are the [natural] products of the waterless lands and burning sands of Isis and Uziris [not sure of the spelling because Khosrow has written them in Farsi, and in Farsi some of the vowels are omitted as understood, instead of being incorporated in the word. And when one does not know the word, one cannot read it properly and therefore one cannot translate it properly either. Suffice it to say that it must be referring to the waterless deserts mentioned in the old and/or new Testaments.]

But the northern migrants were the Meenu-Chehregan: Manuchehr [good looking], Aazaadegan [the free], Moghans [the magi], Raadan [liberals], Radan [gentlemen], the guardians of fire, *Mehr-baanan* who are also the guardian of the rays of sun, for feeding their cattle and locating the pastoral land. Also, *Artesh-taaran* [the army] for repelling the invading tribes.

The prayer of Daryush Shah, or better, Daryush's greatest wish, was this. "*Ahoora Mazda!* (the Knower and the Able!) Guard this Aryan land from three things: droughts, enemies, and lies (untruths, beliefs built on superstition and uncritical thoughts)." This determination of the Aryan people has been endemic in our land, but when all the invaders, even the Turks, saw that Islam meant giving up resistance, and piety meant slavery, they fortified the status quo and ruled the Aryan land for centuries. And in the last 200 years, the southern invaders have kept it under their control and have found it a very suitable tool for governing. But [again] the resistance of people has continued from the early times. Hafez praises, with the best and the most delicate words, the word *Mogh* in his *Divan* fifty times, as a weapon to attack any doctrine based on the slavery of man.

After the above paragraph Khosrow writes all the fifty lines under the title of *Mogh-nameh*, meaning the Book of Moghs. I tried to translate most of it. I did it for those few who would like to know Hafez a little better and deeper. Any one who is not interested can skip these lines and go on to the rest of Khosrow's letter.

Mogh-Nameh

1

Brighten your prayer mat with the glow of wine,

If the Peereh Moghan advised you to do so.

Our guide is not ignorant

He knows the customs and tradition of the Road and the Way.

2

My heart tightens in the loneliness of this Sowme'eh [monastery]

Under the cloak of Saaloos [hypocrisy].

Where is the monastery of the Moghs?

Where is the Naab [pure and clear] *wine?*

5

The reason I am respected in the fireplace of Moghan

Is because of this never-dying flame in my heart

6

My beloved burst into the monastery of Moghan, drunk

With a large cup of wine in hand

Spraying drunkenness with her drunken eyes

On the soul of drinking men.

9

Don't be surprised if you saw the Peer of Moghan as my leader

There is no Sar [head] *in which there is no* Ser [secret].

13

I am the follower of the elder of Moghan

But, don't be upset with me, O Sheikh!

Didn't you promise that wine is to be had in paradise?

18

How the good-looking Mogh *knew about what was going on in our head?*

When he said, "We don't accept cloaks for a cup of wine, anymore".

23

See how nice and forgiving the Peereh Moghan *is;*

Whatever we did in front of him he said we did it beautifully.

24

The ring of slavery to the Peereh Moghan *has been hanging from our ear*

Since the very first day.

We are what we used to be

And will be the same in the future.

26

If I asked for help from the Peereh Moghan, *don't blame me*

Our master said that there is not enough Hemmat [ambition or higher aspiration]

In our own monastery.

27

Let the rules of the Peereh Moghan *govern us all*

The others can come and go

And forget my name.

30

Enough having homemade wine!

Bring me the wine of Moghan

My drinking rival has arrived

Good-bye repentance, good-bye.

32

The door of meaning opened towards my heart

The day I sat at the threshold of the Peereh Moghan.

36

It is now more than forty years that I have been bragging,

"The least among the most obedient servants of the Peereh Moghan *is Hafez."*

38

I see the light of Khoda *in the* Kharaabat *of* Moghan*!*

Such a light in such a place is surprising even for Hafez.

39

The reason I would never stop serving the Peereh Moghan

Is because I don't think it is a good idea.

40

I am the Sufi of the monastery of this sacred universe

But, temporarily, I am destined to demur in the temple of Moghan.

44

Hafez! The place of the Peereh Moghan *is the site of* Vafa *[loyalty],*

You can read your love stories to him

And listen to his love stories.

48

In the bazaar of Moghan

No one is as badly off as Hafez:

My cloak is hostage in one pawnshop

My book in another.

49

Don't turn away from the bazaar of Moghan.

The key for the lock of difficulty is sold over there.

Having praised the elder of Moghan for 49 times, Khosrow terminates his selection with the line in which Hafez dismisses his slavery to anybody, including the much-praised *Peereh*

Moghan, to become the free man or the *Rend* that he is:

50

One hundred Peereh Moghans *are nobody but slaves*

To guard the gate of the palace of Hafez.

Khosrow's letter continues …

About 1400 years after the admixture of north and south in our land, the resulting fusion and confusion of freedom and slavery has affected our culture and our folk literature. The insufficient language of Farsi and the inadequate Arabic script mixed with incomplete knowledge of Farsi and Arabic by most people in Iran, have rendered verbal or written communication difficult, and sometimes misleading. Our beliefs and opinions have become a changing amalgam of the real with the unreal. What is slowing down the spread of truth is not so much ignorance but the pre-existing wrong beliefs. Our society has not profited even-handedly from the advances in science. There are still many scientists who, out of their childhood habits, hold the most superstitious beliefs. Since despots have always ruled our land, to be opportunist, to be joke-telling, and to demand exemption from the rules have become the norm in our behaviour and tools for our survival. That is why, if someone wants to clarify things, one should talk to the *Mardom* [the common people] with the language of *Mardom,* and gently extract the truth out of the confusion of half-real and half-truth, and with the same softness [of voice] condemn wrong beliefs or fanatical opinions.

From the beginning of the Arabs' domination, gradually, some beliefs based on reality entered the domain of the creative imagination. And when these new thoughts and beliefs clashed with the despotic rulers, they were whispered or communicated cryptically among the learned and the interested, sometimes in the form of secrets, sometimes *Erfan* (hence the importance of keeping secrets and "talking behind the curtain" as well as through the *Eehaam* [vagueness] in poetry. Also, the same facts and fears are considered the cause of the development of hidden groups and secret organizations like those of Sufis, *Arefs*, and many more. These are the reasons for the apparent contradiction and duplicity in the expression of my opinions. Our people can understand if one's talk begins from where they know it is real and scientific. One's talk should be expressed in words familiar to them. There is no use in arguing because in an argument the ego of the listener blocks the opening of understanding.

In Iran all the doors are open to you if you quote, in the first place from the Koran, and after that from *Nahj-ol- Belaagheh*, *Mathnavi* of Mowlana, the *Ghazals* of Hafez and the sayings of Sa'di and Ferdowsi. And the listener will accept your views more easily if you respect his or her existing beliefs. In other words, it is effective if one is beside them rather than in front of them.

All of us are in the grip of prejudice and preformed beliefs. Freedom from them is very difficult, especially if we have based our personality on them. This includes being a member of a political party, following a religion, wearing a beard or mustache, receiving recognition and awards for literary work (those whose growth is arrested in one of the stages of creativity and development). The latter are very slow in sensing changing times and understanding the human condition. For example, recall the society of the Soviet Union before its disintegration in 1983. At the time of Andropov, the central committee of Communist Party confessed that "Marxism/Leninism has been transformed to subjectivism" (and therefore all the related theories should be thrown out of the window to be replaced by new theories. The dictatorship of the proletariat had to be revisited, and party members kept out of powerful jobs, like the head of police and army, for the sake of true democracy).

On the phenomenon of *Ghahr*

The breaking of connections with those I used to love is not, unlike your diagnosis, "the genetic residue of cruelty inherited from Agha Mohammad Khan Qajar who made a hill out of the enucleated eyes of the inhabitants of the city of Kerman for having helped his enemy." First of all, I do not have any Qajar gene in me. Secondly, I have broken my connections to prevent possible cruel actions. Any encounter has some bitterness and some sweetness. When the degree of bitterness exceeds that of sweetness, the relationship is better terminated. And I do not wish to remind myself of the bitter past events that have made me reach the decision I have reached.

On the ability to predict

You were surprised when my wife was worried about our two children who had gone to a cinema in Tehran in the pre-revolutionary days and I brought them home through mental telepathy. Telepathy and telling the future are not extraordinary phenomena. In ordinary, everyday life anybody with sufficient information surrounding a thing or an event should be able to predict the near future. But it is difficult to predict big things, like the future of the world. We cannot do it anymore because of the plethora of information and numerous means of communication. We can get to know the past, even though we cannot re-enter it, through those who were there and have documented their observations in their books.

Books, which are the main source of our information, are all about the past. And I painfully recall that since my early youth I have been captivated by the pleasure of reading books. Between the years 1315 to 1320 I read all the 700 rental books in Kheiriyeh book-store near our house, and about 300 of my father's books. Several times, I remember, my father took a book from my hands, tore it, and threw it away to prevent me from reading too much. And from 1320 to 1330, I was busy with my revolutionary friends, reading revolutionary books. And since 1966, when I retired as a pilot, I have been studying all the time and have prepared a library of one thousand hand-picked books (about history, philosophical and belief-related problems, economics and politics, as well as international relations). And, if I can quote myself, "Each one of those books has been boiled down to its viscous residue, with my multiple underlining, markings, and colouring—much more intensely than what you see in this letter. And since 1359, when I totally retired (and haven't made any effort to procure an income) all my time has been spent on study and exercise.

All my worthy friends have passed away, and those who are alive are not accessible due to old age or distance. (The valuable book of history of Esmailieh beliefs, by Dr. Farhad Daftari is one of the books that I've coloured in excess, with many notes written on the margins of its pages.) The speed of my understanding was so fast and my prediction for the changes in the politics was so accurate that most of my friends were surprised. I can only attribute my quickness of reaction to my boxing experience. In boxing one has to react within one-hundredth of a second if one does not want to get knocked out. If you remember, my companion in boxing was Hossein Abdo. He was slightly shorter than I but his arms were longer. He was ten kilos heavier without a gram of fat on his hairy body and was as strong as a bear. He had very good technique and hit like Marciano. I boxed with him for several years and was knocked down several times. To compensate for my inferior power I was forced to adopt unpredictable ways to hit back and hit in quick combinations. If you had been there you would have seen what deadly blows I was receiving. It was so painful that the pain of the prison and pre-prison period were nothing compared to it. It was that experience that made me able to keep my mouth shut under the pain of torture that sometimes pushed me into semi-consciousness or unconsciousness. (This may also explain why I did not go to the funeral of my beloved younger brother, Arsalan. I did not want to step on the bodies of 23 executed, freedom-seeking friends on my way towards the cemetery.) Of course, the main factor [beyond all these book readings and preparatory exercises] is my Esmaili heritage.

Well, let us see. So far, we have talked a little about theology, understanding the universe from its largest to its smallest particle, and the effect of geography on the mind and the views of its inhabitants, compulsory migrations, mixture of races and the amalgamation of various beliefs and inheritances, telling the future, *Ghahr* as a means of preventing violence, versus *Ashti*, and blindness towards distant future. Let us now go to a new page to talk about those who are very dear to me.

Let us begin with the poem of Ghasem Raheemian, whose pen name is Larbon.

In my Sunset

It is a long time since there was light in my lamp

And the song of a bird in my garden.

I, in my sunset, sit in mourning for the lost

Empty cup, broken bottle, longing for a drink

Spreading myself to cover the ground like a shadow

Remembering you is always associated with good things, O wine!

You are the permanent fire and the soul of time.

I am putting all my hope on the shoulders of the wind

Like a straw

So that it lifts me from the depth of this valley to the top of a mountain

To be picked up, perhaps, by a bird from Khaak.

I have attached my heart to the cloud

The heart which is longing for wine.

Dripping beside the plant of repentance

To moisten the dry throat of a thirsty plant

And my footless child lifts its head from the ground.

It is too late.

It is a long time [circled and coloured red by Khosrow]

That no song rises out of the silence of the night

And no music is coming out of the throat of distant garden-streets.

Could it be that the old man, who wandered the city every night,

Has hung up his cloak and gone like a forgotten story?

It is a long time since blood has not dripped from my wound

And tears have not dropped from my eyes to my lap.

I am immobile like a frozen creek

Sitting like a rock

Regard fixed to the road

Waiting for a child to come out of the door of a house

To kick me off the ground.

What was the benefit of [my] coming and going?

Before wetting our lips, we have broken our bottle

There is no hope under this water-coloured, upside-down bowl

Don't depend on the games of the world.

It is a long time since my heart did not palpitate for anybody

The organ is silent

The chest is empty

The bird confined to the cage

Which hand can I grab to take me out of this abyss?

With what hands

And what feet

Can I clap out of joy and kick my heels to the ground?

I, in my sunset, am sitting to mourn for all the things I have lost.

I have crawled to a corner like a shadow

Cut off from everybody,

I have chosen the Khalvat.

The turn of events, dear Nasser, as you know, took twenty-three of our best friends from us. "The turn of the events" took them, not we, even though we were all ready to die. When making our commitment, we knew that our life span was going to be short and it could get terminated at any moment either by an accident as a pilot or by execution by the Army or the anti-revolutionaries in the revolution we were preparing for. This is why we did not look for a permanent soul mate when we looked for a wife. Permanence was a conservative trait, and we were revolutionary. I thought any girl whom I liked and who was ready to live with me during my short and eventful life was good enough to become my wife. My wife and I discussed all these deadly possibilities of our lives, and we married knowingly.

And it was the right way, too. Manuchehr Mokhtari, the dear revolutionary officer in the air force married Star—the daughter of an illiterate middleman in the bazaar—and she made his short life the sweetest possible. The letters of Manuchehr to his wife from prison are among the best and the most delicate literary works in Farsi. My wife, too, was like an angel and a Venus for the first twenty years of our marriage but, as Monavar Khanum said, "unfortunately" I survived, and with my survival gave her time to become what she was born to be, a calculating being with an abacus in hand.

But about my son, as you know, I was in prison when he was born. Now both the son and the mother are dead as far as I am concerned. With her being out of my house and life, I had to stop associating with her side of family, and, being a man without wife, I had to restrict my movements within our own relatives, too, because it is always women who initiate communication among families. The birth of my son was like that of Moses, if you remember, with a similar birth defect.

[Of course I remember. Not only do I know his birth date, I know how and when he was conceived. He was conceived in prison, in a solitary cell, on a Friday, when Khosrow's newly-wed wife went to visit him in prison. The officer on duty on that day was a covert sympathizer of Tudeh Party and let the two stay together for long enough to conceive their first child.]

In prison I was not worried at all that I might get executed. What worried me all the time was the sorrow of my son. But I survived and came out and tried to make up for his short-comings as much as possible. I encouraged him to learn at least one musical instrument, and he became successful in science and art and obtained his license in business administration and became an able musician. The sad saga of my son dried the source of pleasure in my life and removed the joy from it when he misread my feelings and rebelled against me. For me it is mainly the pain of my wife and my son that is imbedded in Larbon's poem. Enough talking about pain; let us talk about *Neekee* and *Shaadee* [goodness and gaiety].

This world is a mixture of gaiety and suffering, goodness and badness. *Ahoor Mazda* and *Ahreeman* are always at war with each other, but *Ahoor Mazda* is always victorious. (*Ahoor Mazda* is the personification of human species.) *Shaadee* is victorious for the simple reason that the human population of the Earth has increased to six billion. If the *Ahreeman* or badness was victorious, humans would not proliferate so readily. Proliferation indicates normality and having a good time. This is a sign of the victory of *Ahoor Mazda*. (Therefore, let us praise him and those who have the thought, the word, and the manner of *Mazda*.)

What is *Neekee* or goodness?

Neekee is that which leads to the betterment of the life of an individual in the present and in the future.

There is no good or bad in the sun or in the stars. Good and bad grow where humans grow. According to the Islamic interpretation they are nicknamed the A*smaa-ol- Hosseinee*— and then abstracted and attributed to *Allah* as *Asmaa'eh Rahmaani* [Godly names]. (Human behaviour, in this system, is divided into the three categories: *Zaatiyeh* [things that happen inside the human body, like thinking], *Fe'lieh* [things that one does], and *Sefatieh* [adjectives; words that Man adds to convey his attitude about things to another man or woman]. All these are guidelines for individual behaviour, but affect the whole world and the totality of humanity. All [of humanity] is summarized in one.

Human lives have a lot in common as far as hunting and eating and defense of family and selfishness are concerned. What makes humans different from animals is the degree with which we become less selfish and do more good for others. In Islam, human adjectives are named *Sefaateh Rahmaani*. They have to do with *Mehr-baani* and always short-changing oneself in the division of goods in favour of others.

For a long time, I kept wondering what the most preferable human qualities were. I eventually found my answer in the Koran, *Aayeh [verse] 17*, the *Sureh* of *Aaleh Emran: (1) Al Saabereen al saadegheen, (2) Al ghaameteen, (3) Val monfegheen, (4) Val mostaghfereen bel'asshaar."*

The number beside each unfamiliar word above is for the following explanation in the same numerical order:

1) *Al Saabereen al saadegheen* means to be patient in fulfilling one's own needs and be impatient in fulfilling the needs of others. *Saaber* [the patient person] tolerates hardships with pain. In other words she or he endures. Better than being *Saaber* is to be *Haleem* (the one who possess helm.) Haleem is a patient person who tolerates hardship with a smiling face. Acquiring knowledge is also better facilitated with *Helm* than with the *Sabr*.

2) *Al ghaameteen.* The one who tolerates life with helm reaches the stage of *Sedgh* [veracity or truth]. (This is well known. You remember the *Sabr* of *Ayyoob* or Jacob's patience in the sacred Book, don't you?) And Ja'far Sadegh (salute to him) represents the embodiment of *Sedgh.* Sheikh Attar in his book, *The Sayings of the Learned*, refers to him [introduces him] in the following paragraph:

"The king of the nation of Mustafa, the proof of [the correctness] of the *Hojjateh Nabavi* [that Mohammad (Salute) is the prophet of God and his wisdom extends to his descendents], that truthful agent, that researcher scientist, that fruit of the heart of the elders, that dear-as-liver to the prophets, the assayer of Ali (Salute), the one who inherited the prophecy, that *Aref* in love, Ja'far Sadegh."

When Ismaili Shi'ehs call themselves Shi'eh-Ja'fary-Esna-ashary [twelve Imami], the Ja'fary of it refers to Imam Ja'far Sadegh.

3) *Val monfegheen.* Those who do not expect rewards for their good deeds, and don't care about becoming famous, and behave like people in love. And the one who symbolizes this attribute is Ali Ebneh [son of] Hossein of Zein ol Abedin, *Seyyed* and *Sajjad*, as well as whoever undertakes a labour of love in serving other people.

4) *Val mostaghfereen bel'asshaar* is the one who gives and forgives without any expectation of reward. The highest level of this is sacrificing one's life for the benefit of the others. And the one who symbolizes this best is Hossein, the son of Ali who was the *Seyyed* [the top man] who sacrificed himself and his family for the good of others.

5) When such a person, who possesses all of these qualities and has passed all the necessary stages of ascent, compares himself with the unreachable perfect man, at the end of the journey, he or she begins to feel inadequate. This inadequacy leads to *Esteghfar*, or self-deprecation and that leads to asking for forgiveness. At this stage, he or she regrets not only the wrongs committed by him or her in the past, but also the good deeds left undone. The person exemplifying this stage of human development is, again, Imam Ali.

Now we have reached the definition of man, *Ensan*, or human being. Let us begin with the female, who is the gentlest, the most sacrificial, and the most loving. Let us talk about woman, the creator of life for all human races, also, the most deprived.

Let us talk first about Monavar to whom you have addressed your letter.

How can I describe someone who has no equal?

With this brain of mine that has not a single conscious vein in it.

She is Monavar the brilliant and the absolute light.

She is the sunshine and the rays of Hagh [truth: one of the one thousand names of God, employed mainly by dervishes].

The shortest way to describe Monavar is to hold a mirror in front of her face. She is the extract of the *Jan* of Modar-jun plus the juice of existence of her grandmother plus the objective existence of the female ancestor of us all, Mehr-Jan Khanum. She is in the continuous line of the living soul of Esmailieh up to Ali and the noble Fatmeh (and like the noble daughter of Mohammad the Prophet, inseparably connected to Ali to become *Noor ala noor* [light over light].

I saw Monavar first at the age of four, in the year 1308 [1929]. The late Hossein was one year old and was not talking yet. I, who was apparently a hyperactive child, suddenly became calm as soon as I saw her. I remember I wanted to talk to her and ask her many questions, but neither could I organize my thoughts nor could I say whatever disorganized thought I had in my mind. Many years passed until 1313 when we came to Tehran. As of that date we became playmates.

In our own house, even though our father was still alive, Ali Gholi Khan was the man of the house, our big brother, and responsible for us, the children. He was always the personalization of *Mehr-baani,* kindness and sensibility.

There was a kind of telepathy between the three of us, Monavar, Daii Ali and me. It happened several times that I was talking to my brother, Morteza, and mentioning her name for some reason, and the phone would ring and when I picked up the receiver I would hear her voice, asking how I was doing. After all those years of hardship and sadness the only place I feel at ease is in her house. Going there is like returning to the period of 1320 to 1330 for me. Monavar is the best and the kindest person to everybody.

She is a scholar, literate, and aware of what is going on. She knows art and does good deeds without advertising them. Their house has become like a sacred temple to me from which *Safa* [smoothness], *Kholoos* [purity], one-facedness, gentleness and *Mohebbat* emanate.

The death of Daii Ali left me severely depressed and sick. I was in a state of confusion and hopelessness for a year. (What can one do?) Daii had the same qualities as Monavar, plus incomparable humour and wittiness. For me these two became the living incarnation of Sardar Abol Hassan Khan and Mehr-jan Khanum.

I noted Monavar had hung two long scrolls of handwritten prayers symmetrically in her guest room. She did it mainly for their decorative value, but I recognized that they were the prayers written in prison in Tehran by Sardar Abol Hassan Khan who was the brother of Agha Khan. He was the one who copied the sacred Koran, seven times, during the seven years he was in prison in Tehran.

A real *Ensan*

You have asked me who I believe is a real *Ensan* in my vicinity. That would be my older brother, Amir Houshang Pouria.

They say the less self you have the better person you are, but my brother, Amir, seemed to have no self at all. He compensated for all the deficiencies of our family that our father had left behind either during his long absences from Tehran or after his death.

After our father's death, Amir was like a father to the children and like a husband to our mother. In school he was always the first in class. He could not continue his studies due to epileptic seizures at the age of 17. Although he started working in the customs department at the lowest rank, he became the head of that institution in a few short years. Customs, as you know, was notorious for bribery and exchange of illegal money, but Amir became the symbol of integrity in that place. Several times thieves conspired to replace him with a more co-operative boss, but his good reputation foiled their plans. He did not mind working long hours, and most nights he worked, either at home or in his office, until past midnight. As an example of his goodness, let me tell you how he sent one of the young civil servants in customs, who was an orphan and responsible for the expenses of his big family, to university to study. Amir told him not to come to work for days in a row, and he [Amir] did his work instead. That man, by the way, became a licentiate in law and a judge in the justice department, and every year at *Now Rooz* he was the first to come to Amir's hand-kissing. On me too, Amir always spent money. One of the surprising games of genetics is that Amir's character is completely like that of our ancestor Zein ol Abedin Ebneh Haaj Ma'soom Mirza-Kuchek, the second to Rahmat-Ali Shah, the *Pole* of *Erfan* at the time of Mohammad Shah and Nasseredin Shah.

The explanation of Rahmat Ali Shah's qualities is in the book of *Bostan ol Siaaheh* by *Mosta'li Shah Sheervaani*, the previous *Pole* and the master of Rahmat Ali Shah. It begins like this: "For about fourteen years, most of the time he sat with the poor and the needy and spent his precious time to satisfy the needs of the poor; … he avoided associating with the rotten and the corrupt" (p 328).

As a child I was Amir's favourite. I respected him so much that several times in front of others, I declared my *Khaak-saary* [utmost humility] and slavery to him by saying, "I am proud to be the slave of this precious brother, for one thousand years." When he passed away, three times, each time for forty days, I sat at his *Chelleh,* meditating on my loss. And I did not find myself for one full year. I became ill, but I did not require medical treatment. This is one brother; the other is your friend, Arsalan, my younger brother whom you had asked about. (It is truly strange that two brothers, in the same family and in the same society show such a contrast in thoughts, deeds, and words.) What can I say about him? Arsalan embodied the reverse of all the good adjectives I have used for Amir, in a serious way. Arsalan was pathologically vain and a show-off. I don't know why he was like that. Of course, in a small house where eight children live—from twenty years old down to two years—all the children suffer [equally] from the parents' lack of attention and clashes among themselves. But he always singled himself out.

Let us pass him and go on.

Somewhere in your letter you had written that Shoja-ol-saltaneh was blinded by his father. He was blinded, but not by his father. The correct version of it is this. Fatali Shah's death occurred in the lunar/Hejri year of 1250, or 1834 AD, Ali-shah Zelleh-Soltan sat on the throne right after his death. Hossein-Ali Mirza Farman-Farma and Hassan-Ali Mirza Shoja-ol Saltaneh went to Shiraz to raise the flag of opposition against this substitute. They were in favour of Mohammad Shah. Mohammad Shah was the elder son of Abbas Mirza who had died six months earlier in Mashad. Fatali Shah had already announced in Tehran that Mohammad Shah was to become his successor. Gha'em Magham (Zelleh Soltan) sent a military troop along with a few English officers from Tehran to Shiraz to capture the two princes and bring them to Tehran. And Shoja-ol-Saltaneh was blinded on the orders of the same man, Gha'em Magham. (And Gha'em Magham too was assassinated later.)

On love

You wrote about love. There are so many things to say about this topic that one becomes more confused by the end of it. What you have taken from Rumi and Hafez is appropriate, but not complete.

Where he [Rumi] says: "*Ey Eshgh*! I am afraid of something else," and receives the reply "that something else is no more," that "something else" is referring to Shams of Tabriz who has departed. And when he says a moon shines in the name of love, he is referring to Hessameddin, his new beloved, the one who is encouraging him to continue his *Mathnavi*. This is perhaps the time that Mowlana has given up the hope of ever finding his lost master and beloved Shams. This is why he tells Hessameddin, "Don't worry. You are not replacing Shams. You are a loving thing in your own right. Don't be afraid."

Maybe this is a good time to stop this letter and not to say anything more, even thought I have a lot more to say. You seem to have just started me up. It is the listener who brings the words out of the mouth of the speaker. I am sending this letter through the dearest of the dears, your sister, Monavar. She is allowed to read it before mailing it to you. I am not under house arrest, but my motion and communication are under supervision.

Signed:

Khosrow

Bee-Nava [the first pen name of Khosrow]

Heidar-Ali [the second pen name]

Rahmat-Ali [the third pen name]

Abri [meaning cloudy; the fourth pen name]

Past political number: 412; T-A-D-A A

Some more comments on Khosrow and his letter: Khosrow's letter ends here. But I want to make a few comments about it before I leave him.

Before translating Khosrow's letter, and therefore reading it more carefully, I had thought that Khosrow had chosen too many pen names for himself, but after reading and translating the letter, I think he has too few. He could have two other pen names: 1—Showgh-Ali, *Showgh* meaning joy, to refer to the amount of joy and elation I could sense in his writings and reading, and 2—*Ein-Ali*, meaning the eye of Ali, since his letter is an eye-opener for me.

Also present in the folder that contains Khosrow's letter and many other letters, there is a cutting from a recent Persian newspaper brought from Tehran by Pari. It is about the interview a reporter had with Khosrow regarding how he rescued the leaders of the Tudeh party from Ghasr prison. In it he explains how they managed, with the help of Lieutenant Ghobadian of the police from the inside of prison, and about a dozen of his friends wearing soldiers uniforms, in one army truck, they went to the prison and took them out. They pretended that they were taking them to another prison. No weapons. They used toy guns inside leather holsters for revolvers on their belts. The title of the article is "It was not done by General Razmara." Maybe before Khosrow's confession, everybody in Iran had thought that the escape was done or facilitated by General Razmara. It is also timely that I add here for the sake of history that General Razmara, while he was the Prime Minister, was assassinated by one of the members of the same group that had assassinated Ahmad Kasravi.

Also I have omitted many of Khosrow's writings about love, and I am unhappy about this because I know Khosrow does not write nonsense. But I had to do it because of the length of his letter.

Khosrow has not forgotten his secret number that was given to him by the military branch of Tudeh Party. I have forgotten mine. And I thank my memory for it.

I did not know that his older brother, Amir, was such a good man. All I remember about Amir was a young quiet man with pale face and the slightest impression of a smile at the corner of his mouth. I don't remember anything he ever told me worth repeating or me having said anything to him. All I knew about him was that he was the only son of General Pouria who had not joined the Tudeh Party. Also I remember that he quit high school and opened a stationery store at the junction of Amirieh with Arfa' Avenue, at the end of which Razi High School and the Museum of Anthropology (Mardom Shenassi) were located. He had a display of good fountain pens behind its tall windows. He closed his shop within a few months because most of his expensive things were stolen one day when he was unconscious after having an epileptic seizure.

That store changed hands many times. Even though its location was good, and numerous students passed by it, it did not last for long. It was the same store to which, many years earlier, my mother had made me return, with shame, the three useless masks I had bought.

One of the things I have omitted from Khosrow's letter is this: "I don't live for myself any more. I don't live at all. I live for my three beautiful granddaughters in my house. Seventy-five percent of my life is spent on them, 25 percent on myself and 25 percent on my books. If it adds up to more than a hundred percent, so be it."

I believe Khosrow. I am sure the crayons he has used to colour some of his words belong to one of his three granddaughters from his rebellious son. I have to write a letter directly to Khosrow to ask him to explain many more things including the connection between Ismaili genes and rebellion.

63

A Letter from Mahmood, My Last Brother

WHILE WE, THE SHOJANIA BROTHERS, are aware of each other's existence and have news about each other, we rarely write letters to each other. If we receive a letter, however, we always reply to it. The letter I am going to translate from my last brother is his reply to my letter that I had written to him after forty years. The reason I had written to him was because I had not talked to him or written to him for almost forty years, seven years of which he was in prison. I have to say right away that the cause of his imprisonment was neither political nor criminal. It was not due to religious differences either, even though it happened many years after the Islamic revolution. The cause of his landing into prison was a cheque that he had written to a friend without a sufficient amount of money in the bank, but the cause of remaining in prison for so long was himself. He liked it there. He could borrow and pay the amount that I am sure was not too much and come out, but he did not. He had tested life outside of prison for long enough to know what he was doing. He lived alone. He had no children. During this time Mehdi had once visited him when he had gone to Iran for a few weeks. When I asked Mehdi how Mahmood was doing, he said he was happy but had put on a lot of weight and seemed to have an unhealthy edema under his eyes. He had free access to the prison's library and had practised calligraphy and drawings, and was spending most of his time there.

I have not seen any of his drawings, but his handwriting has improved so much that I could not recognize my brother in it. It was so perfect that the "To the name of Allah, the compassionate and the merciful" with which he has decorated the top of his letter, is undistinguishable from printed words. To make sure that it was not printed as a heading on the notebook in which he had written his letter, I had to test it with my wetted finger. It is in Koranic style, with more angulated letters than *Nasta'leegh* style with which most Iranians write, and the rest of the letter was written. I will have to print the first page of his letter in my book to show how perfect it is, without being a print. Maybe my unconscious desire wanted to erase the impersonal, honourific, official title of *Jenab* with which my brother had addressed me at the beginning of his letter, rather than a simple "Dear Nasser", or "Dear brother."

Before the translation, I should hasten to add that he writes many poems in his letter, but I can't tell which ones are his, and which ones belong to others. Many of them, if not most of them, are not his. He does not use quotation marks, but the poem on the first page is so familiar that I am sure it is by Forough Farrokh Zad, the poet who lived near As-You-Wish Street. One night we shared a taxi together, coming back from the house of the sister of Siavosh and Iraj Kasraei. (She was the lady who helped raise Shah-naaz Pahlavi, the first daughter of the last Shah by his Egyptian wife, Fowzieh.)

The Letter

To the name of Allah, the compassionate and the merciful

I saw your letter in the hand of the mailman

I fell flat on the ground, like a picture.

This is what happens when you write,

Imagine what would happen when you don't!

Your Honour, Dr. Nasser Shojania, as it is shortly going to be said, and you know it already, Friday evenings are always sorrowful and sad for anybody at any age, and everybody tries to somehow busy himself with something during these gloomy evenings to avoid feeling the passage of time. You go out to the streets only to see that every shop, like the days of mourning an ancient assassination, is closed, except for the florists and sandwich outlets. You return home, you wonder what kind of *Khaak* to spray on your head so as not to feel the rotation of the globe.

The Silent Friday

Deserted Friday

Sorrowful Friday, like old allies

The Friday of ill-conceived, lazy thoughts

The Friday of narrow-mindedness and overstretched yawns

Wait-less Friday

Friday of surrender

Home of emptiness

Home of sadness with the entrance door closed against the invasion of youth

Home of loneliness, augury and doubt.

Home of curtains, cupboards, books and pictures.

Aah, how calm and proud passed my life

Like a distant trickle of running water

Through these silent and deserted Fridays

And those sorrowful vacant houses

Aah, how proud and slow it passed.

Yes, now I am sure; the poem is by Forough. She always complained of boredom. It is also the disease of Mahmood and many of my brothers. Hossein, I remember, on Friday evenings, used to walk around the medallion of the carpet in his room, repeating to himself, "What should I do? What should I do?" Maybe it is a Persian disease, like *ennui,* which is endemic in France. Maybe it is not a disease. It could be physiological, part of the human condition. This is what makes us human. Nothing is good enough for us, for long. Boredom is what separates man from animals. Except for perhaps the gorillas, I have never seen a bored animal in a zoo, and that is perhaps another reason we are genetically remotely related. Before any creative act there must be a period of boredom. God, I dare to say, must have been bored before creation of the universe. This is why He created human beings. He wanted to play hide-and-seek with them. I am sure.

Mahmood continues…

I have to curse a thousand times our Farsi teachers in our high schools for not teaching us how to write a letter to a specialist doctor who—if he abstains from having sour things like *torshi*—has something to say about Persian literature as well. How can I start my letter and end it in such a way that it pleases both God and the reader? The compositions we were told to write were often like these: "Which is better, knowledge or wealth?" or "What would you do if you had a lot of money to spare?" or "Write a letter to your friend and invite him to Tehran." And the most frequent and the most difficult one was this: "Explain the season of spring." And later, when we grew older we found out that none of these compositions helped us in real life and, wherever we looked, instead of spring, we saw the yellow colour of autumn.

Recalling the story of our falling in love;

The first sight of the beloved resembles spring

The heat of desire, its summer

The long hours of waiting, its fall

The coldness of separation, its winter.

Since the time of falling in love has passed

When I am gone

What will remain of me will be only stories.

Your letter arrived on Tuesday the 13th of Khordad [2000?] and I am now writing this letter on the evening of Friday, the 16th of Khordad. Firstly, I want to thank you for letting me know not to write the address of the sender and receiver on two sides of the envelope, so that the mailman does not have to go through extra motion to see who the letter is from, and does not confuse the machines if the letters are sorted electronically. Your criticism did not hurt me. As Sa'di says:

I get hurt by that kind of friend

Who praises my bad habits as good

And my vices as virtues

And my thorns as roses

Where are my enemies to show me my faults?

Blind be the beggar, who, after ten years of begging, still does not remember Friday nights. This humble writer has worked for four years at a sports newspaper, named *Pahlavan* [Athlete] and had my own column under the rubric of "From Every Colour" and was in contact with other agencies by mail and, no matter how dumb, I should have known where the addresses should be written on the envelope.

You may ask why then did I do it, if I knew the right way. It is because more than fifty percent of the people in our country are illiterate and I have seen with my own eyes how they write their letters destined for foreign lands. The writers of these lines, therefore, in accordance with the formula, "if you don't want to become notorious, behave as most people do," wrote the address that way. Also, I did it deliberately so that the postman or woman in the foreign land will notice right away that "talent is found nowhere but in Iran and among the Iranians." In short,

The front and the back of our letters are the same

You have seen my happy days, why ask about the nights?

This line looks like one of Mahmood's own poems. It is too relevant, as if made to fit the occasion. It is not one of those memorized lines to be used when it suits the text. It does not come out of Iran's collective unconscious. It is not a poem. It does not have more meaning than itself. It does not jump off the page.

I, of course, have no claim to being a good writer but a few years ago I wrote an essay in this regard and mentioned some of the common mistakes writers make here.

One was the verb *fowt shodan* [to die] which is often mistakenly written *fowt kardan* [to do dying]. Here is a sentence from your letter, "*Raastee*, three weeks ago, my friend Rastegar in France *fowt kard*." Pay attention to the fact that only those verbs that require the will of the doer can take the auxiliary verb of *kardan*. You can't write, "He ceased doing breathing," for example. You can say his breathing ceased. If you throw yourself from the window, of course, you are allowed to say it the way you have said it. For example, "Hossein threw himself off the balcony."

The second common mistake, also committed by you, is about the word *moshkel*. When you wrote, "Don't postpone the work of today for tomorrow,' which is easy to say but is *moshguel* [difficult] to do." Instead of writing *moshkel*, with *K*, you wrote moshguel, with *gu*.

Translator's note: True. Mahmood is right. The word for *difficult* in Farsi is *moshkel*, with *k*, not with *gu*. I checked just now the *Divaneh* Hafez where he brings this word in the second half of the first line of his first *Ghazal*. It was spelled as Mahmood said, "*moshkel-ha*," the plural form of moshkel.

When I opened the book of Hafez, however, I got distracted by the first line of its first *Ghazal*; the one that half of which, the first half, is in Arabic, the other half and the rest of the divan in Farsi.

O Saaghi! Circulate the cup of wine for the circle of our friends

For love began easily, then came the troubles [Moshkel-ha].

Only recently have I learned from Pari why this is so. That Arabic half line is not from Hafez. He is quoting someone else and that someone else is apparently Yazeed, an Arab who was a contemporary of Ali, but was not as popular among Iranians for what he did to Imam Hossein.

Mahmood and Hafez are right and I am wrong, but I am sure if the Arabic alphabet did have the letter *gu* or *Guaaf*, Hafez would have used it because *gu* is softer than *k*. Compared to Farsi, the Arabic alphabet is more defective. They both have the same number of vowels, six, but Arabic language lacks four consonants, among which is the letter *gu*. This letter in Farsi alphabet is symbolized by the Arabic letter *Kaaf*, with the addition of an extra line over its oblique handle. It is inserted in the Persian alphabet right after the letter *Kaaf* for *k*. I say inserted, rather than placed, because it had to force itself in the tight row of the four letters K L M N that always go together in all or most of the languages derived from the Indo-European root, as well as in Arabic that is supposed to have its own separate Semitic root.

Is it a coincidence that the word for "word" in Arabic is *Kalaam,* or *Kalemeh,* which is made of three of these four always-together letters? I ask myself. "In the beginning," they say the Bible says, "there was word," the Arabic counterpart of word is *Kalaam,* containing most of those letters that go together in many alphabets. Maybe it was the *Kalaam* that got broken up to its constituting consonants to incorporate it into the alphabet when it was being invented in that region of the globe.

Hafez disappointed me, but I am glad that Khosrow Pouria did not. Even though he knows and respects Arabic as much as Farsi, if not more, he has used the world *Moshguel* in his letter, instead of *Moshkel*. I make a note at the corner of his letter to include it in my reply, if I did write one. I would tell him to go and ask Khosrow about it, being certain that Khosrow would give him a convincing answer why *Moshguel* is better. I have to tell him to get his address from Monavar some time he has time, but to see Khosrow he should go to his house only at nights because his house is under surveillance.

Mahmood continues finding faults with my Farsi…

And when you write numbers in the middle of a Farsi phrase, you should remember that in Farsi letters are written in the opposite direction of the way numbers are written. So, instead of writing, "After 8 to 7 years," you should have written "after 7 to 8 years," so that the eye of the reader could continue its smooth motion from right to left.

Now, you can believe Sa'di when he says:

My knowledge has reached to such a high level

That I can tell I am ignorant.

I know the poem, but I don't think it is from Sa'di. I think it by Abu Ali Sina. Sa'di never confessed to ignorance. He was a teacher. Teachers don't confess to ignorance. It is the scientist and the scientifically minded who are ready to confess that they don't know.

Another problem with Farsi writing is punctuation, Mahmood continues. In Iran they use mainly the exclamation and the question marks, often both together.

Raastee, before I forget, convey my *Salaams* to your wife and children. With the every-day problems that people have here no one is thinking of saying *Salaam* to anyone and no one is ready to respond to your *Salaam*. Akhavan was right when he said in his *Zemestan*.

Winter

The pedestrians are reluctant to reply to your Salaam

The air is thick

The doors are shut

The heads are down

The chins are wedged in the V of the neck

Hands are hidden and hearts are heavy with sorrow

The trees are skeletons, studded with crystalline candles

The ground is dead

The sky is low

The face of the sun is as pale as the moon

It is winter.

But let us go on to your questions and comments about my writings and my handwriting that you and Pari and Mehdi have praised so much. Thank you for your kind remarks, but let me tell you frankly what I think about myself, "The smallest particle that does not get counted in any calculation, is me." If you have seen anything good in it is perhaps because "in the city of the blind, the one with one eye is the king." Otherwise, compared to all that Nasser and Mehdi and Pari know, I know very well that I am nobody.

A cat is a lion in front of a mouse

But is a mouse in front of a lion.

Along these lines, let me ask you something. Why don't you and Pari and Mehdi, who have the mind and the guts to write the right things, write something in Farsi so that I could publish it in the newspaper I am currently working for, *Omideh Javan* [The Young Hope]? I have a regular column in it. It is easier for you to write from far away than we can from here. Here, when we want to write something critical, we have to wrap it inside so many layers to hide the main point. The name of our newspaper was once *Omid*, but at the time of the death of the son of our dear leader, Imam Ahmad Khomeini, there was something printed in it that could be interpreted to imply that Seyyed Ahmad Khomeini had been done away with by government agents, and because of that, the privilege of publishing that newspaper was removed, so they changed its name to *Omideh Javan*.

Actually the government was right to be insulted by that unjust accusation. Now we know that the son of Ayatollah Khomeini along with more than three hundred poets and intellectuals, including Daryush Froohar and his wife, both members of parliament, were killed by the psychopath by the name of Sa'eed Imami who was neither on the side of government nor on the side of people. He eventually killed himself. The anti-revolutionaries attributed those mysterious killings to the government, and the government attributed them to the anti-revolutionaries. They both were wrong in their accusations.

I did write something for his column after Mahmood asked me to do so and he did publish most of it, as much he could fit in his thin column. He added only a short paragraph of his own at the beginning of it, as a disclaimer. I do not remember what I wrote in that article. Maybe I talked about the conspiracy theory as the only tool many Iranians have for interpreting political events. Many Iranians, for example, believed—and some still do—that the Islamic Revolution was an American conspiracy.

Mahmood continues …

Despite what people outside of Iran think, Iran is not badly off as far as freedom of the press and democracy are concerned. After all, a few years ago when Canada was chosen the best country to live in, according to the United Nations, Iran was number 75th or 76th among the 150 or so countries of the world, right in the middle. There are, therefore, as many countries that are worse places to live in as there are countries that are better places to live in than Iran. Our friend, who is the man responsible for our newspaper, is like a snake-bitten man. He is afraid of black-and-white ropes.

They keep preaching that waste is profane and therefore prohibited, but each of the candidates for presidency spent millions or even billions of *Tuman* to get elected. I have more to say about this, but later.

A clergy was preaching that if a child, no matter what age, urinated on a carpet, the carpet cannot be cleansed by any amount of washing or any detergent. The dirty portion of the carpet must be cut out. A few days later, when he went home, he saw that a one-square-metre piece was missing from his living room carpet. He asked his wife for explanation. The wife said that their two-year old boy had urinated on that spot and she had done what he had said in the mosque. Her husband got upset and told his wife in a rough voice, "Wife! That was for the people, not for us."

In the attached newspaper column, under the title of *Sha'boon* and *Ramezoon*, if you read, you can see what I mean. The newspaper, *Aftaab-Gardan* [Sunflower] belongs to Gholam Hossein Karbas-Chee who was the mayor of Tehran for six years. Nonetheless they closed his newspaper. He had to pay two million *Tuman* in penalties, too. I am telling you this so that you know that the situation is not so open that one writes whatever one wishes. In short, why should the wise do something to regret it later? One should learn from Sa'di who says:

One should say nothing but the truth

But not every truth should be said.

Now, to answer your question about why the cost of living is so high in Tehran.

It cost the country more than one thousand million *Tuman* to pay for the Imposed War [the Iran/Iraq war]. About 30 million dollars [billion?], with interest, is owed to European countries. Add to this the expenses of the amputees and the wounded and the families of the martyred, then you can see it is a big problem for the government. We have five million single young men who cannot marry because of the high cost of living. The universities graduate many educated young men and women, but there is not enough work for them. Theft, breaking into houses and stealing cars are common occurrences. Worst of all is bribery. Bribery is rampant here.

And people's hope for change and improvement is as unrealistic as the expectation of the legendary blind man about how good his penis looked. Everybody thinks that next year everybody is going to pour into the streets and create chaos and change the government. They ignore the fact that they do not have such courage.

Story

It is said that long ago the cruel ruler of an ancient city issued this ridiculous order. "After tomorrow, anybody who wants to pass through the gate of the city must be sexually abused by one of the guards." For a while, things passed uneventfully, but the waiting line behind the gate was getting longer and longer. When the length of the line got ridiculously long, a man stepped out of the line to object to the way the guards were doing their job. The other people in the line, who were tired of the long hours of waiting in the heat of the summer sun, fell silent to hear what the brave man had to say. "I wonder, Mr. Guard," the man said politely, "if it would be possible to increase the number of guards so that these poor people won't have to wait for such a long time in this heat?"

But, let us jump from branch to branch. You wrote that many years ago a beggar prayed for you to grow old and his prayer has been answered. Interestingly, I too have written something in this regard and it is going to be published in a few days. The title of it is this, "Father, you wanted me to grow old…" and it begins like this:

Father

You prayed that I grow old

Now come and see

The result of your curse

Camouflaged as a prayer.

My story brings to my mind Ahmad Shamloo—the new poet—who recently lost one of his legs to gangrene, at the age of 71. He too shows that long life is not as desirable as one thinks.

Ask the prophet Khezr

[The one who lives forever and his job is to take human life away]

"What profit have you gained

Out of your eternal life

Except for witnessing the death of those you love?"

This is the same poem that my mother quoted to me in reply to my letter of condolences for death of her son, Hossein, a recurrent tragedy for my mother.

In other words:

We are already fed up with this life

Poor Khezr who has to stay here forever!

In short, there are no rules or regulations regarding longevity. Your regular walking and not smoking, and Mehdi's healthy diet won't guarantee a long life for either of you. Even if you look younger, you can't deny the date in your identification booklet.

The old maid [the world]

Took away your fun

One by one

What are you going to do for the lost fun?

Suppose you darkened your grey hair

What are you going to do with the darkness of your vision?

Suppose you cleared your vision with medication or an operation

What are you going to do with your bent posture?

Suppose you manage to keep erect with the help of a cane

What are you going to do with your bent penis?

Regarding me and my health, I have no specific illness that you could diagnose or cure from this long distance. I don't have shortness of breath and I don't need inhalers.

O healer, I know my body better than you

I am burning from faraagh [separateness]

You call it fever.

For a while I limited my diet to *kalbas* and cold cuts and pickles and things like that. My stomach became immensely bloated and pressed against my heart and lungs. In short, I haven't eaten uncooked fruits since my doctor said that I am sensitive to cellulose. I had all the tests, including pictures of my stomach and sonography. Everything was normal and I don't have any internal problem, except for being without a brain. I am afraid I shall hear the news of my brothers' death before I depart for the everlasting world. Generally, people who don't have brains live longer. As the comic newsletter of *Towfeegh* used to have as its motto: *Unlucky the one who is endowed with reason; lucky the one who came as a colt and went as an ass.*

As you know the distance between madness and genius is as little as the width of four fingers, which means most intelligent people like Dr. Massoud Meer-Baha and his brother, and Hamid, were all intelligent but got caught by madness. Mohammad Ghahreman, or better, our own Mohammad Mirza, has a poem:

Oh, madness! It is thanks to you that my mind is at rest

It is thanks to you that wisdom cannot disturb my tranquility.

Even though it is not a good thing to say, I have to confess that when I heard from Monir-jun that you were planning to say something about Daii-jan Sarhang's book, *SOS*, in your book I was worried for a moment that maybe you too were losing your mind. Why are you finding *jerjees* among so many thousand prophets? But then I thought, "It is up to the king to decide what is good or what is bad for his country." Maybe there is something in that book that we did not see.

I see hair; you see the undulation of the hair.

I see an eyebrow; you see the hints of it.

You have informed me that lack of exercise and living a sedentary life shortens one's life as much as smoking a pack of cigarettes a day. I have to say that I am quite active and don't smoke anymore. Actually, it was not I who quit cigarettes, the cigarettes quit me. It happened like this. One day, after smoking a few in a row, I suddenly got disgusted with it and put it out of my life. Regarding physical activities, I have to say that I have a friend, Hassan Moradi, who lives in the lower floor of my apartment with his wife and while I was in prison, took care of my house and would visit me every week. He has a workshop about ten minutes away from my house that repairs electrical automobile parts, like batteries, air conditioners, lights, and starters. From nine in the morning till eight and sometimes eight-thirty at nights I work there. I therefore have no time to exercise or visit with anybody. I don't want to do what Hossein and Khosrow Khalvati did, by frequently visiting our relatives and bothering them with my presence.

You had asked about the general mood of the country. I am sending you a page of the *Ettela'at* newspaper from 1995. It contains the last segment of a series of articles written by Meer Shafiian, a member of the justice department. When you read this you will know how the country is. The waiting lists for trials are almost three years long. Most of the judges are resigning. And so on.

In short, bribery in government offices does *Beedaad* [play havoc] here. In each department there is a division, named Hefaazat and Haraasat, to watch that money does not change hands and that the civil servants behave honestly—and this humble writer has a saying about it that has not been published yet and at the end of it I quote this proverb:

We add salt to prevent our food from going bad

God forbid the coming of the day when salt goes bad!

Were you to ask who got divorced here, I would reply, in chronological order: Shambool, Houshi, Soraya Navab-pour, Mahmood, Feerooz Saramad, and Hormoz Milanian. Houshi's situation is worse than all the others. Since he has never performed his out-of-capital duties and is Baha'i, finding a job for him in Tehran is very difficult. He has not found any work since the revolution, and his attitude is such that people stay away from him.

I just looked at the notepad in which I am writing this letter and realized that no more than one page is left. So, I have to begin to sing the *Ghazal* of good-bye.

In the last few years several times I picked up the pen to write you a letter to ask you a question but each time I postponed it for the next time. As Ferdowsi says, "Never put off for tomorrow what you can do today" [written by Mahmood as is, in English. It is not my translation. It is the only English phrase in his Farsi letter].

The main problem with writing and corresponding by letter is that it creates habits, and all the time one is either waiting for a reply or worried about not having replied.

Sheikh Sa'di was traveling with his son when the highwaymen attacked and took all their belongings. The son asked the father, "Didn't you lose your belongings, father? Then why aren't you sad?" The father said, "My heart was not so firmly attached to those goods to get hurt when they are gone."

Also, another story: Someone sent his son to school to become literate. The teacher asked him to go to the blackboard and write *Aleph*, the first letter of many alphabets. The boy did not move and did not say a thing. The father of the boy was asked to come to school to explain why his son was mute. The father rushed towards his son to punish him for play-acting. The son screamed, "Don't hit me. I am not mute, but I know that as soon as I write or say *Aleph* you want me to write *B* and so on and so on till the end of alphabet." Writing letters to each other is like this, too. If we could stop at this letter, it would be fine. It does not create much love and attachment, and if, God forbid, your coronary arteries began giving you trouble and you left this world, it would not hurt me as much as had you died at the end of a long string of letters exchanged between us.

I don't say that you are not aware of my presence in the world

You are.

What you are not aware of

Is God.

Finally, if you have a few short articles send them here. I might manage to publish them under your own name. As a doctor who has left the country many years ago you might have some interesting observations regarding Iran. Also, let us know how life in exile is.

Before I end, I have one question for you: If it weren't for the children, would you ever return to live in Iran? Or are you happy there, and believe as Sa'di does:

Paradise is where there is no hurt,

And no one has anything to do with anybody else.

I don't think I have left any word unsaid. I have sent my *Salaams* to your family, too, so there is nothing to worry, at least, about that matter; therefore I sing the *Ghazal* of *Khoda-hafezi* [saying good-bye].

We, the pain-familiar and the unfamiliar with self

Tell stories for people and become a story ourselves

We have always been strangers among the familiar

And we will remain so until the end.

Our burning hearts have become candles for the moth

Our burning wishes are flying away from lights

Nasser is wondering who we are

Are we ruins or are we treasure?

Mahmood's letter ends here with no room for *Ghorbanat* or signature.

My last brother has sent an entire notebook to me as a letter. Maybe it is my diary I have been waiting for all these years. Maybe this is a Persian letter.

64

A Prose from a Poet

UNLIKE SOHRAB, my cousin from our mother's side, who was not a poet but lived poetically, Mohammad Mirza, my cousin from our father's side, was a true poet and poetic-looking, but lived a non-poetic, normal life. He made use of his talent to accentuate the pains and pleasures associated with his routine life. We were about the same age and the same size, but we were never classmates of each other because up to the end of high school he was in Khorassan. The only school we attended together was around the *Korsi* in the children's room in the house of Modar-jun. He lived with us during the three years that he attended the Faculty of Law at Tehran University. Many years later, after I had left Iran, maybe in the early 80s, as I was lying on our bed, looking out of the window and watching the same three pine trees on the hilly yard of our distant neighbour, the thought of him came to my mind again for the thousandth time. Trees, for some reason, always remind me of him. So, I wrote him a letter to free my mind from constant chattering with him. Here is his reply, in prose.

4/2/1361 equal to 24 April 1982

Mashad

Nasser-jan, I grew horns out of astonishment and wings out of joy when I unexpectedly received your beautiful letter. First, I thought it was from Fakhr-e-Monir, my younger sister in Vancouver. I know her handwriting and it was not hers. When I used my glasses and looked at the left upper corner of the envelope, my eyes lit up with the light of your name.

You will excuse, I hope, my few days of delay in replying to it.

Well, my dear, I read your letter several times and each time I enjoyed it more. The same beautiful and flowing prose of the years 1327-28, but better cooked. It reminded me of the beautiful composition you wrote which I borrowed it to read for our literature teacher, Dr. Safa. And also the piece you wrote about the waterfall of Pas-ghal'eh in Shemiran that froze in a very cold winter, and I transformed it into a poem! Your letter reminded me of the times of childhood and youth, and the time of freedom from news. You don't know how many scenes of the dead past your letter resurrected in my mind, simultaneously.

As *Saa'eb* says

The news-less time of our chldhood was a little paradise

Pity, a hundred times, that we got to know about it too late.

I have to interrupt the letter of my cousin to say that I already know this line. Maybe I had read it in one of the many books of lesser-known poets that he had spread on the *Korsi* at nights, when he was living with us. Or, maybe he had already quoted it to me on one of those nights. What kind of a poet is he that remembers the past less well than I do? In Farsi a poet is called a *Shaa'er*, Arabic for the present participle of *Sho'ur,* meaning consciousness or awareness. *Shaa'er*, therefore, means "he who is conscious."

…Our mountain climbing on the Triple Summits Mountain (Hassan Ghoul) in Torbat, and those fire-generating rocks which we collected and used to shower our hands with stars when we hit them together, drowned us in a sea of joy. And the little tin toy ship that you brought as a gift for me from Tehran that burnt melted candle wax in a lemonade cap as fuel. Too bad it stopped working so soon. Those few long trips that we made together from Tehran to Mashad and Torbat, and from there to Amir-aabad [the name of their village, so named after Amir Hossein Mirza, their eldest brother, who became a pediatrician and practised all his life in Mashad]; and the disobedient maid of *Naneh-Aagha*…

Naneh-Aagha, I have to interrupt again for the sake of clarity, was the mother of Mohammad Mirza's father. She was an old, thin, ascetic lady who had never travelled out of their village and all her life had breathed its unpolluted air. She was so unaccustomed to the smell of petroleum that she could tell if a truck was passing miles away from their village. "A truck is moving," she would suddenly announce as she was sitting at her simple lunch. Mohammad Mirza and I had to go to the roof of the house to see if she was right, and invariably we would see a black spot pulling a train of dust along the distant horizon.

How well you remembered Almas [Diamond], Naneh Aagha's vicious dog! Like the dogs of Nazi-aabad that do not differentiate between familiar and stranger, it bit my foot through my brand new *Gueeveh* and then, ashamed, put its tail between its legs and moved sheepishly backwards. Naneh Aagha gave it a good beating with a stick, and emptied half a bottle of iodine tincture on my wound that raised my cry to the seventh sky. Still, after the passage of so many long years, Almas's teeth marks are visible on the side of my left foot.

What an unappreciative dog it was! Since it was a puppy, or as the Torbatis say, *Kochok*, Naneh Aagha knew that it wouldn't grow to become a good dog, and wouldn't give anything to it to eat. This is why I would sometimes steal a piece of bread for him or take him to the plains outside of the fortress to catch *Chazz* for it. *Chazz*, if you remember, was a small red insect the size of an average locust. It was green in Port of Gaz in the North, most likely due to adaptation to the green environment near the Caspian Sea. It had a short lifespan. It lived only for one summer, and made a pleasing buzzing sound. The peasant children often caught them and, after plucking their wings, fried them and ate them. In the city of Ghaa'em they catch a lot of them and, after frying, they preserve them for winter, like *Maygoo* [dried locust?]. I don't know the scientific name of it. In Bandar of Gaz they call it *Cher-gherani* to match its sound. In Khorassan it has been known since old times, but a *d* is added to it to become *Chazed*. Asadi Toussi (about 900 years ago) quotes this beautiful line from a poet whose name now escapes me:

Listen to the sound of Chazed *that imitates*

A new Koozeh *submerged in a pool of water.*

(To understand this line the reader should know that a new *Koozeh*, like any non-glazed earthenware, makes a whizzing or buzzing sound the first time that it is submerged in water. This is, of course, the result of water getting into its microscopic pores to release the little air bubbles trapped in them.)

Baary, even though Almas was an unappreciative dog, God, I hope, will make him the neighbour of the inhabitants of the Cave of Kahf. I liked him. Near the end of his life, apparently he had become very vicious and slipped off his rope a few times and attacked a few beggars. The collar around his neck had become too tight but no one dared to get close enough to loosen it. Eventually he left this world with the disease of suffocation! Well, let us pass beyond Amir Aabad and go to Mashad.

I remember the night we were in my brother's house, Dr. Amir-Hossein. Hamid (pity how soon and how *Na-kaam* he left us!) and Majid had gone out. Someone knocked at the door and we, you and I, thinking that it was either Hamid or Majid playing games with us, sang this poem of Sanaei with some alterations. Of course, after each line the knocking at the door got louder:

Your must be Kareem (knock, knock!)

You must be Raheem (knock, knock!!)

You must be Majid (knock, knock, and knock!!!)

You are the representative of wisdom; you deserve our Sana! [Praise].

… … … …

Finally we managed to hear that the knocker was saying with controlled anger and grave manly voice, "Open the door to see who it is!" When we finally opened the door, we almost drowned in our sweat in shame when we saw the man behind the door was our great-uncle, Prince Shoja-ol-Soltan.

[Our uncle must have come to pay a visit to our mother to preempt her visiting him. Traditionally, the newcomer to a city has to sit at home so that the relatives can come to say *Salaam* and welcome, but my mother would not sit and wait. She would go out to visit the others before they came to see her. Or, alternatively, it could be that she had gone to visit the shrine of Imam Reza.]

I also remember the summer of 1328, when we were nineteen or twenty. At nights, when we slept on the rooftop of your house, our eyes, when they got tired of looking at the stars would look into the open window of the neighbour in front of your house and wished we had a wife, too. Also, the incident where we broke a neighbour's window with a *Palakhmoo* [slingshot, in Torbati dialect] and the bitter complaints of the neighbour to Modar-jun.

The nights of Tehran, in those days, were transparent and star-studded, far from smoke and smog. In remembrance of those days! In remembrance of those nights!

It seems that my letter is going to be one of those headless and tail-less ones. This is the way you wanted it, anyway. Whatever word comes to my pen I let it fall on the paper.

Five or six years ago, when I went to Tehran, I heard you had been there a few weeks earlier. I regretted not having seen you. I got your address from Amoo-jan's wife [Modar-jun], but preoccupations and laziness prevented me from using it. Next time—God willing—if you made another trip to this side of the world, please don't leave me news-less. Let me know when you are coming so that if you cannot come to Mashad, I will go to Tehran. What a good thing you've done by writing that letter! Write again and let me know to what stage of life you have reached.

You are probably more or less up to date with my *Haal* and *Roozegar*. Conventionally, I am alive and living, but officially, as Farrokhi Yazdi has said, "I am undergoing gradual degeneration towards death."

It is now more than twenty years that I have been working in the corner of the library of the Faculty of Literature in Mashad. I married Fereshteh (Angel), the granddaughter of our uncle, Rooh-ol-amin Mirza, in 1959. We had two casualties in the first two years of our marriage, one daughter and one son who did not survive. [Most likely due to consanguinity, but it is now too late and too painful to discuss this medical matter.]

The third child, who was a boy, Rooz-beh (Better-day) came into the world in 1351 [1972]. His appearance was healthy and, in the beginning, he made us happy. After five or six months it became apparent that he could not hear. At the age of two, we took him to Tehran for audiometric testing but they did not have the instrument. The next year we took him to Alman, and came back with "arms longer than legs" [empty-handed and disappointed]. He is a boy with extremely good *Adab* [manners] and extraordinary intelligence, but he is very sensitive. This year he is in grade four in the elementary school for exceptional children.

Fereshteh, who is a licentiate in the French language, had transferred herself to his school for his sake. She had been a vice-principal for a few years, and now she has been teaching for about two years.

The second boy, Reza, who, thanks to God, is nineteen months old, is healthy, and has diminished our unease a little. The biggest headache that he has caused me so far is the fact that I had to use up all of my four months of vacation for him and now the faculty owes me no more vacations. Fereshteh worked two weeks in the mornings and two weeks in the afternoon to take care of the child, because we have nobody to take care of him. And I took two weeks of vacation every month to baby sit when Fereshteh was working. I could then work the afternoon shift for two weeks. At any rate, this year is passed, and by the month of *Mehr*, he will be—*Beh-salaamati* [equivalent to "knock on wood"]—two years old. By that time, maybe we will put him in a daycare centre or something like it. Luckily, Rooz-beh likes him very much and they interact nicely with each other. He is beginning to make sentences like *"Maman bia!"* (Come! Mother.) Or *"Baba aamad"* (Father came) and similar things.

Sometimes, he utters meaningless words and disjointed phrases. There is a poet by the name of Najeeb Kaashi (contemporary of Safavid dynasty) who has a *Ghazal* with a line that particularly explains how I am feeling about my conversation with Reza.

There is no rhyme or reason in my words

But, like the babbling of an infant,

It is sweet to the ear.

Baary, our coming to your side of the world is probably impossible. If you can, you should try to come so that our eyes light up with your appearance.

And don't take life too seriously, since its hardship lasts only for its first seventy to eighty years. After that, it gets better! Send me pictures of yourself and the children so that, as Shahriar said, "We saw each other's youth, let us see our old age as well."

You wrote that you have specialized in pathology. It wouldn't be bad if you could dissect us, these moving corpses, too, to find out what is wrong with us.

In recent years I have assembled and corrected the *Divans* of two poets, ready for print, but nothing is published yet. One is the *Divaneh* Shahab Torshizi, who died in Torbat, at the beginning of the reign of Fatali Shah, the other is that of Saa'eb Tabrizi.

Torshizi is an able poet who writes especially good satires, lampoons, and risqué jokes. He is at the same level as Anvari, Soozani, and Yaghmaayeh Jandaghi. The following lines are sample of his milder satire. The poem is about someone whose name was Jom'eh [Friday] and lived in Harat [a city in western Afghanistan] and had not paid the money he owed to the poet. The name of his *Khar-kar*—or as the Tehranis say, his *Kharak-chee* [donkey-man]—was *Aadineh* [another word for Friday or Jom'eh].

Jom'eh one night confided to his wife,

"I suspect there is something fishy going on

Between you and Aadineh"

The wife told the husband,

"Put your double vision aside"

"For me, Jom'eh and Aadineh are the same!"

If this book ever gets published, unfortunately, one will have to replace too many of its satiric words by three dots. And this would fill the pages with so many dots that it would interfere with its correct reading. Even with *Raml* and *Ostorlaab* [Geomancy and Astrology] one would not be able to read them.

From the year 1357 [1978] till now, I have been seriously working on the works of Saa'eb; the master of Hendi style in poetry. I like him with my heart and soul. In addition to my interest, or perhaps because of it, the University of Mashad signed a contract in this regard with me. I finished the whole work, which consists of 75,000 lines, and delivered the work to them on the first day of the month of *Day* in 1980, but due to financial problems, they keep saying today or tomorrow. I finally cancelled the contract a few days ago. Perhaps, as Akhavan (Omid) said, it would help my pocket too if, with the help of friends I publish it myself—life permitting, of course.

You quoted incorrectly my old *Ghazal* about *Kapalieh* (buttocks) on the shore of the Caspian Sea, but your drawing of it, showing smooth waves climbing over each other, was nice. The correct version of it is this: "The Sea was calm, but the shore was waving with buttocks." These kinds of *Koss-o-She'rs* [nonsense] of course belong to the time of our youth. I don't take them seriously anymore.

I have written few poems in recent years, but I won't leave this letter, despite its length, empty. I'm sending you some of my more recent *Ghazals* and also the piece that I have composed a few months ago when Reza began to walk.

By the way, what is Majid Mirza doing and how is he? Is he in the same province as you are or in another province? If you happened to see him or talk to him by phone, give my *Salaams* to him. Yazdan Mirza phoned a few days ago, regarding something. I told him that I had a letter from you. He was glad to hear of your good health and said, "I will write him a letter, if I have time."

Here are my recent *Ghazals*.

(See the next chapter for translation of the *Ghazals*.)

65

TRANSLATION OF THE GHAZALS
OF MOHAMMAD GHAHREMAN

THE SHORTEST DEFINITION OF A POEM that I have heard is this: "A poem is what is left behind after its translation to another language." I am therefore doing a big disservice to my cousin by translating the *Ghazals* he has sent to me as samples of his recent work. And it would be a bigger disservice if I ignored them and did nothing about them. Mohammad Mirza is more than just a cousin. He is no Hafez, but could be among the first three best living *Ghazal*-making poets of Iran. His poems are ten times better than those of Sohrab, but he lives a much less poetic life than that of Sohrab.

Also, being *Ghazal*, they don't have a title so that by translating the title I could at least convey the main idea of the poem in my translation. To make the matter worse, good *Ghazals* —like those that Hafez has made after his maturation—lack coherence in the sense that each line sends the reader to a different direction. The things that pull a *Ghazal* together are the music of the lines—which is the result of the relation of the short and long syllables in Farsi language—and the rhyming of the last word at the end of each line. Also, the grammar being different, it makes the translation more difficult. In Farsi, for example, unlike English, the verb often comes at the end of a sentence and the adjectives come after the noun.

To compensate for some of the above, I will attempt to give a name to each *Ghazal*. And I will choose the name either from the word or idea recurring at the end of each line or from my general feeling about each *Ghazal*. I have to say right at the beginning that I don't promise that my efforts will produce a poetic piece. The uninterested reader, therefore, can skip this chapter and go on to read the rest of the book.

Now, without further Shakespearian ado, here they are:

Ghazal number 1

Bringing the season of spring

Like the good-news breeze

I bring you good news

I've passed over the meadows

I carry the smell of spring.

The older I get

The more desires I grow

Like a fruit-bearing tree

The older I get the more fruit I give.

Talking to me will cloud you with Malaal [ennui]

Clear though I am like a good wine

I give you a headache in the morning

To avoid bruising the rose

I sit away, in the shade of the bush

The gardener cries out

That I am irritating the thorns.

Why tolerate the pains?

Why endure the prison?

Open the book *of a poet*

Open a window.

The wider I cast

From side to side

The fishing net of my regard

The horizon of my desires

Recedes further away from me.

I am living in an eternal autumn

But the blossoming universe

Crowns my head with rose petals

To the eternal autumn, I give the name of spring.

***

Ghazal number 2

Always in sitting position

I am sitting as close to you as me and my mirror

I am with you, yet far away from you, as me and my image.

In the expectation of your appearance, O sunshine of goodness

I am sitting up, waiting for you, like a patient morning.

Like a thirsty desert, twisted under the umbrella of a whirlwind

I am sitting, unmoved, waiting for the moving fingers of a shower.

I am awake with eyes wider than a mirror

I am confused and contorted like the convolutions of a nightmare.

Everybody is exiled only once

By coming into this world

Sitting like a stranger in my house

I feel I am exiled twice.

One may lose one's head for one's country

But one should not forget one's duty:

To sit on one's life

To stand on one's word.

Like the broken waves, our restlessness has a reason;

We are expecting the invasion of a storm.

Every tulip is a candle near the tomb of a martyr

I'm flooded with blood

I am embedded in the cemetery of candles.

The wind of autumn does not help flowers to flourish

This is why we are sitting up, head down, closed lips like a rosebud.

22/Mordad/1352 (1973)

***

Ghazal number 3

Forgive her, O God

Like the cool sunshine of the fall

I have acquired the colour of malaal

Like the morning star

I tend towards Zavaal. [to fade]

I am saddened no matter where I go

To my companion I impart Malaal

From myself I get Malool.

I live with Malaal *no matter where I go.*

In the middle of this salty desert I am spellbound

In the middle of the real world, I think of Mahaal [the impossible].

The future ahead, the past in the back

Caught between the two [non-existents]

How can one think of the Haal? [present time]

I won't mind if both of my wings get broken

As long as my heart is intact.

The reason I keep my head under my wing

Is because my heart is broken.

By mistake or by misreading the signs

I thought I was growing old

When the dust of the passage of time

Settled on my temples.

The green veins of desire

Run through the yellow leaves of autumn

I dream of the impossible spring

I have the thoughts of Mahaal.

Little is left to our hands

And a lot is to be done.

"Is this it?" I ask myself every day

"Or do I still have a little more Majaal?" [leisure time]

Let her pass safely by my grave

Let her pull her skirt off the dusty ground as she goes

She is the one who shed my blood on the Khaak

Oh God! Forgive her

And make my blood on her hand Halaal [kosher].

25/ Day/1356 (1977)

***

Ghazal number 4

Always a loser

The severity of this sorrow

Has made me lose my mind

You have kept me in your sight

But have lost me from your heart!

At nights,

When I sleep with the loneliness of my Malaal

The desire of holding your neck and shoulders

Fills the hollow of my chest and arms.

If, instead of your eyes,

You could see with your heart

A Persian Letter

You would see my silent sighs

Behind my closed lips.

I am fed up with the rotation of this wobbly wheel

That you call the circulating universe

I am fed up with it and everything that it contains

Including the sour face of Saaghi

And the bitter aftertaste of her wine.

It is unbelievable

Darkness and falsehood are over

The true dawn is spraying ash on my temples.

The towering height of the cypress tree

Appears folded compared to mine

Even though

It is me who is carrying the burden of years on my back.

I must be living in exile

Because

Whoever comes to my mind

Is the one who has forgotten me.

I am the cap crowning a wave

I am the whirling wind in the desert

I am the headless and footless flood

I am that homeless rend *who carries his house on his shoulders.*

2/Bahman/1356 (1977)

***

Ghazal number 5

Make me old, make me full, make me free

Oh, Saaghi!

Tie me up with the chain of your wine!

I am thirstier than my eyes

Try your hardest to satiate me.

The rotation of this gigantic wheel

Is going to make us upside down

Balance me by making me inside out

With the recurrent waves of your wine.

O waitress of the restaurant of the world,

Assign me a corner in the land of selflessness

And make my heart reject everything

That can acquire the colour of possession.

For how long should I drink blood in the hope of flourishing?

Remove this desire

Make me in the image of a frozen rosebud

With no hope of ever opening

Old age!

I am mourning the loss of my youth

Make me young again

With the blessing of a Peer.

Make me free, free of reason

A Persian Letter

It has been a long time since the pain of reason has nestled in my head

Make me free from the push-and-pull of reasoning.

Put your lips on my lips like a Nay

I have a chest-full of Faghan (crying)

Remove the desire of affect from me

Make me the governor of the territory of effect.

Like the eyes and the heart of the satiated one

Make me unassuming, indifferent, neutral, immaterial.

The noise of the traffic of desires in my head

Steals the serenity of sleep from my heart.

The wall of the body cannot be kept erect for ever

O Khezr! *Remove the hope of repair from me.*

O healer! Do not try anymore

My heart is gone beyond hope and repair

Don't bother, don't suffer

Just refer my case to the hand of Taghdeer [destiny].

2/Teer/1359 (1980)

***

Ghazal number 6

My child is beginning to walk

My newly footed child is like a new plant

Tender, with fragile stem.

His heels have begun to touch the ground

His head is beginning to grow.

My soul trembles when I think

He can be blown away like a Ghaasedak [little messenger]

By a gentle push

As light as a breath.

With every step that he takes

He falls to the ground.

At every moment

One has to wipe the tears off his cheeks

And dust off his knees.

The shaky legs are teaching him

That one has to step firmly on the ground like a man

With such unsteady gait

One cannot go safely through life.

Until this Sheer [milk]*suckling infant*

Becomes a Sheer [lion] *of a man*

One has to counts weeks

If not months or years.

Since the furnace of this house was ignited by this son

My tongue and the flames of my Ghazals *have been retracted*

One, towards the heart

One, towards the ground.

I've lost everything in this gambling house

I still hope my son will win.

At the bottom of the wine bottle of my life

Nothing is left except for cloudy sediment

The old wounds opened again in the heart

The young desires died again in the chest.

Oh, my little infant

My souvenir

My little one

My little, tender plant

Remember me, when you become a father.

2/Day/1960 (1981)

***

Ghazal number 7

The forgotten

The rotating wheel of time

Erased us from memories.

Like the lines of a bad poem

It is hard to remember us.

I have no attachment

To my roots or my land

Like the branch of a new tree

You can break us easily.

We are the yellow leaves of the autumn

Fallen on the shoulders of each other

In the slaughterhouse of the fall

It is hard to enumerate us.

My life was short and fragile like a bubble

Moving by wind on the surface of the sea

Nothing is left at the bottom of the cup

Except for the sediment of sorrow.

At the bottom of the sea.

The child within me

Never grew up with me;

Toys still deceive me

Games still please me.

This mean turning wheel

Like an aging wet nurse

Is Mehr-*less and milk-less with me.*

This age-gnawing, edentulous Peer [old]

Is chewing away at the child within me

*The cold-*Mehri *of this circulating world*

Froze the elixir of life in my veins.

We are the droplets of blood

Of a martyred love

Dripping on the ground.

You can walk on us

But you can't wipe us out.

We are the droplets of tears

On the face of the orphans

Like the droplets of rain

We are beyond number.

I am down to my bones

I have lost my shirt

With these faceless cards I am getting

There is no hope of winning in this house.

Tell the last breath of life

To get out of my chest

Now that the fire of love

Is extinguished in my heart.

Like a moving shadow on the road

We are bound to the feet of the travelers.

Whoever began a trip

Took us along for fun.

14/Day/1360 (1981)
Mohammad Ghahreman
***

Well Nasser-jan, I have given you a big headache. Say my *Salaam* to your Khanum and I kiss my uncle's grandchildren from a distance. I think I saw Kami when he was almost a year old, when you were living in Tajrish, Shemiran.

Raastee, do your children know Farsi?

I am anxiously awaiting your next letter.

Ghorbanat,

Mohammad

66

AN UN-MAILED LETTER TO A CHILDHOOD FRIEND

BETWEEN SEPTEMBER THE 4TH AND 8TH, 2001, when I was in Boston for my continuing medical education, I found a letter in my briefcase that I had written to Shambool, my childhood friend, while I was in Victoria, dated August 29th, 2000, not mailed for almost a year for some reason. I had a booklet of Canadian stamps in my briefcase, too, and I could have used them to mail the letter through the mailroom of the luxurious hotel, but for some reason—perhaps the intuition of what was going to happen on September the 11th—I did not do that. It would be very suspicious, I thought, if someone, say, from the FBI, happened to be watching me and see that a Middle Eastern-looking man is mailing a letter with Arabic-looking script, bearing Canadian stamps, from America to Iran.

This is the only letter that I have written to Shambool, after 23 years of not having seen him or talked to him by phone. I better have a good reason for not having mailed it for such a long time. This is so unlike me. I never do that. I either don't write a letter, or if I do, I wouldn't hesitate to mail it right away. If anything, I often regret having mailed my letters prematurely.

Maybe the reason I have carried it with me all this time is because Shambool was dying of lung cancer and I wanted to review it at my leisure to make sure it did not contain any inappropriate joke for a dying person. It is difficult to write a funny letter to a dying friend without hurting his feelings. Our friendship was based on fun and jokes only. We had never had a sustained, serious conversation with each other. Now, tonight, after having had my lonely dinner in the dining room and having retired to my room alone, maybe it is the best time to review it and edit it if I must, and mail it when I return to Canada in a few days.

29-August-2000

Victoria, Canada

Shambooleh Azeez, your sister, Nasrin, was here for a few days to find a school for her son. Along with other bad news, she told me that you are coughing these days, but because you know the cause of it, you are afraid to subject yourself to a medical examination, particularly a chest x-ray. What a good idea! If it is cancer it must be too late, anyway. Why bother to confirm it? You are a doctor yourself, and I had told you as well that mixing cigarettes and sorrow is a lethal combination. It is carcinogenic, no doubt about it. Don't learn from me. If I smoke, I do it out of joy, and because there are not too many joyful occasions in life, even in the best of them, I will never get lung cancer.

Baary, now that the diagnosis is almost certain and the prognosis is grave, why don't you close your office, sell everything you have and come here and die beside me?

I will transform my house into a hospice for you and guarantee to make you laugh at least three times a day for two months, or until your death, whichever comes first.

When your father was dying, my father-in-law, Mr. Khazaei, went to see him, despite not being on speaking terms with him in the last few years, for reasons I do not know.

Your father was in the agonal stage. He appeared to be in a coma. His eyes were closed, and his chest was making a drowning sound, but when he heard the lively voice of his old friend, he opened one of his eyes just a little, and smiled a narrow slit, and said to my father-in-law, "the Buffalo Mill!" That must be the name of a secret place that they—and they alone—knew about. But it does not take a genius to guess that they must have had some kind of forbidden fun together in that place, most likely with the help of a nameless woman. I say so because my father-in-law could not have fun in any place without the presence of a woman.

If I come to see you at the time of your death, I am sure you will open your eyes to tell me "*Aab-Gueleh*!" and no one but me would know what you would be referring to. You would be referring to the muddy water in the dugout in the dusty vacant land beyond the railroad station in Tehran, where you and I swam one summer day without the permission of your father or my mother.

We were about ten years old, so the year must have been 1940. You and I went from As-You-Wish Street towards the Thirty-Meter Avenue, headed south to reach the flat land to the west of the travertine building of the railroad station. From there we went beyond the bridge, under which the train went every now and then, and over which occasional cars went towards the slaughterhouse. There was no one around, and there were no plants or bushes as far as the eye could see. The only visible objects on the ground were the scattered rocks with geometric shapes, broken off the slabs used for the facade of the railroad station. We collected some of them.

Suddenly, like the projection of an archeological slide on a screen, a new dugout appeared in the land about the size of our pool, but round, filled with muddy water the colour of coffee mixed with milk. The urge to jump in it came to us simultaneously. We were dressed in our usual white shirts—on which dirt had died, looking off-white even right after they were washed—and our off-white shorts, with nothing under them or over them. We were not allowed to swim in any pool without permission, let alone a muddy one in the middle of nowhere. Even if we had the permission, we did not have extra shorts to wear for swimming. So I suggested we go in naked. You agreed and we took off our clothes and jumped in, wetted our bodies and came out almost immediately, as if our enjoyment was only in the act of our disobedience. We had no towels to dry ourselves. We had to stay naked in the sun for a few minutes before putting on our shorts and shirts and go home in a hurry. We did not tell anybody about it and that fortified our friendship like glue. I would acknowledge your agonal comment with a sad smile and, if you were still alive, I would quote you, "Come back soon, the bean is getting big," from the only letter you wrote to me one summer when we had gone to Mahallat and you were staying in Tehran. Perhaps you were missing me, but did not know how to express your feeling. The bean was planted in our house with the stellate pool, and you were supposed to water it every day while I was gone.

Baary, Nasrin will tell you how nice our house is. It is too good for me. Come, let us enjoy it together. It has a wide view of the Pacific Ocean, looking at St. Juan Island that belongs to America. We are closer to America than to downtown Victoria. I know the hospice. I have worked in one for a short time, but I quit as soon as I discovered that it is harder to work with the dying than the dead.

So, on second thought, maybe it is better if you don't come. Maybe your diagnosis is wrong. Maybe you just have chronic bronchitis. Prescribe some cough syrup for yourself. You will get better. Monavar-jun gave a spoonful of syrup to Ali Gholi Khan, when he was dying. He drank it with no fuss, and when she asked him, "Was it good?" he said, "It was good, *Bah- bah*," like a baby, and died.

Here, they do not die as frequently nowadays, judging by the declining number of autopsies. The coroner does not order as many as she used to, to save money for the government. And people don't seem to die anymore in the hospital, and those few who do don't need autopsies because all their diagnoses were made while they were alive through multiple biopsies. On the very rare occasion where the final diagnosis is still in doubt and the clinician or the next of kin wants an autopsy, there is almost no organ left in the body to perform an autopsy on. The organs are either given away by a prearranged donation, or removed in pieces through multiple biopsies. On the other hand, as you can guess, the number of surgical specimens is going up.

Anyway, try to come here. We might be able to laugh the last few days of your life together. And failing that, let us cry together, like this poem by Shahriar, the master of Old Persian poetry, for Nima, father of the New Persian poetry.

Nima! Express the sorrow of your heart

So that we could cry together, like two exiled

Bring your head closer to my head

So that we could cry together, like two drunkards.

Let them laugh at your disjointed and delirious words, like drunkards

Let us cry for the high fever of the child, like a couple of medicine men.

If you left this world before me, please tell *Khoda* that Nasser is not an atheist anymore. Tell Him that Nasser said, "I wish there was a God."

I hope you remain alive, at least till September 2002, when—God willing—my book will be published. And you would see how much you have contributed to its goodness.

Your life long friend,

Nasser

67

A LETTER FROM SIA

9-April-1997

Tehran, Iran

Salaam Nasser,

I say, "This caravan of life is passing so fast!" This is not my saying and I know it is not a new saying either. Maybe it has been repeated as many times as the number of people who have reached the age of fifty or sixty. It just came to my mind when I received your illuminating letter. As Ali Gholi Khan recently said, "All the children have become seventy years old!"

It was about twenty years ago that you came to Iran and we saw each other for the last time. Since then we have had news about you but no direct communication. Even in those days that we would see each other frequently, it would happen sometimes that we would walk beside each other along a long street without exchanging a single word.

To tell you the truth, when Azeem died I wanted to write you a letter to inform you about it, but when I began the letter I changed my mind, confident that sooner or later someone else will give you the bad news.

As you have said, during these times important changes have taken place in the world, so many and so important that it would have been impossible at the beginning of the twentieth century to predict most of them. This inability to predict is something new. It used to be possible at the beginning of, say, the eighteenth or nineteenth centuries. Even at the beginning of the twentieth century, with a little foresight, one could guess at what stage of development we would be near the end of it, which is now. Let us skip over this subject. It is not relevant to those of us who are descending the last rungs of the ladder of the last century of this millennium.

I saw your brother-in-law, Mozaffar Namdari. He was about to mail you a pair of thick and thin books, the former being the *Divaneh Shams* of Mowlavi, the latter a Farsi-to-English dictionary. He said you have bought a magnificent house. I had heard that your previous house was very nice too, but it is obvious that this last one is something else. I also heard that you said you did not deserve it. I don't know about you. All I know is that many possess castles that they do not deserve, and many deserve houses bigger than they have. That is the way it is. Luckily, we have grown up in families who have always lived, as civil servants, from hand to mouth, and from month to month, with meagre salaries, and we never thought of becoming super-rich when we grew up. It seems our families learned their lesson from this line from Nasser Khosrow.

Don't dirty your dinner mat with other people's bread

As long as you have enough to last you for a night

O heart! O soul! Join the contentment club,

Over there, everything is inexpensive, if not free.

Do you remember, Nasser, these lines from school? Our teachers read them to us and they sounded so sincere with their worn-out suits and frayed sleeves, wearing *Gueeveh* in wintertime.

You and I are lucky that we both have good houses. It was quite possible that we could have worked much harder in our lives without having houses even half as good as we have. Anyway, it is not due to the circulation of the blood of an *Amir* or imam in our veins. It just happens.

You talked about *SOS* and you asked me to read it, too. I have not read it yet. It will be my next book. But I don't know if I should read all of it or only the sections written in small print. I think he [the colonel] was an able man and his aspirations, compared to those of our families that I just described, were high.

He wrote things against the war during the war. Fine, but he was not the first person to do so. Nor was he the first who thought of the United Nations as a remedy for the problems of the world. But this we can tell about him for sure: his thoughts were not an imitation of the thoughts of others. He reached these conclusions mainly by himself. I remember in the days when we were about 11 or 12 years old, and the opinion of people like Dr. Hashem Shojania appeared important to us, we would listen to their discussions when Sharabi visited Dr. Shojania. The two seemed to have accepted each other and agreed to disagree regarding war. Dr. Shojania was of the opinion that war was sometimes necessary for progress.

One reason we laughed at *SOS* was that, as you said, we had not read its small print as well as the main segment of it which was in large print. Sarhang's will was in large print and that was one of the sources of our laughter. He had such an obsession about what should happen to his body after death and where it should be buried. He seems to have had considered all the possibilities, for example, what should be done with his remaining bones if he was found dead in a desert, half eaten by wolves. He wanted his bones be buried under the steps of the future United Nations.

Also, it was partly his own fault if we laughed at his book. For example when pension or retirement income was very low and inflation was not factored perhaps due to the *Rendish* behaviour of the government at the time, a widow of an army sergeant who had been killed in a battle, say, twenty years earlier, received about 30 *Shahi* per month. Now, one of these widows wrote a complaint letter about this and sent it to Sarhang Abdollah Khalvati. Sarhang rightly became very affected by the letter and wrote a long poem about it. Nothing wrong with that so far, but he titled the poem, which was printed as a very thin book, *Nafthat-ol-Masdoor,* an Arabic name that deterred anybody from reading it. Had he called it by its Farsi equivalent, something like *The Sigh of the Chest,* perhaps we would have been less cruel and more sympathetic towards it.

When I read your views on *SOS,* I said, "A hundred bravos to your fault-forgiving eyes." And I told myself, "I have read so many bad books, why not read this *SOS* as well? At least it has a familiar smell."

By the way, after this book he began to write another one, *Dorr dar Guel* [Pearls in Mud]. He read to us some pieces from it, here and there. They were really good. Maybe Sohrab has it. Also his letter in verse to Sadegh Hedayat and its reply are interesting. Or it could be that Sohrab, who is not a stranger to poems and poetry, knows them by heart. At any rate, if I were you, I would not translate *SOS* at all.

Convey my many *Salaams* to Mitra. Many of the people, who have seen you and your family during the years that I have not, give Mitra most of the credit for raising three good children. I think Kami's marriage was only a short time before the wedding of Parham. [Sia's only son. Even though Sia was good-looking and smart and a good human being, those who have seen his son say the son is ten times more so than his father. But I won't believe them until I see him with my own eyes because it is hard to beat Sia's goodness.] We are supposed to become grandparents in a few weeks. I don't know at which stage you are in this regard. Mimi has a lot of *Salaams* for both of you, and of course sometimes she remembers the past in which we spent good time together.

The half-hearted request that I had previously made to immigrate to Canada precluded their giving me a visitor visa. So, I don't think I will be coming to Canada to see you. And

I don't think you are going to come to Iran either, even though I don't know the reason why. The desire to see you once again, however, is always present here.

I end my letter with this line:

"The good time of my life was the days that were spent with friends."

Ghorbanat, Sia

68

A LETTER FROM A NORMAL FRIEND: YOUSEF

YOUSEF AND I WERE NOT CHILDHOOD FRIENDS, nor were we classmates in the elementary school or high school. We became classmates in medical school, Officers' Academy and prison. In the latter two places we were together, not only during the day, but also at nights. Nevertheless, despite being so close to each other, we were not as close as we should have been. This is partly because he was too normal. There was no eccentricity in him. Except for studying medical books, day and night, he seemed to have no external interest, be it literature or politics. Literature, especially new poetry, was almost synonymous with being either a member of Tudeh Party or a sympathizer of it. This is at least what happened to me and many of my friends. Maybe I am wrong. Maybe he was good in covering his feelings. He had to. Being in the military, he could not be a political person. This is why I was very surprised to see him in prison. And when I saw him there, I was a little hurt that he had hidden his political tendency so well from me. But why I am publishing his letter in my book, and by doing so immortalizing him? Because I owe him something, something that was small in the biggining, but has become large with time.

Although we went to prison at the same time, we did not get out together. I was freed a few years earlier, thanks to the mediation of General Hedayat and the tears of my crying sister and the kindness of the Shah of Iran. When I was released I kissed a few hundred prisoners good-bye—in doing so, hurt the skin on my chin for many months to come due to the fact that few of them were cleanly shaven—Yousef asked if I could leave the little square cushion that I had made out of the extra piece of my narrowed mattress, and was using it to sit on during the English class in our room in the prison, for him. And I, so inconsiderately and stupidly, refused. Stupidly, because I thought my mother was anxiously waiting for it to sew it back to my mattress and make it whole again. As if by making it whole again, I would have repaired the prolonged damage and suffering I had caused my mother. My mattress, perhaps, was the last thing on her mind when we met after prison. The pain of this good deed that I have not done hurts me more sometimes than the bad things I have done in the past. I hope this is a good sign of my growth. What is the use of elongating one's life if one does not use the extra time to repair the harms done to others in the past? I don't think I can ever become even with Yousef. Nothing cancels anything. Everything counts. As I am sitting in this hot whirling Jacuzzi pool at the Oak Bay Recreation Centre, I read the quote of the day written with chalk on the green board, "As we live, our deeds shape us into what we are; and everything, really everything, counts at the time of our death."

30-Bahnan- 1362
(20-February-1984)
Tehran, Iran

The dearest and the most precious friend, honourable Nasser: It is not just because I am beginning to write these few lines that I am thinking of you. Just like this moment many more times I have been thinking about you, and each time it has been associated with so much friendship and good feelings.

Of course, all of these belong to the past. Even though in the past we were not very close friends, the few conversations that we did have induced similar warm feelings in me. Anyway, this feeling does not seem to disappear or diminish with years, so much so that I take pleasure when I hear of your successes in life and continual happiness from Dr. Neek-Eteghad [Sia]. I asked him if he knew your address. He did not, but gave me the address of his sister who is the wife of your brother. You are in the same city, as I understood. This is why I am sending this letter through them. Even after having this indirect address I hesitated for a while whether to write or not to write. I did not want to bother you with the worry of having to reply to it. Nasser-jan, at the age of fifty four, I am still enjoying complete health of body and *Jan* [that which animates the inert matter]. About two years ago, I left my part-time job in the Social Services Insurance Organization to become full time at the university. In the beginning I was working with the anatomy group, but now, it is about five years that I have been doing surgery as an associate professor, working in Amir A'lam Hospital. I like it. It is the main factor in the maintenance of my health. With this, I can easily tolerate the inconveniences of life. In the afternoons, I work in my private office, which keeps me busy and satisfied from both economic and scientific points of view. I have a wife who is an anesthesiologist and assistant professor in her department. And I have a 17-year-old daughter and a seven-year-old son. All are healthy and all are living in the authentic environment of a true nuclear family.

During the time that I was doing anatomy, it was impossible not to think of you whenever I passed by that octagonal pool beside the anatomy salon, which you once jumped over when we were in the fourth year, and the whole class clapped for you.

I am planning to send my daughter to my brother in Canada. She is in grade eleven, doing mathematics. She is a talented girl.

Regarding my own continual education, in the years 1978-79, I went to America, sent by the university, for a short course, but it was long enough to become familiar with how to solve some surgical problems. As you see, everything is going nicely and smoothly with us: simple life, uncomplicated family, and warm relationships.

Of our old friends, I sometimes see Dr. Khalil [Sa'adat] and sometimes we have lunch together, and of course we talk about you frequently when we meet.

The thing I know about you so far is that you have become a pathologist. With the intelligence and ability that I know you have, I have no doubt that you are successful and *Sa'adat-mand*. And all these good news about you give me a great deal of pleasure.

You see how fast life passes. Youth goes by so rapidly. The events of the past and their fuzziness seem to become clearer with the passage of the time. One awakens, one sees the real thing, one accumulates experience; still one makes mistakes.

Anyway, I hope you are happy wherever you are. I am glad that through this letter I have spent a few more minutes with you. I would appreciate very much if you—in an appropriate opportunity—without making yourself too committed, wrote me letters sometime—of course, only if you had extra time on your hands and had nothing better to do.

Ghorbanat, Yousef.

***

Luckily, I have a copy of my reply to Yousef. I don't know why I made a copy of it, but here it is in this folder.

Now I remember why. It was about the time that I was writing frequently to my friend Ezzat and had developed the good habit of keeping a copy of my own letters so that I did not repeat their contents in my subsequent letters. Nothing is worse than repeating oneself in a letter to a friend. It would indicate that one has run out of interesting things to say but is obliged to fill the page with something.

Having the copy of my reply, all I have to do is to translate it into English from Farsi. Translating one's own letter, however, is more difficult than translating someone else's letter. It is hard to resist editing one's own writing. But I will try not to change anything. If the translation sounds the same as the rest of the book, it would mean that my writing has not changed much during the writing of this book. A big disappointment for me.

6-March-1984

Victoria

Canada

Dear Yousef, what a good thing you did to listen to your heart and write a letter to me. *Merci*! I know you are right regarding your feelings about me and I know that you do think of me sometimes. I am sure of this because I too think a lot about the past, and my past is rarely without you. It is true that our friendship was of moderate intensity and our encounters were sporadic, yet it must have been something durable; otherwise your words and mine would never see the white face of paper. Actually, maybe it was the very temperate nature of our relationship that has made it durable, since passionate relationships often do not last this long.

These days, one of the lines of the poem I wrote in the Section 4 of Ghasr Prison has become a mantra for my tongue. I keep repeating it loudly to myself, when I am alone, sometimes in my room at home, sometimes in my office at work. It was something like this, but not exactly.

Like a dried flower flattened inside an old book,

The thought of the past still smells for me.

Those days, in the prison, I was happy with the memories of freedom days, and today, here, in the land of freedom, I am happy with the memory of the prison days. Why is it like this? Why don't we appreciate life until it gets woven in the fabric of the past? Why should we always consume stale bread? Why can our stomach not digest fresh bread? The moments of the present are so slippery that as soon as we want to catch them, they slide away through our fingers to join the beaded rosary of the past.

Talking about the past makes me recall the rest of that poem. I don't think you have heard it before. You were not in our section. Your older brother was. You were in another *Band*. This was done for a poetry contest in our room in the section four. Kamal and perhaps Sia participated in it too, as well as two or three others whose names I don't remember now.

An Isolated Tree

Like a self-grown, lone tree

I have grown on the lap of a mountain

My feet stuck in the ground

The wind of gardens circulates in my head

My future is dead before birth

I'm carrying a stillborn infant.

I nourish it with the dead thoughts of the past

that

Like a dried flower flattened inside a book

still smells for me.

If one day you [the Polish girl] *happened to be thinking of me*

Come to see me, unannounced, on a visiting day, and

With your sweet bright smile

Sprinkle sugar on my bitter times.

One good thing about living in my past is that I cannot change it, and therefore I cannot give your place to anybody else.

I have also found out that, despite the past being frozen and always the same, it shifts its meaning depending on the point of view in the present. The past has not died completely. It still has *Jan*. It smells a little. It is part of the present moment, as if the present is not just a slippery moment but a hinge between two long wings, one stretched towards the future, one extended towards the past.

Yes Yousef, you have guessed correctly; I am content with my life. I am as content here with my life as you are with yours over there. As if contentment is not so much dependent on where one lives, but in what stage of life one is. It seems it is more bound to time than space. I sometimes feel so happy that it makes me scared. Scared, because anything, the littlest inconvenience, can make the whole thing crumble.

But you and I should not be too scared. We deserve it. We abstained from badness for 54 years. We listened to whoever made sense, and when the time came we offered to die for it too (not withstanding that our offer was not—thankfully—accepted). Why shouldn't we be free of sorrow for a few days?

Yousef, when I think of so many things that could have happened to prevent our happiness, but did not happen, I consider it a miracle. In fact, living and remaining sane are miracles by themselves, let alone being happy too. You have seen in your anatomy group and in me in the morgue that there is not a big difference between the dead and the living. Any little thing can make a moving body into an immobile corpse, but most of the time it doesn't happen. There are miracles happening every moment of every day; the reason we don't notice them more often is because they happen so frequently.

Yes, I am a pathologist now and working with four or five other pathologists in a 500-bed hospital. I am the vice-chief of the lab and this is as high as I wish to go. There is less responsibility than being the chief. I have not become rich and am not planning to. I have enough for a comfortable life for one medium-sized family. Also, I have found out that "more is never enough." I have a lot of time in the evenings and at nights. I study. I think a lot without becoming a lunatic. I have one wife and three boys, ages 20, 17, and 14. All three study well. Kamran, the first, is in his third year of university, majoring in chemistry and thinking of going into medicine after this year. It is difficult to get in, but he might make it. Who knows? Maybe one day our children will get married to each other!

You mentioned Khalil's name; I miss him a lot. He is another friend we spent our youth with. Read this letter to him at one of your lunch meetings and ask him to pick up his pen and write a letter to me. And leave its reply to me.

When my brother phoned to say, "Come over, you have a letter from Yousef Mohammadi." I felt very bad at first. I thought your situation in Iran had become bad and you wanted my help to immigrate to Canada to practise medicine here. And I was trying to think how I could tell you that your chances of coming here and practising surgery are equal to travelling to the moon and finding life there. When I read your letter, I was relieved that, not only you did not ask me for any application or acceptance or the address of the Royal College, it was full of good news and contentment with life.

Not only your letter was devoid of bad news or impossible requests, it was overflowing with good news and contagious joy. *Merci*, again. It is always said that misery likes companions or *Shareek*; now I see that happiness needs it more. I don't know why God does not have a *Shareek*. By the way, Yousef, S*herk* [Arabic for worshiping someone in addition to God, a serious sin in Islam] is one of the major sins that you and I have never committed. May God remember that. When I can't find one, how can I find two?

I did not know your brother was here. I saw more of him than you in those years when we were all together. It is becoming a small world. Maybe we will see each other again one day, perchance like the lost logs floating on the surface of seas. My chance of meeting your brother is less than the chance of my jumping over the internal walls of the prison to come to see you, even though there are no walls here, just great vastness and astronomical distances.

I was glad to read that you love your occupation. It seems that a job is the most important element in the recipe for happiness. When you don't have a job, even if you are living in the best city in the world with the best climate, it would feel like hell.

Your letter arrived at a good time. You are lucky. I had just finished writing a letter to my friend in France, and my hand had good practice. On normal days I do not write so well.

If you write more letters, I will write more replies. Give my *Salaams* to your wife who is a specialist in "lack of consciousness" [Farsi for anesthesiology] and has enough sense to make life easy for you. And kiss each of your children twice for me, once for not becoming bad kids to ruin your life, and once for becoming someone to be proud of.

Mitra remembers you, but not to the extent that she should. She sends you her *Salaam*, especially to your wife whom she has never met. But be thankful that she does not send you her worst regards because she sadly remembers the day you did not marry her aunt. She was such a kind and motherly nurse. Actually I saw her a few months ago, when my father-in-law was dying. She had aged a little faster than me, so much so that it compelled me to ask her if she knew the secret of longevity. She laughed as pleasantly as in the past, while asking, "Why do you ask me?" We did not talk about you; this is why she did not send *Salaam* to you.

You don't seem to have many friends in this country. Don't ruin your life and don't sell everything just to come here to see me! The maximum that I can make you glad with my presence is a week or two. What are you going to do after that?

I go to university extension courses here to learn French, my favourite language. As a practise to become more fluent in French, our teacher asked every student in our class, "What is the secret of happiness?" All the students had the double problem of finding the answer and saying it in French, except me. When my turn came, I said this, in French: "*Pour être heureux, on doit avoir une passée malheureuse.*" She liked it so much that she wrote it in her notebook, maybe for her future students.

It was so good that you listened to your heart and wrote. Listen again and write more. I have time. I am becoming time-proof. I am becoming *Jaaveed* [eternal]. I am becoming what we wished—in bad faith, of course—for the Shah when we were in the army. I am referring of course to the slogan, "*Jaaveed* Shah!" that we repeated, parrot-like, every evening at the Officers' Academy.

Your durable friend,

Nasser

69

WITH A LITTLE HELP FROM IMAM ALI

LUCKY MEN GO TO PRISON, the unlucky ones to the cemetery. I would be dead if Imam Ali had not helped my lawyer when I was court marshalled for conspiring to overthrow the government of Iran, in the summer of 1953.

Before the trial, we were told we could choose our own lawyer; otherwise the military court would choose one for us. Even if we chose our own lawyer he had to be a military man, preferably an active or a working one. Knowing that I was guilty anyway, I thought there was no point in choosing my own lawyer. So I decided to let the army chose one for me. I had confessed everything without torture. I had confessed so easily that the colonel who was interrogating me felt guilty for not having a chance to use torture on me. This is perhaps why after I replied to his final question he slapped me once with the back of his hand.

The questions and the answers were on paper. His final question was this:

Q – What other information can you add to what we already know?

My answer was this:

A – Your knowledge about our organization is so vast that I cannot add anything to it.

I think he detected some sarcasm in my answer; otherwise there was no need to get rough so late.

The evening before the day of trial a lieutenant colonel came to my cell to introduce himself as my defense lawyer. I thanked him for accepting such an important duty without pay. The next thing he said was that he was not a lawyer and did not know how to defend political prisoners. He was going to base his strategy on my repentance, if I did not mind.

"No, I don't mind," I said. "I am repentant."

"Good," he said, "then you are not going to contradict me."

"No, I won't."

"Also, I am going to read a line from the book of Imam Ali, that I found last night when I was looking for something relevant to your case."

He had a book in his hand when he came to see me. It was a thin green hardcover book, with its title in golden letters, *Nahj-ol-Belaagheh.*

I don't remember exactly what phrase from that book he quoted. I think it was something similar to a Persian proverb that says, "An innocent head may go up to the hanging pole, but never to the top of it." Thanks to his defense I was sentenced to only ten years of prison, instead of being perforated by a shower of military bullets with my hands tied together behind a leafless tree trunk.

Sia was even luckier. He got eight years. He had chosen our retired uncle Colonel Yahya Khalvati as his defense lawyer. I was not quite sure we could choose retired officers; otherwise maybe I too would have chosen him. Maybe God did not want me to. Who knows? Perhaps, unconsciously, I did not want to subject my frail, retired uncle who was the past teacher of most of the colonels who were trying us, to that kind of humiliation. Even though he was Sharabi's brother, he bore no resemblance to him, either physically or mentally. To begin with, he was an extremely cautious man. He had nothing to do with horses or chivalry or doing anything extraordinary. He had warned me, many times, to be more careful about what I was doing when I was wearing military uniform—or a civilian suit for that matter. He was in the infantry. He always talked about the long cannon number 105. All his active life was spent in polishing cannons and teaching trigonometry. Once he warned our mother that living so close to the statue of Reza Shah has its downside, too. We, the children, laughed when he left, but when during the first anti-Shah riot in Tehran they pulled down the solid statue with its horse, with the help of a rope attached to an ugly truck, we realized that our uncle was not too far off in his dire predictions. Another time, I copied a five-*Rial* bill with purple ink and the tip of a fine French pen, so that it resembled real paper money, and showed it to him when he came to our house. He not only did not say anything encouraging, he warned me that fooling around with government documents would entail accountability. When he saw me dancing with the Polish girl at Hamid's wedding, he sent me the message that associating with foreign women could cause problems for military men.

Sia's sentence was reduced to eight years at his second trial. At the first he was sentenced to death—while mine was the same in both courts. The reason Sia's first sentence was so severe was that his trial started a day earlier than mine. And the reason his trial started sooner than mine was because I had given myself up a day after he had been caught.

That one day made a vast difference because, at the time of our trials, one of the many brothers of the Shah, who was also a captain in the army, disappeared. He was apparently the toughest and the bravest among the Shah's brothers, and flew military planes with the same ease as he drove his private cars. The government interpreted his disappearance as a kidnapping by the Tudeh Party to secure our release. So, to show to the Tudeh Party that kidnapping wouldn't soften the government's stance, they sentenced to death anybody who was under trial at that time, including the six medical students, of which Sia was one.

Unluckily, the Shah did not like that brother very much, perhaps fearing a military coup by him one day. I think his name was Shapoor Ali-Reza. He was, they say, more like his father than any of his other siblings. Perhaps the Shah would not have minded if his brother had been killed as a response by the Tudeh Party to the summary executions.

Sia later said that he was so shocked when he heard the verdict while he was standing that he suffered momentary cerebral ischemia and had to sit down. I did not doubt it and attributed the inability of his blood to reach his brain as a consequence of his height rather than the fear of death. Sia is much taller than I. But his tallness is mainly due to his long femoral bones. When he sat on the ground to play chess with a co-prisoner in section four, his right knee was higher than his head. This is why, when I drew his caricature, even though his face was not showing, everybody in the room recognized him.

I was lucky that I was in another court, run by General Fouladi. He made the good decision of cancelling our trials on the day that Shapoor Ali-Reza disappeared. Luckily, the next day he was found, dead, alone, in his plane, which had crashed into a mountain somewhere in the mountainous region of Lorestan where he usually flew. There was no question that it was an accident. There was no evidence of kidnapping by anybody or any organization. So, the next day when the courts reopened, we were sentenced to ten years only. We were the first lucky group who were sentenced to a limited number of years in prison, rather than to life in prison or death.

I thanked my lawyer for his defense. Sia's lawyer had not read anything from Imam Ali, but he had quoted a French general who had said something to the effect that "Any young man who is not revolutionary does not have a heart, and any old man who remains a revolutionary does not have a brain."

Also, Sia said that during the defense, his lawyer's lower lip quivered occasionally. This made me glad that I did not remember to chose him as my defense lawyer. Not only did the lower lip of my lawyer not quiver, he was confident that he could save my life with one phrase from Imam Ali, and he did. So, I owe my early freedom to at least three people: Imam Ali, General Hedayat, and the forgiving Shah of Iran.

70

A MULTICELLULAR ORGANISM CONFINED TO A SOLITARY CELL

IF ONE SURVIVED LIVING WITH ONESELF IN A SOLITARY CELL FOR ONE NIGHT, one is equipped for living with multicellular organisms outside of that cell for the rest of one's life.

I survived. I don't know how, but I did. Maybe it was my belief in all the prophets and the saints. Maybe it was the quotation from Imam Ali that my compulsory council quoted in my defense during the trial. Instead of being taken to the execution square, I was taken to a single cell along the long walls of a dark, narrow corridor. Each cell had a rectangular wooden door with a square hole in the upper half at the eye level for a short guarding soldier.

It was a small room but enough for one person. It was damp. It resembled the change room of a private bath with half of the floor elevated to make a bed or a solid bench. The plaster of the wall near the floor was swollen like edema in the ankle of a catatonic schizophrenic who has been standing in one corner for a long time. One bare cordless light bulb protruded from the ceiling with no corresponding switch on the wall to turn it off. Behind the wall, opposite the door, geese or ducks, were arguing about something. They must have been geese, not ducks, because Colonel Khosrovani, the influential friend of Mansur said, regarding how I was going to be treated if I gave myself up, "They are not going to treat them badly. They will keep them for a few months in the separate place in the prison where I keep my geese, punish their chiefs and release the rest of them after they repent. They are young and prone to mistakes."

He was right. There were geese, but luckily they were kept in the yard. Maybe I had displaced the geese. Maybe that was what the geese were arguing about.

Nothing moved in the room. The closest thing to the room that moved was the face of a soldier passing by the hole in the door at irregular intervals. Sometimes I missed his face when he was late. Once, a familiar face passed. It was the pale face of Vafa'ei, the cheeky classmate and friend of Sia, who was among our group during the trial. He looked into my cell and thumbed his nose. He too had received eight years, not because his lawyer was my uncle, but because he knew professor Adl, the famous surgeon in Iran who also played bridge with the Shah at that time.

Two minutes later Sia passed by the same opening, followed by a soldier. He too looked into my cell, but rather than thumbing his nose, smiled a smile of understanding and sympathy with his large kind eyes that look like the eyes of his sister, Pari, and went on to his own cell.

When the procession ended, I sat on the brick bench to look at the walls. On the moist greenish swollen part of the plaster closest to me, there was a very short, recently scratched line of poetry that I immediately recognized as Shamloo's, probably carved by a previous prisoner, most likely one of the twenty-three who had been executed.

...and I took my heart out of my chest

And raised it above my head and cried to the crowd

Friends! The sun is still alive.

Part of the poem was missing because of either a defect in the plaster or a hole in my memory.

Above those lines, scratched with a different sharp object, probably a fingernail, was written this line to discourage anyone from showing weakness or fear during torture.

The tears of kabob *inflame the fire further.*

Then, suddenly and unexpectedly, the door of my cell opened. First, I thought they had come to take me back for the torture they had forgotten to subject me to before the trial, but I was wrong.

The soldier was a new one, not the one who had been pacing the corridor. He had no gun in his hand and no frown on his forehead. He put down a bulky package and handed me a short note to read and sign as acknowledgment of its receipt. The package contained a pair of soft green, brand new, polka-dotted pajamas, and my own old striped mattress sent by my mother. The note was from my sister, Monavar. It began by congratulating me for having received a prison term instead of being executed and promised that I would stay in prison for much less than ten years. I was surprised how rapidly the news had travelled from the court to the city and the speed with which my family had found my location. Even I did not know where I would be sleeping from one night to the next.

I let the mattress unfold itself on the brick platform of my cell, put on the soft pajamas and covered myself with the army blanket that came with the cell. I don't remember when

I fell asleep, but I remember dreaming my best dream that night. The Polish girl, with whom I danced at Hamid's wedding a week or two earlier —to the envy of the single and married men around us—came to me, laughing pleasantly, and let me rub my cheeks against hers. She asked me politely if she could share my bed.

"I have to think about it," I said, to my own surprise.

"Why? What is it—stupid—to think about?" she said in broken English, distorting her lips and her smooth marble face.

"For many reasons."

"Give me one."

"The first reason is that I doubt that your presence in my room is real. It could be a dream, and I know dreams. The moment you believe them and you want to take advantage of them, they disappear and you wake up. Or you simply wake up and they disappear. I don't want to wake up."

"But this can't be a dream. I know dreams, too."

"What makes you so sure?"

"Because doubts never come into dreams." I can't remember if it was she who said that or me thinking, "doubts, like wishes and desires, belong to the waking hours." This is why Descartes could not convince himself of his own concrete existence when he was sitting and meditating in front of the fireplace. Everything could be a dream he thought, but the moment he realized he was in the middle of doubting, he concluded that it was not a dream. Doubts don't enter the realm of dream. I moved a little to make room for her. I fell off the narrow brick platform and woke up.

In the morning I was taken to section four to live with 13 other prisoners, all young men about the same age and all to become my friends for the rest of my life, except two, one of whom being Manuchehr Mokhtari, who were executed a few months later. Some of them were already my friends, but I did not know they had made the same mistake as I had.

As soon as I met Sia I felt I was out of prison. Sia was known in the family as the smart one. He had entered school at the age of six and occasionally had been the first in his class. If he had chosen the same wrong road as I had chosen, then I could not be so stupid. Naivety transforms to strength when it finds a companion. The first thing that I learned from Sia during the first hour of our cohabitation was that he had been sentenced to seven years in prison, not eight, as I had heard through the walls, after mastering the telegraphic Morse code. He regretted that I would have to stay three more years after his release from prison.

I told him that if I was lucky enough to spend seven years of my life with such a good friend, I should be able to live without him for seventy years. Sia was the kind of person that one could live comfortably both with and without.

The bare electric bulb on the ceiling that was always on at nights and off during the day was the only discomfort that separated our leisurely lives from the ideal. I ameliorated that problem by transforming the Polish girl's silk handkerchief—still in my pants' pocket—with its translucent pale green and pink flowers, into a lampshade. That handkerchief dimmed the light for the nights of fourteen prisoners and ameliorated their dreams, at least for the eighteen months that Sia and I slept there, and beyond. Beyond, because when I had to leave that room, I left it on the ceiling like a cobweb.

So pleasant and short was the time I spent with friends that when the loudspeaker in the corridor announced our early release, it sounded like a recreation bell in the elementary school, ending a ten-minute recess.

At home, when I returned with my narrowed mattress, after the cold embrace by my mother, my oldest brother, Mansur, knowing that I must have no money in my pockets, gave me five hundred *Tuman* to spend on myself. I thanked him for it, but not too much, remembering the day he gave me money to prevent me from seeing Houshi's sisters. Then he said, as if reading my mind, "The Polish girl you danced with has become a famous artist, a painter. People buy her paintings before her brushstrokes are dried. Here is her address." I took the address and thanked him for it, but a few days later, when I decided to go to her place, I found out that I had lost her address.

For no good reason, I did not ask my brother to repeat the address for me. I felt freer after losing that address than when I was released from prison, I don't know why.

At that moment I felt total freedom. Free from love and revolution, prison and political parties, the army and most importantly, free from looking for freedom.

71

A TYPED LETTER FROM MAJID

LIKE ANYTHING ELSE ABOUT MAJID, bringing his letter into my book is the least trouble. Not only it is short, it is typed and it is in English. There is nothing in it that gets lost in translation. And there are no political or religious issues in it that might hurt somebody. He is writing only out of politeness to accompany the money order he had sent to be sent to Iran through me. Majid is not a talkative person. Even his Farsi letters, whether to me or to my mother, were short, especially compared to mine. Our mother often referred to his short letters as prescriptions.

September 10, 2001

Winnipeg

Dear Nasser, I am including the cheque as my share. I am assuming you have already sent the September money to Iran. I am still working, and working hard. Since Brian has left I have to do his work too, which is mainly oncology. Only recently do I have a hematologist colleague who joined St. Boniface General Hospital last September and we share the work both in the lab and in seeing patients. This has reduced my work load to some extent. But I am still working harder than other hematologists and oncologists. They will have a hard time to replace me. I might be working until the age of 75 like you.

Moti is doing fine and she is still part time in University. She keeps writing both prose and poetry but does not publish them because she does not feel they are perfect.

Kaveh is doing well academically in San Francisco. He is involved in research on patient safety and reducing doctors' errors, and his group has just received a $2 million grant for the project. He is also the online editor of Cecil's *Textbook of Medicine*. But, because of his visa problem, he is not making as much money as he should for the important work that he does. And he does not have the luxury of looking for a better job with better pay or position.

Shaheen and Pamela have bought a nice house close to us but we do not see them as much as we should. The two of them are enjoying their baby very much and work as a unit. We don't get to see them and the baby more than once every two or three weeks.

How is everything with you and your family? Is there any prospect of a wedding for Keyvan or Nima, or a baby for Kami and Anna? How is the book coming along?

Give my best to Mitra, Kami, Keyvan and Nima and take my *Salaams* to the Weinermans if you see them.

Khoda-Hafez,

Majid

901 Wellington Crescent

Winnipeg, Manitoba, Canada

Majid's prediction regarding the future of his first son, Kaveh, materialized much sooner than he thought. The other day Nick—our nice colleague and best pathologist—brought in a long page cut out from *The Medical Post*, to my office and said, "I am sure you must know this Shojania."

Half of the page was about Kaveh. The title of the article was "U.S. hospitalists honour Canadian Scholar: The recipient of a National Association of Inpatient Physicians award talks about some of the main advantages of hospitalists' programs."

The article begins like this:

Dr. Kaveh Shojania, a native of Winnipeg and a 1994 graduate of the University of Manitoba, Faculty of Medicine, recently received the Young Investigator's Award from the National Association of Inpatient Physicians (NAIP).

Dr. Shojania pursued his internal medicine residency at the University of British Columbia, completing it at the Harvard-affiliated Brigham and Women's Hospital in Boston. He is now the first-ever hospitalist fellow at the University of California, San Francisco.

Among Dr. Shojania's rapidly growing list of publications is the impressive 645-page evidence report, produced for the U.S. Agency for Health-Care Quality, in the wake of much-publicized Institute of Medicine Report on the prevalence and impact of medical errors in contemporary health care.

Doctors who work full time in hospitals (hospitalists), Kaveh has shown, have slightly better outcome than those who work mainly in their private offices, or work in hospitals only when their own patients are hospitalized. Not that those who work in their private offices are doing a bad job, but statistically speaking, the hospitalists do slightly better. America is pouring a large amount of dollars in research to find out the best system for medical insurance. They want Kaveh to do more research and write more papers, with an almost unlimited grant, but Kaveh has not accepted a new undertaking because he does not have time to do a good job at the moment.

Kaveh would like to come back and practise medicine in Canada. To make his return easy for him, Kamran invited Kaveh to Vancouver to present some of his papers. He came and did it and did a good job. Majid and Moti happened to be there too and they attended his lecture. After the lecture they went to Seattle for a wedding and on their way back they stayed with us in Victoria for two days. I asked both of them about Kaveh's presentation. Majid, who is not prone to talk a lot, especially if it might be interpreted as bragging about his son, just said, "It was good." So I asked Moti. Even though Moti is not a medical doctor (she has PhD in literature), I knew she could explain it better.

Moti said that the title of Kaveh's presentation was "The Cause of Errors in Medicine." Significant mistakes, he said, such as amputating the wrong leg or operating on the wrong side of brain, do happen, but very rarely, and when they happen, it is the result of accumulation or alignment of several small mistakes happening at the multiple sites that the patient has gone through before reaching the operating room. To make his point, he used the example of an un-sliced bar of Swiss cheese. Everybody knows that sliced Swiss cheese has multiple holes, but none of the holes continues from one end of the un-sliced bar to the other end. It would be very rare that the holes of the sliced Swiss cheese fall along each other like a tunnel.

Then Moti said that the reason Kaveh's papers and presentations are interesting and well received by medical communities is because Kaveh was interested and studied philosophy and writing before going to medicine.

Too bad Majid and Moti could not stay a little longer in our house. I had so much to ask and they had so much to see. Moti and Mitra went to see the wooded land we have recently purchased in the Highlands. Moti was quite impressed with Mitra's business mind and her clean, environmentally friendly subdivisions.

Majid looked at the pictures in my album, some of which he did not have. He borrowed the ones he did not have to take to Winnipeg to include them on his CD, and he is going to send me a copy of it, too.

As a sample of my book I showed him the chapter, "Going Home." He read it on the computer screen and at the end he said, "This is good." I was pleased that he approved of it.

I took a digital photo of him while he was sitting on my chair reading my writings with interest.

Moti went to see a friend of hers from Winnipeg who was sick and had come to Victoria to live the rest of her life, and perhaps die. I did not ask who this friend was, but I guess she must be a famous female Canadian writer. Moti respects the privacy of her friends more than doctors do for their patients.

I have not read most of the books of most of the famous Canadian writers. I have only heard short segments of some of their writings on CBC Radio. A few weeks after Moti went to see her friend, I heard samples of very good writing—something that made me feel that I have a very long way to go if I am going to consider myself an author. At the end I heard that the name of the author—if I remember correctly—was Carol Shields. She seemed to know human beings inside out and outside in. Before I fell asleep I said to myself, "I hope she is not the friend that Moti went to see," because at the end of the program she was pronounced dead due to cancer."

72

THREE OPEN WINDOWS

TODAY, A SUNNY VICTORIA DAY IN LATE APRIL, I am having a hard time staying in my office. According to the roster on the wall I am on autopsy duty, but there is no body to be autopsied. Yet I cannot leave my office to enjoy the sunshine. Soon, in early May, we have to move to our new offices in the new building and I have to clear my office of all the unnecessary things accumulated during the past quarter of century. Yesterday, I filled one box with bloodstained papers, representing the provisional summaries of my old post mortems, to be shredded. Also I've filled another box with memos and previous contractual agreements for recycling. Today, I am going to empty my filing cabinet and the drawers of my desk. The filing cabinet will go to the new building, but the desk will stay.

Behind the triple lids of the filing cabinet are three compartments; only the upper part which is for medical articles is alphabetically organized. The other two are filled with softcover books and binders I have brought from educational trips to other Canadian cities and the cities in the United States, mainly Boston.

When I finished sorting out the papers into the boxes for recycling, shredding and garbage, I noticed that I have kept some of them for at least twenty-seven years. A small tree trunk—I calculated—would have been saved had I not received so many memos. Most of the memos are from the old boss. The older one's boss, it seems, the more memos one receives. In fact, I have no memos from the present head of the lab. The present one, if he has anything to say, sends e-mail.

The drawers of the desk take more time than the three compartments of the filing cabinet. Some of the things in the desk have to go into the box marked *H* for home. There are so many expensive happy-birthday cards signed by technologists, secretaries and pathologists, some of them retired or moved to other institutions. Some, having remembered that the day before my birthday is always the Persian New Year, have remembered to congratulate me for that occasion as well. I think I will take these home. The sharp metallic sediment composed of thumbnails, pins, glass slides and disposable blades will have to wait until I have sorted out everything else; then I will pour them in the lidded plastic container marked with the word *Sharps.*

"Where is my crucifix?" I ask, as if someone is standing beside me and looking over my shoulder, though I know there is no one in the room but me. It is not in any of the drawers. Maybe I have already taken it home. I wish it were here so that I could take it and nail it to the wall of my new office, even though we are told, "No holes in the walls of the new offices, not even for a coat hanger." If I could do that then the crucifix would have completed the circle, since it started its journey from the old St. Joseph's, went to the new Victoria General Hospital and from there to the Royal Jubilee Hospital, and now to the most modern building in the city, named the D&T Building.

D&T stand for Diagnostic and Treatment. It includes the lab, the x-ray department and the operating rooms with their attached intensive care units. The building is bigger and better than the rest of the Royal Jubilee Hospital now referred to as "The old town." It is state-of-the-art. It is bigger than the new building of the Victoria Cancer Centre which was finished just a few months ago.

At noon, Marney, the technologist who was here when I arrived in this department many years ago, came to my office to tell me that it was my turn, along with Seamus and Brian, to have an orientation tour of the new building to learn, for example, how to find our way if, in the middle of the night, we were called to make a quick intra-operative diagnosis.

We did. It was nice, spacious and flooded with light, mirrors and glass. It is a five-storey building, each floor being about a third larger than a Canadian football field—and a Canadian football field, I am told, is larger than an American football field, but I don't know by how much. And both the Canadian and American football fields are larger than an international soccer field. The main hall, with its high curved ceiling and the blue neon signs indicating the name of the departments, makes me feel that I am in an airport or a modern shopping mall, if not a cathedral. The operating rooms are cordless, with large floodlights the size of satellite dishes, and invisible laser beams. They look like rooms in a science fiction movie. The operating rooms make me wish that I were the first patient to be operated upon in the new building. My wish did not materialize but my perfectionist friend, Daryush, was the first patient to die in the intensive care unit of the new building after his open heart surgery. His heart had failed as the complication of his long-standing scleroderma, also known as progressive systemic sclerosis. He survived just about a week to read the "Sneak Preview" of my book. He said he liked it.

I promise myself that I will keep my office clean and free from clutter during the three years that I will be working there, until I am seventy-five. Seamus says that he too wants to work until he is seventy-five. I think I have raised the age of retirement in our department by at least ten years.

We will have new computers, and we will communicate by e-mail. Also, for official continuing medical education, so necessary for being able to continue working, we can learn new and old things from the accredited scientific sites on the Internet, instead of going through the trouble of airports and airplanes, just by typing their names after www, including the useful sites from Harvard University and Johns Hopkins hospitals. I've already used this site whenever I go to the Victoria General Hospital, but I have not paid the optional small amount of money required to get credit for my learning.

The tour was tiring and I had more to do when I returned to my office. I had not had lunch yet, and in the doctors' lounge I only had half a cup of coffee and a very short conversation with Dick, the cardiac surgeon.

As soon as Dick had the first sip of his coffee he told me that he has changed his approach to writing and is now trying to write fiction. Just as he said that, the one-way loudspeaker on the wall called him to the operating room. Dick was going slowly and not very enthusiastically. I said, "Go faster, and save some lives for me." He did not go faster, but moved with the same speed while mumbling something like, "I won't say anything to bring God's wrath down on me." I don't think he wants to work until the age of seventy-five. I leave the doctors' lounge right after Dick leaves.

I work the entire afternoon, non-stop, interrupted only by the occasional skin or brain biopsy that my colleagues have left beside my microscope. On the incomplete pathology report beside the slides, my colleagues have written "YOP" meaning, "your opinion please."

Near the end, almost time to go home, I rise from squatting position to straighten my legs and back, somewhat proud of myself for having undone in one day what I had done in so many years. As I continue rising I get taller. When I am tall enough I see a button-like elevation on the upper surface of the dusty horizontal bar that divides each window in two equal halves. Out of curiosity I manipulate it while pushing the lower half of the window upward. Miraculously, the window opens. I do the same with the other two windows. They too open, after flaking off some laminated fragments of paint. After living for twenty-five years or so with three shut windows, now that I have to leave my office I have three open windows. Miracles do happen, but they are either too early, when I am not around to see them, or too late when I am dead. This one happens, exactly when I am leaving.

I stand in front of the open window, looking towards the east. The scenery is almost the same as I have previously described. Maybe the trees have grown a little taller but it does not show. Trees grow so slowly and insidiously that one never sees them grow, unless one looks at them every five years or so. A cold wind comes to my office to go out of the door into the dusty corridor.

Among the papers blown away by the wind is a small yellow page of a note pad that Nima had made at the age of seven for the purpose of selling to office workers. On the top of each page he has printed *"From the Desk of ..."* The three dots represent vacant space to be filled with the name of the owner. At the bottom of each page "NimCo," his trademark is printed. He did not sell many, just enough to recover the money he had paid for the paper. I never made use of the pages of Nima's notepad. Nor did I stain any page of it with coffee coloured rings. I have kept it clean to give it to him as a gift when he opens his own medical office. I am sure he has not kept any for himself.

I stand in front of the open window for a while for no particular reason. Through the transparent blue, a feather-like object comes towards the window in a hurry. When it gets closer I see that it is not a feather. It is a *Ghaasedak,* a little messenger, the one that is mentioned in one of the poems of Omid, "Yes, *Ghaasedak*, what news and from whom you have brought for me?"

I tell the *Ghaasedak*, "If you don't have any good news, better tell me nothing." It does not listen. "Peter Gzowski died last night from shortness of breath," it tells me as it passes by the open windows. "Too bad," I say. "I was hoping he would survive long enough to interview me once again when my book is published." Peter was a reasonable man. The last thing I heard him say was this: "One can live with shortness of breath, but one can live better without it."

73

AMJAD,
AN AMERICAN PATHOLOGIST FROM PAKISTAN

I WOULD RATHER DIE IN A SOLITARY CELL IN IRAN than live forever in a bed and breakfast facility in Boston. It is okay if the meeting one has to attend is taking place in the same facility, but if one has to commute to the centrally located luxurious Four Seasons Hotel to attend the meeting, then staying in a peripherally located bed and breakfast accommodation is a bad idea.

I was not supposed to have fun anyway. It was a business meeting. I shouldn't have expected to mix pathology with pleasure.

The worst part of it was during the two hours of intermission for lunch break, between the morning and afternoon sessions. Two hours was not enough to go back to my room under the roof of an old house, and since I was not registered in the hotel I had no room in it to go and lie down for a while to stretch and digest what I had learned in the morning.

On the second day, during the intermission, I went for a walk, alone, around the hotel where the scientific meeting—Advances in Surgical Pathology—was taking place.

The blue Boston sky with its sporadic cumulus clouds was similar to the ceiling of the conference room in the hotel. The only difference was the presence of multiple cranes on the rooftops, extending their necks like gigantic giraffes towards the sun. Since I did not want to get lost, I limited my walk to the sidewalks surrounding the hotel. I moved in clockwise direction as I came out of the entrance of the hotel.

At the first bend at the first corner of the hotel I had to venture into the street traffic to avoid the deep dugout on the sidewalk. The dugout exposed man-made artifacts, like bundles of cables, rings of wire and broken tubes, instead of the rotting roots of amputated trees.

There is so much history in Boston that one encounters it at every corner. At every corner there is an animated guide or a frozen statue, conveying messages either in spoken words or by arrested gestures. The arrested gestures of the statues sometimes say more than the moving tongue of the tour guides.

Behind the hotel is a tall bronze statue that looks like Abraham Lincoln, standing on a short pedestal, holding his open right hand about a foot above the head of two young black men with rippling muscles, and coarsely granular hair. Nothing is moving, but a magnetic attraction seems to be operating between the hand and the heads because the two men seem to be rising from sitting position towards the hand and the hand appears to be moving upward as the young men rise.

I stopped behind the window of a store selling luxury items for men. I had no intention of going in, but when the owner invited me in, I did not refuse. When I came out I had bought two pairs of cufflinks, each with its own box. They were expensive, but when you pay with Visa, it does not hurt. When I reached the hotel, only an hour had passed. The polite door-man of the hotel recognized me—perhaps from my name tag that was still hanging from my neck—and said hello and moved aside to let me in through the revolving glass and brass door. I thanked him for the offer but with the gesture of my hand I made him understand that I intended to go to the other side of the street to continue my walk. My name tag showed my name and the place I was coming from which was Victoria, Canada. I crossed the busy avenue at a proper crosswalk for pedestrians in front of the overly polite doorman to show him that his respect and politeness towards me were not wasted on an uncivilized person.

There were no buildings or stores along the sidewalk opposite of the hotel. Instead, there was a large, rectangular, scantily treed garden with no walls or fence. Here and there, there were occasional semi-transparent willow trees which did not obstruct the view. The more leafy trees too had shed some of their leaves because of September, making the wavy walk-ways visible up to the other end of the garden. The gravelly and grassy ground was sprinkled with fallen leaves of various shapes and colours, resembling the carpet in the hall next to the conference room in the Four Seasons Hotel.

As I got closer to the junction of the garden with the sidewalk a squirrel approached me expectantly. I put my hand in my pocket to see what I had, if anything, suitable for a squirrel. The only edible thing I found was a hard pink candy with soft interior that I had helped myself to from the cup of candies beside a sweating jug of ice water and an empty glass, placed in front of each registrant in the conference room. I took its wrapping away, but was hesitant to throw it for the chewing creature, fearing that it might cause its teeth to stick together. So, rather than throwing it directly in front of the begging animal I threw half of it away from it, into the open belly of an old tree closest to the sidewalk. The squirrel—as if used to not having its meal always close to its hands—went after it with no difficulty, picked it up and began to chew with no adverse effects. It did it so naturally that made me conclude that it was not its first candy.

I continued my walk along the sidewalk parallel to the park. The next tree trunk that I encountered had a large round ulcer the size of a satellite dish, with a rolled edge resembling a gigantic malignant, ulcerating skin cancer, either a rodent-ulcer, or a well differentiated epidermoid carcinoma. Beyond that, about ten steps or so away, there was a man-sized—or a little larger—statue of a civilized man in civilian suit, separated from the garden on three sides by a low, scalloped row of black chains. The side facing the sidewalk was left open. The bronze statue was standing beside a stone podium, wearing a long, tailed coat. Even though he was a civilian, he had the assertiveness of a military man. His right hand was fisted, resting on an open book. His hanging left hand was holding his leather glove and a short black chain made of the same material as the scalloped chain of the fence. Carved on the slab of marble stone behind him—or maybe in front of him—was a phrase that must have been quoted from one of his own speeches. I don't remember it exactly now, but I think it was close to this:

Whether in chains or laurels

Liberty recognizes no boundary, but victory.

Wendell Phillips: Prophet of liberty; champion of the slave.

I think the surname, rather than the first name, was Phillips, but I am not sure of it. Nor am I sure of its spelling. I will check it the next time I go to Boston. Actually it is going to happen soon, in the early days of May. The conference is not at the same hotel, though. Nevertheless, I will check on it, if it is not too far from where I will be. The reason I don't remember it word for word is that I did not know what laurels meant. Not knowing the meaning of that word has perhaps weakened its adherence to my memory.

I looked around to see if I could find an intellectual looking person who might know the meaning of laurels. For a few minutes, I could not find anybody passing by me, intellectual-looking or otherwise. Eventually I spotted a man coming towards me, as if out of a shopping centre, with a sagging plastic bag in one hand, wearing a white shirt with long sleeves, grey pants, and white skin. He looked like the exact replica of the proverbial "average man on the street," unlikely to know the meaning of that word. Nevertheless, when he got close enough to me, after hesitating for a while—no longer than the hesitation before feeding the wrong food to the squirrel—I asked him, "Excuse me, Sir. Do you know what laurels mean?"

The man, as soon as he came out of the initial shock, switched the shopping bag from his right hand to his left so that with his freed hand he could draw a circle in the air, above and around his head and forehead, while trying to say the word that was stuck at the tip of his tongue, saying, "The thing that the old warriors would put around their head after victory."

"Do you mean palm leaves?" I asked.

"Exactly," he said, as he continued on his way.

"Thank you," I said. "Now I can better understand the literary importance of that quotation." pointing to the writing on the marble wall.

After this, I began to return to the crosswalk to go to the hotel and get ready for the afternoon session. As I was moving towards the hotel I saw a short line of demonstrators was crawling along the curb like a centipede. As I was trying to read their banners to see what they were protesting, a few of those who were closer to the sidewalk invited me with the motion of their hands to join the demonstration. Even though I did not feel good about rejecting an invitation, I declined it with my hand, pointing to the hotel with my thumb, as my reason for not joining. My gesture was meant to look apologetic enough as if I would have joined them if I did not have to go to the conference. It was a lie, of course. I would have never joined them. I don't join demonstrations. I have never done so in Iran or in Canada, let alone in a foreign country. An Iranian going from Canada to demonstrate his displeasure against the American authorities in their country is not only unwise, but utterly stupid if not dangerous.

When I reached the old tree with the cancerous growth, I saw the only pathologist I had talked to during the morning coffee break coming towards me. His name was Amjad, which is derived from the same Arabic root that Majid, the name of one of my brothers, is derived. Majid is also an adjective sometimes used for the sacred book of Koran. This is why Hamid, my other brother, when he was a child, having heard that the name of Majid always came after Koran, once complained to my mother why Majid had a Koran but he did not. Literally, Majid means the praised, but Amjad is the superlative form of it, meaning the most praiseworthy. Amjad is an American pathologist, but he is originally from Pakistan.

I did not know that he had come down just because of me. When he crossed the crosswalk he came straight towards me and said, "I saw you from the lobby on the second floor, and I thought I would come down and walk with you."

"Good," I said. "Let us go in the park and walk on the gravel pathways or sit on one of the benches and talk."

We did that. He asked if I was the only participant from Canada. I pointed to the white-cheeked geese walking along the pool and said, "Only me and these geese, as far as I know." He did not laugh. He was a serious man. Or perhaps he did not know that those walking birds were migrating Canadian geese.

Our friendship had started the day before when I saw him sitting alone at the end of a long sofa in the lobby. I was pacing the lobby to kill time. When I got close to him I told him, out of the blue, that bed and breakfast is a bad idea. He understood what I meant without asking for an explanation. He was not staying in that hotel either, but he was not in a bed and breakfast either. He was staying with his cousin who happened to live in Boston. He said staying with them was even better than being in that luxurious hotel because it made him feel he was back in his original country. "The kitchen and the food we ate as children determine most of our sense of nationality," he said.

"Good observation," I said.

When we reached the tree with cancerous growth, he said, "I saw you were looking at this tree for a while."

"I was trying to diagnose the type of tumour it had." I said, "My differential diagnosis was between a basal cell carcinoma and a well-differentiated squamous cell carcinoma."

He liked the analogy and said, "No wonder you are writing a book in a language other than your mother tongue." He already knew that I was writing a book and that it was addressed to my mother who had failed to teach us her religion.

"So, you don't believe in God?"

"True, but I am still looking for Him."

"How old are you, if I may ask?"

"Seventy years old."

"Do you think you'll have time to find God?"

"Yes I do. I have made a deal with God that He won't kill me until I have finished my book. And I think God has accepted it because my book is a sort of pilgrimage in search of God that will never finish."

"How about your mother to whom you are addressing your book?" Amjad persisted. " Is she a good Moslem and does she do her *Namaaz* regularly?"

"Even more than regularly," I said. "Actually, I believe in *Namaaz*."

"How can you believe in *Namaaz* but not in God?"

"I think *Namaaz* is a good exercise for everyday life, whether you believe in God or not. Its motions are symbolically more important than its words. The way I have described *Namaaz* in my book does better justice to it than the way it is shown on most television programs. On television, whenever they want to show Moslems at *Namaaz*, they always show rows and rows of men with their bottoms towards the sky, while I show a single woman sometimes her forehead is touching the ground in the most humiliating position, sometimes bending like a servant, and sometimes standing tall and erect talking to God like a man."

"Actually there is a mosque in the vicinity of this hotel," Amjad said. "One of our lady colleagues has just gone to find its exact location so that I and a few other Muslim colleagues can go for a noon prayer before the afternoon session. Would you like to join us?"

"That is very kind of you, but I don't know the words."

"That is not a problem if you know the motions. One of us will say the Arabic words audibly so that you could hear and repeat them in your heart as you go through the motions."

"Let us go," I agreed eagerly. These days I have learned not to let lucky coincidences get away from me.

Upstairs, in the hall in front of the conference room under the gigantic chandelier over a fluffy carpet, two other pathologists were standing, waiting for us, smiling, as if Amjad had already given them a thumbnail sketch of my nationality and my peculiar beliefs. The shorter one with a narrow black beard looked like Iraj Arkani from far away. He was from Egypt. His name was Nasser and because of that we smiled a little longer and wider when we shook hands. The taller man, the one whom I thought was an American because of his pale complexion and blond hair was from Lebanon and knew a little Farsi, too, as well as being fluent in English and Arabic.

Time was short, so we skipped the unnecessary pleasantries and useless talk about the weather. Even though each of us was of a different nationality, the fact that we all had the same profession and were attending the same meeting made us closer to each other than if we were from the same country. The other two wanted to have a copy of the chapters of my book that I had read to Amjad the day before. I said that I was sorry that I had left it in my room at a bed and breakfast facility, far from there. But I promised them that I would let them know when my book is published, through Amjad. Amjad and I had already exchanged our phone numbers and addresses.

Like many Pakistanis, Amjad seemed to like and respect Iran and Iranians. The very first day when he found out that I was from Iran, he said that he liked President Khatami's good intentions and he quoted one of his sayings, "We prefer to import western technology, rather than their culture." I agreed with him, saying, "Yes, he is a moderate man. Besides, he knows philosophy and has written books about it and discusses cities and citizenship from the point of view of Plato as well as from his own point of view."

Then, to give an example regarding the good feeling of most Pakistanis towards Iranians, Amjad said that early in the revolution, when in an effort to topple the Saudi regime, some Iranians created chaos in Mecca, the Saudi government asked the Pakistani soldiers to fight the Iranians, but the Pakistani commander refused to order his troop to shoot at Iranians, saying, "We do not shoot at our Muslim brothers."

As we were standing and talking, Amjad kept looking at the dark end of the hall while apologizing that the lady pathologist was not back yet. So we talked about other things that connected us like the richness of our respective countries as far as waterless lands were concerned and the preoccupation of its people with cleanliness. In the middle of our conversation the chandeliers above our heads began to dim to announce the commencement of the afternoon session within one minute. Right at that moment the lady pathologist showed up, walking rapidly from the far end of the hall towards us. She was a tall and delicately built woman with light brown skin, a skin-coloured scarf, a long light brown silk outfit with long sleeves, and a pair of delicate, dark brown shoes with low heels. Amjad introduced us in a hurry, and we shook hands and exchanged smiles. Amjad made a sign that it was time to go for *Namaaz*.

"Sorry, I cannot accompany you," I said. "I am not clean enough for *Namaaz*."

"How come?" Amjad asked, disappointed. "Do you mean bodily or spiritually?"

"Both," I said. "As far as the body is concerned, as you know I am staying in a bed and breakfast accommodation which is far from here. As far as my spirituality is concerned, as you know, I am still looking for God. I don't want to say things, parrot-like, without knowing what I am saying or who I am talking to."

"I understand," Amjad said.

"Thank you," I said, "for your invitation, anyway."

"At least you have an open mind," Amjad acknowledged.

We shook hands and exchanged more smiles as we separated. They went towards the mosque, and I towards the blinking chandeliers inside the conference room.

When I go to an educational meeting, I feel that I have to attend all of it. Even though attendance is not compulsory and all the lectures are given to us in volumes of printed matter, I cannot miss a single meeting no matter how unimportant. I am afraid that if I did not attend the live demonstration, they might say something important that is not in the printed matters we are given and I would never know what I have missed.

74

ALI,

AN AMERICAN PATHOLOGIST FROM IRAQ

DURING THE DAYS OF SEPTEMBER 6 TO 9 OF THE YEAR 2001 I was in Boston for another educational meeting. This time, however, as the result of my bad experience with a bed-and-breakfast facility, I stayed in the same hotel which was the venue of the pathology conference. The subject this time was dermatopathology, rather than general pathology.

The hotel was the ornate Fairmont Copley Plaza Hotel which looked more like a museum than a hotel. The shiny brochures given to the registrants at the registration desk indicated that it belonged to a very rich Arab, probably a multi-millionaire if not a billionaire. The inside of the hotel was even more impressive than the outside. No wall was left flat. The high ceiling of the lobby dwarfs the clients, no matter how tall. There was a wedding taking place at the other end of the lobby, with numerous large bouquets of flowers on the tables, losing their charm under the plethora of plaster flowers around the chandeliers and at the junction of pillars with the ceiling.

This time the registrants were fewer and younger than the previous time for the good reason that this was about advances in dermatopathology and mainly for those who wanted to prepare for their final exam to become a dermatopathologist. Since exams are usually for younger people, they were mostly younger than me, but I did not feel any older. The pathologists who were my age must have either died or retired or perhaps did not come because they thought they knew everything about skin diseases. So, for the first two days I did not talk to anybody. I should not lie. I did. On the second day the young lady doctor next to me asked if I knew Dr. Kaveh Shojania and I said I knew him and she said that they were in the same private school in Winnipeg. She said she knew he was at Stanford sometimes.

Each participant came from a different part of the world or different city of the same country. They didn't know each other and they didn't expect to know. On the third day, a young lady next to me said to the person on the other side that she was from South Korea and was taking this course to pass the exam to increase her chances of getting promoted at the university where she was teaching.

At the lunch break of the third day a young well dressed man who looked like Ez, my Iranian psychiatrist friend in Victoria, joined me at the table, in the semi-empty, unlit restaurant within the hotel. His name tag showed his first name as Ali, and he was a pathologist from New York. I thought he was Iranian, but he said his original country was Iraq. He was clean-shaven, but from the greenish hue of his wide upper lip I could guess that if he had grown a moustache, it would have been, like the mustache of most Iraqi men, much bigger and darker than mine. He was much younger than I, but the deeply engraved lines of his face made him look older than his age. Without asking many questions, we understood each other, as if we knew each other for twenty-five years. Just by having a name like Ali, it was obvious that he was a Shi'eh Moslem from the southern part of Iraq. When he said he was from Iraq, I did not ask him to repeat the name to differentiate it from Iran, and when I said I was from Iran he did not ask me to spell it for him.

When the waitress brought the leather-bound menus for wine and food, seeing that we were so engaged in our conversation, she left the menus on the table and said, "I'll leave these with you and come back later to take your orders."

"That is fine," I said to the waitress, "but bring us each a glass of wine, because we are already in trouble." Referring to the first line of the first *Ghazal* of Hafez where he says, "O Saaghi! Circulate the cup for the circle of our friends; for love began easily, then came the troubles."

Ali smiled a knowing smile and said, "The trouble with trouble is that it always begins easily."

With that saying I thought Ali was familiar with Hafez, but when I asked him, he said that he was not. It was his mother who knew Hafez and when Ali was a child she would murmur some of the *Ghazals* of Hafez to herself sometimes, and Ali would listen, sometimes falling asleep as he was listening.

After looking in silence for a long time at the large stiff menu to choose our meal, I shut the menu and decided to have my favourite food, a pizza.

Ali ordered the same thing, I don't know whether out of politeness or because he too liked pizza as much as I did.

The pizza was thin, crisp, warm and tasty. It was even better than those in Victoria. As we were chewing away on the pizza wedges, Ali asked, "What did you think last night when the fire alarm went off?"

"I did not take it too seriously at the beginning, but when I remembered that the only way to get to our rooms on the first floor was by the elevator, I was worried. Worried, because everywhere it is written, 'Don't use the elevator in case of fire.' So, I went into the corridor to look for some stairs with an exit sign on them. I found some but they did not lead to the lobby. I came back to my room and looked out of the window to see how far I was from the ground. It was not too high since my room was on the first floor. I thought if worse came to worst, I could jump down. Maybe I would break a leg or two, but I would not get burned to death, or suffocate from smoke inhalation. What did you think when the alarm went off?"

His thoughts were the same as mine because his room, like the rooms of the other registrants for the course, was along the same corridor on the first floor.

At the end, the loudspeaker in the corridor announced "all clear", but we never found out where the fire was. The next day someone said that the alarm had gone off by mistake because of some smoke that had come to the hotel from a smoking car in the street.

Everything went fine and uneventfully until the end of our lunch when it was time for paying the bill. Ali insisted that he wanted to pay. I pleaded, "Please don't do that; it is tax deductible anyway. Besides, if one of us has to pay, it should be me because I am older and I have a long moustache. In Iran, the man with the longer moustache has to pay for the table. This tradition is so strict and strong that if someone with shorter moustache pays for the table, there might be blood on the floor of restaurant."

When I came back from the washroom, I found out that Ali had already paid for both of us even before having dessert and coffee.

"It is so Iranian of you!" I said to him to convey my appreciation.

When we finished our coffee, there was still time before the afternoon session, so I invited him to my room to give him a copy of the sneak preview of my book, since most of our conversation had revolved around the book I was writing. In my room Ali sat on the single chair at the desk against the wall and I lay on the bed to read selected paragraphs of the essay. He liked every part of it. He could not believe those words were written by a Muslim pathologist. When it came to *Namaaz*, I asked him if he, being a good Moslem, did *Namaaz* or not. He hesitated to answer right away. He seemed to be weighing his reply, perhaps wondering that I might be hurt if he said no. I reassured him that I would not be hurt if he said no. After my reassurance he confessed, "I respect *Namaaz* and those who do it. I used to do it too, very irregularly of course, as a child, but nowadays, not much."

"Then what do you do when you are not doing pathology?" I asked. "Do you have any hobby?"

"I have a good family life, a good wife and a son and a daughter. I enjoy conversing with them, but my passion is running."

"What kind of running?"

"Marathon"

"Isn't it too hard on your joints?"

"Not really. I don't want to be the first or even among the first ten. I just want to finish the race. Actually this will be my last time. All I am hoping for is to finish the race."

Then I looked at him again and saw that his well-tailored suit had covered up his athletic body.

"How come runners don't look like athletes when they are not running?" I asked.

He laughed.

"I was a champion of wrestling in my weight—64 kilograms—when I was in medical school in Tehran," I said.

"Yours does not show it either," he said, still laughing.

He walked towards the open window, looked down to see once again how far from the sidewalk the room was in case we had to jump if the fire alarm was real. Then he moved away from it to go to his room to get ready for the afternoon session.

"Can I have a copy of your article?"

"You can keep this copy. One day it might become valuable enough to be worth the price of a good pizza."

The afternoon session, the last session of the course, went on uneventfully, and soon after that the participants lined up in front of the check-out counter in the lobby with suit-cases in hand and on the floor.

I was not among those lucky ones. I was not in the line to check out of this hotel because I was not going anywhere. I am condemned to stay in this hotel for two more days, Saturday and Sunday. This is because my wife, who has arranged my tickets and travel, has got me a ticket that would cost me more than staying two extra nights in this luxurious hotel, if I wanted to be home on Friday.

I went to my room as slowly and reluctantly as if going to a solitary cell in prison.

75

A NIGHT WITH SISTER WENDY AND A DAY WITH ALI

THE FIRST FREE NIGHT AFTER THE CONFERENCE, rather than going to town and visit a museum or some art galleries that Boston is famous for, I went to my room to rest and perhaps sleep. When I turned on the television, I was glad to see Sister Wendy was there, talking about some painting in a Boston art gallery. I know her. I know her from Canada. Not that she is from Canada, but because from Canada, when I watch the commercial-free American public channels, I see her in some art shows. She is always dressed like a nun but talks about art. She walks when she talks, but was sitting when she was being interviewed by Bill Moyer. This was her final interview. After that, she said, she was going to quit everything and go into total solitude. Her enlightening comments about the paintings and her positive remarks regarding solitude made me glad that I did not go to town.

In the paintings she would see things that were not there. And they were there as soon as she pointed them out with her interpretation. She would stop, for example, in front of a dark painting displaying an old night scene in which a young mother is nursing her baby with one exposed breast. On the other side of the valley, through the trees, a man in an old-fashioned military uniform is walking while his head is turned towards the woman. Only the central part of the painting is light and that is coming from a bright zigzag line in the sky representing a thunderbolt. There was nothing dramatic in the painting until she pointed out that until a moment earlier, everything was in total darkness, and in a moment everything will return to darkness, and everything, including the momentary joy of the man and the shame of the woman for being caught bare-breasted, will be covered again by the darkness of the night. The artist, she said, has painted a moment of surprise. She did not say it, but one could read between her words that when God said, "Let there be light," and light appeared, a similar surprising scene was revealed. She talked about the nude bodies of women as comfortably as talking about the bleeding body of Jesus Christ. She could tell if the nude body was painted by a male or female artist.

"Is it difficult to go into total solitude?" Bill asked.

"In the solitude I am going to," she said, "I won't be alone. I will be with God."

"What do you have to say about the phenomenon of guilt?" Bill asked.

"It is easy to feel guilty. It is hard to be human. If you have done something wrong and you feel guilty about it, admit it, and go on with your life. You cannot go through life in a supine position. You should go on your tiptoes."

"Is it difficult to remain chaste?" Bill asked with apology and hesitation in his voice. But she answered it so naturally that Bill felt his hesitation and apologies were not necessary. "Not for me," she replied. "I was lucky. When my mother wanted to tell me about the changes the human body undergoes when I reached the age of thirteen, I told her, 'Don't tell me mother. I have made up my mind to become a nun.'"

She had no objection to sex and sexuality. She understood how others understand sexuality, and did not condemn it. "It is a gift from God," she said, "but I have been given the cold gift of asexuality and I am quite happy with it." She knew males and females see the same thing differently, but she had managed to go beyond those differences.

The next morning, Saturday September the 8th, I went down to the lobby to sit on a sofa and think about how I was going to spend my extra time. As the door of the elevator opened, I saw Ali was standing in the lobby. Glad to see him, I asked him for the reason he had not gone home. He said his plane to New York was leaving in the evening, and he had the whole day to wait. Then he suggested we get tickets for the tour of the city from the counter he was standing beside. I agreed immediately. On our way towards the counter I glanced into the salon where the conference was held. There was no one in it except for the unlit chandeliers and rows of empty chairs. It looked deserted and melancholic. It was disproportionately sad, as if all those who were not there anymore were my long lost friends.

We got the tickets and went for the tour. It turned out that going on a tour by a bus was easier than coming back with the same bus. The bus driver was professional and friendly. He was armed with a microphone and narrated the rich history of Boston with accuracy and a sophisticated sense of humour and no bragging about the great achievements of the city or his country. He knew the background of all the big buildings whether old and brown or new and made of glass. He knew the historical connection between the low humble building at the harbor and the famous tea party that sparked the American Revolution and the eventual separation from Great Britain. At the bus terminal where one had the option of continuing the tour by a small boat or returning to the hotel by the same bus, Ali said a second goodbye to me because he did not have sufficient time before his flight, but I, having a lot of time to kill, opted for the continuation of the tour by the boat. I wanted to see the famous silhouette of Boston from the sea side.

464

The destination of the boat was a large, lead-coloured battleship anchored along the hazy horizon. The battleship was not moving, but it carried a lot of history and glory. Unfortunately, as soon as I and a few other tourists reached it, the sailors who were escorting the last tourists out of the ship barred us from advancing by raising the sign, "Closed for the day." We were told that we could go to see the other ship which was a large wooden sailboat with a plethora of ropes and wires and a lot of bloody history behind and beside it. It had gone through battles with metallic ships and had come back wounded but alive each time.

I did that, but I still had a lot of time to kill in that asphalted desert between the two ships. So I sat on a single step at the bottom of a closed door of a single isolated room, a little larger than a washroom, to smoke a cigarette.

The only other structure that was not the colour of lead or asphalt was a windowless, single room made of copper. It was built on a man-made, wooden peninsula extending from the parking lot into the sea. I think it was the studio of a corner-seeking, famous artist, or a memorial to him or her. I got up and moved towards it. Inside, there was a bench in the middle, and a lot of shiny brochures scattered around. Outside the room, an elegant woman in a black dress was sitting at one end of a bench, like a mermaid, looking at the proud silhouette of Boston.

The boat came back as promised, but the bus did not. That was bad enough, but it could have been worse if the reverse had happened. When we were purchasing the tickets, we were not told that the bus drivers do not work after five o'clock.

I got a taxi and gave the driver the name of my hotel. Even though no one was waiting for me at the hotel I don't know why I was so anxious to get there. When the taxi stopped in front of the hotel the bellboy and a well-dressed black man rushed to hold the door of the taxi open. I was surprised by their excessive politeness but when I stepped out I realized that their politeness was not for me. It was for Ali who was standing outside of the hotel with his suitcase. The hotel had phoned for a taxi for him and the taxi happened to be the one that was bringing me to the hotel. I was glad to see him once more. I moved towards Ali, smiling widely. "I thought I would never see you again," I told him as I hugged him goodbye for the third and the last time.

Ali hugged me back as firmly as I did and said, "You will see me again. I might even come to Victoria for my next vacation, with my family."

"Please do that. We have three empty bedrooms since the children have grown and gone."

"I have your address. I will phone you to also let you know about the result of my marathon," he said as he got into the taxi.

I went to the lobby, waited for the elevator to come down to take me to my room. It took the elevator a long time to arrive, but I did not mind waiting. Once in my room, I kept asking myself, with no Sister Wendy in the world and no Ali in the hotel, how am I going to spend my tonight and tomorrow?

76

SUNDAY SEPTEMBER 9ᵀᴴ, 2001

NOT KNOWING THAT TWO DAYS LATER, not too far from Boston, an earth-shaking calamity would occur that would make everybody suspicious of everybody else, I took it easy on the Sunday, my last day in Boston, and ventured for a walk in the little garden adjacent to the hotel. Later, I found out that its name was Copley Square. Copley must be an important name; otherwise the adjacent hotel would not borrow it. It was a rectangular space encased with wrought-iron fences. The moment I stepped out of the hotel, I regretted that I had not brought my camera from Canada. To compensate for the lack of a camera, I made use of the pen and paper that I always carry with myself when I go out and made some notes and drawings.

Now I am thankful for those notes and drawings. Without them, I could not remember anything from that day as the result of the memory-erasing event that would happen two days later.

It was a sunny September Sunday. Except for me, everybody else was in casual dress. The worst-dressed ones were sleeping on the wrought-iron benches in the garden. The best-dressed ones were walking along the sidewalk in a hurry, unaware of the existence of the park, let alone the people in it. They were looking straight ahead of themselves, indicating that they were not tourists. Tourists always look at the skylines and the upper edges of the buildings.

Among my drawings, there is an unfinished drawing in blue ballpoint pen that I made of the Trinity Church, while sitting on one of the benches in front of it. The façade of this building is as wide as the width of the rectangular garden. It is located on its water side, beyond which is the vast blue Atlantic Ocean,

Another drawing, in pencil, depicts the man who interrupted my drawing to supply me with better pen, paper and pencil. This drawing is all in graphite grey except for two small round pink circles, one on each side of his head, each representing the eraser end of the two yellow pencils he had firmly inserted in his hair. The paper used for the drawing was his. He gave it to me. It was partially used by him.

I was sitting in front of the church, amazed by its elaborate convolutions upon convolutions and arches upon arches like waves taking off from waves. To appreciate the troubles the architects and the builders had gone through, I brought out the small notebook that I had brought from the hotel and began to draw its façade. I roughly calculated that if I multiplied my painstaking effort to draw it by ten million times, maybe I would have some idea of how hard the builders had worked to make that building. As I was drawing I heard a man's voice saying, "Sir?" so softly that I thought he was talking to someone else. When he repeated it, I turned my neck towards the voice and I saw it was a young-looking black man wanting to talk to me.

Immediately I hoped that he was not going to ask for money because I had spent almost all my American dollars and had only Canadian money in my pocket, and I did not want to go to the bank again to get American dollars with my Visa just for him.

He came around the bench to face me, sat on a stool that turned out to be his own and said, "Let me show you something."

"Show me," I said as I stopped drawing.

He gave me a special ballpoint pen that wrote more smoothly than the one I was using, as well as his large drawing pad.

"No, thank you, I have a lot of good pens. I am making only some note, for the future," I said.

"No, this pen is environmentally friendly. You have to have it."

"What do you do for a living?" I asked to change the subject as I accepted the pen and the notebook.

"I am not living. I am dying," he said.

He did not look terminal at all. He just looked a little drowsy. He looked healthy enough to withstand some sarcasm, so I asked, "What do you do for dying?"

He got the joke, and said, "I do portraits," and showed me the portrait of a woman he had drawn. It was not bad. It was better than my drawings, but nothing fantastic. It looked amateurish, or at least, it did not look like the drawing by a man who makes a living by drawing portraits. So I asked him, "What were you doing before making portraits?"

"I was a radio announcer."

When he saw a trace of disbelief in my face, he imitated the voice of a radio announcer, saying something very scientific about DNA molecules and genetic mutations. His imitation was convincing and I believed him. Then I asked him to draw me.

At first he agreed to do it. He took one of the two yellow drawing pencils out of his hair, sat on his stool, and went through the motions of drawing, such as measuring the length of my nose with the end of his pencil, from where he was sitting. He made a few lines on the paper then stopped abruptly and said, "I can't do your face."

"Fine," I said, "then, let me draw yours."

He let me, and I did the best I could in those uneasy moments, making sure to leave two white symmetrical circles in his hair, to be later coloured with pink crayon when I go home.

"I am old. I am fifty-one. I am falling apart," my model said, while sitting on the stool.

"You look twenty-five to me," I countered. "Where are your wrinkles? Where are your grey temples?"

"How old are you?" He said.

"I am older. I am seventy-one."

"But you are handsome."

"You too," I said, as I continued to draw. My drawing did not do justice to his face. Once again I wished I had my camera with me.

A younger man arrived, white, with all his belongings in a metallic shopping cart. The two seemed to know each other like residents of a public house.

"Look at his hands! They are so small!" the black man said to his white friend as he was holding one of my hands to show it to him.

When I looked for the first time at his hands, I noticed that he was right. His hands were quite a bit larger than mine.

"What do *you* do for a living?" the black man asked.

"I am a pathologist."

He understood what a pathologist does, and said the usual things about the dead and dissection, but his friend became more interested.

His friend was a small-built boy, younger than him. He reminded me of Shane, the homeless boy that I had once met in Victoria. All his belongings were placed in the shopping cart, mixed with what he was selling. They consisted of a vacuum cleaner with its tube spiraling up a central metallic pole, like a magnified split molecule of DNA. Hanging from the horizontal bar of the pole were wire hangers holding a few new T-shirts and silk scarves the colour of a rainbow. His coat and an extra shirt as well as a few plastic containers were in the main compartment of the cart.

"Can a person with a criminal record become a forensic pathologist?" The young white man asked.

He did not look like a criminal or an ex-criminal. His interest in forensics seemed to be the result of his interest in science fiction.

"Yes, of course," I said. "Why not? But criminals are usually the subjects of a postmortem examination, rather than being the ones who would do it."

"This guy is funny, too," the ex-radio announcer interjected.

"Can you transport a dead body, molecule by molecule, and reconstruct it somewhere else?" the white man asked. It seemed that these were the burning questions he always wanted to ask if he ever met a pathologist.

"Yes, you can. You can break the body down to its smallest particles, and you can transport it somewhere else, but it would be very difficult to reconstitute it. Even if you managed to do it, still it would not be able to function."

"Why?" the young man asked, disappointed.

"For many reasons, the simplest being the fact that the body was dead to begin with."

"How about if you do it to a living person?" the young man dared to ask.

"The result would be the same because you would kill the person during the process of pulverizing the body into its smallest particles."

The white man stopped questioning.

I got up to go. I gave all the loose bills and change I had in my pocket to the black man. It did not even cover the price of his good pen, let alone the large drawing pad. The black man understood that I would have given him more if I had it. When my cigarette package came out of my pocket with the money, he asked what kind of cigarettes they were.

"Rothman's," I said. "I brought them from Canada."

"Can I try one?"

"Try two." I said, as I offered him the package. He took two. I offered the package to the younger man, too, before putting it in my pocket. He politely refused.

77

THE FLAT FAÇADE OF THE BOSTON PUBLIC LIBRARY

THE GREY GRANITE BUILDING FACING THE TRINITY CHURCH is the Boston Public Library. The two buildings bear no resemblance to each other. The convoluted arbutus colour surface of the church makes the flat façade of the library even flatter. The lines of the library are straight and sharp, going either vertically or horizontally. Except for the arches above the entrance doors, there is nothing curved or oblique in this stony building with brown wooden doors. Two symmetrical human statues with angelic profiles and Greek noses are looking at each other, reclining on the stone platforms above the wide inviting stairs, each holding a solid ball in one hand.

Chiseled on the flat forehead of the building are these words all in capital letters: "FREE TO ALL. Public Library of City of Boston: Built by the People and Dedicated to The Advancement of Learning. A.D. MDCCLXXXVIII."

On the face of the granite platforms under the two symmetrical green copper statues, the following names of scientists and artists are carved in groups of four, in four columns, two under each statue:

Newton, Pasteur, Raphaël, Phidias.

Darwin, Cuvier, Titan, Praxitèle.

Franklin, Helmholtz, Rembrandt, Michelangelo.

Morse, Humboldt, Velasquez, Donatello.

People and pedestrians are frequenting the library with the frequency of the clients of a big bank. Since I still had three hours to kill, I got up to go in, watching very carefully not to get run over by a car as I crossed the road. Dying in a car accident in a different country on the last day is worse than dying in a similar way in one's own country.

In the library a young, enthusiastic and knowledgeable intellectual man was leading a group around the interior of the building. I joined the group with his permission. He was doing it for free.

He said Boston is a city which is invading the ocean. It has been expanding into the ocean by transforming water to rocks. The Trinity Church, opposite the library, is built on water.

First he talked a little about the buildings surrounding the square, the library being the last one. From his explanations I learned that my impression of our hotel being like a museum was not too far off. Indeed it was a museum, he said, before it was modified to become a hotel.

If it had been only the church that was built on water, one could believe it because of the miracle of walking on water, but I thought it would take more than a miracle to build that heavy library on water.

As I was thinking that, the guide said the library, too, was built on water. I have forgotten how many tons of rocks and boulders and how many trucks and how many years it took to replace the water with rocks for the foundation of the building, but the guide gave us all the exact numbers at the time. The trucks did not just dump the rocks to sink to the sandy bottom of the sea. They first had to drive heavy pillars deep into the soft bottom of the ocean to reach solid rock, and then they filled the spaces in between the poles with boulders to make just the foundation of the library.

The tiles and tessellations were different in each section, but they were all obsessively accurate and elegant. The guide said he could spend the whole half an hour of the tour just talking about the tessellation of the floor of the small foyer before the main hall. In that foyer, to the left of the entrance door, there was a noble-looking man in bronze, but the guide did not say much about him, mainly because the important things about him were written on a plaque beside him: "Sir Henry Vane, Governor of Massachusetts, 1636 -1662. He believed that God, Law and Parliament are superior to King. He was beheaded."

Also, beside the statue—my inadequate note indicates—was this comment by Winthrop about the statue: "But it pleased God to provide such friends..." And it pleased me, too, to see that the learned Winthrop had begun a sentence with *but*.

The marble of the stairs had come from somewhere else, maybe Italy, the marble of the walls from France. Most of the artists, the architects and the engineers were from Europe. So were the truck drivers, the manual workers, and the project managers.

The whole country seemed to be built somewhere out of this world. This most religious nation seems to be competing with God, as far as creation is concerned. They are modifying nature, as far as construction is concerned. They shape mountains into the form of human heads. They build heavy buildings on the ocean.

Talking about the murals took most of our guide's time.

In the open space, hidden between the buildings and the connecting corridors, there was a rusty green statue of a naked woman in the middle of a pool, covered by a transparent umbrella of water. Our guide spent his last ten minutes talking about that. I have forgotten the exact story, but I think it had something to do with morality, nudity, and freedom of expression, and the Boston Public Library's dilemma regarding these matters—these immaterial matters that have more gravity than the stony building of the library. The statue was not supposed to be used as a fountain in a pool. It was, apparently, an outdoor statue, donated to the library by one or a group of artists to be displayed perhaps somewhere more prominent and with more public traffic, like near the statue of liberty.

The two horns of the dilemma were these. Because of its nudity, which was apparently something new in those days, the recipients of the gift were reluctant to display it in a public square, and because it was art, they did not want to hide it in a closet. Finally, the library came up with the idea of placing it in an open space, pretending that it was a common garden variety of female statue, and veiling it with water to satisfy the public, the artists, and those caught in the middle.

Going out, after we were reminded to be really quiet, we passed through one of the reading rooms, where about forty people, ordinary looking men and women, were sitting behind the long cherry-coloured desks, reading.

The reading room looked like a huge clean classroom with no teacher. It had a high ceiling and was dark. The air was thick with serious thoughts. The floor was divided, longitudinally, by rows of wooden desks. Every reader had an individual green lampshade casting a circle of yellow light just large enough to encompass one open book. The lampshades lined up both longitudinally and horizontally as in a military hall.

Not even one looked up to see who was passing as we passed quietly.

I came out, green with envy.

I went to sit outside on the bench where I was sitting before, even more careful not to be hit by a car as I crossed the road. I don't know why I was so afraid of losing my life on that day. This fear stayed with me in the airplane and did not leave me until our plane landed at Victoria airport.

Before I sat down, I saw the statue of a romantic-looking man on a granite platform, made of the same bluish-green copper that the two symmetrical statues in front of the library were made of. It could have the same age as the Boston Public Library.

The man had long wavy hair like that of a woman and supported his head with his right forearm. His left hand was resting on the edge of a closed book held in an upright position. On the spine of the book was written *The Prophet*. The explanatory plaque said that he was Khalil Gibran, a native of Besharri, Lebanon. He found literary and artistic sustenance in the Denison Settlement House. He had a lot to do with the Boston Public Library, judging by the notes on the plaque. The flowing quotation must have been from one of his books, most likely *The Prophet*: "It was in my heart to help a little, because I was helped much."

I rushed to my hotel to get a taxi to go to the airport. With so much construction going on for the new multi-billion dollar underground highways, I thought I had better start at least one hour earlier than the twenty minutes I was told it would take.

It is a pity that the interesting parts of my trips always happen on the day that I have to rush back.

78

THE CHIVALROUS ACT OF AN INFANTRY OFFICER

I WAS NOT ON CALL, yet Mitra brought the phone upstairs and gave it to me in a manner suggestive of a call from the hospital or the coroner's office. "Who is it?" I asked my wife before getting the receiver from her hand. "It is a Dr. Shojania. I didn't get where he was calling from," she whispered as she gave it to me.

"Alow," I said in the phone, giving the caller a chance to introduce himself, while sparing him the introduction of myself, assuming that he already knew who he was talking to.

"*Salaam*, I am *Jahan-gueer Shojania*, calling from Toronto. I am sorry that after not having talked to you for so many years, I have to call to give you the bad news about Colonel Khalvati."

"What happened? Did he die?"

"Unfortunately, yes."

"Heart attack?" I guessed the cause of his death out of habit. "He did have a bad heart. He had a triple coronary bypass a few years ago."

"Actually a car accident," he corrected with the politeness specific to my cousins on my father's side. "He was at a small party at a friend's house. His friends took him home in their car late at night and dropped him off in front of his house on the other side of the street. As he crossed the street to go home, unfortunately, a truck struck him."

"Too bad," I said. "He is in my book. I wish he were alive, at least until September when my book is going to be published. I wanted to see his reaction to it."

"Are you writing a book?"

"Yes. I have called it *A Persian Letter*; it is a letter to my dead mother in Iran, talking about the past and present. Are you, by the way, the same Jahan-Gueer Shojania who, one summer we came to your village in Feizabad beyond Torbat and we carved our family name on your poplar trees?"

We expected our cousins' family name to be, like the rest of our cousins, Ghahreman, and we were quite surprised to see they were carving Shojania, like ours, on the trees.

"Exactly, and when I and my other brothers carved our family name, as Shojania, you and your brothers thought we were imitating you!"

Later we found out that they were the children of the only cousin who, following the choice of our father regarding family name, had chosen Shojania rather than Ghahreman as his family name. Their father seemed to respect the opinion of our father and considered him unusually smart. The reason I say this is because in one of our earlier trips to Torbat, when we were much smaller, their father—sitting on a large wooden bed over the pool in the middle of the yard with the evening smell of petunia in the air—played a game with us by holding a pebble in one of his two fists, asking us to guess which one contained the pebble. When he saw that Majid chose the right fist several times in a row, he said, "Very smart! Just like his father, Mojtaba Mirza."

"Is your book in Farsi or *Eengleessi*?"

"*Eengleessi*. It is for the people who live outside of Iran, the anIranians."

"You should do it in Farsi too."

"Maybe later. Do you know *Eengleessi*?"

"I hope enough to read your book."

"What do you do for a living these days? Still carving your name on tree trunks?"

"Actually, I met you a few times after you came out of prison. The last time was when you had your clinic in Shemiran, and I came to your office. We sat and talked a lot. I told you that I was a graduate of the medical school in Mashad, and was going to become an anatomic pathologist. I did that for many years. Now I am retired from both the hospital and the university, but still working in a private lab that I think you would recognize the name, Habibi Laboratory."

"Yes, that is the lab in the Shah or Shah Reza Avenue that Dr. Ahmad Chimi—the step-son of our Auntie Pouran, who was adopted and brought up by the only civilian brother of our mother, and grew up to become a veterinary doctor—worked in some evenings when he was not teaching Bacteriology in the Faculty of Veterinary Medicine."

"You remember it very well."

"This is because Dr. Chimi—we called him Ahmad Khan—lived a few years in our house, when he had come from Karaj to teach in the university in Tehran. Do you know that he is still alive? He is more than ninety, I think, but is teaching bacteriology and virology in Melli University. He taught us a lot when he was living with us, especially some of the French language. He gave me money to translate a short article in a French magazine he was reading. It was about Gary Grant and whether it was a good idea that he had decided to play comic rolls instead of the serious ones he was playing till then."

Then I asked if I could go to Iran and do a locum in that lab after my retirement. There came a few moments of silence. Then my cousin said, "Actually I was going to ask you if there is any work there that suits my expertise, something in research for example. I don't need the money. I just can't remain idle."

"Forget it. Don't waste your time looking for it. No one will tell you 'no,' but after you fill out all the applications, repeating your age and your birth place a hundred times, and passing the exams, "The tail of the proverbial camel has reached the ground like that of the legendary fox." Age is important in this country. The less you have of it, the better off you are. You might manage to work a few years longer if you were already working here, but you cannot begin to work here in your advanced age. What are you doing in Toronto anyway?"

"I've come to see my son. I'll be back in Iran soon. By the way, I often have lunch with some of the doctors who were with you during your years of incarceration, like Drs. Kheir Mohammadi and Diba."

"I remember the first one. He was one year ahead of us in medicine, but don't remember Diba."

"He has changed his name."

No wonder. I did not ask for his original name. When someone changes his name, one should not try to remember the discarded one.

"How come, by the way, it is you who is giving me this bad news, rather that the usual Pari or Layli who are in Vancouver and closer to both me and Sohrab?"

"I don't really know. I heard it from Massoud, the son of Mehdi Mirza."

"Strange! It is very strange. I never thought Sohrab would go back to Iran to get run over by a truck."

"It is not Sohrab I am talking about. I am sorry if I have misled you. I am talking about his brother, Colonel Manuchehr Khalvati, your brother-in-law, Monir Khanum's husband."

I exhaled a long sigh of relief.

Then I became ashamed of my sigh of relief and immediately tried to phone my sister and Sohrab to convey my condolences and apologize for my initial sense of relief, but none of them was home.

Manuchehr had become totally deaf in the last few years of his life. He was a year older than Sohrab but looked five years older due to his unhealthy diet. He read a lot of books in the last twenty years of his life. He always sent his *Salaam* to me at the end of the letters that my sister wrote me—or at least my sister said so.

In the end Monir took care of him like her first baby, the flabby baby that came to the world and went out of the world without having said or heard a word. She had named her Sheerin, meaning sweet. I thought my sister would be as sad for her husband as when she lost her first Sheerin. Perhaps more so because she replaced the lost Sheerin with another Sheerin the next year but could not replace an old husband with another one.

Were I successful with my phone call to Sohrab, I wanted to tell him that what a good thing he did when he invited his only brother to France to see each other one more time before either one of them died, despite being short of money. Sohrab could have been home but had turned off his hearing aid.

More information about the circumstances of Manuchehr's death reached my ears when Mehdi came with an older, but new, friend who was a friend of our stepbrother, from Vancouver to rent his house to new tenants. The friend had suffered a lot during the first few days after the revolution, but had not ended up in prison. As Mehdi was leaving for the last ferry, he smiled and told me more details about the fatal accident of our brother-in-law and the beneficial consequences of it for our sister.

When Manuchehr was dropped off by his friends at the intersection near his house, the traffic light for the crossing was green. As he began walking towards it, a truck pulled around the corner and, because the driver's seat was quite high and Chehry was short, the driver did not see him and struck him. The driver stopped after the accident and took him to a hospital. He died after a few hours without ever regaining consciousness. The hospital phoned our sister and Sheerin, and they, along with the grandchildren, went and saw him for the last time. They said his face and his watch were badly broken.

The truck driver's insurance company paid ten million *Tuman* to his wife as compensation and the Islamic government of Iran doubled the money. The reason the government doubled the money was not because my sister had suffered for a long time in silence from her husband, but because it is in their policy that whoever suffers an unjust death during the sad month of Moharram—the month of mourning for the unjust death of Imam Hossein— to double the award automatically. And the accident happened in that month, that Arabic month that has caused many Persian Muslims to cry for more than a thousand years and will do so forever.

This untimely death of my brother-in-law goes a long way toward washing away the bitter taste of the cream puff he never bought for us.

Let me tell you what happened, and bear with me one more time, if you have heard it before. We were living in As-You-Wish Street. Sohrab and Chehry and my two sisters were playing a card game, Belott, which is a simplified version of bridge with two pairs of partners playing against each other. We, the children, were not part of the game. We were just watching without caring which pair would lose or win because the lost money was to be collected in a cup and, at the end of the game, Chehry was to go and buy cream puffs with it for everybody, including the children. He was supposed to go by his friend's car that he had borrowed for the night. The pastry shop was at the Laleh-Zar Street in the northern part of Tehran. He went out of the house with stellate pool around eight o'clock at night and did not come back until nine-thirty the next morning, empty handed.

"What happened, Chehry?" everybody shouted, bitterly.

He told this story. "A friend of mine who was crossing Laleh-Zaar Street, drunk, was hit by a car. I had to stop and take him to a hospital. Meanwhile I hurt my wrist and ran out of gas and, unfortunately, I had to pay the money I had taken from here for the gas." He told this story while he had a bandage around his left wrist to make us believe that he really did go to a hospital for his own injury too.

His story did not fool the children, let alone my sister who was to become his future wife.

But I knew my sister would miss him a lot. Besides, Chehry was not just a husband. He was a good hunter, a boxer, and, despite all his roughness, had a kinder heart than any of the Shojania brothers. When my mother died, they say Chehry cried like a child. Except for Chehry, I have never heard a grown man cry like a child for the death of his aunt who happened to be his mother-in-law as well.

Chehry, like many tough military men, had a good and strong handwriting, but did not write much. He had not inherited the gene for it from his father. Nor had he inherited the gene of frugality from his mother. He was a very generous man, and because of that he soon ran out of money and suffered for the rest of his life for not being able to show his generosity towards his friends. He was interested in women and horses, but unlike his father and brother, he lost his money and his share of his inherited village, as they say here "on slow horses and fast women." Actually, it was by watching this deterioration in him that his father wrote a chapter in his book to say that military life is deleterious to man's morality, especially if one begins it at grade one.

Right after registering Manuchehr in a military school at grade one, Sharabi regretted his action and decided not to do the same with his second son, Sohrab. But Sohrab wanted it so badly that apparently he made a very passionate and patriotic speech on the first opportunity that he met the Dean of the Officers' Academy that the general recommended to Sharabi that he had to put Sohrab in military school too.

I sometimes wonder what kind of a person I would have become had I started my education as a cadet in the army instead of the Namoos School for girls. I am sure I would be a very different person, but I am not sure if that person would be better than me, or worse. Unlike my uncle, I don't think military life damages one's morality. Sohrab went through the same system and turned out very different from Chehry. Could it be that the difference was due to the fact that one brother always dealt with horses and became chivalrous while the other with cannons?

Not necessarily, because, Colonel Yahya Khalvati, the twin brother of our mother was an infantry officer and dealt with canons all his military life and we never saw him on horseback, yet remained morally intact and died a noble and natural death. When he died, among his papers there were pages in Farsi representing his translation and interpretation of selected segments of Koran, yet we never saw him reading that sacred book or doing *Namaaz*.

79

CARRYING THE *SALAAM* OF MAJID TO THE VICTORIA CANCER CENTRE

WHENEVER MY BROTHER MAJID WRITES ME A LETTER, he asks me to convey his *Salaams* to Dr. Brian Weinerman, the clinical director of the Victoria Cancer Clinic, now the Victoria Cancer Centre, since they have moved to the new building. Majid and Brian have been friends since Brian was in Winnipeg. They were the only two oncologists who handled all the cancers in Winnipeg, if not in the entire province of Manitoba. Majid was treating mainly the malignancies of children, Brian the adults. But not necessarily, because now that Brian has left Winnipeg, Majid is handling the malignancies of both the adults and children.

I usually don't leave my office to carry the *Salaams* that I have been asked in letters, from friends to friends, but if I happened to see the person to whom a *Salaam* is sent, I might give it to him or her if I have nothing better to say.

I happened to see Brian one evening, not long after Majid's letter, and shortly after September 11, at one of the basic science lectures in the new building, where pizza and refreshments were also being served. They had to serve dinner because the time of lecture coincided with the time of dinner. Besides, the lecture was so basic that had very little to do with the causes or cure of cancer and for this reason it required some incentive for people to attend.

Even though I saw Brian before the lecture and we did have a short conversation, I did not convey to him the *Salaam* of Majid because both our minds were preoccupied with something else that had happened somewhere far beyond cancer and the cancer centre. Mine, I remember, was preoccupied with the twin implosions at the World Trade Center in New York, and Brian's with the recent death of his father.

He had just come back from Winnipeg. He had gone there to see his dying father and luckily his father was still alive when he reached there and they managed to exchange their last words. Brian said that he happened to see Majid in the elevator of the hospital in Winnipeg and they talked to each other as long as the ascent lasted.

Brian appeared too sad and subdued, somewhat more than is required for the natural death of one's aging father. He looked depressed and somewhat fearful for the future, as if something worse was going to happen. To make him feel a little better, without commenting about the death of his father or giving him the *Salaam* of Majid, I told him, "Brian, mark my words, this will be the last tragedy. As of now the world will become a better place for many and a worse place for a few."

"I hope you are right," Brian said without being reassured, as he rushed to start the meeting. He did not ask what I was talking about, but I am sure his mind was preoccupied with the same thing that my mind was. The tone of his voice and the fact that his mood did not improve indicated that he did not completely share my optimism.

That night, when I went home, I made a long poem out of that short conversation, and incorporated Brian's comment in it as its recurrent theme. I named it "An Agnostic's Prayer" and subtitled it "A Peaceful Prophecy."

That poem also terminates my book. My hope was to continue the book up to 100 chapters, but the tragic event of the Twin Towers truncated it to 81 or 82 segments. The book finished but the poem developed the life of its own. A night or two after I finished it I phoned Moti and Majid to talk about the recent trip I had made to Boston where I had visited Moti's sister, Soheila, and her educated and educating family. But soon, without saying enough about how nice she was and how helpful she was in encouraging me to finish my book, I said that I had written a poem about the calamity of September the 11th and asked if they wanted to hear its first page. Moti said yes right away, but Majid did not say anything. His silence, however, did not worry me much because he is always silent. Besides, I wanted to hear Moti's reaction more than Majid's. If Moti approved of it, I would know that it was a good poem.

I read the first page over the phone. Both were so silent during my reading that I had to interrupt myself to ask if they were still there. "Yes, yes, read on," Moti and Majid immediately said together, and I read all of it for them. At the end Moti said, "This should be read or heard by as many people as possible." I said, "I know. After thinking a long time about where to publish it, I have decided to publish it in an American journal. I have sent it to *The New Yorker*. I think they deserve it the most."

It took about three months to get my poem back in the same envelope on which I had written my address. It contained the long poem and a short note on the smallest square piece of paper, as if cut out of a pocket notebook, with the heading *The New Yorker*. It read, "We regret that we are unable to use the enclosed material. Thank you for giving us the opportunity to consider it. The Editors. Best Wishes."

It had no signature, but the last two words, the "Best Wishes," were printed in blue to resemble handwriting.

This was my first rejection paper, yet it did not hurt as much as I had thought it would. Actually, I was glad to receive it. It had taken so long to come that I thought maybe my envelope was not even opened by their editorial staff. The time was a doubtful time. It was the time of suspicion and mistrust. It was at the time of the anthrax scare and it was possible that they had decided, as a precaution, not to open any mail from strangers until it was found out who was mailing the germs. In short, I understood the reluctance of *The New Yorker*. It was in mourning. The cover of the post-September issue was black. One could see only a faint silhouette of the Twin Towers in the distance.

I told Moti about the first rejection I had experienced in my short period of writing. After a few weeks she suggested another magazine, also published in New York, by the name of *Persian Heritage* to which Moti had sent some of her own poems and they had published them. I sent it to them and followed it with a phone call. Its editor happened to be an Iranian from a city not far from Torbat. He was pleased with it and promised to publish it in their September issue which was to be dedicated to the tragic event of September 11 on the occasion of its first anniversary. I phoned him a few days before September 2002, to tell Kia, their chief editor, that I had revised it and had a new and improved version of it, if they had not published it yet. She said I was late. It was already sent to the printer.

80

"An Agnostic's Prayer and a Peaceful Prophecy"

Listen!

Everybody

The uprooted

The imploded

And the distanced from the beloved

Anyone with a lacerated chest or a wounded heart

Come closer to me and sit down on the ground, cross-legged, like my mother

And wipe the tears from your face with your sleeve, like a child

Listen to my peaceful prophecy and pray that I am right:

After this the world will become a better place for many and a worse place for a few.

Tragedies happen

Tragedies happen to good people

Since the world has more good people in it than bad

It is bound to happen

But mark my words and pray that I am right

This will be your last tragedy

After this the world will be a better place for the good and a worse place for the bad.

A Persian Letter

Listen! You too:

The inhabitants of those dusty distant lands

With stationary waters and running sand

Rusty mountains

Fields of poppies

Droplets of blood

The land of drought, apricots and cracked pomegranates

Crying sons, smiling daughters, faceless mothers

The land of extreme climates, extreme men, and extremely moderate women

After this the world will be a better place for you too

And a worse place for a few among you.

Everybody lost something big on that morning

I lost my newfound God

Under the columnar rubble of the Twin Towers

I don't know which one.

Everybody was in the middle of doing something good when it happened

I was in the middle of writing a letter to my dead mother in Iran

When I saw a silent bang, and then another one

Out of the blue came two aluminum matchsticks

To turn the Twin Candles of the world into a pair of crumbling chandeliers

"Oh, no!"

"My God!"

"My God!!"

Glowing skeletons

Progressive collapse

Pulverized bone

Stardust, burning stationery

Flaming fire in shadowless sunshine

Cumulus clouds

Mirror images

Metallic eagles

Silver cufflinks

Tearless candles

Melting steel

Wavy mirrors

Distorted foreheads

Collision

Collapse

Telescoped

Lightless glassless windows.

This was big

This was bad

This was bigger than the Big Bang

This was the second Big Bang

The true Big Bang

The first Big bang was misnamed:

When there is no human

There is no consciousness

Therefore no bigness or smallness.

When there is no eardrum

There is no loudness or softness

When there is no human there is nothing

No good, no bad, no construction or destruction

And no element of uncertainty.

The first does not count

The first mistake is either to be forgiven.

Or corrected

By the second appearance.

The time that began right after the first Big Bang

Made slaves out of men

After the second Big Bang

Man will become the master of time

When man becomes the master of time

He will rewind it like a video

And let the frozen river of the past to run again.

Instead of the future the past will unfold

The future will be whatever we make with our hands

When the tears are dried and the rubble are removed

Man will build on their solid foundation

A new clocktower, taller than the fallen two put together

Much taller than the Big Ben, with a happier face

For the whole universe to watch.

After this, trust will reign in the world

Rebellion will no longer be confused with patriotism

And the frozen fish of terror will no longer swim

In the lukewarm waters of sympathy

Laced with ignorance.

After this the young will obey the elders

And the old will learn from the young

Violet will lose its violence

And grey wisdom will acquire a purple hue;

The wisdom of Sohravardi

The Islamic Persian theologian

The one who polished the pre-Islamic Persian icons

The one who was strangled for his inflammatory remarks.

There are always a few who dance at the wrong time

To the wrong tune

In the wrong place

But mark my words;

From now on the wise will dance

Strangers with strangers

The way Rumi wished to dance

At the intersection of Islamic bazaars

With a cup of wine in one hand

In the other, the undulating hair of the beloved.

The root of the Islam of my mother was *Tasleem*:

To surrender

To give up

To *Tavakkol*:

To put one's will in the hands of God.

Time is on the human side

Things will improve as time goes on

In addition to the God and all the prophets

My mother also believed in twelve Imams

The twelfth Imam neither died nor became martyred

He disappeared to reappear one day as the Saahebeh Zaman

Literally the Master of Time

He would get rid of all the bad and badness

To make the world populated by good people only.

Don't worry if the liberator becomes strong

Worry if the liberator becomes weak.

Leave your fear at home and go out of the door

Either to work or for a walk

And I will go to finish my interrupted letter to my dead mother in Iran.

If everybody's mother had behaved like mine

The world would have been already a better place for many and a worse place for a few.

Nasser Shojania
Victoria, Canada
15-September-2001

81

PHOTOS, NOTES AND DOCUMENTS

Fig. 1 — Nayyer Ashraf (Khalvati) Shojania, 1900-1989,
the recipient of *A Persian Letter.*

Judging by the official seal next to her face, this photograph must be from her identification booklet. Judging by the familiar black blouse she is wearing, the date of this picture must be the winter of 1936, the year her husband died. For further explanation see chapter 24," Going Home."

Fig. 2 — My father, Mojtaba-Mirza Shojania.

A gentleman farmer from Torbat, Heidarieh. He was the husband of two wives, father of eight sons and two daughters. He had good handwriting but never wrote a book. He had collected the *divan* of most of Persian poets but never made a poem, except for one line: "Every science is *Sharif* (noble), but medicine is *Ashraf* (the noblest),"written in a letter to his first son in Paris to dissuade him from law and persuade him to enter medicine. He was not overtly religious, but he had the sacred books of Islam, Christianity and Judaism at home. He "mixed himself with the poets," as my mother said in one of her letters. In this regard my father resembles me a lot. It is too bad that he died so early, before I could find out how many more things we had in common.

The photograph must have been taken with a primitive box camera in the courtyard of our house in Sanguelaj District in Tehran where he died, judging by the gilded plaster work on the wall. He does not look sick enough to have died within a year, but he did. The position of the hands on the knees speaks of his good manners. The sharply demarcated white lock of hair is a benign medical syndrome whose name escapes me now. I can look it up. The wide space between the index and the middle fingers of the left hand has no special meaning except that he smoked cigarettes.

Fig. 3 — The Shojania Siblings.

Seated in the front row, from left to right: Monavar Saramad, Dr. Hashem Shojania, and Monir Khalvati.

Standing in the back row, not in chronological order, the seven full bothers, known as *the Shojania Brothers*, from left to right: Mehdi, Hamid, Hossein, Mansur, Nasser, Mahmood and Majid.

Time: the summer of 1953—A few weeks before Nasser lands in prison. Nasser is wearing a civilian suit because of the occasion; otherwise he would be in military uniform.

Place: the guest room in the house of Colonel Vokhshur in Shemiran, Iran.

Occasion: the wedding of Hamid.

In a few seconds the bride and three other sisters-in-law will join the picture.

Fig. 4 — Ten Shojania siblings and four sisters-in-law.

Seated on the ground, from left to right: Pari-vash (Vokhshur) Shojania, the bride, Afsar Shojania, wife of Dr. Hashem Shojania, Farangueece (Vokhshur) Shojania, wife of Mansur.

The fourth sister-in-law is Pari-rokh (Neek-Eteghad) Shojania, wife of Mehdi, pregnant with their first son, Mohsen.

Fig. 5 — The cover of *SOS* (original in colour).

Designed by an Armenian artist, perhaps Avanecian. The skeleton standing next to the imaginary United Nation's building is the author of the book, Colonel Abdollah Khalvati. It is a self-explanatory picture: Make peace and with the money saved from not making weapons, build the building of the United Nations. The line of poem going across the picture is by the colonel himself, saying,

"This very page represents my wish

And the summary of all I want to say."

Signed: Sarhang Abdollah Khalvati, "*La* Sharabi"

The cover must have been made early during the writing of the book, when the colonel did not like the nickname *Sharabi*—the wine-stricken—given to him by the inhabitants of Tehran. This is why he has put the short word *La*, (a negative Arabic word) in front Sharabi to negate it. At the end of the book, however, he changes his mind and is proud of that nickname, confessing that he is eternally drunk, but with the wine of love for humanity.

در خدمت پدرم . اوقاتی که ۶۸ سال ازسنشان میگذشت .

شادمانی روان پدر بزرگوارم را ازدرگاه ایزد متعال خواستارم و بمناسبت
دریافت مربای تربیت وجود بی‌همتای بزرگوارشان بنام « محمد ابراهیم خان
خلوتی» (صدیق خلوت) مباهات مینمایم .

Fig. 6 — from the book *SOS*
Sharabi, as a child, is standing beside his father.

Translation of the Farsi caption is as follows:
"At the service of my father at the age of 68.
I wish the happiness of his soul from God and I am proud of the up-bringing
I received from him. Mohammad Ebrahim Khan Khalvati (Seddigh Khalvat)."

از داشتن مادری چون «خانم بزرگ ، بی بی گرشــب بانو بیگم»
فرق مباهات برافراشته ، شادی روان آن یگانه زن که باعث افتخار نوع خود بوده‌اند
از پروردگار عالم خواسته و از تربیت مادرانهٔ وجود نازنیشان سپاسگزارم .

Fig. 7 — From *SOS*

Mother of Colonel Abdollah Khalvati

Translation of the Farsi caption:
"I am proud of having a mother like
'Khanum Bozorg (Great Lady), Bibi Garshasb Banu Bigom'
and I wish the happiness of the soul of that unique woman who was the source of
pride for her species and I thank her for the motherly upbringing I received from her."

یش انبوه برف مانندس سرازیر شد ۱
بوای که فرستاده
اب فراهم آورد
بایستی خیلی تو
میتوانستم توروی
ـل، خانم فرمودند
ت ها را براتون
ض کنید: تا حالم
کشید چون نهار
نم بخورم و بمن
شما خیال نکنید
ـعادارم بی مضایقه
ـ بیاورید. خود
کمالتتان خیلی
وال شما را از
تبه آدم فرستادم

« آقای سید محمد نجار »

علاقمندی دارم و شمارا مرد بزرگواری میدانم تمنا دارم
ائید برایتان بزنند و ازمن رودر وایسی نکنید » گفت :

Fig. 8 — from *SOS*

Mr. Seyyed Mohammad Najjar

The proud carpenter in the Little Bazaar of Asheikh Hadi, always sitting in front of
the house of Colonel Sharabi.
He never confessed that as a young man he was working in the garden of the father of
Sharabi.

بانو بی‌بی‌فخرالتاج درسن بیست و نه‌سالگی پس‌ازهفت‌سال از عروسی ۰ این عکس
بوسیلۀ یکی ازبستگان گرفته شده، در آن ایام بواسطۀ حجاب داشتن وتدّین
اسلام راضی نمیشدند عکاس نامحرم از ایشان عکس بردارد لهذا
ما عکس ایام‌عروسی‌را نداریم، با دوربین عکس‌های فوری
کوچك گرفته شده بعداً عکس‌را بزرگ نموده اند

Fig. 9 — from *SOS*

Lady Bibi Fakhrettaj at the age of 29 after seven years of marriage.

"This picture is taken by one of her relatives. In those days, due to the Islamic requirement to wear the *hejab* and to avoid beeing seen by strange men, my wife did not let a professional photographer take her picture. This is why we do not have our wedding picture together. This picture is enlarged from a group picture taken at her home with an ordinary camera."

Fig. 10 — from *SOS*

"A page from the identification booklet of my wife
In 1942—almost at the time of our discussion."

Colonel Sharabi printed this photograph of his wife in his book to show how young she looks at the age of 40 and attributes this preservation at least partly to her obsessively following the rules and regulations of her religion.

عکس ایام عروسی ، « ثور » ۱۲۹۸
کامروائی یا تابستان عمربا رتبهٔ نایب اولی .

Fig. 11 — from *SOS*

"Photo from wedding days
Times of pleasure or the summer of my life
When I was a first lieutenant."

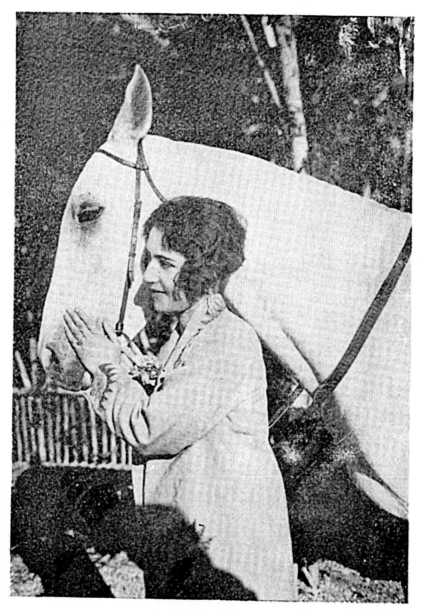

بهترین تسخیر من .

بانو « بی بی فخرالتاج » خانم واسب «پری زاد». (توسط زنی عکاس عکس برداری شده است.)
(شرح در تعلیقات)

Fig. 12 — from *SOS*

"My two best conquered:
Lady Bibi Fakhrettaj and horse 'Pari-zad.'"

This photograph was taken by a female photographer. See explanation at the end of *SOS*.

ثمرۀ وجودم یاگلهای بی خارم .

Fig. 13 — from *SOS*

"The fruits of my life or my thornless flowers"

Manuchehr and Sohrab at the age of seven and six. This is the picture that made us laugh at the book of our uncle when we were children. As children we thought the adjective "thornless" was quite inappropriate for them, especially for Manuchehr who was quite thorn-full.

ایشان خواستند بمن بفهمانندکه داشتن اولاد دست انسان نیست
اسبابی فراهم میگردد که بر خلاف دلخواه تعداد
اولاد زیاد میگردد و به من فرمودید:«چند اولاد
داری؟»از اتفاقات من دو اولاد داشتم لهذا خداوند
متعال نخواست مجاب شده سببی فراهم گردید
که توانستم بهتر و کاملتر بذکر مطالب پرداخته
دلائل خود را برای ایشان تشریح کرده باشم.

❀ ❀ ❀

مربوط به صفحات: ۳۹۵–۳۹۷

شکستن شمشیر: آمال من آن بود که تا آخر عمر با
ملبوس نظامی بوده باشم و چنانچه در این کتاب
نوشته شده بقول سعدی :

« لازم بکلاه تَرَکی داشتنت نیست

زمستان عمر رسیده ، در
اواخر سر ازیری از کوه عمر
صحرای مقابل را با چشم
میبینم .

درویش صفت باش و کلاه تَتری دار .»

Fig. 14 — from *SOS*

"The winter of life has arrived and from the downhill slopes of the mountain of my life
I can see the plain in front of my eyes."

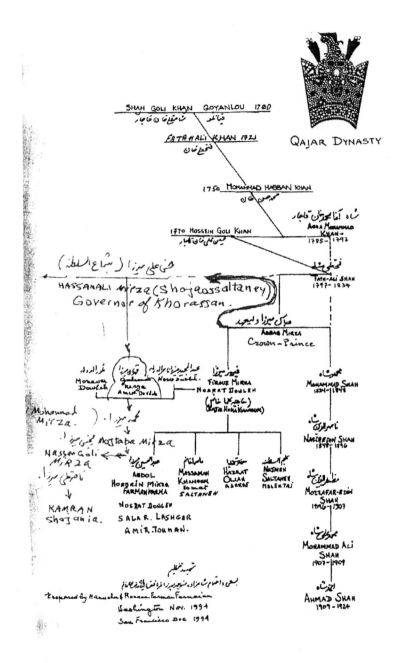

Fig. 15 — A branch of the family tree of descendents of Qajar
showing Farman-farma family.
It is from the book, *Oil and Blood.*

Without permission, since we are related, I have badly grafted the branch of Shojania
and Ghahreman to show the connections.

1- Mohammad-Hassan-Khan Ghajar   3- Hassan-Ali-Mirza   5- Mohammad-Mirza
2- Fath-Ali-Shah Ghajar   4- Ghahreman-Mirza   6- Mojtaba-Mirza

Fig. 16 — Six generations of my ancestors from father's side.

The first three are photographs from paintings; the second three are true photographs.

The first, from left, is the father of Fatali Shah—or perhaps the father of Agha Mohammad Khan, the founder of Qajar dynasty. He was not a king, even though he is wearing a small crown.

The second is Fatali Shah who ruled Iran for 35 years.

The third is Hassan Ali-Mirza (Shoja-ol-saltaneh). The *Shoja* of my family name comes from him. Written in Farsi on the left upper corner of the painting is, "The days of blindness."

The fourth is Ghahreman Mirza. This photograph used to be on the wall of Dar-ol-fonoon, the first high school in Tehran. He had unusually good handwriting. Figure 17 shows his handwriting on the inside of the cover of an astronomy book.

The fifth is Mohammad Mirza. I know nothing about him except for a line in a long poem in his praise, indicating, "The importance of the city of Torbat depends on two things: its noble *Khaak* and the presence of Mohammad Mirza in it."

The sixth is my father, Mojtaba Mirza.

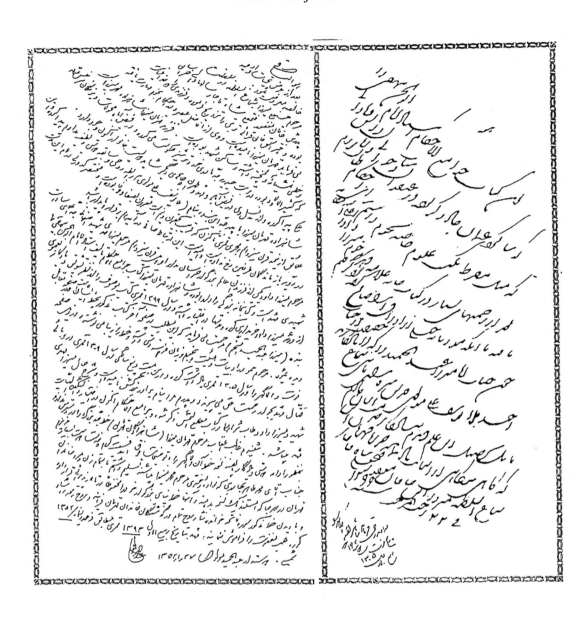

Fig. 17 — The flawless and dotless handwriting of Ghahreman Mirza.

On the right is the handwriting of Ghahreman Mirza; on the left is the explanatory note about it by Mr. Abdol Hamid Mowlavi.

Mr. Mowlavi found this handwriting on the inside of the cover of an astronomy book in the main library of Mashad.

The style of the handwriting is "broken" type. It is also dotless; this is why it is difficult to read. The very learned men in those days omitted the dots from the words. The reason for that omission was that if someone is so unfamiliar with the words that they need dots to know what they are, they better forget about reading. Also, if in the classroom a student objected to the lack of dots in a piece of writing, he or she would be called, *"Molla noghati"* a dotty Molla indicating "not very educated."

I have tried to read it several times with the help of Farhad Mirza and other cousins. We have figured most of the words out, but not all of them. At the very top, in the centre, is the word *Hoo,* which is not an interrogative pronoun or a question. It is a name, one of the more than one thousand names for God.

What can be read by me from the beginning of the page is this:

"This book of Javame-ol-ahkam of the Master Abolhassan Bayhaghi, who was the student of Othman the Magician, and has been studied by me at the time of my youth when I was very interested in science, especially Astronomy, is offered to you [Mr. Yousef Mowlavi?] even though it is partly eaten by termites...."

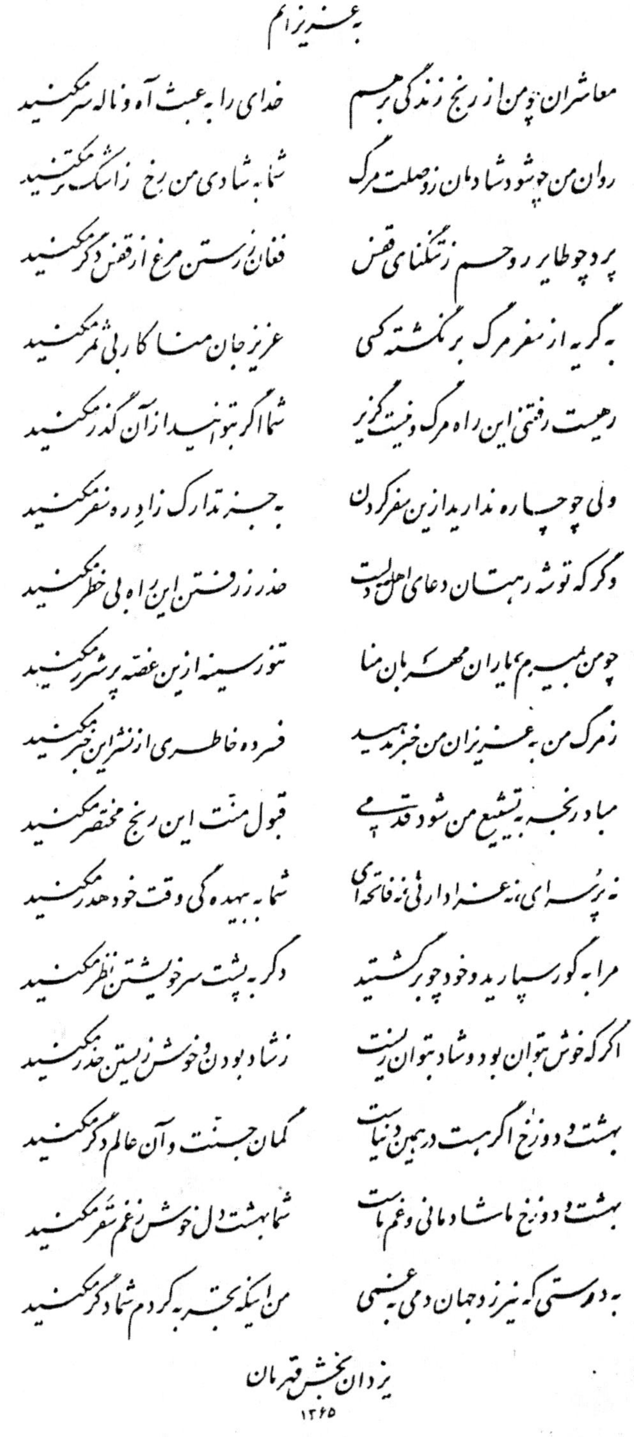

به عزیزانم

معاشران چو من از رنج زندگی برهم   خدای را به عبث آه و ناله سر مکنید

روان من چو شود شادمان ز رحلت مرگ   ثنا به شادی من رخ ز اشک تر مکنید

پرد چو طایر روحم ز تنگنای قفس   فغان ز رستن مرغ از این قفس دگر مکنید

بگریه از سفر مرگ برنگشته کسی   عزیز جان من این کار بی ثمر مکنید

رهست رفتنی این راه مرگ و نیست گزیر   شما اگر بتوانید ازآن گذر مکنید

ولی چو چاره ندارید ازین سفر کردن   به جز به تدارک زاد ره دگر مکنید

وگر که توشه رهستان دعای اهل دل است   حذر ز رفتن این راه بی خطر مکنید

چو من بمیرم یاران مهربان منا   تو را ز سینه ازین غصه پر شرر مکنید

ز مرگ من به عزیزان من خبر بدهید   فسرده خاطری از این تر خبر مکنید

مباد رنجه بتشییع من شود قدمی   قبول منت این رنج مختصر مکنید

نه پرسه ای نه عزا داری نه فاتحه ای   شما به بیهوده گی وقت خود هدر مکنید

مرا به گور سپارید و خود چو بر گشتید   دگر به پشت سر خویشتن نظر مکنید

اگر که خوش بتوان بود و شاد بتوان زیست   ز شادی بودن خوش زیستن حذر مکنید

بهشت و دوزخ اگر هست در همین دنیاست   گمان جنت و آن عالم دگر مکنید

بهشت و دوزخ ما شادمانی و غم هاست   شما بهشت دل خوش ز نغم تیره مکنید

به دوستی که نیرزد جهان و می عیشی   من آنکه تجربه کردم شما دگر مکنید

یزدان بخش قهرمان
۱۳۴۵

Fig. 18 — The last poem of Yazdan-bakhsh Ghahreman, telling his friends not to cry or be sad when he is gone (dead). It is a good example of his poems, made of simple words, strong melody and flawless logic. It cannot be translated without losing a lot of its good points. This is for Iranians only, whether they can read English or not.

Fig. 19 — One of the postpartum letters by my mother. It was written in 1934 from Mashad to Auntie Pouran in Tehran. This is translated in the book.

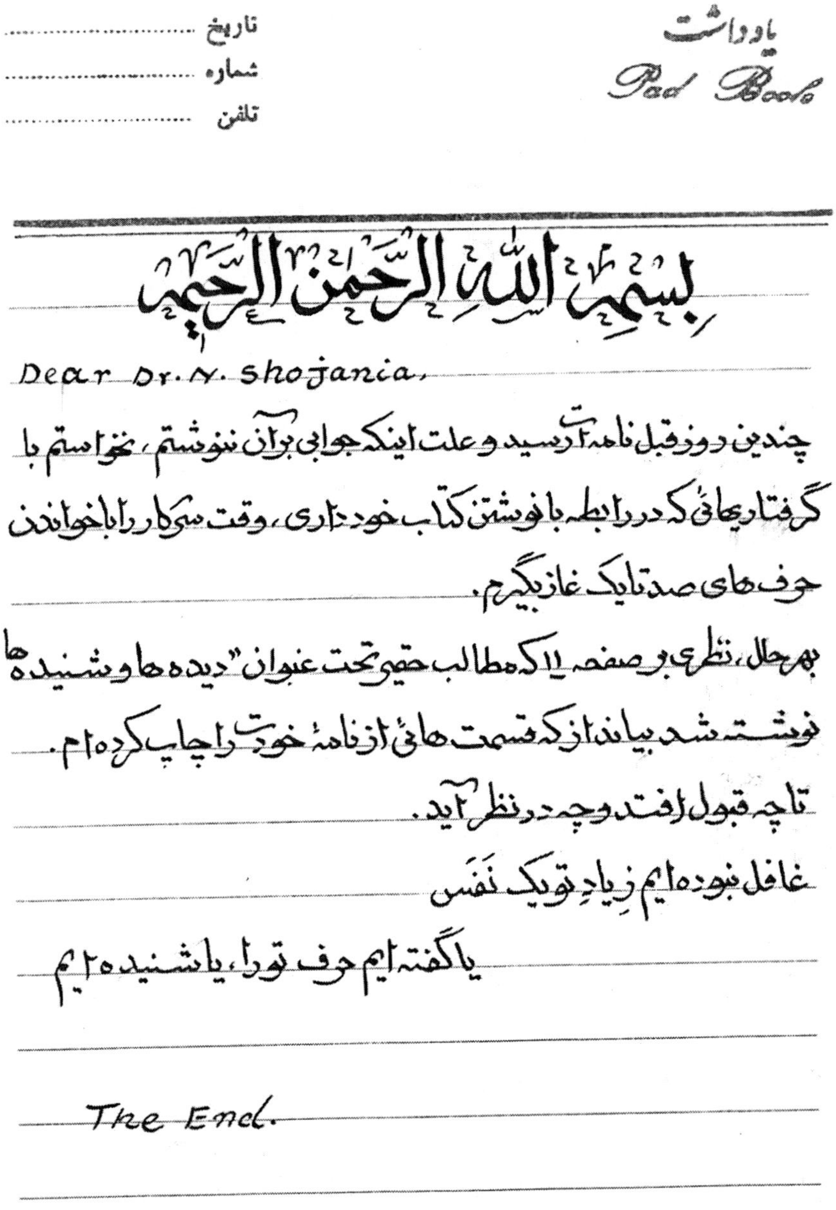

یادداشت
Pad Book

تاریخ ....
شماره ....
تلفن ....

بِسْمِ اللَّهِ الرَّحْمَنِ الرَّحِیمِ

Dear Dr. N. Shojania,

چندین روز قبل نامه ات رسید و علت اینکه جوابی بر آن نوشتم ، خواستم با

گرفتاریهائی که در ارتباط با نوشتن کتاب خود دارم ، وقت سرکار را با خواندن

حرف های صدتایک غازی بگیرم .

بهرحال ، نظری بر صفحه ۱۱ که مطالب حقیر تحت عنوان "دیده ها و شنیده ها"

نوشته شده بیانداز از که قسمت هائی از نامه خودت را چاپ کرده ام .

تا چه قبول افتد و چه در نظر آید .

غافل نبوده ایم زیاد تو یک نَفَس

یا گفته ایم حرف تو را ، یا شنیده ایم

The End.

Fig. 20 — A short note from Mahmood.

Sent to me along with the recent Persian newspaper in which he has written an article for the column "The Seen and the Heard."

His flawless handwriting, in both Farsi and Ghor'ani (Arabic), has improved so much since his release from prison that I cannot recognize my brother in it.

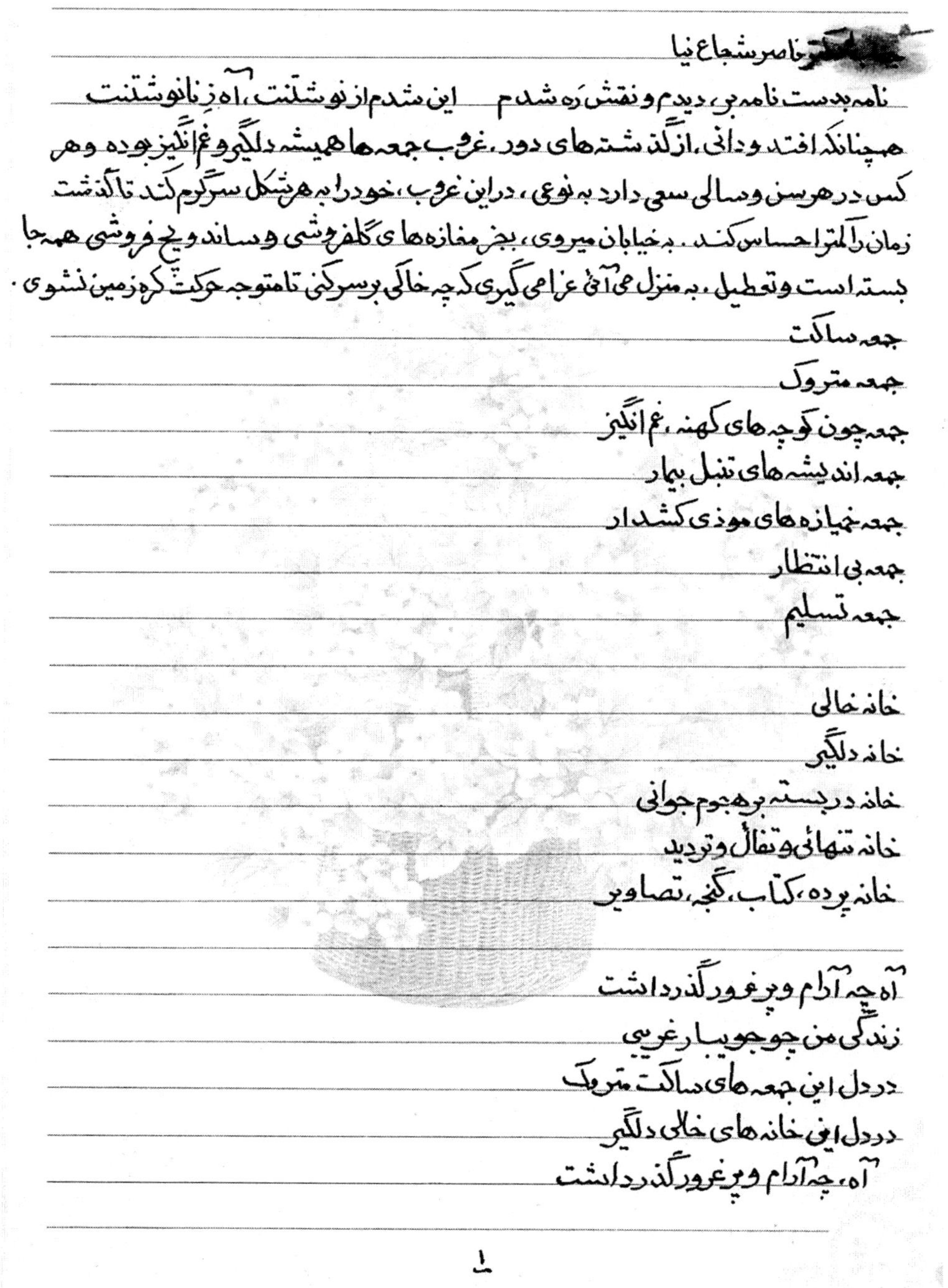

نامه ..... امیر شجاع نیا

نامه بدست نامبر، دیدم و نقش زه شدم   این شدم از نوشتنت، آه ز نانوشتنت

همانند افتد و دانی، از آن نشته های دور، غروب، جمعه ها همیشه دلگیر و غم انگیز بوده و هر

کس در هر سن و سالی سعی دارد به نوعی، در این غروب، خودرا به هر شکل سرگرم کند تا گذشت

زمان را کمتر احساس کند. به خیابان میروی، بجز مغازه های گلفروشی و سماندویچ فروشی همه جا

بسته است و تعطیل. به منزل می آئی عزامی گیری که چه خالی. پر سرکنی. تا متوجه حرکت که و زمین نشوی.

جمعه ساکت

جمعه متروک

جمعه چون کوچه های کهنه، غم انگیز

جمعه اندیشه های تنبل بهار

جمعه خمیازه های موذی کشدار

جمعه بی انتظار

جمعه تسلیم

خانه خالی

خانه دلگیر

خانه دربسته بر هجوم جوانی

خانه تنهائی و تفال و تردید

خانه پرده، کتاب، گنجه، تصاویر

آه چه آدم ویرغور گذر داشت

زندگی من چو چویبار غریبی

در دل این جمعه های ساکت متروک

در دل این خانه های خالی دلگیر

آه، چه آدم ویرغور گذر داشت

۱

Fig. 21 — The first page of the long reply by Mahmood to my first and only letter after his release from prison. The first word is smudged by my saliva. I wanted to test it to see if the page was a print or written with ink.

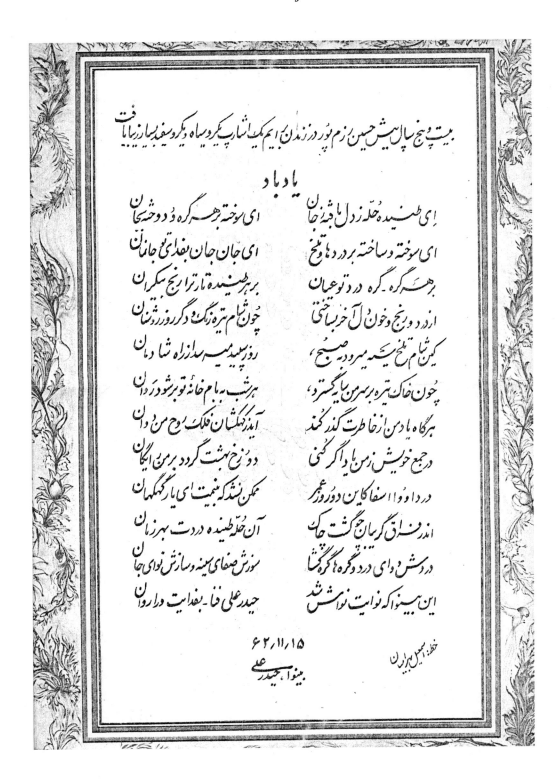

Fig. 22 — A poem by Khosrow Pouria for his executed friend, Marzban, who had made a lacy scarf with black-and-white sewing thread for him while they were both in prison. The poem was written in 1983, twenty-five years after the event.

Fig. 23 — Agha Khan and his wife came to Tehran in the early 1940s. They are surrounded by his relatives. Modar-jun is standing right behind Agha Khan. Aunt Seddigheh is talking to Agha Khan. General Javadi and his wife with sun glasses are between the two sisters. Monir, Mansur, Monavar, Feri, and many others are there. I and most of my brothers—from Mehdi down—are not there, not because we were not invited, but because at that time we did not consider the occasion important enough to attend! Also, not present in this gathering are the Pourias.

Fig. 24 — Agha Khan looking at some document.

The lady on his left is Bibi Zibandeh Khanum, the mother of Naadereh Khanum, the mother-in-law of Colonel Vokhshur. Mansur, Ali Gholi Khan, and Monavar are behind Agha Khan. Next to Monavar is Farzaneh, the daughter-in-law of Zohreh Khanum. Next to her is Estephan, the Polish wife of Sohrab, the mother-in-law of General Nassiri, the last head of SAVAK. Next to Estephan is Monir, and next to Monir is Alieh Khanum, the mother-in-law of Mr. Jahan-Shahi.

Fig. 25 — Ezzat Rastegar

My friend, my mentor and "the silent *Aref*"
who has enriched my book by his sayings and writings.

Fig. 26 — Nasser Shojania in his second year of medical school.

It is the summit of my innocence.

I don't belong to any political party, and I am not in love with anybody except for sport, literature, my country and most of the people in it.

I was wearing this uniform, by the way, when the soldiers, along the road on our way to bury Colonel Sharabi, mistook me for a general and saluted me.

Fig. 27 — summer of 1963

Mitra and Nasser at their wedding.

Times have changed. Unlike Colonel Sharabi, who could not have a photograph with his wife at their wedding night, I have many. This is one of them. The reason is that we were married in a different time. In our time my wife had no objection to a male photographer taking our picture together.

Fig. 28 — Siavosh Kasraei, pen name Kowli,
friend and guest at our wedding.

Fig. 29 — Mitra, my wife, about forty years after our marriage.

This photo was taken at home with an ordinary camera. Like the wife of Colonel Sharabi, my wife too has kept her initial beauty and freshness and perhaps has improved on it despite not being obsessed with religion.

Fig 30 — Standing at the Night-Time Ceremony

in the yard of section 4 of the Ghasr prison in Tehran.

The year must be 1954. I am the first in the front row, on the right. I do not remember the names of many, including the one who is standing next to me. I know, however, the one who is standing next to him. He is Hassan Shokoohi. He had good handwriting. He wrote the last draft of *Medical Emergencies* that I was translating in prison. He had a wide black moustache, bushier than his eyebrows, but he shaved it as soon as he landed in prison. Sia is standing on the top row, the third from right. He is the tallest one. Several others I recognize by their faces, but I don't remember their names. (It must be pruning season because the trees are just pruned.)

Fig. 31 — Houshi, inserted between four brothers.

From left to right: Hamid, Hossein, Houshi, Nasser and Majid.

Fig.32 — Birth of Nasser

This photograph was brought to me by Mansur when he came to Victoria from San Diego, for the memorial service of our mother, in the fall of 1989.

Mansur told me that the newborn under the hand of our mother, underneath the white sheet, is me.

I believe him because the other five children who were born ahead of me are there.

Mansur and Monir are sitting on chairs in front. Mehdi is standing beside the bed. Hossein and Monavar are behind the bed. The lady without a head is the mother of Modar-jun.

The time must be 22, March, 1930, because this is the date I have been telling everybody is my birthday.

The place must be the house of our grandmother in the street, Hammam of Shazdeh in Tehran, near Sanguelaj District. Thank you, Mansur, for having kept this picture for so long.

Also, thank you, Mother, for covering my face at this critical moment.

It was as warm under the aerodrome as it was in your womb.

And thank you, Nima, for taking this picture out of your album and mailing it to me so that I could print it here. I will bring it back to you when I come to Vancouver to see my first grandson, Alexander Justin Shojania, the newborn baby of Kamran and Anna.

Fig. 33 — Modar-jun near the end of her life

This photograph is taken by Farrokh Saramad, her grandson from Monavar.

The negative of this picture reached my hand exactly two weeks after I spoke about her as "a good Moslem" on the occasion of World Religions Day. Judging by the time it takes for a letter to reach my hand from Tehran, I concluded that it must have been mailed to me while I was speaking about her. Since the negative image looked like the image of her soul, I took it as her permission for what I was doing.

It was printed in Victoria by Dr. Joe Kiss, my friend who is a radiologist at Victoria General Hospital. Joe is also an artist and an amateur photographer. Joe has the enlarged black-and-white pictures of his mother and father in his office. They are from Hungary. His father wears a chapeau. His mother wears a scarf like my mother.

Fig. 34 — Nasser in 2001, by a Canadian artist in Victoria named Dean Lewis.

This book may be available directly online at www.apersianletter.com.

It is also available through Trafford Publishing

(see order form next page).

ISBN 141203075-7